Praise for *The Encyclopedia of Jewish Myth, Magic and Mysticism*

"An erudite and lively compendium of Jewish magical beliefs, practices, texts, and individuals. Geoffrey Dennis serves up a delicious smorgasbord of the irrational, demonstrating that Judaism has been and is not only a rational and legalistic monotheism, but also a rich storehouse of magical traditions that Jews often fail to recognize. This superb comprehensive encyclopedia belongs in every serious library."

—Richard M. Golden,
Professor of History and Director of the
Jewish Studies Program, University of North Texas, and
editor of the *Encyclopedia of Witchcraft: The Western Tradition*

"How many books must one browse through to find some simple explanation of an obscure or cryptic concept or terminology while exploring the vast seas of ancient Jewish mystery wisdom? Answer: more books than years in our lives. Solution: *The Encyclopedia of Jewish Myth, Magic, and Mysticism* by Rabbi Geoffrey Dennis. Rabbi Dennis has performed a tremendously important service for both the scholar and the novice in composing a work of concise information about aspects of Judaism unbeknownst to most, and intriguing to all. Even if you don't know enough to know what subject or name to look up in this user-friendly encyclopedia, just flipping through the pages will bring you more on-the-spot knowledge than an hour of watching *The Discovery Channel*. How this modest rabbi managed to stump even me, an expert in Jewish myth and mysticism, is as magical as the book's title claims to be. I am humbled by this work and by the mere thought of what it took to write it, and by the wealth of information it contains."

—Rabbi Gershon Winkler,
author of *Magic of the Ordinary: Recovering the Shamanic in Judaism*

The Encyclopedia of

Jewish

myth, magic
and mysticism

About the Author

Rabbi Dennis has studied in Jerusalem and earned a Master's Degree in Hebrew Letters and ordination from Hebrew Union College, the oldest Jewish seminary in the Americas. He also has degrees in nursing and in education. A working rabbi since 1996, he is currently rabbi of Congregation Kol Ami in Flower Mound, Texas, and faculty in the Jewish Studies Program at the University of North Texas, where he teaches courses on Kabbalah, Talmud, and Midrash.

He is an energetic and engaging teacher and has been a popular lecturer in congregations, universities, and national conferences. His articles on a variety of topics appear in periodicals like *Parabola: The Magazine of Myth & Tradition* and *Healings Ministries*. He is a major contributor to *Encyclopedia Mythica*, an online resource devoted to world myth and folklore.

He is married and the father of two children.

To Write to the Author

If you wish to contact the author or would like more information about this book, please write to the author in care of Llewellyn Worldwide and we will forward your request. Both the author and publisher appreciate hearing from you and learning of your enjoyment of this book and how it has helped you. Llewellyn Worldwide cannot guarantee that every letter written to the author can be answered, but all will be forwarded. Please write to:

Rabbi Geoffrey W. Dennis
℅ Llewellyn Worldwide
2143 Wooddale Drive, Dept. 0-7387-0905-0
Woodbury, MN 55125-2989, U.S.A.
Please enclose a self-addressed stamped envelope for reply,
or $1.00 to cover costs. If outside U.S.A., enclose
international postal reply coupon.

Many of Llewellyn's authors have websites with additional information and resources. For more information, please visit our website at:
www.llewellyn.com

The Encyclopedia of

Jewish

myth, magic
and mysticism

Rabbi Geoffrey W. Dennis

Llewellyn Publications
Woodbury, Minnesota

First Edition
First Printing, 2007

Cover design by Kevin R. Brown
Interior illustrations by Llewellyn art department

Llewellyn is a registered trademark of Llewellyn Worldwide, Ltd.

Library of Congress Cataloging-in-Publication Data
Dennis, Geoffrey W.
    The encyclopedia of Jewish myth, magic and mysticism / Geoffrey W. Dennis.
       p. cm.
    Includes bibliographical references.
    ISBN-13: 978-07387-0905-5
    ISBN-10: 0-7387-0905-0
      1. Mysticism—Judaism—Encyclopedias. 2. Jewish mythology—Encyclopedias. 3. Magic, Jewish—
      Encyclopedias. I. Title.
    BM723.D46 2007
    296.1309436'03—dc22

                                      2006048789

Llewellyn Publications
A Division of Llewellyn Worldwide, Ltd.
2143 Wooddale Drive, Dept. 0-7387-0905-0
Woodbury, MN 55125-2989, U.S.A.
www.llewellyn.com

Printed in the United States of America

CONTENTS

Concerning everything that cannot be grasped, its question is its answer.
—Ketem Paz

To my sons, Avi and Micah, who love secrets.
To Robin, the greatest angel I know.

ACKNOWLEDGMENTS

My deep appreciation to my classmates and friends Rabbi Martha Bergadine, Rabbi George Gittleman, Dr. Dana Kaplan, Rabbi Max Weiss, and Rabbi Stan Zamek for taking the time from their busy lives to read the manuscript and offer insights and suggestions. Their contributions greatly improved the final product.

Thanks too to my brother John, to Charles Gregory, and to Scott and Kelley Snowden. Though non-experts in matters Jewish, they also read the book and helped me see it through the eyes of a general reader.

My gratitude also goes to Dr. Richard Golden. He unwittingly triggered the creation of the *EJMMM* and then graciously offered me encouragement once I finally owned up to what I was doing.

I want to acknowledge my teachers at Hebrew Union College-Jewish Institute of Religion, for teaching me the tools I needed to research this book: Rabbi Steven Balaban, Dr. Marc Bregman, Rabbi Chanan Brichto *z"l*, Dr. Alan Cooper, Dr. Susan Einbinder, Rabbi Ben Hollander, Dr. Adam Kamasar, Dr. Robert Katz *z"l*, Dr. Steve Kaufmann, Masha Klein, Dr. Michael Klein *z"l*, Dr. Barry Kogan, Dr. Paul Liptz, Dr. Michael Meyer, Dr. Eugene Mihaly *z"l*, Dr. Alvin Reines *z"l*, Hannah Saggi, Dr. Richard Sarason, Rabbi Julie Schwartz, Ezri Uval *z"l*, Dr. Ben Zion Wacholder, Dr. Mark Washofsky, Dr. David Weisberg, and Dr. Isaac Yerushalmi.

I want to thank Natalie Harter, Karl Anderson, and all the editors at Llewellyn, both for taking an interest in an unsolicited proposal from an unknown author, and also for being the nicest and most pleasant people I've yet encountered in the publishing world.

My greatest and eternal thanks must go to my wife and soulmate, Robin, who encouraged my vision and gave me the confidence to write this book. Not only did she read and help revise countless manuscripts, but she has been more patient and forgiving of me during the years of writing this book than I deserve or merit. May her reward be waiting in the World-to-Come, because she's stuck with me until then.

INTRODUCTION

Judaism is one of the oldest living esoteric traditions in the world. Virtually every form of Western mysticism and spiritualism known today draws upon Jewish mythic and occult teachings—magic, prayer, angelology, alchemy, numerology, astral projection, dream interpretation, astrology, amulets, divination, altered states of consciousness, alternative healing and rituals of power—all have roots in the Jewish occult.

But for millennia, many of these core teachings have been unavailable to the general public, concealed by barriers of language and by the protective principles governing the teaching of Kabbalah, which has both nurtured and guarded such knowledge. Now, however, many more traditional texts of Jewish mysticism and magic are being translated into English and many more almost-forgotten manuscripts of Jewish esoteric teachings have been recovered and identified. At the same time, people of all backgrounds are thirsty for the kind of wisdom that can only be drawn from ancient wells. This confluence of factors inspired me to write a book like *The Encyclopedia of Jewish Myth, Magic and Mysticism*.

> When Adam HaRishon, the First Man, sinned, he blemished all the *nitzotzot* (Holy Sparks)
> . . . causing them to become immersed in the *kelipot*. . . . The *kelipot* are the husks or shells
> [of impurity, evil, and entropy] that imprison the fallen Holy Sparks.[1]

This is a book full of husks and sparks: of things concealed and revealed, lost and then recovered. This encyclopedia focuses exclusively on the esoteric in Judaism—the fabulous, the miraculous, and the mysterious. In this book the reader will find many *kelipot,* husks from the ancient and shattered world of Jewish occult teachings: the seemingly eccentric, the offbeat, the peripheral, and the outlandish. Much of it will strike a modern reader as dark, strange, and alien stuff indeed—husks.

Because so much has been lost over the past two centuries of what we term "modernization," even many Jews will be puzzled by the contents of this book. And to be frank, most Jews can live very satisfactory spiritual lives never having known, or never knowing, much of what can be found in these pages. So be forewarned: this is not a

---

1. Sefer ha-Gilgulim, 3, as translated by Yitzchak bar Chaim.

primer on Judaism, providing a conventional perspective on those beliefs and practices most people associate with Torah and Jewish faith. On the other hand. . . .

Concealed within these many husks there are *nitzotzot,* Holy Sparks. Since Jewish esotericism is the oldest and most influential continuous occult tradition in the West, shaping everything from angelology to the zodiac, this book contains lore that can spiritually enrich the lives of anyone, Jewish or not, who wishes to understand the mysteries that underlie our universe. The reader who looks carefully into this book will glimpse flashes of insight, glimmers of inspiration, and sparks of wit and wisdom. For Jews, this book uncovers aspects of Judaism that have been lost to most of us until recently. For every reader, this book is meant to be a portal into an exotic alternate spiritual world, for this is a book about three things that have profoundly shaped human experience: myth, magic, and mysticism.

Already, with the word "myth," the puzzlement begins and our modern prejudices take over our thinking. For is not a myth a kind of fairy tale, a fantastic account about something that never really was? Modern Jews are constantly taught that Judaism is a religion without mythology, a faith unburdened by fanciful and grotesque "adventures of the gods." To that claim I answer, "Well, yes and no."

First of all, let us clear something up: a myth, a really good myth, is not a story about something that never happened. It's a story about something that happens all the time. Myths are archetypal tales, fabulous stories told to help us fathom important truths— truths about ourselves, our universe, and how things really are. And while it is true that Judaism (mostly) lacks stories about "God as action-hero," it nevertheless revels in mythological tales about those things which are, to paraphrase the Psalms, "little less than God"; angels and demons, primeval monsters, magicians and miracle-workers, agents of good and evil. After all, what are the first eleven chapters of Genesis, if not a carefully crafted mythic account of exactly what human beings are and how our world came to look the way it does? The simple fact is that Jewish tradition overflows with myths of deep complexity and singular wisdom.

It is much the same with regard to the magical. Modern Jews like to imagine that magic has been swept into the dustbin of history by the long, inexorable progress of rationalism. More than that, Jews have been taught from our youth that Judaism has always possessed an essentially naturalistic worldview and that magic, merely a marginal Jewish preoccupation at most, was just an anomaly resulting from our being situated (and corrupted) by the superstitions of our neighbors. But that's not entirely accurate. It is only in the last two centuries Jews have fully embraced science, but we have always been looking for ways to change the world for the better, whether it be through science, medicine, or "practical Kabbalah."

Even today, rationalism has not completely displaced our sense that there is a mystical potential at work in the world; Occam's razor has never been able to fully overpower the Sixteen-Sided Sword of the Almighty.[2] Millions of people, both Jews and gentiles, continue to believe that the stars influence our lives. Most Americans believe in the reality of angels. Jewish techniques of dream interpretation and for combating the evil eye are still widely practiced today. When you read the entries of this book on topics such as these,

---

2. See **Sixteen-Sided Sword of the Almighty** in the "S" section.

you will realize that magical thinking and enchanting deeds have always had a place in Judaism and, however much some might want to dismiss Judaism's miraculous and wondrous traditions, the presence of Jewish magic in Jewish life has merely been eclipsed, never uprooted; it still has the potential to empower us.

Mysticism, the quest for an intimate encounter with God, has fared little better in modernity than Jewish myth or magic, but for different reasons than those discussed above. For despite a long retreat from its disciplines among many Western Jews from the eighteenth through twentieth centuries, Kabbalah has continued to have its champions and its practitioners.

Instead, there is a terrible irony that haunts the contemporary seeker in regard to Jewish mysticism. For it was in the middle of the last century, just at the time when sparks of renewed interest in Kabbalah were released in the world, that a terrible demonic force, Nazism, arose to engulf and extinguish the lights emanating from the countless spiritual centers of Jewish mysticism in eastern Europe. The Nazis slew many, if not most, of the precious teachers and disciples of Jewish mysticism in its monstrous campaign to blot out all things Jewish from the world. Because of the scope of that crime, those of us who would use Kabbalah in our soul journey, or who long to storm the gates of heaven, have been left with few teachers to guide us. Thus many of us have had to rediscover the ancient paths to supernal wisdom without accomplished masters to guide us on our way.

Thankfully, as we enter into a new millennium, new teachers have arisen and this generation has yielded many new devotees. Students of Kabbalah, inspired by a small but vigorous circle of self-educated leaders, have shown themselves determined not to let such divine mysteries slip into oblivion and they have recovered and reclaimed much. Moreover, as this generation has come to better understand the wisdom and power of Kabbalah, that recovered knowledge has also helped inspire interest in related Jewish traditions—mythic traditions and occult traditions, other holy sparks, that are now included in this encyclopedia.

As I said at the beginning of this introduction, this book is a combination of *kelipot* and *nitzotzot*, of husks and sparks. While I have learned many divine lessons from these traditions, lessons that have both enriched my understanding and influenced my life, many more of them remain still trapped in their husks; I apprehend them but do not yet understand or appreciate what they are trying to teach me. Moreover, in teaching this lore to my congregants, to my university students, to Jews and to non-Jews alike, I have come to understand that holy sparks do not always reveal themselves to everyone at the same time, or even reveal themselves at all. Spiritually, the student has to be ready to see a spark before it can shine forth. Some teachings that I find enlightening or empowering continue to remain dark and inert for my students. Other teachings that I fail to appreciate myself, my students find illuminating. Therefore my philosophy in writing this book has been to include all the Jewish mystical, occult, and fabulous teachings I have found—even those I neither fully understand nor accept—in the hopes that a reader somewhere will perhaps find a spark in something I cannot (yet).

It has also been my approach in writing these entries to describe more than I interpret, and to interpret more than judge. At times, some interpretation is called for, and I give it my best effort, trying to be clear without oversimplifying. At other times, judgment of some sort is also appropriate, and at such occasions, I offer mine; the reader is welcome to disagree with me—in fact I encourage it. And on occasion I include comments that reflect, as one early reader called it, an "insouciant sense of humor." I feel it is right to do this because humor has always been an honored method of Jewish wisdom development. The Bible, rabbinic literature, and Kabbalah are all filled with sayings, stories, and teachings that are supposed to make us laugh. Furthermore, I hope that it will be clear to the reader that I use humor in a spirit of love, for I do love this lore, all of it, even those practices and ideas that puzzle me, trouble me, or seem at odds with my own philosophy of Torah.

How to Use This Book

The *Encyclopedia of Jewish Myth, Magic and Mysticism* is the first and only comprehensive one-volume reference guide to the lore of the great Jewish esoteric traditions. For the first time, a reader has ready access to ancient mysteries and powerful practices. The *Encyclopedia* provides over one thousand A to Z entries, running from a single sentence to article length, on virtually every aspect of Jewish Kabbalah and occult lore.

In addition, each entry is cross-referenced to multiple related topics elsewhere in the *Encyclopedia*, weaving together the many Jewish esoteric concepts, terms, and practices, in order to give the reader the fullest possible understanding of the depth of Jewish wisdom and the interconnected nature of Judaism's occult teachings. Such cross-references are signified by a word appearing in **bold** font. I have also included a *Quick Reference Glossary of Frequently Used Terms* in the back to help individuals with the Hebrew and historical terms frequently used in the *Encyclopedia*. It might even be wise for the reader to begin there.

As a rule, I have tried to use the English translations of terms, making the entries easier to use for those not so familiar with Hebrew. Thus, one will find the major entry on the day of rest under "Sabbath" rather than "Shabbat." I break with this convention when I deem that a Hebrew term will be more familiar to the reader than its translation: "dybbuk" rather than "clinging spirit," "Sefer Zohar" rather than "Book of Splendor." I apply the same rule when there simply is no adequate English translation of a term, such as "sefirot."

Yet, even as much as the *Encyclopedia* reveals, much more remains concealed. For while the *Encyclopedia* explains a great deal, there is so much more to be learned by reading the original sources. Moreover, Jewish occult traditions have always been deliberately elliptical, forcing students to do further searching on their own, requiring the disciples of the wise to draw their own conclusions and form their own practice. I feel obliged to honor that approach, for it is based on sound pedagogy and admirable caution in dealing with deep matters. There is no "lazy man's path to enlightenment" in Jewish tradition. For this reason, I have provided copious citations taken from the full scope of Jewish tradition, sources both familiar and obscure; from the Bible, the Dead Sea Scrolls, apocalyptic, magical, rabbinic and Kabbalistic literature, and beyond. I provide these citations in the expectation that any true seeker after wisdom will have the discipline to go deeper in his or her pursuit of insight and empowerment. The footnotes and bibliography at the back of the book serve as similar resources; there is much more that can be learned on all these topics from the teachers, books, and articles listed there.

These entries, intentionally, are only finger posts pointing a way. It is up to you, dear reader, to decide if you will continue on the places where they point. As is said in Jewish spiritual circles, *ha-maskil yavin*, "the enlightened will understand."

Some Remarks on Hebrew Usage

In writing this book, I have adopted a transliteration system that is user friendly to a general reader. It mostly follows modern Israeli-Sefardic pronunciation. The guttural *chet* and *chaf* are represented by a "ch" in the Latin alphabet; that's "ch" like "Ba<u>ch</u>," not "<u>church</u>." Since many other translators today opt to transliterate the Hebrew letter *chet* as "h," let the reader be aware: the now-common transliteration "Hasidim" will appear in this work as "Chasidim."

I have avoided most of the diacritical marks used in scholarly transliteration of Hebrew, with the exception of the occasional (') to signify a syllable stop.

Names generally follow older English usage—Abraham rather than *Avraham*—unless it is a word that has no tradition of an Anglicized name. Thus the biblical *Yaakov* is "Jacob," but the angel *Yehoel* is not changed to "Jehoel" because no one (I know) bothers to do that.

The Hebrew *fayh* is transliterated as "f" rather than the older convention of "ph," so in the *Encyclopedia*, phylacteries will appear as "tefillin," not "tephillin," and the Kabbalistic diagram of divine emanations as "sefirot," not "sephirot."

All "a" sounds are "ah," as in "father."

In this encyclopedia the Hebrew *kuf* is (usually) transliterated as "k" rather than the more linguistically justified "q," though I use a "q" if it appears in a familiar name like "Qumran." Defying any linguistic consistency, I use "Kabbalah" when referring to the Jewish mystical phenomenon, but "Qabbalah" when referring to the Christian/Spiritualist offshoot. Wondering why? This would be a good time to look at the entry **Qabbalah**.

A

Aaron: The brother of **Moses** and **Miriam**, Aaron was both a prophet and the first High Priest. In Jewish tradition, he exemplifies the virtues of duty and peacemaking.

Alongside Moses, he performed various miraculous deeds and signs before Pharaoh and his court. Aaron transformed his **rod** into a **serpent**, which consumed the serpents created by Egyptian magicians (Ex. 7). The first three of the ten **plagues** (**blood**, **frogs**, and lice) were initiated by Aaron at God's command (Ex. 7–8).

In his role as High **Priest** of the new sacrificial cult of God, Aaron enjoyed supernatural protection. He survived a trial by ordeal when his authority was challenged by **Korach** and his kinsmen. His status as High Priest evidently immunized him from divine punishment (Ex. 34; Num. 8) and he was instrumental in checking a plague sent by God among the Israelites by performing a rite with **incense** from the **altar** (Num. 17:1–15). According to the **Bible**, Aaron died by the will of God before entering the Land of Israel.

Rabbinic literature describes miraculous events surrounding the death of Aaron. God placed one mountain on top of another to mark where Aaron would be buried, which is why the Bible calls his burial place *Hor ha-Har* ("Mount Mountain"). Aaron was laid to rest on a couch in a luminous **cave** on Mount Hor by **angels**. He was then enveloped by a **Cloud** of **Glory** and he died by the **kiss** of God (Yalkut, Chukkat 764; Lev. R. 10; Mid. Teh. 83.1).

In the mystical theosophy of the **sefirot**, Aaron symbolizes the emanation of **Hod**, divine glory. He is also one of the **ushpizin**, the spiritual ancestors invited to sit in the sukkah with the living during the holiday of **Sukkot**.

It is interesting to note that despite the many theurgic-religious elements in the biblical accounts of him and the magical attributes of his rod, unlike Moses, Aaron is not widely portrayed as a magician in non-Jewish circles.

Aaron of Baghdad: A mysterious, possibly mythical figure, whom early medieval mystics in Western Europe credited with bringing Jewish esoteric traditions to them from the **East**.[1] A number of miraculous tales about him have been preserved in books such as **Sefer Yuhasin**.

1. Scholem, *Major Trends in Jewish Mysticism*, 41, 84.

Abaddon: "Destruction." One of the compartments of **Gehenna** (Masekhet Gehinnom). In the book of Job, it is **Death** personified. The New Testament identifies Abaddon as the "Angel of the Abyss" (Rev. 9:11).

Abba: "Father." A Talmudic holy man who, although not an ordained **rabbi**, has shown spiritual or healing powers. The word is also applied in various ways to the mystical Godhead. *SEE* PARTZUFIM; SEFIROT.

Abbahu, Rabbi: Talmudic Sage (ca. 3rd–4th century). He experienced clairvoyant dreams. An avid collector of lore, both legal and legendary, he preserved a number of stories of how angels intervened in the life of biblical figures (PdRE 16, 43).

Abbaye: A Talmudic Sage and folk healer. Abbaye once tricked Rabbi **Acha** into exorcizing a **demon** from his house of study (Shab. 66b).

Abbreviations: The use of abbreviations appears in Hebrew writings as early as the 2nd century BCE. Variously called **notarikon**, *siman*, or *rosh tevot*, abbreviations have been widely used for the functional purpose of saving space at a time when writing materials were costly and scarce. But even though the origins of the practice are obviously utilitarian, this method of writing is, in fact, a kind of **encryption**. As such, abbreviations can also be a form of esoteric communication. Over time, certain kinds of abbreviations, such as acronyms (words formed from the first letter or syllable of other words) and **acrostics** (verses arranged so that a particular letter from each line, taken in order, spells out a word or phrase), came to be regarded as dynamic sources of secret knowledge and power to Jewish mystics and to magical practitioners of all persuasions.[1] Thus the name for the month preceding the High Holy Days, *Elul*, is seen as an acronym for **A**ni **L'**dodi **V'**dodi **Li** (I am my beloved's and He is mine). In another example, **Be**RESHIT (Gen. 1:1, "In the beginning") is understood to be an acronym for *Bara Rakia, Eretz, Shamayim, Yam Tahom*, "He created the firmament, land, heaven, sea, and abyss."

In Kabbalah, abbreviations are sometimes called *tzeruf otiyot,* or letter combinations. Perhaps the most famous of these is related to the Talmudic story (Ber. 55a) of the **four Sages** who entered **Pardes** (Paradise). Tradition teaches that *pardes* ("orchard") is an acronym for the four methods of **Torah** interpretation: *Pashat, Remez, D'rash,* and *Sod* (plain meaning, allegoric, homiletic, and esoteric). In other words, the living may find entry to Paradise by penetrating into the mysteries concealed within the Torah text.

Abbreviations are also an almost universal feature on **amulets**. One talismanic acronym is the word **Shaddai** (shin-dalet-yud) that appears on a **mezuzah**. The word itself is a biblical **name of God**, but also stands for *Shomer Delatot Yisrael* (Guardian of the doorways of Israel). The presence of this acronym-incantation helps give the mezuzah its protective power. **Magic squares** and diagrams constructed from different kinds of abbreviations dot medieval Jewish books on mystical knowledge, **magic**, and **alchemy**.

Names of worthy figures are sometimes held to be abbreviations of esoteric teachings. Thus the name **Jacob**, *YAaKoV*, is actually made up of four titles of God, **Y**otzrecha, **O**secha, **K**onecha, and **B**orecha (your Former, your Maker, your Owner, your Creator), revealing God's special relationship with Jacob, and through him, his descendants. The most notable and widespread name abbreviation custom to this day is the various methods adopted for writing an abbreviation for the **Tetragrammaton** so that it may not be pronounced and to thereby prevent the erasure or destruction of God's written name. *ALSO SEE* ANAGRAM; HAFUCH; ISRAEL; TEMURAH; TZERUF.

1. Singer, *Jewish Encyclopedia*, vol. 1, 39–43.

Abdiel: An angel mentioned in **Sefer Raziel**.

Abihu: The brother of Nadav. *SEE* NADAV AND AVIHU.

ABiYAh: This word is a mystical acronym for the **four worlds of emanation**: **Atzilut**, **Beriyah**, **Yetzirah**, and **Asiyah**.

Ablution: *SEE* IMMERSION; MIKVAH; WATER.

Abner: The commander of Saul's army. The Philistines were not the only ancients who employed **giants**. Abner was so enormous that while he slept, David was able to crawl beneath his crooked knees and so escape a trap Saul had set for him (Eccl. R. 9:11; Yalkut Jer. 285; AbbS). He was the son of the **Woman of Endor** (PdRE 33).

Abracadabra: The archetypal *voce magica*, magical word. Many claim it to be of Jewish origin reading it as a kind of fractured Aramaic, *ab'ra k'dabra*, meaning, "I will create according to the word." This is very plausible, assuming the Aramaic syntax has undergone corruption. It is also plausible that it is of non-Jewish origin. *SEE* HEBREW ALPHABET; INCANTATIONS; MAGIC.

Abraham: (Hebrew: *Avraham*). The progenitor of the Jewish people, Abraham is also considered in rabbinic tradition to be a natural philosopher, mystic, and a prophet second only to Moses. He personifies loving-kindness, devotion, and faithfulness.

In the **Bible**, Abraham not only responds to the direct command of God to leave his homeland for Canaan, he has several encounters with **angels** (Gen. 18, 22). In the **Midrash**, he is granted many miracles. To save him as an infant from the wrath of evil King **Nimrod**, he is secreted away in a cave, where the angels feed and minister to him. According to the text Ma'asei Avraham Avenu, God later delivers him from a fiery martyrdom planned for him by Nimrod.

In several sources, he is celebrated as an astrologer (Book of Jubilees; B.B. 16b). In one Midrash, he sees his infertility is written in stars, but comes to learn that God has power over even the astral influences. This then explains God's decision to change his name from Abram to Abraham (Gen. 15), for in changing his name, God also changes his fate. From this experience, Abraham gives up the practice of astrology (Zohar III: 216a; Aggadat Bereshit).

The reason God commands him to circumcise himself (Gen. 17) is that this act of self-perfection will make the spirit of prophecy more accessible to him (PdRE 29; Tanh., Lech Lecha 20).

In the **Zohar** he is credited with the knowledge to create a **golem** (I: 79a), a knowledge alluded to in the biblical text (Gen. 12:5). This tradition springs from a single reference to him in the final chapter of **Sefer Yetzirah**. Because of this same reference, some mystics also regard Abraham to be the author of that work. Abraham also possessed a miraculous healing stone, the **tzohar**. After his death, God suspended it from the sun, enhancing the sun's healing powers (B.B. 16b).

In early Kabbalah, Abraham comes to be regarded as an archetype, a personification of sefirotic attributes. In later works this logic is reversed, with Abraham being treated as a divine attribute whose dynamic function in the world is expressed allegorically through the Abraham saga found in the Torah. He represents the sefirah of Chesed, pure love. (Pes. 118a; Gen. R. 38, 61; Seder Eliyahu Rabbah, 1:13; Zohar, Bahir). SEE PATRIARCHS AND MATRIARCHS; RIGHTEOUS, THE.

Abraham, Apocalypse of: A 2nd-century-CE document that contains revelations of future history and a vision of heaven, probably of Jewish origin but also now including Christian glosses. It exists today only in Slavic language translation.

Abraham Azulai: Kabbalist (Moroccan, ca. 17th–18th century). He wrote Avraham L'chesed and an influential commentary on the Zohar. One source credits him with performing wondrous deeds, but as there are at least three prominent Abrahams in the Azulai family, this cannot be verified.

Abraham ben David of Posquieres: Mystic and polemicist (Provencal, ca. 12th century). He experienced a visitation of **Elijah** (Commentary on Yad ha-Chazakah).

Abraham ben Moses: Kabbalist (Egyptian, ca. 13th century). Rabbi Abraham, a mystic influenced by Sufism, is most notable for being the son of **Maimonides**.

Abraham ben Simeon: Magician, alchemist, and world traveler (German, ca. 14th century). Abraham is the author of *Cabala Mystica*, "The Mysterious Tradition" (or alternately, *Segullat Melakhim*, or "The Book of Sacred Magic"). Abraham not only told tales of how he enjoyed royal patronage from many European princes, he even claimed to have given two popes occult advice. Much of what we know about Abraham is in doubt—the veracity of these stories themselves, or even whether Abraham was actually a Jew or a Christian of Jewish parentage.[1]

1. Patai, *The Jewish Alchemists*, 271–89.

Abraham ibn Ezra: SEE IBN EZRA, ABRAHAM.

Abraham, Testament of: The Testament is a 2nd-century-CE apocalyptic text describing Abraham's **ascent** into heaven. It appears to be a Jewish text heavily glossed by Christian copyists. It survives only in Greek.

Abraxis: An **angel** mentioned in the Gnostic tradition that appears in later Jewish **amulets** and in Medieval Jewish angelologies.

Abu Aharon: Healer and wunder-rabbi (Italian, ca. 10th century), he performed **exorcisms**, broke the spells of **witches**, and combated **zombies** (Sefer Yuhasin).

Abulafia, Abraham: (1240–1291?). Medieval Spanish Kabbalist, self-proclaimed prophet, and failed **messiah**. Abulafia practiced and taught a sophisticated and novel form of ecstatic (or as he called, "prophetic") Kabbalah that, until recent times, has not received much general attention, no doubt due to his controversial personality and career. In his own lifetime, his claims and unorthodox teachings earned him condemnation from rabbinical authorities. Fortified by belief in his own messianic identity, Abulafia at one point sought an audience before Pope Nicholas III in order to convert him. Not surprisingly, he was imprisoned for spreading his "gospel." More surprising is that he actually survived the ordeal, outliving the Pope in question. His teachings are enjoying a revival on two fronts: renewed scholarly research, and the revival of his techniques within contemporary meditative circles.[1] *SEE* MEDITATION; TZERUFIM; VISIONS.

> 1. Scholem, *Major Trends in Jewish Mysticism*, 120–46; Kaplan, *Meditation and Kabbalah*, 57–71. Also see Idel, *The Mystical Experience in Abraham Abulafia*.

Abyss: (*Tehom*). The name for the primordial waters that preceded Creation and are now trapped below the crust of the earth (Gen. 1; Gen. R. 13:13; Ps. 104). In **Temple** times, the ritual of the **water libations** was performed to draw up these tellurian waters to help to moisten and fructify the earth (Tan. 25b).

It can also refer to the realm of the dead, the place where evil spirits and wicked souls dwell. In later Jewish eschatology, it is one of the seven compartments of **Gehenna** (Masekhet Gehinnom). *SEE* CHAOS; WATER.

Academy on High: *SEE* YESHIVA SHEL MALAH.

Acha ben Jacob: Talmudic Sage (ca. 4th century). He was a storyteller, folk healer, and exorcist. He once defeated a **demon** in the form of a seven-headed hydra (Kid. 29b; B.B. 75b).

Acherit ha-Yamim: "The End of Days." *SEE* JUDGMENT, DAY OF; ESCHATOLOGY; MESSIAH.

Acrostic: *SEE* ABBREVIATIONS; NOTARIKON; HAFUCH; TEMURAH; TZERUF.

Adam: (*Adam Rishon*). Adam is the first human being and an archetype for all humanity. One Kabbalistic teaching reveals that the word *ADaM* is a mystical abbreviation for the essence of human nature: **A**damah (earth), **D**ibur (speech), and **M**a'aseh (action).

God placed him in the Garden of **Eden**. According to **Alef-Bet of Ben Sira**, he was wed first to **Lilith**, whom God had made simultaneously with him. When they argued, she flew off to become the queen of **demons**. Only after that did God create **Eve** (AbbS).

He also had numerous other dealings with **angels** and demons. **Gabriel** and **Michael** were the witnesses at his wedding to Eve. Not only was he later tricked by the **serpent**, but he was also seduced by **succubae**, generating demonic offspring (Eruv. 18b; Gen. R. 20:11; PdRE 20). Before his expulsion from Eden, Adam was clothed in divine **Glory**. After the fall, God made miraculous **garments** for both Adam and Eve that never wore out. Adam also received from the angel **Raziel** the **tzohar**, a gemstone holding the primordial **light** of Creation. Along with Eve, he was laid to rest in the **Cave** of Machpelah in the middle of the Garden of Eden, where their bodies lie concealed from mortal sight in a state of luminescent and fragrant preservation. The **Zohar** teaches that at the hour of death every person sees Adam (Num. R. 19:18; Gen. R. 17; B. Eruv. 18b; A.Z. 8a; Sot. 9b; Tanh., Bereshit; Zohar I: 127a–b). *SEE* GARMENTS OF ADAM.

Adam Baal Shem: Mysterious Kabbalist who performed healings, magically defeated anti-Semitic plots, and eventually transmitted secret teachings of the Torah to the **Baal Shem Tov**. He is probably Adam of Bingen, a wonder-working rabbi who enjoyed some notoriety in the court of the Holy Roman Empire.[1] He makes several appearances in Jewish folktales.

> 1. Rabinowicz, *The Encyclopedia of Hasidism*, 8.

Adam, The Book of: An eccentric reading of Genesis 5:1, "This is the book of the generations of Adam . . ." inspires the tradition that there is a Book of Adam, separate from Genesis, which contains a genealogy of all the human generations that will ever exist. Some equate it with **Sefer Raziel**. Separate from the legendary book, there is an actual apocryphal book entitled "The Book of Adam." (B.M. 85b–86a; Gen. R. 24:1; Sanh. 38b).

Adam Kadmon: "Primordial Man." Also called *Adam Elyon* or *Adam Ila'ah*. Not to be confused with the frail figure of Adam in the Genesis account who is formed from clay (Gen. 2:7), Adam Kadmon is the supernal, first creation of God that is made in the divine image (Gen. 1:26–27). Drawing on Platonic notions of "forms," the teachings about Adam Kadmon explain that he is the true "image of God," a majestic vessel of divine **Glory**, the ideal human (PdRK 4:4, 12:1; Lev. R. 20:2). All earthly humans are in *his* image. We are an image of an image, as it were (B.B. 58a).

According to the **Midrash**, Adam Kadmon is androgynous, incorporating all the aspects of both genders. He is also a macrocosm, extending from one end of the universe to the other and containing all Creation. When he was created, in fact, he was so awesome the **angels** mistook him for God and began to worship him (Gen. R. 8:1; Lev. R. 14:1, Chag. 12b, 14b).

The "heavenly man" becomes a prominent aspect of many Kabbalistic systems. In some, Adam Kadmon signifies the totality of the **sefirot**. Often, the ten sefirot are shown superimposed on the figure of the Adam Kadmon to represent his mediating role between God and Creation—he is literally the embodiment of divine attributes as well as the place of the universe. In Lurianic Kabbalah, he is the light that fills primordial space after the light of God is withdrawn. Luria sees the Jewish project as bringing a restoration of humanity to the state of Adam Kadmon. **Chayyim Vital** sees Adam Kadmon as a kind of "world soul" and finds repetitions of him at each stage of the chain of Creation (Gen. R. 8:1, 10; Sanh. 38a; Zohar II: 48a, 70b; Etz ha-Chayyim). He also teaches that various facets of all the subsequent human souls are derived from different "limbs" of Adam Kadmon and that the traits and qualities in a given soul reflect the location from which they were derived (Sefer ha-Hezyonot).

Some scholars regard **Gnosticism** as the source for the Jewish tradition of Adam Kadmon.[1] Christian Scriptures also allude to the tradition of Adam Kadmon, linking the idea to Jesus (I Corinthians 15:45–50). This idea reappears in the heretical sect of Shabbateanism, which holds **Shabbatai Tzvi** to be both the messiah and the incarnation of Adam Kadmon.

The concept of Adam Kadmon has served mystics in their efforts to exalt and elevate the status of humanity (in potential) and emphasize the divine aspect of man. *(SEE APPENDIX FIGURE 3.)*

1. Couliano, *The Tree of Gnosis*, 99–100, 113, 165–66.

Adam Rishon: *SEE ADAM.*

Adamah: "Earth." In the **Zohar**, it is the third of the seven material worlds. This is where humans and demons interacted freely (Sitre Torah, Zohar I: 253b–254a).

Adar: This month in the Hebrew **calendar** falls in the spring. Its **zodiac** is **Dagim**. The minor holiday of Purim occurs in Adar. As the last month before Nisan, the month of Exodus, before the events of Purim it was considered an ill-fortuned month.[1]

1. Erlanger, *Signs of the Times*, 245.

Adat El: "Divine Assembly." The Bible describes the God of Israel as presiding over a conclave of divine and numinous beings (Deut. 32; Ps. 82; Job 1). The assembly gathers in a sacred tent atop a cosmic **mountain** (Ps. 15; Isa. 14:13). The construction of the **Tabernacle** by the Israelites is meant to provide God with a parallel earthly abode (Ex. 24–25).

In the later books of the Bible and post-biblically, this image is refined into the concept of the angelic court attending upon God, who is envisioned as a divine monarch who consults with the court, but is not bound by their opinions (Sanh. 38b; Gen. R. 8:4). Coinciding with the creation of a permanent earthly **Temple**, the same sources start to re-envision the sacred tent of assembly as a heichal, a "**palace**." *SEE ANGELS; HOST OF HEAVEN.*

Adiriron Adiron: "Mighty of the Mighty." A divine title, originally a euphemism for the **Tetragrammaton** but later regarded as a magical name in its own right, used on **amulets** (Miflaot Elohim).

Adonai: "My Lord." A Jewish appellation for God that gradually became a euphemism commonly used in order to avoid saying the **Tetragrammaton** (Yoma 39b–40a). The word *Adonai* eventually developed an aura of mystery itself. As such, it became a name of power, alongside the Tetragrammaton, attractive to both Jewish and non-Jewish magical practitioners. Consequently, it frequently appears in spells, **amulets**, and other magical devices. *SEE* NAMES OF GOD.

Adonaiel: An angel mentioned in the **Testament of Solomon**.

Adversary, the: *SEE* SATAN.

Af and Chemah: "Wrath" and "Anger." Found in the seventh level of heaven, these two angels of monstrous proportions are chained together with bonds of black and red **fire** (Gedulat Moshe). In other texts, Chemah is listed among God's punishing angels.

Afikoman: *SEE* PASSOVER; UNLEAVENED BREAD.

Afterlife: *SEE* DEATH; ETERNAL LIFE; KINGDOM OF GOD; RE-INCARNATION; RESURRECTION.

Aggadah: "Story/Narrative/Legend." This is the catchall term for all the non-legal materials in rabbinic literature—narratives, interpretations, poems, theology, etc. Most mythic, fabulous, and occult teachings are found embed-ded in the aggadic portions of Jewish literature.

AGLA: An acrostic name of God constructed from the Hebrew phrase, *Attah gibor l'olam Adonai*, "You are eter-nally mighty, O Eternal." It was often used in exorcism rites, Christian as well as Jewish.

Agrat: *SEE* IGRAT.

Agriculture: *SEE* FERTILITY; FIRSTBORN; FOOD; ISRAEL, LAND OF.

Ahijah: A prophet who lived in the time of King Je-roboam. The teacher of **Elijah**, he was a master of the es-oteric **Torah** (J. Eruv. 5:1; Sanh. 102a; Mid. Teh. 5:8). Long after death, this biblical figure reappears as the **mag-gid**, the spirit guide, to the **Baal Shem Tov**.

Ahimaaz, Megillat or Sefer: *SEE* YUHASIN, SEFER.

Ahimaaz ben Paltiel: Adventurer and **wunder-rabbi** (Italian, ca. 11th century). His magical deeds and the deeds of his family are recorded in **Sefer Yuhasin**.

Aish M'tzaref: "Fire of the Refiner." A 16th-century tractate on **alchemy** and **Kabbalah**.

Akatriel-YaH: Super-angelic figure mentioned in Talmud tractate Berachot (7a–b). In this passage he is seen sitting on the **Throne of Glory** and the voice of God speaks through him. This enigmatic passage has been subject to much interpretation; some scholars regard Akatriel-YaH to be yet another name for **Metatron**, while others theo-rize that perhaps Akatriel is a personification of God's **Glory**. Extra-Talmudic texts only deepen the confusion. One angel-adjuring text includes Akatriel in a list of seven angels. On the other hand, a **Cairo Geniza** fragment clearly regards Akatriel-YaH to be a **name of God**.[1] *SEE* MALACH-ADONAI.

1. Abrams, "From Divine Shape to Angelic Being," 46–63.

Akiba (or Akiva) ben Joseph: Talmudic Sage, biblical exegete and mystic (ca. 1st–2nd century). He is arguably the most celebrated figure in the **Talmud**. He was the only one of the **four Sages** who entered **Pardes** and returned unscathed. His prayers were credited with end-ing a drought. He encountered a **ghost** and subsequently exorcised it by teaching the dead man's son the daily lit-urgy; this is credited by some with establishing the tradi-tion of reciting **Kaddish** for the dead (Seder Eliyahu Zuta). As one of the **ten martyrs**, his willingness to die for the sake of God's honor prevented God from undoing Creation (Midrash Eleh Ezkarah).

Akkum: "Akkum" is an acronym formed from the words *Oved Kochavim U'Mazilim*, "worshipper of stars and con-stellations." As such, it serves as a standard Talmudic term for a pagan. Some Christians claimed it stood for *Oved Kristos U'Miriam*, "worshipper of Christ and Mary" (highly improbable, since it involves conflating Greek and Hebrew) and that all negative references to pagans found in the Talmud were actually directed at Christianity, a belief that re- sulted in widespread Christian censorship of the Talmud in Europe.[1]

  1. Singer, *The Jewish Encyclopedia*, vol. 1, 312.

Akrav: "Scorpion." The **zodiac** sign for the month of Cheshvan. This is the weakest of the signs, a water sign, and it is associated with the forces of decay, melancholy and disorder. It is the month during which the **Flood** occurred and the Matriarch **Rachel** died.[1]

  1. Erlanger, *Signs of the Times*, 145–58.

Alchemy: The Hermetic tradition, one part theosophy, one part **astrology**, and one part experimental science, was first expounded in writings attributed to the Egyptian Hermes Trismegistus. Emerging in late antiquity, alchemy was a profoundly spiritual pursuit, a quest to uncover the potential for transformation of the natural order through the study of transformation in certain iconic natural sub- stances—metals. Some alchemists even envisioned their rit- ualistic chemistry as a kind of sacrificial rite.[1]

Alchemy has been associated with Jews since antiquity. **Moses** is credited with being the teacher of Hermes him- self, but this may also represent a conflation of the biblical Moses with the figure of **Moses of Alexandra**, an Egyp- tian-Jewish alchemist of antiquity. Some traditions credit the Patriarchs with transmitting alchemical knowledge (along with the **philosopher's stone**) that was learned from **Adam**. **Bezalel**, the builder of the **Mishkan**, is said to have been an alchemist (Ex. 31:1–5). Late traditions as- sociate **David** and **Solomon** with the Hermetic arts, based on the biblical account of how David gave Solo- mon stones, assumed by later readers to be philosopher's stones (I Chron. 22:14). One ancient alchemist even in- terpreted the sacrifices made in Solomon's Temple as na- scent alchemical rituals. By far the most important and influential historical Jewish alchemist of ancient times is **Maria Hebraea**.

Medieval alchemists, both Jewish and gentile, frequently claimed occult knowledge of Kabbalah. The **Zohar** of **Moses (Shem Tov) de Leon** and the writings of **Abra- ham Abulafia** show a familiarity with alchemy. Direc- tions for the making of **gold** appear in several Kabbalistic works, and Jewish scholars debated whether such transfor- mations were actually possible.

Because Kabbalah was so widely applied by Christian alchemists to their work, by the dawn of the modern era alchemy and Jews were uniquely linked, though this ap- pears to be more perception than reality. So ingrained was this perception that, in order to give their ideas more gravitas, a number of treatises on alchemy were evidently published by non-Jews using Jewish pseudonyms.

Actual Jewish practitioners include Jacob Aranicus (French, ca. 13th century), Isaac and John Isaac **Hollander** (Dutch, ca. 15th century), Modecai Modena (Italian, ca. 16th century) and **Samuel de Falk** (English, ca. 18th cen- tury). Even Baruch Spinoza expressed an interest in it. Oddly, however, few Hebrew language alchemical texts authored by Jews have survived to the present.[1]

  1. Janowitz, *Icons of Power*, 109–22; also see Patai, *The Jewish Alchemists*.

Alef: The first letter of the **Hebrew alphabet**, it is a si- lent letter, taking on the sound value of whatever vowel is assigned to it. In gematria, it has the numeric value of 1. It is the first letter of the first word in the **Ten Com- mandments**. One tradition claims this silent *alef* was the only sound actually pronounced by God at Mount Sinai, but even that "silent sound" was too much for the mortal listeners, who were slain by the power of God's voice and had to be revived with angelic kisses (S of S R. 5:16). Its very shape is made from the fusion of other letters, two yods and a vav, whose combined numeric value is 26, the same value of the **Tetragrammaton**. Alef is therefore a symbol of God's utter unity and God's mystery. In the writings of **Moses Cordovero**, alef flows from Keter, the highest of the sefirotic emanations.[1]

  1. Munk, *The Wisdom of the Hebrew Alphabet*, 43–54.

Alef-Bet of Ben Sira: (*Otiyyot ben Sira*). Also called "Pseudo ben Sira," it is a satirical **Midrash** composed in the Middle Ages arranged in twenty-two sections to mir- ror the twenty-two letters of the **alphabet**. According to this book, Joshua ben Sira (the author of the work, Ben Sira) was both the child and grandchild of the prophet Jer- emiah. This is possible because a gang of villains forced Jeremiah to masturbate in a pool and his semen later en- tered into his daughter as she bathed. The rest of the nar- rative about ben Sira's life continues on in a similar tone.

The whole book satirizes biblical figures, Jesus, and even God. Parts of the book were so offensive that even the scribes who took the time to copy it felt the need to censor it. Perhaps the most famous passage is its unique version of the **Lilith** legend. In the context of this work it is clearly meant as yet another parody on traditional Jewish teachings. Yet since its inclusion in 19th-century anthologies of Midrashim, it came to be widely regarded as a legitimate part of Jewish esoteric lore.[1]

1. Dan, *The 'Unique Cherub' Circle*, 16–29.

Alef-Bet of Rabbi Akiba: (*Otiyyot de Rabbi Akiba*). A collection of **Merkavah** teachings, including elements of **Shi'ur Qomah**, compiled sometime between the 7th and 10th centuries CE. It includes many magical traditions.

Aleinu: This prayer of the Jewish liturgy is effective against spirit possession if recited seven times, forward and backward (Zanfat Pa'aneah). *SEE* INCANTATIONS; REVERSAL.

Alemanno, Johannan: Magician and Kabbalist (Italian, ca. 15th century), Alemanno was a tutor to Pico della Mirandola, the Renaissance-era **Christian Qabbalist**.

Alexander the Great: When Alexander (356–323 BCE) came to Jerusalem during his conquests, Simon the Righteous came out to meet him and Alexander bowed down to him, to the amazement of his servants. Alexander told them that a vision of Simon's image appeared to him in battle and made him victorious. Alexander also saw God's name written on Simon's diadem, remembered it, and thus introduced the gentiles to the **Tetragrammaton**, God's name of power (Josephus, Ant. 6:317–39; Yoma 69a).

Alitha: A fantastic beast capable of extinguishing any fire (Midrash ha-Gadol).

Alkebetz, Solomon: Mystical poet (Turkish, ca. 16th century). Author of the mystical liturgical poem *Lecha Dodi*, Alkebetz was a spiritual practitioner of **gerushin**, a mystical soul-projection technique achieved by **incubation** on the graves of saintly individuals.

Almoli, Solomon ben Jacob: Oneiromancer (Turkish, ca. 16th century). He is author of **Pitron Chalomot**, "The Interpretation of Dreams," the most comprehensive text on oneiromancy written by a Jew. *SEE* DREAMS.

Almonds: (*Shaked*). With their fruit encased in a shell and their eyelike shape, almonds are a symbol of concealed wisdom and divine favor. They seem particularly linked to the priesthood. The oil cups on the **menorah** were almond shaped (Ex. 26). Aaron's **rod** was made of almond wood and sprouted blossoms during his **ordeal** with other contenders for the High Priesthood (Num. 17). Almonds are eaten in order to ward off the **evil eye**.

Alphabet, Hebrew: *SEE* HEBREW AND HEBREW ALPHABET.

Alphabet, Magical: A set of symbols consisting of lines terminating in circles that was a popular feature in ancient and medieval magical inscriptions and **amulets**. Scholars sometimes refer to these symbols as *brillenbuchstaben*, "eye-glass" symbols, because the circles at the ends of the characters resemble monocles. The number of magical signs found on Hebrew magical texts far exceeds the twenty-two letters of the **Hebrew alphabet**, so evidently talisman makers assigned their own phonetic or hieroglyphic values to these symbols. Consequently, no definitive system for their translation or interpretation is available to us.[1]

1. Naveh and Shaked, *Magic Spells and Formulae*, 109; Trachtenberg, *Jewish Magic and Superstition*, 140–42.

Alroy, David: False messiah (Iraqi, ca. 12th century). Alroy claimed to be the **Messiah** ben David and declared war against the Seljuk Sultan. He was an accomplished sorcerer, performing many wonders for his followers, and even once escaping captivity by magical means. According to one legend, he met his end by telling his followers to decapitate him, so that he could be resurrected. The first phase of his plan worked perfectly (Benjamin of Tedula; Shalshelet ha-Kabbalah).

Altar: (*Mizbei'ach*). A surface used for **sacrifices**, usually elevated upon a pillar of stone(s). Throughout the **Bible**, altars are erected at the sites of divine appearances or revelations (Gen. 15, 22, 28), which were considered numinous places from that time forward. The presence of an altar therefore constituted a shrine. In later Jewish thought, the altar represents a harmonizing principle between God and humanity.

Israelite altars were made of a pillar of unhewn stones supporting a square platform with "horns," or projections rising at each corner (Ex. 22, 29). Israelite practice featured two different kinds of altars, one for the animal and meal offers, and another for the burning of incense.

The word itself, *Mizbei'ach*, is regarded to be an acronym for *Mehila, Zachut, Berachah, Chayyim*: "forgiveness, merit, blessing, and life."

Once found on innumerable high places across the land, such altars disappeared when all sacrifice was centralized in Jerusalem as a reform measure to curb idolatry and syncretistic practices. Licit sacrifices in the cult of the God of Israel, according to the Bible, included **incense**, kosher **animals**, meal, **oil**, **salt**, and even **water**.

There is evidence that Jews living far from their homeland erected altars to the God of Israel, despite the prohibitions stipulated in the Bible. For example, the Jewish garrison in Elephantine, Egypt had one, but also engaged in syncretistic worship of local deities alongside the God of Israel. There is also an episode reported in **Talmud** in which a sacrifice was made even without an altar (Zev. 116b). Over time this kind of practice was extinguished and anything even remotely resembling an altar in form or function was purged from Judaism. Thus any use of an altar from that period forward only occurs in occult or illicit rituals. The use of such an unsanctioned altar is mentioned, for example, in **Sefer ha-Razim**.

In the absence of the cult, the Rabbis declared the kitchen table (i.e., the Jewish home) to be the "small altar" of God.

Aluka: "Leech." This is a traditional Hebrew term for a **vampire**. Some texts also identify it as a name for one of the seven compartments of **Gehenna** (Gedulat Moshe 41; Sefer Chasidim).

Amalek: The tribal and metaphysical nemesis of Israel. Deuteronomy commands Israel to "blot out" Amalek—originally identified in the **Bible** as a tribal people who massacred vulnerable Israelites coming up from Egyptian slavery—from under heaven, for God "will be at war with Amalek throughout the ages" (Ex. 17, 18; Deut. 25). The later failure of Saul to kill Agag, the King of the Amalekites, alienates God from him.

Because of Saul's error, descendants of the Amalekites continue to threaten Israel across the ages. **Haman** was a descendant of Agag. The Romans were also identified as children of Amalek. Since rabbinic times it has been idiomatic to describe any implacable enemy of the Jews as "Amalek" (Ant. 11; MdRI; Ex. R. 26; PdRK 27).

Amemnar: Sorceress mentioned in **Talmud** (Pes. 110).

Ammi: Talmudic Sage, folk healer, and diviner (ca. 3rd century). His remedies appear in Horayot 12a and Avodah Zarah 28a–b.

Ammon of No: Variations of this name appear in lists of fallen angels and demons across Jewish literature. He is the angel/demon governing **alchemy**, **dreams**, and **Christianity**.[1] *SEE* REINA, JOSEPH DELLA.

1. Schwarz, *Kabbalah and Alchemy*, 108.

Amtachat Binyamin, Sefer: An 18th-century compilation of segullot, formulae for making **amulets**, and medicinal prayers and treatments, composed by the Baal Shem Binyamin Binush.

Amulet: (*Kamia*, "Binder"). An amulet or charm is an object or device, usually with writing on it, which provides protection against harm, whether of natural or supernatural origin. The use of amulets and charms is virtually universal across human cultures and across time, and Jews are no exception. Jewish amulets have been used to ward off a variety of ills: disease, mishap, dangerous animals, sorcery, and/or malevolent spirits. They can also serve as love charms. They have been particularly used by Jews to induce **fertility**, protect women during pregnancy, and to shield newborn infants. For many Jews, amulets signified human empowerment in the face of unseen and malevolent forces in the world.[1]

Amulets take many forms throughout the different periods of Jewish history. The use of amulets to ward off evil spirits and/or disease was pervasive in the cultures that surrounded ancient Israel, and numerous examples of Canaanite, Phoenician, Assyrian, and Egyptian origin have been recovered. The use of amulets by biblical Israelites is specifically criticized in Isaiah 3:18–20. It is unclear from the context whether amulets qua amulets are being condemned, or whether they are merely included in a list of vanities and luxuries associated with women. Only two physical examples of amulets from the biblical era have been uncovered so far. The first is a tomb inscription found at Khibet el Qom dating to the 8th century BCE asking for the protection of YHWH and his **Asherah**. The second is also a tomb artifact, but this one consisting of two rolled-up copper plates inscribed with the Priestly Blessing (Num. 6:24–25) found at Ketef Hinnom and dating from the 7th century.[2]

Evidence for the use of amulets grows dramatically post-biblically. II Maccabees 12:40 reports disapprovingly of slain Jewish warriors found wearing amulets with foreign gods inscribed on them. Again, it is unclear whether the author objects to talismans in general or to just these syncretistic examples. Of course, the **tefillin** worn by Jews on the head and arm to fulfill the commandment (Deut. 6:8) are regarded as having talismanic properties by some Jews, thought that is not their formal function. The Latin word for *tefillin*, *phylactery* ("safeguard") highlights this perception. Likewise, in some circles the **mezuzah** put on the doorpost of Jewish homes is also regarded as a charm against misfortune.

The Sages are largely at ease with the use of amulets, saying that "anything that effects healing is not considered witchcraft" (Shab. 67a), and discussing their use to protect people (particularly children), animals, and property. Amulets were considered a regular part of the medical response to illness and the Sages speak of experienced *kamia* makers who have a proven track record of making efficacious amulets. They also discuss the criteria for judging a good medical amulet (Shab. 61b; Yoma 84a). They do, however, place limits on the sanctity with which amulets may be treated, even ones with God's name inscribed on them (Shab. 115b). The Babylonian Talmud distinguishes between written amulets and folk amulets, the latter being called *kamia shel ikrin* and being made from roots (rather like a medicine bag). We have a number of written metallic amulets, mostly in Aramaic, from that era. Features of these charms include biblical phrases, **names of God**, and strings of *nomina barbara*, or nonsense words and phrases. **Atbash** (letter substitution) codes are sometimes used. Often foreign loan words appear and, on occasion, unpronounceable divine and angelic names. Diagrams, magical **alphabets**, and crude illustrations are common but not constant features. Many written amulets were rolled up and inserted in **metal** tubes, the same way a *mezuzah* is protected and displayed (Sanh. 63b; Pes. 111a–b).

Of the sample of amulets from late antiquity that have been found, perhaps the most intriguing are **incantation bowls**: pottery dishes painted with incantations and then buried under the doorpost of a house to trap underworld spirits who attempt to enter.[3]

Beginning in the Middle Ages, amulets appear that are designed to protect against the *ayin ha-ra*, the **evil eye**. Many more physical examples of amulets from the medieval period have survived, giving us a clearer picture of the forms, as well as the logic behind them. Many examples of silver, lead, and pewter amulets have come down to us, so metal is apparently a preferred material for amulet making, though it may also be that metal's durability means more examples of these types of charms have survived.[4]

Despite the ridicule of a few rationalists like **Maimonides**, amulet making was considered a worthy religious undertaking by most Jews. **Eleazar of Worms** and **Moses Zacuto** were both advocates for them. **Sefer Chasidim** even permits the limited use of amulets made by non-Jews (247, 1114). Quite a number of amulet recipe books have survived, but by far the most influential was **Sefer Raziel**, which describes their manufacture in detail and prescribes specific times on certain days when engraving amulets will make them potent. Innumerable Jewish amulets have been preserved that were based on the models found in the 1701 printed version. Most controversies about the use of amulets arose not over their effectiveness, but about whether individuals were selling amulets with false claims, or over whether certain amulet designs may have originated in heretical circles, such as that of the false messiah, **Shabbati Tzvi**.

With the advent of modern printing and stamping techniques, amulets have been mass-produced in both metal and paper as pendants, small sheets, or broadsides. The most famous of these is the Middle Eastern tradition of the **Shivitti** talisman, using the words from Psalm 16:8 "I have placed the Eternal always before me." Select amulet makers, like Chayyim Azulai (ca. 18th century), became celebrated figures. The Chasidic community has been very enthusiastic about their use from the very beginnings of their movement (ShB 23, 107, 187), which actually may have dampened the enthusiasm for amulets in the Orthodox community at large because of their distaste for all things Chasidic.

Even today, amulets enjoy widespread use in some traditional Jewish circles, especially among the Chasidic and Oriental (Asian and North African) communities. More modern amulet makers will often use the same kind of animal skin parchment and ink that is used in making a **Sefer Torah**. These modern amulets, sometimes called **segullot**, feature either verses from Scripture with perceived protective properties, or permutations of the names of God. Often these words and anagrams are arranged in **magic squares**, **circles**, **hexagrams**, and other enclosed patterns (either to block out or to trap the malevolent forces) to enhance their power. These also have mathematical associations, being grouped in threes, nines, or other significant numbers.

Popular images appearing on amulets include the protective hand or **chamsa**, **menorahs**, **fish**, and **angels**. A few examples even have crude pictures of the very demonic forces the amulet is meant to ward off. One suspects that the primitive quality of these demonic illustrations is deliberate—yet another way of degrading the power of the evil spirits—because many amulets are designed with attention given to aesthetics and are quite beautiful.

Beyond the materials used, there are rituals of power that must be observed when creating an amulet. Thus the maker will subject himself to a period of purification, usually three days, following the example of the Israelites who purified themselves for three days prior to receiving the **Torah**. Amulet-making manuals list prayers and incantations that must be recited while constructing the *kamia*, along with those spells that will be written on it.

Certain days and times are better for making amulets, and these are carefully observed (Sefer Raziel).

SEE ANGELS; BIRTH; CIRCLES; HEALING; INCANTATION; MAGEN DAVID; MAGIC SQUARES. *(SEE ALSO APPENDIX FIGURES 4 AND 5.)*

1. Klein, *A Time to Be Born*, 37–38, 151–52.
2. Mazar, *Archaeology of the Land of the Bible: 10,000–586 B.C.E.*, 522–26.
3. Naveh and Shaked, *Amulets and Magic Bowls*, 15–20.
4. Roth, *Encyclopedia Judaica*, vol. 1, 907–14.

Anafiel: A princely **angel** who appears in Merkavah literature (III Enoch 6, 18; Hechalot Rabbati). He guards the heavenly palace of **Zebul**. He wears a crown and holds the "signet ring" of God (serves as God's vizier). His status resembles that of **Metatron** in other texts.

Anagram: SEE HAFUCH; NOTARIKON; TEMURAH; TZERUF.

Anak, Anakim: Human-angelic offspring, a race of **giants** related to the Nefalim (Deut. 2:12–21), especially associated with the city of Hebron (Josh. 14:15). They resettled in Philistine territory after the Israelite conquest, accounting for Goliath and his brother (Josh. 11:22).

Ancestors: The belief in the continuing presence of the dead and their influence on the living has been, in different forms, a feature of Jewish belief from earliest times. This has led to venerating the ancestral dead, and even cults dedicated to them. The **Bible** itself refers to such practices as ensuring the dead are gathered together with the clan on ancestral land (Gen. 50:24–25), caring for the dead spirits (Deut. 26:14; Isa. 57:6), and consulting them for occult knowledge (Deut. 18:11; Isa. 8:19–22, 19:3; I Sam. 28:3–25).

It is clear that ancient Israel venerated its dead (Deut. 10:15). Many scholars also believe that the Children of Israel inherited a cult of the ancestral dead, possibly even deified dead, from their Semitic milieu and that it remained a popular belief among Israelites despite the opposition of the prophets. References in the Bible to the *ob*, (a familiar spirit apparently derived from the same Hebrew root as "father") have been considered part of that covert tradition. Other scholars argue that a cult of the beneficent dead was introduced by influence of the Assyrians, who were obsessed with **necromancy**, in the 8th through 7th centuries BCE. From this perspective, all seemingly earlier references found in the Bible are actually anachronisms introduced by later editors.[1] Contrary to the proscription of the **Torah**, the only clear example of a biblical figure who consulted the ancestral dead for guidance is that of **Saul** summoning the dead spirit of the prophet **Samuel** (I Sam. 28:4–25). The account clearly illustrates that the author of Samuel believed necromancy was real, though the end results for Saul were personally disappointing.

With the prophetic verse Jeremiah 31:15–16 serving as *locus classicus*, "A cry is heard in Ramah, wailing, bitter weeping, **Rachel** weeps for her children, she refuses to be comforted . . . ," the Sages of Talmudic times believed that their ancestors were aware of what transpired on earth and would plead before God on behalf of their descendants (Tan. 16a; Men. 53b). Midrash Lamentations Rabbah includes a description of biblical figures like **Abraham**, **Moses**, and Rachel interceding before the Divine Throne when God's judgment is being pronounced against Israel (Lam. R. 24). In time, this idea of the positive influence of the beneficent dead expanded into the doctrine of **zechut avot** (the merit of the ancestors), which became canonized in the daily liturgy with the Avot prayer ("You remember the faithfulness of our ancestors and therefore bring redemption to their children's children . . ."). **Sefer Chasidim** describes how the dead pray for the living (452). As late as the **Zohar**, we find the theme of being reunified with one's relatives is still a prominent expectation of the afterlife (Va-yehi 218b). In later Kabbalah there is a shift from veneration of biological ancestors to "soul" ancestors (see **Reincarnation**).

Under the influence of Christian and Muslim saint veneration, the doctrine of zechut avot eventually evolved into a more direct veneration of the meritorious dead, with practices such as praying to them for their intercession in personal matters. The purported graves of many luminaries—biblical (Rachel's tomb in Bethlehem), rabbinic (**Simon bar Yochai** in Meron), Medieval (**Meir ha-Baal Nes** in Tiberia), and modern (**Nachman of Bratzlav**)—have become the focus of pilgrimages and prayers for divine intervention among the ultra-Ortho

dox. Even the tombs of Jews who would have scoffed at such behavior, like **Maimonides**, have become destinations for Jewish pilgrims and supplicants.

The custom of graveside veneration endures and thrives to this day in some sects of Judaism, and is extended even to such 20th-century figures as the Moroccan faith healer **Baba Sali** and the seventh CHaBaD rebbe, **Menachem Mendel Schneerson**. SEE DEATH; GHOSTS; IBBUR OR DEVEKUT; RIGHTEOUS, THE.

1. Schmidt, *Israel's Beneficent Dead*, 132–263.

Ancient Holy One or Ancient of Days: (*Atik Yomim; Atik Kadisha; Atik ha-Aatika*). Another idiom for God, based on Daniel 7:9. In Talmud, it is that aspect of God that will reveal esoteric teachings to the wise (Pes. 119a; Ber. 17a). In the **Zohar** this term is used to specifically refer to the most hidden aspect of God, either **Ein Sof** or **Keter**. SEE PARTZUFIM.

Androgyny: According to the rabbinic interpretation of Genesis 1:27, the first human, **Adam Kadmon**, was initially created androgynous, with both male and female aspects. Thus man was truly "one," most closely resembling God. Later, God decided that Man needed to be bi-sexual and more like the other creatures. Only then did God divide Adam into two persons, one male and one female (Gen. R. 8:1; Ber. 61a). When people enter into a fit **marriage**, the complete, primeval human is reconstituted through the union (Yev. 63b; Gen. R. 17:2; Zohar I: 85b). Though this myth strikes us today as odd, it conveys the idea that God conceived humanity in essential gender equality, regardless of historical social realities.

Angels and Angelology: (*Malach, Irin, Cheruv, Saraf, Ofan, Chayyah, Sar, Memuneh, Ben Elohim, Kodesh*). In Judaism, an angel is a spiritual entity in the service of God. Angels play a prominent role in Jewish thought throughout the centuries, though the concept has been subject to widely—at times wildly—different interpretations.

A number of numinous creatures subordinate to God appear throughout the Hebrew **Bible**; the *Malach* (messenger/angel) is only one variety. Others, distinguished from angels proper, include **Irinim** (Watchers/High An gels), **Cherubim** (Mighty Ones), **Sarim** (Princes), **Serafim** (Fiery Ones), **Chayyot** ([Holy] Creatures), and **Ofanim** (Wheels). Collective terms for the numinous beings serving God include *Tzeva*, (Host), *B'nai ha-Elohim* or *B'nai Elim* (Sons of God), and *Kedoshim* (Holy Ones). They are constituted into an **Adat El**, a divine assembly (Ps. 82; Job 1). A select number of angels in the Bible (three to be precise) have names. They are **Michael**, **Gabriel**, and (assuming it's a proper name) **Satan**.

Angels can come in a wondrous variety of forms, although the Bible often neglects to give any description at all (Judg. 6:11–14; Zech. 4). They appear humanoid in most biblical accounts (Num. 22) and as such are often indistinguishable from human beings (Gen. 18, 32:10–13; Josh. 5:13–15; Judg. 13:1–5), but they also may manifest themselves as pillars of fire and cloud, or as a fiery bush (Ex. 14; 3). The Psalms characterize phenomena that we regard today as "natural," like lightning, as God's *melachim* (Ps. 104:4). Other divine creatures appear to be winged parts of God's throne (Isa. 6) or of the divine chariot (Ezek. 1). The appearance of cherubim was well enough known to be artistically rendered on the Ark of the Covenant (Ex. 25). Perhaps the most ambiguous creature is the **Malach Adonai**, an angel that may or may not be a visible manifestation of God (compare the wording of Ex. 13:21 to 14:19).

Biblical angels fulfill a variety of functions in the lower worlds, including conveying information to mortals (Zech. 1–4), shielding (Ex. 14), rescuing (Gen. 21), and smiting Israel's enemies. It is interesting to note that by-and-large, biblical angels have responsibilities but no authority. This begins to change with the biblical book of **Daniel**. Daniel includes a number of ideas about angels that are elaborated upon in post-biblical texts, including named angels and guardian angels. Most significant for future Jewish angelology, Daniel posits that all the nations of the world have their own angelic prince, that angels are arranged hierarchically, and that angels have actual, if limited, spheres of authority over mortal realms (also see Deut. 32).

In Job, God grants temporary authority over Job to Satan (chapter 1). Angels seem to have a particularly prominent role in those biblical books written by, or under the influence of, priests (Genesis, **Isaiah**, **Ezekiel**, and **Zechariah**).

Jewish sources of the Greco-Roman period add considerable detail to the traditions of angels found in the Hebrew Scriptures (Jubilees 2:2; Ben Sira 16:26–30). We especially see the first systematic organization of biblical **host of heaven** into a hierarchy of different castes of angels governing and serving on different levels of heaven. Zechariah's reference to the seven **eyes** of God (4:10), for example, is understood to refer to either seven archangels, or the seven angel hosts in the **seven heavens** (I Enoch 61; Testament of the Patriarchs, Levi).

We also see a "quasi-polytheistic" view of the divine order recast in monotheistic terms. Now instead of having minor gods with specific spheres of power, lists of angels appear, all subordinate to God, but each designated with their sphere of authority (III Enoch). This is accompanied by a proliferation of named angels. For the first time we hear of **Uriel**, **Raphael**, Peniel, **Metatron**, and many, many others (I Enoch; Tobit; IV Ezra).

There is also an awareness of an affinity between angels and mortals. Already hinted at in the Bible, it is made clearer post-biblically that the boundary between human and angelic states can be quite permeable. Elaborating on cryptic passages found in the **Bible** (Gen. 5:24; II Kings 2:11), it is taught that exceptional mortals, such as **Enoch**, **Elijah**, and **Serach bat Asher** may be elevated to angelic status (I Enoch; Zohar I: 100a, 129b; T.Z. Hakdamah 16b).

A sense of dualism, stronger than what is found in the Hebrew Scriptures, starts to find expression in late antiquity and leads to angels being divided into camps of light and darkness, as exemplified by the angelology in the **War Scroll** and the **Manual of Discipline** found among the **Dead Sea Scrolls**. The mythic allusion to the misadventures of the **Sons of God** in Genesis 6:2 becomes the *locus classicus* for this belief in evil angels. Thus the legend of **fallen angels** first appears in the pseudepigraphic writings (I Enoch 6, from the section sometimes called the **Book of the Watchers**). The mythos of fallen angels, central to the dualistic priestly mysticism of the **Qumran** sect, eventually becomes a major theological motif in Christianity, but remains largely in the background in rabbinic Judaism, exerting far less influence over subsequent Jewish angelology. It is here also we first see the idea that angels envy humanity, a theme that continues in rabbinic and medieval literature (Sanh. 88b–89a; 109a; Gen. R. 118:6; ChdM). The belief that angels may be invoked and employed by human initiates, later a staple element of **Ma'asei Merkavah** mysticism, first appears at this time (Testament of Solomon).

Generally speaking, rabbinic literature de-emphasizes the importance of angels when compared with their role in the priestly Qumran, apocalyptic, and mystical traditions. For the first time, the idea is suggested that angels have no free will (Shab. 88b; Gen. R. 48:11). But they do have intellect and an inner life; they argue and are capable of errors (Sanh. 38b; Midrash Psalms 18:13). Most angels exist to do a single task (B.M. 86b; Gen. R. 50:2) and exalted as they may be, angels are subordinate to humanity, or at least the righteous (Gen. R. 21; Sand. 93a; Ned. 32a; Deut. R. 1).

Still, references to angels in rabbinic literature are almost as vast as the **host of heaven** themselves.[1] Many divine actions described in Scripture were now ascribed to various angels (Deut. R. 9; Gen R. 31:8; Sanh. 105b). Contrary to this trend, however, the Passover Haggadah pointedly denies that angels played any role in the pivotal event of delivering Israel from Egypt (Magid).

Angelic functions are revealed to be even more varied and their role in the operation of the universe even more pervasive. The figure of *Mavet* (Death) in the Bible is now identified as the *Malach ha-Mavet* (the **Angel of Death**). The Early Jewish concept of a personal angel, of **malach sharet**, **mazal**, or **memuneh**, "ministering" or "guardian" angel and an angelic "deputy," also comes to the fore in rabbinic literature (Rashi on Meg. 3a; Mid. Prov. 11:27; SCh 129, 633, 1162). The idea that the angels form a choir singing the praises of God also captures comment and speculation by the Sages (Gen. R. 78:1). While rabbinic writings offer no systematic angelology comparable to that coming out of contemporaneous Christian, mystical, and magical circles, certain parallel notions can be seen. Thus we learn in Talmud that **Michael**, the angelic prince over Israel, serves as High Priest in *Yerushalyim shel malah*, the heavenly **Jerusalem** (Chag. 12b). Legends concerning the prophet-turned-angel Elijah (Ber. 4b) become one of the most commonplace angelic tales. Elijah frequently appears among mortals, bearing revelations from heaven and resolving inscrutable questions.

That all angels (and not just serafim and cherubim) have wings is first mentioned during this period (Chag. 16a; PdRE 4). The size of angels may vary from small to cosmic (Chag. 13b). Angels also move at different speeds, depending upon their mission (Ber. 4b).

There also emerges a fundamental disagreement about the nature of angels. Some consider angels to be God's "embodied decrees," while others regard them to be elementals made of fire, like an Islamic *ifrit*, or from an impossible combination of fire and water (Sefer Yetzirah 1.7; S of S R. 10; J. R.H. 58; Gedulat Moshe). Others regard them as immaterial, disembodied intellects. Likewise, there seems to be an ongoing controversy about what, or whether, angels eat (Judg. 13; Gen. R. 48:14; B.M. 86b; Zohar I: 102b).

Angelology is a major element in **Merkavah** mysticism. Any practitioner wishing to ascend through the palaces of the heavens and achieve a vision of the divine **Glory** needed to know how to get past the angelic guardians (usually by knowing and invoking their names) at each level (III Enoch). Perhaps even more important to this mystical tradition, angels can be summoned and brought down to earth to serve a human initiate. Many rituals and practices devoted to this end have been preserved in the **Hechalot** writings. Starting in late antiquity, angels are increasingly related to and seen as part of the everyday life of individuals and the functioning of the world. Thus, the names of angels have protective properties and frequently appear on **amulets**, magical inscriptions, and formulae. In the bedtime ritual **Kriat Sh'ma al ha-Mitah**, the angels Michael, Gabriel, Uriel, and Raphael are invoked for protection through the night.

Unlike the biblical writers, the Sages allow themselves to speculate on the origins of angels. They teach, for example, that angels did not pre-exist Creation, but were formed as part of the heavens on the second day (Gen. R. 1:3, 3). Another Rabbi posits that they came into existence on the fifth day, along with all "winged" and "gliding" (bird and fish) creations. Later traditions reconcile the different positions by asserting different kinds of angels came into being at different stages of Creation (Chag. 14b; PdRE 4). The **Zohar** teaches that all angels are the products of specific **sefirot**—angels of love emanate from **Chesed**, punishing angels emanate from **Gevurah**—and each type came into existence coinciding with the emergence of the sefirah that is its source (I: 46a–b). Gradually, a distinction emerges between named angels, which are enduring, and anonymous ephemeral angels, which are constantly coming in and going out of existence (Chag. 14a; Gen. R. 78:1).

Medieval Midrash reiterates and further develops earlier teaching about angels, but it is during this period that individual philosophers start to offer systematic and idiosyncratic interpretations of angels. **Maimonides**, for example, talks about them at length in his Mishneh Torah, in Hilchot Yisodei ha-Torah (Laws of the Foundations of the Torah). While he meticulously classifies angelic rankings (there are ten) in his rationalistic system, Maimonides equates them with the Aristotelian "intelligences" that mediate between the spheres. As such, they are conscious and govern the spheres in their motion, but in his Aristotelian context Maimonides is saying they are forms of natural causation rather than supernatural beings. He also expands his definition to include natural phenomenon and even human psychology (he refers to the libidinous impulse as the "angel of lust"). He also denies that angels ever take corporeal form; the encounters described in the Bible are only the dream visions of the **Patriarchs and Matriarchs**.

By contrast, other thinkers, like the **German Pietist Eleazer of Worms**, adhere to esoteric and unapologetically supernatural angelologies. Because of the exalted status of **Torah** study among Ashkenazi Jews, rituals for summoning angels, especially angels who could reveal secrets of the Torah, like the **Sar ha-Torah** and **Sar ha-Panim** (The Prince of the Torah and the Prince of the Presence), became widely known.

The early medieval magical work **Sefer ha-Razim** catalogs hundreds of angels, along with how to influence them and use their names in constructing protective amulets, throwing curses, and otherwise gaining power. The Zohar continues the tradition of angelic taxonomy, ranking them according to the **four worlds of emanation** (I: 11–40), as well as assigning angels feminine as well as masculine attributes (I: 119b).

Visitations by angels were widely reported among medieval Kabbalists. The mystic-legalist **Joseph Caro** wrote of his **maggid**, the spirit of the Mishnah, who visited him in the night and taught him *Torah ha-Sod*, the esoteric Torah (Maggid Mesharim).

Despite the more traditional view of some Chasidic masters like the **Baal Shem Tov**, who characterized angels as "the garments of God," the most novel contribution of Chasidic thought to angelology was a distinctly anthropocentric, even psychological, interpretation of angelic nature. Elaborating upon the teachings of **Chayyim Vital**,[2] some Chasidic masters held that ephemeral angels, like **demons**, were the direct result of human action. Goodly deeds created good angels, destructive behavior created destructive angels, etc. In other words, most angels are the creation—really a byproduct—of humans rather than God.[3] Thus the balance between the angelic and demonic forces in the universe is a direct result of human decision and action: ". . . man stands upon the earth and his head reaches to the heavens, and the angels of the Eternal ascend and descend within him" (Ben Porat Yosef 42a). Despite this, or perhaps because of it, the Chasidic masters emphasize the value of seeking the help of angels. Again, a more psychological interpretation would be that they are calling on Jews to draw strength from their own past good deeds. The most comprehensive Chasidic meditation on angelology is Sichat Malachei ha-Shareit ("Meditation on the Guardian Angels") by Tzadok ha-Kohen Rabinowicz.[4]

In the last quarter of the 20th century, there has been renewed interest in angels throughout the Jewish community as evidenced by a boom in books from a Jewish perspective on the subject.

1. Lauterbach, "The Belief in the Power of the Word," 293–300.
2. Werblowsky, *Joseph Karo, Lawyer and Mystic*, 79.
3. Steinsaltz, *The Thirteen-Petalled Rose*, 10.
4. Rabinowicz, *The Encyclopedia of Hasidism*, 23–24.

Angel of the Covenant: *SEE* ELIJAH.

Angel of Death: (*Malach ha-Mavet, Mar Mavet, Malach Ahzari*). God's agent of death in the world and the most dreaded of all numinous beings. First mentioned in biblical literature simply as *Mavet* (personified Death), *ha-Mashchit* (the Destroyer), **Malach Adonai** (Angel of the Lord), and in at least one place as multiple "messengers/angels of death," in later literature the title "Angel of Death" becomes conventional. God created the Angel on the first day, along with light. Some traditions fuse **Satan** and the **Yetzer**

ha-Ra with the Angel. Others give the Angel the name **Samael** ("The Gall of God").

Death is the slowest of all the angels, except in times of epidemic, when he is the fastest. The *Malach ha-Mavet* is monstrous in appearance, full of eyes that see all creatures (Ber. 4b), and he can appear with seven **dragon** heads (**Testament of Abraham**). He is robed in a mantle that allows him to change appearance. Death can command hosts of demons (Gen. R. 26). Some traditions hold the Angel was created on the first day, along with **darkness**, while others say he arose after the first sin (PdRE 13; A.Z. 22b; Zohar I: 35b).

Despite the piety and cleverness of such extraordinary mortals as **Abraham**, **Moses**, and **David**, who delayed their demise, no one can resist this angel forever. A select righteous few, like Moses, die directly from the **kiss** of God, rather than through the harsh agency of the Angel. Supposedly the biblical city of **Luz** was immune to death, and the Angel could only strike those who left the confines of the city (Sot. 46b). At the moment of death, the Angel hovers at the head of the dying with a sword dripping gall. Seeing the Angel causes the person to open his mouth in terror, and the gall enters the body, killing it (A.Z. 20a–b).

A number of people are said to have had dealings with the Angel while still alive, including David, **Solomon**, and a number of Talmudic Sages, most famously **Simon (Shimon) ben Halafta** and **Joshua ben Levi** (Ket. 77b). The greatest mortal nemesis of Death, until to the coming of the **Messiah**, has been **Moses**, who had many dealings with it during his own life and was able to thwart it in various ways. Either God, or the Messiah acting as God's agent, will slay the Angel of Death at the end of time (Passover Haggadah; Isa. 25; PR 161b).

The teachings about the Angel found in the whole expanse of Jewish literature are quite diverse and hard to reconcile into a coherent whole. There exists, for example, an isolated tradition that there are actually six *malachei ha-mavet*, with each one empowered to slay a different category of creature. Another strand of tradition teaches that the same angel that brings a soul into the world is also the one who will bring it back to the higher realms. There are also traditions concerning **Domah**, the angel of the grave, who pronounces the initial judgment against the soul while it still clings to the body. In some texts, Domah functions exactly as the Angel of Death does.

Fearful that the Angel will use a person's **name** to "find" him or her, some Jewish parents will not name newborns until the day of their circumcision or synagogue naming, when they will enjoy the added protection of Jewish **ritual**. Symbolically "selling" an ill child, changing its name, or giving away its clothing to someone else can confuse the Angel. It is customary that the prayers for **Rosh Chodesh** are not recited on the month of Tishrei in order to mislead the Angel about the coming High Holy Days, the time when it is determined who will die in the coming year. The giving of **charity** and the study of Torah has the power to postpone death, but not prevent it (Gen. R. 21:5; Ex. R. 30:3, 38:2; Num. R. 23:13; Tanh., Bereshit 11; Me'am Loez, Bereshit).

Angel of the Lord: *SEE* MALACH ADONAI.

Angelic Script: An alphabet that appears in **Sefer ha-Razim**, **Sefer Raziel**, and on medieval amulets. *SEE* ALPHABET, MAGICAL.

Angelification: In early Jewish mysticism, the experience of *unio mystica*, mystical union with God, was most often expressed in the notion that a human could, either temporarily or eternally, achieve angelic status and become part of the divine assembly. The archetypal figure for this kind of transformation is **Enoch**, who was transubstantiated into **Metatron** (III Enoch 3). According to a medieval Midrash, nine people entered Paradise alive (and, by implication, underwent transformation into angels): Enoch, **Elijah**, the **Messiah**, **Eliezer** (the servant of Abraham), **Ebed Melech**, **Batya** (the daughter of Pharaoh), **Hiram** (who built Solomon's Temple), Jaabez (son of R. Judah the Prince), and **Serach bat Asher** (Derekh Eretz Zuta 1).

The priests who contributed to the **Dead Sea Scrolls** also apparently believed they enjoyed a transitory fusion with the angels when they performed their mystical liturgy, the **Songs of the Sabbath Sacrifice**. **Ma'asei Merkavah** mystics sought a similar kind of angelic experience on a personal level through their practices of mystical **ascent**.

Medieval Judaism preserved a variant form of this idea in teaching that the **righteous** are elevated after death and dwell among the angels (El Malei Rachamim prayer). *SEE* PURIFICATION; THRONE OF GLORY; YORED MERKAVAH.

Animals: The term *chayya*, "living thing," usually refers to land creatures, birds and fish being traditionally classified separately. Jewish tradition teaches that all animals, regardless of intelligence, constantly praise God through their voices, sounds, and characteristic behaviors and gestures (Perek Shirah; Mid. Teh., End). But while the **Bible** clearly regards animals to have consciousness, the question of whether animals have souls begins in the Middle Ages, with the earliest rational philosopher, Sa'adia Gaon, responding in the positive. Jewish mysticism, with its belief in **reincarnation**, embraced Sa'adia's position early on. Solomon Aderet taught that animals and humans share souls. **Chayyim Vital** argued that souls transmigrate between humans, animals, plants, and even inanimate objects. Numerous Chasidic masters claimed the Jewish tradition of showing compassion toward animals, *baal chayyim*, was partly based on the knowledge that animals were transmigrated souls. Consuming meat slaughtered according to the rules of Jewish ritual law, *kashrut*, allows those souls to be properly released and permits the consumer to absorb the **nitzotzot**, the holy sparks contained in the flesh (Meirat Einayim 279; Tanya 7).

Animals possess innate wisdom from which human beings can learn (II Kings 5; Job 12). Animals naturally acknowledge the Creator and his messengers (Num. 24; Pss. 65, 148; Yalkut, Ps. 150). Certain enlightened humans, such as **Solomon** and Hillel, can commune with the animal world (Sof. 16:9).

Normally regarded as mundane aspects of God's Creation, Jewish sources nevertheless include stories of fantastic creatures and animals with supernatural abilities. The Bible credits two ordinary creatures with the human capacity of speech: the serpent in the Garden of **Eden** (Gen. 3) and the **ass** of the gentile prophet **Balaam ben Boer** (Num. 24). While the Bible explicitly accounts for the speech of the ass (it is a temporary angelic gift), no clear explanation is given for why the **serpent**, of all God's other creatures, has the ability to speak. A subsequent tradition fills in this lacuna by proposing the animal was re-ally **Satan** in disguised form, an interpretation that later became central to Christian exegesis.

Fantastic animals mentioned in the Bible include **Leviathan** (Isa. 27:1), Nehash (Isa. 27:1), and **Rahav** (Isa. 57:9), mighty sea monsters, which have their roots in the pagan traditions of the Babylonian chaos monster Tiamat and/or the Canaanite sea god, Judge River. Like their pagan counterparts, these mythic beasts threaten the cosmos and must be subdued. Two others, **Behemoth** and **tanin**, may in fact be references to mundane creatures, the buffalo and crocodile, but in later tradition become regarded as a monstrous giant oxen and a **dragon**, respectively.

A number of fantastic creatures borrowed from pagan mythology appear in Jewish writings of antiquity, most notably the **phoenix**. The **Apocalypse of Baruch**, for example, incorporates the phoenix into its description of how heaven operates. The sphinx is also mentioned in III Baruch.

While animal fables were a staple element of rabbinic literature, tales of fantastic creatures actually believed to exist are less common. The most famous such creature is the **shamir worm**, the stone-eating creature the Rabbis claim allowed **Solomon** to build the **Temple** in **Jerusalem** without resorting to using **iron** tools, which God had prohibited (Ex. 22). Tales of Leviathan and Behemoth multiply, including a description of Leviathan as God's pet and an oft-repeated tradition that these two beasts will be the main course at the messianic **banquet**, their slaughtering being a metaphor for the final triumph of God over the forces of chaos at the end of time. **Ziz**, a gigantic bird, appears along with Leviathan and Behemoth as being created on the fifth day of Creation (Midrash Konen).

The Jews of Medieval Europe included in their bestiaries those creatures widely held to exist by their non-Jewish neighbors, including unicorns and **barnacle geese**.[1] Animals also feature prominently as symbols in Jewish dream interpretation. *SEE* BIRDS; DIVINATION; DOGS; DREAMS; EAGLE; FISH; SOUL.

1. Ruderman, "Unicorns, Great Beasts, and the Marvelous Variety of Things in Nature in the Thought of Abraham ben Hananiah Yagel," in Twersky and Septimus, *Jewish Thought in the Seventeenth Century*.

Anointing: *SEE* MESSIAH; OIL.

Apocalypse of Abraham: SEE ABRAHAM, APOCALYPSE OF.

Apocalypse of Baruch: SEE BARUCH, APOCALYPSE OF OR BOOK OF.

Apocalyptic Literature: A genre of Jewish religious writing mostly composed between the 2nd century BCE and the 5th century CE. A few apocalyptic texts appear in the **Bible** (specifically the book of **Daniel**, parts of **Zechariah**, **Isaiah**, and **Ezekiel**), but the bulk of the writings considered apocalyptic, such as the **Apocalypse of Baruch**, the **Apocalypse of Abraham**, the **Testament of Levi**, the Ascension of Isaiah, and the **Books of Enoch**, were never included in the biblical canon. The vast majority of them were not even preserved in the sacred Jewish languages of Hebrew or Aramaic, but instead have survived only in Christian revisions, having been translated into a variety of Western and African languages. Some never even existed in Hebrew/Aramaic, but were originally composed by Greek-speaking Jews.[1]

Inspired by biblical prophetic traditions, apocalyptic literature sees itself as the continuation of **prophecy**, but there are certain features that distinguish it from classical Hebrew prophecy. These documents are usually (but not uniformly) characterized by:

1) Occultism: The revelation in these works is purportedly a "secret." Unlike prophecy, it is meant to be revealed only to a privileged few, usually the "elect."

2) **Pseudepigrapha**: Being cast as the work of some figure of the ancient biblical past, often a figure that is rather peripheral in the canonical Scriptures, such **Levi**, **Baruch**, or **Enoch**.

3) Cosmic revelation: The books often provide a revelatory tour of heaven, hell, the primordial past, and/or events at the end of time.

4) Symbolic images: The events portrayed will be presented in heavily encoded figurative images including **hands**, bowls, **scrolls**, **angels**, or **dragons**, which must be interpreted in order to understand their import. **Gematria** and word mysticism is also a frequent feature.

5) Angel- and demonologies: The denizens of the divine spheres play a far more prominent role in apocalyptic texts than they do in most canonical biblical prophecy or in rabbinic literature. Often an angel is a mediumistic figure, called the *angelus interpretus*, in the text who explains the meaning of the revelation.

6) Dualism: These books are starkly dualistic, more so than the Bible, with forces of good and evil, light and darkness, clearly and diametrically opposed to one another.

7) Determinism: This genre features a marked sense of fatalism. The prophetic sense of contingency, that the future could change based on human moral decision and action, is largely absent in apocalyptic works. Instead, history is seen as a vast, cosmic machine moving toward an inevitable conclusion. The only role of human free will is in making the decision of which cosmic force to ally with.

Recent scholarship suggests that apocalyptic literature may have largely been a product of priestly circles in Early Judaism.[2] During the later corruption of the Temple and then after its destruction, these writings flourished as a mystical visionary alternative to the lost earthly sanctuary. This also explains its decline. It began to fade with the progressive loss of priestly prerogatives and the rise of rabbinic influence. Christianity and, to a lesser extent, Islam inherited and continued to produce and study apocalyptic traditions for centuries after they had lost their currency in Jewish circles. Still, these works continued to have an influence in Judaism, shaping the language and practices of the **Ma'asei Merkavah** and **Hechalot literature**, which pursued apocalyptic and occult visions, but muted or discarded their eschatological and dualistic preoccupations.[3]

1. Metzger and Coogan, *Oxford Companion to the Bible*, 34–39; Gruenwald, *Apocalyptic and Merkavah Mysticism*, 2–23.
2. Barker, "Beyond the Veil of the Temple: The High Priestly Origins of the Apocalypses," 34–48.
3. Elior, *The Three Temples*, 259.

Apocrypha: A collection of religious writings from Early Judaism that have some canonical status in the Church, but none in Judaism. The collection includes both **Apocalyptic** and **Pseudepigraphic** writings.

Apple: *SEE* FRUIT.

Apple Orchard, the Holy: An idiomatic phrase appearing in the **Zohar** drawn from the imagery of the **Song of Songs**. It refers to the state of union of human beings with the **Shekhinah**, the ultimate attainment of communion with the divine.

Aravot: The seventh and highest heaven. It is the location of the **Throne of Glory** (Chag. 12b).

Archangel: (Greek, "chief messenger/principal messenger"). Archangels are a class of princely angels with authority over heavenly realms, earthly nations, or other angels. The term "archangel" does not actually exist in Jewish literature until almost modern times. Instead, it is a default translation for several Hebrew angelic terms such as **Irin** (Watcher), **Sar** (Prince/Archon), or Sharet (Ministering angel). Angels with names, such as **Metatron**, **Michael**, or **Gabriel**, are often styled as "archangels." *SEE* ANGELS AND ANGELOLOGY.

Arelim (or Aralim): An angelic rank listed in the **Zohar**. *SEE* ERELIM.

Arfiel: In **Hechalot** texts, this is the angel who guards the heavenly palace **Rakia**.

Ari, ha- or Arizal: *SEE* LURIA, ISAAC.

Arikh Anpin: "Long Visage." *SEE* PARTZUFIM.

Ark of the Covenant: (*Teiva ha-Eidut*). A portable chest that served as the repository for the **Ten Commandments** and the thirteenth **Torah** scroll written by Moses (the other twelve went to each of the tribes). More importantly, the Ark served as a locus of God's presence among the Children of Israel. At God's commission, the biblical wonder-craftsman **Bezalel** built the Ark while the Israelites sojourned in the desert.

The Ark was a box plated in **gold** inside and out, mounted with two carrying poles and adorned with two **cherubim**. The wings of these cherubim came together to form the "mercy seat" of God and from there God spoke with Moses (Ex. 25). As the "Strength and the Glory of God," the Ark was carried into battle by the Israelites (Josh. 6:6–15; Judg. 20:27; I Sam. 4:3–5), where it served as a sign that *YHWH-Tzevaot* (The Lord of Armies) was present.

The Ark was imbued with numinous holiness so profound that mortals risked death simply by touching it (II Sam. 6:6–8). When the Philistines briefly captured it, its power was such that they were afflicted with boils (or hemorrhoids, the Hebrew being uncertain) and vermin, and their idols humiliated. It is last mentioned during the reign of Josiah and is not accounted for after the Babylonian exile.

According to the **Talmud**, the Ark could flatten the hills where it was carried (Ber. 54a–b) and destroyed all snakes and scorpions along its path. It was also extradimensional and did not actually occupy physical space at all (B.B. 99a). Its very presence also caused great **fertility** (Yoma 30b). The cherubim on it would rotate as an **omen**; when Israel earned God's favor, they would embrace, like lovers (B.B. 99a; Lam. R., Mavo; PdRK 19).

Some traditions claim it was taken into captivity in **Babylon** along with the people, while another tradition claims it was buried on Mount Nebo. Still another teaches it was secreted on the **Temple** grounds, filled with **manna**, anointing **oil**, the **Rod** of **Aaron**, and the treasures of the Philistines, where it awaits rediscovery in the time of the **Messiah** (PR 26:6; PdRK 13:114b).

Ark, Holy: (*Aron, Teivah*, or *Heichal*). A niche or cabinet in a **synagogue** for the storage of the **Torah** scrolls. Mounted on the **east** wall (toward Jerusalem), it functions as the visual focal point of the sanctuary.

Protective and miraculous powers begin being attributed to the ark by the late Talmudic period, coinciding with the rising status of the synagogue as the holy place, par excellence, in rabbinic Judaism. People would on occasion sleep before the ark in order to receive a revelatory **dream** or in the hope of experiencing a miraculous **healing**. **Amulets** were sometimes placed inside the ark for a period to enhance their power. *SEE* INCUBATION.

Arka: (Aramaic, "Earth"). One of the seven underworld realms mentioned in the **Zohar**. The descendants of Cain, monstrous humanoids, dwell there (Sitre Torah; Zohar I: 253b–254a).

Arkiel: A fallen angel who taught humanity **geomancy** (I Enoch).

Armageddon: (*Megiddo*). Christian tradition identifies this ancient city in Israel as the place of the final conflict between God and the forces of Satan. The city does not have the same dramatic role in Jewish **eschatology**. SEE ARMILIUS BEN BELIAL; GOG AND MAGOG; MESSIAH.

Armaros: Fallen angel who taught mankind **magic** (I Enoch).

Armilius ben Belial: The eschatological nemesis of the Messiah. The tradition of Armilius is medieval in origin, first surfacing textually during the 8th century. While there are several variations, the core story is that Armilius is a king who will attack **Jerusalem** in the last days, killing the Messiah, son of Joseph. In turn the Messiah, son of David will counterattack and slay Armilius, either with the breath of his mouth (an allusion to Isa. 9) or by **fire** raining from heaven. **Sefer Zerubbabel** reports he will be the offspring of sexual congress between a beautiful Roman statue (the Virgin Mary?) and **Satan**. Armilius thus is a monstrosity with green skin, gold hair, and two heads who thinks himself God. Amilius narratives can be read as a counter-narrative (or parody) of Christian eschatological beliefs (Sefer Zerubbabel; BhM 1:56, 2:51, 3:141).

Armisael: A guardian angel with power over the womb and childbirth. He can be **summoned** by reciting Psalm 20 while invoking his name.

Artapanus: Egyptian-Jewish writer (ca. 2nd century BCE). He wrote that Abraham taught astrology to the priests of Heliopolis and that the mysterious figure of Hermes Trismegistus, founder of the alchemical arts, was actually Moses.

Aryeh: "Lion"/Leo. Astrological sign for the Hebrew month of Av. This signifies tragedy, power, destruction and redemption. The First and Second Temples were both destroyed in the month. Other disasters have befallen the Jewish people under this sign.[1]

   1. Erlanger, *Signs of the Times*, 87–108.

Arzaret: The mythical land beyond the **Sabatayon River** where the **ten lost tribes** dwell until the time of the messianic restoration.

Asaf ha-Rofe, Sefer: "The Book of Asaf the Physician." This medieval magico-medical manual claims to be based on traditions received from "Shem the son of Noah," linking it to the mysterious lost Book of **Noah**. Some of the material clearly draws upon the ancient Book of **Jubilees**, especially chapter 10.

Ascent, Heavenly: The mystical experience of projecting oneself into higher realms while still alive. Both **apocalyptic literature** and the New Testament (II Cor. 12:3) make it clear that soul ascensions were known and accepted in Early Judaism.

Apocalyptic traditions tend to limit ascents to the mythic past; only biblical worthies merited such experiences, figures such as **Enoch**, **Abraham**, and **Moses**. There is little or no indication in apocalyptic writings, however, that the experience is accessible to the contemporary reader. By contrast, the **Dead Sea Scrolls** suggest for the first time that mingling with angelic realms is possible, at least for the priestly elite.[1]

Later **Hechalot literature** radically "democratizes" (for lack of a better word) the possibility of mystical ascent—any intellectually and spiritually worthy person can now do it, though it is exceedingly dangerous—and offers descriptions of some of the rituals and preparations necessary for such ascents.[2]

The **German Pietists** and early Kabbalists preserved and continued these practices.[3] **Sefer Chasidim** also reports a near-death ascent (270). Famous post-biblical practitioners of ascent include Rabbis **Akiba** and **Ishmael**, **Isaac Luria**, the **Baal Shem Tov**, and Abraham Joshua Heschel of Apt.

Terminology for the experience of entering divine realms changes over Jewish history, being known variously as *Nichnas Pardes* (Entering Paradise), *Yored ha-Merkavah* (Descent to the Chariot), **Yichud** (Unification) and **Devekut** (Cleaving). SEE MEDIUM; TRANCE.

Techniques for ascent in Jewish sources include ritual **purification**, **immersion**, **fasting**, study of sacred and mystical texts, sleep deprivation, reciting word mantras (especially divine names), self-isolation, and even self-mortification.

The purposes of heavenly ascension can include various forms of *unio mystica*, sometimes in an ineffable experience, other times by a visionary enthronement before God or **angelification**, receiving answers to questions, gaining inspiration (for composing liturgical songs), or obtaining an apocalyptic **vision** of the future (Chag. 14b–15a; Mid. Teh. 19:4; Gen. R. 2:4). SEE MA'ASEI MERKAVAH; MEDITATION; THRONE OF GLORY.

1. Schiffman and VanderKam, *Encyclopedia of the Dead Sea Scrolls*, 26; Elior, *The Three Temples*, 180–83.
2. Schafer, *The Hidden and Manifest God*, 146–47.
3. Dan and Kiener, *The Early Kabbalah*, 2–4.

Asenat: The Egyptian wife of Joseph. Rabbinic legend identifies her as the daughter of Dinah who survived being abandoned by her grandfather Jacob through the agency of an **amulet** inscribed with God's name. An **angel** carries her to **Egypt** where she is adopted by Potiphar and later marries her uncle **Joseph** (PdRE 38).

Asherah: Either (a) a totem-pole-like pagan symbol or (b) the local Canaanite version of Astarte, the consort goddess of Baal.[1] Most references found in the **Bible** are meant in the former sense, though two extra-biblical inscriptions found in modern Israel prove that at least someone thought of Asherah as a consort goddess for YHWH (Khirbet el Qom and Kuntillet Arjud inscriptions).[2] Because of the very ambiguous way the Bible treats the term, the exact relationship between the pole and the goddess is subject to considerable contemporary scholarly debate.

Some students of the occult believe that Asherah "went underground" in increasingly monotheistic Israelite religion, eventually morphing into the quasi-divine feminine figures of **Wisdom** and/or **Shekhinah**. Evidence to sustain this thesis can be found in the **Zohar**, where Asherah makes a startling reappearance in post-biblical Jewish mysticism as another name for the sefirah of **Malchut** (I: 245b), bringing the pre-Israelite idea of a divine consort back almost full circle.

1. Metzger and Coogan, *Oxford Companion to the Bible*, 62.
2. Smelik, *Writings from Ancient Israel*, 152–60.

Ashes: Ashes are closely linked to death and nonbeing in Jewish thought. The ashes that are the byproducts of certain rituals and sacrifices have power over death. Thus, in the priestly purity system of ancient Israel, the ashes of a red heifer sprinkled upon a person have the power to take away the impurity that comes from contact with a corpse. Certain kinds of ashes (of cat placenta, for example), appear as ingredients in magical formulae and healing remedies (Key of Solomon; Likkutim 86a).

Asimon: Either a demon or punishing angel mentioned in the **Zohar**. He torments those who transgress on the **Sabbath**. He is multi-hued and has eight wings (I: 14b, II: 249b).

Asirta: An evil spirit who serves **Lilith** (Zohar II).

Asiyah: "[World of] Action." The "lowest" of the **four worlds of emanation**, the four-fold structure of Creation derived from Isaiah 43:7, Asiyah is the material plane, the place of the world as we experience on a day-to-day basis, though it also contains select spiritual forces as well.[1] The **ofan** angels, for example, govern this world. It corresponds to the physical dimension of human experience, as well as the divine capacity for speech.[2] (Massechet Azilut, Bahir, 197). Most of the **kelipot** came to rest in this dimension after the **Breaking of the Vessels**. The other three spiritual worlds are **Atzilut**, **Beriyah**, and **Yetzirah**. SEE EMANATION; SEFIROT.

1. Scholem, *Kabbalah*, 118–19.
2. Schwartz, *Tree of Souls*, 16. Also see Steinsaltz, *The Thirteen Petalled Rose*, 4–6.

Aslai: "Spirit Possession." A demonic possession illness reported among the Jews of Moroccan cultural background.[1]

1. Goldish, *Spirit Possession in Judaism*, 352–53, 356–58.

Asmodeus: (*Ashemdei*). An evil spirit. The name Asmodeus may be derived from the Zoroastrian *Aesmadiv*, the "spirit of anger" who serves Ahriman, the Persian god of evil. Asmodeus is first mentioned in the apocryphal book **Tobit**, where he slays seven grooms of a young girl before being bested by the hero. He also appears in the **Testament of Solomon**.

In Pesach 110a he is dubbed the "king of **demons**." The *locus classicus* for Asmodeus is the wonderful Talmudic tale of how he usurps the **throne of Solomon** (Git. 68a–b) after the king initially binds him to service by means of a magical **ring**. Surprisingly, the demon is treated rather sympathetically. He both morally instructs Solomon and provides him with the **shamir worm**. His foreknowledge of human destiny is credited to his daily Torah studies in heaven. The tale may reflect an effort by the Sages to reconcile their belief in the demonic with monotheism, portraying evil spirits as yet another tool of God's inscrutable will. The passage also highlights the belief that magical practitioners can **summon** and "bind" demons and use their powers for their own purposes, a staple belief of medieval sorcery.

In Kabbalistic works such as **Treatise of the Left Emanation**, Asmodeus is portrayed as a deputy, or even the offspring off **Samael**. He is also assigned a consort demoness, **Lilith** "the lesser."

Like rabbinic literature, medieval Jewish tales link Asmodeus with august Jewish figures, such as **Simon bar Yochai**, the Talmudic mystic. In one such story, Asmodeus is portrayed as doing what he does in order to serve the Sage and God. The Bar Yochai story and other references to Asmodeus in Kabbalistic texts, where his name is invoked to beneficent purposes, reflect the ongoing effort among Jews to reconcile the existence of demons with pure monotheism. *SEE* DEMONS; EVIL; SITRA ACHRA.

Ass: Several fantastic traditions about donkeys and asses appear in Jewish history. Balaam's talking donkey is one (Num. 24). There is a tale in the **Talmud** of a man who is turned into an ass and then sold to a Sage. The Sage takes the ass to **water**, where the purifying influence undoes the charm.

Even more bizarre has been the accusation, first popularized by ancient Greek and Roman anti-Semites, that Jews worship an ass. According to the Roman writer Dem-

ocritus, Jews venerate a golden bust of an ass, and regularly sacrifice a gentile victim to it.[1] This constitutes the first ever appearance of the **blood libel** myth. The calumny may have its roots in a certain Gnostic sect who evidently did use a donkey as an important symbol. This Gnostic group used elements of biblical tradition in its teachings, thus providing the connection.

Sefer ha-Razim mentions the magical use of donkey blood and flesh. A Hebrew magic formula found in the **Cairo Geniza** uses an ass's shoulder bone for a **hate spell**. *SEE* ANIMALS.

1. Schafer, *Judeophobia*, 55–62.

Assembly, Divine: *SEE* ADAT EL; HOST OF HEAVEN.

Astrology: (*Chavirah; Chochmat ha-Mazzalot*). Belief that the heavens influence human affairs and may be consulted for purposes of divining the future has been popularly accepted in virtually all cultures in which Jews have lived. While condemnation of its practice, on a variety of grounds, is a common theme throughout Jewish religious literature, it is also true that belief in the influence of the heavens has been prevalent among Jews and has been practiced by very prominent Jewish historical figures.[1]

Astrology is a very ancient art among Semites. Ugaritic texts from Syria dating from the second millennium BCE include a list of omen interpretations of the moon.[2] Though there are Toraitic prohibitions against worshiping celestial objects (Ex. 20:4; Deut. 4:19–20), evidence for the actual practice of astrology appears relatively late (the 7th through 6th centuries BCE) in the biblical record. This may reflect the rising influence of Assyrian culture, which had well-developed and sophisticated astrological sciences. Astral cults, along with their priests, were reportedly introduced into the Temple in Jerusalem during this time. This cult included the worship of the *Tzeva ha-Shamayim*, the host of heaven; *Baal*, the storm god; *Shemesh*, the sun; *Yareach*, the moon; and *Mazzalot*, the constellations, or as some scholars translate it, the **zodiac** (II Kings 23:4–5).

When King Josiah initiated a reform of the **Temple**, symbols of celestial worship found there, like a **chariot** representing the journey of the sun god, were purged. It is during and after this period that we find specific prophetic condemnation of astrological augury (Jer. 10:2; Isa.

47:13–14). The experience of exile among the Babylonians, who were avid astrologers (called **Chaldeans** in Daniel), only served to expand Jewish exposure to this form of **divination** (Dan. chapter 2). The fact that Daniel was made the supervisor of all astrologers, sorcerers, and wizards (Dan. 2:48) may have helped legitimize the practice to later generations of Jews.

Astrology continued and expanded during classical antiquity, though its practice remains a point of controversy among Jews. Josephus reports that Jews looked to the heavens for favorable signs in their war against Rome (War 4:5). The testimony of the **Sibylline Oracles**, on the other hand, lauds the Jews for eschewing astrology entirely, while I Enoch regards it as one of the sins of primordial humanity (8:3). The **Book of Jubilees** has Abraham discredit the astrologers of his time (12:16–18). And yet, a tale that runs counter to that attitude is a passage in Tosefta that claims one of God's blessings to the Patriarch was the knowledge of astrology (Kid. 5:17). Both of these attitudes are replicated in rabbinic stories about Abraham (Gen. R. 44:10; Shab. 156a).

Several of the rabbinic attitudes toward astrology can be found in **Talmud** Tractate Shabbat, particularly in one passage, 156a–b. Belief in the influence of the stars was mostly accepted among the Sages of Talmudic times (Shab. 53b; B.M. 30b), which should not be so surprising, given the Babylonian milieu in which so many Rabbis lived. There are also multiple accounts of astrological predictions that are given credence, though, in best Talmudic tradition, contrary evidence and skeptical remarks are preserved alongside them (Sanh. 65a–b. See also Sif. D. 171; Sifra, Kedoshim 6). Intriguingly, a few Sages steered a middle course between the two opinions, claiming God granted Israel special immunity from celestial influence, though they conceded the stars had power over the rest of mankind (Gen. R. 37:1, 44:12, 79:2). This idea was later developed more fully in the **Zohar** as part of a theology of Jewish uniqueness (3 Pinchas 216b). At least one Sage, Mar Samuel, actively practiced astrology. King **Solomon** is identified as a master of the science (Eccl. R. 7:23:1).

Many well-educated Jews studied and practiced astrology well into the modern era, it being an accepted part of medieval medicine and sciences.[3] No philosophic education would have been considered complete without some knowledge of how the stars affect the sublunary realms. Examples of horoscopes written by Jews have been found in the **Cairo Geniza**. A wide array of famous scholars, ranging from mystics to rationalists, wrote treatises on the topic, including Sa'adia ben Joseph, **Abraham ibn Ezra**, **Nachmanides**, Levi ben Gershon, **Judah Loew** (the Maharal of Prague), and the **Vilna Gaon**. Rationalist philosophers Maimonides, Crescas, and Albo were among the few skeptics, attacking its validity and condemning it as forbidden by Scripture. On this point they were largely ignored.

Starting with **Sefer Yetzirah** and its commentaries and continuing through the **Zohar** and beyond, astrology plays a significant role in many Kabbalistic systems. It was a central concern of a wide array of lesser works and commentaries.

The applied magical use of astrological forces is an interest of many Jewish astrological texts, such as **Sefer Raziel**, **Sefer ha-Chayyim**, and **Sefer ha-Razim**. The increasing influence of Hermetic theories of astrologically based magic in the Renaissance become evident in the writings of several contemporary Jewish writers, especially **Johannan Alemanno** and **Abraham Yagel**, who sought to fuse Jewish angelic theories of planetary influence with gentile "natural" alchemical/astrological magic.[4]

A number of Jews identified as astrologers have had at least parts of their work survive down to today, including Masha'allah (Sefer She'elot), and Abu Da'ud (Sefer Nevuot). A few, such as **Abraham Zacuto** (Sefer Yuhasin) and Jacob ben Emanuel (Prognosticum), achieved a fame that extended beyond the Jewish world.

Since the rise of scientific astronomy, the more negative assessments of astrology have become normative, and even most traditional Jews shy away from it. Still, a number of Jewish customs have their basis in astrology, such as selecting propitious days for initiating a project and wishing one another "**Mazal tov**" (literally, "A good star").[5]
(SEE APPENDIX FIGURE 6.)

1. Ness, *Astrology and Judaism in Late Antiquity*, chapter 4, 1–14.
2. Hallo and Younger, *The Context of Scripture*, vol. 1, 290.
3. Zimmels, *Magicians, Theologians, and Doctors*, 15.
4. Ruderman, *Kabbalah, Magic, and Science*, 89–101; Idel, "Jewish Magic from the Renaissance Period to Early Hasidism" in Neusner, *Religion, Science, and Magic*, 82–117.
5. Roth, *Encyclopedia Judaica*, vol. 3, 788–95.

Asuta: (Aramaic, "healing"). The word most used to describe a miraculous or theurgic **healing**. It appears frequently on **amulets** and **incantation bowls**. SEE MAGIC; SEGULLOT.

Atbash: A letter-substitution code, perhaps the oldest system of **encryption** on record. It involves a "mirror" code of the alphabet. The first letter has the value of the last letter, the second letter the value of the second to last, and so on. The name *ATBaSH* itself is an acronym constructed from the methodology of the code: *Alef* = *Tav*, *Bet* = *SHin*. Making their first appearance in the **Bible**, *atbash* codes are a ubiquitous feature on **amulets**, especially in the form of encoded divine names.[1] SEE ENCRYPTION; HAFUCH; HEBREW ALPHABET; TEMURAH; TZERUF.

    1. Metzger and Coogan, *Oxford Companion to the Bible*, 64–65.

Atik Yomin: (Aramaic, "Ancient of Days"). A divine figure that appears to Daniel in a vision (Dan. 7:9, 7:13). In classical Kabbalah, he is identified with **Keter** and signifies the most transcendent aspect of the accessible Godhead. SEE NAMES OF GOD.

Atzilut: "Emanation." The highest of the **Four Worlds** created by the divine emanations, a realm of pure spirit and intellect. The world of Atzilut is closest to the Infinite Light of **Ein Sof**, even though it is not united and identified with it. Atzilut is the first plane or world of immanence, of structure separable from or "outside" God.

Automatic Writing and Speech: SEE XENOGLOSSIA.

Avodah B'gashmiyut: "Worship by [mundane] Action/ Actualized Worship." Judaism has always emphasized "deeds over creeds" and taught that service to God is best realized through bringing a higher consciousness (**kavanah**) to the ordinary tasks (eating, drinking, labor, sex, bodily functions) of living.[1] SEE COMMANDMENTS; TIKKUN.

    1. See Buxbaum, *Jewish Spiritual Practices*.

Awan: The sister of Cain and, later, his wife (Jubilees 4:1).

Ayin: Sixteenth letter of the **Hebrew alphabet**, vocalically it is only a glottal stop. Numerically it has the value of 70. The word for the letter, *ayin*, means both "eye" and "fountain." Ayin signifies vision, insight, consciousness, and the world. The number seventy reminds one of the seventy nations, the seventy languages, and seventy names for God (Baal ha-Turim; Num. 11:16). In the traditional text of the **Torah**, the *ayin* that appears in the word **Sh'ma** (Deut. 6:4) is enlarged, signifying that all Israel must be an *aid*, "witness," to God's oneness.[1]

    1. Munk, *The Wisdom of the Hebrew Alphabet*, 171–79.

Ayin ha-Ra: "Evil eye." A malevolent form of **witchcraft**. SEE EVIL EYE.

Azariah: The name the angel **Raphael** uses when he travels in disguise on earth (book of Tobit).

Azariah, Menachem: Kabbalist (Italian, ca. 16th century). His teachings, that the Torah is actually a narrative of the divine *dynamis* rather than about mortal deeds, connect the seven biblical prophetesses—**Sarah**, **Miriam**, Deborah, Channah, Abigail, **Huldah**, and **Esther**—to the seven lower sefirot.

Azazel: Azazel is a term of considerable controversy, referring either to (a) an evil power, or (b) a location. Even the meaning of the name is a topic of considerable controversy. If we assume the spelling has undergone some kind of corruption, it most likely means "Wrath of God."

    Azazel features prominently in the **Yom Kippur** ritual described in the Torah known to modern readers as the "Scapegoat" ritual. In this ceremony, the High Priest transfers the sins of the people onto a **goat**, and then releases it into the **wilderness**, "to Azazel." It is not clear, however, if the word refers to an entity or a place, perhaps an infernal realm, to which the scapegoat is dispatched (Lev. 16:8–10). Some scholars believe that the term refers to a barren, rocky zone in the desert. Others theorize that Azazel was a goat-demon, or **satyr**, a remnant of premonotheistic Israelite beliefs (Lev. 17:7).

    Both interpretations of the word continue to have currency post-biblically. The expression "L'Azazel" becomes a colloquialism for "go to hell!" On the other hand, given the general Near Eastern belief that the desert/wilderness was the dwelling place of demons, it is not surprising to see Azazel appear as a **fallen angel** or a demon in various post-biblical texts, such as the **Dead Sea Scrolls** (**Damascus Document**, II) and in the **Apocalypse of Abraham** and **I Enoch**. The most famous tradition identifies him as one of the angels that fell from heaven because he became enamored with mortal women (Gen. 6:2). In I Enoch, he is the angel who taught mankind the impure arts of war, lapidary, and cosmetics. In the end, he is exiled to the desolate wilderness (9, 10, 13).

Aside from etymological discussions of the meaning of the word, Azazel appears as a **demon** in Talmud (Yoma 67b; RaSHI commentary) and medieval Midrashic sources, such as **Yalkut Shimoni**. In one text, Azazel is regarded to be the serpent that tricked Adam and Eve into sin. Some claim Azazel is an alternate name for other demonic personalities, such as **Samael**. In one Midrash, the goat offering to Azazel on Yom Kippur is a bribe that God requires Israel to give **Satan**/Samael every year in order that he will deliver a good report about Israel's conduct when called to the celestial court (Me'am Loez, Achrei Mot-Kedoshim). *SEE* FALLEN ANGELS.

Azriel of Gerona: Mystic (Provencal, ca. 13th century). Azriel was a student of Isaac the Blind and the teacher of **Nachmanides**. Along with his contemporary Ezra ben Solomon, his teachings regarding the ten **sefirot** provided the foundations of speculative Kabbalah.

Azulai, Chayyim: Rabbi and Kabbalist (Turkish, ca. 18th century). Azulai was one of the leading rabbis of his generation and he held important positions among the Jews of the Ottoman Empire. He was also a famed amulet maker and those samples that survive have been prized for their efficacy.

Azzah: A fallen angel appearing in III Enoch. *SEE* UZZA.

B

Baal: "Lord/Master/Husband." The chief active god of the Canaanite, Ugaritic, and Phoenician pantheons. A god of thunder and fertility, several biblical authors considered him YHWH's chief rival for the loyalties of the people Israel. The Bible sometimes speaks of "baalim" in the plural. This may reflect the common custom of identifying a local spirit with Baal. Thus, in different places, the Bible mentions a Baal Hadad and a Baal Pe'or ("The lord god of Hadad," "the lord god of Pe'or").

Baal ha-Chalom: The angel of **dreams** (Otzer Geonim, 4). In Talmud, it can also refer to a professional oneiromancer (Ber. 56a–b). *SEE* ANGELS; DIVINATION; DREAMS; SAR HA-CHALOM.

Baal ha-Sod: "Master of Secrets." It is a general, nontechnical moniker for a teacher of Jewish esoteric traditions.

Baal [Baalat] Ov: "Master [Mistress] of Ov." A necromancer. This term first appears in the Bible in a list of forbidden occupations (Deut. 18). An *ov* is a familiar, a term that may be derived from Akkadian. It is also possible, though less likely, that an ov is a dead ancestral spirit. In that case the word is being derived from the Hebrew *avah*, "father," the Arabic *aba*, "return," or *aabi*, Hittite for "grave."[1] According to the **Talmud**, a Baal Ov is a medium who causes the dead to speak, either through his own body or, in the Mesopotamian custom, through a skull (Sanh. 65b; Shab. 152b–153a. Also see Josephus, Ant. 4:4). *SEE* DEATH; DIVINATION; GHOSTS; MEDIUM; NECROMANCY; POSSESSION, GHOSTLY; XENOGLOSSIA.

1. Schmidt, *Israel's Beneficent Dead*, 150–52; Roth, *Encyclopedia Judaica*, vol. 3, 114.

Baal Shem: "Master of the [Divine] Name." An informal title given to wonder-workers and/or saints. From earliest Judaism it was believed that the names of God, but most often the **Tetragrammaton**, could be manipulated for theurgic or magical purposes. The Talmud also teaches that truly **righteous** persons have the power to bend God's will to their own (M.K. 16b). Such people were sometimes called *anshei ma'aseh*, "men of [wondrous] deeds."

The term "Baal Shem" for a wonder-worker, however, is early medieval in origin. Though it was sometimes applied to religious poets, most people designated a Baal Shem were either folk healers who used **segullot** cures, or the manufacturers of **amulets**. Some achieved fame as exorcists.[1]

Many writers used the term pejoratively, as synonymous with "quack" or "charlatan." Even a marginal figure like **Abraham Abulafia** looked down upon them. Some books of their cures and incantations, such as Miflaot Elohim (The Wonders of God), have been published in the modern era. The most famous of all *Baalei Shem* is **Israel ben Eliezer**, the founder of **Chasidism**.

1. Scholem, *Kabbalah*, 310–11.

Baal Shem Tov: *SEE* ISRAEL BEN ELIEZER.

Baba Sali: Kabbalist and **wunder-rabbi** (Moroccan, ca. 20th century). He was famous for his **healing** powers. His gravesite in southern Israel is still a popular place of pilgrimage.

Babel, Tower of: *SEE* TOWER OF BABEL.

Babylon: (Akkadian: *Bab-ilum*, "Gate of Heaven"). A city-state empire centered in what is now Iraq. Supposedly founded at the command of the god Marduk, this city became the place of Jewish exile after 586 BCE. Babylon was a culture permeated with supernatural beliefs and magical practices. Under its hegemony in the years following the destruction of **Jerusalem**, Jews became increasingly preoccupied with such matters. **Astrology**, **divination**, the use of **amulets**, and the practice of **magic** in a variety of forms, all became more pervasive folkways among Jews living in Iraq and Persia. Referring to the country as *Bavel* or *Shinar* interchangeably, the Bible repeatedly ridicules the pretensions of the Babylonians, especially in the fable of the **Tower of Babel** (Gen. 11).

Bachya ben Asher: Mystical Bible commentator (Spanish, ca. 13th–14th century). A student coming out of the circle of **Nachmanides**, his works include many occult teachings and esoteric interpretations of biblical episodes. Bachya particularly believed in the theurgic power of the **commandments**—that their proper performance empowered God, while sin weakened God's power in the world.[1]

1. Idel, *Kabbalah: New Perspectives*, 162–64.

Backwards: *SEE* REVERSAL.

Bahir, Sefer ha-: "The Book of Illumination." This document is the most influential early book in what would become the classical **Kabbalah** of the Middle Ages. Though written in a Midrashic style and credited with great antiquity, it is more likely the work of early medieval Provencal mystics. Like the earlier **Sefer Yetzirah**, the Bahir is deeply immersed in the supernal power of words and letters. The first description of the sefirotic **tree of life** appears in its pages. It is also one of the first

works to treat the mundane *nomina* of the Bible as allegories for metaphysical realities. Thus, according to the Bahir, "Abraham" is really the divine attribute of love, and his saga recorded in Scripture is actually an allegory for how God's love functions in the created realms. It expounds on divine names and their magical uses, as well as how to theurgically activate divine power through the performance of commandments.[1]

1. Dan and Kiener, *The Early Kabbalah*, 28–31; Green, *Guide to the Zohar*, 16–18.

Bakol: The daughter of Abraham. Her existence is derived from reading the verse, "And God blessed Abraham with *ba-kol* [everything]," as a pun: how could he have everything if he didn't have a daughter? The Bahir (78) regards her to be a divine creature (B.B. 16b; Gen. R. 59:7).

Balaam ben Beor: Ancient gentile seer from Transjordan. An extended story about Balaam appears in Numbers 22–24. Balaam is summoned by the King of Moab to collectively curse the Israelites. Being on good terms with YHWH, Balaam initially refuses, but is eventually induced to go help the king. Riding on an ass to join the king, he is confronted by a sword-wielding **angel** (See **Animal**). Once he arrives, rather than cursing Israel, he is instead possessed by God and pronounces four extended blessing oracles upon them.

Gnostics declared Balaam to be a prophet of the High God of goodness, and an enemy of the God of Israel, whom they equated with the evil **Demiurge**. They interpret the conflict of these two deities as the cause of Balaam's various reversals of fortune. In the Midrash, Balaam is described as everything from a magician to a prophet. One legend even declares him the greatest of the seven prophets God sent to the non-Jewish nations, the gentile counterpart to Moses (Num. R. 10). He is generally, but not consistently, portrayed as a wicked conspirator against Israel. Another tradition treats him as the most evil practitioner of witchcraft; he even derived his power by **bestiality**—copulating with his donkey (Sanh. 105a–b; Zohar I: 126a).

It was commonly held in the Middle Ages that Balaam was also a master of **astrology**. Renderings of him in illuminated manuscripts often showed him holding an astrolabe. **Sefer Raziel** claims he knew the workings of the Divine **Chariot** (B.B. 15b; Tanh., Balak; A.Z. 4a–b; Avot 5).

Baladan: "Not a Man." A dog-faced **demon** mentioned in rabbinic literature (Sanh. 96a) and the Zohar (I: 6b). Isaac Safrin may also be referring to these same imps when he speaks of the "evil dog" who works against humanity (Megillat Saterim).

Balsam: (*Bosem*). The juice of this plant is extracted for medicinal and perfumery uses. It may also have been an ingredient in the **incense** burned in the **Temple**. In the **World-to-Come**, thirteen streams of balsam oil will flow for the pleasure of the **righteous** (Tan. 25a; Gen. R. 62:2; Zohar II: 127a). *SEE* HERBS AND VEGETABLES; PHARMACOPOEIA.

Baneman: (Yiddish, "changeling"). A wood-and-straw doll that demons substitute for a living infant. The parents are enchanted so as to perceive the doll as living, while the actual infant is taken and raised to serve infernal forces (Toldot Adam, sect. 80). *SEE* BANIM SHOVAVIM; CHANGELING.

Banim Shovavim: "Mischievous sons." Originally used to describe wayward children (Chag. 15a), it took on a supernatural interpretation, being used to refer to changelings who are the offspring of human-demonic couplings. These creatures are a threat to the mortal children of their fathers. At the time of a man's death, these demonic children also besiege the newly deceased soul and the demonic offspring must be redeemed by means of a graveside ritual of **incantations** and magical **circles** (*Tikkun Shovavim*).[1] *SEE* DEMONS; NOCTURNAL EMISSION.

1. Scholem, *On the Kabbalah and Its Symbolism*, 154–56.

Banquet, Messianic: (*Seudah shel Livyatan*, "The meal of Leviathan"). One of the most popular mythic images of the reward awaiting the **righteous** in the **World-to-Come** is the messianic banquet (PdRE 10). There the great **chaos** monsters, **Ziz**, **Behemoth**, and **Leviathan**, will finally be slaughtered for the enjoyment of all. In one version of this legend, there were originally two Leviathans. God killed the first in primordial times and salted

away the meat for the banquet. The other sea monster will be served fresh (B.B. 74b; PR 16:4, 48:3; Mid. Teh. 14:7).

The subtext of this myth is that in messianic times the last forces of destruction, chaos, and entropy will finally be swept away, and the world will achieve its perfect state.

Bar Hedya (or Hadaya): Talmudic oneiromancer (ca. 4th century). He is portrayed as a man of doubtful character whose interpretations depended on the amount of money paid him. The story of Bar Hedya also features a humorous episode about one of his predictions that came to pass: Rava was told by Bar Hedya that his **dream** signified he would be hit twice with a club. The Sage is in fact later attacked, but averts a third blow by declaring to his attacker, "Enough! I saw only two [blows] in my dream!" This suggestive story may help explain Bar Hedya's maxim, "All dreams follow the interpretation." In other words, dream interpretations are no more than self-fulfilling prophecies (Ber. 56a–b).

Bar Jesus: A Jewish magician mentioned in the Christian Scriptures (Acts 13).

Bar Nifli: (Aramaic, "Son of the Clouds"). Messianic figure, based on the book of Daniel (7:13), described in IV Ezra, Babylonian Talmud, and Targum.

Bar Shalmon: This Jewish Odysseus made his way to the infernal realms after fleeing from punishment for a false oath he had sworn. There he came under the protection of **Asmodeus**, king of demons, to whom he taught **Torah**. He fell in love with Asmodeus's daughter, and they were wed. He eventually abandoned his wife and escaped back to the land of mortals, but was slain by his spurned wife and her minions for failing to keep his vow to her. This story, which has its origins among Arabic-speaking Jews, appears in the collection **Ma'aseh Yerushalmi**.

Bar Yochni: A gigantic bird mentioned in **Talmud** (Bik. 57a). Some stories of this bird overlap those of the **Ziz**.

Baradiel: The angel of hail (I Enoch).

Baraita de Yosef ben Uziel: This esoteric commentary on **Sefer Yetzirah**, pseudepigraphically ascribed to the authorship of the mysterious Joseph ben Uziel, grandson of the prophet Jeremiah, was an important text created within the mystic **Circle of the Unique Cherub**.[1]

1. Dan and Kiener, *The Early Kabbalah*, 24; Also see Dan, *The 'Unique Cherub' Circle*, 59–79.

Baraita mi-Pirkei Merkavah: "Tradition from the Chapters of the Chariot." A book of **Ma'asei Merkavah**.

Barakiel: The angel of lightning first mentioned in I Enoch.

Barminan: (Aramaic, "Far from us!"). An expression meant to ward off the **evil eye** (think in terms of the prayer of the rabbi in *Fiddler on the Roof*: "God, bless and keep the Czar—far away from us!"). It can also be used as a euphemism for a dead body.

Barnacle Geese: Fantastic birds thought to metamorphose from shells. Christians used this creature as an allegory for Jewish conversion to Christianity (a humble shellfish can be transformed into a beautiful bird). Jewish versions of the barnacle geese legend have them growing on trees (Zohar III: 156).

Barrenness: *SEE* FERTILITY.

Baruch, Apocalypse of or Book of: A cluster of pseudepigraphic works, with different versions existing in Greek and Syriac, claiming to be **Baruch ben Neriah**'s firsthand accounts of the destruction of the earthly **Jerusalem** and his ascension to the heavenly Jerusalem. In one vision, Jerusalem is actually destroyed by angelic forces rather than Babylonians. Then the sacred vessels of the Temple are secreted away, after which the spirit of **prophecy** seizes Baruch and he experiences eschatological visions. This is how the Syriac version ends. The Greek version picks up with Baruch ascending bodily into the **seven heavens**, where he sees fantastic visions of the past, the future, hell, and the celestial workings. Both versions, though evidently of Jewish origin, have been so heavily reworked by Christian writers that it is difficult to tell what is original and what has been superimposed on the text over time.[1]

1. Metzger and Coogan, *Oxford Companion to the Bible*, 76–77.

Baruch ben Neriah: Secretary to the prophet Jeremiah (ca. 6th century BCE). Like many other peripheral characters that appear in Scripture, Baruch becomes a prominent figure in Jewish occult tradition. He becomes the protagonist of the **Apocalypse of Baruch**. The Rabbis identify him with the character **Ebed Melech** mentioned in the book of Jeremiah, making him an Ethiopian (PdRE 53). Counted as a prophet by some Sages, later legends claim his body experienced a saintly death untouched by decay. His grave was a place of highest sanctity; like the **Ark of the Covenant**, those who touched it died. Other stories have him ascend bodily into heaven, like **Elijah**. (Meg.14b, 15a; Sifrei, Num. 99; II Baruch). *SEE* RIGHTEOUS, THE.

Bat: Not mentioned in the Bible, in rabbinic literature the bat is a shape-shifting creature that takes a number of forms over time but eventually morphs into a demon (B. K. 16a). *SEE* ANIMALS.

Bat Kol: "Daughter of [the] Voice." A minor form of revelation described in **Talmud** and later Jewish literature. Not prophetic in the prescient sense, instead it proclaims God's will or judgment. It appears most famously in the miraculous duel between Rabbi Eliezer and the Sages (B. M. 59b; J. Ber. 2). It sometimes is heard extolling the **righteous** at the time of their death. *SEE* PROPHECY; VISION.

Batya: "Daughter of the Eternal." The daughter of Pharaoh, she adopted the infant Moses. She had the spirit of prophecy in her and knew she was raising an agent of God. She is one of the select few who ascended to heaven without tasting death. In **Eden** she rules over one of the **palaces** of the righteous dead (Sot. 12b; Meg. 13a; Ex. R. 1, 18; Lev. R. 1:3).

Beard: *SEE* HAIR.

Beelzebub: A demon. He is first mentioned as a Phoenician god in II Kings 1. His name probably derives from Ugaritic "Lord Baal," though it is often translated as "Lord of Flies." By Greco-Roman times he is a demon lord and he is mentioned in Christian Scriptures (Matt. 12:24–27). He may be the same as Belzebouel, who appears in the **Dead Sea Scrolls**.

Beer Shachat: "Well of Destruction." One of the seven compartments of **Gehenna**, it is the destination of the "ten wicked nations." **Kushiel** is its principle angel (Masekhet Gehinnom).

Behemoth: A mythical beast mentioned in Job 40:15–24 and Psalm 50:10, which calls him the first of God's creations. Other sources insist he was created on the sixth day (Midrash Konen). Behemoth drinks up all the waters that flow from Paradise (PR 16:4, 48:3). He is so big he sits on a thousand mountains (Zohar I: 18b). His bones are hard as tubes of bronze and his limbs are like iron rods.

At the end of time he will do battle with **Leviathan**, a battle neither will survive. In the **World-to-Come**, he will be an entrée at the messianic **banquet**. Behemoth is often portrayed in medieval Jewish illuminated manuscripts as an ox of gigantic proportions (II Esdras 6:52; B. B. 74b; Lev. R. 13:3, 22:10; PdRE 11). *SEE* ANIMALS.

Beinonim: "The in-betweens/the doubtful." Starting in III Enoch, it is the designation for those who are neither pious nor evil. The bulk of humanity, the *beinonim* are those whose fate in the afterlife is still in question.

Beit ha-Midrash, heavenly: *SEE* YESHIVA SHEL MALAH.

Beli Ayin ha-Ra: "No evil eye!" *SEE* EVIL EYE.

Belial: "Worthless." Belial is a demon mentioned in the **Dead Sea Scrolls**, apocryphal books, and the Gospels. Based on the Book of Jubilee's description of him as the accuser and tempter, Belial may be an alternative name for **Satan**. In some medieval works, Belial gives birth to **Armilius**.

Belimah: A term used in **Sefer Yetzirah** to refer to the **sefirot** prior to their unfolding, it means either "containment/restraint" (the divine restraint that pre-existed the emanation) or "silence" (the cosmic silence that preceded God's first words, "Let there be light").[1] Later interpretations, treating it as a **notarikon**, divide it into two words, *b'li-mah*, "without whatness," in the sense of "without substance." Thus *Belimah* becomes associated with **Keter**, the first emanation.

Other works, such as **Baraita de Yosef ben Uziel**, understand it as a reference to the ten metaphysical concepts the average Jew is forbidden to contemplate: what is before Creation, after the judgment, the reward of the righteous, the punishment of the wicked, and the remotest ends of what is up, down, east, west, north, and south.

1. Green, *Guide to the Zohar*, 54; Kaplan, *Sefer Yetzirah*, 25–26.

Bells: Bells appear in a significant role only during biblical times, when the High **Priest** was required to wear them on the hem of his ephod (seventy-two of them according to the **Talmud**). Whether they were merely aesthetic or also served a protective function against malicious spirits is a matter of speculation. Unlike Christian-based theurgic practices, bells do not appear to have been used much by Jewish practitioners.

Belomancy: The casting of arrows for the purposes of **divination** is well attested to in Semitic cultures surrounding Israel. Not only do Akkadian and Arabic documents refer to it, but archaeologists have found bronze arrowheads with the inscription *chetz* (arrow) on them. Since inscribing an arrow with the word "arrow" seems pointless, at least one scholar speculates that the word is meant as a pun of the Ugaritic word for "luck."[1]

The practice of belomancy is explicitly mentioned twice in Hebrew Scriptures, once with condemnation (Ezek. 21:26), the other as a legitimate way for a prophet to discern the future (II Kings 13:14–19). It is alluded to in another passage (I Sam. 20:19–22). This third passage may be meant as satire, showing it (and the interpretation of word **omens** in general) to be nothing more than a sleight-of-hand trick to convey messages already known to the practitioner.

The methods of belomancy vary. According to Ezekiel, a bundle of arrows is shaken and then cast down, possibly in front of an idol. The pattern in which they fall was presumably interpreted, I Ching fashion, by the *baru* (diviner). Arab sources suggest that arrows (usually three, just as described in the I Samuel passage) were shot, and the message then derived from the pattern of their landing.

1. Singer, *The Jewish Encyclopedia*, vol. 2, 307; Roth, *Encyclopedia Judaica*, vol. 3, 114–15.

Ben Azzai, Simon: Talmudic Sage and mystic (ca. 2nd century). He is one of the **four Sages** who entered Pardes. According to the account in Chagigah 14b, "He looked and died." **Genesis Rabbah** takes this as a sign of his piety, for he is credited with saying that the pious see the rewards awaiting them in the moments before their death. The Jerusalem Talmud records that when Ben Azzai expounded **Torah**, the flames of **Sinai** enveloped him (Lev. R. 16:4).

Ben Stada: A practitioner of **witchcraft** mentioned in **Talmud** (B. Shab. 104b). He derived his knowledge from **Egypt**, one of the great sources of arcane knowledge.

Ben Temalion: A beneficent **demon** that helped a group of Jews, led by **Simon bar Yochai**, sent as emissaries to Rome. He did this by first possessing the daughter of Caesar, only to have Bar Yochai perform an **exorcism** on her. When Ben Temalion finally left her body, Bar Yochai earned Caesar's gratitude and his cooperation (Meg. 17b).

Ben Zoma, Simon: Talmudic Sage and mystic (ca. 2nd century). He is one of the **four Sages** who entered **Pardes**. The experience drove him mad (Chag. 14b). Prior to this misadventure, Ben Zoma was noted for his obsession with **Ma'asei-Bereshit**, the mysteries of **Creation**.

Beree: The **angel** of **rain** (Job 26:7; Tan. 25b).

Bereshit: "When God created. . . ." This first word of the book of Genesis serves both as the Hebrew name for the biblical book and as an idiom for "Creation." SEE CHAOS; CREATION; MA'ASEI BERESHIT.

Beriyah: "Creation." The second of the **four worlds of emanation**, this is the level in which positive existence emerges. Some traditions associate this with the **Throne of Glory**, which functions as the first **garment** concealing the supernal light of **Creation**. It is a realm of pure intellect and the place from which human reason emanates. Jewish word mysticism also associates it with the first letter *hay* in the **Tetragrammaton**, the four-letter name of God.

Beruchim, Abraham: Kabbalist (North African, ca. 16th century). He advocated the mystical discipline of **midnight** prayer and study. He was such a severe advocate of repentance that he was believed by many to be the **reincarnation** of the prophet **Jeremiah**.

BeSHT: *SEE* ISRAEL BEN ELIEZER.

Bestiality: Sexual relations with animals are explicitly forbidden by the Torah (Lev. 18). Stories of inter-species intercourse do, however, appear in Jewish literature. The most famous of these is a Talmudic reference to **Eve** copulating with the **serpent** (Shab. 146a). There is also a more obscure tradition that Adam first gave vent to his libido with God's other creations, a story that serves as an etiological rationale as to why God felt compelled to create a female partner for him. One Midrash claims that antediluvian people engaged in bestiality with all the land creatures, thereby contributing to the absolute corruption of all Creation, requiring the great **Flood** to purge the earth of this obscenity (Gen. 6; Eruv. 18b). Interestingly, as in Greco-Roman religions, such tales of bestiality are mostly set in the mythic past.

Bestiality is closely associated in the Talmudic imagination with **witchcraft**, and the Sages believed that it was through intercourse with animals that **Balaam** gained his infernal powers (Sanh. 105a–b; Zohar I: 126a).

Thus in **Talmud**, there are several apparently earnest discussions as to whether a Jew should let a pagan serve as a bailiff for Jewish livestock, out of fear the animals will be used for immoral/infernal purposes. It would be easy to assume that these are simply cases of Jews stereotyping their neighbors, but the fairly frequent representation of human-animal coupling on Greek pornographic urns suggests that the Talmud's concern was more realistic than we might imagine today.[1]

    1. Deacy and Pierce, *Rape in Antiquity: Sexual Violence in the Greek and Roman Worlds*, 69–96. See also Mathieu, *Sex Pots: Eroticism in Ceramics*.

Bet: Second letter of the **Hebrew alphabet**. It has the numeric value of 2. It is the first letter appearing in the **Torah**. According to **Genesis Rabbah**, the shape of the letter (closed above, below, and on one side, with only one side open) is meant to teach that a person should not engage in speculation about what is above, below, or precedes Creation; a lesson respectfully but more or less completely ignored by the author of this book. According to Deuteronomy Rabbah, the *bet* at the beginning of Torah (with its value of 2) teaches us about the inherent duality of Creation (2:31).[1]

    1. Munk, *The Wisdom of the Hebrew Alphabet*, 43–54.

Beth (or Beit) Alfa: This archaeological site of an ancient synagogue (ca. 4th–5th century CE) is most notable for the richly decorated mosaic floor consisting of numerous Jewish motifs surrounding an elaborate **zodiac** at the center. The most puzzling element of this display is that **Helios**, the Greek god of the **sun**, is clearly represented there in the hub of the design.[1]

    1. Avi-Yonah, *The Encyclopedia of Archaeological Excavations in the Holy Land*, 187–90.

Beth El: (*Beit El*, "House of God"). The location, near biblical **Luz**, where Jacob had his dream of a stairway to heaven (Gen. 29). It would later become a sacred center for the early cult of YHWH.

Beth El Circle: A fellowship of Lurianic mystics that convened in Jerusalem in 1737. Made up mostly of Sefardic Kabbalists, its members included Gedaliah Hayon and Shalom Sharabi. The circle continued into the 20th century.[1]

    1. Jacobs, *The Jewish Mystics*, 156–169.

Betulah: "Virgin"/Virgo. The zodiac sign for the month of Elul. This sign signifies the earth, night, sensuality, materiality, and the feminine principle.[1]

    1. Erlanger, *Signs of the Times*, 99–120.

Bezalel: "In the Shadow of God." The Israelite craftsman, "filled with the spirit of God," was primarily responsible for the construction of the **Tabernacle** (Ex. 24–25). Bezalel was identified as a gifted artisan in the Bible, and legends of his fantastic skills multiplied.

So great was his insight into God's intention that the Sages dubbed him the *R'aiah*, the Seer, along with other honorific names. Bezalel built the Tabernacle according to a heavenly pattern shown to him. He could do this because he knew how to manipulate the **Hebrew alphabet** to unleash its supernal powers, just as God used them to create the universe (Ber. 55a; Zohar I: 9a). This legend is related to the widely held belief that the Tabernacle was itself a model of the cosmos (Num. R. 12:13). The medievals credited his talent as a metallurgist to his knowledge of **alchemy**.

Bible: (*TaNaKH*). TaNaKH is an **acrostic** for the three divisions of the Hebrew Scriptures: *Torah*, *Neviim*, and *Ketuvim* (Pentateuch, Prophets, and Writings). This arrangement also roughly reflects the decreasing degree of divine inspiration credited to each book, with **Torah** being the most direct of God's revelations and the Writings generally credited to the more modest influence of the **Ruach Elohim**, the "Holy Spirit." The Hebrew Scriptures consist of thirty-nine canonical books (there are other methods of counting the collection, including treating the twelve minor prophets as a single book). The authoritative collection emerged out of a little-understood and mysterious process of canonization, a canonization not completed until at least the end of the 2nd century CE.

The Bible also mentions within its pages several other mysterious **lost books**. These include The Book of Jashar, The Book of the Wars of the Lord, and the royal chronicles of both Judah and Israel.

Aside from the many accounts of **miracles, angels**, and other spiritual forces documented in its pages, the Bible is widely regarded to be filled with occult secrets and powers not meant for the masses. These secrets are concealed in the laws and stories by means of hints, allusions, allegories, and are even encoded into the very language itself.

This occult dimension of the Bible is illustrated in a famous legend that the earth trembled when Onkelos the Proselyte and Jonathan ben Uzziel first translated the

Scriptures from the Holy Tongue (**Hebrew**) into popular Aramaic. When Ben Uzziel further dared to make explicit the esoteric meanings in his translations, a heavenly voice ordered him to stop (Meg. 3a; En Yaakov).

Evidence that the words of Scripture were held to have protective powers already begins in biblical times, as indicated by the discovery of metal **amulets** inscribed with the **Priestly Blessing** (The Lord bless and guard you . . .) dating from the Monarchy period. **Tefillin** and **mezuzahs**, both of which contain biblical texts, were similarly credited with having protective powers (Ber. 23b; S of S R. 3:7, Num. R. 12). Reciting Psalm 91 came to be regarded as the first line of defense against demons. In the Middle Ages, a scroll or book of Scriptural verses would be placed at the head of a crib to protect an infant.

Despite the words of Rabbi Akiba, who declared that all who use Bible verses for spells have no place in the **World-to-Come** (M. Sanh. 10:1), many biblical verses, such as Ex. 15:26, were used as healing **incantations**. In order to heal a seriously ill person, one might look in a book of Scripture, take the first word the eye falls upon, and add that word to the ailing person's **name**. And of course, biblical names, words, and phrases appear on virtually every inscribed amulet. Perhaps the most frequently used verses in a theurgic context are Genesis 49:18, Zechariah 3:2, and Numbers 6:24–26. **Psalms** were particularly popular in this regard. An entire book, **Shimmush Tehillim**, "Useful Psalms," is devoted to cataloging verses for treating various conditions.

Passages would also be recited over crops to increase **fertility** and over property to protect it. According to **Chayyim Vital**, one can read and pronounce Scripture in such a way that it draws down an **angel** that grants the summoner further revelations of secrets contained in the text (Sha'ar ha-Nevuah 2).

In classic magical fashion, verses were often read both forward and in reverse, or in **permutations**. Scriptures can also be used for purposes of **divination**. SEE BIBLIOMANCY; CODES; HEBREW ALPHABET; PSALMS; TEMURAH; TORAH; TZERUFIM. *(SEE ALSO APPENDIX FIGURE 5.)*

Bibliomancy: (*Sheilat Sefer*). Using Sacred Scriptures as a means of **divination**. Above and beyond the familiar interpretative tradition that finds references to current events in the words of the **prophets**, a verse can also be selected at random in the hopes of receiving an ominous message (Chag. 15a; SA, Yoreh Deah, 179:4). (This kind of interpretation can be found in the *pesher* commentaries found among the **Dead Sea Scrolls**. And, of course, it is still a popular way to interpret the book of Revelations among some contemporary Evangelical Christians.) Some Sages believed in the mantic science of **kleidon**, treating the serendipitous overhearing of verses recited by school children as **omens** (Git. 58a). The **Baal Shem Tov** compares the Bible to the **Urim and Thummim** as a potential source of mantic knowledge (Sod Yakhim u'Vo'az).

Binah: "Understanding/Insight." In the sefirotic system, Binah is the offspring and complement to **Chochmah**. It is the dark receptacle of Chochmah's light, the female counterpart to its masculine principle. As such, it is also called *Ima*, "Mother," and *Heichal*, "Palace." It is the womb of God's **light**, giving birth to all the "lower" **sefirot**. Binah is one of the root aspects of the **Tree of Life**.

Birds: (*Tzipor; Oaf*). Birds are a symbol of immortality and the **soul**. Studying the behavior of birds was a form of **divination** most popular among the Hittites.[1] Since biblical times, Jews have also regarded birds as portending the future. According to one strand of tradition, human souls take the form of birds in heaven (Baruch Apocalypse 10; Seder Gan Eden). The **Vilna Gaon**, in his mystical interpretation of the book of Jonah, also teaches that a dove symbolizes the transmigrating human soul. SEE ANIMALS; HOOPOE; MILHAM BIRD; PHOENIX; ZIZ.

1. Hallo and Younger, *The Context of Scripture*, 206; Roth, *Encyclopedia Judaica*, vol. 3, 114.

Bird's Nest: SEE PALACE OF THE BIRD'S NEST.

Birth: As the first commandment found in the Torah (be fruitful and multiply), procreation occupies a special place in Jewish thought (Gen. 1). Being a liminal time when forces of life and death potentially conjoin, it has attracted considerable occult interest.

According to the Torah, giving birth brings with it a state of uncanniness or weirdness (in the Old English sense of the word). That plus the ample amount of **blood** and other bodily fluids expelled meant that a woman was rendered *tamei* (impure) following childbirth, thirty-three days for a male infant, and twice that for a female (a blood-expelling event that yields a blood-expelling child). At the end of the period, sacrifices must be brought (Lev. 12:1–2). Beyond these, no other ritual or theurgic practices regarding childbirth are preserved in the TaNaKH. In the Scriptures, there are a number of births associated with miraculous circumstances, including the births of Isaac (Gen. 18–23) and Samson (Judg. 13).

By the time of the Rabbis, **angels**, **demons**, and **witchcraft** began to be associated with birth (Ber. 8a; RaSHI on Sot. 22b; Zohar II: 264b, 267b). In the face of the many threats to a woman in childbirth, there developed local theurgic customs and protective rituals. A copy of Leviticus might be put in the crib (SCh 1140), or magic **circles** drawn around the birthing bed, which would also be draped with **amulets** called *kindbet* in Yiddish, "child's crib," or *chamsa* in Arabic, "five [fingers]." In Poland, there arose the custom of "womb blessing" in the presence of a Torah scroll. In some communities, a Torah might be brought into the room to ensure a safe birth. Psalms or germane biblical passages (Gen. 21; I Sam. 1) would be recited.[1] In an example of analogous magic, all the doors of the house would be opened and all the knots and bows of the woman's garments would be undone to ease the birth process. Alternately, some women would wear a sash, amulet belt, or even a Torah binder around the abdomen.[2]

Mother- and/or child-protecting amulets and prayers were often mass-produced in Europe after the advent of the printing press. In Oriental communities, charms made of precious metals (silver in particular, including coins) still continued. Many of these contained binding **incantations** or pleas that protective angels or meritorious ancestors drive off the lilot and/or destructive demons attracted by the birth. Many Chasids still use a **red** string, either blessed by a living rebbe or taken to a dead tzadik's grave, and then tie it on either the woman or the bed. Vigils called *tachdid* are still practiced by Oriental Jews in Israel to this day.

1. Klein, *A Time to Be Born*, 148–52.
2. Ibid, 111–15.

Birth Pangs of the Messiah: The various tribulations and disturbances—political, social, and cosmic—that precedes the coming of the Messiah.

Bitachon, Sefer ha-: This esoteric work by the little-known **Iyyun Circle** includes passages on the creation of a **golem**.

Bitter Destruction: (*Ketev Meriri*). The demon of catastrophe (Pes. 111a–b) is identified from biblical passages (Deut. 32; Ps. 91). His power is greatest between the seventeenth of Tammuz, the date when the walls of Jerusalem were breached by the Romans, and the ninth of Av, the day the Temple was destroyed. He is scaly and hairy and rolls about like a ball. His gaze brings instant death. (Num. R. 7:9; Me'am Leoz).

Bittul ha-Yesh: "Nullification of the Ego/Selfhood." Since the ego stands as an impediment between the soul and God, Chasidic teachings encourage the spiritual seeker to sublimate or overthrow the self in order to achieve **devekut**, unification with the true reality that is God.[1]

1. Rabinowicz, *The Encyclopedia of Hasidism*, 48; Green, *Jewish Spirituality*, vol. 2, 181–91.

Black: SEE COLOR.

Blasphemy: In Jewish tradition the offense of blasphemy is limited to one who pronounces the Tetragrammaton (YHWH) for the purpose of profaning it (Lev. 24; Sanh. 56a). The punishment could vary from a flogging to death. The Gospel accounts that claim Jesus was condemned by a Jewish court for "blasphemy" for calling himself **Son of God** has no basis in any known Jewish law (M. Sanh. 7:5), suggesting the charge may be the Gospel writer's own invention.

Blessed Holy One: (ha-Kadosh Baruch Hu). A title for God popularized in Talmudic times, in Kabbalistic thought "The Blessed Holy One" designates the specifically male aspect of the Godhead and it is identified with the sefirah of Tiferet. SEE NAMES OF GOD; SEFIROT.

Blessing: (*B'rachah*). The capacity to bless something belongs foremost to God (Gen. 1, 12). A human may also bless, but with the understanding, either explicitly stated ("May it be Your will . . .") or implied, that the power of blessing comes from the Deity. Because a blessing in fact comes from God, even if humans utter it, Jewish literature regards blessings to have real consequences (Gen. 28, 48). Once said, the blessing has a reality independent of the one who spoke it, as exemplified by the saga of Esau and Jacob. Though Isaac intended the blessing he spoke over Jacob for Esau, once it was given, it could not be rescinded. In this sense a blessing is also more like an adjuration or decree of destiny than a prayer. The fact that humans have the capacity to bless is a sign of our exalted status in the cosmos (Meg. 15a; Ber. 7a; Chag. 5b). SEE CURSE.

Blood: (*Dam*). Blood is considered the essence of life and the handling of blood is of tremendous concern to God (Gen. 9). For that reason, many taboos and laws concerning blood are found in Jewish law (Lev. 17:11, 19:26; M. Ker. 5:1; Yad, Ma'achalot Asurot 6:2). The sprinkling of blood from the sacrifices upon the altar was an element in the rituals of atonement and purification. It is the first of the plagues God unleashes upon Egypt—every body of water, from the sacred Nile to the cooking kettles, was turned to blood and defiled. Blood also has protective power against numinous forces, as demonstrated during the Exodus from Egypt (Ex. 12:7, 12:22–23). The Jewish awe regarding blood continued to have a paranormal aspect—one medieval tradition held that menstruating women who gaze into mirrors will leave blood marks on the glass.

According to priestly law, blood from sacrifices and food slaughtering must be poured out on the ground and covered. Subsequent Jewish law requires that Jews go to great lengths to extract blood from animal carcasses, first hanging the animals for draining, then soaking and salting the flesh afterward to draw out any additional blood. This taboo about eating blood has meant that blood is not a regular *materia magica* used in Jewish magical formulae, rituals, or potions. Occasional exceptions appear in magical manuals such as **Sefer ha-Razim**, where we learn lion's blood, mixed with wine and rubbed on the soles of the feet, gives one persuasive power over princes. Later religious authorities, usually drawing from non-Jewish sources, start to permit blood as an ingredient in therapeutic formulae (Shevut Yaakov II: 70).

Ironically, the Jewish attitude of aversion to blood may have inspired Christian anti-Semites to regard Jews as blood obsessed and even blood lusting. Among American folklorists, the custom of hanging slaughtered animals and draining the blood practiced among Hispanics of the Southwest is taken as evidence of Crypto-Jewish occult folkways.[1] SEE BLOOD LIBEL.

1. Neulander, "The New Mexican Crypto-Jewish Canon," 140–58.

Blood Libel: The claim that Jews kill gentiles motivated by ritual/demonic impulses. While accusations of Jews engaging in ritual murder go as far back as the 1st century CE (Against Apion 2, viii 95), in what amounts to a remarkable disregard of all the evidence that Jews loathed the consumption of **blood**, medieval Christian superstition held that Jews, vampire-like, craved the blood of innocent Christians. This accusation, now known as a "blood libel," enjoyed great currency in Christian circles from the Middle Ages until well into the 20th century, though it was sporadically debunked by Church authorities.[1]

Early versions of the libel claimed Jews would steal the consecrated host from church sacristies and then perform satanic rituals upon the bread in order to make it bleed. Because Easter was the time of Jesus's death, the rumor then arose that Jews ritually reenacted the death of Christ by killing an "innocent," usually a child, and using the child's blood for the making of **matzah** for **Passover**. The first such accusation occurred in Norwich, England, in the 12th century. A long series of similar accusations arose across Europe in the centuries that followed. The purported Christian victims were frequently beatified, while the Jews accused mostly met manifold gruesome ends, the manners of death being limited only by the local imagination. During the Black Death plagues of the 14th century, it was widely believed that Jews were spreading the contagion by poisoning the wells used by Christians, leading to numerous savage persecutions across Europe. Actual trials of Jews for ritual murder peaked during the 18th century.

A Russian, Menachem Mendel Beilis, was the last Jew tried for the crime of ritual murder in 1911 (he was acquitted). In the 19th and early 20th centuries, Catholic newspapers revived the charge against Jews as part of a campaign to combat the liberal, socialist, and democratic ideas then sweeping Europe (Jews were seen as central players in these infernal ideologies). Partly as a result, accusations continued to arise in Catholic countries in the first half of the 20th century.[2] Gleefully promoted by the Nazis in the 1930s–40s, the blood libel is enjoying a new life in the Arab world, where the media and leaders in Syria and Saudi Arabia periodically claim that demonic Jews are filled with (literal) blood lust directed at non-Jews.[3]

1. Trachtenburg, *The Devil and the Jews*, 140–58.
2. See Kertzer, *The Pope vs. The Jews.*
3. Al Manar TV, Nov. 11, 2003; *Al-Riyadh*, March 10, 2004.

Blue: *SEE* COLOR.

Body: (*Guf*). The body is both a precious vessel for the soul and a mirror of higher realities (Lev. R. 34:3). Generally speaking, Judaism does not view the body as inferior to the soul, as did the Greeks, Gnostics, and some sects of Christianity. Rather, all material things are, as God describes them in the first chapter of Genesis, intrinsically "very good." The mystic Isaac of Akko likewise taught that the body is *the* necessary vehicle for human spirituality.

For this reason, the preeminent concept concerning the afterlife is that of **resurrection**, of having the body (perhaps in a more perfected form) reunited with the soul. Thus the body comes close enough to God's ideal that we can expect to be reunited with it in the **World-to-Come**.

From Early Judaism onward, the body is regarded as a **microcosm**, a replica of the universe in miniature (AdRN 31:3). According to many Sages, to study the human body is to gain insight into the nature of God. Kabbalists find the **sefirot** manifest in the organization of the body, associating its limbs and members with each of the ten aspects of God's emanations (Pardes Rimmonim, Sha'ar Hatzinorot). Illustrations superimposing the sefirotic tree of life on a human form are commonplace. Others, like **Abraham ibn Ezra**, see the human form as analogous to the **Temple** and its furnishings. All such comparisons only serve to highlight the sacred nature of the body, its status as a precious vessel of divine purpose, and as a potential receptacle of divine power. *SEE* ADAM KADMON; BONE; FINGER. (*SEE ALSO APPENDIX FIGURE 3.*)

Boel: An angel mentioned in **Sefer ha-Razim**, he is the principle angel who governs the "seventh camp of the first firmament." He is probably a Judaized version of the Greco-Egyptian god Bouel.

Bone: (*Etzem*). Rabbinic tradition identifies 248 bones in the human body, equaling the number of positive commandments found in the Torah. This number may be purely symbolic, or may be the result of actual empiricism. Counting teeth along with the 200+ bones classified by modern physiologists helps shrink the gap between what the rabbis claim and what is known today.

In the Bible, God uses bone as the starting point in creating (or recreating) a living person (Gen. 2; Ezek. 37). These last remains of the dead are regarded as having an enduring connection to the spirit. Joseph asks that his bones be brought up from Egypt to Israel, apparently not out of mere sentimentality, but in order than he might eventually dwell with the society of his dead ancestors (Gen. 50:25). This also may be the reason for the particular distress and pathos regarding the death of Rachel, whose bones must be left in a roadside grave, far from the ancestral tomb at **Machpelah** (Jer. 31:15–16).

Skulls were used to commune with the dead in Assyrian and Neo-Babylonian necromancy, but even the few incidents of necromancy reported in the Bible do not make mention of this practice. In the Midrash, however, the **terafim** mentioned in Gen. 30 are explicitly linked to this practice, claiming the terafim stolen from **Laban** were actually shrunken heads that spoke auguries (PdRE 36).

The Midrash speaks of a bone called the **luz** that, like the soul, is indestructible. It is from this bone that God will resurrect the body (Lev. R. 18:1). It was believed that postmortem diagnosis of a person's habits could be made by examining their bones (Gen. R. 89:2). One tradition goes further, claiming on the basis of Ps. 38:4 and Ezek. 32:27 that the sins of mortals are inscribed on their bones (Masekhet Kallah Rabbati 3:1).

A late Kabbalistic tradition holds that after death the bones that bear the marks of iniquity (see above) are transformed into demons (Kitzur Shelah). This is a variation on the idea that would emerge in **Chasidism** that angels and demons are the byproduct of human moral actions. *SEE* ANGELS; BODY.

In the priestly system of purity, human and animal bones are ritually impure. This severely curtails the use of bones in Jewish magic. An exceptional example found in the Talmud involves an incantation **ritual** for freeing a bone lodged in the throat by placing a similar (non-human) bone on the top of the head (Shab. 67a). Archaeologists have found finger bones buried beneath the thresholds of the Dura-Europos synagogue (ca. 3rd century) in Syria, evidently a prophylactic custom also attested to in neighboring pagan shrines. A magical text from the **Cairo Genizah** (T-S K 1.15) prescribes burying a dog or donkey shoulder bone under the houses of two people you want to alienate from each other. The bones of kosher animals could be incorporated into medical treatments (Shevut Yaakov, III: responsum 77).

The fingernails, while not technically bones, play an important role in the Kabbalistic imagination, because they represent the **kelipot**, the "husks" of impurity that attach themselves to and obscure the divine nitzotz/spark (Zohar, Shemot). Therefore it is customary in Kabbalistic/Chasidic circles for people to clip their nails on the eve of Shabbat as an act of purification. *SEE* BURIAL; FINGER.

Book of Formation: *SEE* YETZIRAH, SEFER.

Book of Illumination: *SEE* BAHIR, SEFER HA-.

Book of Jashar: *SEE* YASHAR, SEFER.

Book of Life: (*Sefer ha-Chayyim*). The heavenly book in which the names of individuals are recorded for life in the coming year. Not being recorded in the book signifies that the person will die in the next twelve months. The names are written in the Book starting on each Rosh ha-Shanah, and the Book is then sealed on Yom Kippur. The concept appears in the Bible in various guises; it may be related to the concept of the *Tappim Shimtu*, the Mesopotamian "Tablets of Destiny" battled over by the gods (Ezek. 2:8; Zech. 5:1; Jer. 17:1; Malachi 3:16; Enuma Elish).

Exclusion from the Book means a death sentence in the coming year. The Book of Life is a major theme in the High Holy Day liturgy, a way of reminding the wayward to repent (High Holy Day Machzor; R.H. 16a; Ex. R. 45:6; PR 8).

Book of the Pious: *SEE* CHASIDISM, SEFER.

Book of Radiance: *SEE* ZOHAR, SEFER.

Book of Raziel: *SEE* RAZIEL, SEFER.

Book of Secrets: *SEE* RAZIM, SEFER HA-.

Book of the Wars of the Lord: *SEE* MILCHAMOT ADONAI, SEFER.

Book of the Watchers: *SEE* ENOCH, FIRST BOOK OF.

Bor: "Pit." The Underworld. Going there is not a good thing (Ezek. 26:20). A biblical synonym for **Sheol**, in later Jewish literature it becomes the name for one of the seven levels of **Gehenna**.

Bor She'on or Bor Sh'on: "Pit of Turmoil." One of the seven compartments of **Gehenna** mentioned in the Talmud (Sotah 10a; Eruv. 19a).

Botarel, Moses: Sorcerer and failed messiah (Spanish, ca. 15th century). Botarel was a magician who used **amulets**, sacred names, and angelic summonings. He wrote an eccentric commentary for **Sefer Yetzirah**. After a visitation from **Elijah**, he declared himself messiah, but the claim came to nothing.

Bow: Biblical rhetoric often envisions God as a cosmic warrior with a bow (Zech. 9, 10). The **rainbow**, of course, is a sign of God's peaceful intent toward the world after the Flood, having "hung up" the bow (Gen. 9). Starting in Talmudic times, the "bow" takes on a sexual association, becoming a euphemism for a penis (Gen. R. 87:7; Chag. 15a; Sanh. 92a; Zohar I: 58a).

Bratzlav Chasidim: The so-called "Dead Chasidim" first formed around the charismatic and enigmatic **Nachman of Bratzlav** in the first decade of the 19th century. Unable to move past his death, they have been unique among Chasids for having no living **rebbe** to lead them. Their particular practices and outlook have provoked suspicion and hostility from other Jewish groups. They have even been suspected of being secret **Frankist** heretics.

Today they are among the most open, if undisciplined, of the Chasidic sects, attracting many seekers from the larger Jewish world.

Bread: (*Lechem*). Bread is the archetypal sustenance in Judaism. The use of bread for **ritual** purposes extends back to the beginnings of the people Israel.

In the biblical age, bread was one of the acceptable forms of offerings in the sacrificial cult. The afternoon offering was even coined *minchah*, meaning "meal offering." Theurgic practices included the display of *lechem ha-panim*, the "Bread of Presence/show bread," twelve loaves that were set in the sanctuary of the Temple and replaced on a weekly basis. Unleavened bread, or **matzah**, also plays a central role in the rites and observance of **Passover**. **Manna** was the miraculous bread that fell from heaven, feeding the Israelites for their forty-year sojourn in the Wilderness.

Chief among the purely ritual uses of bread is *challah*. A small amount of it is pulled from the dough and burnt, in commemoration of the portion set aside for the **priest**. An additional ritual use is the ceremony of *tashlich*. Some say this custom is based on the notion that sins could be "transferred" to a substance which led to the custom of casting bread upon a natural water source.[1] In authoritative interpretations this act is purely symbolic, but some apparently believed there was a metaphysical efficacy to this custom and that they were literally casting away their sins through the agency of the bread. Medieval customs included setting a loaf of bread beside a dying man, perhaps as sustenance for the soul's journey after death.

Overtly magical traditions include the belief that bread and salt given to a newlywed couple or the family moving into a new house will deter the **evil eye**. Based on the wording of Ex. 23:25, it was believed that bread and water hung in a home would prevent the spread of disease (Ta'amei ha-Minhagim III, p. 142). A wounded vampire could fend off destruction if she (Jewish tradition only mentions female vampires) could obtain and consume the bread and salt of her assailant (Testament of Judah the Pious). Cakes decorated with magical incantations would be consumed by people to "absorb" the magical result (Machzor Vitry; Sefer Rokeach). This practice is most associated with magical methods for improving memory and the mastery of Torah texts (Sefer ha-Rokeach, Sefer Raziel). SEE AFIKOMAN; MANNA; SUBSTITUTION; UNLEAVENED BREAD.

1. Frankel and Platkin Teutch, *The Encyclopedia of Jewish Symbols*, 24–25.

Breaking of the Vessels: (*Shevirat ha-Kelim*). The primordial dissolution of the cosmos. According to the cosmogonic theory of **Isaac Luria**, God is the totality of all things, and it is the nature of God's abundant goodness to want to give. This divine desire to give immediately created a receptacle (the primordial universe) to receive that abundant goodness, in the form of light, flowing out from God. God created intermediate vessels to contain the supernal light emanating from **Adam Kadmon**. However, these vessels initially could only receive the divine overflow but not return it or discharge it, so they filled to capacity and shattered. The universe therefore suffered a cosmic disruption, or misalignment (Etz ha-Chayyim, Sha'arei ha-Melachim 5; Sha'ar ha-Gilgulim 3; Tanya 25).

In order to bring it back into balance, God reformed the structure of the universe into vessels that could both give and receive. Often this new structure is called the **Partzufim**. Therefore the universe now contains unevenly distributed areas of abundance and areas of lack, with **nitzotzot**, scattered divine sparks, which need to be gathered and given back so the original order can be restored. Those sparks of the divine light that fell deepest into Creation, however, were encased in **kelipot** (husks) of impurity, evil, and entropy.

This then is the Lurianic rationale for the Torah and commandments: it is by the correct performance of these acts that we unleash the divine sparks trapped in every aspect of worldly existence and, in partnership with God, restore the divine order (Sha'ar ha-Gilgulim). Various Chasidic writers, such as **Nachman of Bratzlav** and **Sh'neur Zalman of Laydi**, have offered refinements and elaborations of this metaphysical model. This myth is perhaps the most overt expression of **Gnosticism** found in Jewish mysticism. SEE TIKKUN.

Breastplate: (*Hoshen*). The breastplate of the High Priest of the cult of YHWH. It had both symbolic and spiritual significance. It consisted of either a gold plate or gold threads interwoven with scarlet, purple, and blue fabrics and mounted with twelve precious and semiprecious stones, each one engraved with the name of a tribe, arranged in four rows across. There may also have been a pouch behind it, made from folded fabric. According to one rabbinic tradition, the engraving on the stones was done by the **shamir worm** (Git. 68a–b).

One of the functions of the *hoshen* was divining YHWH's will, and as such it was sometimes referred to as the *hoshen mishpat*, the "Breastplate of Judgment." If and how it was used, and its exact relationship to the **Urim and Thummim**, is unclear. Perhaps they were used in conjunction with each other. Or perhaps the title "Breastplate of Judgment" simply derives from the fact that the *hoshen* held the Urim and Thummim when not in use. Others believe that the High Priest gazed into the gemstones and received oracles from the patterns of light refraction (lithomancy). Another tradition holds that it functioned like a Ouija board, with the priest scrying the letters in order to form word messages (Yoma 73b). *SEE* EPHOD; GEMSTONES; PRIESTHOOD.

Bride of God: While the Bible gives no indication that the God of Israel has a divine consort, a piece of biblical-era graffiti reveals that there were people who held that YHWH was linked to Asherah. In the prophetic imagination, the people of Israel are the bride of God (Jer. 2:2; Hos. 21:22).

Rabbinic and mystical literature amplifies this teaching until it becomes a major metaphor for the relationship between God and the Jews (Pes. 106b; Sanh. 7a; PdRE 41; MdRI, 3; Deut. R. 3:12; PR 31:10; Bahir, 196; Sha'ar ha-Pesukim). The Zohar also speaks of the Shekhinah as the "bride of God," though this may be a distinction without a difference, since the Shekhinah is regarded to be both the feminine side of the Godhead and the collective soul of Israel (Zohar I: 120, 202a–203a; II: 175b; III: 74b). Mostly startling of all is the Zohar's claim that during this time of exile and evil ascendant, Lilith has become God's consort (II: 118a–b; III: 97a).

Brit Milah: *SEE* CIRCUMCISION.

Brontology: A method of divining the future from meteorological and astrological observations. A genre of writing very popular in late antiquity, there is one Jewish example, an Aramaic fragment, which has been found among the **Dead Sea Scrolls**.

Broshah: A child-stealing demoness.

Burial: The period immediately following death is regarded in many cultures as a liminal time in which the soul must be assisted by the living to find its way into the afterlife. The consequences of failing to properly do this include displacement of the soul as a **ghost** or other distressed spirit, or the bringing of evil upon those living who did not fulfill their obligations to the dead.

Hints of this thinking are evident in the Bible, yet despite a few allusions to *rafaim* (ghosts), the texts tell us only the most minimal facts about how the Hebrews buried their dead. Specifically, we find the use of **caves** for family/clan burial, or barring that, the construction of a cairn with an upright stone pillar. The desire of **Joseph** to have his bones transferred to Israel may reflect a belief that his spirit would be in a kind of afterlife exile unless he was buried alongside his kin (Gen. 50:25).

For a brief period of time Jews practiced secondary burial, which involved first allowing the soft tissue to decay away and then reinterring the **bones** in an ossuary or bone chamber with the bones of other family members. While there is one mention of cremation in the Scriptures (I Sam. 31:12), the burning of bodies is never accepted as normative and is forbidden in Jewish law.

In the more expansive rabbinic literature, however, many more beliefs and practices surrounding burial, including beliefs about the soul and its needs, are recorded. Bodies were buried with their feet directed toward **Jerusalem**, so that in the moment of resurrection they would arise facing the way home. Tradition mandates a body be buried quickly, for to leave it to decay is sign of disrespect. On the other hand, the bodies of the **righteous** do not decay (B.M. 84b; Zohar I: 4a). According to **Sefer Chasidim**, those who die bearing a grudge will seek vengeance against the living after they are gone, so it is best to settle any disputes with a dying person (708).

Many customs relating to fear of the **evil eye** are written down during the Middle Ages. The formal existence of *Chevraot Kadisha*, communal burial societies, helped preserve many of these. Examples include not allowing a child to follow the coffin or even attend the funeral (there was already a prohibition that applied to the sons of priests based on the rules of priestly purity). Mourners in some communities shattered a pot in front of their door when they left for a funeral, evidently to frighten away the evil eye. Sephardic Jews were known to throw **coins** around the coffin of the dead in order to "pay off" evil spirits who might otherwise attack the vulnerable spirit of the deceased. A grave should not be left dug and empty overnight, lest the evil eye see it and cause another death. All the water in the house would be poured out, either because the dead soul may have used it to perform **ablutions** in preparation for its journey to the afterlife, or because the **Angel of Death** might have used the water to wipe clean the knife used to slay the deceased. Water would be poured over the threshold of a house in mourning to prevent the spirit of the newly deceased from entering his former abode. Those who accompany the body need to perform various rites, such as the *Tikkun Shovavim*, to protect against evil spirits drawn to the death. These might include ritual ablutions and interrupting the processional to and from the grave (S.A. Yoreh Deah 339–75; Ma'avar Yabbok).

Modern preparations of the body for burial have become increasingly elaborate. Shards of pottery are placed over the eyes of the dead. The thumb of the corpse is often bent to form the hand in the shape of the letter *shin* and bound in place with *tzitzit*. Some burial societies place a stick or a fork in the hand of the dead so that it may symbolically dig its way to the Holy Land for the **resurrection**.

The dread of burying a person alive does not seem to have preoccupied Jews. Thus when, as a response to this anxiety, European gentile authorities started requiring bodies be kept above ground for three days, many Jewish communities resisted. This was a controversy of metaphysical significance to those who believed a delay in burial meant the soul could not successfully transmigrate to its next incarnation.

The **Baal Shem Tov** was credited with being a kind of spirit guide to the disoriented souls of the newly dead, guiding them to their reward on the eve of the **Sabbath**. Pious Jews to this day will congregate into *Chevra Tehillim*, "Psalm fellowships," reciting Psalms post mortem in order to ease the transition for the dead. Many of the customs mentioned above, or variations of them, continue to be observed in various traditional communities. *SEE* BANIM SHOVAVIM; DEATH; GHOST; POSSESSION, GHOSTLY; SOUL; WORLD-TO-COME.

Burning Bush: (*Senah*). The fiery bush from which God's angel made himself manifest to **Moses**, and from which God gave Moses his commission to deliver the people Israel (Ex. 3–4). It symbolizes both God's concern for Israel and God's presence in even the lowliest part of **Creation**.

Ex. R. (2:5) includes a debate whether the angel of the bush was **Michael** or **Gabriel**. Despite the fantastic nature of this apparition, the burning bush has not received a great deal of esoteric interpretation. Whether the bush should be regarded as belonging to the motif of the "cosmic tree" found in both pagan and Jewish cosmology is a matter of debate. St. Catherine's Monastery in the Sinai claims to have the original bush preserved in its courtyard as a holy relic.

In a classic example of magical **paradox**, the word *senah* can be recited over and over to combat **fever** (Shab. 67a). In more elaborate ceremonies, a bush is actually cut down as part of a fever-combating **ritual**. *SEE* FIRE; TREES.

Burnt Offerings: *SEE* SACRIFICE.

C

Cabala Mystica: "The Mysterious Tradition," or sometimes referred to as "The Book of Sacred Magic." An alchemical text composed by Abraham ben Simeon. Variant manuscripts survive in Hebrew, French, and German. It shows a broad knowledge of Jewish sources, but given its multiple references to Christian ideas, it is unclear whether the author is a Jew or a Christian. *SEE* ALCHEMY.

Cain: The first child of **Adam** and **Eve**. According to the Bible, Cain was exiled from his family after he murdered his brother, Abel (Gen. 4). God marked him so that all creatures would know not to kill him. According to one rabbinic legend, God marked Cain by giving him a **horn** growing out of his forehead. In old age, his vision-impaired grandson, Lemach, killed Cain when he mistook him for a game animal. According to another tradition, the letter *vav* (one of the letters of the **Tetragrammaton**) was inscribed on his forehead, granting him theurgic protection (Ginzberg, *Legends of the Jews*, 1:111).

Pirkei de-Rabbi Eliezer 21 calls him a "spawn of **Satan**," reflecting a tradition that Cain was actually the offspring of the coupling of Eve and the **serpent**, rather than with **Adam** (Targum Pseudo-Jonathan, Gen. 4:1; Shab. 146a; Zohar I: 34b, 54b–55a). One tradition considered all his descendants up to the time of **Noah** perverse—it was his daughters whose allure ensnared the **fallen angels** (Gen. 6)—but his line ended with the bulk of humanity during the **Flood**, which his progeny helped trigger (Wisdom of Solomon 10:3–4; Chokhmat ha-Nefesh 26v).

In **Kabbalah**, Cain is the personification of the fallen state of mankind, the symbolic representation of spiritual alienation between man and God, while Tubal-Cain, **Enoch**, Noah, and **Abraham** each signify a progressive restoration of the divine-human relationship. The taint of Cain, passed down from his serpent-demon sire, persisted with humanity until the giving of the **Torah**.

Cairo Geniza: A *geniza* is a repository for damaged or discarded texts that contain divine names, where they await eventual burial, like a human corpse. In the ancient synagogue of Fostat, Egypt, outside of Cairo, the Geniza there had not been emptied for some 1,200 years when Western scholars discovered its existence at the end of the 19th century. This collection of texts dates from as early as the 8th century of the Common Era. Along with biblical, rabbinic, and liturgical texts, the Geniza includes a number of astrological and magical documents such as the **Testament of Solomon**, **Sefer ha-Razim**, **The Book of the Responding Entity**, and **The Book of Guidance**, books which include incantations to invoke **angels** and to control and expel **demons**. **Amulets**, herbal preventatives, spells for combating illness, and mantic techniques, such as **lecanomancy**, are also found among the documents. A partial list of magical texts in the Geniza include:

> **Oxford MS. Heb. C 18/30:** A fragment of **Sefer ha-Razim**. There are multiple fragments of ShR found in the Geniza.

T-S K 1.15: A Hebrew-Arabic fragment of a magical handbook. It contains formulae for **birth**, **love**, and **hate** magic, and **curses**.

T-S K 1.19: A fragment of magical spells for **fertility**, for birth, "for opening everything closed . . . ," for use against forgetfulness, and for protection against **poison**.

T-S K 1.57: A fragment of spells for winning the favor of powerful people and for protection against harm on a journey.

T-S K 1.58: A text of spells for silencing enemies, and for protecting against scorpions and against **witchcraft**.

T-S K 1.80: A fragmentary text of adjuring spells for angels to subdue enemies, for augury, and protection.

T-K 1.91: A text of spells for **healing**, **sleep**, household tranquility, counteracting curses, silencing enemies, and for preventing stillbirth and miscarriage.

T-K 1.132: A fragment of incantations for **divination**, love, creating enmity, learning, and gaining influence.

T-K 1.171: Spell text with formulae for learning **Torah**, protection from scorpions, creating divine fire, and influencing others.

There are many more magical texts among the Geniza collection, most little more than scraps of material, which have some magical, mystical, or occult purpose.

Calendar: (*Luach*). Since biblical times, the Hebrew Calendar has been based on the cycles of the **moon**, corrected to the solar year, with the *moled*, the "birth" of the new moon, signaling the start of each month. The Babylonians had a significant influence on the organization of the Hebrew calendar because of the Jewish exile in their midst. The current names for the months are all, in fact, Babylonian names. The year-numbering system is based on the years from **Creation** (PdRE 8).

The exact operation of the calendar has been a point of sectarian controversy throughout Jewish history. Some, like the priests who collected the **Dead Sea Scrolls**, adhered to an alternative solar calendar and despised the lu-

nar system as an impure and wicked artifact of the **fallen angels**.[1] At times the Samaritans, who also possessed an alternative calendar, even attempted to interfere with the announcement of the Jewish **New Moon**, which was determined by direct observation and then publicized using hilltop beacons (R.H. 22a). *SEE* ENOCH; MOON; NUMBERS; SUN; ZODIAC. *(SEE ALSO APPENDIX FIGURE 6.)*

1. Elior, *The Three Temples*, 54–57.

Candles: *SEE* LAMPS; LIGHT.

Candlestick: *SEE* MENORAH.

Cannibalism: The only accounts of cannibalism in Jewish literature are to be found in accounts of starvation during sieges and famines (Lamentations; En Yaakov).

Carmel, Mount: Mountain on the coast of north Israel, where the city of Haifa now exists. In biblical times, Carmel was evidently regarded as a holy high place dedicated to the God of Israel. **Elijah** fought his wondrous duel with the prophets of **Baal** and **Asherah** there (I Kings 27:30), winning the argument when a miraculous fire from heaven consumed his offering. It was later, while hiding in caves there, that he was able to destroy troops of King Ahab, also by means of a flame strike. *SEE* FIRE; MOUNTAIN; SACRIFICE.

Caro, Joseph: Legalist and mystic (Turkish, ca. 16th century). Caro authored the Beit Joseph and **Shulchan Aruch**, the two most influential digests of Jewish Law in history. He also kept, over much of his adult life, a personal mystical diary in which he records his regular encounters with his **maggid**, or spirit guide. Caro sometimes identified this figure as the Mishnah personified. Other times he called it the **Shekhinah**. The maggid revealed its *sod ha-Torah*, its secret Torah, to Caro via **xenoglossia**. The authenticity of this mystical testimony, published after his death in the collection Maggid Mesharim, has been regarded as suspect. Many found it hard to believe that such an acute legal mind also had such a bizarre esoteric inner life. Still, given that there are independent accounts of Caro's spiritual possessions written by his contemporaries, most scholars today accept the Maggid Mesharim as genuinely from Caro's hand.[1] Caro also performed **exorcisms**. Some have argued his is the first recorded example of a Jewish exorcist who dealt with ghostly (as opposed to demonic) **possession**. *SEE* IBBUR OR DEVEKUT; MEDIUM; VISIONS.

1. Jacobs, *Jewish Mystical Testimonies*, 123–51.

Cats: Cats do not appear in Jewish literature before the Greco-Roman period. Attitudes towards cats (lucky, unlucky) varied from one Jewish community to another, and may have been a reflection of how cats were viewed in the larger communities. One Kabbalist believed that the soul of one who misuses the **Divine Name** is reincarnated as a cat.

Offering menstrual blood to a cat, accompanied by the appropriate spell, can render a man impotent (Shab. 75b). Sprinkling the ashes of a female fetus of a black cat on one's eyes makes demons visible (Ber. 6a). In medieval Jewish communities, cat's **blood** was used for medicinal purposes (though was not in a potion to be consumed). Surprisingly, cats are never mentioned in **Sefer ha-Razim**, which provides one of the most exhaustive lists of Jewish *materia magica* preserved. *SEE* ANIMALS.

Caves: (*M'arah*). Caves are archetypal symbols of the womb, death, and the underworld. Several caves are mentioned in Scripture, including the caves where **David** hid himself from Saul and the cave where **Elijah** dwelt on Mount Horeb prior to his theophany from God (I Kings 18). The cave most associated with supernatural events, however, is the **Cave** of Machpelah outside of Hebron, where Abraham's family interred their dead (Gen. 23; PdRE 39).

The Sages describe Machpelah as a nexus point of power, or even as the entrance to **Eden**. **Abraham** stumbles upon Machpelah accidentally, only to discover the perfectly preserved and radiant bodies of **Adam** and **Eve** inside. This is what inspired him to buy the cave, despite the exorbitant price (Gen. R. 58:8; Mid. Teh. 92:6).

The most famous cave in rabbinic tradition is the cave where **Simon bar Yochai** and his son hid from the Roman authorities. According to legend, God miraculously provided them with a carob **tree** and a well to sustain them, and their clothes never wore out. They dwelt there for twelve years. Elijah finally appeared to them to announce the end of the Roman persecutions, but when they went outside, their gazes incinerated any impure thing they looked upon, whereupon God ordered them back to the cave for another year. They came out more reconciled to the flaws of the world, and Bar Yochai performed many **miracles** after that (Shab. 33b; Gen. R. 79:6; Eccl. R. 10:9; PdRK 11:16). The **Zohar**, it is claimed, was written while Bar Yochai was in the cave.

Cemetery: (*Beit ha-Kevarot; Beit Olam; Beit Chayyim*). A communal repository for the dead. As the repository of corpses, the cemetery is regarded as *tamei*, an "unclean," or better translated, an "uncanny" place. As the abode of the dead, the cemetery is frequently regarded as a portal between this world and the next. As such, communion between the living and the dead is more possible there than in other locations.

In the Bible, the prophet Isaiah gives testimony to the practice of **incubation**, of people sleeping on a grave overnight with the goal of having a mantic or veridical dream (Isa. 8:19–22, 19:3). In rabbinic literature, the voices of the dead and/or actual ghosts are encountered there. It was also a place where **demons** and **unclean spirits** would lurk. Such traditions multiply in later Jewish writings. **Eleazar of Worms** (ca. 13th century) describes the "lights" of dead souls wandering around cemeteries at night, engaging in some of the same activities as when they were living, such as conversation, prayer, and Torah study (Sefer Rokeach 313; SCh 35, 452). Shabbatei Horowitz (ca. 18th century) recommended reciting Psalm 91 to drive away demons before entering a graveyard.

Like their non-Jewish neighbors, Jews of antiquity consulted the dead for advice, effectively ignoring both biblical and rabbinic prohibitions. **Sefer ha-Razim** provides a **ritual** for ghost summoning in a graveyard. Like their German neighbors, Jews of the Middle Ages believed that herbs gathered from cemeteries had great medicinal powers. One ritual recorded involves gathering them while reciting Psalm 19.[1]

There is little evidence that human body parts were used by Jews for medical or magical purposes, though archaeologists in one exceptional case have found human finger bones imbedded in the walls of an ancient synagogue in

Dura-Europos. *SEE* BLOOD; BODY; BONES; DEATH; LAMP; NEC-ROMANCY; YICHUDIM.

1. Trachtenberg, *Jewish Magic and Superstition*, 207.

Census: *SEE* COUNTING.

Centaurs: Centaurs were among the demonic offspring of the corrupt generations starting with Enosh. Centaurs were wiped out by the Flood (Eruv. 18b; Gen. R.11:5, 23:6).

CHaBaD: Also known as the Lubavitch Chasidim, CHa-BaD is the second largest Chasidic community in the world, after the Satmars. The word "CHaBaD" is an acronym derived from the Hebrew words *Chochmah-Binah-Da'at*, "Wisdom-Insight-Knowledge," the first triad of the **sefirot**. CHaBaD espouses one of the most complex mystical theosophies found among the Chasids, which is largely enshrined in the **Tanya**, written by CHaBaD's first **rebbe, Sh'neur Zalman of Laydi**. CHaBaD is also notable because, in contrast to most Chasidic groups, it maintains a strong culture of outreach to other Jews, making it one of the most accessible ways for nontraditional Jews to learn Chasidic teachings. In recent years, the group has become highly controversial because many of its members insist their deceased rebbe, **Menachem Mendel Schneerson**, will return from the dead as the **Messiah**. Some Chabadniks have even gone so far as to declare Schneerson a divine being, advocating a kind of quasi-Christian heresy.[1]

1. Berger, *The Rebbe, the Messiah, and the Scandal of Orthodox Indifference*, 104–5, 159–74.

Chafetz Chayyim: Rabbi and ethicalist (Israel, 1838–1933). Rabbi Meir Kagen, universally known as the Chafetz Chayyim, dabbled in the occasional spiritual **exorcism**.

Chai ben Sherira Gaon: Leader of Babylonian Jewry (Iraqi, ca. 9th century). His writings on the nature of **Ma'asei Merkavah** mysticism and **Hechalot literature** inform Jewish understanding of these ideas and practices to this day (Otzer ha-Geonim).

Chaldean: A Babylonian. Later Jewish usage rendered it synonymous with "astrologer."

Chalomot She'elot: "Dream questions." A **divination** ritual involving questioning **angels**. *SEE* DREAM; SAR HA-CHALOM.

Chamsa: (Aramaic, "Five"). A hand-shaped **amulet**. *SEE* HAND.

Chanameel: Cousin of the prophet Jeremiah (Jer. 32), a prophet in his own right, and a master of esoteric powers. He could adjure **angels**. During the siege of Jerusalem, he summoned armies of them to fight the Babylonians. Since this contravened God's will, God changed the angelic names. In response, Chanameel summoned the *Sar Olam*, the "Prince of the Universe," to lift Jerusalem into heaven, where it waits to be brought down with the coming of the Messiah (Eikah Zuta, Lam. R. 2).

Chanina ben Dosa: Mishnaic wonder-worker (ca. 1st century). Called an *ish ma'aseh*, a "man of [wondrous] deeds." Many miraculous stories of him revolve around his abject poverty. Because of his piety, God replicated the miracle of the manna just for him. When a shrewish neighbor sought to humiliate Ben Dosa's wife because of their poverty, God filled her oven with savory bread (B. Tan. 25a). So poor he was able only to bring a polished rock to the Temple as an offering, God sent angelic porters to him, who then teleported him there instantaneously. In another legend, his wife prayed for some of his heavenly reward to come to them while they were still alive. A golden table leg miraculously appeared. But when Ben Dosa dreamt of a table in heaven with only three legs, he made her return it to its heavenly source.

He once caused the beams of his neighbor's house to grow by means of a magical incantation constructed from the person's name. He had the power to stop and start the rain with a **prayer**. He also made vinegar burn like **oil**. Such was the power of his saintliness that he could overcome **Igrat**, a **queen of demons**. Other **miracles** are credited to him (Pes. 112b; En Yaakov). *SEE* RIGHTEOUS, THE.

Chanina ben Pappa: Talmudic Sage (ca. 4th century). Demonic forces periodically tormented him. He was once confronted by evil spirits while delivering charity at night, but drove them away with words of Scripture. On another occasion, his body spontaneously erupted into sores in order to fend off a seduction. When **witchcraft** was used to cure them, he was forced to flee to maintain his modesty, only to end up in a haunted bathhouse (J. Pe. 8; Kid. 39b, 81a). He also received **dreams** that guided him in his teaching of the **Torah**. He was a close acquaintance of the **Angel of Death**, whom he was able to outfox for a month. Before he died, he was shielded by a pillar of **fire** and only died when he willingly acquiesced (Ket. 77b).

Chanina ben Tradyon: Talmudic Sage (ca. 2nd century), he was one of the **ten martyrs** of the Roman persecutions. According to RaSHI, Ben Tradyon knew how to use the power of the forty-two-letter **name of God** so well that he could obtain whatever he desired. Though a pious man, his martyrdom was punishment for abusing his occult knowledge (A.Z. 17b). Burned to death while wrapped in a Torah scroll, he told his watching disciples that he saw the letters of the text flying off to heaven (BhM 2:64–72).

Chanting: Chanting is a spiritual practice that has occupied a central place in Jewish worship from time immemorial. The **Torah** and the rest of Scripture are chanted when read liturgically, following an ancient method known as *ta'amim*. The **Merkavah** mystics likely chanted divine names and word permutations to achieve an altered state of consciousness. Chasids also use chanting, especially the distinctive musical form of the *niggun*, a wordless melody, to achieve states of **ecstasy**. *SEE* CHASIDISM; MUSIC.

Chanukah: A minor Jewish holiday celebrated for eight days beginning on the twenty-fifth of Kislev. The centerpiece of the holiday is commemorating the miracle of **oil**, when a single day's worth of **olive** oil burned for the eight full days required to rededicate the **Temple**, which had been desecrated by Israel's enemies. This small wonder becomes the basis for many legends and folktales of miraculous events occurring at the Chanukah season. *SEE* MENORAH.

Chaos: (*Tohu* or *Tohu va-Vohu*). The primordial state of existence before the creation of the cosmos. In the Bible, God is the tamer of Chaos, forcing it to conform to His will. God's words reshape Chaos, usually imagined as a watery void, into sky, oceans, and land (Gen. 1; Ps. 104; Job 38). In ancient pagan cosmogonies, the gods must battle personified chaos in order to create the universe. Personified chaos creatures, represented by **Leviathan**, **Rahav**, and **Behemoth**, are still found in Jewish mythology, but they are both figuratively and literally domesticated, becoming yet another of God's creations, and in some interpretations, God's actual pets (A.Z. 3b). Still, some biblical passages hint that chaos is a constant threat, a power that lurks at the periphery of the cosmos, and there is a danger it can be unleashed again, as it was in the Noah epic (Gen. 6–9). Even if physical chaos is restrained, moral chaos is still a force in the world (Ps. 44, 74). Chaos is also the antipode of life, and is often associated with death, a form of chaos that humanity reintroduced into God's universe (II Sam. 22:5–6; Gen. 2–3). In the **End of Days**, God will finally and completely subdue all residual chaos, perfecting the world morally and defeating death utterly (Isa. 2; Isa. 25:8).[1]
SEE ABYSS; DEATH; EVIL; FOUNDATION STONE; OLAM HA-TOHU; WATER; WATER LIBATION; YETZER HA-RA.

1. See Levenson, *Creation and the Persistence of Evil*, 3–47.

Charba de Moshe: *SEE* SWORD OF MOSES.

Chariot: (*Merkavah*). These vehicles of ancient elites were also envisioned as the transport of the gods. The Canaanites described **Baal** riding on a chariot of clouds. Astral cults envision the orb of the sun as being the wheel of a celestial chariot. Sometime in the 6th century BCE, a representation of a sun chariot was installed in the **Temple** in Jerusalem, a move condemned by the prophets (II Kings 23:11–12).

God also rides a supernal chariot (Hab. 3:8). Like Baal, it is sometimes envisioned as a cloud (Ps. 104:3). One passage suggests God maintains a fleet of vehicles (Ps. 68:18). Elijah is transported to heaven in such a cosmic chariot.

In the most detailed, albeit confusing, biblical description of God's celestial chariot, it appears to be made of numinous creatures: **chayyot**, **ofanim**, and **cherubim** (Ezek. 1, also see chapter 10). Many of the features of Ezekiel's chariot correspond to the objects and colors found in the Temple sanctuary, suggesting that God's chariot is the pattern for the figures and implements found in and around the **Holy of Holies**. A heavenly chariot, with **Helios** steering it, also appears in Jewish synagogue art.

According to Talmud, a mighty angel, **Sandalfon**, stands behind the chariot at all times, while **Metatron** stands beneath its wheels. Many of these traditions overlap with the **Throne of Glory**, and the relationship between the two divine conveyances is confusing. Many scholars simply speak of God's "Chariot-Throne."

Some Sages declare the Patriarchs Abraham, Isaac, and Jacob to be the "chariot" of God, inspiring the mystical-ethical teaching that we likewise should strive to be God's chariot in the world (Gen. R. 47:6). SEE ANGELS; ARK OF THE COVENANT; CHERUB; MA'ASEI MERKAVAH.

Charity: (*Tzedakah*). Proverbs 10:2 declares "Charity saves from death." Many Jews have taken this admonition quite literally and generous giving to the poor and needy is perhaps the single most frequently prescribed preventative and protective remedy in all of Jewish folklore. Generous giving in this world also ensures **resurrection** in the **World-to-Come** (PdRE 33).

The appearance of a beggar or poor person is even regarded as a "gift" to the person encountering him, for God is providing an opportunity for the donor to gain merit (R.H. 16a; B.B. 10a; Zohar I: 104a; Sefer ha-Yashar 13). Based on Psalm 111:3, Isaac Luria taught that giving charity leaves an enduring mark on the soul. **Chasidism** celebrates self-sacrificing charity and has numerous stories praising Chasidic masters who lived charitably and died penniless. SEE COINS; RIGHTEOUS, THE.

Charms: SEE AMULETS.

Chashmal or Chashmalah: The mysterious substance or entity illuminating the heart of Ezekiel's chariot vision (Ezek. 1). The Talmud treats the word as a **notarikon**, the division of which reveals two words, "words" and "quiet." Thus the heart of divinity is a matrix of silence and speech from which Creation emanates (Chag. 14b).

According to Midrash Konen, Chashmal is the fiery substance that makes up the **pillars** on which the world rests. Noting that the Bible offers both a masculine and feminine spelling (Ezek. 1:4, 1:27, 8:2), some mystics think it signifies the masculine and feminine principle present simultaneously in divinity.[1] Gematria yields several different equivalences: *dimyon tzivonim*, "image of colors," and *ki zohar aish*, "Like a fiery splendor," neither of which are terribly edifying. But even these cryptic analyses can only approximate the truth. Those who truly comprehend the significance of Chashmal place themselves in mortal danger (Chag. 13a). Hechalot Zutarti and Midrash Konen (2:25) attempt to resolve the confusion by designating Chashmal as yet another class of angelic being. In modern Hebrew, *chashmal* is the word for "electricity." SEE CHARIOT; EZEKIEL; FACE OF GOD; VISIONS.

1. Wolfson, *Along the Path*, 2–3.

Chasidei Ashkenaz: SEE GERMAN PIETISTS.

Chasidim, Sefer: "Book of the Pious." This 13th-century book of ethical, esoteric, and occult teachings was the main and most influential work of the **German Pietist** movement. It was written by **Judah ben Samuel ha-Chasid**. It includes many fabulous beliefs and tales of the paranormal, including descriptions of **witches**, **vampires**, and visitations from **ghosts**.

Chasidism: While the word "Chasid" can refer to any pious Jew, in modern times Chasidism has come to mean a pietistic movement within Judaism that was founded by **Israel ben Eliezer**, the Baal Shem Tov, in 18th-century eastern Europe. It began among Jews who were reacting to the domination of Jewish community life by an elite culture of rabbis and to the upheaval following the collapse of the messianic hopes raised by **Shabbatai Tzvi**. Chasidism stresses the superiority of religious enthusiasm and devotion over study and intellectualism. Many Jews found this message inspiring and the movement quickly spread through eastern and central Europe.

The Baal Shem Tov taught largely through parables that stressed humility and purity of heart. He also drew heavily upon Jewish mysticism, particularly the teachings of **Isaac Luria**. He was also widely regarded to be an exceptional "wunder-rabbi," performing many miracles and supernatural feats, as his title of **Baal Shem** suggests.

His immediate successors created a dynamic and charismatic movement of tremendous spiritual power and intensity, while later generations began institutionalizing these teachings. Divisions gradually arose, and leadership evolved into dynastic families, the heads of which were known as **rebbes** (masters) or *tzadikim* (righteous ones).

The Chasidic groups that survived the Holocaust (and many did not) differ in the degree to which they combine an intellectual emphasis with their spiritualism, which is now known as *Chasidut*. As the last truly premodern movement, they also hold to the accumulated supernatural and occult teachings of traditional Judaism. Most Chasidic groups today live in Israel and the United States.

While Chasidism is remarkable for its agenda of popularizing mystical/theurgic teachings and practices, perhaps the most unique feature of the Chasidic movement within Judaism is the exalted status of the rebbe, the charismatic leader of a Chasidic "court," who is perceived as a kind of perfected human who serves as a conduit between the Chasids and God. The Chasids assume, as a matter of course, that such spiritual enlightenment is accompanied by a mastery of spiritual and miraculous powers. Many disciples of a rebbe will appeal to him for prayer and spiritual intervention on their behalf, so the rebbe plays a shamanistic role for many of his followers. Most Chasidic communities are rife with tales of **miracles** that follow a **yechidut**, a spiritual audience with a *tzadik*: barren women become pregnant, cancer tumors shrink, wayward children become pious. Many rebbes dispense **segullah** charms and healing folk remedies. The spiritual power of the *tzadik* is such that after death in this world, the proper name of a *tzadik* can be treated as a quasi-divine name and has **healing** powers. Therefore, the name of Chasidic masters may appear on **amulets**.

There is an enormous library of Chasidic metaphysics, philosophy, and mystical speculation that has been produced, the vast bulk of which remains untranslated from Yiddish.[1]

1. Rabinowicz, *The Encyclopedia of Hasidism*, 188–95. Also see Roth, *Encyclopedia Judaica*, vol. 7, 1383–88.

Chatom ha-Merkavah: "Seal of the Chariot." A fragmentary text of **Merkavah** Mysticism found in the **Cairo Genizah** collection.

Chayyei ha-Olam ha-Ba: "The Life of the World-to-Come." A mystical/theurgic manual by **Abraham Abulafia**.

Chayyim, Sefer ha-: "The Book of Life." Composed in the 13th century, this text includes mystical teachings on **astrology**, the divine **chariot**, and theurgic rituals, such as making a **golem**. Not to be confused with the celestial **Book of Life**, a legendary book which has the same Hebrew name.

Chayyot: "[Holy] Beasts." Angelic entities that pull the divine **chariot**. Sporting four wings and formed of fire and light, they sing praises to God, but also have flaming breath that is a threat to other angels. According to **Hechalot Rabbati**, each day they **dance** and cavort before God at the times of prayer. They can smell when a living human enters the precincts of heaven. (Ezek. 1; Chag. 13b; Gen. R. 2:2; Ex. R. 47:5; Midrash Konen; Zohar I). *SEE* ANGELS.

Chelm: A mythical city of fools, not to be confused with the actual city of Chelm, Poland. Hundreds of Jewish parables, jokes, and short stories are devoted to the misadventures of the ironically dubbed *Khelmer Chacham*, "wise men of Chelm," whose deeds, springing from daft premises, silly rationales, and logic run amok, serve as proverbial examples of how reason and wisdom are not synonymous.[1]

1. Frankel and Plotkin Teusch, *The Encyclopedia of Jewish Symbols*, 32.

Chemai, Rabbi: This minor Talmudic Sage is the purported author of the mystical tract **Sefer ha-Iyyun**.

Chemdat Yamim: This digest of Kabbalistic practices, a kind of mystical **Shulchan Aruch**, promises its rituals will affect **tikkun** both on earth and in the Godhead.

Cherem: "Ostracization/Excommunication." This is normally a form of legal punishment not to be confused with the biblical concept of **karet**, being spiritually cut off. Yet in esoteric circles it is a term often used in **incantations** directed against **demons**, in effect legally excommunicating them. It is the theurgic equivalent of a "restraining order" on evil spirits.[1] *SEE* EXORCISM; GET; POSSESSION, DEMONIC.

　1. Naveh and Shaked, *Magic Spells and Formulae*, 129.

Cherub, Cherubim: (*Keruv*, "Mighty One"). A winged numinous being in the service of God. A common motif in both Israelite and pagan iconography, a cherub is a hybrid creature with a human head, avian wings, and a beastly body, usually that of a lion. Such was a stereotypical way of illustrating a supernal entity in the Ancient Near East, much like the modern convention of showing a glowing halo around the head of a spiritually enlightened being. The Israelites may have regarded them as the animating spirits of winds and clouds (II Sam. 22:11). Josephus declares that their exact appearance was no longer known in his time. In the Talmudic accounts their appearance is more varied and less stereotypical (Sukkah 5b; Gen. R. 21).

Cherubim guard the entry to the Garden of **Eden**. They were a repeated decorative image on the curtains in the **Temple** (II Chron. 3:14), and two statuary cherubim sat upon the **Ark of the Covenant**, their wings coming together to form a "mercy seat," or throne, for God. The voice of God would emanate from there (Ex. 25–26). The fact that cherubim are associated both with Eden and the Temple suggests that the inner sanctum of the Temple was perceived, either symbolically or mystically, as corresponding to the primordial Garden. Cherubim also served as the steeds or chariot of God (II Sam. 22).

Cherubim are incorporated into the elaborate and systematic angelology of Early Judaism. They played a prominent role in the priestly spirituality of the Dead Sea Scrolls sect (Song of the Sabbath Sacrifice; 4Q385). Ranked above mere angels, I Enoch assigns them to the sixth and seventh heavens.

According to Talmud, when Israel offered its prayers, the cherubim on the Ark of the Covenant moved in response. They would either turn to face each other or away from each other, depending on Israel's state of sin (B.B. 99a). In Yoma 54a, Rabbi Katina goes even further, claiming the cherubim were actually sculpted in a posture of sexual union, signifying the mystery of God's passionate love for Israel. Other Sages reject this legend. Still, the writings found among the Dead Sea Scrolls also hint at the idea that the paired cherubim on the Ark somehow signified life and fertility, perhaps even a *hieros gamos* (4Q405, frag. 19).

Intuiting the intention behind their hybrid appearance, the medieval Kabbalists described the cherubim as symbolizing the union of heaven and earth (Zohar, Terumah 2). The **Zohar** further teaches that the two cherubim on the Ark represent the masculine and feminine divine attributes.

The idea that the cherubim serve as the creatures that pull the divine chariot and/or guard the **Throne of Glory** is a major theme in Kabbalah. Some writers even regard the cherubim as synonymous with the chariot itself (Ezek. 1; Gen. R. 21:9; Yoma 54a). *SEE* ANGELS; CHARIOT; CHERUB, THE UNIQUE.

Cherub, the Unique: (*Keruv ha-M'yuchad*). A medieval metaphysical concept of the divine **Glory** as forming a kind of anthropomorphic apparition visible to mortals. This was also the favored **meditation** technique, akin to creative visualization, practiced by the **Circle of the Unique Cherub** mystics. It consisted of forming a **vision** of deity (referred to as the "Unique Cherub") during prayer, to serve as a bridge to the true, invisible Godhead. This practice is unique, in that it is virtually the only example in Jewish tradition in which one is encouraged to imagine what God looks like. *SEE* CHERUB; FACE OF GOD; GLORY OF GOD; PESEK HA-YIRA'AH V'HA-EMUNAH; REIYAT HA-LEV; VISION.

Chesed: "Love/Kindness." The fourth of the **sefirot**. Chesed is born out of **Binah** and is the principle of boundless divine mercy, grace, and blessing manifest in **Creation**. It is part of the "right side," the masculine, positive divine energy. The limitless love of Chesed is balanced over against the power of **Gevurah**, God's justice and power. An excess of either degrades reality and threatens the existence of the universe. It is especially linked to the Patriarch **Abraham**, who personified Chesed in the world of action. It is sometimes called *Gedulah* and is symbolized by the **color** white.

Chet: The eighth letter of the **Hebrew alphabet**. It has the vocalic value of "kh/ch," the gutteral "h." It symbolizes transcendence and grace.[1]

> 1. Munk, *The Wisdom of the Hebrew Alphabet*, 112–16.

Chibbut ha-Kever: "Torments of the Grave." The individual who has not led an exemplary life can expect to find the separation of the soul from the body extremely painful (SCh 30). Some teach that this pain is the result of the soul (specifically the **nefesh**) remaining close to the body and being forced to experience its gradual decay and disintegration (Job 14:22; Ber. 18b). Others hold that punishments worse than what will be experienced in **Gehenna** befall the newly dead: floggings with whips of fire and iron, dismemberment by punishing angels and the like. **Domah**, the angel of the grave, comes to the soul to pronounce the judgment of Chibbut ha-Kever. Normally a soul can expect to be bound to the body for seven days (Zohar I, II). During this time the soul can also expect to revisit the episodes of its earthly existence (Tan. 11a). A medieval tractate, Masekhet Chibbut ha-Kever, gives a detailed account of the process. SEE CEMETERY; DEATH; ETERNAL LIFE; JUDGMENT.

Childbirth: SEE BIRTH.

Children: Children are highly vulnerable to spiritual attack, so considerable thought and energy has been given in Jewish tradition to protecting children from **demons** and **witchcraft** through protective **prayers**, **incantations**, and **amulets**.

Children can also be a source of mantic knowledge. The Talmud declares that prophecy has been "given over to children" (B.B. 12b). While the Talmud probably meant this as a dismissive remark, some Jews have taken it seriously. Specifically, overhearing the biblical verses a student recites at his studies can be interpreted as **omens** (Chag. 15a; Git. 57a).

Likewise, from time to time there has appeared in Jewish literature the idea of child prodigies—that a child, either consciously or unconsciously, can have a special gift for **prophecy**. A child prophet arose in Spain during the 13th century, and another among the Jews of Poland in the 15th. SEE DIVINATION; EVIL EYE; KLEIDON; LILITH.

Children of Darkness: As described in the sectarian literature of the **Dead Sea Scrolls**, the Sons of Darkness are the demons and their mortal minions of evil and impurity who work to undermine the authority of God. The priesthood in control of the Temple during the latter part of the Greco-Roman period is evidently the human side of this evil conspiracy. SEE WAR SCROLL.

Children of the East: Fabled magicians and astrologers. SEE EAST; NAMES OF IMPURITY.

Children of God: (*B'nai ha-Elohim*). A term for the heavenly host; **angels** (Gen. 6; Job 1). The singular term, *Ben Elohim*, son of God, is also an honorific given to Israelite kings of the Davidic line based on II Samuel 7 and Psalm 2. This is not to be confused with the Christian doctrine that Jesus is the "only begotten Son of God." The Children of Israel are also called God's "firstborn son." SEE ANGELS; DAVID; RIGHTEOUS, THE; SON OF GOD.

Children of Light: This term, which appears in the nonbiblical materials of the **Dead Sea Scrolls**, refers to the good angels and their priestly supporters who faithfully serve God and battle against the impure, demonic **Children of Darkness**. The conflict of the Children of Light and Darkness is a centerpiece of the dualistic mystical theology of the sectarian priests of Qumran. SEE WAR SCROLL.

Chiromancy: Palm reading. This form of augury first appears in Jewish circles in the **Dead Sea Scrolls** (4Q186). Examples of chiromantic diagrams in Hebrew have been preserved.

Chitzon, Sefer: "Outside Book." The rabbinic term for any book of antiquity that appears intended to be taken as authoritative, but is not included in the Jewish scriptural canon. These books include works that claim to be written by biblical figures (**Pseudepigrapha**), such as the **Testament of Levi** or the **Books of Enoch**, as well as **apocalyptic** literature and those books that offer "revised" accounts of those found in canonical books, such as **Jubilees** (which reworks Genesis) and the **Temple Scroll** (a revisionist version of Exodus-Deuteronomy).

Chiyya, Rabbi: Wonder-working Talmudic Sage (ca. 3rd century). He could make the wind blow and the rain fall by his prayers. The Talmud hints that he could even raise the dead if he so wished (B.M. 85b).

Chochmah: "Wisdom." The second of the sefirot, it emerged from the primordial power of **Keter**. It in turn is the source of **Binah**. It is the first "being" to exist "outside" of God. It is equated with **Torah**, the blueprint through which God makes the universe. It is also called **Abba**, "father," reflecting the fact that it is the first expression of the binary/dualistic nature of Creation. SEE WISDOM.

Chok I'Yisrael: An 18th-century collection of verses—biblical, rabbinic, and Kabbalistic—that are believed to be able to effect divine **tikkun**, repair of the cosmos. Jews are encouraged to recite these verses daily.

Choleim Chalom: "Dream diviner." An oneiromancer, linked to false prophets (Deut. 13:2). Yet based on the examples of **Joseph** and Daniel, in post-biblical Judaism dream interpretation is regarded as a respectable form of manticism. SEE DIVINATION; DREAM.

Choni ha-Ma'agel: "Choni the Circle-Maker." Wonder-worker (ca. 1st century BCE). This rainmaker was famous for his close relationship with God. Several stories about his using magic **circles** to make **rain** appear in rabbinic literature. His contemporary, the great Sage and witch hunter Simon Ben Shetah, expressed his great displeasure with Choni's theurgic antics, but in the end conceded that Choni had a unique relationship with his Creator. He once slept for seventy years (Tan. 19a, 23a). SEE RIGHTEOUS, THE.

Chozeh: "Seer." This person may be synonymous with a *roeh*; someone who experiences premonitory or veridical visions. SEE FACE OF GOD; PROPHECY; VISIONS.

Christian Qabbalists: As part of the Renaissance project to recover the teachings of the classical non-Christian past, a number of 15th-century Christian scholars be-came interested in Kabbalah and studied it under Jewish teachers. The most famous of these men is Pico Della Mirandola, but this number also includes Johannes Reuchlin, Pietro Gallatius, Francisco Giogio, and Egidio da Viterbo. These men translated parts, even whole books, of Jewish mysticism for the use of Christian scholars, esoterics, and alchemists. Some even tried to use the doctrines of Jewish Kabbalah to prove the validity of Christian doctrine.[1]

Eventually these translated works were read and used by 19th- and 20th-century theosophists, influencing a variety of modern esoteric movements. Much of what is published under the rubric "Qabbalah" today is derived from these Christian Kabbalists. Such theosophical works are made up of metaphysical ideas stripped of their Jewish assumptions and teachings, often conflated with Christian and Hermetic teachings, and bearing little resemblance to the Jewish mystical tradition it purports to explain. SEE CHRISTIANITY.

1. Scholem, *Kabbalah*, 196–201.

Christianity: A religion emerging from Judaism in the 1st and 2nd centuries CE. From very early on, Christianity and Judaism were faiths competing on similar ground. Ideologically, both shared in the heritage of Israelite religion and its texts and both participated in the esoteric traditions of Jewish apocalypticism. In the matter of esoteric praxis, both engaged in spiritual **healing** and both had traditions of demonic **possession**. Other parallels, whether obvious or subtle, meant that even as critical ideological differences drove them apart, certain affinities remained. Religious leadership on both sides sought to keep those attractive elements of the competing faith at arm's length. Both groups regularly accused the other of engaging in **magic**, a term which already had a pejorative connotation in Roman times.[1] Thus, for example, in the Talmud we have one incident of a rabbi who is criticized for seeking a healer among the Christian community.

Likewise, despite the obvious Jewish roots of the spiritual healings performed by Jesus, early Christian leaders despised Jewish remedies and faith healing and equated them with **witchcraft** and devilry (Dialogue with Trypho 85:3; Council of Laodicaea, Canon 35–37). **Joannes Chrysostomus**, for example, railed endlessly at their

Christian congregants who sought medical or spiritual help in the synagogues. Chrysostomus in particular carried on about the "synagogue of Satan" where demons found refuge (Homilies against the Judaizers 1:6). This attitude became so pervasive that medieval Christians became convinced that Jews in general were practitioners of **sorcery**, and even simple Jewish customs and protective acts, like opening doors at a time of death, or casting earth at a funeral, were perceived as malevolent witchcraft and could bring dire consequences.

For a brief period during the Renaissance, Christians showed a renewed interest in Jewish Kabbalah and theurgy.[2] But that same heightened consciousness of Jewish occultism yielded a harsh backlash against Jews during the Reformation period, especially given the witch-hunting hysteria of the 16th and 17th centuries. This pervasive and often destructive Christian stereotype of Jews helped contribute to the collective decision in the 18th and 19th centuries by the Jewish community to distance itself from the bulk of Jewish esoteric traditions and practices. And it is only in the last half century, when Christian opprobrium has been muted, that many Jews have again shown renewed interest in their own mystical and occult heritage. *SEE* BLOOD LIBEL; CHRISTIAN QABBALISTS; HOST DESECRATION.

1. Levine, *The Ancient Synagogue*, 274.
2. Langermann, "Magic and Astrology," in Grendler, *Encyclopedia of the Renaissance*, vol. 3, 21, 23.

Chrysostomus, Joannes: Early Church Father and savage anti-Semite (ca. 3rd century). His anti-Jewish polemics proved very influential on subsequent Christian attitudes toward Jews and Judaism. Deeply offended by the good relations he observed between the Jews and Christians of his time, he authored a series of ferocious sermons directed at the Jews. Among the things he objected to were the Christian use of Jewish faith healers and attendance of the Jewish holidays. Chrysostomus called the synagogue an "assembly of Satan" and declared Jews to be in the thrall of the demonic.[1] *SEE* CHRISTIANITY.

1. Trachtenberg, *The Devil and the Jews*, 21, 58.

Circles: (*Iggul/Ma'agal*). As a symbol of centrality and infinity, images of circles appear frequently in Judaism— the Temple, Jerusalem, and Israel are concentric circles of holiness in the world (MdRI, be-Shallach). As a sign of protection, magic circles first appear in Jewish tradition in the Bible, when Joshua encircles Jericho seven times in order to collapse its walls.

They also appear in **Talmud** and **Midrash** with the many stories of **Choni ha-Ma'agel**, Choni the Circle-Drawer, a charismatic figure who could cause rain. It is a matter of debate whether the "heave offering" described in the Torah involved waving the offering in a circle. Certainly the custom of **kapparah** involves waving a chicken in a circle before it can become a substitute bearer of the sins of the individual. The use of protective circles, so familiar in medieval sorcery, also starts to appear in Jewish practice. Such circles were also used to protect the birthing bed of pregnant women (**Sefer ha-Chayyim** 2.8). Smaller circles drawn around a wound or area of illness on a body presumably exorcised the malaise-causing spirit.

The book Zera Kodesh ("Holy Seed"), written in the 16th century, describes making concentric circles on the ground (usually three or seven) with an iron blade, often with an inscription or the names of angels added. The magical handbook **Key of Solomon** describes the use of magic summoning circles in some detail. The **Baal Shem Tov** once defeated a priest-witch by making a protective circle with his staff (Megillat Setarim).

Performative circles, created by walking or linking hands around someone to ward off the **evil eye**, came to be part of both Jewish weddings and funerals. They are used in a variety of ways to treat illness.[1] European Jewish women would circle a cemetery in a ritual of divination (Sefer ha-Chayyim; Maavar Yabbok).[2] To animate a golem, an adept must circle the form 462 times while reciting the necessary incantations of animation (Pseudo-Sa'adiah).

1. Zimmels, *Magicians, Theologians, and Doctors*, 147.
2. Fine, *Judaism in Practice*, 61.

Circle of the Special (or Unique) Cherub: A modern term for the largely anonymous school of mystics (ca. 13th-century Rhineland) who focused their esoteric teachings on **Sefer Yetzirah**. Only Avigdor ha-Tzarfati and Elchanan ben Yakar have been linked by name to this mysterious group. They devote a great deal of their esoteric speculation to the meaning of the **cherub** that supports (or is) the **Throne of Glory** and is the mechanism through which the prophets and mystics experience **visions** of God in physical form.

They are the likely authors of several mystical tracts, but most notably what is now known as the "Pseudo-Sa'adia" commentary on Yetzirah (it was mistakenly ascribed to the 10th-century-CE Babylonian philosopher Sa'adia Gaon).[1] *SEE* BARAITA DE YOSEF BEN UZIEL; CHERUB, THE UNIQUE; PESAK HA-YIRA'AH V'HA-EMUNAH; PSEUDO-SA'ADIA.

1. Dan, *The 'Unique Cherub' Circle*, 56–75.

Circumcision: The rite of circumcision (*brit milah*), performed on a male child on the eighth day after birth, is regarded to be a "sign of the covenant" between Jews and God. It symbolizes the human role in perfecting God's Creation. It renders the males who undergo it *tam*, "perfected" (Gen. 17).

In at least one enigmatic biblical passage (Ex. 4:24–26), circumcision thwarts a supernatural attack. Moses had failed to circumcise his son, Gershom, and the Talmud explains that as a result, Moses is all but swallowed up by an angelic/satanic force (versions vary: **Satan**, **Uriel**, **Gabriel**, and the team of **Af and Chemah** all are proposed in different texts) in the form of a **serpent**, but it is unable to go past "the sign of the covenant." When his wife **Zipporah** sees that the creature cannot engulf Moses's penis, she intuits the meaning of the attack. She immediately performs the rite on her son, and the attack ends (MdRI, Yitro 1; Ex. R. 5:8; Ned. 31b–32a).

In the case of **Abraham**, circumcision overrides his **fate** as revealed in the stars (Ned. 32a). So awesome is the power of circumcision that in the **World-to-Come**, Abraham sits at the gates of **Gehenna** and does not allow any circumcised Jew to be taken there. **Domah**, the angel of the grave, is powerless to punish those who bear the mark of the covenant (and honored it in life by restraining their lustful impulses) (Gen. R. 48:8; Zohar I: 8b). Since medieval times, when a *brit milah* is performed, a chair is set aside for **Elijah**, the "Angel of the Covenant," who is believed to be present at every *brit milah*.

The Book of Jubilees calls the uncircumcised "sons of **Belial**." In rabbinic literature, certain exemplary figures were born already circumcised, especially **Adam** and **Noah**.

The **Zohar**, not surprisingly, finds supernal secrets underpinning the rite of circumcision. **Moses de Leon**, its author, was deeply engaged, if not obsessed, with the numinous significance of circumcision. For example, de Leon, expanding on a Midrash appearing in **Pirkei de-Rabbi Eliezer** (29), posits that it is only through circumcision that a human is able to receive prophecy and experience full *unio mystica*, mystical union with God (I: 97b–98a; also see Gen. R. 12:8; Tanh., Lech Lecha 20).

More than that, in the Zohar and in subsequent Kabbalistic thought, the human penis is a reflection of the divine structure, the **sefirot**. This is based on the principle that what exists above is mirrored below. Thus God has a supernal "phallus," of sorts, but this aspect of God actually is androgynous, encompassing both the male and female principle; it is in itself combined to make the *hieros gamos*, a schema that (more or less) keeps this mystical doctrine within the bounds of Judaism's monotheism. While the shaft (**Yesod/Tiferet**) is male, the corona, as the phallic counterpart to the clitoris, is considered female (**Shekhinah/Malchut**). Therefore the act of human circumcision reveals the feminine aspect in the human male; *brit milah*, it seems, is an act of ritual androgynization (Mashiv Devarim Nekhochim 193–96; Zohar I: 29b; Shekel ha-Kodesh 67). *SEE* ORLAH; PHALLUS.

Cloud: (*Anan*). As visible heavenly objects, clouds are often associated with supernatural phenomena. God rides upon the clouds (Ps. 104:3). When God becomes manifest on earth, clouds obscure what is happening (Ex. 19–21; Job 22:13; Ex. 19; Lev. 16:2). **Angels** also manifest themselves as clouds, most famously the pillar of cloud that guided the Children of Israel during the day on the Exodus (Ex. 13:21, 14:19–24).

According to rabbinic tradition, a cloud is a sign of the **Shekhinah**, the feminine divine Presence (Gen. R. 1:6, 1:10). Such clouds hovered over the tents of the Matriarchs (Gen. R. 60:16). Clouds (called "Clouds of Glory" by the Sages) not only led the Israelites, but actually transported them, surrounding them on all sides and protecting them from the harsh desert environment (MdRI, Bo 14; PR 20; Targum Shir ha-Shirim). These clouds had supernal letters written on them, serving as banners for each tribe. Moses ascended into heaven to receive the Torah wrapped in clouds (Men. 29b; Shab. 88b–89a).

A pillar of cloud became manifest over the altar of the **Temple** on **Yom Kippur**, and its appearance was an augury of the future (Yoma 21b). The presence of these clouds diminished and eventually disappeared due to the accreted sins of Israel. **Bar Nifli**, "son of a cloud," is a title for the Messiah, who will appear riding one, according to the book of Daniel (7:13). Virtuosos of Kabbalah, such as **Moses Cordovero**, sometimes had pillars of cloud appear over or around them (Sefer ha-Hezyonot).

Cock: Domesticated among Jews first during Greco-Roman times, roosters were a symbol of fertility. A cock would be carried before a newlywed couple on the way to the bridal chamber. According to some sources, the cock derives its knowledge of the sun's rising from the stirring of the **phoenix**, which, being a fellow avian, was detectable by the rooster. The cock is also the only animal who hears the cries of the soul at death (Tanhuma, Pekudei 3).

Given that one word for a cock is *gever*, which also means "man," it is not surprising that roosters came to be used as magical substitutes. Thus a cock is used by a man to perform the **substitution** ritual of **kapparah**. A rooster can also be used for divination, by studying either the changes in its comb or the pattern of scratches it makes on the ground. It can also be used to make rain (Hor. 12a; Sefer ha-Raziel).

Codes: *SEE* ENCRYPTION.

Coins: Coins have several magical uses. They can be included in amulet bags (silver being repellent to evil spirits), made into magical rings, used as bribes for witches and even demons, or for divination (either flipping the coin or as part of more elaborate rituals). During the Middle Ages, Jews taught methods for using a **divining rod** to locate buried coins.

Color: Color has important symbolic meaning in Judaism. Most familiar are associations such as purple (*argaman*) with royalty, deep blue (*tekelet*) with heaven, white (*lavan*) with purity, and black (*shachor*) with mourning. Adam was

created by the combination of dust of different colors—we are, in effect, a kind of animate sand-painting (Ginzberg, *Legends of the Jews*, 1:55). In dreams, all remembered colors are a good omen, except for blue (Ber. 57b).

Colors have a more powerful role in Kabbalistic thought. The **sefirot** each have assigned colors.[1] Concentrating on colors was also a meditative prayer device promoted by the **German Pietists**. Colors are incorporated into sympathetic rites of practical Kabbalah with the goal of activating those sefirotic qualities in the material world (Pardes Rimmonim, 32.2). Part of activating a particular divine attribute is imagining that particular color in one's meditations, or even dressing in that color while performing the ritual (Kedushat Levi, Yitro). This is also part of making an efficacious amulet (Pardes Rimmonim, 10:1). Colors of particular significance include:

> *Black*: In Kabbalah it signifies Malchut/**Shekhinah**, the **speculum** "that does not shine." It is the color of mourning.
>
> *Blue*: The color of heaven is also the color of the Throne of God (Chul. 89a), God's **Glory** (Ex. 24:10; Num. R. 14:3), and **Chochmah**. It is the color of the special thread that is part of ritual **fringes** a Jew wears. Blue was a featured color in the **Tabernacle**. Blue is a good luck color and in the Mediterranean, Jews paint their doors and window frames blue as a defense against the **evil eye** entering.
>
> *Gold*: Gold symbolizes **Din**, the quality of divine judgment. It is also a symbol of Jerusalem, the "city of gold."
>
> *Green*: This color is associated with **Tiferet**.
>
> *Purple*: The color of royalty, purple was one of the colors God mandated be part of the Tabernacle. It is the color of **Chesed**.
>
> *Red*: As the color of blood, life, and alarm, red is often the preferred color in anti-demonic amulets. A scarlet cord hung in the **Temple** on **Yom Kippur** that turned white when Israel was forgiven. It is the color of **Gevurah**, God's attribute of power.
>
> *Silver*: A sign of purity, it also has anti-demonic properties.

White: The color of light, holiness, purity, compassion, and the **moon**. Kabbalists engaging in mystical ascents, summoning of angels, or other rituals of power will don white as part of their preparatory purification rituals.[2] Likewise the shroud a corpse is wrapped in after purification rites are performed is white. It is the color of the sefirot **Tiferet** and/or **Chesed**.

1. Idel, *Kabbalah: New Perspectives*, 103–11.
2. Idel, *Hasidism: Between Ecstasy and Magic*, 198.

Comets and Meteors: Heavenly bodies that appear only irregularly, such as comets and shooting stars, are understood either as **omens** or as heavenly responses to events on earth (Hor., Berachot 58b). Rabbi Israel Isserlein, for example, took the appearance of Halley's Comet in 1456 to be a prodigy of God's judgment against the Hapsburg Kings. *SEE* BRONTOLOGY.

Commandment: (*Mitzvah*). According to rabbinic exegesis, the Torah contains 613 commandments from God. These divine instructions are the structural framework of Jewish religious observance and morality.

Community Rule or Rule of the Community: A document of the **Dead Sea Scrolls** that exists in several manuscript versions (4Q5; 1QRule; 1QS). Community Rule lays out the organization of the sectarian priestly group at Qumran. It also explains the group's dualistic ideology, the community's role at the End of Time, and teaches about the dual messiahs, the Aaronide and Davidic kings. *SEE* CHILDREN OF DARKNESS; CHILDREN OF LIGHT.

Conception: While a human soul is waiting to be born, the angel of conception, **Lailah**, teaches the soul all the Torah. The soul is also shown the full breadth of the universe, the Garden of **Eden**, and **Gehenna**. When the time for birth arrives, Lailah strikes the fetus on the upper lip. This creates the dimple beneath the nose. More importantly, all that the soul has learned enters the sub-conscious and is forgotten until it is relearned in the world. When that soul is ready to return, Lailah is the angel that escorts it back (Tanhuma Pekude 3). The **Tanya** offers a different, very elaborate metaphysical model of conception in which the soul is a poly-psychic entity composed of elements from different spiritual source points.

Copper Scroll: Found among the **Dead Sea Scrolls**, the Copper Scroll consists of three copper sheets riveted together, now broken into two. Inscribed upon it is a list of hidden treasures buried around Jerusalem. The treasures listed, taken together, amount to tons of gold and silver. Some theorize that it is a record of the **Temple** treasury, concealed for the duration (or such was the plan) of the Jewish Revolt in or around 66 CE. So far, none of the purported treasures it described have been located.

Cordovero, Moses: Ethicalist and Kabbalist (Turkish, ca. 16th century). A student of **Joseph Caro**, he is the author of **Pardes Rimmonim**, **Tomar Devorah**, and other works. He taught a comprehensive and, at times, obtuse mystical theology. He received visitations from **Elijah** and was said to be the biblical **Eliezer** reincarnated. He was a teacher of **Isaac Luria**, though Luria developed a very different mystical worldview. According to one account, a **pillar** of **cloud** or **fire** hovered over his body during his burial.

Corpse: *SEE* BODY; BURIAL.

Countenance, Divine: *SEE* FACE OF GOD.

Countenance, Prince or Angel of the [Divine]: (*Sar ha-Panim* or *Malach ha-Panim*). Sar ha-Panim is an angel, or angels, that serve as a visible manifestation of God. The belief in this particular angel is based on Exodus 33:14, which, translated literally, has God telling Moses, "My Countenance will go [with you] but I will depart." This angel is mentioned explicitly in Isaiah 63:9.

Metatron is the angelic figure most associated with the *ha-Panim* title. Other angels, such as **Suriel** and Tzakadhazy, are also called by the title *ha-Panim*, leading to some confusion. Are all these angels actually different names for Metatron, as one tradition suggests, or are the *ha-Panim* really a whole class of angels, of which Metatron is only the most famous? There is no definitive answer.

Counting and Census: The numbering of people is a sensitive issue in Jewish tradition. God repeatedly punishes the Israelites for taking any unauthorized census (II Sam. 24; II Chron. 21). In later Jewish tradition, counting people invites the unwanted attention of the **evil eye**. In order to make sure a **minyan** (ten people) is present for a public service, it is customary to have each recite one word in a ten-word phrase, such as "Deliver Your people and bless Your Heritage, sustain them forever." When there are enough present to complete the phrase, the service is ready to begin. Another solution is by simply reversing what one says, as in "not one, not two, not three. . . ."

Covenant, Angel of the: *SEE* ELIJAH.

Creation: One of the principle cosmological teachings of Judaism is that the universe is created by God. Rabbinic teachings include much more information about the origins of the universe than are found in the biblical account.

Personified Torah is God's "architect" in the design of Creation (Gen. R. 1.1). In the course of God reshaping the primordial **chaos**, some of the six days of Creation have special significance. The second day, Monday, is the only day of Creation that God does not bless. This is because God created **Gehenna** on that day (Gen. R. 4:6; 11:9). It is therefore a bad luck day. On the other hand, the third day is blessed twice by God, making it a propitious day, especially for beginning a new enterprise, like a marriage. According the **Zohar**, since the word for "light" in Genesis 1:14, *me'orot*, is lacking one letter, this reveals a deficiency in that light of the fourth day, signaling the emergence of evil in Creation (without the *vav* normally present, the word can be read as *me'erot*/"curses") (Tan. 68b; PdRK 5:1; Zohar I: 12a, 33b).

The waters of the **abyss** that preceded the Creation are now trapped beneath the earth, held at bay by the *Even ha-Shayitah*, the **Foundation Stone**. God removed this stone for the great **Flood** of Noah's time. The design of the **Tabernacle** and the **Temple** that followed it are **microcosms** of Creation (Ex. R. 35:6; Num. R. 12:13). The human body also embodies the entire universe in microcosmic form.

Mystical works such as **Sefer Yetzirah**, **Midrash Konen**, and particularly the teachings of **Isaac Luria** detail the intimate structure of Creation, the metaphysics of the divine speech that created the world, and the powers of creation that human beings can access.

The Chasidic philosophy of **Tanya** (219, 320) teaches a kind of "subjective acosmism": while we experience the reality of Creation, from God's perspective there is no beginning to the universe, as it were, and all distinctions made manifest through Creation are not "seen" by the Creator—it all remains undifferentiated "oneness."[1]

The mystical project is to restore to humans the capacity to see the world from God's perspective, at which point Creation will reverse itself and all "being" will revert to "no-thing-ness." *SEE* ADAM KADMON; EMANATION; MA'ASEI BERESHIT; TWILIGHT.

1. Green, *Jewish Spirituality*, vol. 2, 160–63; Rabinowicz, *The Encyclopedia of Hasidism*, 74.

Crimson Cord: *SEE* SCARLET CORD.

Crown: Crowns are a symbol of authority and power. There are four crowns in Jewish tradition: the crown of royalty, the crown of priesthood, the crown of Torah, and the crown of a good reputation (Avot 4:17).

Both the king and the High Priest wore types of crowns. In some Jewish communities, brides and grooms are crowned at the **wedding**. The only fabulous crowns mentioned in the aggadah are the one million, two hundred thousand crowns placed on the heads of Israel (two for each male—God assumed they would share with the women) by angels at Mount Sinai. Those crowns were taken back by God after the **Golden Calf** incident (Shab. 88a).

Crown of God: The crown of God is constantly being woven by the angel **Sandalfon** from the prayers of Israel. It bears the **Tetragrammaton** on its front. It is multihued, reflecting the many different prayers offered to God. There is one description of God wearing ten crowns, which the mystics take as a reference to the **sefirot** (Ber. 55a; Chag. 12a, 13b; Ex. R. 21:4; Mid. Teh. 88:2; Zohar I: 132a, 168b).

Crypto-Jews: Jews (mostly from the Iberian Peninsula) who, after coerced conversion to Christianity, secretly maintained Jewish practices.

Crystal: *SEE* GEMSTONES.

Cures: *SEE* HEALING.

Cures, Book of: A powerful tome of healing mentioned in the **Talmud**. King Hezekiah hid it away because of the impiety of his people. (Pes. 56a; M. Pes. 4:9; RaDaK's comments).

Curses: A verbal invocation to bring harm, evil, or detriment on another. More than a threat or a wish, a curse is assumed to have the power to make the desired harm a reality.

Two elements make up the logic of cursing: a magical/symbolic view of causality and "formalism," the belief that a speech-act has power, regardless of intention, justification, or authority.[1] While some assume that the "power" of the speaker underpins the efficacy of the curse (Num. 22:3), because of formalist assumptions in rabbinic thinking, even curses uttered unintentionally by ordinary people have the potential to be detrimental (Meg. 15a–b, 28a).

God has the power to both bless and curse Creation. Both powers are demonstrated in the first three chapters of Genesis. Humans also have the power to curse individuals and whole classes of people. Some biblical authors simultaneously try to limit the use of curses and undermine their formalist assumptions by claiming unjustified curses will have no effect (Prov. 26:2). Curses can be absolute or conditional. An absolute curse is meant to be immediate (Gen. 4:11; II Sam. 16). A conditional curse only become efficacious when certain conditions are met or violated (Deut. 27–28). A notable form of conditional curse that appears in the Bible is the conditional self-curse (I Kings 19:2, 20:10). Often included in an oath, this curse was placed on oneself accompanied with a symbolic act of destruction—shattering a pot, chopping up an animal, or some other deed that signified what would happen to the one making the vow if he or she should fail. Even God uses a form of this when making a covenant with Abraham (Gen. 15:7–21).

The Sages elaborate upon these biblical beliefs (Mak. 11a; Eruv. 18b–19a; Tem. 3b–4a; Mak. 16a). **Demons** as well as human beings can utter curses. Using a curse can actually invite unwanted demonic attention on the person uttering the curse. The Talmudic Sage Rav reportedly had the power to curse others with sterility (Shab. 108a). At least one Sage, **Joshua ben Levi**, had the power to curse crops. In the Jerusalem Talmud, Tractate Chagigah, we read that the curse of Simeon ben Shetah's son was considered so potent that eighty witnesses recanted their perjury rather than see his curse realized.

In Hebrew magical texts of late antiquity, several aggressive or "binding" spells are to be found. Most are aimed at demons, but a few are directed against other human beings. Texts such as **Sefer ha-Razim** and **Sword of Moses**, which have moved beyond the constraints of rabbinic prohibitions, are the most flagrant in the kind of curses they record. ShR, for example, teaches that the "angels of *Chimah*" (wrath) that occupy the second camp of the first level of heaven will carry out a variety of curses at the command of the properly prepared adept: they will inflict "combat and war and are ready to torment and torture a man to death." Specific curse formulae include capsizing a boat, collapsing a wall, sending someone into exile, breaking bones, blinding and/or laming, even undermining business dealings.

Medievals believed that even reading those portions of the Torah that recount God's curses against disobedient Israel (Deut. 27–28) could result in those curses being realized, so those portions were read rapidly in a whisper, a custom still observed today in many congregations.

The exact mechanism of cursing varies. As noted above, a curse can follow simply because of an utterance. Jewish magical texts, however, generally require more effort. ShR, aping Greek pagan magical practices, requires *materia magica* along with specific rituals and incantations. Timing and astrological influences can also increase or mitigate the power of a curse.

The practice of cursing is still with us. In a much publicized event during the 1994 Israeli elections, a Kabbalist put a *pulsa denura* (lashes of fire) curse on candidate Yitzchak Rabin because he supported territorial compromise with the Palestinians.[2]

1. Lauterbach, "The Belief in the Power of the Word," 287–89. Also see Brichto, *The Problem of "Curse" in the Hebrew Bible*.
2. *The Jerusalem Report*, Nov. 16, 1995.

Curtain: *SEE* PARGOD; TEMPLE.

Curtain of Heaven: Sometimes identified as the first of the **seven heavens**, the curtain of heaven conceals the **Throne of Glory** from the sublunary spheres. According to the Talmudic Sage **Resh Lakish**, the curtain of heaven is drawn back at dawn and spread each evening, producing the effect of day and night. It is rolled up during the passing of **comets**, briefly revealing the firmament in all its glory. **Angels**, **demons**, and **ghosts** can hear the decrees and conversations of the divine court from behind the heavenly veil. *SEE* PARGOD; RAKIA.

D

Da'at: "Knowledge/Union." In the **Torah**, *Da'at* can mean a variety of things, from simple understanding to sexual intercourse (as in Genesis 3, ". . . and he *knew* his wife and she conceived . . ."). In Jewish mysticism, Da'at is a mysterious (even for Kabbalah) harmonizing principle that is sometimes included as part of the sefirotic system. In some systems, it is an aspect of **Keter**, balancing **Chochmah** and **Binah**. Thus Da'at is the priniciple of *hieros gamos*, unifying the higher sefirot Chochmah and Binah in their purpose of giving birth to the lower sefirot and directing the effluence from the higher **sefirot** into the lower ones. Some Kabbalistic models, on the other hand, do not speak of Da'at at all.[1]

1. Scholem, *Kabbalah*, 107; Idel, "Sexual Metaphors and Praxis in Kabbalah," 209.

Dagim: "Fish"/Pisces. The **zodiac** symbol of the Hebrew month of Adar. It signifies opposites, disparity, night, moisture, and the ascendance of the feminine principle. The festival of Purim falls under this sign. The arch-villain of the Purim story, **Haman** (book of Esther), used his knowledge of **astrology** to choose Adar to implement his plan to eradicate the Jewish people because, as the last month of the biblical calendar, it was a time when the Jews were particularly vulnerable. His plans went awry because he did not understand the special providence of Israel that protects it from the adverse influence of the stars. The fact that Haman was undone by a woman, **Esther**, would be characteristic of the feminine power manifest under this sign.[1]

1. Erlanger, *Signs of the Times*, 245–63.

Dalet: The fourth letter of the **Hebrew alphabet**. The word "dalet" means door. It is associated with the sefirah of **Malchut**, the "lowest" of the **sefirot**. Thus dalet can signify lowliness, humility, and poverty. It has the numeric value of 4 in **gematria**.[1] *SEE* NUMBERS.

1. Munk, *The Wisdom of the Hebrew Alphabet*, 78–84.

Damascus Document: Versions of this mysterious sectarian text have been found only among the ancient **Dead Sea Scrolls** and the medieval **Cairo Geniza**. Scholars remain puzzled over this long history (over a thousand years) of otherwise invisible transmission. Who cherished this document enough to continue copying it for a millennium? Why are there no other traces of it during that time span, or beyond? It was clearly important to the Dead Sea Scroll community (fragments of eight copies were found at **Qumran**) and reflects the priestly ideology of that group, but it is never quoted or cited in traditional Jewish sources, so what group of Jews continued to use this document, unknown to the Jewish world at large? A number of theories have been floated, none of them terribly satisfactory.

Beyond a series of arguments about Jewish law and custom that are pointedly at odds with the way they are treated by rabbinic Judaism, the most notable occult ideas found in the Document are a dualistic doctrine that the world is divided between **children of light** and **children of darkness** who are in perpetual war, the teaching that God has deliberately led the gentiles of the world astray, and the belief that there will be two messiahs, an Aaronide, or priestly **messiah**, as well as a Davidic, or royal messiah.[1]

1. Schiffman and VanderKam, *Encyclopedia of the Dead Sea Scrolls*, vol. 1, 166–70.

Dan: The biblical tribe descended from Jacob's fifth son. Guilty of **idolatry** (Judg. 18) and other faults, according to the biblical accounts, Dan became associated with sinister and malevolent forces. Some texts of **apocalyptic literature** and **Midrashim** regard Dan as a source of darkness and conflict. Early Christian tradition, evidently picking up on this theme, expresses the idea that the Antichrist will be a Danite. On the other hand, in the **Talmud**, tractates Sanhedrin and Shabbat contain a tradition that the general of the Messiah's armies will be from the tribe of Dan. SEE ESCHATOLOGY; MESSIAH.

Dance: (*Machol, Rikod*). "Praise Him with timbrel and dance" (Ps. 149:3). Dance is a spiritual technique used by humans across the globe, particularly for inducing altered states of consciousness. Ecstatic dance is a very ancient Jewish practice, being mentioned several times in the **Bible**, particularly in the books of Samuel (I Sam. 10:10–11, 19:20–24; II Sam. 6:14–16).

There are multiple theurgic uses for dance. According to **Pseudo-Sa'adia**'s commentary on **Sefer Yetzirah**, dancing in **circles** is a necessary element in the animating ritual for a **golem** (42b). Dance and **incantations** for protection are part of the ceremony of the **New Moon**. Dance can also be therapeutic. Women would dance and sing for those suffering from spirit **possession**.[1] In the medieval text Ma'avar Yabbok, it is explained that ten pious men can destroy any demonic offspring made by a man in his lifetime if they dance in a **circle** seven times around his corpse.

Basing the practice on the verse "All my bones shall say, 'Who can be likened to You?'" (Ps. 35:10), **Chasidism** has a celebrated tradition of dance as a spiritual discipline. Some Chasidic masters taught mass group dances of **yichudim** (unification) meant to draw down the **Shekhinah** and the presence of **angels** (ShB 61). Acrobatic dancing at weddings and other celebrations is also a noted Chasidic custom. Dance continues in modern Judaism, mostly associated with the holiday of Simchat Torah, when Jews gather to dance with the Torah scrolls.

Even the angels dance; each day the **Chayyot** dance before the **Throne of Glory** during the hours of prayer (Hechalot Rabbati). Dance will continue in the **World-to-Come**, as described in Song of Songs Rabbah (End), when the righteous shall join God in an eternal dance of joy. SEE MUSIC.

1. Zimmels, *Magicians, Theologians, and Doctors*, 83.

Daniel: Carried off into exile as a child and raised in the Babylonian court, Daniel is the protagonist of the biblical book of Daniel. Daniel is one of only two figures (the other being Joseph) associated with **magic** that the biblical authors view in a favorable light. It may be significant that both men's extensive involvement with magical practices occurs in the context of exile to a foreign court.

According to the book of Daniel, because of his extraordinary ability to scry the king's **dream** without being told its content, the King of Babylon appoints Daniel "chief prefect over the wise men of Babylon" (2:48). This elicits tremendous jealousy among the professional magical class of the court. Interestingly, the book of Daniel never actually credits Daniel with another miraculous act, though miraculous things happen for his benefit, such as God shutting the mouths of the **lions** when he was cast into their den. His chief talent seems to be **oneiromancy**, interpretation of dreams, and he is vouchsafed a series of highly symbolic **visions** of apocalyptic content. Puzzlingly, unlike other biblical figures, the Sages do not elaborate much on the biblical accounts of Daniel, nor do they credit him with many additional supernatural feats. SEE APOCALYPTIC LITERATURE.

Dargesh: A *dargesh* is a good luck charm for a house, apparently a bench or bed. It was believed that a bed not slept in overnight was a good **omen**, so a dargesh (or sometimes, a "bed of Gad") provided perpetual fortune (B. Ned. 56a; M.K. 27a). Ancient Mesopotamians would keep a "ghost chair" in their homes, so perhaps the *dargesh* was likewise intended to signal to beneficent spirits that the home was a welcoming rest spot. The "Chair of Elijah" present at a circumcision conveys a similar message. In Sefer ha-Hezyonot 22, we learn that spirits expect seating to be provided when they visit the living. SEE ELIJAH; GHOSTS; HOSPITALITY.

Darkness: (*Choshek*). The original state of the universe before God brought forth the cosmos, darkness is also a creation of God (Isa. 45; PdRE 3). Darkness is often a symbol of ignorance, dread, or evil, especially in eschatological imagery (Am. 5). Darkness is one of the ten **plagues** that afflicted **Egypt** during the **Exodus**. It is the lurking place of evil and **unclean spirits**, which is why both the **Bible** and the **Talmud** teach that night is a spiritually dangerous time. Demons even dwell in certain kinds of shade—that of a lone palm tree, a jujube, a caper, and thorny bushes with edible fronds (Pes. 111a–b). In the Kabbalistic work **Galya Raza**, the fact that darkness preceded light signifies that evil has dominance over good in Creation, a remarkably pessimistic worldview for a Jewish document.

Just as often, however, darkness is understood dialectically, as a complement to **light** and is exalted and celebrated, as evidenced by the daily prayers *Yotzer Or* and *Ma'ariv Aravim*. In the Zohar, darkness is a fiery primordial substance and a manifestation of the sefirah of **Gevurah** (I: 16b, 112b). Complementing "darkness" is "night," which signifies **Shekhinah**, the lowest sefirah that does not emit its own supernal light, yet is critical to the harmony of the cosmos. Darkness has its own governing angel (PR 20:2, 53:2). SEE CHAOS; MIDNIGHT; NIGHT; SEFIROT; TWILIGHT.

David ben Jesse, King: Warrior-poet and Israel's archetypal king. While the biblical accounts of King David are decidedly naturalistic and almost completely (with the exception of his encounter with an angel described in First Chronicles) bereft of supernatural events, many legends of the fantastic are told about David's life in other Jewish literature.

According to **Midrash**, when **Adam** was shown the generations that would descend from him, God revealed to him that David was destined to die shortly after **birth**. Adam was so saddened to see this great soul cut short that he gave up seventy years of his own life span for the future king of Israel (Gen. 5:5; PdRE 19).

Like **Samson**, David was exceedingly strong, and slew many wild beasts with his bare hands (Mid. Sam. 20). His extraordinary musical gifts were Orpheus-like, and he possessed a magical **harp** that played by itself (B.B. 3b–4a).

During his battle with the giant **Goliath**, he performed several **miracles**. The five stones he selected actually came to him of their own accord. When he touched them, they merged into a single wondrous and deadly missile. During their face-off, David cast the evil eye on Goliath, paralyzing him. After Goliath fell, an angel helped David in delivering the coup de grâce, as the shepherd was too small to lift the giant's weapon by himself.[1]

He encountered other fantastic beasts during his life, including the brothers of Goliath, a giant **re'em**, and talking **animals**. When he was elevated to kingship by

Samuel, the oil of his anointing turned to **gemstones** as it dripped from his head (Mid. Teh. 22:22, 34:1; Sot., 42b; Lev. R. 10:7, 21:2; Ruth R. 4:1; Tanh., Emor 4; Mid. Sam. 20:106–8; Zohar III: 272b).

David had an ongoing spiritual association with stones. Later, he would uncover the **Even ha-Shetiyah**, the foundation stone of the cosmos, and on that stone his son **Solomon** would build the **Temple**. There are several legends revolving around David and the foundation stone.

Numerous miracles are recorded in rabbinic literature surrounding his military campaigns. His death, which was foretold to him, had to be carefully contrived by the **Angel of Death** in order to outwit him. According to one legend, David studied **Torah** continuously and Death had to create a distraction before he could seize David's soul (Shab. 30a–b). Another claimed David actually fled to the mystic city of **Luz**, where the power of Death did not extend, and the Angel had to trick David into leaving the sanctuary of the city. In a unique legend, he never actually left the city, and lives on there to this day, like King Arthur in Avalon. This is at odds with the bulk of tradition, which records his death in detail. At his funeral, his son Solomon summoned **eagles** to gather and use their wings to shield his body from the sun (Ruth R. 3:2).

On the **Day of Judgment**, he will arise from the grave and once again sing his Psalms, which will be heard from one end of the universe to the other. Those sinners in **Gehenna** who respond "Amen" to his words will be redeemed instantly (Ruth R. 1:17; PdRE 19; Mid. Teh. 92:10; Num. R. 14:12).

David is destined to be the biological ancestor of the **Messiah**. In later Kabbalistic circles, it became accepted that the Messiah will in fact be David reincarnated. This belief is reflected in the popular messianic song *David Melekh Yisrael*, "David, King of Israel," which includes the refrain, *Chai, chai, v'kiyyam*, "[he] lives, lives, and endures." In the system of the **sefirot**, David represents **Malchut**, the tenth sefirah.

1. Ginzberg, *Legends of the Jews*, vol. 3, 537–38.

Day: In the **Zohar**, "days" is a Kabbalistic term for the "lower" seven **sefirot**.

Day of Judgment: SEE JUDGMENT, DAY OF.

Day of the Lord: *SEE* JUDGMENT, DAY OF.

Dead Sea Scrolls (DSS): An ancient library of scrolls found in various caves between 1947 and 1964 around the ruins of Qumran in the area of the Dead Sea. The collection was hidden away by an unknown collective of Jews, probably sectarian priests who had been driven from power in the **Temple**, possibly the group known as the **Essenes**, in the centuries before the destruction of Jerusalem in 70 CE.

The collection consists of both biblical and non-biblical documents. The DSS are far and away the biggest and most ancient collection of Jewish documents in existence, and their importance is hard to overestimate.[1] The documents are now largely translated, after many decades of delay, and each document is usually known by a number-letter designation, based on the cave in which the text was found. For example, 4Q561 means [Cave] 4, Q[umran, document number] 561. Larger finds were occasionally given names by their translators, such as the **Community Rule**, the **Damascus Document**, or the **War Scroll**. Some smaller, damaged fragments still need to be read, assembled, and interpreted.

Many of the non-biblical works in the DSS reveal aspects of ancient Jewish spirituality previously unknown to the world. The documents also contain myths, traditions, practices, and other information that gives us new perspective on the Hebrew Scriptures we have today, and even add background to the ideas found in the Christian Scriptures, though there were no actual Christian texts found among the DSS. Because of this potential to create controversy over the history of Judaism and, especially, the origins of Christianity, the fact that the documents largely remained in the exclusive control of a small circle of scholars for the first forty years spawned multiple conspiracy theories and rumors of the shocking revelations they contained. Since their full publication in the 1990s, many of the grander paranoid theories have evaporated, but the DSS still contain many things of interest to the student of the esoteric.

Among the non-biblical texts, there is a particular affinity for stories of **Enoch**, a human who ascends into heaven to become an angel and, conversely, for the **fallen angel** traditions of divine beings that come down to cor-

rupt humanity, suggesting the authors championed a kind of dualistic angel mysticism.[2] There is also a pronounced number mysticism revolving around groups of fours and sevens. The authors of the Dead Sea Scrolls were advocates for a solar **calendar** they believed was given to humanity by the angels, and opposed the lunar-based calendar being used by the rest of the Jewish community.[3]

Besides the documents of priestly spirituality and mysticism, among the texts in the DSS collection there exist several magical books—books of spells (4Q510, 4Q511, 11Q11), divination (4Q561), and astrology (4Q318). 4Q560, for example, is a fragmentary text of magical adjurations against injurious spirits. 4QCryptic, also known as 4Q1861, is a fragmentary work of **physiognomy** (divining based on a person's physical features).[4] Angelologies and demonologies are present in many documents, along with several elaborate accounts of the eschatological battles to be expected at the end of time. *SEE* BRONTOLOGY; HOROSCOPE; PSALMS, APOCRYPHAL; SONGS OF THE SABBATH SACRIFICE; SONGS OF THE SAGE.

1. Schiffman and VanderKam, *Encyclopedia of the Dead Sea Scrolls*, vol. 1, vii–x.
2. Ibid., 249–52.
3. Ibid., 108–16.
4. Ibid., vol. 2, 502–4.

Death: (*Mavet*). Death entered existence through the sin of the first humans, who by their disobedience lost access to the **Tree of Life** (Gen. 3). Initially, people lived for many hundreds of years each, but God shortened the life span because of the long-term human inclination to devolve into violence (Gen. 6).

According to the **Talmud**, there are 903 ways to die. The Bible speaks repeatedly of *karet*, being "cut off," a heavenly punishment, and *al pei Elohim*, death by the **kiss** of God. Sudden death is a sign of divine displeasure, as is death before age fifty. The Sages do not consider child deaths in the same way (Shab. 32b). No righteous person dies until another is born.

Omens of death include the barking of dogs and the appearance of owls, ominous **dreams**, and seeing human shadows that lack the head. The dying can see **Adam**, the **Angel of Death**, and/or the **Shekhinah**. If a man dies smiling, or with his face uplifted, it is a good omen that he will have ease in the afterlife, as is dying while facing people, on the eve of the **Sabbath**, or at the conclusion of **Yom Kippur**. If a person dies weeping or with the face downcast, it is a bad omen. Likewise, if one dies with the face turned away from people, at the end of the Sabbath, or on the eve of Yom Kippur, it is a bad sign. **Rain** at the time of death and/or burial is a sign of divine pleasure, and it is a good omen for the deceased (Hor. 12b; SCh 1516).

Some who are dying achieve a capacity for clairvoyance or **prophecy** (Gen. 49, 50:24; Deut. 31:28–29; Testament of the Twelve Patriarchs; Testament of Job).

The soul of the dead escapes through the mouth and at that moment its voice can be heard from one end of the universe to the other (Gen. R. 6:7). The windows in the place where a corpse rests should be opened to allow the spirit to move freely. Based on Job 14:22, the Rabbis teach that the **soul** remains conscious, some say until the interment, while others claim the dead can hear the living until the final decomposition of the body (Shab. 152b). Some teach that the disoriented soul hovers about the body for three days (others claimed seven) seeking to reenter it (Lev. R. 18:1; PdRE 34). According to the **Zohar**, the soul of the newly dead wanders between its earthly residence and its grave (I: 226b).

Since the souls of the dead stay close to their bodies until their transition to **Eden**, ghosts are mostly limited to the confines of the cemetery (Shab. 152b). The soul's separation from the body is a painful one, a process called **chibbut ha-kever**, "the torment of the grave." One Sage asserts that worms feel like needles to the dead (Ber. 18b). This tradition is based on the belief that the grave itself is atonement for the sins committed in life (Ket. 111a).

Kabbalists who taught the doctrine of **reincarnation** believed that the souls of the dead, or at least parts of a soul, transmigrate from one living body to another, and the souls of the disturbed dead can possess the body of a living being. The souls of the **righteous** can be temporarily recalled to this world to help the living (Kav v'Yasher; Sha'ar ha-Gilgulim).

Despite the belief in moral accountability through death, because Jews have not been burdened with the fear of "eternal damnation," Jewish teachings have generally viewed death with great equanimity. The Kotzker Rebbe compared death to "moving from one home to another." A. J. Heschel spoke of it as a "homecoming." *SEE* BURIAL;

DYBBUK; ETERNAL LIFE; GHOST; IBBUR OR DEVEKUT; POSSESSION, GHOSTLY; WORLD-TO-COME.

Decrees, Divine: In the imagination of the Sages, God's decisions resemble royal decrees. Each decree written on high is sealed. A decree may be nullified by repentance, **prayer**, and **charity** (R.H. 16b). The piety of the **righteous** is so great that they have the individual power to reverse a divine decision (Suk. 42a). Thus, playing on the epithet for Moses, *Ish Elohim* (which can mean "Man of God" or "Husband of God"), Midrash Psalms notes that Moses could nullify God's decrees, just as a husband can nullify his wife's vows (90:5).

If God's decision is sealed, however, then the matter is fated, and humans cannot change its outcome (Eleh Ezkarah). If the righteous pit themselves against a fated decree, it can place the very existence of the world in jeopardy, so in all such cases the pious have chosen to accept the divine judgment rather than uproot the world (R.H. 16b, High Holiday Machzor; Aggadat Esther; Midrash Eleh Ezkarah). *SEE* JUDGMENT, DAY OF; ROSH HA-SHANAH.

De Falk, Samuel: *SEE* FALK, CHAYYIM SAMUEL JACOB.

Demiurge: "Craftsman." The evil creator god of Gnostic myth. Derived from the philosophy of Plato, the Gnostics reimagine him as a malevolent force that imprisons spirit in the material world. Some Gnostic thinkers (Valentinus, Maricon) claim the demiurge is none other then the God of the Hebrew Scriptures.[1] *SEE* GNOSTICS AND GNOSTICISM, ANCIENT.

1. Couliano, *The Tree of Gnosis*, 115–116, 125.

Demons: (*Sheid, Mazzik, Ruach Hara, Se'ir, Malach Mashchit*). Demons are spirits that act malevolently against human beings, usually in the form of disease, illness, confusion, or misfortune. The Bible makes repeated mention of evil spirits (Lev. 16:10; I Sam. 16:14–16; Isa. 34:14), including satyrs and night demons, but does not provide a great deal of detail.

More elaborate stories about demons appear during the Greco-Roman period. The Gospels, which provide us with a picture of Jewish life in 1st-century Palestine, record several accounts of confrontations between Jesus and demonically possessed people.

The existence of demons, while widely accepted, has always presented a theological difficulty for Jews. Since all things are ultimately the creation of the one God, the question of why evil spirits should exist has greatly exercised Jewish thought. Drawing upon the cryptic passage about the "sons of God" found in Genesis 6:1–4, **apocalyptic literature** offers the first attempt to explain their existence in a monotheistic context by claiming demons are really **fallen angels**, or the offspring of the union between humans and fallen angels.[1] This explanation introduces a larger strand of thought, recurrent throughout Jewish literature, that demons are actually somehow the byproducts of human beings.

Rabbinic literature, particularly the **Talmud**, provides the most extensive source for Jewish demonology, though the information is scattered through many sources, and throughout those sources several explanations for the existence of demons are offered (Pes. 111a–111b; Ber. 5a, 60b; Git. 70a; Shab. 151b; Sukkot 28a; Eruv. 100b; B.B. 73a).

The Talmud begins by asserting that they are a creation of the twilight of the sixth day (Avot 5.6). The Talmudic sources do not specify whether demons are an independent creation, or whether they first appear as a result of the sin of **Adam** and **Eve**, which in some traditions also happened at twilight of the sixth day. Whatever the case, they cannot procreate on their own, so they used semen from Adam in order to make more of their own kind (Eruv. 18b). An elaboration on this tradition is that **Lilith**, the first woman, having transformed herself into a witch-demon using the **Tetragrammaton**, takes the nocturnal emissions of men she seduces to procreate demons (AbbS). Eve was also seduced by incubi, producing a line of malevolent offspring, beginning with **Cain** (PdRE 21; Targum Pseudo-Jonathan 4:1).

Midrash Tanhuma regards them to be souls without bodies, creations that were as yet unfinished when the day of rest commenced (Bereshit 17). Pirkei de-Rabbi Eliezer (34) teaches that demons are the disembodied souls of those who died in the Flood (also see Yalkut, Isaiah 429). Another strand of tradition asserts that the sins of a person are inscribed on their bones, and when they die, demons are a kind of postmortem metaphysical emission, like the release of the soul (SCh 770, 1170; Kitzur Shelah). The **Zohar** also claims that some demons *are* the souls of the wicked dead (I: 28b–29a, 48a; II: 70a; III: 25a).

One anonymous medieval rationalist even attempted a more naturalistic interpretation of demons, describing them as a noxious product of the interaction of sunlight with smoke and vapor that then clings to the body, causing illness (Sefer ha-Atzamim). Menachem ben Israel also argues for what we would describe today as a "naturalistic" explanation of the demonic.[2]

In classic Kabbalistic thought, the demonic is a necessary part of Creation, a product of the **Sitra Achra**, the "other side" of the divine emanations (specifically **Gevurah**) in the material universe (Treatise of the Left Emanation). Medieval mystics would often characterize demons as "destructive" or "punishing angels," a way of emphasizing that demons, too, are part of God's Creation and subject to the divine will. Mystics also clarify and elaborate on the Talmudic position that demons are the byproduct of human sin.

Demons occupy an intermediate place between mortals and angels. According to Chagigah 16a, they resemble angels in three ways: they have wings, they can fly throughout the universe, and they hear what transpires in heaven. They also resemble mortals in that they procreate, eat, and die. They are invisible, except under special conditions.

Tractate Berachot has perhaps the most information on demons of any part of the Talmud. There we learn that demons tend to dwell in the wilderness, in ruins, and in other places not frequented by people (Isa. 13:21). It also describes a "diagnostic" ritual for detecting the presence of the demonic: Ashes spread around one's bed at nighttime will reveal demon tracks in the morning, and demons can be rendered visible by grinding up the ashes of a black cat's afterbirth and then sprinkling the powder in one's eyes (Ber. 6a).

RaSHI makes an early attempt to classify demons, distinguishing between *Ruchin*, *Mazzikim*, and *Lilin*. The German Pietist **Judah he-Chasid** taught that demons actually study **Torah** and adhere to Jewish law. Based on this understanding, demonic attacks can occur only when the victim has transgressed in some way (Sefer Ohr Zarua). It is interesting to note how much Judah's teaching parallels medieval Islamic ideas about the spiritual life of djinns.

The malevolent effects of demons are many: they cause illness and death, especially for the vulnerable (children, women in childbirth), they trouble and deceive the mind, and they cause contention in the community of mortals.

The appearance of demons varies, but is always terrible. In keeping with Ancient Near Eastern beliefs about evil spirits, demons have bird talons for feet in addition to wings. At night, demons can appear in human form (Meg. 3a).

Demonic power waxes and wanes according to the time of day, the week, the seasons, meteorological conditions, topographical features, and other natural factors (Yalkut Chadash, Keshafim 56; Num. R. 12:3; Pes. 3a–b, 112a; Shab. 67a). The informed person can use this information to minimize the threat of this power.

Around human habitations, they frequent rooftops, out-houses, and drainage gutters. Strangely, demons are attracted to synagogues. The **Angel of Death**, for example, is said to keep his tools there. There are even stories of Sages doing night battles with demons in the **synagogue** (Shab. 66b).

Prominent demons have names, usually derived from their particular power. Reshef, for example, means "pestilence." Some demons, like **Samael**, have theonymic names like angels. Occasionally demons can have surprisingly mundane names, like "Joseph." The name Lilith means either "air" (Akkadian) or "night" (Hebrew) and has its roots in Mesopotamian aerial spirits called "lilu."

Reciting certain **psalms** repels evil spirits (Pss. 29:91, 121), as do other key verses of Scripture (Num. 7:4–6). Magical phrases and **incantations** have also been recorded that can combat their malevolent effects (Pes. 100a; 112a). The **bells** on the skirt of the High **Priest** evidently drove them away. Drinking water only from white containers turns away night demons (Pes. 3a). **Mezuzah**, **tefillin**, and ritual **fringes** are credited with the power to ward off evil spirits (Ber. 5b). The Jews of Mesopotamia additionally protected their homes with **incantation bowls**. Temporary protection can be obtained through the use of magic **circles**. **Amulets** of nearly infinite variety have been created across Jewish history to combat demonic assault. Demons can be bribed with food or money (PdRE 46; Tosefta Shab. 7:16; Ber. 50b), or frightened off with **shofar** blasts, unpleasant smells, or **spitting**. Guardian angels are the best defense, and are acquired every time one performs a **mitzvah** (Ex. R. 32).

Intriguingly, there is a strand of tradition that holds a mortal can work constructively with demons, if one knows the proper rituals of power to control them. This idea is first articulated in stories about Solomon controlling demons (**Testament of Solomon**). One Sage in the Talmud permits demon summoning, provided one does not violate Torah in either the manner of the summoning or what is asked of the spirit (Sanh. 101a). **Eliezer of Metz** (ca. 12th century) permitted the use of imps in spells and amulet writing: "Invoking the demons to do one's will is permitted . . . for what difference is there between invoking the demons and angels?" Demons can be turned against other demons (Lev. R. 24). Rabbi Judah Loew of Prague permitted communication with demons, but solely for the purpose of **divination** (B'er ha-Golah 2).

Sometimes the demon will help a human willingly (Pes. 106a), but usually spirits must be controlled magically, captured, and coerced to do the will of the adept. By the same token, anything that smacks of demon veneration or worship, such as making offerings or burning **incense** to a demon, is expressly forbidden (Sanh. 65b). *SEE LAW AND THE PARANORMAL.*

1. Nickelsburg, "The Experience of Demons (and Angels) in I Enoch, Jubilees, and the Book of Tobit," 1–20.
2. Dan, "Menasseh ben Israel's Nishmat Hayyim and the Concept of Evil in Seventeenth Century Jewish Thought," in Twersky and Septimus, *Jewish Thought in the Seventeenth Century*, 71.

Demon Queens: *SEE* LILITH; IGRAT; MALKAT; NAAMAN.

Depository: (*Machon*). One of the **seven heavens**, it is the level that warehouses all celestial precipitations: **rain**, snow, **hail**, **dew**, as well as the winds, storms and vapors (Chag. 12b–13a).

Destiny: *SEE* FATE.

Devekut: "Clinging/Cleaving." The experience of mystical union with God, usually as an outcome of meditative prayer or spiritual exercises. The term can also express a more mundane notion of binding oneself to God through good deeds and meticulous ritual practice (Deut. 11:22), but it is most intimately associated with mystical ecstatic practices. Devekut is not to be confused with monastic mysticism or any other kind of denial of worldly life. **Chasidism** both affirms the need for everyone to pursue devekut and the need to be engaged with the world by teaching that the ordinary tasks of living are, with the right intention, *the* stepping stones to greater attachment with God.

Moses Cordovero also described a magical-theurgic dimension to devekut, in that the act of "clinging to God" can be used to influence the direction of divine forces in the higher worlds (Pardes Rimonim 75d). Chasidism sometimes uses it as a term for beneficent spiritual possession.[1] *SEE* ASCENT; AVODAH B'GASHMIYUT; IBBUR OR DEVEKUT; MEDIUM; YICHUDIM.

1. Goldish, *Spirit Possession in Judaism*, 257–304.

Devekut B'otiyot: "Cleaving to the Letters." A mystical **prayer** technique taught in early **Chasidism**. It involves carefully and fervently articulating each syllable of the words of prayer. The effect is to create a mantralike chant with little or no interruption in sound.

Dever: "Pestilence." The **demon** of **plagues**. Some **Bible** commentators regard the ten **plagues** described in Exodus to each be a demon unleashed by God, Dever being one of them.

Devir: The innermost compartment of the **Temple**. *SEE* HOLY OF HOLIES.

Dew: (*Tal*). Dew is more than mere precipitation in Jewish tradition, it is a symbol and a metaphor for divine **emanation** (Shir ha-Kavod; Zohar I: 88a).

There are dews of beneficence and dews of destruction stored in **Machon**, the sixth level of heaven. In the seventh heaven, **Aravot**, there resides the very special *tal shel techiyah*, the "dew of resurrection," which will revive the dead on the **Day of Judgment** (Chag. 12b; Shab. 88b; J. Ber. 5:2; PdRE 34). God has had to deploy this dew once already, at Mount Sinai, when the whole people of Israel died of fright from hearing God speak (S of S R.; Targum S of S).

Though it seems understood in most texts that dew is a precipitation from the sky, in some Jewish teachings, dew is part of the underworld waters—it rises from the earth (Gen. 2:6). As such, it is the "feminine" waters, the counterpart to the "masculine" rainfall. Only when the two waters combine can the earth truly fructify. In the **Zohar**, dew signifies all manner of divine emanations from on high, including **manna**, which is a kind of dew (I: 95b; II: 61b).

Din: "Judgment." The divine attribute of strict justice. In rabbinic teachings, God's attribute of Din is associated with the divine name **Elohim**. In biblical stories that refer to God by that name, the power of severe justice is most present in the world during those episodes. It is from the attribute of Din that the rigorous, harsh, and even demonic aspects of the world emanate.

In Kabbalah, Din is synonymous with the sefirah of **Gevurah**. It is personified by the angel **Gabriel**. *SEE* SEFIROT.

Dina: "Law/Religion." Another name for the angel of the Torah. *SEE* YEFEIYAH; YOFIEL.

Directions: Each of the cardinal compass points is overseen by a princely angel: **Michael** (south), **Gabriel** (north), **Uriel** (east), and **Raphael** (west). East is the source of light, north of darkness, west, the snow and hail, and south, the rains and dew. (Num. R. 2:10; Zohar I: 149b). God assembled **Adam** from earth taken from the four corners of the world (Tanh., Pekudei 3). *SEE* EAST; NORTH; SOUTH; WEST.

Disease: The prevalent attitude found in the Hebrew **Bible** is that disease, like all other things, comes from the will of God. Some passages in the Torah also show God using disease as a retribution for sin. At the same time, God also declares "I am the one that heals you" (Ex. 15:26). Though this aspect of the Bible could have led Jews to believe, like Christian Scientists, that human intervention in disease is a violation of God's will, that is not how Judaism has dealt with the issue. The Sages, for example, blame some disease on demonic forces and therefore permit the use of virtually any remedy, whether natural or supernatural. Today, virtually all Jews accept scientific theories of natural pathology. It is promised that in Messianic times, all disease will be curable with the "living waters" that will flow from Jerusalem (Zech. 13–14). *SEE* DEMONS; HEALING.

Divination: (*Simanut, Nichush, Kesem, K'shafim*). "Who is wise? He who foresees the results of his deeds" (Tam. 32a). Across human cultures, it has been widely believed that the gods and spirits close to them (the dead, for example) have privileged knowledge of what will unfold in the mortal realms. The ability to gain such supernatural insight has been prized by humans since (and probably before) the dawn of written history. All divination can be divided into the quest for one of two kinds of knowledge: knowledge of the future (manticism) and knowledge of present, but hidden, events (clairvoyance).

Jews are no exception in their desire for this knowledge, and throughout history many Jews have accepted the reality of divinatory events and experiences. Moreover, Jews have been practitioners of many different diviner's arts across time and geography. Starting with the testimony of the Hebrew Scripture, however, Judaism has manifested an ambivalent attitude toward divination and from earliest times Jews have struggled to distinguish between licit and illicit forms of divination.

The generic biblical words for divination are *kesem* and *nachash*. In the Ancient Near East, three types of divinatory practices are documented: serendipitous **omens**, impetrated omens, and mediumistic divination. The first consists of the reading and interpretation of omens and prodigies in naturally occurring phenomenon, such as the weather, abnormal births, or astral signs. The second practice consists of asking questions by means of divinatory devices, such as casting lots or reading entrails, and the third involves the consulting of human oracles or divine forces channeled through a person, such as **prophecy**.

Within these general rubrics, the books of the Hebrew Scriptures make reference to myriad forms of mantic practices, both licit and illicit. Among the accepted means of divination are prophets and seers of YHWH (Deut. 18:14–22; I Sam. 9:6; II Kings 3:11), **oneiromancy** (dream interpretation) (Gen. 37:5–9; Daniel), **Urim and Thummim**, the casting of **lots** (I Sam. 23:10–12), **music** (II Kings 3:15), **lecanomancy** or **hydromancy** (reading patterns in liquid) (Gen. 44:5), and word omens (I Sam. 14:9–10).

Illicit methods, condemned by biblical authors, include **terafim** (consulting idols; Zech. 10:2), hepatoscopy or extispiciomancy (reading animal entrails, Ezek. 21:26), **necromancy** (communing with the dead; I Sam. 15:23), **belomancy** (casting or shooting arrows; Ezek. 21:26), and **astrology** (Isa. 47:13; Jer. 10:2). At times, the biblical witnesses are not always in agreement about what constitutes legitimate mantic practice. Thus, for example, despite the cases of exemplary practitioners like Joseph and Daniel, the prophet Zechariah condemns oneiromancy along with other forms of divination (10:2). II Kings 13:15–19 recounts a case of what appears to be prophetically endorsed belomancy.

Clairvoyant divination (revealing a hidden current reality) is less common, though veridical dreams are acknowledged as a way for mortals to understand God's will. (Gen. 20:3; I Sam. 3:3–10; I Kings, 3:5–15). Other acceptable forms of clairvoyance include the casting of lots to determine who enjoys God's favor (I Sam. 10:20–24) and conferring with a seer to find a lost possession (I Sam. 9:6), though the evidence is more ambiguous here; given their narrative context, careful readers must decide whether we are meant to regard these two practices as efficacious, or merely ruses by the prophet to further God's inscrutable purpose.

Many types of diviners are mentioned in Scripture. Under the general category of oracular prophets, there is the *navi* (prophet), the *roeh* (seer), and the *ish elohim* (man of God). There are also several terms for mantics separate from the Israelite institution of prophecy, all of them being targets of condemnation: **baal ov**, **itztzim**, **kosem kesamim**, **menachesh**, **meonen**, and **yeddioni**. The exact meaning of these terms is tentative, as the usage and meaning may well have changed within the time frame of the thousand years over which the **Bible** was composed. And, as in English, some terms may not even reflect technical distinctions, but are merely synonyms, often borrowed from other languages.

The Talmudic Sages were extremely sensitive to serendipitous omens, and were avid observers of the stars, the **trees** (Suk. 28a), and the behavior of **birds** (Git. 45a) and other selected animals. Biblical verses elicited from **children** can be read as signs. All the same, the Rabbis condemned those forms of operational divination they associated with *Kesem/Nachash* (**sorcery/witchcraft**). An extended discussion of witchcraft and divination appears in Sanhedrin 65b. In that passage, "performance" or impetration, such as the use of **divining rods**, is the primary criteria for determining that a form of manticism is illicit. The Sages are not consistent on these points, and the line between licit and illicit forms of divination is often blurred beyond useful distinction.

The medieval **Sefer Chasidim** continues with this ambivalence, condemning forms of impetrated divination while recording dreams and omens and teaching their interpretation (237, 441, 729, 1172). In his book *Chokmat ha-Nefesh*, **Eleazer of Worms** lists a variety of bodily omens and their meaning. **Chayyim Vital** consults witches, sorcerers, and visionaries in dizzy variety in his quest to confirm through paranormal means his own spiritual genius (Sefer ha-Hezyonot). The dead continue to be regarded as an excellent source of mantic knowledge, even though necromancy is roundly condemned. Here the distinction seems to be that when the dead initiate the communication, it is acceptable, but if the living attempt to initiate a séance, it is not (this too changes under the influence of Spanish Kabbalah).[1] **Astrology**, **lamps**, **cocks**, **Bibliomancy**, and **mirrors** were all acceptable sources of advanced knowledge by the Middle Ages. Though condemned by the **Talmud**, the use of divining rods was also tolerated by the late Middle Ages.

Most specifically, Jewish divination practices have all but vanished from modern communities, though some pietistic groups still practice the custom of scrying the fingernails at Havdalah (*SEE* FINGER) and/or employ Bibliomancy. Most Jews who are interested in such things today make use of techniques popular in the general culture, such as horoscopes and Tarot cards. Jews can still be very attentive to serendipitous omens. *SEE* GEOMANCY; MEDIUM; NECROMANCY; PROPHECY.

1. Chajes, *Between Worlds*, 13–18, 30–31.

Divining Rod: Sticks or staves can be used for purposes of divination (rhabdomancy). It is a very ancient practice. The art of **belomancy**, the use of arrows for determining a course of action, is an example of rhabdomancy mentioned in the **Bible**. The first mention of a Jew actually using a staff as a divination rod appears in the Talmud, where the technique is for a diviner to hold it up-

right and release it. The direction in which it falls determines the course of action. The Talmud condemns this as **witchcraft**. Nevertheless, divining rods resurface among European Jews amidst the craze for dowsing buried treasure that seized Europe in the High Middle Ages. Jewish magical recipes exist that explain the type of tree to be used (usually hazelwood or **myrtle**), when the rod is to be harvested, and the **incantations** and rituals surrounding its use. *SEE* DIVINATION; ROD.

Divri ha-Yamim shel Moshe: "Chronicles of the Life of Moses." It is a medieval collection of tales about Moses that includes many more miraculous details than are found in the biblical accounts.

D'li: "Pail"/Aquarius. The zodiac sign for the month of Shevat, the late winter month in the Land of Israel. It is a sign of purification, wealth, benefit, and the Torah. The holiday of Tu B'shevat, the "New Year of Trees," is celebrated this month, when the winter rains are falling and helping fructify the earth. This reflects the wealth and abundance associated with this sign.

Dogs: Like many peoples of the Near East, Jews have historically not had a favorable opinion of dogs. The few images of dogs found in the **Bible** are negative. Only the apocryphal book Tobit offers a positive portrayal of a dog.

The book of Deuteronomy specifically prohibits the religious use of the "wages of a dog." In the past this obscure law has been regarded as an oblique reference to male sacred prostitution. Recent archaeological digs, however, have uncovered an enormous **healing** cult among the Philistines that involved the sacrifice of dogs. It seems more likely that Deuteronomy is referring to this phenomenon.

Dogs were regarded as highly sensitive to the presence of the spirit world. Thus both the **Talmud** and medieval Jewish literature regard the behaviors of dogs as ominous. Frolicking dogs signify good tidings, and may even signal the presence of **Elijah** in the vicinity. Barking dogs mark the presence of the **Angel of Death**. Witches and demons can take on canine form. Dog fur is listed among items to be used for medicinal amulets in the Talmud. In the **Zohar**, "dogs" is a circumlocution for demons (I: 6b).

The souls of the wicked are often transmigrated into dogs (ShB 108). Many of the later supernatural beliefs about canines appear to come directly from the folk traditions of non-Jewish neighbors (Baba Kamma 60b; Sefer Chasidim 1145–46). *SEE* ANIMALS.

Domah or Dumah: "Silence." The angel of the grave. Domah is a punishing angel of the afterlife (Ber. 18b; Shab. 152b; Sanh. 94a). He comes with an angelic court to visit the soul of the dead once the body is interred. At that time, Domah, wielding a flaming scepter, asks the soul its Hebrew name, reviews its deeds while living, and pronounces the first judgments upon the dead (PR 23:8). In the Zohar, he is one of the principal angels of Gehenna (I: 8a–b, 94a, 102a). *SEE* ANGEL OF DEATH; BURIAL; CHIBBUT HA-KEVER; DEATH; NAME, HEBREW.

Donmeh: A secret heretical sect, once scattered across the Ottoman Empire, which arose from the followers of **Shabbatai Tzvi**. Outwardly maintaining the practice of Islam, the Donmeh cling to many Jewish observances and the belief that Tzvi is the Messiah. Once virtually moribund, the group has found renewed life on the Internet as "Neo-Sabbatean Kabbalah."

Doubles: *SEE* PAIRS.

Dove: (*Tor* or *Yonah*). The dove, specifically the turtle-dove, is a symbol of purity, peace, the **Messiah**, the people Israel (S of S R. 2:14), and the **Shekhinah**. According to the **Vilna Gaon**, the dove is also a symbol of the **soul** (Commentary to Jonah, 1).

It is a dove that brought an olive sprig, a message of hope to **Noah** that he would find refuge on dry land. Thus it becomes a symbol of future redemption. A dove is one of the clean animals that may be offered in sacrifice in the **Temple**. *SEE* DOVE, GOLDEN.

Dove, Golden: Based on the imagery of Psalm 68, the Messiah becomes identified with a celestial golden dove, which serves as his messenger (B. Yoma 44b; Zohar III: 196b). This same idea appears, in variant form, in the Christian Gospels associated with Jesus (Mark 1). *SEE* BIRD'S NEST.

Dragon: (*Tanin; Teli*). An archetypical monster, usually resembling a serpent. With only a few vague references in the **Bible**, the term *tanin* is open to various interpretations, the most mundane being the crocodile. More imaginative readers understand it to refer to a monstrous serpent or dragon that dwells in water and is a menace to navigation (Neh. 2:13; Isa. 27:1; B.B. 74a–b). At times the word becomes synonymous with **Leviathan**. Daniel is credited with battling a dragon and killing it by filling its mouth with pitch (Bel and the Dragon). In the apocalyptic literature, there is a dragon of monstrous dimensions in **Sheol** that feeds on the souls of the wicked (III Baruch 4–5). Demons can take the form of dragons (B. Kid. 29b), and some demons, such as **Samael**, are given the title "serpent." In **Kabbalah**, a cosmic blind dragon, **Tanin'iver**, serves as the steed of **Lilith**. (Daniel, Septuagint version; III Baruch; Treatise on the Left Emanation).

In medieval writings *teli* becomes another idiom for a dragon, and in some texts it becomes the term for the Milky Way, because of its sinuous, elongated appearance (Zohar I: 125b).

Drash: To "inquire [of God]." *SEE* DIVINATION.

Dream: (*Chalom*). Clairvoyant and prophetic dreams have a long and honored role in Judaism. The **Bible** identifies numerous Patriarchs, kings and prophets who have dreams of ominous import (Gen. 28:12, 31:10, 37:5–9; Dan. chapter 2; Zech. 1:8). Prophets and dreamers, in fact, are often listed together (I Sam. 28:6; Deut. 8:2). It also acknowledges certain individuals, such as Joseph and Daniel, as having a talent for interpreting dreams. The Bible assumes that both dreams and the ability to interpret them come from God.

The Sages of the **Talmud** express diverse attitudes towards the mantic potential of dreams. While there are several examples of Sages who dismiss their ominous value, the overwhelming bulk of the Rabbis take dreams quite seriously. The most popular notion (Ber. 57b) seems to be that dreams are "one-sixtieth of prophecy." Dreams are also considered "one-sixtieth of death," and it is interesting to note that both prophecy and death are phenomena that the Sages believe give a person access to the divine mind.

By the same token, the Sages note that "Neither a good dream nor a bad dream is completely fulfilled" (Ber. 55a, 57b). There is some suspicion that dreams have mixed sources, and therefore mixed reliability—good dreams come from the agency of angels, while false dreams are the work of demons (Ber. 55b).

There is considerable rabbinic material concerning the meaning of dreams, including the stories of individual Sages and a short list of dream symbols and their meanings (Ber. 56b–57b). The Talmud even mentions a professional dream specialist, the *Baal ha-Chalom*, who is necessary because interpreting one's own dreams is discouraged (Yoma 28b). There is also an angel in Jewish tradition called **Baal ha-Chalom**. There are multiple stories in rabbinic literature of the dead returning to address the living in their dreams. An unsolicited dream vision of the dead apparently does not violate the prohibition against necromancy, and such visions are generally treated as a valid source of occult knowledge (SCh 237, 705, 708–10, 729, 1129).

The **Zohar** is cautious about the value of dreams, seeing them as an admixture of prophecy and the dark forces of the **Sitra Achra** (I: 149a). A major interest of Jewish mystical/magical literature is how to induce revelatory dreams. Various **Hechalot** texts include **incubation** practices for receiving dream revelations. **Sefer ha-Razim** has an entire section devoted to dreams and getting dream questions answered; doing so involves a period of ritual **purification**, going to a body of **water**, burning **incense**, and performing an incantation to the **Sar ha-Chalom**, the angel of dreams. After three nights, the angel will appear and answer questions.

Medieval works, such as **Sefer Chasidim** and fragments of the **Cairo Geniza**, continue this interpretive tradition. **Chayyim Vital** kept a diary of veridical dreams (both his own and the dreams of others) concerning himself. The most complete Jewish work of dream interpretation is **Pitron Chalomot** by the Turkish rabbi **Solomon ben Jacob Almoli**.

Chasids considered dreams to be very important. There are innumerable stories of dead Chasidic masters appearing to their families and/or disciples in dreams, dispensing advice and revelations. Some masters also recorded their own dreams, relating them to their followers with appropriate interpretations. Chasids frequently bring their own disturbing dreams to their rebbes for interpretation and counsel in dealing with their ominous implications.

There are several traditions about the angel who is in charge of dreams, the Sar ha-Chalom. This angel is sometimes identified with **Gabriel**, the angel of revelation (Zohar I: 149a).

There are various remedies for bad omens revealed in dreams, including **fasting** (Shab. 11a; Tan. 12b; SCh 226, 349), giving **charity** (B.B. 10a), or reciting talismanic verses from Scripture upon waking (Ps. 30:12; Jer. 31:13; Deut. 23:6; Zech. 10:2). There is also a prayer for defense against ominous dreams, *Hatavat Chalom*, that is recited before a priest while he is pronouncing the Priestly Blessing (Ber. 55b). Based on a popular belief that a dream comes true "as it is interpreted," an individual may enlist three friends to magically nullify a bad dream by relating the dream and reciting the phrase, "It is a good dream," to which the friends respond, "Yes it is good, may it be good, may God change it to good." *SEE* BAAL HA-CHALOM; DIVINATION; INCUBATION; NECROMANCY; TA'ANIT CHALOM.

Dumah: "Silence." An alternative name for **Domah**, the angel of the grave. It is also a name for one of the compartments of **Gehenna** (Ps. 94:17).

Dumiel: Guardian angel of the Persians and/or a gate guardian of heaven (Yoma, Hechalot Rabbati).

Dwelling: (*Maon*). One of the **seven heavens**. It is the level that holds all the lower ranks of **angels** and the heavenly choir. Here Israel's praises are sung before God every day (Chag. 12b–13a).

Dybbuk: (Yiddish, "Clinging/possessing spirit"). A *dybbuk mi-ruach ra*, a "clinging of an evil spirit," is a **ghost** or disturbed transmigrated **soul** that possesses the body of a living person. While demonic possession has a long history in Judaism, the first reports of dybbuks only start to appear in the 16th century. The term "dybbuk" itself is even later—early accounts simply speak of *ruchim*, "spirits." Dybbuk accounts coincide with the spreading belief in **reincarnation** among Jews.

According to pre-Lurianic Jewish mysticism, the dybbuk is a sinner who is seeking refuge from the punishments of the afterlife or who for some reason has been unable to continue its journey to its resting place in the Treasury of Souls. In Lurianic Kabbalah, the dybbuk phenomenon is more closely linked to the biblical fate of **karet**, being "cut off," and because of its sin the dybbuk has been exiled from its next proper stage of reincarnation. Thus it finds refuge in a living victim and must be exorcised. In Luria's teachings, **exorcism** is a doubly therapeutic event, both relieving the possessed person and releasing the dybbuk to continue its journey into the afterlife (Sefer ha-Brit). Dybbuks mostly attack those who are spiritually vulnerable. It enters, for example, into a home with a neglected **mezuzah** because it knows someone resides there who is lax in spiritual practice and development. Dybbuks are also disproportionately male and disproportionately possess **women**, though there are also accounts in Jewish legal literature of men being possessed (Darkhei Teshuvah 4, no. 52). In some accounts, there is a sexual dimension to the dybbuk's choice of victim.[1] *SEE* DEATH; GHOST; POSSESSION, GHOSTLY.

1. Bilu, "Dybbuk and Maggid," 348–66. Also see Goldish, *Spirit Possession in Judaism*, 45–54, 64–68, 313.

E

Eagle: (*Nesher*). The eagle is a symbol of divine Presence and favor, as well as a creature of mystery (Prov. 30:19; Midrash Prov.). Scripture compares God to an eagle that guards her young (Deut. 32). It also signifies **Chesed** in sefirotic theosophy.

An eagle is one of the four faces that **Ezekiel** sees among the holy creatures that make up God's **chariot** (Ezek. 1). Eagles served **Solomon** and performed many wondrous deeds in service to him. The **Ziz**, a mythical bird, is sometimes described as an eagle of giant proportions (B.B. 73a–74a). Protective words and phrases arranged in the image of an eagle occasionally appear on Jewish amulets.

Earring: In the biblical period, earrings were either **amulets** or symbols of devotion to pagan gods, as indicated by Jacob's decision to bury them along with some idols in his possession (Gen. 34:4).

Earth: (*Eretz, Adamah, Tevel, Archa*). Earth is one of the four elements that make up the **world** (Chag. 12b). In Israelite cosmogony, the earth was created on the third day. It rests upon mighty **pillars** and floats above a watery **abyss** below its crust (Pss. 74:4, 104:5). The earth was conceived as flat (Isa. 40:22), with an *axis mundi*, or navel (Ezek. 38:5; Jubilees 8; PdRE 11) and the edges or "ends" lined by mountains (MdRI 1). **Sefer Yetzirah**, following Job 26:7, understands the earth is suspended in space. According to the Sages, there are actually seven dimensions of the material world: *Eretz, Adamah, Arka, Harabah, Yabbashah, Tevel,* and *Heled*. An alternate list gives *Neshiyya* and *Tziyya* in

place of *Harabah* and *Yabbashah*. (Lev. R. 29:11; SY 4:12; Zohar III: 9b–10a). Mankind, being a **microcosm** of the world, is made from dirt drawn from the "four corners" of the earth (PdRE 12).

According to the **Bible**, the earth is cursed by both the disobedience of Adam and Eve and the crime of Cain (Gen. 3). Still, the earth manifests God's will. It fails to yield produce for those who ignore God's will and can even swallow up those who offend God, as it did **Korach ben Izhar** and his supporters (Num. 16:32). And it continues to have a sacred status: in order to enter a zone of holiness, Moses must first shed his sandals, walking on the earth without a barrier (Ex. 3).

According to the Sages, the earth can also protect those whom God would save. Thus in one legend, the Hebrew babies in **Egypt** were delivered from Pharaoh's decree by the earth opening up and hiding them from their would-be killers (Sot. 11b; Ex. R. 1:12).

The Land of **Israel** is holy and the earth of that land possesses special power. **Creation** began at the **Temple Mount** and radiated out from there, making Jerusalem the center of the world (Tanh., Kedoshim 10; PdRE 35). It is the soil from the grounds of the future Temple that God used to make Adam (Targum to Gen. 2:7). Soil from Israel binds a believer to the Holy Land and to God (II Kings 5). When **Jacob** experienced his veridical dream promising him the whole Land of Israel (Gen. 28:13), God enfolded the entire Land of Israel and placed it beneath his body (Chul. 91b). Being buried in the Land of Israel has some atoning power and so is a factor in **resurrection**. For that reason, pious Jews will insist on being buried with a small amount of dirt from Israel scattered in their coffin (Ma'avar Yabbok; commentary to Maimonides Hilchot Melachim, V).

Some conceived of the earth as having awareness or intelligence through its own principle angel (Num. R. 23:6). According to legend, King **David** once unleashed the waters trapped beneath the earth by moving the *Even ha-Shetiyah*, the **Foundation Stone**, which is found beneath the bedrock of the **Temple**.

Soil within the precincts of the Temple possesses special power. It is used in the trial by ordeal described in Numbers 5:17 to divine whether a wife has been unfaithful to her husband (Sot. 2:2). In the **golem** traditions, the creature must be partly constructed from earth within the confines of a **synagogue**. Ordinary earth stuffed in the mouth of a **vampire** that has died will prevent it from becoming the undead. Earth thrown over the shoulder after a funeral discourages the **evil eye**. SEE BURIAL; DIRECTIONS; MOUNTAIN.

East: (*Kedem, Mizrach*). The east is a symbol of spatial, temporal, and spiritual antiquity. Like the sun, time and primeval forces emerge from the east. Thus **Eden** (and therefore Paradise) is in the east and it is from there that primordial man migrates to Israel, which is at the center of the **earth** (Gen. 2, 11). It is therefore also a realm of power. It was a measure of Solomon's power that he "surpassed the wisdom of the children of the East" (I Kings 5:10). The people of the East were famed for their knowledge of magic and astrology (Eccl. R. 7:23; PdRK 4:3; Tanh., Chukkat 6).

Kabbalah treats the word for "east," *MiZRaCH*, as an acronym: *Mi-tzad Zeh Ruach Chayyim*, "From this side comes the spirit of life." The **Bahir** calls the east the "seed," the place from which generativity flows. The **Zohar** associates it with the sefirah **Tiferet** (I: 85a). It is personified in the angel **Uriel**.

The wind that parted the sea for Moses and the Israelites blew from the east. The ancient **Temple** faced east, with the **Holy of Holies** oriented to the west, so the rays of the rising sun would enter the building as it ascended. Jewish homes often have a "Mizrach," a printed amulet with protective images and verses, sometimes in **microscript**, which is mounted on the eastern wall of the house, in the direction of **prayer**. SEE DIRECTIONS.

Ebed Melech: A foreign courtier, an Ethiopian, in the court of King Zedekiah. One tradition claims this is just another name for **Baruch**, the prophet Jeremiah's secretary. According to the Greek Apocalypse of Baruch, the righteous gentile Ebed Melech slept through the entire sixty-six years of the Babylonian exile. Rabbinic legends credit him with entering heaven alive, like **Elijah** and **Enoch** (Yalkut 2:367).

Eclipse: Both lunar and solar eclipses are considered ill omens (Isa. 3:26, 13:10). Because the **moon** is a symbol of the Children of Israel, a lunar eclipse is particularly ominous for Jews, while a solar eclipse bodes ill for gentiles. On the other hand, the **Talmud** expounds that the **sun** is eclipsed when a great rabbi dies and is not honored, indicating Jews are in a state of spiritual decline, for Baba Batra 75a compares "the face of Moses to the face of the sun." So a solar eclipse signals an "eclipse of the [spiritual] sun."

In Talmud, Tractate Sukkah teaches that the appearance of an eclipse, along with its exact location in the sky, can be read to know the specific type of blight (famine, war, etc.) and/or the population who will be most affected. SEE ASTROLOGY; DIVINATION; OMEN.

Ecstasy: (*Hitpaalut; Hishtapchut ha-Nefesh*). A state of transcendent exaltation; enthusiasm. In the **Bible**, it is associated with the prophetic experience (Num. 19; I Sam. 19). In Talmudic times, ecstatic dancing was a central part of rituals such as the **water libation ceremony**. Later Judaism considers it a desirable state of mind for prayer and worship. **Chasidism**, especially, creates worship services and spiritual gatherings (**Tish** and **Farbrengen**) conducive to ecstatic worship. Jewish spiritual practices for achieving a state of ecstasy include **chanting**, **dance**, **music**, **weeping**, and **meditation**. SEE JOY AND HUMOR.

Eden, Garden of: (*Gan Eden*). The mythic realm of primordial humanity, over time the term has become synonymous with "Paradise."

In the **Bible**, God situates the Garden on earth between four rivers: the Tigris, Euphrates, Gihon, and Pishon (Gen. 2:8). The Garden is technically **east** of Eden. At its center grew two cosmic trees, the **Tree of Life** and the **Tree of the Knowledge of Good and Evil**. After the sin of **Adam** and **Eve**, humanity is expelled from the Garden, and the route back is barred by two **cherubim** armed with a single fiery sword (swords evidently being in short supply).

In the rabbinic writings, Eden, like Jerusalem, is simultaneously located on earth and within the precincts of heaven (M. Ber. 5:3). The Sages describe an earthly Garden, *Gan Eden shel ha-Aretz*, which mirrors (imperfectly) the heavenly Garden, *Gan Eden shel Malah* or *shel Elyon*. Eventually there evolves an idiomatic and symbolic distinction between *Gan* and *Eden*. *Gan* is the earthly portion, while *Eden* is the locality where the dead reside (Shab. 119a; Ber. 18a; Ket. 103a; Zohar III: 182b).

The **Cave** of Machpelah is the entryway to the higher Eden (Mid. Teh. 92:6). Its entrance is guarded by myriads of angels, who welcome the righteous dead, garbing them in glory. Each dead soul rests beneath their individual canopy and partakes in delicacies. Each heavenly day, the person undergoes a complete life cycle, being a child in the morning, a youth in the afternoon, and a mature adult in the evening. Every variety of fruit and spice tree grows there, each of unsurpassed beauty and fragrance (Yalkut; Ber. 34b).

The medievals elaborate on the image of the celestial Garden, describing it as a walled enclosure of astronomical proportions, filled with precincts and palaces. There are many such realms, usually seven (corresponding to the **seven heavens**), each serving as the residence for different categories of meritorious souls. Thus there is a palace for those who were martyred, another for the young, and another for those women who cared for the ill and aged for many years (Yalkut; Seder Gan Eden). There angels attend upon the dead, who are refreshed by the fragrance emanating from the **Tree of Life**.

In addition to imagining Eden as a garden, rabbinic literature often describes it as a **yeshiva shel malah**, an academy on high, where the dead study Torah and where the secrets that eluded our understanding in life are revealed at last (Gen. R. 49:2; Num. R. 17:6).

Gehenna abuts directly on the Garden. *SEE* ADAM; ETERNAL LIFE; EVE; GUF HA-DAK; HECHALOT LITERATURE.

Edom: The name of the tribal nation dwelling southeast of Israel, regarded in Israelite tradition to be the descendants of **Esau**. In rabbinic literature, the word became an encoded term, an occult reference first for the Roman Empire, and later for Christendom that arose in its place.

Egg: (*Beitzah*). Eggs are virtually universally seen as symbols of life, immortality, and mystery and are therefore filled with magical potential. Two eggs produced by the same hen on a single day is a bad omen (it is certainly a bad omen for the chicken, as the quickest remedy for averting that particular prodigy is to kill the hen that laid them).

Eating the roasted egg that is part of the **Passover** Seder plate brings good luck. Eggs were used in folk medicine, as well as the preparation of protective talismans. For the latter, the egg would be inscribed with a magical formula and then consumed, either as a means of purification for the **amulet** maker, or as part of the amulet-making process itself (Sefer Rokeach).

Eggs were an important ingredient in **love** potions and memory incantations. They could be consumed or buried near the target person or at a location of power, such as a crossroads. Eggs are also aphrodisiacs, stimulating virility. Eggs have a guardian spirit that may be consulted for purposes of divination. Presumably, this involves breaking the egg and studying the pattern created (Sanh. 101a).

Egypt: (*Mitzrayim*). "Ten measures of witchcraft were given to the world; nine measures went to Egypt" (Kid. 49b). The land of Egypt has been associated with mystery and the occult since earliest Jewish history, with tradition viewing it as a breeding ground for **witchcraft**. The biblical contest between **Moses** and Pharaoh's sorcerers (Ex. 7:10–13) sets the tone for all subsequent Jewish attitudes toward Egypt.

Because of its biblical associations, as well as its exotic status in the Greco-Roman imagination, Egypt continues to be regarded as a place of sorcery and arcane knowledge throughout Jewish tradition. Two of the most famous Jewish alchemists, **Maria Hebrea** and Moses of Alexandria, hail from there. The Sages characterize Egypt as the "capital of witchcraft" (Gen. R. 86:5). The fact that the Neo-Platonic theurgists—precursors to the practical Kabbalists of the Middle Ages—first appeared in Egypt only reinforces the image of the country as a place of magic and supernatural power.

Ein Sof: "Without End." *Ein Sof* is the term used in **Kabbalah** for the true but hidden essence of God, which is entirely unknown and unknowable to humans. All human knowledge of God is really knowledge of the ten emanated **sefirot**, which are "outside" Ein Sof. *SEE* ELOHIM; FACE OF GOD; NAMES OF GOD; PARTZUFIM; TETRAGRAMMATON.

Eldad and Medad: Two elders in the Israelite camp who become seized with the spirit of **prophecy** (Num. 11:26–29). According to rabbinic tradition, their prophecies included apocalyptic visions concerning the Messiah and Jerusalem (Sanh. 17a). These were purportedly recorded in an apocryphal work bearing their names, but that text has not survived.

Eleazar: Talmudic Sage (ca. 1st–2nd century). Eleazar was a great spiritual virtuoso. He could make food (cucumbers, to be precise) magically materialize. He met with **Elijah**, who introduced him to the Messiah. He had many insights into the higher worlds, and when he expounded on them, he was engulfed in supernal fire. He was also a clairvoyant who could interpret when the actions of animals revealed them to be messengers of heaven (Sanh. 68a; Zohar I: 98; Zohar II: 28; Zohar Chadash).

Eleazer, Abraham: Alchemist (Unknown nationality, ca. 15–18th century). Author of **Uraltes Chymisches Werk**. Despite the influential nature of this work, it is impossible to fix the dates of his life. But since his book was published in 1760, yet it contains quotes from known alchemical treatises from only as late as the 14th century, the window of his lifetime can be narrowed to roughly a 300+ year period. *SEE* ALCHEMY.

Eleazar bar Shimon: Talmudic Sage and mystic (ca. 2nd century). The son of **Simon bar Yochai**, he lived in a **cave** with his father for thirteen years, studying the secrets of **Torah**. When he finally emerged, his vision had become so purified that it burned any imperfect thing he saw on the outside, so he was forced to return to the cave (Shab. 33b–34a; Gen. R. 79:6; J. Shev. 9:1).

Eleazer ben Judah of Worms: Ethicist and mystic (German, ca. 13th century). Also know as Rokeach, Eleazer was a leading light of the *Chasidei Ashkenaz*, the **German Pietist** mystics. He experienced **visions** and could perform great acts of theurgy. He used his knowledge of divine names, for example, to slay an evil gentile prince who threatened the Jewish community (Meisa Buch). He wrote numerous works pertaining to **mysticism**, **gematria**, and **magic**, including **Sefer ha-Chayyim**, **Sefer ha-Rokeah**, and a commentary on **Sefer Yetzirah**.

Elect of God: (*Bechir Eloha*). A mysterious figure mentioned in the **Dead Sea Scrolls**. He is a mantic figure, with secret knowledge of the **zodiac**, occult books, and Scriptures.

Eliezer: The servant of **Abraham**. A former prince, he bore a remarkable resemblance to his master (PdRE 16; Gen. R. 59:8). He had many fantastic adventures in the service of Abraham during which he demonstrated heroic wit and cleverness (Sanh. 109b). The angel **Michael** accompanied him on his journey to find a bride for **Isaac** (Gen. R. 59:10). He is counted as one of nine people who entered Paradise without having to undergo death. In one surprising tradition, he is identified as the giant **Og** (Sof., add. 1:2).

Eliezer of Metz: Talmudist (German, ca. 12th century) and author of Sefer Yereim. He is virtually unique among rabbinical authorities in his granting legal permission for Jews to summon both **angels** *and* **demons** to achieve benevolent purposes.

Elijah: Also frequently called *Eliyahu ha-Navi*, "Elijah *the* Prophet," this prophet of ancient Israel (ca. 9th century BCE) is one of the most celebrated heroes in Jewish lore. In his earthly mission he performed numerous miracles in his war against Israelite idolatry (I Kings, chapters 17–21). He was carried from earth in a fiery chariot (II Kings 2).

Rabbinic literature elaborates on many of his feats. He never died (B.B. 121b; Gen. R 31;5), instead, having ascended to **heaven** on a divine **chariot**, he became one of only a few select mortals who have been elevated to the status of an **angel**, and is henceforth known as the "Angel of the Covenant" (Mal. 3:1; Ber. 4b; Zohar Chadash Ruth 2:1). Unlike **Enoch**, however, Elijah retains his material body. On high, he fulfills essentially the same function that Peter does in popular Christian imaginings, directing the souls of the dead to their proper destinations (Seder Olam 7; PdRE 15).

Another Jewish tradition claims he has always been an angel, specifically **Sandalfon**, and he only briefly takes human form (Yalkut Reubeni; Pardes Rimmonim 24:4; Emek ha-Melekh 175c). A cognate tradition holds that he has had multiple earthly incarnations, most famously as **Phinehas**, the zealous grandson of **Aaron** mentioned in the book of Numbers, a figure who predates the historical Elijah by hundreds of years (PdRE 29).

In countless Jewish stories, Elijah appears wandering the earth, performing wonders, intervening on behalf of the poor, teaching, and giving divine insight to those who recognize him (B.B. 121b; B.M. 59b). He is present at every circumcision, and a chair is set aside for him, to welcome him (PdRE 29; SCh 585; SA 265:11; Zohar I: 13a). In the absence of the spirit of **prophecy**, it is a visitation of Elijah, along with the **Bat Kol** and the **Ruach Elohim**, which now provides humanity with knowledge of the divine will (PdRE 1). The phenomenon of xenoglossia is sometimes understood to be an Elijah visitation.[1] He also appears to people in visions and dreams. Kabbalistic texts frequently cite him as the source for various mystical teachings (Zohar I: 2a).

Based on the verse in Malachi mentioned above, Elijah is understood to be the herald of the **Messiah**, as well as the figure who will restore the power of **prophecy** to the people Israel. Therefore his presence is invoked at every **Passover** Seder (Haggadah). It is he who will sound the great **shofar** of salvation, marking the start of the Messianic Era. One tradition states he will perform seven wondrous feats at that time: resurrecting **Moses** and the Generation of the Wilderness, bringing up **Korach** from the earth, resurrecting the **Messiah** ben Joseph, restoring the **Ark of the Covenant** and the other vessels of the **Temple**, displaying God's scepter, flattening the mountains in fulfillment of Isaiah's prophecy, and resolving the many unanswered questions and unresolved disputes concerning Jewish tradition. His permanent return to earth is a recurring theme in Jewish prayer and liturgy (Eruv. 45a; M.K. 26a; PdRK 9:76; Gen. R. 21:5).

1. Bilu, "Dybbuk and Maggid," 355.

Elijah ben Solomon: *SEE* VILNA GAON.

Elisha: Israelite prophet and disciple of **Elijah** (ca. 9th century BCE). He received the mantle of Elijah (literally), as well as a "double portion" of his spirit. He performed numerous miracles, many of them variations on the miracles performed by his master, including feeding the poor, purifying water, healing a leper, and resurrecting the dead. A little testy about his personal appearance, he had a group of boys mauled by she-bears after they ridiculed his baldness, though **Sefer Chasidim** reports he was punished with a chronic illness for this particular misuse of his prophetic power. Even his bones had miraculous powers (II Kings 13:20–21). The **Talmud** claims he did exactly twice as many miracles as Elijah.

Elisha ben Abuyah: Talmudic heretic (ca. 1st–2nd century). Also known by the euphemism *Acher*, "The Other," this student of the wise lost his faith and is remembered as a provocateur and enemy of Judaism. The **Talmud** contains a couple of versions of his apostasy, but by far the most intriguing is the cryptic account of his involvement in the incident of the **four Sages** who entered **PaRDeS**/Paradise (Chag. 14b). The Talmud credits his apostasy to seeing the angel **Metatron** sitting on a throne and concluding, "There are two powers in heaven" (Chag. 15a). Chagigah declares Elisha *kofer ha-ikkar*, "cut the root," possibility meaning he rejected the essence of faith (the oneness of God) because of that experience. When he died, he was doomed to a state of limbo. He was not punished in **Gehenna** for his sins, but neither was he allowed to enter the **World-to-Come**. His disciple R. Meir finally used his spiritual merit and power to burn his body. Smoke rose from his grave for many years, until R. Yochanan used his spiritual merit to release him into the World-to-Come. (Chag. 15b; M.K. 20a; Nazir 44a). *SEE* CHIBBUT HA-KEVER.

Elohim, El, Eloha: "God." The generic Hebrew word for divinity, it appears thousands of times in the **Bible**. The use of this name for God in a biblical passage is understood to denote that God's attribute of strict justice is forefront in that moment. In sefirotic metaphysics, *Elohim* is equated with **Gevurah**, the attribute of strict justice. Oftentimes, mystical texts will speak obliquely of *Elohim* being subordinate to **Ein Sof**, or of *Elohim* being the first creation of Ein Sof.

The most common form of the word *Elohim* has been the subject of much sectarian and polemical speculation and overinterpretation because it is in the plural form ("gods"). This is actually not a problem linguistically, as there are other examples of a "collective singular" form in Hebrew, such as *mayim* ("water") and *shamayim* ("sky"). *SEE* NAMES OF GOD.

Emanation: (*Atzilut; Shefa*). In classical Kabbalah, the material world comes into existence through the unfolding emanation of divine **light**, involving a progressive series of shielding or reducing that light in order for discrete bodies to emerge from the undifferentiated oneness of divine being. Duality and multiplicity as we experience it is only possible because the supernal light is increasingly "clothed" in **garments** of lower reality. This notion of divine "concealment" is fundamental to Jewish occult thought (Pardes Rimmonim 5:4, 25d; Ketem Paz 1:124c). It is markedly different, however, from the Lurianic teaching of **Tzimtzum**, in which positive existence emerges in the "absence" of divinity, rather than in its concealment.[1] Later disciples of **Isaac Luria** craft elaborate accounts trying to reconcile the classical doctrine of emanation with their master's myth of divine withdrawal. *SEE* ADAM KADMON; CREATION; FOUR WORLDS OF EMANATION; PARTZUFIM; SEFIROT. *(SEE ALSO APPENDIX FIGURE 2.)*

1. Blumenthal, *Understanding Jewish Mysticism*, vol. 1, 162; also compare Matt, *The Essential Kabbalah*, 90–91 to 92–93.

Emek ha-Melekh: "Valley of the King." An influential book of **Kabbalah** written by Naftali Bacharach.

Encryption: Much of Jewish religious literature has features to it that can be characterized as "encoded," from its often terse and elliptical style to its pervasive use of **anagrams**, **acrostics**, **notarikons**, and symbolic **numbers**.

One form of systematic encryption found in Jewish writing, called **atbash**, consists of inverting the values of the letters of the alphabet, "mirror" style. Thus, in an atbash word, Alef stands in for Tav, Bet stands to Shin, etc. This may in fact be the earliest recorded method of encryption. It is already evident in the **Bible**, where the

name Sheshach (Jer. 25; 51) is "Babel" (Babylon) in *atbash* code.

There is another method of alphabetic substitution mentioned in **Talmud** known as the "Alef-Bet of Chiyya" (Sukkah 52b) that was used to secretly teach Judaism during the time of Babylonian persecution. Later this method would be known as **temurah**. The use of "invisible ink" for sending secret messages is also discussed (Shab. 104a–b).

Of course, **gematria**—finding hidden meaning in the numeric value of letters, words and phrases—is the most famous and prevalent form of code in Judaism. *SEE* HAFUCH; MYSTERY; TZERUF.

End of Days: *SEE* ESCHATOLOGY.

Endor, Woman of: Often incorrectly described as "the **Witch** of Endor," this **necromancer** performed a séance for King Saul, despite his own royal prohibition against such practices (I Kings 28). The episode is cryptic and short on details, but evidently the woman performed the ritual at night using an underworld god to raise the spirit of **Samuel** from the grave, who then spoke either through her or as a disembodied voice. Samuel pronounces doom upon Saul, confirming his worst fears that divine favor had withdrawn from him.

According to the rabbis, a necromancer can see the summoned spirit, but only the one seeking an augury can hear its message. They also posit that she recognized Saul as the king because spirits arise differently for royalty than they do for commoners. The **Midrash** identifies the woman as Zefaniah, the mother of **Abner**, David's general (Lev. R. 26). *SEE* DIVINATION; NECROMANCY; WOMEN.

Enoch: (*Chanoch*). One of the primordial ancestors of humanity. He was, significantly, seventh in the first ten generations of humans listed in Genesis. According to Scriptures, Enoch was the most righteous of the antediluvians and "went with God . . . and he was not, for God took him." From this minimal information, much is extrapolated. He appears as an important figure in a slew of apocryphal works (**I Enoch**; **Jubilees**; **Book of Giants**). He is credited with the creation of writing, astrology, and receiving from **angels** the solar calendar so precious to the priests who collected the **Dead Sea Scrolls**. To them, he was the prototype of all scribes, sages, and priests (I Enoch 12, 14, 80, 81–82, 106–7; Jubilees 4). He was also an oneiromancer (**Book of Giants**). In places, his role is so exalted that he functions as the principle conduit of divine knowledge to mortals.

Some Jewish traditions held that Enoch ascended bodily into heaven, where he was transubstantiated into the princely angel **Metatron** (III Enoch), though there is at least one tradition that rejects this claim (Targum Onkelos, Gen. 5:24; Gen. R. 5:24). Along with the name change, his material body is consumed and replaced with a body of supernal **fire**. He is known by several angelic titles and names, including **Sar ha-Panim**, the Prince of the Divine **Countenance** and/or *Bar Enosh*, "Son of Man." Hebrew texts about Enoch and his angelic translation include **Sefer Hechalot**, **Hechalot Rabbati**, and Sefer Chanoch. *SEE* ENOCH, BOOKS OF.

Enoch, Books of: Multiple books exist in Greek, Hebrew, and Aramaic associated with the name of Enoch, such as **III Enoch**, the **Book of Giants**, and Sefer ha-Razin de Chanoch. Several others have been preserved only in translations (Slavonic and Ethiopic). There are many variations between the texts, and some contradict one another, but the cluster of elements that overlap in different versions are the story of his earthly role prior to the **Flood**, his ascension into heaven, his experience of apocalyptic revelations there, his involvement in the affairs of (fallen) angels, and his translation into an angel. *SEE* APOCRYPHA; ASCENT.

Enoch, First Book of: (I Enoch). A book that exists only in two variant translations, Greek and Ethiopic. The Hebrew original is not known to exist anymore, though we have found Hebrew/Aramaic fragments among the **Dead Sea Scrolls**. The Ethiopic translation is an apocalypse that is divided into five books: the Book of the Watchers, the Book of Similitudes, the Book of the Course of the Heavenly Luminaries, the Book of Dreams, and the Epistle of Enoch. It includes the legend of the **Fallen Angels**, **dream** visions, visions of the final judgment, and other literary flotsam and jetsam. The Greek version shares some texts, and is only one-third the size of the Ethiopic version.

Enoch, Second Book of: (II Enoch) A Jewish pseudepigraphic work, probably written in Egypt, from the 1st century CE. Only Old Slavonic manuscripts (in two versions) have survived to this day. This rather cryptic book is also an apocalypse, revealing the workings of heaven, hell, and the end of the world. The book is one of the first to expound on the **seven heavens** and to give a detailed description of the pleasures of Paradise (and the first to associate the heavenly afterlife with **Eden**) for the righteous dead.

Enoch, Third Book of: (III Enoch). Also known as Sefer ha-Hechalot, Sefer Chanoch, or "Hebrew Enoch," it describes the process of mystical **ascent**. Unlike the early Enoch books, which reflect more purely a priestly spirituality, this work is also clearly rooted in rabbinic Judaism. A Talmudic Sage-Priest, Rabbi **Ishmael ben Elisha ha-Kohen**, is the central figure, and the work is most likely a product of **Merkavah** mystics. It has been lumped together with the other, earlier Enochean books primarily because R. Ishmael encounters Enoch in heaven, in his angelic form of **Metatron**. This text narrates the mystical ascension of Rabbi Ishmael into the **seven heavens** and his encounters there with angelic beings. It details the steps of **angelification** and transubstantiation of Enoch. It includes a description of the **Guf ha-Briyot**, the Treasury of Souls, and the **transmigration** of souls. *SEE* HECHALOT LITERATURE; HECHALOT RABBATI.

Enoch, Fourth Book of: (IV Enoch). A fragmentary Aramaic work found among the **Dead Sea Scrolls**, it includes many parts of other Enochean books, and may in fact be the earliest version of these works that we now have. The **Book of Giants** may also belong to the Enochean library.

Ephod: An embroidered garment of blue, red, purple, and gold (perhaps a short tunic or poncho) worn by the High **Priest**. The Ephod was made from the interweaving of cloth with threads of gold metal, giving it a somewhat rigid, mail-like quality (Ex. 28:6–30). The High Priest's **breastplate** was mounted on its front. It was evidently important that the High Priest wear it while fulfilling his oracular duties (I Sam. 21–23; 30). *SEE* URIM AND THUMMIM.

Ephraimites: The tribe descended from Jacob's eldest grandson. The prophets among the Ephraimites enslaved in Egypt miscalculated the time of God's deliverance by thirty years. When they attempted to leave, they encountered the Philistines, who slew 200,000–300,000 of the men (PdRE 48). *SEE* EXODUS.

Erelim: A class of angels, the genius of all foliage, mentioned in Midrash Konen 2:25.

Eretz: "Earth." Conventionally a term for "land" or "earth," but in the **Zohar**, Eretz is the second of the seven worlds. **Adam** was expelled there from the Garden of **Eden**. It is a realm of **darkness**. Adam was released from there when he repented his sin against God.

Erotic Theology: *SEE* BRIDE OF GOD; PHALLUS; SEX; ZIV-VUGA KADISHA.

Esau: Son of **Isaac**, brother of **Jacob** (See Genesis, chapters 25–34). According to the **Midrash**, he possessed the magical **garments of Adam**, which gave him power to slay or capture any animal (PdRE 24). Because of this, an **angel** had to interfere in his hunting expedition (Gen. 28) in order to give Jacob more time to pull off his deception of Isaac and receive his father's blessing. Later, filled with bloodlust, Esau attempts to kill the returning Jacob by biting him in the neck and sucking his blood (PdRE 37), but is foiled when God turns Jacob's neck to ivory (or marble). Later, he attempted to seize control of the **Cave** of Machpelah from Jacob and was slain by Chushim, the son of Dan, in the ensuing confrontation (PdRE 39).

In time, Esau comes to be regarded as the archetype of Israel's enemies, particularly Rome. Many Midrashic stories featuring Esau are actually encoded criticisms of Rome and Romans. The **Zohar** calls him "a true offspring of the serpent," a demonic figure (I: 145b). *SEE* PATRIARCHS AND MATRIARCHS.

Eschatology: (Greek, "Study of end things"). Eschatology is the branch of esoteric knowledge involving the end of the world, usually encompassing the final divine intervention into history, the apocalyptic fate of Israel, the es-

tablishment of the **Kingdom of God**, the **resurrection**, and the **Day of Judgment**.

One of the beliefs that distinguished Israelite religion from the pagan religions of the Ancient Near East was the novel Israelite notion of time, that history not only goes in cycles, but also advances to a unique conclusion.[1] By contrast, most polytheistic peoples had a notion of mythic time, in which history moves purely in reiterating cycles, with little or no concept of an unfolding future that was essentially different from the past. The biblical prophets taught that history was advancing toward an end that would be unlike that which had preceded it.[2] They also taught that there will be a divine realm transcending earthly existence in which all humans would participate.

Major biblical sources for eschatological teachings include **Daniel**, **Zechariah**, the last quarter of **Ezekiel**, and **Isaiah** chapters 40–66. As expounded in numerous post-biblical writings (most famously in the many **apocalyptic** books of late antiquity, but also in the **Dead Sea Scrolls**, **Talmud**, **Midrash**, and Kabbalistic texts), the exact details of the end are very much up for grabs.

Jewish accounts of "the end" encompass four related themes: personal salvation and national redemption in this world (Resurrection and Messiah), the fate of the soul, and the collective afterlife beyond this world (**Eternal Life** and the World-to-Come).[3] Most classical Jewish writings on these themes are impressionistic and episodic. Themes and descriptions often overlap, or are conflated together, giving the impression that various teachers and texts contradict one another. It was not until well into the Middle Ages that commentators would provide comprehensive and summary descriptions of Jewish eschatological teachings. The many nuances of individual visions and variations among the teachers of Israel are too numerous to catalog. *SEE* MESSIAH; WORLD-TO-COME.

1. Kaufmann, *The Religion of Israel*, 358–59.
2. Koch, *The Prophets*, vol. 1, 1–6.
3. Raphael, *Jewish Views of the Afterlife*, 18–20.

Esdras, the Books of: Apocryphal books of the Greco-Roman period attributed to the scribe Ezra. Keeping track of the various texts is a discipline unto itself. I Esdras is also known as III Esdras. II Esdras is also known as IV Ezra. This confusing situation arose when early Church

Fathers designated the biblical books Ezra and Nehemiah to be "I and II Esdras." Thus I and II contains the biblical accounts of Ezra. III and IV (or I and II) Esdras, on the other hand, are apocalyptic texts full of eschatological visions, including the fate of Israel, the return of the **ten lost tribes**, and a calculation of the end of times. *SEE* APOCALYPTIC LITERATURE.

Essenes: (Meaning uncertain; possibly either Aramaic, *Chasayya*, "Pious Ones," or Greek, *Hosiotes*, "Holy Ones"). A mysterious Jewish sect of the Greco-Roman period mentioned by the contemporary writers Philo, Josephus, and Pliny. Their respective accounts of the Essenes are somewhat contradictory, and while the Dead Sea Scrolls offer us new possible understandings of the sect (assuming they were the owners of the DSS library), there is still much we do not understand about them. The sect was a closed society, dominated by hereditary **priests**, requiring a period of initiation and trials before being accepted through oaths and ritual **purification**. The full teachings of the group were a secret, with discipline being enforced by a court of one hundred initiates. At least some initiates were celibate and lived in communal quarters.[1] Essene teachings include a profound interest in **angels** and **eschatology**, the latter of which centers on a priestly messianic figure, the "Teacher of Righteousness." They were masters of **divination** and in the making of medicines and potions (War 2:119–61; Ant. 18:11, 18–22). *SEE* COMMUNITY RULE; DEAD SEA SCROLLS; MANUAL OF DISCIPLINE.

   1. Martinez, *The Dead Sea Scrolls Translated*, lii–lvi.

Essingen, Samuel: Baal Shem (German, ca. 18th century). He was a folk healer, amulet maker, and exorcist.

Esther: This savior of Persian Jewry, a central figure in the biblical book bearing her name, was vouchsafed many **miracles** during her life. One of the four most beautiful women in all history, she was an orphan taken in by her uncle **Mordecai**. God gave Mordecai the ability to nurse the baby from his own breast. Once the King singled her out from among his harem to be Queen of Persia, the **Holy Spirit** enhanced her already legendary beauty (Targum Esther Sheni). To bring about a favorable outcome in her efforts to save the Jews, **angels** orchestrated her encounter with King Ahasuerus to plea for the life of her people. She

retained her beauty throughout her life and never appeared to age (Esther Rabbah).

Esther, Apocrypha of: This Greek language account of the events of the biblical book of Esther includes descriptions of Esther's prophetic **dreams** not found in the **Bible**.

Esther, Book of: The Sages debated whether to include this profane book, which never mentions God, in the biblical canon, but did so anyway. By contrast, the book of Esther is the only biblical book not found among the **Dead Sea Scrolls**. Perhaps, given the **Qumran** community's obsession with ritual purity and ambivalence toward sexuality, a book that makes a heroine out of a Jewish woman who willingly becomes a concubine and then queen to a gentile was just too much to accept.

Estrie: *SEE* VAMPIRE.

Et: The direct object indicator in Hebrew, spelled *alef-tav*, it is never translated. Thus in Genesis it reads, "When God began to create [et] the heavens and [et] the earth . . ." This purely grammatical device that appears thousands of times in the **Bible**, however, has been interpreted to be of occult significance. Rabbi **Akiba** insisted that in the case of Genesis, the *et* refers to all the created things in heaven and on earth that are not explicitly mentioned in the Creation accounts, like **angels** (Pes. 22b; Chag. 12a).

In early Jewish mystical thought, *et* symbolizes totality, because *alef* is the first and *tav* the last letters of the Hebrew alphabet, so *et* encompasses everything in between. In the **Zohar**, it signifies **Shekhinah** (I: 29b, 53b, 247b).

Eternal Life: Jewish tradition has always taught that mortals have, or will have, a continued existence after death. In Isaiah 25, the prophet promises that a time will come when **death** will disappear entirely. The **Bible** describes an underworld realm of the dead called **Sheol** (grave), where souls dwell in dark silence. In Greco-Roman times the first descriptions of a *heavenly* afterlife start to appear in Jewish literature.

In rabbinic imagination, **Torah** is synonymous with the **Tree of Life**, which was lost as a consequence of the sin of **Adam** and **Eve**. Thus, the giving of the Torah at

Sinai restores the possibility of human immortality. In addition to this, because of their immersion in Torah, saintly men are also immune from most (but not all) forms of death (Shab. 55b). The souls of the **righteous** are escorted to their reward by three companies of **angels**, each uttering their own message of comfort. For the wicked, three myriads of destructive angels serve as escort, quoting Scriptural verses of reproach (Ket. 104a).

The quality of the afterlife an individual has is based on moral criteria: the righteous will enjoy eternal favor and ease, the wicked face annihilation, and those of us in between, the **beinonim**, must face trials and punishment for our sins, to ensure that in the end we will enjoy reconciliation with God. Descriptions of what eternal life entails vary across Jewish tradition and sources.

The belief in **resurrection**, the bodily restoration of the dead in the End of Days, is based on Ezekiel 37, Daniel 12:2, and Isaiah 65:17. Resurrection has been the predominant way that Jews understand and envision the afterlife (II Maccabees, **Talmud**, and the Gevurot prayer of the daily liturgy). Exceptionally righteous figures, however, can be translated directly into heaven, where they become celestial luminaries and **angels** (I Enoch 102). Examples of such individuals include **Enoch**, **Elijah**, and **Serach bat Asher**.

Under Greek influence, there also arises a belief in a disembodied eternal existence (Jubilees 23; I Enoch 103–4; IV Maccabees 14). Later rabbinic tradition eventually reconciles these competing traditions of bodily resurrection and disembodied heavenly existence.

Finally, Jewish mysticism teaches that there is a mechanism involving transmigration of souls that is also part of the journey towards eternal life. SEE BURIAL; CHIBBUT HA-KEVER; DEATH; EDEN; ETERNAL LIFE; JUDGMENT; REINCARNATION; WORLD-TO-COME.

Etrog: A citron. An etrog is one of the *arba minim*, the **four species** Jews are commanded to gather for the celebration of the holiday of Sukkot (Lev. 23:40). As the spherical element in the otherwise linear/phallic **lulav** bouquet, the etrog symbolizes the female aspect of fertility joined to the three branches representing the male force.

Etrogim (pl.) have multiple magical uses. Pregnant women eat etrogim that have already been used during Sukkot to protect them and ease their pain during childbirth. The stem from an etrog is sometimes placed in the bed to help with a difficult labor. **Sefer Raziel** advises using an etrog in the **purification** ritual before the preparation of an **amulet**. To accomplish this, a magic formula is written on the etrog. The message is then wiped off with wine and the etrog consumed.

Eve: (*Chavah*, "Living thing"). The mother of all humanity (Gen. 2–3:20) was not the first woman God created; according to **Alef-Bet of ben Sira**, **Lilith** came before her. The bulk of Jewish tradition, however, does not ascribe to the Lilith tradition. Instead, it teaches that God created Eve by dividing the androgynous **Adam** in half, separating his masculine and feminine aspects (Ber. 61a; Eruv. 18a; Gen. R. 8:1; Sefer Ha-Likkutim 5b). God erected ten bejeweled canopies to serve as her bridal chambers. **Angels** were the witnesses and musicians at her **wedding** to Adam (PdRE 12). The demon **Samael**, in the form of a **serpent**, seduced her both mentally and physically while her guardian angels were away (Sot. 9b; Shab. 196a; AdRN 1:4). The corruption he ejaculated into her continued on down through the generations, adversely affecting humanity until the giving of the Torah. He persuaded her to eat from the **Tree of the Knowledge of Good and Evil** and to induce Adam to do the same. She bore **Cain** and Abel on the same day; Cain was the child of her demonic lover, while Abel was the child of Adam. After the birth of Abel, she and Adam separated for 130 years. During that time, incubi had intercourse with her in her **sleep** and she bore them many **demons** (Gen. R. 20:11). Some traditions hold that her third son, Seth, was actually her first child by Adam (Gen. R. 22:2, 23:5; PdRE 13). She was buried with her husband in the **Cave** of Machpelah (PdRE 20).

Even ha-Shetiyah: SEE FOUNDATION STONE.

Even Maskit: A demoness, the concubine of **Rahav**.

Even Numbers: SEE NUMBER; PAIRS.

Evil: (*Ra*). The most persistent conundrum for monotheism is the question, "Why is there evil?" If there is only one supreme power in the universe—God—and God is beneficent, how is it possible for evil to exist? There are really only three solutions to this mystery, and arguably they can be collapsed into just two. Answer number one is that God's power is not supreme, whether by God's own will or some outside necessity, so evil is the manifestation of something outside God. This answer has the problem of walking a slippery slope toward dualism, and many monotheists have fallen hard down that slope. Thus some Christian sects explain evil through the existence of the Devil, whom they regard to be effectively a kind of "anti-God," operating independently of God's will. Most Christian theologians are aware of this trap, and avoid taking the logic of the devil quite so far, but many rank-and-file Christians have difficulty with the notion that God actually controls the devil on some level.

Most Jews (at least since late antiquity) have remained firmly monotheistic and almost universally rejected this argument. Judaism does not concede that any independent force can exist outside of God's power—leaving the problem of evil intact.

A second solution is to regard evil as a byproduct of human free will. Some would argue that that is really just a more elegant version of the "God is not the only power" argument. This argument posits that God has conceded some power to humanity by granting us free will. As such, we can choose to behave evilly if we wish. God's power is constrained for our sake, but the reason for God doing this is a great mystery. Variations of this argument are found in Jewish circles, particularly among rationalist thinkers.

The third (or second) position argues that the appearance that evil has an independent existence is illusionary and all that appears "evil" from a human perspective is in fact truly subordinate to God, serving God's purpose in some inscrutable way. Thus in most forms of Jewish mysticism, evil is a part of Creation, a byproduct from the "other side," or **Sitra Achra**, of the divine emanation. "Evil is the chair for the good," as the Baal Shem Tov put it, and suffering, misfortune, and sin are necessary outcomes of existence. Even evil entities, such as demons, are really subject to, and agents of, God's purpose. Thus Chasidic teaching emphasizes that there is no absolute evil. It is common for mystics to call demons "destructive angels" to emphasize that they remain obedient to God in

some sense. For this reason, one can read in Jewish literature of demons studying Torah, adhering to Jewish law, and even helping pious Sages. It is based on this also that a few Kabbalistic authorities say it is permitted to summon demons in order to have them perform beneficent services for humanity. At the same time, humans are not permitted to willfully participate in evil or bring evil into being.

In concert with such notions of the demonic, Judaism teaches that humanity's own evil impulse, the **yetzer ha-ra**, serves a critical function in God's universe and for this reason the Sages teach that humans should not try to destroy or negate our selfish and destructive desires, like ambition, lust, or revenge. Rather, we should sublimate them and harmonize them with God's intention (Daat v'Emunah 10). Thus ambition becomes creativity, lust becomes a desire for marriage and children, and revenge is redirected toward the goal of ensuring justice is done. In interpreting "It is not good that man should be alone; I will make a helpmate for him" (Gen. 2:18), the Koretz Rebbe offered this: "There can be no goodness in man while he is alone, without a *yetzer ha-ra* within him; I will endow him with the ability to do evil, and it will be as a helpmate to him, to enable him to do good, if he masters the evil nature within him." *SEE* DEMONS.

Evil Eye: (*Ayin ha-ra*). The "evil eye" is the reification of envious desire; the spiritual manifestation of jealousy and ill will. Belief in the evil eye extends across many cultures. As the most universally accepted example of **witchcraft** found in Jewish culture, the evil eye is a man-made force that can have grave negative consequences for any good circumstance or event (Num. R. 12.4; Pes. 50b; Eruv. 64a–b; B.M. 30a), even physically harming or killing the person subject to this envious urge (Yev. 106a; Lev. R. 17:3; Gen. R. 53:13, 56:11). Some regard the evil eye as the source of disease, while one Sage in the **Talmud** claims that "ninety-nine out of one hundred die from an evil eye" (B.M. 107b).

Attracted by praise or positive events that draw its attention, the types of situations that can trigger an attack of the evil eye are legion: **weddings**, **births**, a religious ritual, **sex**, even good news or a simple compliment. Some individuals, such as menstruating women, are more likely to inflict the evil eye on a person. Like demonic forces, the evil eye can be coerced to serve good ends by certain religious virtuosos (B.B. 75a; Shab. 34a; M.K. 17b; Chag. 5b; Ned. 7b). It is also the case that the evil eye has no power over select righteous people, like Joseph (Ber.).

There are numerous prophylactic things that can be done to fend off the evil eye, including avoiding ostentatious behavior (especially "double" events: double weddings, two uninterrupted toasts) that will attract envy, delivering a compliment only by means of a circumlocution, or in a characteristically Jewish habit, expressing joy in a **reversed** or ironic way, like "It could be a lot worse." Some people will follow an account of good news with the phrase *keynahora* (*kein ayin ha-ra*), "Let there be no evil eye." **Spitting** or simulating spitting three times is also widely practiced (SCh 1182; Nishmat Chayyim 3:27).

Amulets are a common defense against the evil eye (Num. R. 12:4) and can be as simple as a **red** thread tied to the body of a person, or as elaborate as a plaque or pendant made up of protective verses and representations of the eye itself, **angels**, or even **fish** (because fish, living in the ocean, are "concealed" from its view). Painting vulnerable areas of a home, such as the doors and windows, blue or hanging herbs in the house also thwart the eye.

Once the evil eye is unleashed, there are also countermeasures that can be taken, such as a reversal **incantation**, activated by putting the opposing thumb over each eye (Ber. 55b). Alternately, one can recite a positive verse with the word "eye" in it, such as, "But Noah found grace in the eyes of the Eternal" (Gen. 6:8). A **gemstone** placed between the eyes will also counteract the effects (Tosefta Shab. 4:5).

Evil Impulse: *SEE* YETZER HA-RA.

Excrement: Proper care in eliminating bodily wastes is considered a religious obligation, part of the commandment to guard and care for the body (Ber. 60a; AdRN 41; Lev. R. 34:3). Jewish tradition even has a blessing, the *Yatzar et-ha-Adam*, for bodily functions (Siddur).

While excrement, especially human excrement, was a popular element in Greco-Roman and European magical formulae, it appears only rarely in Jewish magical compounds. The biblical injunction commanding the proper disposal of human excrement (Deut. 21) is no doubt a factor in limiting its use. Animal excrement, however, is used in Jewish medicinal products as well as in magical potions. One **curse** found in the **Cairo Geniza** involves using wild donkey dung to inflict an enemy with flatulence.

Exile: (*Galut*). The exile of the people Israel from the Land of Israel is more than just a historic tragedy, it is a cosmic catastrophe, for it resulted in the **Shekhinah** also going into exile along with Israel, creating a "fracture" in the oneness of God, as it were.[1] At times, Jewish thought conflates the historic exile of the Jewish people with the mythic exile from **Eden**. Kabbalah regards exile to be part of the divine plan of **tikkun**, rectification. Offering a metaphysical interpretation of the rabbinic dictum that exile was given in order that converts from all nations could be gathered to Israel (Pes. 87b), "converts" is mystically understood by some Kabbalists to refer to the sanctification of all alienated aspects of the self and Creation.[2]

Chasidic writing, in particular, read exile simultaneously as a psychological, national, historical, and cosmic reality and makes the state of exile a centerpiece of their metaphysics. Chasidic mystical "yichudim" meditations that precede certain blessings explicitly refer to this. The **Tanya** emphasizes the illusionary nature of exile, that it only seems like exile from human perspective. The mystical quest is to see past that illusion, and in doing so, redeem the world.

1. Idel, *Kabbalah: New Perspectives*, 173–91.
2. Scholem, *The Messianic Idea in Judaism*, 39–48. Also see Breslauer, *The Seductiveness of Jewish Myth*, 19–25.

Exodus: The biblical account of the flight of the Israelites from **Egypt** is full of fabulous elements: the confrontation between **Moses** and the Egyptian magicians, turning staves into **serpents**, the ten **plagues**, the parting of the Reed Sea, and the pillars of fire and cloud that led and guarded the Israelites. Rabbinic literature elaborates upon these, with Rabbi **Akiba** going so far as to demonstrate homiletically that there were not just ten, but really 250 plagues (the Haggadah). There are also stories of God's interventions to protect the Israelite people against the worst Egyptian abuses during their slavery; when Pharaoh ordered the massacre of the Israelite boys, **angels** stood in the midst of the Nile and caught the infants being cast in (S of S R. 2:15; Ex. R. 23:8). Angels also shielded the child

Moses until he could mature into the deliverer of the people. When **Pharaoh** refused him an audience, Moses was **teleported** into the palace. *SEE* PASSOVER.

Exorcism: (*Gerush, Cherem, Reigash Sheidim*). A ritual of power performed in order to drive an evil spirit, whether demonic or ghostly, from a possessed person, location, or object. The Christian scholar Origen credits Jews with a special talent for exorcising **demons** (Against Celsus, book 4).

The first allusion to exorcism appears in the **Bible**, in the youth narratives of David (I Samuel). But while the biblical David seemed to be able to effect a temporary expulsion of Saul's evil spirit using music, the book of Tobit contains the first explicit description of an (informal) exorcism. Josephus recounts incidents of possession and exorcism in his Antiquities of the Jews (2, 5, 8, 45–48). In his description, exorcism involved burning herbs and immersing the possessed person in water. The New Testament also reports **Jesus** to have performed numerous exorcisms of demonic spirits in 1st-century Palestine (Matt. 12; Mark 5, 6, 13; Luke 8).[1]

The **Dead Sea Scrolls** include several exorcism **incantations** and formulae, mostly directed against disease-causing demons. The DSS **Psalms** collection in particular (11Q5) has "four songs for the charming of demons with music." People who fell under the influence of false prophets and mediums were thought to also require the exorcism of possessing evil spirits (the false prophets and mediums themselves were subject to death, a sure cure for most possessions, see Zechariah 13).

The **Midrash** mentions the procedure, though at times in a tongue-in-cheek manner (PdRK 1:4, Num. R. 19.8). An extended story in Leviticus Rabbah 24:3 tells of the exorcism of a well of water involving **iron** implements and shouted formulae. **Simon bar Yochai** exorcises a demon that assists him in getting the cooperation of Caesar in lifting an oppressive decree against the Jews. In a medieval Midrash, **Chanina ben Dosa** is credited with exorcising an evil spirit haunting an old woman. Intriguingly, in the last two accounts, the Sages exorcise demons, even though each of the evil spirits actually behaved in a beneficial fashion.[2] By the late Middle Ages, whole texts dedicated to countering demons started to appear.

Key to any Jewish exorcism is having a truly pious man, an **abba**, **baal shem**, **rebbe**, or a **rabbi**, conduct the ceremony. This is in contrast with Mesopotamian and Greco-Roman practices, which generally use a physician. The process usually starts with the exorcist ritually purifying himself, either according to traditional Jewish practice, or by special means, such as anointing himself with water and oil. Some exorcists may invoke the presence of a *maggid*, or beneficent spirit, to assist them.

Many exorcisms were public events, either performed in a **synagogue**, or at least requiring the presence of a **minyan**, a minimum of ten men that normally makes up a ritual quorum (Divrei Yosef). Various somatic symptoms (swellings, paralysis, markings, and bodily sensations) were sought in the victim for diagnostic purposes (Sha'ar ha-Gilgulim). Most techniques include interviewing the demon and/or **dybbuk**, taking a personal history, as it were, in order to understand what is motivating the spirit and so better effect the removal (Shalshelet ha-Kabbalah). Many possessing spirits are evidently quite forthcoming and loquacious. At times cooperation was coerced from the demon by "fumigation," exposing it to smoke and **sulfur**, a sympathetic invocation of the infernal realms (Igrot ha-Ramaz). The goal of the interview is to eventually learn the name of the evil spirit.

The exorcist then uses the power of the demonic spirit's own name to "overpower" it, by round after round of scripted ritual actions involving threats and rebukes, getting more intense and invasive with each effort. A few ceremonies on record reached the point of actually "beating" the demon out, but most simply involved verbal coercion.[3]

Jewish exorcisms are usually "liturgical," using protective passages from the **Psalms** and other sacred texts. Anti-demonic psalms have been found among the **Dead Sea Scrolls**, though whether they were used in actual exorcism is impossible to know. The same idea resurfaces in the Middle Ages, with Psalms 10, 91, and 127 particularly being lauded for their power against evil spirits. (See **Psalms**; **Shimmush Tehillim**). **Sefer ha-Gilgulim** instructs the patient to recite Psalms 20, 90, and *Ana Bokoah*, an acrostic prayer made from a **name of God**. Rituals accompanying the recitations can include sounding a **shofar** or the use of other Jewish objects, such as candles, Torah scrolls, **kvittles**, **tefillin**, or **lamps** (Sha'ar Ruach ha-Kodesh 89; Ma'aseh shel Ruach be-Kehillah). Later exorcism reports include the use of **amulets** (Minchat Yehudah 47a).

According to Lurianic **Kabbalah**, exorcism of a possessing dybbuk involves the **tikkun**, or "repair" of the ghostly soul. The tzadik/exorcist accomplishes this by promising the dybbuk salvation, then extracting all its goodness, restoring those resources to the root soul or Treasury of Souls, until the estranged evil consciousness withers and is annihilated. Thus the Lurianic Kabbalist is acting on behalf of both the victim and the dybbuk. The primary sign of a successful exorcism was a bloody fingernail or toenail, the point by which the dybbuk enters and leaves the body. Occasionally there are reports of spirits violently leaving through the throat, vagina, or rectum. A sudden and dramatic change in the victim's behavior is also a sure sign of recovery (Igrot ha-Ramaz 24b). Interestingly, Jewish exorcisms occasionally fail. Apparently, reports of misadventures are virtually non-existent in Catholic tradition. Jews, as always, are highly self-critical.

In a related tradition, it is believed righteous individuals have the power to gather up lost souls who are trapped in this world and release them so they may continue their journey into the afterlife. Figures such as the **Baal Shem Tov**, Rabbi **Nachman of Bratzlav**, and Rabbi Chayyim ben Attar were famous for doing this. Reports of exorcisms continue to come out of traditional communities both in the United States and Israel, though there has been a marked decline in the number over the past century. *SEE* DEMONS; GHOSTS; POSSESSION, DEMONIC; POSSESSION, GHOSTLY; WOMEN.

1. See Twelftree, *Jesus the Exorcist*.
2. Bar Ilan, "Exorcism by Rabbis: Talmud Sages and their Magic," 1–9.
3. Chajes, *Between Worlds*, 57–96.

Expanse: (*Rakia*). One of the seven levels of heaven. It is the level that holds all the celestial bodies: **moon**, **sun**, stars, and **planets** (Chag. 12b–13a).

Explanation of the Four-Letter Name: A brief tract on how the prophet Jeremiah used the forty-two-letter **name of God** to construct a **golem** with the help of his son, Sira.

Explicit Name of God, the: (*Ha-Shem, Shem Hayah, Shem ha-Miuchad, Shem ha-Meforash, Shem Kodesh, Shem Shamayim, Shem ben Arba Ottiyot*). In most esoteric contexts, the "explicit name" carries the connotation of "the name [of God as it is] fully pronounced," meaning with its correct vowel sounds. Since these vowels never appear in writing, the correct pronunciation of all divine names is transmitted orally, from esoteric master to disciple (Kid. 71b). The term "explicit name" is usually referring to the **Tetragrammaton**, but this is not always the case. In some texts it is also synonymous with other occult **names of God**, such as the forty-two-letter name of God.[1]

1. Cohen, "The Name of God, a Study in Rabbinic Theology," 587–92.

Eybeschitz, Jonathan: A 17th–century German rabbi and amulet maker. A highly controversial **Baal Shem**, Eybeschitz invoked the power of the false messiah **Shabbatai Tzvi** in the wording of his amulets, embroiling him in a very public controversy that eventually required the intervention of gentile authorities to protect him.

Eye: (*Ayin*). The eye is a powerful symbol of sight, both normal and paranormal. Depending on the context, the eye can be regarded as a positive or negative force. Naturally a covetous eye is bad and may bring about the malevolent force of the **evil eye**. The **Angel of Death** is covered in eyes, allowing him omniscient sight.

On the other hand, the eye is also a symbol of the all-seeing God of Israel. Zechariah had a reassuring vision of supernal **menorah** covered in eyes. Chamsa amulets often feature an eye in the center of the palm, invoking God's constant guardianship.

Ezekiel ben Buzi: The great prophet-priest of the Babylonian **exile** experienced apocalyptic visions and miraculous encounters. His **vision** of the **Merkavah**, the divine **chariot**, is the starting point for all Jewish mysticism (Ezek. 1; 10).

In chapter 37, Ezekiel describes his vision of the dry bones. The **Talmud** (Sanh. 92b) relates that this was more than just a vision, that the prophet in fact resurrected six hundred thousand Israelites killed by the Babylonians. Other traditions say he resurrected the Ephraimites who died trying to escape Egypt prior to the **Exodus**. After his death, his burial place in Kifil, Iraq, became a place of pilgrimage, and many miracles are the result of the power of his grave (Sanh. 92b; PdRE 33).

Ezekiel Shem Tov David: (Indian, ca. 19th century). His Judeo-Arabic commentary on the **Psalms** includes a description of each psalm's theurgic uses, ranging from combating **demons** to treating snakebite.

Ezra, Apocalypse of: *SEE* ESDRAS, THE BOOKS OF.

Ezra, Fourth Book of: This book provides perhaps the most elaborate description of heaven and hell found in apocalyptic literature. *SEE* ESDRAS, THE BOOKS OF.

Ezra of Gerona: Kabbalist (Spanish, ca. 13th century). A leading figure among the Gerona mystics, he wrote a mystical commentary on the **Song of Songs** and an explanation of the mystical significance of the **commandments**.

F

Face: Medieval Jewry developed techniques for interpreting character from lines of the forehead and facial features. *SEE* METOPOSCOPY; PHYSIOGNOMY.

Face (or Countenance) of God: (*Pani Elohim; Partzuf*). There is a tension, beginning in the Bible and continuing through Jewish literature, as to whether it is actually possible to "see" God. The Bible itself gives contradictory testimony. In one passage we are informed, "For no man shall see Me and live" (Ex. 33:20). Yet in contrast we are told, "I saw the Eternal sitting upon a throne" (Isa. 6:1). Some interpret Exodus 33 to indicate that there are aspects of God that can be apprehended with the senses, just not God's "countenance" (literally, "face"). Exodus 33:14 also offers the possibility that the "countenance" is an angel, rather than a divine feature. Yet, a passage later in the Torah (Deut. 34) describes Moses as one who knew God *panim el panim* ("face-to-face"). This tension carries into the post-biblical period; the Midrash declares that not even the angels may see God (Num. R. 14:22) and that God sees all things yet is not seen (Mid. Teh. 91:1; Num. R. 12:3). However, Hechalot texts indicate that the well-prepared adept can view what is even unseen by the angels who surround God's throne (Hechalot Rabbati).

So Jewish prophetic and mystical texts bequeath to the tradition three types of mystical encounters with God: the aural encounter, involving hearing divine voices; the ineffable encounter, in which there is no sensory comparison to be made; and the visionary encounter, in which God is manifest to the eyes, often in a **dream**. Yet even those who believe in the possibility of the last type still suggest that such manifestations are more a product of **reiyat ha-lev**, of mortal imagination, than an accurate reflection of the appearance of God. The **German Pietists** make the distinction that what is seen is the divine **Glory**, rather than God in essence. This distinction is often described in terms of God's "clothing" and is helpful in making sense of the many detailed yet diverse images of God that appear in both Scripture and mystical literature—the visionary sees only what surrounds God and these "garments" are borne of his or her own imagination. What is more, the image chosen is almost always an anthropomorphic one, hence God's "face."

Lurianic Kabbalah also describes divine faces, the **Partzufim**, though these are not visible per se, and they may be something akin to the divine **speculum** described in other sources. Two of the countenances especially, **Arikh Anpin** and **Zer Anpin**, reflect the divine effluence through the channels of the **sefirot**. This is the feedback mechanism God builds into Creation after the **sherivat ha-kelim**, the collapse of the primordial vessels of light. *SEE* COUNTENANCE, PRINCE OF THE; GLORY; GODHEAD; IMAGE, DIVINE; VISIONS.

Fae: Mischievous fairy creatures mentioned in medieval European Jewish texts. Like the name, the concept is of non-Jewish origin. Jews fuse the tradition of fae as changelings with the rabbinic legend of Adam's sexual dalliance with demons during a period of separation from Eve. *SEE* BANIM SHOVAVIM; KESILIM.

Falk, Chayyim Samuel Jacob: Alchemist and magician (Polish-English, ca. 18th century). Known in English as

Samuel de Falk, he was also referred to as the **Baal Shem** of London. The Polish-born Falk had to flee Germany because of accusations of **sorcery**. He settled in London in 1742 and was famed as a wonder-worker and alchemist. He had a sidekick, Hirsch Kalish, who kept a record of his exploits. SEE ALCHEMY.

Fallen Angels: The tradition of a revolt in heaven ending in the expulsion or fall of the rebellious angels is a major theme in Greco-Roman Jewish writings. Hints of this are found first in Genesis 6:14, with a brief report that divine beings copulated with mortal women, producing the primeval giants and superheroes. Psalms 82 also has been interpreted as recounting an angelic expulsion from heaven.

In **apocalyptic** works like **I Enoch** and the **Book of Giants**, these cryptic passages are expanded with fuller accounts of angelic disobedience and divine punishment. These books also teach that it is from these angels that humanity first learns many occult and impure crafts: **sorcery**, the lunar **calendar**, and **astrology** (I Enoch 6, 8, 10; Jubilees 4–5). These angels are central to the dualistic theology of the sectarian priests of Qumran (Community Rule II, III; Damascus Document II; War Scroll XIII).

Because of their expulsion from heaven, these angels become the principal **demons**, thereby offering a rationale for why there are infernal forces at work in a **Creation** that is wholly the work of a beneficent God. The fallen angels most singled out by name are **Samael**, **Shemchazi**, and **Azazel**, though I Enoch names eighteen "Princes."

While both Christian and Gnostic traditions embrace and elaborate on these stories (Isaiah 14, for example, is interpreted as an account of the fall of Satan), the main stream of Jewish thought marginalizes the pre-rabbinic notion of fallen angels, though the theme reappears in snippets of Jewish Midrashic and mystical literature (Gen. R. 26; PdRE 22; BhM 5; Yalkut, Gen. 44; Zohar I). SEE ANGELS; FLOOD, THE; GIANTS; GIANTS, BOOK OF; SATAN.

Farbrengen: (Yiddish, "Gathering"). A kind of spiritual-communal rally held by CHaBaD **Chasids**. Functionally identical to the rebbe's **tish** practiced by other Chasidic groups, the *farbrengen* features long discourses on mystical teachings of Torah, interrupted by **chanting**, song, and dance.[1] The crowd is also loosened up by a liberal supply of liquor present at all such events. SEE REBBE.

1. Rabinowicz, *The Encyclopedia of Hasidism*, 125.

Farfir Lichter: (Yiddish, "purple/attractive light"). A mischievous spirit that misleads nighttime travelers. They can be thwarted by reciting Job 2:2 three times.

Fasting: Fasting is a traditional sign of penitence, as well as a method of spiritual purification in both religious and magical rites (Ex. 34; I Sam. 28). **Solomon** fasted in order that God would grant him exceptional wisdom (Mid. Mish. 1:1). During Talmudic times, whole communities would undertake fasting for rain—an entire tractate of the Talmud, Ta'anit, is devoted to the issue. Sages would fast in order to be granted better retention of the Torah lessons they learned (B.M. 85a). Fasting was also a spiritual preparation for performing mystical **ascent** (Otzer ha-Geonim 4). Fasting is regarded as a remedy for a range of evil **omens** and supernatural threats, such as bad dreams or dropping a Bible. Since it is most associated with negative circumstances, fasting before a joyous occasion, such as a wedding, is practiced as a way to deceive the **evil eye**. (Shab. 21b; Ta'anit).

Fat: Animal fat was a featured part of the offerings made to God in the sacrificial cult. After the sacrificial services ended, fat continued to have a role in the making of medicines, potions, and magical formulae (**Sefer ha-Razim**). Unlike their Christian and pagan counterparts, Jewish magicians avoided the use of human fats in potions and remedies, both because of issues of ritual purity and because of Jewish attitudes toward the respectful treatment of corpses.

Fate: (*Garol, Mazzal, Hashgacha, Te'udah*, Yiddish: *Beshert*). While belief in free will is the bedrock of Judaism (Deut. 30), various fatalistic beliefs are found in Jewish tradition. The belief that there is a person one is destined to marry is one example (Sha'ar ha-Gilgulim 8). Belief that poverty or prosperity is fated to certain people is another. A general belief in providence, both general and individual, is evident throughout Jewish thought. Humans, however, have the power to change their doom. Thus in the High Holiday liturgy it is declared that God records "who will live and who will die" each **Rosh ha-Shanah** in the **Book of Life**, but also it affirms that "Prayer, repentance and charity avert the severe decree." Rabbi Akiba expresses it as a **paradox**: "All is foreseen, yet free will is given" (Avot 3:15).

Belief in fate is also evident in Jewish thought through **astrology**, and even the Talmudic Sages occasionally remark that the stars determine some human circumstances. And as for the ultimate form of fate, death, the fundamental belief that there is a universal doom attached to being mortal is implicit in all Jewish thought—but even this destiny is undermined, or at least mitigated, by the possibility of **eternal life**. (M.K. 28a; Tan. 25a; Suk. 53a; Meg. 25a; Nid. 16b).

The priests who authored some of **apocalyptic literature** and, especially, the **Dead Sea Scrolls**, had a particularly fatalistic worldview. They spoke of *te'udah*, of preordained heavenly statutes that not only determined the cycles of the seasons and the order of nature, but also determined history (Thanksgiving Hymns, XII). *SEE* FREE WILL.

Fertility: Fertility, both agricultural and human, was a major concern of all peoples of the Ancient Near East. Pagan religions universally featured fertility rites and rituals. Fertility-related gods, such as **Baal**, enjoyed special prominence. In Israelite religion, YHWH is the guarantor of life and its continuation. Though the earth is rendered less fertile by the transgressions of primeval man (Gen. 3), the earth retains its fundamental capacity to be fruitful. Human barrenness and fertility is a recurrent theme throughout the Hebrew Scriptures. Much of the **Abraham** saga, for example, can be read as telling of YHWH's fulfillment of the promise to make the barren Abraham and **Sarah**, and all their progeny after them, a wellspring of fecundity (Gen. 15, 22). The need to have a child has had such a grip on the Jewish mind that childless men in the Middle Ages would engage in a legal fiction of symbolically "purchasing" a child from another family in order to avoid any divine opprobrium arising from not fulfilling the mitzvah of being "fruitful and multiplying."

Thus, despite this guarantee of fertility to the Jewish people, the use of **amulets**, **incantations**, and fertility symbols have been widespread.[1] Specific foods and herbs, such as **eggs**, **fish**, milk, **mandrake**, and **garlic**, are con-

sidered aphrodisiacs or sources of potency. Medieval Jewish tradition includes many examples of theurgic rituals, primarily name magic involving **angels**, **astrology**, and the **zodiac**, for ensuring the fertility of people, of agricultural lands, and of cattle. Numerous medieval texts provide love **incantations** and recipes for **love** potions.

A mystical **sex** manual, **Iggeret ha-Kodesh**, emphasizes that time of day, state of purity, state of mind, and even the orientation of the bed (a kind of Jewish tantric feng shui) have an influence over fertility. A major focus of the miraculous powers of **Baal Shems** has been their gifts for overcoming infertility, usually through the method of **segullot**.

The Jewish holiday most intimately engaged with themes of fertility is **Sukkot**, with its prayers for **rain**, the waving of the lulav, the **four species**, and the (now defunct) **water libation** ritual.

In the **World-to-Come**, the hyper-fertility that once existed in **Eden** will be restored. Women will, painlessly, bear children every day. The Sages have even more to say about the fruitfulness of the earth in messianic times: trees will bear ripe **fruit** daily, and even wild trees will become fruit bearing. Wheat will grow as high as palms, and wheat grains as big as kidneys. A single grape will require a wagon to move and people will simply tap them for juice as they would a keg (Ket. 111b; Shab. 30b; Nid. 31b; EY; Sefer ha-Raziel; Iggeret ha-Kodesh).

1. See Klein, *A Time to Be Born*.

Fevers: The common (but often deadly) fever has been interpreted as a form of demonic attack, perhaps because of the link between **demons** and the infernal regions. Consequently, considerable Jewish pharmacology, remedies, and **healing** incantations are devoted to their treatment.

Fevers can be treated by reciting biblical verses, especially Moses's plea for the recovery of Miriam (Num. 12:13) and/or the verse, "there was a bush all aflame, but it was not consumed" (Ex. 3:5). The Talmud offers folk remedies for many different kinds of fevers, almost all of which include magical elements (Git. 69a–70a). One recipe, using analogous magic symbolism, involves using iron, string, and a bush (think "burning bush") (Shab. 67a).

Hebrew magico-medical manuals found in the **Cairo Geniza**, like the Talmud, distinguish many types of fevers

Fig 94

and offer different treatments for each.[1] One medieval text recommends a **reversal** incantation, reciting the word *Ochnotinos*, reducing the word one letter with each repetition, thereby reducing the fever (Sefer Chasidim).

1. Naveh and Shaked, *Magical Spells and Formulae*, 177, 185–87, 199, 202, 221.

Fig: *SEE* FRUIT.

Finger: The fingers of the human hand have a number of occult associations. According to the **Testament of Solomon**, **demons** will vampirically suck the thumbs of children, causing them to waste and die. The use of fingernails for the purposes of **divination** is a longstanding Jewish practice—one uses the light of the **Havdalah** candle (used for a ceremony marking the end of the Sabbath) to gaze into one's own nails. Young girls do so in hopes of seeing the face of the man they will marry, but earlier authorities held that all kinds of **omens**, for good or for ill, could be detected in the reflection. Conversely, there is a belief that cutting one's nails can adversely affect memory unless a specific order of trimming is followed: starting with the left hand, begin with finger four (ring) and end with one (thumb), and avoiding doing any two in sequence; right hand two to five. Fingernails can be used in magical formula and, most dangerously, in **witchcraft**. The careful disposal of trimmings is therefore imperative.

If a pregnant woman comes in contact with fingernail parings, the impurity adhering to the parings will adversely affect the fetus. White spots on the nails are considered a good omen. *SEE* HAND.

Fire: (*Aish*). Fire, one of the four elements in classical physics, is both a symbol of beneficence and destruction, as well as a manifestation of the numinous. It is also a symbol of passion and regeneration. Fire was first introduced to humanity at the end of the Sabbath, when God taught Adam how to use a flint (Pes. 54a; Sanh. 38b).[1]

Fire is frequently a manifestation of divine wrath, but also of divine Presence (Deut. 5:4). God makes the promises to Abraham in the form of fire (Gen. 15). Sodom and Gomorrah meet a fiery end (Gen. 19). God appears in a **burning bush** (Ex. 3), rains fiery hail down upon the Egyptians (Ex. 8), and sends a fiery angel to protect the Is-

raelites from pursuit by their former masters (Ex. 13) and later to guide the people in the desert. **Elijah** is closely linked to fire, being able to smite soldiers of King Ahaziah (I Kings 1) and ignite offerings (I Kings 18) with heavenly fire.

According to one rabbinic tradition, fire was created on the second day of Creation. Another tradition claims that a primordial fire preceded light, and gave birth to it. Talmud teaches that there are "six varieties" of fire, some natural and some supernatural (Yoma 21b).

The theurgic sacrificial offerings of ancient Israel were performed using the medium of fire. *Aish zara*, "alien fire," however, was forbidden in the sacrificial cult. The exact nature of this fire, whether it was fire introduced from an outside source or fire offered at unsanctioned times, is not clear. Its use by **Nadav** and **Abihu** triggered their fatal punishment by divine fire from heaven (Lev. 10:1–2). According to the Midrash, subsequent to this disaster, the altar fire descended from heaven to consume the sacrificial offerings (Yoma 21a–b). This celestial fire transferred to the **Temple** and burned uninterrupted, rain or shine, until the apostasy of King Manasseh, a positive manifestation of the same power that killed Nadav and Abihu. Sages experiencing revelatory moments appear to be ringed in fire (Lev. R. 16:4; Zohar II: 14a–15a).

The Bible describes God as a "consuming fire." In the **seven heavens**, fire serves in the place of matter as the fundamental substance that gives form to reality. The divine chariot is wreathed in fire. Many **angels**, such as **Metatron** and **Gabriel**, are composed of fire. There is even a special class of fiery angels called **serafim**, and the sweat that pours from them in their labors creates the **River of Light** that flows around heaven. The palaces of heaven are made of supernal fires. Even the primordial **Torah** itself is made of white fire and letters of black fire. Torah study is compared to fire in that one who stays too far from it freezes, but one who draws too close is burned. When a person has a revelatory experience, that event may be accompanied by manifestations of supernal fire (Deut. 5:4; III Enoch; Zohar III: Naso; Lev. R. 16:4; Chag. 14b; Zohar I: 94b).

On the infernal side, the fire of **Gehenna** burns sixty times hotter than earthly fire. There are five different kinds of fire in Gehenna: fires that consume but do not drink;

fires that drink but do not consume; fires that drink and consume; fires that neither drink nor consume, and a fire that consumes fire (BhM 1:147). **Demons** also can have a fiery appearance, while RaSHI claims that fire is one of the things demons eat for sustenance.

Fire may be used as part of a cursing ritual (burning up the written name of the intended victim) or for **divination**. As a source of light, fire drives away demons. Salamanders are a creature born out of fire and, according to some traditions, their blood provides protection from burns (Pes. 54a, 118a–b; Zev. 61b; Sanh. 38b; Ber. 57b; PdRE 4; Chag. 27a; Ex. R. 15:22; Num. R. 2:23; J. Shek. 6:1; SCh 547–48). *SEE* ANGELS; DEMONS; LAMPS; LIGHT; PHOENIX; SACRIFICES; SALAMANDER.

1. Frankel and Platkin-Teusch, *The Encyclopedia of Jewish Symbols*, 53–54.

Fire, the Seven Angels of: According to the **Book of the Great Name**, there are seven angels of fire: TRMWM, **Uriel**, Afiel, **Gabriel**, Nuriel, Paniel, and Serafiel. Invoking them will protect the adept against being burned. *SEE* SERAF.

Firmament: (*Rakia*). God placed a firmament between the waters of earth and the waters of heaven to separate them (Gen. 1). Some say there are two firmaments, based on a biblical verse (Deut. 10:14), but most teach that there are seven. Later traditions identify the word *rakia* as referring to just one of the **seven heavens**, the level that holds the heavenly bodies (Chag. 12b). *SEE* CURTAIN OF HEAVEN.

Firstborn: (*bechor; reishit*). God was forced to destroy the firstborn males of the Egyptians, both cattle and human, on Israel's behalf (Ex. 12). All of the ten **plagues** are interpreted as a response to some aspect of the suffering endured by the Israelites during their enslavement, and the plague of *machat bechorim*, of slaying the Egyptian firstborn, is retribution for a crime mentioned explicitly in the Exodus narrative: the slaying of Israelite boys on Pharaoh's orders (Ex. 2). Still, because God is required to destroy a part of Creation for Israel's sake, God acquires title to the firstborn males of Israel, animal and human, in perpetuity. This means that every male creature that

"opens the womb" must either be given over to the sanctuary, destroyed, or redeemed from God in a cultic ritual. In the ceremony of **Pidyon ha-Ben**, a firstborn son is brought on the thirty-first day after **birth** before a priest and "redeemed" with a donation of money to charity (also see B.M. 61b on God's concern with knowing the firstborn).

Fish: Fish are a symbol of both good luck and fertility in Judaism. They are considered a good luck food to eat on the **Sabbath**. This is based on the language of Genesis 1, where God uses the identical wording to bless the fish as is used to bless the Sabbath. In Zohar II: 30b, fish are understood to be a symbol for **angels**. A fish is also a good **omen** since a sea creature, **Leviathan**, will be the main course at the messianic **banquet**. These associations also make fish popular food on the Sabbath, which itself is a foretaste of the **World-to-Come**. A mystical tradition teaches that the souls of the **righteous** are sometimes reincarnated as fish (Megillat Setarim; Yismach Moshe 29b; ShB 108).

In accordance with the **food** prohibitions found in the Torah, only fish with fins and scales are considered fit to eat. It was also held in Talmudic times that eating fish and meat in combination could bring on **leprosy**.

Ever since the account found in the book of Tobit, where the hero defeats a **demon** by burning the heart and liver of a rotten fish (Tobit 6), fish are also considered a potent defense against evil spirits and the **evil eye**. The evil eye, in particular, has no power over them because they dwell in the sea and so are covered from its view (Ber. 20a). For those reasons, fish images frequently appear on **amulets**. For the same reason, European families often gave their sons the name Fishl as a protection against bad luck. Fish parts also are required in a variety of folk remedies. Because fish are so numerous, they are also considered a **fertility** food. Fish are also used in segullot (folk remedies). Perhaps the most unusual involves placing a live fish under the sole of the foot as a treatment for jaundice (Shemesh Tzedakah, no. 23).

Five: *SEE* NUMBERS.

Flies: Flies symbolize decay and corruption. They constitute one of the ten **plagues** God inflicts on Egypt during the Exodus. Flies are also linked to the demonic; **Beelzebub** is sometimes known as "Lord of the Flies."

Flood, the: The biblical account of God flooding the entire world in response to the wicked devolution of Creation (Gen. 6:5–9:17). God is effectively reversing the creative process, releasing the watery **chaos** that was contained in the Creation account of Genesis.

It is a wholly miraculous tale. Its supernatural aspects include not only the rain, but also the marvelous assembly of all the earth's animal species and forty days of continuous rain.

Apocalyptic and rabbinic literature adds many fantastic details. The corruption was so complete that even animals sought to have sex with different species. The generation of the Flood felt no need to repent, because they believed their mastery of **magic** would protect them. Later they made various attempts to prevent the flooding, including plating the earth in iron and using a miraculous sponge (I Enoch 6:2, 7:5; Gen. R. 30:7; Tanh., Noah 5, 12; Sanh. 108a–b). The race of **giants** refused to repent because they believed they could simply stand above the floodwaters (PdRE 22). Some giants did in fact survive, most notably **Og** of Bashan. God mingled the rain water (which is male) with the water of the abyss (which is female) to procreate even more floods. The Land of Israel, however, was spared from the flood waters (Gen. R. 26; PdRE 22; MhG; Zeb. 113a; Nid. 61a). *SEE* FALLEN ANGELS; GIANTS; NOAH.

Foetor Judaicus: Among the many pernicious myths circulating about Jews in the Middle Ages, the claim that Jews have a particular repugnant odor was one of the most popular.[1] Sometimes this smell is identified as sulfur and brimstone, the odor of hell. In popular Christian imagination, baptism resolves this particular hygiene problem permanently (Martin Luther, *That Jesus Christ was Born a Jew*), but evidently bathing in Christian blood also gives temporary relief (Franciscus of Piacenza, *Sermons*). This latter explanation also conveniently helps resolve the problem of why some Jews actually lack this congenital stink—Jews who don't smell are ritual murderers.

1. Maccoby, *Judas Iscariot and the Myth of Jewish Evil*, 84, 110.

Food: Food is emblematic of life. The Jewish rules of *kashrut* (fitness) are the most extensive set of food taboos found in any culture, rivaled perhaps only by the Hindu Laws of Mani. Most attempts to explain these laws appeal either to rational explanations, such as hygiene, or to holiness, the effort to distinguish Israel from the surrounding peoples. Though it is rare that Jewish interpreters offer occult explanations for these rules, from the beginning it has been clear that food has metaphysical significance. A good example would be the biblical teaching that the life-vitality of an animal resides in its blood, so that blood had to be spilled rather than consumed, in order to return the life force to God (Gen. 9).

Certain foods can affect people in ways beyond mere nutrition. Too many olives, for example, can adversely affect memory. On the other hand, foods eaten at certain propitious times can have positive influence over one's fortune. Thus the Talmud advises eating pumpkin, fenugreek, leek, beets, and dates at the **New Year** (Hor. 12a). Pomegranates eaten on the New Year will enhance **fertility**. The consumption of sweets at special occasions (bar mitzvahs, weddings, and the like) portend of success and happiness; the cradles of newborns are sometimes sprinkled with sugar and sweets before the child is first placed in it.[1]

Food is also used for medicinal purposes. **Herbs** especially were used in Jewish folk **healing**. While the fitness of a food has always been an issue, from the time of the Mishnah on, any food thought to be of medicinal value, even forbidden food, should be part of the healer's arsenal (M. Yoma 8; Shab. 67a). Thus a healing poultice or remedy could include noxious foodstuffs. **Abraham Yagel** even prescribed crawfish cooked up in a potion to treat a mental illness.

The Talmud teaches that food left out unattended attracts **demons** and evil spirits. **Isaac Luria** and his followers also taught that the prohibited foods were manifestations of the **Sitra Achra** and, unlike kosher foods, their **nitzotz**, their holy "spark," could not be released through consumption. Chasidic teachings include the belief that a damaged soul may be reincarnated as an **animal** or plant, toward the eventuality that the food made from those things will be eaten by a saintly person, at which point the soul achieves release (Likkutai Torah; Tanya; Megillat Setarim; ShB 108).

Mystical sources find great metaphysical power in the act of eating, usually inspired by the example of the sacred meal eaten by Moses, Aaron, and the Elders in God's presence on Mount Sinai (Ex. 24). In texts such as the **Zohar**, there appear many mystical food rituals. Thus the food on the **Sabbath** (the day when Israel received double **manna** in the desert) takes on great importance. One must eat three meals over the course of the day in order to receive the additional soul granted each Jew on the Sabbath and to draw closer the angelic realms. A precise ritual, even involving the arrangement of the foods on the table in relationship to each other, must be followed for each meal. Failure to do the rituals correctly puts you at the mercy of the demonic.[2] Eating food from the **tish** of a **righteous** man is also considered a source of supernatural blessing and protection.

Providing food for the poor, an important biblical obligation, also serves the **sefirot**, keeping the male (giving) and female (receiving) aspects of God in balance (Zohar I: 17b).

At least one Sage, **Eleazar**, could make food (cucumbers, to be precise) magically materialize (Sanh. 68a). In **Sefer ha-Razim**, foodstuffs are used for a variety of magical purposes, medical and otherwise. *SEE* FASTING; HEALING; HERBS AND VEGETABLES; PHARMACOPOEIA.

1. Trachtenberg, *Jewish Magic and Superstition*, 184, 213.
2. Hecker, "Food Practices in the Zohar," in Fine, *Judaism and Practice*, 353–63.

Footstool: A footstool was a symbol of status in the ancient world. The Bible regards the world to be the footstool of God. **German Pietists**, by contrast, regarded the Torah to be God's footstool. This myth conveys the idea that the Torah is, as it were, the part of the **Throne of Glory** that projects into this dimension, providing the rationale for liturgical bowing in the direction of the Torah during a service (Ps. 99:5; SCh 1585).

Foreskin: *SEE* ORLAH.

Fortis, Abraham Isaac: (Polish, ca. 18th century). Physician and amulet maker. Professionally trained in Western medicine, yet conversant in amulets and segullot, Fortis was a celebrated doctor who embraced both Jewish folk healing practices and the emerging naturalistic theories of medicine.

Fortunetelling: *SEE* DIVINATION.

Forty: *SEE* NUMBERS.

Forty-Two Part Name of God: *SEE* NAMES OF GOD.

Foundation Stone: (*Even ha-Shetiyah*). This rock is the capstone of Creation. Under this stone God trapped the floodwaters of the **abyss** (Isa. 2:2), the source of the entire world's **water**. All the world's winds also originate from there (Otzer Maasot, 121). This stone sits under the **Temple Mount**. The stone is actually a piece of God's **Throne of Glory** (Tanh., Kedoshim 10; Zohar II) and inscribed with the **Tetragrammaton**. A chunk of the stone was used by God to make the two tablets of the **Ten Commandments**. God moved this stone only once, to unleash the Flood of Noah's day. When King **David** tried to move the stone into the **Holy of Holies**, **chaos** was unleashed and it was only by using the theurgic power of reciting the **Psalms** that he was able to drive the waters of the abyss back to their proper place (Suk. 49a, 53a). Other traditions claim the rock levitates in a cave beneath the Temple Mount, and when it finally falls the coming of the Messiah is imminent. (Suk. 53a–b; J. Sanh. 29b; M. Yoma 5:2; J. Yoma 5:4, 8:4; Yoma 54a–b; PdRE 35).

Fountain of Elisha: A spring, also called the "Eye of the Sultan," found outside of Jericho that was miraculously cured of tainted water by the prophet (II Kings 2).

Four: *SEE* NUMBERS.

Four Kingdoms: The four beasts that appear in Daniel's dream (Dan. 8) are allegories of four empires that oppressed the Jews, but exactly which four is debatable. Most lists choose from among these five due to their historic roles in oppressing Jews: Assyria, Babylon, Persia, Greece, and/or Rome.

Four Sages: Tractate Chagigah 14b relates a cryptic story of four Sages who entered Paradise. The four Sages were **Ben Azzai**, **Ben Zoma**, **Elisha ben Abuyah**, and **Akiba ben Joseph**. Exactly what "entering *Pardes*" means is the greatest of all the mysteries associated with this story. Some say it involved mystical ascent. Others say it involved esoteric interpretations of the Torah (see **PaRDeS**). Whatever the reality behind the event, it proved catastrophic for three of the four men. Ben Azzai "looked and died." Ben Zoma "looked and lost his senses." Ben Abuyah "cut the root," and became known only as *Acher* (the Other), while Akiba alone emerged "whole/in peace." Much speculation of the nature of mystical **ascent** springs from this legend (Gen. R. 2:4; Lev. R. 16:4; S of S R. 1:10).

One tradition elaborates on the story thusly: Ben Azzai was so captivated by what he saw he could not give it up and refused to return to his body. Ben Zoma became so immersed in the mysteries he had seen that he ceased to be able to function in life. Ben Abuyah saw **Metatron**. Thinking he had seen another deity besides God, he declared "there are two powers in heaven" (he embraced **Gnosticism**) and turned against the Torah (Chag. 15a; J. Chag. 77; Lev. R. 16; S of S R. 1:10).

Four Species: (*Arbaah Minim*). The Torah commands that four plant species be gathered for the celebration of the Sukkot harvest festival (Lev. 23). The Torah is not explicit as to the identity of two of the species, but the Sages have established the four species as the palm, the willow, the **myrtle**, and the citron. The branches of the first three species are bound together to form a *lulav*, while the citron is called the **etrog**. During the holiday, these four species are used in a mysterious ritual: the species are held together in two hands and waved toward the four compass points and up toward the sky, then down to the earth.

A number of homiletic explanations are given for this ceremony, but there are also some *sodot*, esoteric explanations, usually based on the belief that these four species symbolize and activate different forces of the divine sefirot. The most prominent of these esoteric interpretations highlight the phallic appearance of the bouquet when the lulav and etrog are held together; in doing this ritual, humans participate in bringing together the feminine and masculine forces in the Godhead in a kind of *hieros gamos*, a sacred union (Bahir 198). This interpretation is quite overt in Kabbalah, where the lulav is a symbol of **Yesod** and/or **Tiferet**, the male sexual dimension of the Godhead (Zohar III: 121a, 255a).

Many traditional Jews keep the lulav and etrog after the holiday season, believing that their ritual use has now imbued them with *kedushah*, a usable spiritual power. They are subsequently used as talismans and in folk medicine.

Four Worlds of Emanation: According to classical **Kabbalah**, the universe is a progressive unfolding resulting from an overflow of divine energy from the **Ein Sof**. Four "worlds" or supernal realms result from this emanation: **Atzilut** (Emanation), **Yetzirah** (Formation), **Beriyah** (Creation), and **Asiyah** (Action). Different traditions elaborate on each of these, relating them to the structure of the soul, the angelic hierarchies, and various spiritual and material realities. *SEE* EMANATION; KABBALAH; PARTZUFIM; SEFIROT.

Fox: (*Shual*). This most cunning of animals frequently appears in Jewish fables as a trickster. Its appearance on a person's left side also portended an ill **omen**. A fox tail wards off the **evil eye** (Tos. Shab. 4:5). Its tooth was used as a treatment for insomnia, although the Sages do not elaborate on the specific method to be followed (Shab. 67a).

Francesa Sarah of Safed: Medium (Turkish, ca. 16th century). Francesa was famed for her prophetic visions and was frequently consulted by leading rabbis and even Kabbalists (Sefer ha-Hezyonot 18; Divrei Yosef, 264–366).

Frankincense: (*Levunah*). An aromatic incense used in the Temple cult. It is a resin extracted from the *Boswellia Thurifera* bush found in Arabia, Somalia, and India. It also has psychotropic properties and was used to sedate individuals facing execution (Sanh. 43a).

Frankists: A Jewish occult sect that arose among the Jews of Poland in the 18th century. Evidently influenced by the Kabbalistic teachings of **Shabbatai Tzvi**, a Polish Jew named Jacob Frank claimed to be the **reincarnation** of the Patriarch **Jacob** and created a secret circle of followers. Frankist ritual gatherings appear to have involved the conscious violations of the **commandments** in order to fulfill Frank's teaching that "One must nullify the Torah in order to fulfill it." These violations included, most sensationally, sexual rites and rituals. Only slightly less outrageous was the belief that Frankists should convert to **Christianity**, because this would allow the Frankists to conquer the Christians from within. Although placed under a **cherem**, the Frankists found sympathetic gentile authorities that protected them for a while. The group did eventually convert en masse to Christianity, only to find themselves in trouble with the Church for their continuing bizarre and heretical activities. Though Frank served an extended prison term for his Christian apostasy, his influence continued throughout the rest of his life. His daughter continued as the sect leader after his death, and though the group perpetuated the belief that Frank never actually died, the Frankists gradually declined and disappeared by the late 19th century.[1]

1. Rabinowicz, *The Encyclopedia of Hasidism*, 133; Scholem, *Major Trends in Jewish Mysticism*, 315–18.

Freemasons: A secretive fraternal society. Though Freemasonry espouses an ideal of universal brotherhood and a nonsectarian notion of God, acceptance of Jews varied from country to country, and in some places, like Prussia, Jews had to form their own segregated Jewish lodges.

The pernicious myth that Freemasonry was an arm of the "Jewish conspiracy" for world domination emerged in Europe in the mid-19th century. This may be the combined result of Masonry's reputation as a "secret society" and its liberal ideology of universalism that favored the efforts of Jews to gain full rights and equal status in Europe. This conspiracy theory of a "Masonic-Jewish" alliance was first widely disseminated during the Dreyfus Trial in France in 1870. This supposed plot was enshrined in the **Protocols of the Elders of Zion** and has been a staple of anti-Semitic paranoia ever since.

Free Will: (*Ratzon*). Freedom of will is one of the distinctive characteristics of the God of Israel, because unlike the gods of pagan theology, God's freedom is not impinged upon by **fate**, *shimtu*, norns, or any other notion of destiny. In mystical theology, will is a function of the highest of God's attributes, **Keter**.

Human free will is a critical way in which we bear the "image of God" (Deut. 30). But how human autonomy is to be reconciled with God's omnipotent authority remains an intellectual puzzle, and there are multiple Jewish answers that would take us far beyond the parameters of this book. *SEE* FATE.

Fringes: (*Tzitzit*). God commanded the ancient Israelite men to wear *tzitzit*, "fringes," on the corners of their outer garment, or *tallit* (a togalike wrap). These fringes are both symbols of devotion and, more magically, receptors of spiritual energy and inspiration. Each fringe consists of eight strands made from four strings, five knots, and four groups of twists between each knot; the four groups consist of seven, eight, eleven, and thirteen windings. One thread was to be blue, the rest white. Today, when all clothing is tailored, observant Jews will wear their fringes on a special garment, a square prayer shawl also called a *tallit* and/or a poncholike undergarment called a *tallit katan*.

The required blue (*techelet*) strand had to be made from a special source, from the extract of a creature known as the *chilazon*. When the identity of this animal was lost, sometime during the disruptions between the Byzantine and Islamic empires, the use of a blue thread ceased. The chilazon is probably the *Murex trunculus* shellfish found off the coast of Lebanon. Until recently, it was only known how to extract a purple dye from the creature, but a method for turning the purple dye a deep sky blue has been recovered, and it may be possible once again to restore the ancient blue thread to the *tzitzit*.[1]

One esoteric teaching holds that the dangling threads represent both the undone work of Creation and the divine shefa, or emanation, which flows "downward" into the **Four Worlds**. Therefore the fringes are actually a kind of metaphysical conduit, directing divine energy to the wearer from on high. The knots represent the power of the commandments to "bind" sin, or even **demons**. Based on this, the Sages occasionally credit the fringes with a supernatural ability to prevent one from sinning. In one tale, the fringes literally slap their wearer in the face when he is about to transgress. In at least one example, a tallit has been credited with producing miraculous healings and was kept by an eastern European community for several generations. A seriously sick child will be wrapped in the tallit with the hope of a cure (Bachya's comments on Num. 15:38; Num. R. 17:9; Zohar I: 23b; Sifrei Num.

15:41; Men. 44a; Etz ha-Chayyim, Sha'ar ha-Chashmal 2).
SEE HAIR; KNOTS; ZER ANPIN.

> 1. Kaplan, *The Aryeh Kaplan Anthology*, 166–223.

Frogs: The second plague God sent against the Egyptians in the **Exodus** story. **Rabbah bar Channah** claimed to have seen a frog the size of a castle.

Fruit: Various fruits symbolize supernal higher realities in Judaism. **Kabbalah** frequently refers to human souls as the "fruits" of the **sefirot**, the "tree of life" (Bahir 14; Zohar I: 15b, 19a, 33a). Other associations with Jewish occult lore include the following:

> *Apples*: Apples are a symbol of occult knowledge; the mystics and philosophers speak of secret wisdom as "golden apples concealed in silver filigrees." The state of enlightenment is known as the **orchard of holy apples**.
>
> *Figs*: Fig is the fruit most widely regarded by the Sages to have been the forbidden fruit from the **Tree of Knowledge of Good and Evil** eaten by **Adam** and **Eve**. This is because only a few verses later it is described how God made **garments** of fig leaves (Gen. 3:7). According to Talmud, Berachot 40a, consuming the leaves of the Tree of Knowledge is the source of the knowledge of **sorcery**. **Hechalot** text includes a ritual for summoning the **Sar ha-Torah** that involves writing an incantation on a fig leaf and then eating it.

> *Grapes*: According to some, grapes were the forbidden fruit Eve ate in the Garden. More notoriety comes with **Noah**, who was the first to plant vines and brew wine from its fruits (Gen. 9). The twelve spies sent by Moses into Canaan brought back a cluster so big that two men had to carry it (Num. 13). Because of that association, grapes are a symbol of bounty and joy, and as a result, grapes are one of the foods that has been given its own blessing to be recited before it is eaten. In the **World-to-Come** each grape will grow so large it will require a wagon to transport it. People will tap each grape as one would a barrel and no less than thirty kegs of wine will flow from each (Ket. 111b).
>
> *Pomegranates*: The pomegranate is a symbol for the **Torah**, because it supposedly contains 613 seeds, equaling the number of commandments in the Five Books of Moses (Chag. 15b). Pomegranates decorated both the **Temple** and the robes of the priests. It is eaten during the High Holidays in the hope that the coming years will be as full of blessings as the fruit is full of seeds.

Fumigation: A technique for **exorcism**, entailing exposing the spirit to **incense** or a noxious smoke, such as sulfur.

G

Gabirol, Solomon: Philosopher and poet (Spanish, ca. 11th century) Jewish occult tradition credits him with creating either a **golem** or a mechanical automaton.

Gabriel: "Mighty One of God." One of the four high angels that surround the **Throne of Glory**, Gabriel stands at the left hand of God. He is the **angel** of revelation, a role he fills in Christian and Islamic traditions also, as well as the Prince of Fire (I Enoch; Deut. R. 5). He and **Michael** functioned as the witnesses at the wedding of **Adam** and **Eve**, and he is one of the three angels who appear to Abraham bearing news of the birth of Isaac (Gen. 18; Mek. 86b). Of those three, it was Gabriel who destroyed **Sodom** in a rain of **fire** (Gen. R. 50:2; B.M. 86b). He also had a role in the Tamar-Judah affair in Gen. 38 (Sot. 10b).

Some traditions (though not all) identify him as the angel who wrestled **Jacob**. In one tradition, he is the angel who establishes Rome as a punishment for Israel, while in other versions of the same legend it is Michael (Shab. 56b; Sanh. 21b). He participates with Michael in Daniel's revelations (Daniel chapters 8–9). He can also function as a guardian angel; he nursed the infant **Abraham** through his finger, protected Israel in Egypt, and aided the infant **Moses** (Yalkut Exodus; Sot. 12b). He has other roles in human affairs also (Sanh. 45b; Shab.55a).

He is one of the four guardian angels invoked for protection in the bedtime ritual of the **Kriat Sh'ma al ha-Mitah**. The color **red** is linked to Gabriel, signifying that he is a manifestation of God's judgment (Sitre Torah, Zohar I: 99a).

Gad: This Hebrew word can have two fundamental meanings:

1. "Luck" or "fortune." Personified as a deity by the ancients, devotees would make food offerings to him (Gen. 30:11; Isa. 65:11). Invoking the power of Gad continued among Jews even after this idolatrous associate was forgotten, much like we today still speak of "luck" as a force or entity.

2. One of the twelve tribes of Israel. There are no esoteric or legendary traditions involving Gad that this writer has found to date.

Gad the Seer: Advisor to King **David**. He is the purported author of a book of heavenly revelations. *SEE* WORDS OF GAD THE SEER.

Galgaliel: "Cycle of God." The Angel of the **Sun** (I Enoch).

Galgalim: "Cycles/whirlwinds." A class of angels mentioned in **Hechalot Rabbati**.

Galitzur: An **angel** known as "the revealer of the meaning of Torah" mentioned in **Sefer Raziel**. He is one of the angels that ministers before the **Throne of Glory**. His wings protect the other attending angels from the fiery breath of the **Chayyot** (PR 20:4). *SEE* SAR HA-TORAH.

Galya Raza: "Revelation of a Secret." A Kabbalistic tract on **reincarnation**, this anonymous 16th-century work provides an elaborate Gnostic-flavored theory of Creation and the dominion of **evil** over the universe as a framework for its teachings about transmigration of souls. It contains perhaps the most pessimistic interpretation of **Creation** to be found in a Jewish religious work.[1] *SEE* GNOSTICISM; REINCARNATION.

1. Fine, *Essential Papers in Kabbalah*, 243–69.

Garden of Eden: *SEE* EDEN.

Garlic: Medievals included garlic, a multipurpose herb, in remedies to treat toothaches and epilepsy. Roasted garlic is an aid for virility. Garlic also has demon-repelling qualities—some could be hung in the doorway of a house (along with a rooster head) as an amulet to protect a newborn.[1] **Chayyim Vital** included it in a formula for making silver.

1. Zimmels, *Magicians, Theologians, and Doctors*, 145.

Garment: (*Beged, Malbush; Chaluk*). "Garment" is the term used in **Kabbalah** to refer to the barriers that protect the material world from being dissolved by the power of greater spiritual realities. Thus the **Zohar** teaches that the **Torah** we have on earth, consisting of texts, stories, laws, etc., is really only the "garment of Torah." The real, spiritual Torah is simply beyond the grasp of material beings, so it needs to be "clothed" for us to experience it (I: 134a; III: 36a).

God, too, has "garments," variously identified as God's **Glory** or **Chashmal** (the untranslatable substance Ezekiel sees at the center of the divine **chariot**). God is described in the Bible as wearing **light** as a garment (Ps. 104:2; Isa. 6). Hechalot Rabbati describes a divine robe of light that is covered all over with the **Tetragrammaton**. The Sages link this idea of God's garment to **Creation**, suggesting that somehow God "wears" the universe (Gen. R. 3:4; Ex. R. 15, 22; PdRE 3; PdRK 22:5; Zohar III: 273a).[1]

There are a few references in tradition to magical garments among humans. There are, for example, the legendary **garments of Adam**, but there is also a mysterious cape or mantle described in **Sefer ha-Malbush**, "The Book of the Garment." The mantle, made from deer skin and covered in divine names and then activated in an occult ritual at water-side, grants the adept magical powers. Practical Kabbalists sometimes dress in colored garments appropriate to the sefirah they are attempting to magically

access.[2] *SEE* EMANATION; FRINGES. *(SEE ALSO APPENDIX FIGURE 2.)*

1. Green, *Jewish Spirituality*, vol. 2, 169. Also see Ginsburg, *The Sabbath in Classical Kabbalah*.
2. Idel, *Hasidism*, 198, 369–70.

Garments of Adam: These miraculous clothes, made by God, allowed anybody wearing them to hunt and capture animals at will. They were permeated with the fragrance of **Eden** and never wore out. God gave them to **Adam** and **Eve** after they were stripped of the protective **Glory** they wore in the Garden of Eden (Gen. 3:21; PdRE 14). Since the **Bible** describes the garments as made out of unspecified "skins," one legend claims they were made out of the skin of **Leviathan**. They passed from Adam through his descendants to King **Nimrod**. **Esau** took the garments from Nimrod when he slew the king (Gen. R. 63:13, 65:16; PdRE 24; Zohar I: 74b). These were the same garments that **Jacob** wore to fool his blind father, **Isaac**, into thinking he was Esau. Even then, the garments still bore the unique scent of the Garden of Eden, which helped in the deception. Jacob was the last recorded owner of the garments (Gen. 27:27; Gen. R. 65:11; Tanh., Toldot).

The **Zohar** regards the garments of Adam to be allegorical, a reference to the **sefirot** (I: 142b). *SEE* GARMENTS.

Gate: (*Sha'ar; Delet*). A gateway is emblematic of access to celestial and underworld realms (Gen. 28:7; Pss. 24, 78). There are five gates by which one may enter the divine realms and three that lead to **Gehenna** (Zohar I: 1a). Heaven is filled with doors through which prayers and deeds ascend (Gedulat Moshe).

Doors and gates are also liminal points by which demons and spirits may enter a home (Gen. 4:7). In the **Exodus**, smearing **blood** on the doorways of a dwelling created a barrier between the spirit of destruction able to move freely in the world and human habitations. Since the giving of the **Torah**, scriptures affixed to a doorway in a **mezuzah** serve the same function (J. Pe. 15d; A.Z., 11a). **Incantation bowls** would be buried under a threshold to prevent entry by demons.

Gate of Mercy: (*Sha'ar Rachamim*). Known as the "Golden Gate" to the Arabs, it is a walled-over entryway on the east wall of the **Temple** platform. There is another passageway next to it known as the **Gate of Repentance**. At the end of time, **angels** will finally open them both. Another tradition teaches that the original gate of Solomon's Temple sank below the earth and will rise up along with the resurrected souls at the end of time (Lam. R. 2:13). Through this gate the Messiah will enter **Jerusalem**.[1]

1. Vilnay, *Legends of Jerusalem*, 54–56.

Gathering Spirits, Book of: (*Sefer Kevitzat ha-Ruchot*). This short book is an early medieval manual for gathering and controlling demons.

Gay: "Valley." In the Zohar, it refers to a mysterious underworld dimension of the material world that links the earth to the punishing afterlife (Ps. 23; Sitre Torah, Zohar I: 253b–254a).

Gedi: "Kid." The Hebrew word for the **zodiac** sign Capricorn. It is linked to the month of Tevet, which is a winter month in the Land of **Israel**. A fast day is observed on the tenth of the month, marking the beginning of the siege of **Jerusalem** by the Romans. It signifies sleep and dormancy, but also renewal and new birth (Mid. Tanh. 1). It is also the sign associated with **Jacob** (Es. R. 7:11).[1] *SEE* GOAT.

1. Erlanger, *Signs of the Times*, 199–226.

Gedulah: "Greatness." Another term for the sefirah of **Chesed**. *SEE* SEFIROT.

Gedulat Moshe: "Greatness of Moses." A medieval text describing the afterlife. In it, **Metatron** and other angels give Moses a tour of **Gehenna** and the **seven heavens**.

Gehazi: The servant of the prophet Elisha was a man of bad judgment and weak faith. When the prophet commissioned him to take his **rod** and go resurrect the son of the Shunammite woman, Gehazi first tested the staff on a dead dog. The staff worked, but then lost its power, forcing Elisha to go personally to perform the miracle (II Kings 5). Gehazi was punished by being afflicted with **leprosy** (Mid. Aseret ha-Dibrot). Later he helps King Je-

roboam commit the sin of building golden calves for his sanctuary in the northern kingdom of Israel (Sot. 47a; MdRI, Amalek 1). For this offense he was reincarnated as a **dog** (Shivhei ha-BeSHT).

Gehenna/Gehinnom: (Hebrew, derived from *Gay Hinnom*, "the Valley of Hinnom"). Hell; the punishing afterlife.

Originally the word referred to the valley on the west side of the Old City of **Jerusalem**. Because in biblical time the valley was the site of pagan worship, including the **tophets** for child sacrifice, the term has become synonymous with **evil**, and it is imagined to be the location of a gate to hell, *Gehenna*.

Aside from the book of Daniel, the Hebrew Bible is virtually silent on the topic of punishment in the afterlife. **I Enoch** gives the first detailed description of Gehenna as an abysmal furnace where the wicked are fettered in burdening chains and tormented by fire. Interestingly, Enoch provides conflicting testimony as to the duration of this suffering. Some passages suggest that the punishments of Gehenna will last until the final judgment, when it will give up its dead, while other verses indicate the wicked are eventually completely consumed by its fires and annihilated (51, 63, 56).

The exact nature of Gehenna varies from tradition to tradition. It should come as no surprise that a fiery furnace (inspired by a description in Daniel) filled with coal, pitch, and sulfur is the most popular image. One text claims there are no less than five different kinds of **fire** burning there. Bitter cold and pervasive darkness is also a common motif, a theme first appearing in II Enoch, which distinguishes between compartments of fiery and icy retribution. Rabbinic literature describes the punishments of Gehenna as alternating fire and ice (PdRK 10:4; J. Sanh. 10:3).

Gehenna came into existence on the second day of Creation, which is why that is the only day which God does not declare "good" (Pes. 54a, based on Gen. 1; Ned. 39b). There are three **gates** to Gehenna, guarded by three angelic princes: **Kipod**, **Nasagiel**, and **Samael**. One gate opens to the desert, another to the **sea**, and the third to the valley of Ben Hinnom outside Jerusalem (Eruv. 19a; BhM 2:30). In the Zohar, Gehenna is a byproduct of the **Left Side** of the sefirotic emanations. According to **Gedulat Moshe**, Gehenna is a living entity that eternally hungers for the souls of the righteous, a hunger that can never be sated.

According to **Masekhet Gehinnom**, Gehenna is divided into seven precincts (*madori*) or palaces. The seven compartments of hell are **Sheol**, **Abaddon**, **Beer Shachat**, **Bor Sh'on**, **Tit ha-Yeven**, **Domah**, and **Tevel**. The *Nahar deNur*, the **River of Light** that flows from under the **Throne of Glory**, separates Gehenna from the **seven heavens**. Many other rivers—streams of gall, pitch, and poison—flow from precinct to precinct (Sot. 10b; Mid. Teh. 11:6–7; Zohar I: 62b).

Each compartment contains its own team of punishing **angels** headed by a princely angel, and each has its own unique punishments intended for specific kinds of sins: those who denied succor to the poor dwell in icy misery, slanderers hang by their tongues, etc. Some souls experience repeated cycles of horrific destruction and painful reconstruction, but everyone is spared for the duration of the Sabbath (except the Sabbath desecrators) (PR 23:8). Some precincts are reserved exclusively for the sinful gentile nations, such as the seven Canaanite nations and the Romans.

The **Talmud** specifically limits the time that most souls must spend in Gehenna to a maximum of twelve terrestrial months (Ed. 2:10; Gen. R. 33:7; Seder Olam ha-Ba), though a very few thoroughly wicked souls will never rise up from there at all (R.H. 17a). In tractate Berachot, the Sages can only think of seven individuals of the biblical period that would merit such harsh treatment. After many excruciating months of purgative suffering, the souls are finally reduced to ash and their purified essence now awaits the **resurrection**. Sometimes famous biblical evildoers, for whom there is no redemption, are associated with a specific level of Gehenna.[1]

In III Enoch and subsequent writings, souls are divided into three categories: the **Righteous**, the Wicked, and the **beinonim**, "in-betweens," the bulk of humanity who have both merits and sins recorded in the **Book of Life**. The conditions and duration of the soul's sojourn in Gehenna depends on which category one belongs to. It is interesting to note that the righteous must appear there, but just long enough to plead on behalf of the sinners and use their merit to ease their punishments (B.B. 84a; Tam. 32b; Shab. 152b; Suk. 32b; Ex. R. 51:7; PR 41:3; Mid. Ruth 79b; Tanh., Noah 1, Bo 2).

1. Patai, *Gates of the Old City*, 277–81; also see Raphael, *Jewish Views of the Afterlife*.

Gematria: (Greek, "Calculations/numerology"). Gematria is a complex hermeneutic technique in which numbers are used to reveal messages in texts and thereby derive insight into the order of the universe.

In the **Hebrew alphabet**, each letter possesses a numeric value: *alef* = 1; *bet* = 2; *gimel* = 3; *dalet* = 4; *hay* = 5; *vav* = 6; *ziyan* = 7; *chet* = 8; *tet* = 9; *yud* = 10; *kaf* = 20; *lamed* = 30; *mem* = 40; *nun* = 50; *samech* = 60; *aiyin* = 70; *payh* = 80; *tzadi* = 90; *kuf* = 100; *resh* = 200; *shin* = 300; and *tav* = 400. Some methods also assign additional numeric values to the "final forms" of the letters *mem*, *nun*, *tzadi*, *payh*, and *kaf* (in Hebrew orthography, the shapes of these five letters change when they appear at the end of a word). Gematria involves calculating the value of letters, names, words, and phrases, and then deriving homiletic or occult meaning from the numbers, often by matching them to words and phrases of equivalent value.

Interpretation via numerology is accepted among the thirty-two hermeneutic rules of the **Torah** laid down by the Talmudic Sages. The theosophical basis for gematria is first articulated in **Sefer Yetzirah**. There it is taught that numbers, like the Hebrew alphabet, are the hylic matter from which God constructs the universe. Therefore numeric relationships, especially those that appear in the language of Scripture, are not accidental or coincidental. Rather, such equivalencies reveal key interrelations in the structure of God's universe and hidden creative potentials.

A preoccupation with hidden number relationships is clearly evident in the Torah itself. Thus, for instance, there are precisely seven words in the first verse of Genesis, equaling the seven days of Creation. Perhaps the most famous example is found in Genesis 14:14. There we are told that **Abraham** took 318 retainers with him to rescue his nephew Lot from an army of marauding kings. The number stands out because it is unlike the stereotypical **numbers** that appear elsewhere in Scripture, such as 12, 40, or 70. Early on, interpreters noted that the name of Abraham's servant, **Eliezer**, also has the numeric value of 318, suggesting that in fact Abraham took only Eliezer with him. The extraordinary nature of this correlation is further enhanced when one realizes that "Eliezer" is a theophonic name meaning "My God is a help," implying that Abraham rescued **Lot** from the armies of four kings with only God's aid alone.

More sophisticated methods of finding meaning in Scripture soon emerged. From the first words of Exodus 35:1, Rabbi Nathan derived that there are 39 categories of forbidden labor on the **Sabbath**. Another Sage notes that since there are 613 commandments in the Torah yet the word "Torah," only equals 611, that reveals to us that the first two commandments God spoke at Mount **Sinai** were heard directly by the people, while all the rest came through the agency of Moses.

While rabbinic use of gematria was relatively infrequent, it was much more appealing to the medieval mystics, the **German Pietists**, and the Kabbalists, for gematria appealed to their interest for occult revelation.

The medieval text **Tikkunei Zohar** endorses four hermeneutic methods of calculation: absolute values (straight equivalency), ordinal values (valuing each letter 1–22, thus mem = 12, shin = 21), reduced values (letters with values of 1, 10, or 100 are revalued at "1"; 2, 20, or 200 at "2," etc., so that there are only nine values), and integral reduced values (each letter of a word is valued at one, up to a maximum of 9 for a nine-letter word). Together these four methods coincide with the four-letter **name of God** and the **four worlds**. Later traditions listed even more methods, as many as seventy-five.

While gematria has little authority in determining Jewish law, it plays a significant role in Jewish esoteric teachings and is a staple element of **Kabbalah**. The German Pietists had a deep interest in the numeric values concealed in both Scripture and Jewish prayer texts. They also devoted much reflection to the numeric values of angelic and divine names. It is interesting to note that occult interest in numerology helped spur the standardization of the wording for the **Siddur**, with spellings being fixed, in part, based on the gematria value that they yielded.

Classical Kabbalah elaborates even further on these practices. Works by mystics like **Joseph Gikatilla** and **Abraham Abulafia** also overflow with numerology. **Chasidism** found much value in numerology, and many Chasidic sermons and writings hinge on numerological interpretations.

Gematriaot, Sefer: A medieval book of protective magical procedures. It includes the prophylactic and theurgic use of Scriptural verses, magical formulae, and the **healing** power of **gemstones**.

Gemstones: Precious and semiprecious stones have been used as sources of occult power throughout human history. The ancient Mesopotamians spoke of an *elmeshu* stone that the gods used for **divination**.[1] Alchemists claim the legendary **philosopher's stone** made it possible to turn lead to gold. Jews, too, have many occult traditions related to gemstones, and their power is suggested in the Latin proverb, *Judaeos fidem in lapidibus pretiosis, et Paganos in herbis ponere* ("Jews put their trust in precious stones and Pagans in herbs").

The most famous gems mentioned in the **Bible** are the twelve stones, set in three columns of four rows, in the **breastplate** of the High **Priest**. Miraculous properties have been ascribed to the twelve stones, primarily as tools in divination. Since the exact translation of Bible mineralogical terms is now lost, there are multiple conflicting lists for the stones that were actually used. This list comes from the medieval text **Sefer Gematriot**:

> *Odem* (Ruby) has many benefits for fertility—it enhances male potency, prevents miscarriage, and eases labor pangs.
>
> *Pitdah* (Topaz) combats fevers and is also useful in **love** potions and rituals.
>
> *Bareket* (Carbuncle) sharpens the mind and combats the effects of old age.
>
> *Tarshish* (Beryl) helps digestion.
>
> *Nofech* (Jade, Emerald, or Carbuncle) enhances strength and courage.
>
> *Sapir* (Sapphire) has medicinal value, especially in treatment of the **eyes**.
>
> *Yahalom* (Emerald) is a good luck charm and a sleep-aid.
>
> *Leshem* (Jacinth) can be used for scrying.
>
> *Shebo* (Agate) keeps a person secure and stable on foot or on horseback.
>
> *Shoham* (Onyx) is a charm that will gain favor for the wearer.
>
> *Ahlamah* (Amethyst) increases physical courage and is a phylactery against evil spirits.
>
> *Yashfeh* (Jasper) is useful in keeping one from revealing secrets and in curbing ardor.[2]

Other gems of power also appear in Jewish narratives. Jonah, for example, discovered a pearl that gave off light, illuminating the interior of the fish that swallowed him. Perhaps the most famous gemstone is the **tzohar**, a fragment of supernal light given to **Adam** and his descendants. Those who possessed it could access many occult powers. Some legends claim the First **Temple** was studded in gems, while many images of the heavenly **Jerusalem** and **Eden** describe the walls and structures of these places as being built from precious stones. *SEE* URIM AND THUMMIM.

1. Rawlinson, *Cuneiform Inscriptions of Western Asia*, vol. IV, 18, no. 3.
2. Trachtenberg, *Jewish Magic and Superstition*, 265–67.

Genesis Rabbah: (*Bereshit Rabbah*). One of the most influential collections of the **Midrash**. Entirely devoted to the book of Genesis, the work contains many fantastic traditions concerning Creation, the mythic past, and biblical figures and events.

Geomancy: (*Goral ha-Chol*). Divination using rocks, pebbles, and/or sand. Stones are cast on a smooth surface—paper or a tabletop—and the resulting patterns are interpreted. Chayyim Vital describes a consultation with a witch who used geomancy to summon divinatory demons (Sefer ha-Hezyonot 21). An anthology of geomancy divination texts, collectively known as Sefer ha-Goralot, have survived from the Middle Ages. Some of these works are attributed to notable figures such as Sa'adia Gaon and **Ibn Ezra**. Most of these documents combine the practice with either **astrology** or **gematria**. *SEE* GEMSTONES; ROCK; URIM AND THUMMIM.

German Pietists: (*Chasidei Ashkenaz*). This mystical pietist sect of 12th–13th century Rhineland was one of the most important esoteric movements in Jewish history, as well as a major source of Jewish magical and occult traditions. Drawing inspiration from the **Hechalot literature**, **Sefer Yetzirah**, and the esoteric teachings of the **Talmud**, the German Pietists expounded many secrets of **Torah**, but especially concentrated their mystical speculations on the statutory prayers. These teachings were closely bound up with the numeric mysticism of gematria. They also had a keen interest in **angels** and **demons**, **dream** divination, and practical **theurgy**. Key figures include **Samuel ben Kalonymus he-Chasid**, **Eleazer ben Judah of Worms**, Abraham ben Azriel, and **Judah ben Samuel he-Chasid**, the last being the author of the major work of the Pietist tradition, **Sefer Chasidim**, the "Book of the Pious." Many of their teachings have subsequently become integral parts of European Jewish occult tradition. *SEE* GEMATRIA; TOSAFISTS.

Gerona Kabbalists: The city of Gerona in northern Spain became the center of mystical teachings during the 13th and 14th centuries. It produced the influential mystics **Azriel** and **Ezra of Gerona**, **Nachmanides**, and Jacob ben Sheshet Gerondi.

Gerushin: A meditation technique espoused by **Moses Cordovero** entailing long periods of isolation at the graveside of a righteous man to achieve mystical insights (Or Yakar 13:75). *SEE* DEATH; INCUBATION; MEDIUM; POSSESSION, GHOSTLY.

Gervasius, Julius: German Alchemist (ca. 18th century). Some historians claim that, writing under the nom de plume of **Abraham Eleazer**, Gervasius composed "Uraltes Chymisches Werk," a famous book of **alchemy**. This theory, while interesting, really has no more going for it than the more straightforward conclusion that the named author of the book is also the actual author.

Get: "Divorce certificate." Intriguingly, a number of Jewish **exorcism** techniques use the language of Jewish Law in their dealings with the demonic. Thus there are several **incantation bowls** inscribed with **incantations** written in the form of a *get*, a certificate of divorce.[1] Such "spirit gets" are directed against any **Lilith** or succubus that has been sexually tormenting a male victim. *SEE* JOSHUA BEN PERACHYA.

1. Naveh and Shaked, *Magic Spells and Formulae*, 17–18, 27, 159–61.

Gevul, Sefer ha-: A commentary on the **Zohar** by **Judah ben Samuel he-Chasid**.

Gevurah: "Power/*dynamis*." The fifth sefirah and the principle of divine justice, power, fear, and even terror.

This is also the source of the "**left** side"—evil, destructiveness, cruelty, and the demonic in Creation. It must be balanced by the forces of **Chesed**, abundant love. It is a feminine principle yet is personified, ironically, in the lower worlds by the Patriarch **Isaac**. He is so linked to it because he willingly accepted the severe **decree** that he be sacrificed by his father. It is symbolized by the **color** red. *SEE* SEFIROT.

Ghost: (*Rafa, Ruach, ha-Met*). The idea that spirits of the dead can continue to dwell among the living is an ancient Jewish belief. Most ghosts in Jewish tradition are either souls of the dead who have not yet made the transition into the **World-to-Come**, or are spirits that are somehow disturbed or summoned by the living. The only ghost story found in the **Bible** describes how the ghost of the prophet **Samuel** is temporarily summoned from the realm of the dead for the purposes of a séance (II Sam. 28).

Rabbinic literature, by contrast, is replete with ghost stories. It is possible for the pious among the living to hear the ghosts of the dead conversing in the **cemetery** at night (Ber. 18b). The dead can communicate with both the living (B.B. 58a; Pes. 113b; M.K. 28a) and the divine realms (B.M. 85b). They are a source of knowledge for all that transpires in the world (PdRE 34). In rabbinic and medieval accounts, ghosts are usually limited to appearing in a **dream** or lurking within the confines of a graveyard (SCh 452, 709–10, 728), though there is one exceptional story in which the spirit is free to come to visit the living wherever they may be (SCh 170). Later belief held that ghosts could move more freely, but needed to find a living host, thus becoming an **ibbur** or **dybbuk** (Sefer ha-Hezyonot 22–24; Nishmat Chayyim III: 11; IV: 10). Ghosts can take a variety of forms, human or animal (Ma'asei ha-Shem). **Chasidism** has many tales of dead spirits visiting and dwelling among the living (ShB 100). *SEE* ALSO BURIAL; DEATH; EXORCISM; MEDIUM; NECROMANCY; POSSESSION, GHOSTLY.

Ghoul: *SEE* CANNIBALISM; VAMPIRE; WEREWOLF.

Giants: (*Nefalim, Refaim, Gibborim, Emim,* and *Anakim*). Many stories of an ancient race of giants appear in Jewish tradition. A part of the traditions of **fallen angels**, giants are the offspring of intercourse between angels and mortal women. Collectively known as the *Nefalim* and *Anakim*, famous giants found in the **Bible** include King **Og** of Bashan, **Orpah**, **Goliath**, and his brother **Ishbi-benob**. Rabbinic texts identify many more, including Hiva and Hayya, the sons of the angel **Shemchazi**.

The giants are consistently portrayed as violent and defiant of God. They were cannibals and, in one tradition, they were so berserk with lust that they copulated with every kind of land beast (I Enoch 10). They were, in any case, very destructive, consuming whole herds of animals at a sitting and generally terrorizing mankind (III Maccabees 2:4; I Enoch 6:2–7:5; Mid. Abkir; **Book of Giants**). It was such behaviors that helped trigger the **Flood**.

Most giants were subsequently wiped out in the deluge, but some survived, as evidenced by their continuing presence among the Canaanite and Philistine peoples. They managed to survive the Flood because Og (later king of Bashan) persuaded Noah to allow him on the Ark. Og finally died at the hand of Moses when he tried to destroy the Israelite encampment in the desert by hurling a mountain onto it. God caused the hollowed mountain to fall on him like a yoke, and Moses was able to slay the encumbered giant (Num. R. 21; Tanh. B. 55; Ber. 54b). David and his mighty men slew the brothers Goliath and Ishbi-benob and their giantess mother, Orpah (Sanh. 95a; Gen. R. 59).

The exact dimensions of giants vary from tradition to tradition. Minimalist accounts, like those of Goliath, put them at the 9–10 ft. mark, while later rabbinic literature often describes them in much grander terms (by one account twenty-three thousand ells—almost one hundred thousand feet). Often they are described with monstrous features: extra fingers and toes, multiple rows of teeth, and the like (Deut. R. 1; Chul. 60a; I Enoch 7). Some accounts break them into three classes, on the assumption that the different biblical names reflected meaningful distinctions. The Rabbis considered gigantism a potential problem even in their own days (Bik. 45b).

Giants, Book of: (*Sefer ha-Giborim*). Apocryphal work that gives an expanded account of the race of **giants** produced by the sexual intercourse between **fallen angels** and mortals mentioned in Genesis 6:1–4. A copy of the text in Hebrew, preserved in fragmentary form, has been found among the Dead Sea Scrolls. The Jewish text is believed to be the source for a more widely dispersed and influential Manichean/Gnostic version that is known by the same name. That intact Gnostic version includes an account of a war between the giants and the **host of heaven** prior to the Flood.

Gihon: One of the four primordial rivers that flowed from the Garden of **Eden** (Gen. 2). It is identified with a spring that wells up in the Kidron Valley of Jerusalem and that has always been the city's main water source. It was rerouted by King Hezekiah. A later legend claims it was stopped up until **Chayyim Vital**, who divined its location from a ghostly visitation of his teacher, **Isaac Luria**, reopened it. In the time of the Messiah, it is presumably the waters of Gihon that will flow both east and west out of Jerusalem, gradually expanding to gargantuan volumes, sweetening the waters of both the Mediterranean Sea and the Dead Sea (Ezek. 47:1–12).

Gikatilla, Joseph ben Abraham: Kabbalist (Spanish, ca. 13th century). A student of **Abraham Abulafia**, Gikatilla composed several highly influential Kabbalistic works, including Ginnat Egoz, Sha'arei Orah, and Sha'arei Tzedek.

Gilgul: "Rolling [souls]." In early Jewish literature, this refers to a notion that there are underworld conduits by which the dead "roll" to the Land of **Israel** (Ket. 111a). In later writings (Bahir; Sefer ha-Gilgulim) this becomes the Hebrew expression for **reincarnation**. A soul may undergo *gilgul* many times.

Gilgulim, Sefer ha-: "Book of Reincarnations." A treatise by **Chayyim Vital** on reincarnation and on the metaphysics of the various components of the soul. Not to be confused with another book on the same topic by the same author, **Sha'ar ha-Gilgulim**.

Gimel: The third letter in the **Hebrew alphabet**, its name, *gimel*, is linked homiletically to the word *gimilut*, which means "bestowal/reward," an act of beneficence. Thus it signifies **charity** and kindness. Its shape represents the divine flow of goodness that pours down to the universe from on high (Magen David). Its numeric value is 3.[1]

1. Munk, *The Wisdom of the Hebrew Alphabet*, 55–70.

Glory of God: (*Kavod*). The manifest presence of God (Ex. 33). There are several different ways the term "Glory of God" is interpreted. Inspired by the biblical words of the **serafim** praising God, "The whole world is full of Your Glory" (Isa. 6), some regard it to be a kind of divine emanation, perhaps synonymous with the **Shekhinah** and/or the **Holy Spirit**—the immanent, indwelling presence of God in **Creation**.[1] Others associate it with the **Torah**. Sa'adia Gaon regards it to be a quasi-natural phenomenon, "second air," that yielded the visual manifestations seen by the prophets (Emunah v'Daat).

Many esoteric writings seize on Sa'adia's idea and regard the Glory to be a **vision** of a divine form created by the invisible, formless God—a manifestation of God that is actually visible to the human eye.[2] According to the Kabbalistic work Sod ha-Egoz, God uses nine different kinds of appearances—corresponding to the nine times God uses the phrase "Jacob my servant" in the Hebrew Scripture—while becoming visible/apprehensible to Jews. These different forms include **light**, **clouds**, **angels**, and humanoid body parts, such as a hand (Leviticus Rabbah 1:14). This may be related to the concept of divine **speculum**, which are also nine in number.

Perhaps the least understood of these is the appearance of an angel that *is* God. This is the **Malach Adonai**, a phenomenon that occurs several times in the **Bible** (Gen. 18, 22:15–16; Ex. 3:2) and is the basis for those angels mentioned in Talmudic and mystical tradition, such as **Akatriel-YaH**, which have names incorporating the Tetragrammaton and are, at times, identified as the "God of Israel" (Ber. 7b; Ma'aseh Merkavah). Some medieval mystics continue to recount visions of an anthropomorphic Glory. The adepts of the **Circle of the Unique Cherub**, for example, go so far as to claim that the human body is actually made in the image of God's Glory. SEE CHERUB, THE UNIQUE; DREAM; FACE OF GOD; MALACH ADONAI; METATRON; PROPHECY.

1. Levenson, "The Jerusalem Temple as a Devotional and Visionary Experience," in Green, *Jewish Spirituality*, vol. 1, 32–41.
2. Wolfson, *Through a Speculum that Shines*, 125–32.

Gnostics and Gnosticism, Ancient: Ancient Gnosticism was a dualistic religious ideology with occult characteristics. Scholars identify two types. Mesopotamian Gnosticism (Zoroastrianism, Manichaeism) taught that two forces, good and evil, were eternal and in eternal conflict over control of Creation. The second type, Mediterranean Gnosticism, teaches that good and evil are the result of a cosmic disruption of a primordial harmony.[1] The latter form flourished around the Mediterranean basin in the Greco-Roman era. This second variety of Gnosticism may have grown out of Judaism, though too little is known to draw any conclusions. Whatever the case, Judaism and Gnosticism are linked together in the ancient world because many Gnostic traditions are dependant on the Hebrew Scriptures and their traditions, especially through Gnostic-flavored interpretations of Genesis and Ezekiel.

The fundamental belief shared by ancient Gnostic systems was that there are actually two divine powers: a good but remote deity who utterly transcends the material universe, and an evil creator god, most often called the Demiurge and usually equated with the God of the Hebrew Scriptures. The Demiurge creates material existence for his own ends, trapping spiritual entities and imprisoning them in bodies of flesh. Because of this, according to the ancient Gnostics, the world as we experience it is the result of a dreadful accident at best and an evil conspiracy at worst. Most humans do not understand the true nature of things because the Demiurge deludes them into accepting the world as beneficent. It is only through being initiated in the esoteric "gnosis" of the higher, immaterial god that a person can hope to be saved from the burden and torments of material existence.[2] Along with a disdain for the material world, ancient Gnosticism devalued the body and particularly sexuality, which was the mechanism by which new souls are imprisoned in flesh by the Demiurge and his minions, the Archons. Thus Gnosticism exhibited a strong ascetic streak, often embracing celibacy and bodily mortification.[3]

On account of its dualism, its hostility for the Creator god, and its distain for physical creation, the Rabbis were vociferous in their opposition to the ancient Gnostics and their teachings. In fact, most references to heretics and heretical ideas found in Talmudic and Midrashic literature seem to be directed toward Gnosticism in its various forms (Chag. 14a–16a; Gen. R. 1:4; Sanh. 94a).

Gnosticism was gradually extinguished in the West by the hegemony of the Church, which viewed it as a Christian heresy, but it continued to flourish in the East for several centuries, mostly in the Manichean religion. The spread of Islam eventually undermined its viability in the Middle East and Central Asia. Gnostic ideas, however, continued to pop up throughout the Middle Ages in groups like the Bogomils and Cathers. Many modern scholars have recognized that there are Gnostic elements present in classic **Kabbalah**. The mystical system of **Isaac Luria**, with its emphasis on the notion that the world as we know it is a cosmic accident that needs correcting, comes the closest to a full-blown re-emergence of Gnosticism within Judaism.[4]

1. Jonas, *The Gnostic Religion*, 112–46, 237.
2. Couliano, *The Tree of Gnosis*, 50–145; Rudolph, *Gnosticism*, 59–67.
3. Williams, "Divine Image—Prison of Flesh: Perceptions of the Body in Ancient Gnosticism," in Feher, *Fragments for a History of the Human Body*. Also see Idel, "Sexual Metaphors and Praxis in Kabbalah," 212.
4. Scholem, *Major Trends in Jewish Mysticism*, 260; Fine, *Physician of the Soul, Healer of the Cosmos*, 144–46.

Goats: The goat is symbolically linked to Jacob, who had three significant events in his life involving goats—his deception of his blind father Isaac in receiving his blessing (Gen. 27), his deception of his father-in-law Laban while in his service (Gen. 30), and his being deceived by his sons in the incident surrounding the selling of **Joseph** (Gen. 37). In what may be a continuation of this "deception" motif, a goat (known as the "scapegoat") is also offered "to **Azazel**" every **Yom Kippur** as part of the atonement ritual for Israel (Lev. 16), a ceremony that parallels the Babylonian *Akitu* ritual. For all these reasons, the goat has become emblematic of sudden **reversal** and change of fortune. A goat kid is also the symbol of the zodiac sign **Gedi**.

The **Talmud** credits several extraordinary feats to the goats of righteous men, including the killing of bears and wolves. Goat's milk has multiple medicinal uses, including the treatment of angina and ailments of the spleen. The **Midrash**, Me'am Loez, gives an elaborate explanation that the Yom Kippur scapegoat offering is a bribe given to the accusing angel **Satan/Samael**, in order that the angel will withhold his criticism before God (Achrei Mot/Kedoshim).

It was once popular to serve goat's head at the **Rosh ha-Shanah** festive meal as a good luck charm of future prosperity. The practice is still observed by some Sephardic families in Israel and the Middle East.

To medieval Christians, a horned goat was a symbol of **Satan**. Jews, regarded as allies of Satan, were stereotypically portrayed in Christian polemical illustrations as riding astride a billy goat, often sitting backwards. *SEE* ANIMALS; SUBSTITUTION.

Godhead: According to Maimonides, God has no body and is essentially unknowable. Mystics, by contrast, make a distinction between the unknowable aspect of God, the **Ein Sof**, and that aspect of God that intersects with Creation. This knowable part of God can be graphed, as in the **sefirot**, or even envisioned as quasi-anthropomorphic forms (MdRI, Shirata 4; R.H. 17b; PR 21). Sefer Bahir describes God as having seven "forms": right and left "legs," right and left "arms," a "torso," a "head," and an androgynous **Zer Anpin**. *SEE* CHERUB, THE UNIQUE; FACE OF GOD; MALACH ADONAI; PHALLUS; SEFIROT; SHI'UR QOMAH.

Gog and Magog: First mentioned in Ezekiel 38–39, Gog is the "Chief Prince" of Magog. He will be involved in the eschatological wars with Israel at the end of time. He will be defeated by God and his corpse buried in the Land of **Israel**.

In rabbinic writings, Gog and Magog are understood to be synonyms and are linked to the traumatic events around the coming of the **Messiah**. Later sources identify the king of Gog as **Armilius**, a monstrous offspring of **Satan**. Eventually the two words become the archetypal term for a war of evil against God, and serve as the closest Jewish analogy to the Christian notion of Armageddon (A.Z. 3b; PdRK 79; Ed. 2:10; Shab. 118a; S of S R. 8:4).

Gold: (*Zahav, Paz, Charutz, Ketem*). Because of gold's untarnishable surface, it is a symbol of eternity (II Enoch 8:4). It also has a number of occult associations. Gold is the most frequently mentioned metal in the **Bible**. According to **Talmud** Yoma 44b, there are seven kinds of gold listed in Scripture. Gold comes from *Havilah*, a mythical land bordering the Garden of **Eden** (Gen. 2:11). The instruments of the Temple sanctuary, itself a symbolic Eden, were made from or plated in gold. In sefirotic theosophy, gold is the color of **Din**, the attribute of justice.

Along with gentile practitioners, Jewish alchemists were very interested in obtaining the knowledge to transmute other substances into gold. Gold has many magical uses. It is a surprisingly common ingredient in medicinal potions. Various methods of **divination** using gold are known to Jews, such as using gold coins in making divination rods for hunting treasure, or the use of gold divination discs. For good measure, such discs can serve as **amulets** afterward (**Sefer ha-Razim**; **Shimmush Tehillim**, Ps. 16). *SEE* COLOR; METAL.

Golden Calf: At precisely the moment that God was with **Moses** atop Mount **Sinai** giving the instruction that the Israelites were not to make idols, the people were sinning below by building a golden calf and calling it the "God of Israel." Aaron, the brother of Moses, played a crucial role in letting this offense happen (Ex. 34).

In their close reading of the biblical account, the Rabbis note that the **Bible** hints that the Israelite women refused to surrender their jewelry for the project. Because of this loyalty, God granted women an extra monthly day without work, at each **New Moon** (Tosafot to Rosh Hashanah 23a).

When Moses saw what had happened, he smashed the tablets of the **Ten Commandments** and the supernal letters on the stones immediately flew back to heaven. Some commentators claim Moses broke the tablets not out of anger, but for the sake of "plausible deniability"; if the people never actually saw the Commandments, they would be less culpable in God's eyes.

In some later mystical thought, the Calf became synonymous with the dangers of mystical speculation. According to this interpretation, the Israelites witnessed the same divine **chariot** described by **Ezekiel**, but misinterpreted the angelic "oxen" face to be that of God, thus inspiring them to build the calf. *SEE* IDOLATRY; TEN COMMANDMENTS.

Golem: "Form/Humanoid." A man-made being, usually an anthropoid, animated through the creative power of the **Hebrew alphabet**. Belief that one could make artificial humans was widespread among magical practitioners of antiquity. Though there is a possible allusion to the idea in Scripture (Ps. 139:16), the specific basis for this is found in **Sefer Yetzirah**, which teaches that man may become a "lesser creator" by learning to manipulate the occult power of the alphabet when combined with divine names (6, Long Recension). This is possible because God used the alphabet in the work of making the cosmos (Gen. R. 4:2, 12:10; Bahir 59).

Some commentaries to Sefer Yetzirah claim biblical figures made golems. **Abraham** used Sefer Yetzirah's power to "make souls" (Gen. 12); the prophet **Jeremiah** also made a golem. Two anonymous Talmudic Sages were able to create a "one-third" size calf for Sabbath meals (Ber. 55a; Mid. Teh. 3). More cryptic is the report that Rava "created a man," who he then sent to **Rabbi Zeira**, who caused the creature to return to dust (Sanh. 65b). By the Middle Ages, belief in the ability of mystical adepts to make a golem from a combination of dust and occult power was well established.[1] The medieval savant Solomon ibn Gabirol used his wisdom to create a maidservant for himself.

By most accounts, the golem had no free will or the power of **language**, though some stories have the golem utter words of warning from heaven. As a soulless entity, the golem is not required to fulfill the **commandments**. Since the animation came from using the secret name of God, the golem could then be returned to inanimate earth by saying the divine name in **reverse**. Alternate traditions require not only the use of God's name in the formation ritual, but also that the word *emet* (truth) be written on the forehead of the creature. Erasing the letter *alef* would leave only the word *met* (death), thereby slaying the golem (Sanh. 55a, 64b; Sefer Gematriot).

The golem became a staple of Jewish folk legends in Europe, the most famous golem being the one created by Rabbi **Loew of Prague** to protect the community against anti-Semitic violence. Like many other golem tales, over time the Prague golem grew in power and in unpredictable behavior and the creator was forced to destroy his creation, thus curbing his own hubris and teaching him humility.

The outline of the creative process is this: after a period of **purification**, the adept enters a **synagogue** and there molds a humanoid form from unploughed mountain **earth** and living **water**. He then animates each limb by means of **tzeruf**, combining the **Tetragrammaton** with a series of 221 or 231 permutations of the Hebrew alphabet, as described in **Sefer Yetzirah**. It is not clear whether the permutations are simply spoken or actually written on the limbs. One method also requires a circle **dance** be performed around the inert form of the creature (B. Sanh. 38b; Gen. R. 24:2; PR 23:2; MhG 96; Pseudo-Sa'adia). This procedure is meant to mimic the Midrashic description of how God created **Adam**.

1. Idel, *The Golem*, 54–72.

Goliath: Goliath of Gath was a biblical **giant** exceeding nine feet in height. He was probably killed by the youthful **David** using a sling. The word "probably" is necessary because the **Bible** itself gives contradictory testimony as to whether David actually did this feat (II Sam. 21:19). Although ostensibly a Philistine, he is identified as one of the *Refaim*, a race of biblical giants who were the descendants of **fallen angels**. According to the Sages, David and Goliath were related, for Goliath was the child of Orpah, the sister of Ruth, who was David's great-grandmother. Orpah bore three other giants besides Goliath (Mid. Tanh., Vayigash 8). David used occult powers to overcome him, striking him first with the **evil eye**. An **angel** then helped the diminutive David by smothering Goliath's face in the ground after the boy toppled him with the sling stone (Lev. R. 21). Goliath had a giant brother, **Ishbi-benob**, who was slain by one of David's warriors.

Goral: "Lots." *SEE* LOTS.

Goralot, Sefer ha-: "Book of Lots." A late medieval book of demonology and spirit possession.

Grapes: *SEE* FRUIT.

Grass: Every blade of grass has its own angel who compels it to grow (Mid. Konen 2:24). Mourners at a funeral throw grass over their shoulders as they leave the grave to signal to the spirit of the dead person that it is to remain with the body for now. *SEE* ANGELS; BURIAL; DEATH; GHOST; MEMUNEH.

Graves: *SEE* BURIAL; CEMETERY.

Great Name, Book of: Modern title given to an anonymous text of **Hechalot literature**. It has sometimes been published as part of **Hechalot Rabbati**.

Green: *SEE* COLOR.

Grinder: (*Shechakim*). Third of the **seven heavens**. From this level of heaven comes the **manna** and all other miraculous sustenance (Chag. 12b).

Guardian Angels: There are **angels** who oversee nations and individuals. According to the Midrash, the angels Jacob witnessed ascending and descending were the changing watches of guardian angels (Gen. 28:12). Every person has two such angels watching over him or her, one who assists when the person strives to do right, the other who clears the way if the person chooses to pursue sin (TdE 3:4). The most famous of these are the two angels that escort each person on the **Sabbath**, but there are many varied traditions about the role of angels in the life of individuals (Tan. 11a; Chag. 16a; Shab. 119b; Sefer ha-Gilgulim 1). *SEE* NATIONS.

Guf ha-Briyot: "The Body/Vessel of Creatures." Souls are said to originate in a celestial reservoir called the *Guf*, from which they enter the earthly realms in order to animate bodies. The **Messiah** will not come until the Guf has been emptied of all its souls (Yev. 62a). After death, these souls return to the spiritual realms and are deposited in the *Otzar* or **Tzror ha-Chayyim**, the Treasury of Souls, which is beneath the **Throne of Glory**. (A.Z. 5a; Ned. 13b; Shab. 152a; PR 2:3; Bahir 126; Zohar I: 119a).

Guf ha-Dak: "Sheer body." This is the Kabbalistic concept, also called the *tzelem*, of a containing field that surrounds the soul after it has separated from the physical body; it is the physical body as it is manifest on spiritual planes. Different from an aura, this is the body the soul dwells in while it resides in **Eden** and/or **Gehenna** (Zohar I: 7a, I: 224a–b, II: 11a; Seder Gan Eden). It conforms to the contours of the physical human shape.

Gufei Torah: "Embodiments of Torah." At first used as an expression for "the essential teachings" of the **Torah**, in mystical parlance *gufei Torah* refers to the "external" or obvious aspects of the Torah—its laws, narratives, and plain meanings. This is in contrast to the "soul" of the Torah, which refers its esoteric interpretations (Zohar I).

Guidance, the Book of: (Arabic, *Kativ Alahudah*). A magical handbook, written in a mix of Hebrew, Aramaic, and Arabic, found in the **Cairo Geniza** (T-S K 1.143). It contains many magical formulae, including spells for **love**, **divination**, influence, **healing**, **birth**, subduing **demons**, and **amulet** making.

H

Note: The Hebrew letters *Chet* and *Chaf* are often transliterated into English as "H." Thus one frequently finds transliterated words like "Halom." This encyclopedia transliterates these letters as "Ch," resulting in spellings like "Chalom." Thus some words the reader is seeking in this chapter will appear under the heading "C."

Habakkuk: The biblical prophet was the boy whom **Elisha** miraculously resurrected (Zohar I: 7b). He was a master of esoteric knowledge (Mid. Teh. 7:17, 77:1; Bahir 46–47).

Habitation: (*Zabul*). Fifth of the **seven heavens**. In it exists the heavenly **Jerusalem** and **Temple**. **Michael** is both the angelic Prince and High Priest of this precinct (Chag. 12b).

Habraham (Abraham) the Jew: A 15th-century French alchemist and author of *Livre des Figures Hieroglifiques*, "The Book of Hieroglyphic Figures." It is unclear whether Habraham was an observant Jew, a convert to **Christianity**, or simply a pseudonym for an anonymous alchemist who wished to give his writings greater gravitas by linking them with the Jewish occult. *SEE* ALCHEMY.

Hadraniel: "Acclaim of God." An angelic guard who first challenged, then guided, Moses in his ascent into heaven (PR 20; Zohar II: 258a). Lightning springs from his mouth (BhM I: 59). He also appeared to Adam to caution him about revealing the secrets of a book of power, either **Sefer Raziel** or the **lost book** of Adam (Zohar I: 55b).

Hadriel: "God is my Glory." A **punishing angel** of **Gehenna**.

Hafuch: "Turn [around]." A word or phrase revealed by rearranging the letters of another word; an anagram. For example, *Mishnah* (the Oral Traditions of the Torah) can be rearranged to spell *nishama* (soul), teaching that learning the Oral Torah is the key to **Eternal Life**. Perhaps the earliest recognized anagram is in the name *Noach*, (Noah), which not only means "comfort," but when its Hebrew spelling is reversed (*chet-nun*), it means "grace," both themes central to the **Noah** saga.

By Talmudic times, finding an anagram in a word was an accepted hermeneutic strategy for reading Scripture. It also became a feature in medieval poetry. Anagrams appear frequently in Kabbalistic thought and can also be referred to as **temurah**. Thus in Lurianic systems, the **names of God** are combined and recombined into meditative phrases. *SEE* ABBREVIATION; ENCRYPTION; GEMATRIA.

Hagar: The handmaiden of **Sarah** (Gen. 16–22). She encountered an **angel** after she was expelled out of Abraham's encampment. According to the **Midrash**, she and Abraham were reunited at Sarah's death, for the Rabbis identify her with the woman named **Keturah** mentioned in Genesis 22. *SEE* ABRAHAM.

Hail: (*Barad*). Hail is emblematic of divine punishment. It emanates from storehouses in the heavenly abode of **Depository**. Different texts identify either Yurkami or

Baradiel as the Prince of Hail. The hail which fell as a plague upon Egypt was a "miracle within a miracle," being ice of burning **fire** that neither **water** quenched nor heat evaporated. In **Gehenna**, it hails continuously half the year (Ex. R. 51:7). *SEE* RAIN; SEVEN HEAVENS; WATER.

Hair: (*Se'ar*). Hair is a symbol and source of power in Jewish tradition.

Based on the image of the lover in Song of Songs (chapter 5), which is interpreted as an allegorical description of God, God is often referred to as having "hair" or "locks." The **dew** of **resurrection** clings to God's hair; one day God will shake it off, reviving all the dead (PdRE 34; Shab. 88b).

The description found in Daniel of God as **Atika Yomim**, the Holy Ancient One, also elevates the symbolic importance of beards. God has thirteen "curls" in His divine beard, representing the thirteen merciful attributes (Zohar III: 289b). These curls are the conduits by which those qualities flow into Creation (Likutei Torah). Some sources identify the **Zer Anpin** first described in the **Bahir** as "God's beard." **Moses Cordovero** spoke of the "mystery of the beard."

For mortals, hair symbolizes identity, compassion, and vanity. In the case of men, it conveys virility and strength. The **Bible** forbids Israelite men to "round" the corners of their hair (Lev. 19). Most interpret this to mean men should remain bearded, though others see it as requiring lengths of uncut hair, known as *payot*.

Nazirites, biblical devotees who desired a higher level of commitment to God, could not cut their hair at all (Num. 6:1–21). **Samuel** and **Samson** are two examples of biblical Nazirites. In the Samson narrative, of course, his hair was the reservoir of his supernatural strength (Judg. 16). In Jewish folk custom, the hair of a male child is not cut for the first three years of life, evidently with the idea that it gives the vulnerable child an added measure of protection, and is then only cut for the first time in a ritual, preferably at a place of power, like the tomb of a saintly person. Many Chasids consider the side curls and beard to be so important that they are ready to be martyred rather than allow theirs to be cut.

A woman's hair is also a source of potency, but in a different way. It is seen as the most visible sign of her sexual power, and therefore must be concealed from all but her husband after marriage (Ket. 2:1; Ber. 24a). Thus the image of **women** with unbound hair becomes a stereotype for wantonness and danger. In medieval tradition, **vampires** have the power to fly once they release their hair.

The **Zohar** uses hair in the practice of **physiognomy** and regards hair to be a reflection on personal disposition and character (Zohar II: 70b–71a). Borrowing from Greco-Roman practice, hair could be used as an ingredient of magical formulae. The most fearsome example of such use would be a **curse**, or binding ritual, which would require a lock of the victim's hair. Therefore, the proper disposal of hair is critically important.

Ha'itmari, Elijah: Rabbi and exorcist (Turkish, ca. 18th century). This rabbi-spiritualist interviewed a poltergeist who revealed many secrets of the spirit world to him (Midrash Talpiyot).

Ham: One of the sons of **Noah**. According to the Midrash, Noah cursed him after Ham and his brother Canaan either castrated or sodomized their father (Sanh. 70a; Gen. R. 36). *SEE* SEX.

Haman: Advisor to the Persian king Ahasuerus and villain of the book of **Esther**. As a descendant of the Amalekite King Agag, he was possessed by a metaphysically rooted hatred of Jews, leading him to seek the extermination of the Jews of Persia. According to the Midrash, he was an astrologer who selected **Adar** as the month for the massacre because no Jewish holiday fell in that month to grant the Jews protective good fortune. **Angels** nevertheless helped trip him up in the disastrous (for him) wine party with Queen Esther. When his plan failed, he was sentenced by King Ahasuerus to hang, but of all the **trees** in the world, only the reviled thorn tree would allow him to be hung from its branches. *SEE* ASTROLOGY; LOTS.

Hamnuna Sava, Rav: In **Talmud**, he is merely another of the Sages. According to the **Zohar**, on the other hand, he is a heavenly being who descends to earth disguised as a humble ass-driver and reveals secrets of the Torah to righteous initiates prepared to hear his wisdom. He is evidently the offspring of a monstrous sea creature, perhaps **Leviathan** (I: 5a–7a). He dwelt in heaven until sent to earth, where he is fated to walk until the coming of the Messiah, when he will serve as the Messiah's footman. He is the author of a **lost book**, *Sefer Hamnuna Sava*, which is cited several times in the Zohar (II: 146a–b). *SEE* SAR HA-TORAH.

Hamsa or Chamsa: (Aramaic, "Five"). A hand-shaped **amulet**. *SEE* HAND.

Hamshakhah: "Drawing down." *Hamshakhah* is tapping into the divine effluence of the **sefirot** for theurgic purposes through the performance of a Jewish ritual, especially through the act of reciting a statutory blessing over a person or phenomenon (Ginnat Egoz; Pardes Rimmonim). Unleashing this theurgic power in a Jewish rite is usually a matter of **kavanah**, of bringing the right state of mind to the **ritual**.[1] *SEE* THEURGY.

1. Idel, *Hasidism*, 71.

Hand: The hand is a symbol of strength and action. The **Bible** speaks of both the hand and fingers of God, though most readers understand that to be figurative language. Still, the hand is a symbol of godly potential. God's right hand is the manifestation of divine power (Deut. 33:2; Pss. 118, 139). When God's hand is extended in love, it is the source of deliverance, protections, and revelation (Ex. 6:6, 33:22). Once the Egyptians had experienced the ten plagues, Pharaoh's counselors declared it the "finger of God." The Sages take this to mean that when God's entire "hand" is raised against the wicked, fifty plagues are unleashed against them.

Even the number of fingers and joints in the hand conceal secrets of the divine nature (Zohar I). According to **Pirkei de-Rabbi Eliezer**, **Adam** and **Eve** were initially protected by a skin made of nail, which disappeared when the first couple sinned, leaving them naked (14).

Ritual **immersion** of the hands before eating is a fixed rabbinic practice, but in the Zohar it takes on metaphysical consequences: those who fail to wash allow the **evil eye** or **unclean spirits** an opening, while washing elevates one to the status of an **angel**, with all the protection that entails.

Many Jewish communities arrange the fingers of a corpse awaiting burial to resemble Hebrew letters that appear in the **names of God**.

Magical uses of the fingers and hand include both rituals and signs to be used against the evil eye. For example, squeezing the thumb with the opposing hand is a prophylactic act (Ber. 55b). While **chiromancy** is described in the **Dead Sea Scrolls** and the **Zohar**, palm reading such as is familiar to us today is a form of **divination** mostly derived from non-Jewish sources, but is given credence in some later writings (Nishmat Chayyim III, Ma'aseh Book).

The **Chamsa**, a representation of an open hand, is one of the most ancient of Jewish **amulets**. It is sometimes called the "hand of Miriam" (among Jews) or the "hand of Fatima" (among Muslims). These amulets often incorporate other protective devices, such as verses of Scripture in **microscript** and/or **eyes** embedded in the palm. *SEE* FINGERS.

Hanganot: "[Spiritual] Practices." Special spiritual and devotional practices, above and beyond the usual requirements of Jewish tradition, that are taken on by an individual for the purposes of cultivating a higher consciousness.

Hanganot Tzadikim: This book contains the collected **hanganot** of the spiritual giants of **Chasidism**.

Harp of David: David is known as "the sweet singer of Israel" and there are several legends concerning his harp or lyre. With it, he temporarily exorcised Saul's evil spirit (I Samuel). It would play by itself each **midnight**, rousing David to pray and compose (PdRE 21). The strings of the harp were reputed to be made from the sinews of the **ram** that **Abraham** sacrificed on **Mount Moriah**. (Ber. 3b; EY). As a sign of eschatological hope, it is taught that this harp, symbolizing God's promises to Abraham, will be played by **David**, progenitor of the **Messiah**, at the **resurrection** to awaken the dead. *SEE* DAVID; MUSIC.

Hashbaah: "Swearing/Adjuration." A magical adjuration, usually for protection, often recited at **Havdalah**, when the week is beginning.[1] *SEE* INCANTATIONS; LECH-ISHAH; SEGULLAH.

1. Ginsburg, *The Sabbath in Classical Kabbalah*, 11.

Hate Spell: A particular type of **curse** that creates enmity between two people targeted by the adept. Evidently these curses were used to undermine rivals, particularly rivals for love. If one could create hostility between a rival and the person the practitioner desired, this would be advantageous. One can think of it as a kind of aversion-conditioning love spell. The few examples found in Hebrew magical texts (**Sefer ha–Razim**; **Cairo Geniza** fragments) are by and large identical to such spells appearing in Greco-Roman magical spell books, so the technique may well have been borrowed. *SEE* CAIRO GENIZA; GREEK PAPYRI; INCANTATION; LOVE.

Havdalah: "Separation." A ceremony performed to mark the end of the **Sabbath** at sunset on Saturday. It involves a cup of **wine**, inhaling aromatic spices, and a candle that is extinguished in the wine to mark the end of the holiday. The origins of the ritual are said to go back to **Adam** who, experiencing terror at the first sunset, received from God the gift of **fire**, over which Adam uttered the first blessing. The **Messiah** will first appear at Havdalah.

As the end of Shabbat and the beginning of the week, Havdalah is a time of transition, an ideal time to utter supplications and incantations for protection, healing, and good fortune (Havdalah de Rabbi Akiva).[1] Young women who gaze at the **light** of the havdalah candle reflected in their wetted fingernails can see the face of their future husband. Touching those same hands to the eyelids brings good luck. Allowing the candle to burn down entirely before extinguishing ensures a good spouse for a daughter. Wine used in havdalah can heal ocular ailments (Mid. Teh. Ps. 32). Sprinkling the wine on the table ensures a week of bounty. It can also have detrimental effects if abused. *SEE* RITUAL.

1. Ginsburg, *The Sabbath in Classical Kabbalah*, 257–63. Also see Kanarfogel, *Peering through the Lattices*.

Havdalah de-Rabbi Akiva: A guide to theurgic ritual to be used during the **Havdalah** ceremony, it contains angel-invoking anti-demonic spells similar to those found on **incantation bowls**.

Hay: The fifth letter in the **Hebrew alphabet**. It has the numeric value of 5. It is one of the three letters that form the **Tetragrammaton**. According to **Kabbalah**, God created the earth with the letter *hay*. When God changed Abram's name to Abraham by adding a *hay*, it signified that the world was created for the sake of Abraham coming into it (Zohar, Pinchas). Similar name changes occur for Sarah and Joshua.[1]

1. Munk, *The Wisdom of the Hebrew Alphabet*, 85–93.

Head: *SEE* FACE; FACE OF GOD; PHYSIOGNOMY.

Healing: (*Refuah*). "Whatever is effective as a remedy is not witchcraft" (Shab. 67a). Preventing and curing illness and disease is a universal human preoccupation. Jews have been tremendously influential in the history of Western medicine and their reputation as formidable healers reaches back into classical antiquity.

In the **Bible**, God is the most often identified source for disease and healing (Ex. 15:26), and the most common cause for God sending disease is sin (Deut. 28:27). God flatly declares, "I wound and I heal" (Deut. 32:40). It would have been logical, therefore, to conclude that human medicine and healing are actually contravening the divine will.

Jewish tradition does not accept this line of argument, however (Shab. 82b), and instead argues that the human attempts at healing are analogous to the human cultivation of the earth: a necessary activity if human life is to thrive (Midrash Samuel). The appropriateness of healing incantations is also debated, one side arguing that a variety of healing practices are *de facto* magic prohibited by the Torah, while others permit any remedy meant for healing or the protection of health (Hor. 13b; Shab. 67a–67b; Tos. Shab.7:21; J. Shab. 6:9). Just as Jews believed that illness can have supernatural origins, it can likewise be treated via magical, theurgic, and other supernatural means. In practice, all this has meant that **amulets**, spells, exorcisms, and potions were a regular part of the healer's arsenal of treatments.

In the **Dead Sea Scrolls**, evil spirits are regarded as the source of many illnesses, an idea that finds parallels in the Gospel accounts of Jesus's healing ministries. Among the Dead Sea Scrolls, there exists a fragmentary text (4Q560) that is a collection of protective formulae for fending off demonic attack. Specifically, it deals with protection against fevers, tuberculosis, chest pain, and the dangers of childbirth. Other texts (4Q510–11; 11Q11) deal with the binding of disease-causing **demons**.

In rabbinic writings the word for epilepsy, *nikhpeh*, means to be "possessed." Exorcizing spells are therefore included along with other treatments. The **Talmud** regards demons as the cause of ocular diseases, food poisoning, and other ailments (Pes. 111b–112a). **Witchcraft**, spiritual attack by another human being, was also an accepted explanation for disease. In the Talmud an opinion is recorded that "ninety-nine out of a hundred die from an **evil eye**" (B. M. 107b).

Jewish literature preserves a vast list of theurgic and magical methods of healing illnesses, whether or not such illnesses are ascribed to attack by evil spirits. Along with conventional folk remedies involving diet, curative **food**s (Git. 67b; Eruv. 29b; Git. 69a–70a; A.Z. 28a–b; Ket. 50a; Yoma 83b–84a), exercise and healthful practices, the Sages would prescribe the recitation of Scriptural verses (Deut. 6:4 [the Sh'ma], or Ps. 29, for example) and **incantations**, called *refuot* (healings). Talmud Shabbat 66b–67a and Gittin 67a–69a record examples of such healing incantations.

The very act of studying Torah serves as a treatment for illness, according to Rabbi **Joshua ben Levi** (Eruv. 54a). Rabbi Judah declares sacred study "a drug for the entire body."

Angels, or in a few cases demons, could be invoked to effect a recovery (Shab. 67b; Sanh. 101a). Tractate Shabbat lists the names of the healing angels: Bazbaziah, Masmasiah, Kaskasiah, Sharlai and Armarlai. Demons, presumably the sources of a given affliction, could be summoned in order that they might be adjured, bound, and/or exorcised.

Amulets and talismans were frequently used both as preventatives and as remedies (Shab. 67a), though again, some Sages strongly disapproved of such devices. Tractate Shabbat discusses whether one may go in public on the Sabbath with healing charms (one is permitted only to carry a limited number of things on the day of rest), including locust eggs (for an earache), **fox** tooth (for sleep disorders), or a nail from a gallows (for an inflammation).

Items imbued with *kedushah*, spiritual power, such as leftover **wine** from holiday **Kiddush**, or **olive oil** blessed for use in a Chanukah **menorah**, were also felt to have extra medicinal power. This also raises the point that particular foods and **herbs** were often suggested to counteract illnesses. In rare instances, this even included nonkosher meats. Mishnah Yoma 8 sets the precedent that nonkosher food

may be consumed if it has a medicinal purpose. Examples are given in the commentary to that Mishnah (Yoma 84a) of treatments that include donkey flesh (for jaundice) or dog liver (for rabies).

In the Talmudic age, remedies were mostly based on the principle of *similia similibus curantur*, using natural materials and treatments that seemed to have some analogous/symbolic association with an illness. An example of this homeopathic approach would be using parts of a bush—think of "burning" bush—to obtain a cure for a fever (Ket. 50a; Git. 69a; Shab. 67a).

This use of material chosen for its "logical" suitability as a treatment dominates in both early Jewish medicinal and magical texts. Occasionally, rabbinic literature will describe a medicinal recipe containing noxious ingredients, such as animal **excrement**, **earth** from a grave, or gall. Poultices, curative broths, and topical mixtures, again frequently crafted from the most unlikely materials, were also common (Git. 68b–69a).

Cupping and bloodletting, well-established traditional treatments of antiquity, continued to enjoy favor, even though the **Talmud** itself expresses serious doubts about the efficacy of the former.

Faith healing—the belief that certain people had the power to heal residing in their touch—also appears in a famous passage in Tractate Berachot. Two Rabbis in particular, **Chiyya** and **Yochanan**, were famous for having this healing power (Ber. 5b).

The **synagogue** of antiquity was not only a place of sacred assembly, but also a center for healing. Some early Church Fathers railed bitterly because their congregants were entering Jewish places of worship in search of treatment for their ailments. These complaints were often accompanied by accusations of Jewish **sorcery**, which suggests that various forms of spiritual and/or magical healing were common practice.[1]

By the medieval period, Jewish medicine was increasingly based on naturalistic premises, which is to say that Jews were educated in the Galenic principles of the "four humors" as etiological theory and as a diagnostic tool. Treatments that were more empirically grounded, as opposed to magical and homeopathic, were becoming a larger part of medical practice. In fact, Jews became famous and sought-after as practitioners of scholarly Greek-style healing. Still, whether provided by folk healers or scholastic healers, most medicine continued to be based on a hodgepodge of natural and supernatural assumptions and a mélange of natural and magical treatment regimes.[2]

Jews were enthusiastic in applying the Arab elaborations on the Greek methods of medicine during the Middle Ages and began making their own unique contributions using the new methods. Outstanding Jewish physicians, like the philosopher Maimonides, championed naturalistic theories of disease etiology and treatment over more fantastic traditional assumptions.

Jews embraced the subsequent scientific revolutions in medicine and as a result, traditional folk healing has been pushed to the periphery of Jewish life in recent centuries. Now it is mostly the domain of communities who resist the influences of modernity, such as the Chasids, or among Oriental Jewish communities who are still only a generation or two away from more traditional folkways. Interest in non-Western healing methods, however, is on the rise, and many Jews are re-incorporating traditional Jewish healing practices of prayer, healing touch, and herbal medicine into their treatment. SEE PHARMACOPOEIA; SEGULLAH.

1. Levine, *The Ancient Synagogue*, 274.
2. Ruderman, *Kabbalah, Magic, and Science*, 26–34. Also see Zimmel, *Magicians, Theologians, and Doctors*.

Heart: (*Lev*). In Hebrew thought, the heart is the seat of intelligence rather than emotion. It also symbolizes harmony and the center. The **Holy of Holies** was called the *lev ha-olam*, the "heart of the world." Israel is described as the "heart" of humanity, while the other peoples are the limbs (Ha-Kuzari). Surprisingly little esoteric or paranormal teachings about the heart are found in Judaism, aside from the Zoharic idea that **Tiferet** is the "heart" of the **sefirot**. SEE BODY.

Heaven: (*Shamayim*). The abode of God and God's celestial court. Sometimes, but not always, it is thought also to be the place of Gan **Eden**, the afterlife abode of the righteous dead.

The notion that the heavens are structured into a hierarchy of seven compartments is a common belief in classical and late antiquity. It may have its roots in the seven obvious heavenly structures: the moon, the sun, the planets visible to the naked eye, and the stars, though Jewish descriptions of the seven layers do not generally conform to this purely astronomical scheme of the heavens. Thus in Jewish writings, the planets and stars are generally confined to a single level. Rather, Jewish traditions of the heavenly hierarchy are based on either angelology—segmenting the heavens according the class of angel that inhabits it—or parsing it according to the many unseen heavenly functions and phenomena, like the sources of precipitation, the abodes of the dead, and the celestial residences.[1]

The idea of heaven being divided into seven precincts first figures in the **Apocrypha** and in the sectarian writings of the **Dead Sea Scrolls**, especially in the work **Songs of the Sabbath Sacrifice**. The names of the seven heavens that are given in **Talmud** are **Vilon**, **Rakia**, **Shachakim**, **Zevul**, **Maon**, **Machon**, and **Aravot** (Chag. 12b; AdRN 37). Each level is separated from the other by a distance of five hundred years (Gedulat Moshe).

Re'uyot Yehezkel, an early work of **Hechalot literature**, offers its own list: *Shamayim, Shemei Shamayim, Zevul, Arafel, Shachakim, Aravot,* and *Kisse ha-Kavod*. Yet another list gives the following seven with one add-on: *Rakia, Shemei ha-Shamayim, Zevul, Arafel, Shachakim, Machon, Aravot,* and *Kisse ha-Kavod*. According to this text, the eighth heaven is where God abides while not sitting on the **Throne of Glory** in the seventh palace/heaven. In one aggadah, there are actually seven chariot/thrones, one in each level.

In the Zohar, the seven heavens are equated with the lower seven **sefirot** (Zohar I: 32b, 86a). SEE PALACE.

1. Elior, *The Three Temples*, 77–78.

Heavenly Academy: SEE YESHIVA SHEL MALAH.

Heavy Clouds: (*Aravot*). The highest of the **seven heavens**, it is the location of the **Throne of Glory** and the **host of heaven**. It is the storehouse for righteousness, justice and mercy, as well as the treasures of life, peace and blessing. It also contains the Treasury of Souls yet to be born (Chag. 12b–13a; EY).

Hebrew and Hebrew Alphabet: Called the *Lashon Kodesh*, "the Holy Tongue," Hebrew is a supernal **language**, the language of heaven. One Sage goes so far as to say that angels do not recognize prayers said in other tongues (Shab.

12b). Hebrew is the language of theurgic power par excellence. The first key to the power of the language, Jewish mystics teach, lies in the Hebrew alphabet.[1]

The Hebrew alphabet consists of twenty-two letters, all of them consonants (an additional system of vowel symbols was adopted in the Middle Ages). The Hebrew letters have always been accorded special power because God brought the universe into existence through a speech-act (Gen. 1; Ps. 33:6). In the **Bible**, adding or changing even a letter to a person's name had the power to change their destiny (Gen. 17:5, 35:15).

According to the **Talmud**, not only did God create the world using the letters, but **Bezalel** was selected to build the **Tabernacle**, which was a microcosm of the universe (Num. R. 12:13), precisely because he also knew how to manipulate the alphabet (Ber. 55a; Tanh., Bereshit 5). Many other passages find supernal meaning in the alphabet and even in the shape of its letters (Gen. R. 1:10; Tanh., Bereshit 11). One legend, in which the letters of the Ten Commandments reportedly fly back to heaven when Moses destroys the tablet, illustrates the divine nature of these characters (Pes. 87b).

Sefer Yetzirah further explores the ideas about the supernal nature of language that are found in Talmud. Possibly influenced by Pythagorean mysticism, it teaches that the alphabet, along with the decimal base numbers, are the very building blocks of Creation and that mastery of their esoteric power allows the initiate to likewise create new realities, even animate matter. The esoteric significance of letters is the major concern of several other early mystical texts, such as **Shi'ur Qomah** and **III Enoch** and continues as an ongoing feature of Kabbalistic writings.[2] In the **Zohar**, the Hebrew alphabet is equated with **Shekhinah**. Out of this, an exalted "word mysticism" emerges:

> "Just as there are twenty-two letters of the Torah and prayer, so there are twenty-two letters in all the existent things of matter and body, because the world was created by their means . . . but the letters are clothed in matter . . . and within the letters, there the spiritual force of the Holy One, blessed be He, is dwelling . . ." (Toldot Yaakov Yosef).

In other words, letters are not just instruments, but actual forms of the divine. The unique sanctity and power of the Hebrew alphabet becomes a basis for defending the custom of prayer in Hebrew, even though Jewish law permits prayers to be recited in any language. For the same reason, Hebrew letters are considered important vehicles for **meditation**. Combining the idea of the alphabet as cosmic building blocks with the belief that each human is a **microcosm**, **Chasidism** teaches that every person is made up of the twenty-two letters. Given this reality, when properly "arranged," a person becomes a *logos*, an embodiment of God's word (Sefat Emet, Ekev). SEE SPEECH. *(SEE ALSO APPENDIX, FIGURES 1 AND 5.)*

1. Idel, *Hasidism*, 65, 70, 156–57. Also see Lauterbach, "The Belief in the Power of the Word."
2. Janowitz, *Icons of Power*, 33–61.

Hechalot Literature: "Palaces/temples." The first distinctly mystical movement in Jewish history, **Ma'asei Merkavah**, appeared in the late Greco-Roman period. The Hechalot writings are the literary artifacts of that movement. The central elements of all Hechalot writings are accounts of mystical ascents into heaven, divine visions, and the **summoning** and control of angels, usually for the purpose of gaining insight into Torah. The *loci classicus* for these practices is the Chariot vision of Ezekiel (chapter 1) and the Temple vision of Isaiah (chapter 6). It is from this, and from the many extracanonical **apocalyptic writings** of heavenly visitations, that Hechalot literature emerges.

The title, "Hechalot," derives from the divine abodes seen by the practitioner. In their visions, these mystics would ecstatically project themselves into the higher realms and journey through the seven stages of mystical ascent: the **seven heavens** and seven throne rooms.

Such a journey is fraught with great danger, and the adept must not only have made elaborate **purification** preparation, but must also know the proper **incantations**, **seals**, and angelic **names** needed to get past the celestial guards, as well as know how to navigate the various forces at work inside and outside the palaces.

The literature sometimes includes fantastic and baffling descriptions of the precincts of heaven and its awesome denizens. The highly literal and overly explicit images of heavenly objects and their numbers (". . . four thousands of thousand of fiery chariots and ten thousand fiery torches amidst them . . .") common to this literature are actually meant, *reductio ad absurdum*, to convey the truly ineffable nature of the ecstatic experience.

At times, heavenly interlocutors will reveal secrets of the **Torah**. In some texts, the mystic's interest centers on the heavenly **music** and liturgy, usually connected with the angelic adorations mentioned in Isaiah 6:3. Both those who wrote Hechalot texts and those who later used them in their ascents would describe the music and prayer language they heard while in the heavens. The mantralike repetitive nature of many of these compositions seems meant to encourage further ascent.

Literary works that have survived in whole or in part include **Hechalot Rabbati, Hechalot Zutarti, III Enoch, Ma'aseh Merkavah, Massechet Hechalot, Chatom ha-Merkavah, Otiyyot Rabbi Akiba**, and possibly **Re'uyot Yehezkel**. In addition, there are many fragmentary manuscripts that seem to belong to this genre, along with some magical texts, but the exact relationship of such texts to Ma'asei Merkavah mysticism and to each other is often not clear. *SEE* PALACE.

Hechalot Rabbati: "The Greater Palaces." This is perhaps the most intact surviving document of **Merkavah Mysticism**. This work describes the methods and experiences of ascending into the **seven heavens**. The work gives a detailed account of the perilous progress of a living soul negotiating its way through heaven, including descriptions of the angelic guards and how to get past them, the many hazards, and what one could expect to see. In this work, the princely angel **Anafiel** serves as the guide to Rabbi **Ishmael ben Elisha**, the narrator and presumed author. Hechalot Rabbati concludes with an apocalypse in which heavenly mysteries are revealed. Some versions have an additional material on the **Sar Ha-Torah** appended. This book has been highly influential in some branches of Jewish mysticism, particularly on the **German Pietists** and on the Spanish Kabbalist, **Joseph Gikatilla**. *SEE* BOOKS OF ENOCH; III ENOCH; HECHALOT LITERATURE.

Hechalot, Sefer: Alternate name for **III Enoch**. *SEE* ENOCH, BOOKS OF.

Hechalot Zutarti: "The Lesser Palaces." A work of **Merkavah Mysticism** that has survived only as manuscript fragments and quotations found in other writings. Its major theme is expounding on the account of the **Four Sages**. *SEE* HECHALOT LITERATURE.

Helios: The Greco-Roman god of the sun makes several surprising appearances in Jewish contexts. Most notably, he is clearly represented at the center of a mosaic **zodiac** on the floor of the Beta Alfa synagogue, an excavated Byzantine synagogue in northern Israel. Just as puzzling, Helios is included in adjuration texts that appear to be part of the **Hechalot** corpus, most famously in **Sefer ha-Razim**. Scholars are divided on what the presence of Helios means. Some argue this indicates that the Jewish communities that produced these were out-and-out syncretistic polytheists, fusing the worship of the God of Israel with Roman paganism. Other scholars, perhaps the majority, think these references to Helios signal a kind of tolerant Jewish "inclusive monotheism," prevalent in late antiquity, in which pagan deities are demoted to the status of **angels**, but are still counted as parts of the **host of heaven**.

Hephzibah: The mother of the eschatological Messiah. Mentioned only in **Sefer Zerubbabel**, she is credited with playing a significant role at the end of times (beyond giving birth to the Messiah). A messianic warrior in her own right, she will slay two kings by wielding the wondrous **rod** of Aaron.

Herbs and Vegetables: As in most world cultures, Jews have used herbs for far more than dietary supplements and flavoring. Selected herbs are common ingredients in medicines, potions, and poultices (Pes. 42b; J. A.Z. 2:2). Medicinal uses for herbs found in the **Talmud** include the following:

Asparagus: beer or broth made from it is beneficial to both heart and eyes

Bitter vetch: good for the bowels

Black cumin: eases chest pain

Dates: for hemorrhoids and constipation

Radishes and lettuce: aid digestion

Small cucumbers: laxative

Garlic: improves virility, increases circulation, and kills intestinal parasites

Milt: for teeth

Lentils: prevent croup

Mustard and asparagus: general preventatives

Beets and onions: good for general healing

In addition to these, some herbs were thought to have influence over supernatural forces. Fennel, for example, was prized for driving away evil spirits. Jewish magical texts of antiquity, like their Greco-Roman counterparts, used herbs in magical concoctions (Sefer ha-Razim). Mandrake has been an ingredient in love potions since biblical times (Gen. 30).

While most modern Jews no longer look to the herbal healing methods of their ancestors, there is a renewed interest in the topic, and some herbal treatments are enjoying a revival. SEE FOODS; HEALING; PHARMACOPOEIA.

Hermes, the Books of: A collection of forty-two books attributed to either Hermes/Thoth, the Greek God, or Hermes Trismegistus, the mythic founder of the discipline of **alchemy**. Most, if not all, of the books so identified were actually composed by anonymous theurgists, mystery cultists and mystics, some of which may have been Egyptian Jews.[1] SEE ALCHEMY.

1. Patai, *The Jewish Alchemists*, 403.

Heschel of Opatov, Abraham Joshua: Chasidic master (Russian, ca. 18th–19th century). Rabbi Joshua was a noted Chasidic Kabbalist who taught the doctrines of **reincarnation** and regarded himself to have been reincarnated several times, including one incarnation as a High Priest of ancient Israel.

Hexagram: Six-angled or six-cornered shapes are used throughout the world as a talisman against evil. In Judaism, the six-pointed **Magen David** is the religion's most distinctive modern symbol and a frequent seal incorporated into protective **amulets**. SEE SEAL, MAGICAL. (SEE ALSO APPENDIX FIGURE *4*.)

Hezekiah: King of Judah of the Davidic Dynasty (726–697 BCE). One of the few kings to earn God's favor, Hezekiah enjoyed the counsel of the prophet Isaiah and merited a miraculous deliverance from the Assyrian armies of Sennacherib, which were smitten by angelic forces (II Kings 17).

Hezyonot, Sefer ha-: "The Book of Visions." A kind of spiritual memoir and dream diary of **Chayyim Vital**, it contains some of Luria's teachings on **reincarnation**, along with Vital's accounts of ghostly **possession**, his personal visions, psychic experiences, encounters with mantics, and other mystical phenomena.

Hillel Baal Shem: (Russian, early 18th century). An itinerant folk healer and amulet maker. He is the author of the magical manuscript, Sefer ha-Cheshek.

Hiner Bet: A deathlike trance state. Certain people would be seized by a *hiner bet*, only to awaken with occult knowledge about the sins and transgressions of neighbors in the community. Demons and punishing spirits were assumed to be the source of this secret knowledge (Sefer ha-Hezyonot, ShB 20).[1]

1. Ben Amos and Mintz, *In Praise of the Baal Shem Tov*, 34–35; Goldish, *Spirit Possession in Judaism*, 259–261.

Hiram: King of Tyre (ca. 7th century BCE), he is not to be confused with the donor/architect of the same name who constructed Solomon's **Temple**. He is condemned by Ezekiel for claiming to be god. Yet according to the Sages, the King Hiram of Solomon's time and the King Hiram of the 7th century condemned in Scriptures were in fact one and the same.

According to **Midrash**, God had granted him exceptionally long life, but this only led the king to think of himself as a deity. In time his hubris drove him to build a fabulous structure upon the sea, an inverted pyramid, which he dubbed the **seven heavens**. God's punishment for his arrogance was that he was overthrown by his own son-in-law, Nebuchadnezzar, who then forced Hiram to eat pieces of his own flesh until he died. The structure he built, on the other hand, was drawn intact down into the sea and will re-emerge in the Messianic Age. Another legend tells of him being brought alive into heaven like Elijah, only to be expelled into **Gehenna** after he showed the poor judgment to declare himself a god once he got there (Gen. R. 9:5; B.B. 75a; Yalkut; BhM 111–12).

Hisda, Rabbi: Talmudic Sage (ca. 3rd–4th century). The leading oneiromancer in the **Talmud**, he expounds many of the axioms that have become the principle assumptions of Jewish **dream** interpretations (Ber. 55a).

Hitbodudut: "[Self] isolation." This term can refer to either physical isolation or mental concentration. In both cases, it is used in relation to meditation techniques.

Hitkasherut: "Attachment." This is the spiritual practice of concentrating on words in order to unleash their spiritual and/or theurgic potential. *SEE* KAVANAH.

Hod: "Majesty." One of the lower sefirot, it works in concert with **Netzach** to bring forth **prophecy**—knowledge of divine purpose—in the lower worlds. It is personified by **Aaron**.

Hollander, Isaac and John Isaac: Alchemists (Dutch, ca. 15th or 16th century). These two men, known only through their writings, *De Triplici Ordine Elixiris et Lapidis Theora* and *Opus Saturni*, were highly influential on later practitioners of the Great Art. Their collected writings were published in the 17th century under the title *Isaaci et J. I. Hollandi Opera Universalia et Vegetabilia sive de Lapide Philosophorum. SEE* ALCHEMY.

Holy of Holies: (*Kodesh Kodeshim; Lev ha-Olam; Devir*). The Holy of Holies is the innermost sanctum of the **Temple**, where the **Ark of the Covenant** resided. It was hidden behind a curtain and the High Priest alone would enter it, and then only once a year, for the **Yom Kippur** ritual. When King David moved the **Foundation Stone** into the Holy of Holies, the Sages feared that people might learn how to pronounce the **name of God** inscribed upon that rock, so they created two bronze guardian **lions** on pillars by the doorway. When someone entered with the intent of learning the name, the lions would roar, and the terror of the experience would blot the Name from the person's memory (PdRK 148a). The lions were no longer part of the Second Temple edifice, which is why it was possible for **Jesus** to steal the **Explicit Name of God** and use it for magical purposes (Toldot Yeshu). The Holy of Holies takes on an erotic connotation in the Midrash, which describes it as the "wedding chamber" of God and Israel (Tanh. B., folio 17; S of S R. 3:15–19).

Holy One, Blessed or Blessed be He: (*ha-Kadosh Baruch Hu*). In rabbinic parlance, this is a common honorific for God. Often it is abbreviated as *HKB'H*. In the **Zohar**, however, the term specifically refers to the masculine dimension of the Godhead and is the divine name referring to the sefirah of **Tiferet**.[1]

> 1. Green, *Guide to the Zohar*, 47.

Holy Sparks: *SEE* NITZOTZ.

Holy Spirit: (*Ruach Elohim*). The immanent presence of God in Creation and in the individual; enthusiasm (in the original Greek sense of the word, "filled with divinity"). It is the divine Presence that inspires individuals, such as **David** and **Bezalel**, to create sacred words and art. It can also be a conduit for divine power; those who are possessed of the Holy Spirit have the power to revive the dead (M. Sot. 9:9; A.Z. 20b). Various forms of Jewish mysticism equate it with different aspects of the Godhead. **Sefer Yetzirah** links it with divine speech and the upper **sefirot**, the **Zohar** equates it with **Shekhinah** (Me. 7a; PdRE 4; PR 3:4; SY 1:6–9; 6:1; Zohar I: 79a). *SEE* GLORY; RUACH ELOHIM.

Hoopoe: A mythical ferocious bird that guarded the **shamir worm** until **Asmodeus** helped **Solomon** steal it (Git. 67a–b; Ginzberg, *Legends of the Jews*, 32–33).

Hormin: A **demon**, one of the children of **Lilith**. He was executed by the demonic authorities for making his presence visible to mortals (B.B. 73a).

Horn: (*Karan*). In Judaism, a horn is a symbol of power, of alarm, and of otherworldliness. In rabbinic tradition, **Cain** sprouted a horn from his forehead; this is the "mark" that God gave him to protect him. As a result, Cain's semi-blind grandson **Lemach** accidentally killed him because he mistook Cain for a game animal.

In early Christian tradition, **Moses** was thought to have horns, an idea derived from the language of Exodus 34:29. This idea is even enshrined in Michelangelo's statue of the prophet. Evidently this is based on a Latin mistranslation of the Hebrew word *keren*, which can mean either "horn" or "radiate" in Hebrew. This otherwise quaint confusion took on darker overtones during the Middle Ages when Jews were widely regarded to be minions of the Devil. The popular superstition that Jews concealed horns under their hats only added to the atmosphere of contempt and hatred that Jews had to endure. In fact, medieval Jews were required to wear a *pileum cornutum*, a "horned hat" (it resembled a Chinese "coolie" hat with a spiked peak). In some Christian countries, Jews were further required to affix horn-shaped figures on the doors of their **synagogues**, or horns were part of the "Jew's badge" worn on outer garments. All of which served as a kind of dark echo of the myth about the horned murderer, Cain, to whom Jews were constantly compared by Christian exegetes.[1]

1. Trachtenberg, *The Devil and the Jews*, 44–52

Horoscope: Records that use the appearance of the heavens and track the influence of celestial forces as a means to determine one's character, predict one's personal future, or diagnose illness. While there is one possible example of a horoscope (4Q186) among the **Dead Sea Scrolls**, and the **Talmud** makes passing reference to **birth** predictions (Shab. 156a), Jewish interest in casting formal horoscopes is more clearly evident by the medieval period, when examples can be found in the **Cairo Geniza**. The mania for horoscopes (especially medical horoscopes) that marked the High Middle Ages and Renaissance is also evident among European Jews. *SEE* ASTROLOGY; ZODIAC.

Hospitality: Hospitality is highly valued in Judaism. It is important to show hospitality to spirits. Abraham is famed for the welcome he extended to the three angels (Gen. 18). There are many legends concerning **Elijah** that relate the consequences resulting from how particular people treated him when he appeared on their doorstep. The Babylonian Jewish custom of having a **dargesh**, a spirit bed, in one's home was a part of this belief. The Jews of the Ottoman Empire would welcome visiting **ghosts** by

setting out chairs for them (Sefer ha-Hezyonot 22). There is also the **Sukkot** tradition of **Ushpizin**, of welcoming the spirits of the ancestors into the sukkah.

Even **demons** need to be treated well, if only to prevent them from doing ill to the host. Thus, some **amulets** actually use the language of hospitality in their adjurations: "If you are hungry, eat! If you are thirsty, come drink! . . . but if you are not hungry or thirsty . . . go back the way you came . . . !"

Host Desecration: The pernicious myth that Jews would steal the sacred wafers of the Roman Catholic mass in order to compulsively reenact the passion of Jesus was a popular medieval superstition, one that ultimately claimed several thousand Jewish lives and caused untold Jewish suffering over the centuries. The whole concept grew out of the doctrine of Transubstantiation, the Catholic belief that the wafer, once consecrated, actually became the flesh of Christ. And as actual flesh, it was popularly believed, it would presumably bleed and feel pain if stabbed or misused.

According to the narrative of Host desecration stories, Jews would steal or purchase wafers through bribes and then stab, crucify, or burn the bread in the service of **Satan**, their master. Between 1215 (when the doctrine of Transubstantiation was affirmed) and 1600, scores of such accusations were made in communities across Europe, with the result that suspected Jews, even whole Jewish communities, found themselves subject to inquisition, torture, and capital punishment. The Church hierarchy made several attempts to repudiate the calumny, but such efforts had only limited success. The accusation is closely related to the **blood libel**.

Host of Heaven: (*Tzeva ha-Shamayim*). A term that can refer either to the stars and constellations or to the angelic court and army. It appears several times in the **Bible**, often with indeterminate meaning. In the book of Joshua, Moses's successor actually encounters the **Sar Tzevaot**, angelic commander of the host outside of Jericho (Josh. 3), which in different traditions is identified as either **Metatron** or **Michael**.

Hechalot literature starts to fuse the two ideas and by late antiquity, a number of Jewish texts talk about angels as the animating genii of stars and planets. In time, this would lead to the amalgamation of native Jewish angel magic with **zodiac**-based gentile Hermetic magic. In texts like **Sefer Raziel**, there is an almost complete fusion of angelic identities with stars and their influence. *SEE* ADAT EL; ANGELS.

House of Study on High: *SEE* YESHIVA SHEL MALAH.

Huldah: This female prophet appears in II Kings and helps identify a forgotten book of the covenant, probably the book we know today as Deuteronomy. According to the Sages, God gave her the particular mission to prophesy to the women of Israel.

Hydromancy: The use of **water** for purposes of divining the future. There are multiple ways to use water in impetrated **divination**, such as combining it with **oil**, dropping foreign objects in it (think tea leaves), or studying reflections on the surface of lakes and rivers for images, **angels**, or omens. *SEE* DIVINATION; LECANOMANCY; RIVERS; SUMMONING.

Hyena: (*Tzavua* or *Napraza*). In the **Bible**, hyenas appear alongside satyrs and *lilot* (**Liliths**) in a list of evil creatures (Isa. 34:14). According to the **Talmud**, the hyena is a shape-shifting animal that evolves first into a **bat**, and finally into a **demon** (B.K. 15b; J. B.K. 2).

I

Ibbur or Devekut: "Impregnation/Cleaving." These are generic terms for spiritual possession, usually beneficent, but not always. Also called a **maggid**, it is related to, but is not to be confused with, a **dybbuk**. An ibbur coexists inside a living body, which already has a resident **soul**, usually for a short period of time (Sefer ha-Hezyonot 46; Sha'ar ha-Gilgulim). Some souls of **righteous** saints are able to do this for the benefit of mankind, either to perform a special task through, or to reveal a vital teaching to, the possessed individual. Sometimes the ibbur does this on its own initiative, but more often a worthy mystical seeker deliberately induces the possession. To achieve this, a period of **purification** and preparation is necessary. In some ibbur tales, wearing a "sign of the covenant," such as **tefillin**, is a prerequisite to such possession. Usually there is some kind of ecstatic practice involved. **Isaac Luria** preferred using an **incubation** ritual. A few **Safed** mystics wrote down testimonies of their ibbur possessions. It also marked early **Chasidim**.[1] SEE MEDIUM; POSSESSION, GHOSTLY; SUMMONING; XENOGLOSSIA.

1. Goldish, *Spirit Possession in Judaism*, 101–19, 257–304, 404.

Ibn Ezra, Abraham: Biblical commentator and astrologer (Spanish, ca. 11th century). Most famous for his rationalist and linguistic commentary on the **Torah**, Ibn Ezra was also an avid devotee of **astrology** and wrote a number of works about the influence of the stars over the sublunary plane. He was convinced of the power of the stars over the lives of mortals, and believed astrology belonged among the canons of scientific knowledge. He incorporated his theories into his Torah commentaries, including the novel proposal that

the **Urim and Thummim** of the High Priest was actually a kind of astrolabe. His fame in these matters was such that a few of his astrological works were translated into Latin. He also offered a naturalistic interpretation of **demons**. Though Ibn Ezra taught virtually no esoterica aside from his beliefs in astrology, many legends concerning him as a master of the occult appeared throughout the Middle Ages after his death. There is, for example, at least one tradition claiming Ibn Ezra made a **golem**.

Ibn Yachya, Gedaliah: Rabbi, Talmudist and exorcist (Italian, ca. 16th century). He is the author of Sefer Shalshelet ha-Kabbalah. It contains fantastic and supernatural traditions concerning the heavenly bodies, Creation, the soul, magic, and evil spirits.

Idol, Idolatry: (*Pesel, Elil, Teref, Shikutz*). A physical representation of deity. The refusal to make a visual image of divinity is called "aniconism," and is most evident in the traditions of Judaism and Islam. Physical representations of the gods were critical to the religions of the Ancient Near East, so the Israelite rejection of any physical image of divinity was one of the most revolutionary aspects of the cult of **YHWH**. It was so incomprehensible to pagans that some Greco-Roman writers even accused Jews of being atheists.[1]

The misunderstanding was mutual. It is clear from the biblical testimonies that the prophets believed pagans worshipped the idols themselves *as gods*. This religious phenomenon, believing an object to be an actual genie or spirit, is called *fetishism*. Clearly, many early ancient "pagans in the pews" believed this to be the case, with some actually thinking that the idols "ate" the offerings brought to them, and ascribing miraculous powers to the idolatrous object itself.[2]

More sophisticated classical pagans, however, understood an idol to be something different—more than a mere representation of a god, but less than the actual god itself. The purpose of making a physical image of a god was, for the sophisticated pagan, *to attract that god's attention.* An idol was a kind of "god magnet," meant to invite the god's presence into the shrine, home, or whatever locale where the idol was erected. Another way of imagining an idol is as somewhat akin to a **voodoo doll**. Whatever happened to or for the idol would be telegraphed to the actual god. Thus, cleaning and clothing the image, burning pleasant smelling incense, making offerings of food, or even human lives, before an idol would please and comfort the god it represented, making him or her more positively inclined toward the devotee.

This is the logic behind the **Golden Calf** incident (Ex. 34). The Israelites did not simply decide to make up a new and different god. They were still intent on worshipping YHWH, but they felt compelled to make an idol of God in the form of a calf (a bull, really) in order to attract the attention and ensure the continuing presence of YHWH in their midst, which they felt was missing during the absence of **Moses**.

From ancient texts of the cultures surrounding Israel, it is clear that for an idol to function, one had to do more than merely construct the image. Idols were "activated" by means of initiation rituals. Thus, in both Mesopotamian and Egyptian magical texts we have a ceremony called the "opening of the mouth" rite by which the idol was activated and the presence of the god was drawn to it.[3]

The Hebrew **Bible** is clearly most concerned with the actual making and veneration of images as described above. Yet as religious idolatry has fallen out of fashion in the West, the idea of "idolatry" has taken on a more figurative meaning, being equated with the worship of anything outside God (money, success, sports, and even religious objects) that should not be of ultimate concern.

The impulse toward fetishism, however, remains a universal human preoccupation, and as is evidenced by some of the entries in this book, it is still an issue for some Jews.

1. Schafer, *Judeophobia*, 21, 23.
2. Kaufmann, *The Religion of Israel*, 17–20.
3. Kugel, *The God of Old*, 73–85.

Idra: The Aramaic term for a "threshing floor" (*goren* in Hebrew). There has been some supernatural import to threshing floors since biblical times. Threshing floors are favored locations for God or angels to become manifest (I Chron. 13:9; II Sam. 24:16). The latter site becomes the eventual location of the **Temple**. In the **Zohar**, an idra is a mystical assembly, or a conclave of members of a mystical brotherhood that gathers when one of their number is dying and supernal secrets are about to be revealed.

Iggeret ha-Kodesh: "The Holy Letter." A medieval mystical **sex** manual attributed to **Nachmanides**. It teaches about spiritual intention while having sex, sexual positions and their relative merits, even the direction to be oriented while having sex. *SEE* BODY.

Iggeret Sod ha-Geullah: A 16th-century anthology of supernatural and folk tales about the Jewish community written by Abraham Eliezer ha-Levi.

Iggulim v'Yosher: "Circle and Line." A Kabbalistic term which refers to the "marriage" of divine masculine and feminine attributes. *SEE* ZIVVUGA KADDISHA.

Igrat: (Alternately, Agrat). The night demoness of harlotry, she is a **succubus** who seduces men in their sleep and gathers their nocturnal emissions. In **Kabbalah**, she is listed among the **four demon queens**, the mothers of all demons. Reflecting the rabbinic belief that evil spirits procreate, this demon is sometimes mentioned with a proper matronymic Hebrew name, *bat Malkat*, "daughter of Malkat." One tradition proposes that she herself was the product of a human-demon coupling.

She had intercourse with **David**, and from his royal semen she gave birth to both the gentile kings who would become his enemies (not unlike Morgan LaFaye and Arthur) and to **Asmodeus**, the King of Demons. She is mentioned in the **Talmud** as a demon who communes with **witches**. The spiritual intervention of **Chanina ben Dosa** and **Abbaye** curbed her malevolent power over humans (Pes. 110a and 112b; Num. R. 12:3; Bachya's comments on Gen. 4:22).

Illusion: (*Achaia Aynayim*). Some Sages ascribe the magical feats seen among the gentiles to feats of illusion—what we today call stage magic. Others regard such wonders to be real, but inferior to the miraculous feats credited to biblical and rabbinic heroes (Sanh. 65a). The **Talmud** concludes that those who use only sleight of hand to perform magic are not technically wizards, and therefore not subject to the penalty for **witchcraft**. *SEE* LAW AND THE PARANORMAL; MAGIC; SORCERY; THEURGY.

Image, Divine: (*Dimyon*). According to Genesis 1, humanity shares a commonality with God not found in other parts of God's Creation; humanity is made in God's likeness (*demut*) and image (*tzelem*). Almost all schools of Jewish mysticism teach that there is a unique affinity between God and man, that there is more continuity than disjuncture between divine and human nature.

Still, the exact nature of the divine "image" that God granted humanity is a matter of debate in Jewish occult tradition. While non-esoteric rabbinic texts focus on the soul as an analogy for God (Berachot 10a—the soul fills and animates the body just as God fills and animates the universe), **Sefer Yetzirah** seems to regard speech, and the capacity that grants us for creativity, to be the unique way man mirrors God. **Shi'ur Qomah** implies that the actual physical shape of humanity is a kind of homunculus of the divine form. The **Circle of the Unique Cherub** similarly considered the human form to be made in the image, not of God proper, but in the image of the divinely emanated image of the **Unique Cherub** (**Baraita de Yosef ben Uziel**). Only slightly less anthropomorphic, the **Zohar** regards the human shape to be a **microcosm** of the **sefirot**, the divine emanations, rather than of God in actuality.[1] **Eleazer of Worms** claims there are ten divine features in every human being: the soul, facial expressions, the senses of sight, hearing, smell, touch, speech, walking upright, wisdom, and insight (Sefer Sodei Razaya). *SEE* ADAM; ADAM KADMON; BODY; FACE OF GOD; GODHEAD; VISION.

1. Dan, "Imagio Dei" in Cohen and Mendes-Flohr, *Contemporary Jewish Religious Thought*, 473–78. Also see Wolfson, *Through a Speculum that Shines*.

Imagination: To the Jewish rational philosophers, the imaginative faculty is inferior and (should be) subordinate to the intellect. In some cases, they even regarded imagination to be a problem, an impediment to accurate theological understanding (Moreh Nevukhim, I: 73; II: 34). For the Jewish mystic, however, imagination is the key to the ecstatic experience.[1] It is through imaginative visualization, sometimes called **reiyat ha-lev**, that the practitioner is able to comprehend the true nature of the **sefirot** and to experience **visions** of divine **Glory** (Zohar I: 103a; Shir Ha-Kavod; Ber. 6a). *SEE* CHERUB, THE UNIQUE; FACE OF GOD; MEDITATION.

1. Hartman, "Imagination," in Cohen and Mendes-Flohr, *Contemporary Jewish Religious Thought*, 452–72. Also see Wolfson, *Through a Speculum that Shines*.

Immersion: (*Tevilah; Mikvah*). Immersion in **water** for the purposes of ritual purity is part of the system of priestly purity outlined in the Torah, which includes partial (the hands) and total body immersion, as well as the immersion of objects used in **ritual** contexts. Originally, being in a state of ritual purity was important only in the sacred areas of the Israelite camp in the desert and to the **Tabernacle** at its center. Such places were, in effect, an extension of heaven (or the Garden of **Eden**) that intrudes into mundane space, so one had to be pure enough to operate in these heavenly spheres (Yalkut Reubeni 31b). Initially such rules of immersion mostly affected the **Priests** and Levites who had to work in these zones. The one exception was that the whole Israelite community was required to immerse in anticipation of receiving the Torah. In time some aspects of ritual purity were applied to other Jews (Yev. 47b; Tractate Niddah).

Mayim chayyim, or living water, is necessary to effect such **purification**. In practice this means either a natural body of water (**sea**, lake, or **river**) or a **mikvah**, a ritual pool drawing part of its water directly from a natural source, like rainwater. The fact that human hands do not draw such water, that it flows uncontaminated directly from the higher realms, is the source of its power. Thus contact with this heavenly flow cleanses one and prepares one for contact with other heavenly forces.

Chasidism adds to this other interpretations, such as that the water signifies the **sefirot**, the divine overflow, or that it represents the totality of undifferentiated oneness. It also stands for the womblike watery **Olam ha-Tohu**, "world of concealment," prior to new birth/creation (Reshit Chochmah, Sha'ar ha-Ahavah 11; Sefer Ha-Chinuch 173).

The underlying logic of ablution, that one must be in a state of purity when in contact with divine space or things, was eventually extended to both the quest for mystical union with the divine and even the encounter of the soul with God in the afterlife. Thus in the **Hechalot literature**, an initiate seeking to ascend into **heaven** would undergo ablution as part of the ritual purification beforehand. The process of **tahorah**, purifying a corpse in preparation for burial, follows the same logic.

Ablution for the **soul** as well as the body is also a feature found in some mystical and noncanonical Jewish documents. According to these texts, souls of the dead must go through purification by ablution in the *Nahar Dinur*, the celestial **River of Light**, before entering Paradise (Reshit Chochmah chapter 11, #30; I Enoch 17:5).

Ritual immersion can also be used for magical purposes beside preparatory purification (Hechalot Rabbati; Sefer Ha-Malbush). It also has magical properties. One Chasidic tradition teaches that if a man immerses himself while his wife is in labor, he will ease her **birth** pangs.[1]

1. Klein, *A Time to Be Born*, 93, 144.

Incantations, Spells, and Adjurations: (*Kishuf; Kesem; Chever; Lachash; Mashiva*). An incantation or spell is a spoken word, phrase, or formula of power, often recited as part of a larger **ritual**, which is recited in order to effect a magical result. Most cultures have some idea about words having supernatural constructive powers, but nowhere is this belief stronger than in Judaism.[1] Both the **Bible** and Jewish mysticism emphasize that God created the universe by means of a series of "speech acts." Humanity is the only one of God's mortal creations with the power of speech, implying that our words can, under certain conditions, have the same constructive (and destructive) power.[2]

Jewish belief in the efficacy of spells, or "constructive language," is premised on three assumptions:

1) There is special power inherent in the **names of God**.[3]

2) There is special power in the words and phrases that God speaks, i.e., the words of the **Torah** and the Hebrew Bible.[4]

3) The **Hebrew alphabet** itself is supernatural in origin, which means that using Hebrew letters in certain combinations is a source of special power, even when it has no semantic value to the adept.[5]

Spells may be either "theurgic" or "magical" in character. Usually, the belief underlying the use of theurgic spells is that God has in some way delegated that power/authority to the adept.

Truly magical incantations, by comparison, are "autonomous"; they do not involve spiritual entities at all. Often a magical spell or incantation is simply addressed to the object to be influenced. Thus, a truly magical incantation most closely parallels the word power of God Himself.

Incantation phrases are also a form of "heightened speech," not unlike poetry. As such, there are a number of distinctive stylistic features present in incantations. These can include: repetition, rhythm, reversals, nonsense words, foreign words, and divine names of power.

Repetition, usually done three or seven times, or by another number symbolically relevant to the issue at hand, is the premier aspect of constructive words of power (Shab. 66b). Thus we find a teaching in the **Talmud**, for example, that reciting a verse containing the phrase "Voice of the Lord" seven times thwarts evil spirits at night.

An incantation meant to undo the effects of a given event or phenomenon will often include elements of **reversal**, reciting a word or phrase backwards in some fashion. An example would be this one for dislodging a bone in the esophagus: "One by one, go down, swallow/swallow go down, one by one." In Pesachim 112b, we read that one afflicted with an ocular disease should recite the word *shabriri* (blindness) repeatedly in the phrase "My mother has cautioned me against *shabriri*." With each repetition, the speaker should reduce one letter from the word: *shabriri, shabrir, shabri, shabr, shab, sha. . . .* The magical ritual of reducing the word is intended to yield a parallel reduction in the severity of the illness.

Spells can include rhymed or nonsense phrases that have minimal or no semantic value (*voces mysticae*). Rather, rhythmic meaningless arrangements of words and phrases are used for the illocutionary or mantralike effect, or for a sympathetic result, or because these words are understood to be meaningful to heavenly powers, if not the adept.

For example, to fend off an evil water spirit, the **Talmud** recommends intoning this: "*Lul shafan anigeron anirdafon*, I dwell among the stars, I walk among thin and fat people" (Pes. 112a). While the second clause of this spell is strange enough, the first clause of the spell is neither Hebrew nor Aramaic; by all indications it is just gibberish. This feature, common to Greco-Roman magic, emerges in Jewish circles in late antiquity.[6]

Akin to nonsense phrases, incantations often include *nomina barbara*, the use of foreign words and phrases. This feature of Jewish spells goes back to the Babylonian tradition of using archaic Sumerian words in their incantations, and becomes characteristic of Jewish incantations by the Greco-Roman period. With the later decline of Hebrew and Aramaic as a spoken language, these languages themselves become *lingua magica* for many spellcasters, both Jewish and gentile. RaSHI explains that an integral part of spellcasting involves reciting words that may be incomprehensible to the enchanter (Commentary, Sot. 22a).

The use of names of power is a pervasive aspect of all Hebrew/Jewish spells. The **names of God**, angels, the righteous dead, even one's mother, are considered critical to giving an incantation efficacy (Shab. 66b). Often the names are encrypted in **atbash** form or in other occult methods. Spells from late antiquity are often promiscuous in the powers they invoke, freely mixing Jewish and pagan entities. One Greco-Egyptian spell calls upon "First angel of [the god], of Zeus, Iao, and you Michael, who rule heaven's realm, I call, and you, archangel Gabriel. Down from Olympus, Abrasax, delighting in dawns, come gracious who view sunset from the dawn."

Magical incantations that appear in the Talmud (and are therefore presumably sanctioned by at least some Sages) mostly serve the functions of **healing** and protection. In Tractate Shabbat 67a–b, one Sage gives explicit sanction to the use of magic if it is done solely for the purposes of healing. Outside the Talmudic/Midrashic tradition proper, there are spells for **summoning** angels, **love** spells, and "binding" spells intended to **curse** or thwart a rival in love, business, or other personal matters. While rabbinic authorities have never endorsed the latter forms of incantations, they are more tolerant of spells that enhance goals the Sages endorse, such as healing, or spells meant to enhance the learning of Torah. These latter two types are perhaps the most common in Jewish literature.

Tolerance for the use of spells can also be regional. The Babylonian Talmud preserves several examples of spells (see especially tractates Pesachim, Shabbat, and Berachot), while the Palestinian Talmud has virtually none. We know that at least some Jews in Palestine engaged in spellcasting, because we have magical texts from that region and period. Evidently, the difference between the two Talmuds reflects something of the respective "official" attitude among the Sages of those regions toward spellcraft.

The types of incantations recorded continue to expand in number and variety of purpose throughout the Middle Ages. In theurgic manuals like the **Book of the Responding Entity**, there appear an increasing number of spells based on astrological power (what Renaissance adepts would dub "natural magic"). In expressly magical texts, like **Sefer Raziel**, there appear incantations to "receive all desire." These spells often completely parallel gentile magic, involving magical materials, fire and water, invoking the names of governing angels, and throwing something of value with magical names and phrases inscribed on it into the proper element (fire, seas, etc.). Treasure-locating spells also appear in medieval magical manuals. What status many of these spells had in "normative" Jewish circles is hard to judge. Again, spells recorded in the works of later religious authorities tend to be limited to the same areas tolerated by Talmudic authorities: incantations for better memorizing Torah, invoking an **angel** or **ibbur**, and for protection against medical or supernatural misadventure. SEE AMULETS; LANGUAGE; MAGIC; SEFER HA-RAZIM; SEFER RAZIEL; SEGULLAH; SORCERY; SWORD OF MOSES; WITCHCRAFT. *(SEE ALSO APPENDIX, FIGURE 1.)*

1. Lauterbach, "The Belief in the Power of the Word," 287–89.
2. Scholem, *On the Kabbalah and Its Symbolism*, 166–67.
3. Dan, *The Heart and the Fountain*, 101–4.
4. Janowitz, *The Poetics of Ascent*, 85–87.
5. Janowitz, *Icons of Power*, 45–61.
6. Miller, "In Praise of Nonsense," in Armstrong, *Classical Mediterranean Spirituality*, 481–504.

Incantation Bowls or Demon Bowls: These are **amulets** used by the Jews of Mesopotamia and Israel in late antiquity to protect their homes from evil spirits. The bowls that have survived to this day are ceramic and covered with magical incantations, usually in Aramaic, but sometimes in Hebrew, Mandaic, or Arabic. They are usually made for a specific individual or family, and all the people to be protected are named in the text of the incantation. Often the home and property are also included. The incantations usually consist of **curses** against **demons**, spirits of illness, the **evil eye**, **witches**, and/or all generic misfortunes.[1] In these spells, God and/or a variety of protective angels are adjured to enforce the curse and guarantee the efficacy of the protective charm. Usually written in a spiral pattern on the inside surface of the bowl, permutations of the **names of God** and/or **magic squares** and **circles** are often part of the protective formulae. Some bowls will have crude illustrations of demonic figures, often portrayed as shackled or otherwise trapped. The exact rituals by which these bowls were created and activated are now lost, but there is a hint that preparation may have involved using a cemetery, either as a source for the clay or as the grounds on which the bowl was prepared.

Some of these caldrons have been discovered by archeologists buried under the doorways of excavated homes. They were either buried inverted, or made in pairs and buried against each other lip to lip, evidently creating a space to "catch" any **demons** rising from the underworld. Other rituals associated with the bowls apparently involved writing the name of an offending demon on the bowl with a series of binding adjurations and then breaking it.

Even though the custom of burying demon bowls has ceased, stepping on a threshold is still considered bad luck, reflecting an ongoing anxiety about liminal zones, such as doors and windows, places of transition where malevolent forces can gain entry.

1. Naveh and Shaked, *Amulets and Magic Bowls*, 15–20, 124–98.

Incense: (*Ketoret; Bosem*). Incense had a significant role in the sacrificial cult of YHWH. Part of its function was symbolic, recreating the **clouds** that once blanketed Sinai God was revealed there. In the **Temple**, the cloud of incense also served as a protection against the High **Priest** seeing too much of God's **Glory** (Ex. 30; I Kings, 7; M. Suk. 4:5; Suk. 43b).

According to the **Talmud**, the incense used in the Temple was made in quantities of 368 *maneh* (measures); one measure for each daily offering during the year, with three extra measures for **Yom Kippur** (Ker. 6a). The Book

of **Jubilees** describes it as made up of seven ingredients: frankincense, galbanum, stacte, nard, myrrh, costum, and spices (16:21–31). An alternate list from apocryphal literature is: saffron, spikenard, reed, cinnamon, myrrh, frankincense, and mastic. Rabbinic tradition specifies twelve (M. Tam. 6:2; Yoma 1:5). Any attempt to duplicate the Temple formula for incense was forbidden after the destruction of the sanctuary by the Romans.

Incense also served as a component in theurgic rituals. In the book of Numbers, **Aaron** used incense in his effort to combat a supernatural pestilence that was decimating the Israelites (chapter 17). Since incense seems to be attractive and soothing to evil entities, it is sometimes used for both demon summoning rites and **exorcisms**. This very reason is sometimes given as the rationale for why Jews should not wear perfumes during the period of mourning—mourners are spiritually vulnerable to demonic attack, so one should avoid doing (or emitting) anything to attract demonic interest.

Incubation: The practice of sleeping, usually in a sacred location, in order to induce a divinatory or veridical **dream**, or for the purpose of communing with a numinous entity. Those seeking to commune with God, angels, divine voices, or the dead, use incubation techniques to do so (Gen. 15).

In ancient times, Israelites would sleep in the **Tabernacle** compound in order to experience a dream revelation from God (I Sam. 3). Zechariah experienced dream visions, but it is unclear whether he elicited them (Zech. 4).[1] Apparently some Israelites also used incubation for the purposes of **necromancy** by sleeping on or at graves. The prophet Isaiah roundly condemns this practice (Isa. 8:19–22, 19:3).

The Talmudic Sages believed that omens and revelations could be derived from dreams, but did not encourage or document any methods for intentionally producing such experiences. By contrast, Jewish mystics have always been avidly interested in inducing dreams and they record several incubation techniques. The **Merkavah** mystics would invoke **Sar ha-Chalom**, the Prince of Dreams, or the angels Azriel, Ragsiel, and/or Rabyoel, to answer **she'elot chalom**, dream questions. A number of such incubation techniques are recorded in the **Hechalot** literature and they were replicated and elaborated upon by medieval Kabbalists. Magical handbooks, like **Sefer ha-Razim** and the **Sword of Moses**, include similar angel-adjuration techniques.

After the destruction of the Temple, incubations were sometimes attempted by sleeping overnight in a **synagogue**, though most practices do not specify a particular location (SCh 80, 271, 1556). By the high Middle Ages, incubation techniques included the previously illicit practice of sleeping on or about the graves of the meritorious dead. **Isaac Luria**, in particular, was an avid practitioner.[2] It was also accepted practice among European Jews in the early modern era (ShB 1, 7).

Preparatory techniques for incubation include **fasting** and **immersion**, the reciting of **prayers** and **psalms**, **summoning** angels, and **incantations**. SEE DIVINATION; POSSESSION, GHOSTLY.

1. Flannery-Daily, *Dreamers, Scribes, and Priests: Jewish Dreams in Hellenistic and Roman Eras*, 269.
2. Fine, "The Contemplative Practice of Yihudim in Lurianic Kabbalah," in Green, *Jewish Spirituality*, vol. 2, 70–98.

Incubus: A male spirit who copulates with human females, usually while they sleep (Nishmat ha-Chayyim, III: 16, 52c–53b). Often the demon will appear in a familiar form, usually the husband (but sometimes not) in order to get the woman's cooperation (She'elot u'Teshuvot of Meir Lublin, #116). Demonic offspring can result, as well as **banim shovavim**, impish children or changelings. The most famous example in Jewish tradition involves women having intercourse with the **fallen angels**.

Intercession: The request that a saint, **angel**, or other spiritual intermediary intervene with God on one's behalf.[1] **Hechalot Rabbati** describes a class of angels who plead the Jewish people's case before God. In medieval Europe, there arose a custom of professional intercessors studying Torah on behalf of a pregnant woman as a means of prophylaxis. Intercessory prayer has been present in Judaism since late antiquity, but has become more accepted over the centuries, possibly because of exposure to Christian and Islamic saint veneration. Chasidism, for example, seeks the intercession of both living and dead *tzadikim*. SEE ANCESTORS; RIGHTEOUS, THE.

1. Klein, 37, 145–46.

Invisibility: The power to vanish is only occasionally mentioned in Jewish literature. Both Isaac Luria and the Baal Shem Tov reportedly could render themselves invisible (Toldot ha-Ari; ShB 180).

Irin: SEE WATCHERS.

Iron: (*Barzel*). Evil spirits are believed to have an aversion to metal, particularly silver and iron. Thus we read in one **Midrash** that a Sage summoned locals with iron tools to drive out a demon that had haunted a well (Lev. R. 24). Iron objects, such as knives, are also used in rituals to combat fevers (Shab. 67a). To this day, some Jews will carry a small iron object, such as a safety pin, to ward off malevolent spirits.[1] The supernatural power of iron is derived from its Hebrew name, *BaRZeL*, which is believed to be an acronym for the four Matriarchs of the twelve tribes: **B**ilhah, **R**achel, **Z**ilpah, and **L**eah. Their merit imbues iron with its protective quality.

1. Trachtenberg, *Jewish Magic and Superstition*, 46, 49, 160.

Isaac: Isaac was the second son of Abraham, the only son by Abraham's beloved wife Sarah. He was the bearer of all God's promises to Abraham to make his descendants a mighty nation. Isaac himself was born of a miracle, being conceived decades after Sarah's menopause. Three angelic visitors, later identified as **Michael, Gabriel**, and **Raphael**, came to Abraham's camp and heralded Isaac's conception (Gen. 18). God later commanded **Abraham** to sacrifice Isaac, his beloved son, and only the intervention of an angel prevented him from doing so (Gen. 22).

Rabbinic literature adds more miraculous details to Isaac's life. His birth triggered the sun and moon to shine more intensely, a phenomenon not to be repeated again until the Messianic Era. Moreover, the blind regained their sight, the deaf could hear, and barren women became fertile. A general sense of well-being, unknown since **Eden**, swept the world (Tanh., Gen. 37; Gen. R. 3). Sarah's breasts were filled with such bounty that she not only nursed **Isaac**, but all the children that attended his weaning party.

According to some **Midrashim**, God ordered the offering of Isaac in response to Satan's taunting, much like the incident in Job. On the basis of the **Bible**'s own chronology, the Sages conclude Isaac was actually thirty-seven at the time of his binding, that Isaac submitted willingly to God's test, and that he actually underwent death at the hands of Abraham, only to be resurrected afterward (Lam. R., petichta 24; PdRE 31; Tanh., Vayera 23; Seder Olam). During the period of his demise, his soul ascended to heaven, where he studied Torah (which had yet to be given to humanity) in the **Yeshiva shel Malah**, the heavenly academy (Gen. R. 56; PdRE 31; Sefer ha-Yashar 43a–44b). Having done so, he returned to his body with an extraordinary knowledge of its contents. When he was about to be sacrificed, the angels starting crying; some of those tears fell in Isaac's eyes, leading to his eventual blindness. Another version has the blindness result from Isaac looking directly at the divine **Glory** (described in Gen. 28; Gen. R. 65:10; Deut. R. 11:3; PdRE 32).

When he finally did die, his body did not decay and was not consumed by worms. Like the others laid to rest in the **Cave** of Machpelah, his body was perfectly preserved (B.B. 17a–b).

In the system of **sefirot**, Isaac is the manifestation of **Gevurah**, of God's strict justice.

Isaac ben Jacob ha-Kohen: Kabbalist (Spanish, ca. 13th century). He wrote several mystical treatises. His **Treatise on the Left Emanation** was a groundbreaking study of demonic metaphysics and paved the way for the **Zohar**.

Isaac ben Samuel of Acre: Kabbalist (Israel, ca. 13th–14th century). Isaac is most remembered for his travels and contacts with other notable mystics of his day. He wrote Otzar Chayyim, a spiritual diary of his experiences and practices, especially the use of **Tzerufim**, word and letter combinations, as a meditative device.

Isaac ben Samuel of Dampierre: Talmudist (French, ca. 12th century). Rav Isaac approved of the summoning of spirits for purposes of **divination** and benevolent **magic**. His disciples believed that he himself received his insights from angelic instruction.

Isaac, Testament of: Apocryphal work about the death of Isaac. On his deathbed, God grants him a revelation of the afterlife. It includes what may be the first reference to the *Nahar Dinur*, the **River of Light** that flows between **Eden** and **Gehenna**.

Isaac the Blind or Isaac the Pious: Isaac ben Abraham of Posquieres was a Kabbalist (French, ca. 12th–13th century). As the possible author of the **Bahir**, he can be regarded as the first of the classical Kabbalists. He was also the teacher of the first generation of great mystical writers of the Spanish/Provencal tradition. One tradition claims **Elijah** was his angelic teacher. He is the first to openly teach the concept of **reincarnation** in Judaism. Some of his writings also offer mystical insights on colors and light, suggesting that his blindness came later in life.

Isaiah: This prophet of ancient Israel is credited with the longest prophetic book in the **Bible**, the eponymously named "book of Isaiah." In it, the prophet-priest records a spectacular (and typically priestly) **vision** of God that appears to him in the **Temple** in which he sees YHWH seated on a throne in Glory, attended by **serafim**. This revelation becomes the archetype for subsequent Jewish **Hechalot literature**.

In a famous sign from God given to King Ahaz of Judah, Isaiah predicts that a pregnant woman known to both men would bear a son (Isa. 7–8). In II Kings, Isaiah foretold that God would smite the Assyrian army of Sennacherib besieging Jerusalem, an event that unfolded as predicted shortly thereafter, relieving the city. Aside from these, there are no supernatural events associated with the life of Isaiah in either the Bible or rabbinic literature.

Iscah: Another name for Sarah (Meg. 14a; Sanh. 69b).

Ishbi-benob: A biblical **giant** (II Samuel) and one of the four brothers of **Goliath**. According to the **Midrash**, he once captured **David** and devised an ingenious **death** for him, but God miraculously delivered David (Sanh. 95a; Gen. R. 59; Yalkut).

Ishchak ben Yacub Ovadiah Abu Isa Al-Isfahani: Failed messiah (Persian, ca. 7th century). He led a revolt against the early Islamic Caliphate (the Ummayyads), a venture that ended in total defeat and the death of Abu Isa.

Ishim: "Men." A class of angels with bodies half of snow, half of fire (Gedulat Moshe).

Ishmael: The son of Abraham and Hagar, in the **Bible**, Ishmael's life is saved by God, who sends an **angel** to intervene when he and his mother were dying in the wilderness. In rabbinic literature, his vulnerability in the desert was the result of **Sarah** putting an **evil eye** upon him (Gen. R. 53:15). The well that the angel shows them is in fact the miraculous well God created on the sixth day of Creation, the same one known as the **Well of Miriam** that would move with the Israelites during their forty years of wandering (Avot 5:6).

Ishmael ben Elisha ha-Kohen: Mishnaic Sage and mystic (ca. 2nd century). After his mother struggled many years to conceive, Ishmael was born because of the intervention of the angel **Gabriel** (another tradition claims it was **Metatron**) and at his birth he was recognized as one of the seven (or ten) most beautiful infants in the world. He was one of the **ten martyrs** killed by the Romans and the unjust killing of this righteous soul nearly caused the foundations of the earth to crumble. Seeing his beauty, the daughter of Caesar asked that he be spared. Instead, Caesar ordered that his face be peeled from his head and presented to her. When his soul finally departed, Gabriel escorted him to his eternal reward (Mid. Eleh Ezkarah; BhM 2:64–65). The face of Rabbi Ishmael went on to become the source of miraculous healings. This may be the only example of a relic taken from the body of a martyr in Jewish tradition.

Ishmael is regarded as a virtuoso in the methods of mystical **ascent** and the **Ma'asei Merkavah**, having learned the proper techniques from **Rabbi Akiba** (Ma'aseh Merkavah). As such, he appears in a remarkable passage of the **Talmud** (Ber. 7a) having a conversation with **Akatriel–YaH**. In this divine manifestation, Akatriel-YaH asks Ishmael to *bless him*. After having experienced something like that, it is not surprising that Ishmael is the central figure in a number of mystical texts, including **Ma'aseh Merkavah**, **Pirkei Hechalot**, and **Sefer Raziel**. *SEE* DECREE, DIVINE; RIGHTEOUS, THE; YORED MERKAVAH.

Israel: "Yisraeil." This term can refer to several esoteric concepts:

1. The people Israel: The name bestowed upon **Jacob** after he wrestled with a divine being. The name, along with its power, becomes the title of his descendants, the *B'nai Yisraeil*, the "Children of Israel." The name can be translated as either "God wrestler," "Prince of God," or "Upright of God," but using **gematria**, the name *YiSRAeiL* can be read as *YeiSH* 231, "There are 231 [gates]," referring to the 231 power permutations of the **alphabet** described in **Sefer Yetzirah**. The name is also numerically equal to the phrase *sechel ha-poel*, "understanding the workings." This teaches that Israel has theurgic authority—both the capacity and the occult knowledge to use the alphabet for creative purposes, imitating what God did in creating the world, as well as commanding spirits (Ginnat Egoz 57b). The people Israel are God's "inheritance" and "portion" (see Deut. 30–34). While the celestial governance of other peoples is delegated to **angels**, God rules over Israel directly. *SEE* ISRAEL, LAND OF; NATIONS; RIGHTEOUS, THE.

2. An angel of the heavenly firmament. The name of Israel is inscribed on his forehead, and each day he greets the dawn singing God's praises, paralleling what the people Israel do on earth (**Pirkei Hechalot**). This angel may in fact be the transubstantiated Patriarch Jacob, who is identified in several texts as a quasi-divine being (Mid. Teh. 8:6; PdRE 35, 36).

Israel ben Eliezer (the Baal Shem Tov or BeSHT): Mystic and founder of the Chasidic movement (Ukrainian, ca. 18th century). He became known as the *Baal Shem Tov* (Master of the Good Name) or the BeSHT, by his disciples. Many legends, healings, and miracles are attributed to him, including curing barrenness, combating werewolves and demons, shifting mountains, and others too numerous to mention. He was a clairvoyant and an **amulet** maker, a practice associated with Chasidism to this day. The power of his amulets, interestingly enough, derived not from the use of God's name, but from his own name in their construction (Shemot ha-Tzadikim). He wrote little himself except for some letters, and almost everything we know of his teachings were written down by his followers in collections like **Shivhei ha-BeSHT** (ShB), which overflow with stories of the paranormal and fabulous. The one collection of letters that is widely credited to him does include his description of experiencing a **Ma'asei Merkavah**-like mystical **ascent**.[1]

1. Rabinowicz, *The Encyclopedia of Hasidism*, 234–38. Also see Jacobs, *Jewish Mystical Testimonies*, 182–91.

Israel, Land of: (*Eretz Yisrael, Eretz ha-Kodesh, ha-Aretz*). The Land of Israel is holy. It is God's own earth, just as the people Israel are God's own special allotment, and people may dwell there as tenants only so long as their righteousness merits their presence. Eventually the land vomits out the wicked. The Canaanites lost their right to the land for this very reason (Gen. 12), and though the land has been promised to the Children of Israel in perpetuity, actual occupation of the land is still contingent on the people's moral condition. The **earth** of Israel is full of spiritual power, and many believe that to be buried with a bag of earth from Israel will ensure that a Jew, wherever he or she may be buried in the **world**, will be resurrected on the **Day of Judgment** to forgiveness and vindication (Toldot Chachmei Yerushalyim). According to Kabbalist **Abraham Azulai**, there is an umbilicus connecting heaven and Israel that bypasses all the **four worlds**. The land is, in effect, the gateway between heaven and earth (Chesed L'Avraham). The **righteous** that die in exile undergo **gilgul**, "rolling"; they journey via underground causeways to the Land of Israel, where they will experience immediate **resurrection**.

Itztzim: "Medium/necromancer." The root of this term is the Hebrew word for "bone." Most likely it comes from the Akkadian *etzemmu*, "[one who knows a] dead spirit, ghost." *SEE* DIVINATION; MEDIUM; NECROMANCY; POSSESSION, GHOSTLY.

Iyyun Circle: A mystical school of southern France (ca. 13th century). The group produced some thirty texts, though most of them still exist only in manuscript form. **Sefer ha-Iyyun** is the most well known and most studied of these.

Iyyun, Sefer ha-: "The Book of Speculation." A text of mystical theosophy. It builds much of its teaching around the version of the **Tetragrammaton** that appears in the theophany at the **burning bush** (Ex. 3), eHYeH, "I will be."

J

Jachin: One of the two bronze **pillars** on the exterior of Solomon's **Temple**. Along with the other pillar, Boaz, it was erected (apparently free-standing), before the door to the sanctuary. The function and/or symbolism of these pillars are never explained in Scripture. Oddly, while these mysterious objects have been the subject of considerable occult speculation in Christian, Hermetic, and other gentile traditions, Jewish esotericism has shown remarkably little interest in them.

Jacob (also Israel): Biblical Patriarch, the son of Isaac. He was father to twelve sons who would be the founding fathers of the twelve tribes of Israel. In the **Bible**, Jacob experiences two major supernatural events, his **dream** vision of the ladder between heaven and earth (Gen. 28) and his mysterious nighttime wrestling match with a man/angel by the river Jabbok (Gen. 32), at which time he is renamed "Israel" (one who wrestles with God).

In rabbinic legend, there are even more supernatural dimensions to Jacob's life. Given the biblical account, it is not surprising that most of them revolve around **angels**. When Jacob stole the birthright by deceiving his blind father Isaac, Isaac tried to **curse** him, but angels prevented this. At this time, Jacob purloined the **garments of Adam** which were then in Esau's possession. When he wore them, they emitted the scent of **Eden** (PdRE 32; Zohar I: 142b).

When Jacob had his dream-vision of the heavenly ladder, he also received apocalyptic revelations. In one version, he actually ascended to the top of the ladder and from there caught a glimpse of the celestial **Temple** (Gen. R. 56:10, 79:7; Sifrei Deut. 352; PdRK 21:5; Tanh., ve-Yetzei).

When Jacob wrestled with the angel, it was Esau's guardian angel he battled (Gen. R. 77:2; Tanh. Va-yishlach). Another tradition claims it was his own guardian angel, **Israel** (PdRE 36). Angels also served as Jacob's messenger to his brother **Esau** at the time of their reconciliation. Esau was so intimidated by this manifestation of the heavenly host that he immediately abandoned his plans to kill his brother. Later in life, Jacob's arrival in **Egypt** brought an end to the famine his son Joseph had been battling. He died by the **kiss** of God.

The **Zohar**, building upon a tradition that Jacob resembled **Adam** (B.B. 58a), goes further in suggesting that Jacob took on all the most beautiful of Adam's features—and perhaps he was even a reincarnation of the first soul (Zohar I: 142b).

In early Jewish mysticism, Jacob is considered the most perfect of the **Patriarchs**, almost angelic (Ps. 134:5; Gen. R. 76:1; PdRE 35; Mid. Teh. 8:6). For that reason, his image is inscribed on the **Throne of Glory**, a fact alluded to in the Bible: "And upon the likeness of the throne was a likeness of a man" (Ez. 1:26). **Midrash** ascribes to him divine status in God's eyes (Meg. 18a; Zohar I: 138a). All this, plus the fact that there is an angel with his name (Israel), suggests there may be a now-forgotten tradition of Jacob undergoing angelification.

The Zohar regards him to be the personification of **Tiferet**, the balancing force between the **Chesed** of **Abraham** and the **Gevurah** of Isaac (Gen. R. 74:17; Tos. Sot. 10:9; B.B. 17a; Zohar I).

Jacob ben Jacob ha-Kohen: Kabbalist (Spanish, ca. 13th century). Along with his brother, **Isaac ben Jacob**, he is the author of a popular mystical tract on the power of the **Hebrew alphabet**. *SEE* KABBALAH.

Jacob Isaac the Seer of Lublin: Chasidic master and wonder worker (Polish, ca. 18th–19th century). A celebrated figure in his own lifetime, he possessed the power to predict the future. He could also recount the past incarnations of the souls of the people he met. Because of these divinatory feats he was called the "Urim v'Thummim." Unfortunately, his powers escaped him at a critical moment, for he believed the Napoleonic Wars signaled the **End of Days**. *SEE* CHASIDISM; PHYSIOGNOMY; RIGHTEOUS, THE.

Jacob of Marvege: Mystical diarist (Rhenish, ca. 13th century) who collected legal and spiritual answers about Jewish practice from the angels by means of **incubation** and published them in a text, **She'elot u–Teshuvot min ha-Shamayim** ("Questions and Answers from Heaven"). These legal opinions were widely accepted, despite their paranormal origins. *SEE* DREAM.

Jannes and Mambres: *SEE* JOCHNES AND MAMRES.

Jashar, Book of: (*Sefer Yashar*, "Book of the Upright"). A **lost book** of ancient Israel quoted only briefly a few times in Scripture, virtually nothing is known about its dimensions, content, or authorship. Based on the few quotes excerpted, the only useful thing that can be said is that it was probably poetic in genre. Based solely on its title, some Sages claim that it is the book of Genesis, but none of the quotes taken from the Book of Jashar appear anywhere in Genesis. There is a medieval mystical book by the same name.

Jehovah: Christian scribal misinterpretation produced this name for God from YHWH. The name has no religious significance to Jews. *SEE* EXPLICIT NAME OF GOD; TETRAGRAMMATON.

Jekon: One of the leaders of the **Fallen Angels** (I Enoch).

Jephthah: A biblical Judge/Chieftain appearing in the book of Judges. As punishment for following through on his foolish vow to immolate his daughter (Judges 11), God cursed Jephthah that his flesh should fall away bit by bit, so that no one spot would be his final burial place (Gen. R. 60:3).

Jeremiah: The biblical accounts of the prophet Jeremiah are effectively bereft of supernatural elements. The Rabbis have little else to report in this regard, other than a legend that the prophet was born circumcised (AdRN 2). According to a medieval legend, however, he created a **golem** using **Sefer Yetzirah** (Sefer Gematriot).

Jeremiel: A destructive angel who rules one of the compartments of **Gehenna** (MG). In II Esdras, he is an Archangel.

Jerusalem: (*Yerushalyim, Ir David, Ir ha-Kodesh*). The city, originally a Jesubite stronghold, became David's capital around 1000 BCE. He modestly renamed it the City of David, but its ancient name continues to overshadow all subsequent names given by it conquerors, including *Aelia Capitolina* by the Romans and *Al Quds* by the Arabs. Often it is simply referred to as "the Holy City." It is the holiest of the four holy cities of Israel (Hebron, Tiberius, and **Safed** being the others).

The creation of the world began at the point where Jerusalem now stands. Before the Fall, **Adam Kadmon** made his offerings before God on a hilltop where one day the city and Temple would be built (Gen. R. 8:20). It is first mentioned in the book of Genesis as "Salem," when the mysterious priest of the city, **Melchizedek**, visits Abraham (chapter 14). The **Temple** of YHWH is built there on **Mount Zion** by **Solomon**. The city has been destroyed twice, once by the Babylonians and once by the Romans, and conquered many times by different empires. Whenever it has been permitted by its rulers, Jews have lived in the city.

It is the location of many miracles and regarded to be the nexus point between the material and all spiritual planes. There is a celestial Jerusalem (*Yerushalyim shel Malah*) that is the ideal counterpart of the earthly Jerusalem (*Yerushalyim shel Mattah*) (Tanh., Pekudei 1). In the celestial Jerusalem, the **Temple** there continues to offer sacrifices to God, overseen by the angelic High Priest, **Michael** (Tan. 5a; Zohar III: 15b, 68b, 147b). The earthly Jerusalem is also the center of the world (Tanh. Kedoshim 10).

Biblical Jerusalem was the epicenter of many fabulous phenomena. The entire city smelled like cinnamon (Shab. 63a). During the time the Temple stood, no woman ever miscarried, no one ever experienced demonic attack, there were never any accidents, the buildings never collapsed, the city was fireproof, no one was homeless, and no one was parsimonious (AdRN 35). As the "gate of heaven" (Gen. 28), all varieties of good and blessing flowed down from heaven through the city to benefit the world (Lev. R. 24:4). The Temple compound, as befits its unique metaphysical status, at times defied the laws of physics by providing infinite space for worshippers (Avot 5).

In the **World-to-Come**, the celestial Jerusalem will descend to earth and the city will spread out in every direction to encompass all the returning exiles (Ber. 49a; B. B. 75b, Sifrei 1; Zech. 2–12). Messianic Jerusalem will be of astronomical proportions and unsurpassed splendor, encompassing thousands of gardens, pools, towers, and citadels, and only the righteous will be permitted entry. The gates and building will be made of precious **gemstones**, its walls of precious metals, and its glow will be visible to the ends of the earth (Isa. 54:12; Mid. Teh. 87:2; B.B. 75b; PdRK 299; BhM 3:74–75). Its towers will rise so high that it will merge with heaven (BhM 3:67; PdRK 466). God's **Glory** will reside there and experiencing it will become commonplace (Zech. 2).

A great tent will be made from the skin of **Leviathan** and all will gather under it to feast on its meat in a messianic banquet. The hidden vessels of the Second Temple will be recovered, the Temple will function again, and the waters of the **abyss**, now tamed, will issue forth from under the messianic Temple, growing into mighty streams that will freshen the waters of both the Dead Sea and the Mediterranean (Yoma 77b–78a; Zech. 14; Ezek. 47:1–12). **Clouds** will convey the pilgrims of all nations to Jerusalem on a regular basis, where they will worship at the Temple in universal harmony.

Jesus: Itinerant Galilean holy man and failed **messiah** (ca. 1st century). In the Gospel accounts, Jesus is a miraculous figure, born of a mortal woman and the **Holy Spirit**. He has the power to heal, cast out demons, multiply food-

stuffs, walk on water, and perform many other miracles. Christian dogma declares him the "only begotten son of God" and "God incarnate," claims that Jews reject.

The Rabbis rarely mention Jesus or Christians in the centuries following his death. From the few unambiguous comments about him found in **Talmud** and **Midrash**, it is clear they knew very little about Jesus, and what little they did know came mostly from Christian sources. Often what appears in rabbinic literature is convoluted tidbits from the Gospel accounts. Thus a figure called Ben Stada—who may or may not be Jesus—gained magical skills as a result of spending his youth in **Egypt** (Shab. 104b). Whether or not the Shabbat passage is actually referring to Jesus, elsewhere it is clear some Rabbis believed Jesus was really a magician (Sanh. 104b). The medieval polemical tract **Toldot Yeshu** claimed that Jesus obtained his magical and miraculous powers by stealing the knowledge of the **Tetragrammaton** from inside the **Temple**. He wrote the **name of God** on parchment and inserted it into an incision (or a tattoo) in his skin. Jesus then used the power of God's name to fly and to perform miraculous healings.

Jews were also highly skeptical of the Christian claim of his resurrection and ascension. Rather than ascending bodily into heaven as the Gospels claim, Toldot Yeshu asserts his body was stolen by a gardener who used it for his own purposes. References to this "body theft" story also appear in pagan and Christian apologetic literature about Jesus. Most of the more colorful Jewish legends appear in Toldot Yeshu.[1]

1. Roth, *Encyclopedia Judaica*, vol. 10, 10–14; vol. 15, 1208.

Jethro: The father-in-law of Moses. According to **Midrash**, for a time Jethro served as a sorcerer in the palace of Pharaoh. He saw **Joseph** use the **rod** of power the Patriarchs had inherited from **Adam**, so when Joseph died he took it and planted it in the garden of his home in Midian. There it remained, unmovable, until **Moses** appeared and drew the rod out of the **earth**. When he saw this, Jethro knew Moses was the man destined to deliver Israel, and he gave his daughter **Zipporah** to him in marriage (PdRE 40).

Jewelry: *SEE* CROWN; EARRING; GEMSTONES; RINGS; TZOHAR.

Jezebel: Queen of Israel through marriage to King Ahab. The Bible taught that she was a **witch** who used her powers to lead Ahab astray (II Kings, chapter 9).

Job: The Rabbis call him one of the "seven gentile prophets." In the pseudepigraphic Testament of Job, Job fights a protracted face-to-face contest with **Satan**. At the end of his life, Job gives his daughters miraculous belts that grant them power over **angels**.

Jochnes and Mamres (alternately, Jannes and Mambres): The chief magicians of Pharaoh who battled **Moses** in **Egypt**. They foresaw the coming of Moses by means of **divination** and so instructed Pharaoh to kill the Israelite firstborn sons. As the two sons of **Balaam**, they were true **witches**; they could fly and make themselves invisible. Later they joined the Israelites in the Exodus as agent provocateurs and incited the people to construct the **Golden Calf**. They also assisted Balaam in his efforts to curse Israel. Eventually they were slain using the power of the divine name (Men. 85a; Tanh. Ki Tissa 19; Yalkut, Ex. 168; Zohar I).

Joel: An **angel** mentioned in the **Testament of Solomon**.

Jonathan, Rabbi: SEE YOCHANAN.

Jonathan Shada: A **demon** mentioned in the **Talmud** (Yev. 22a).

Joseph: Patriarch and son of **Jacob**. Joseph was a celebrated oneiromancer, with a special God-given capacity to interpret **dreams**. On three occasions he demonstrates this talent in the **Bible** (Gen. 37, 39, 41). He was also a diviner, engaging in the practice of **hydromancy** by use of a ritual cup. This cup becomes the occasion for one episode in the reconciliation of Joseph and his brothers (Gen. 43–44).

According to the **Midrash**, the pit his brothers cast him into was populated by poisonous snakes and scorpions, but like Daniel, he was miraculously protected (Shab. 22a; Gen. R. 84:16). Later, **Gabriel** taught Joseph all the world's languages while he languished in prison. After his death, the Egyptians had his body sealed in a metal coffin and sunk in the Nile in order that his bones would bless the river (MdRI Bashallach; Ex. R. 20:17). With the help of **Serach bat Asher**, Moses was able to raise the coffin from the deep in order to fulfill the promise made to Joseph, on his death bed, that his bones would be buried at **Machpelah** (Sot. 13a–b; MdRI Be-Shallach; PdRK 11:12). The descendants of Joseph are immune to the **evil eye** (Ber. 20a).

Joseph ben Ephraim Caro: SEE CARO, JOSEPH; MAGGID.

Joshua: The successor of **Moses** as leader of the Israelites, Joshua meets an **angel** outside of Jericho, the commander (**Sar**) of the **host of heaven**, which later tradition identified with **Michael** (Josh. 5:13). He commanded the sun to stand still for thirty-six hours (Yalkut, Lech Lecha). Joshua eventually married **Rahab**, and the prophets **Jeremiah** and **Huldah** were their descendants (Num. R. 8; MdRI, Yitro).

Joshua ben Levi: Talmudic Sage (ca. 3rd century). He was a confidant of the angelic **Elijah**. Elijah was Joshua's **maggid**, or spirit guide. Joshua accompanied Elijah on some of his earthly missions (Mak. 11a; Gen. R. 35:2; BhM 2). Elijah also granted him an interview with the Messiah (Sanh. 98a). Rabbi Joshua is most famous for having toured the seven levels of **Gehenna** and the **seven heavens**. There are multiple versions of his visions in both rabbinic and medieval texts. In one case, it is told that he first tricked the **Angel of Death** into giving up its sword before Joshua jumped over the wall to **Eden**. Once in Paradise, he refused to give the sword back until God intervened, and then only after extracting a promise from the Angel that it would henceforth no longer display the fearful weapon to his victims (Ket. 77b; Ber. 51a; Eruv. 19a; BhM 2, 5).

Joshua had the power to make it rain (J. Tan. 3:4). He also practiced oneiromancy and taught methods for interpreting and averting ill omens that appear in **dreams** (Ber. 56b). He provided sage advice on how to avoid attracting the Angel of Death (do not take a shirt directly from someone's hand in the morning, do not allow someone who has not washed their hands to wash yours, and don't stand close to a woman who has just returned from caring for a corpse) (Ber. 51a). His son Joseph also had the power to see **visions** (Pes. 50a; B.B. 10b).

Joshua ben Perachya: Early Sage (ca. 1st century BCE–1st century CE). He was one of the *zugot*, the scholars who formed the leadership of the Jewish community in the third through first centuries BCE. He is credited as being a teacher of **Jesus** while he lived in exile in **Egypt** (Sanh. 107b). Evidently, there is a legend (this writer cannot identify the source) that Joshua once used a **get** to exorcise a **succubus**. For this reason, his name will sometimes be invoked in the text of **amulets** and **incantation bowls** that likewise use the language of divorce to exorcise **liliths** and female demons.[1]

> 1. Patai, "Exorcism and Xenoglossia among the Safed Mystics," 225; Naveh and Shaked, *Amulets and Magic Bowls*, 17, 159–61.

Joy and Humor: "Serve God in joy" (Ps. 100:3). Judaism emphasizes that joy and laughter are spiritual tools that draw one close to God (Avot 4:1; Ben Porat Yosef 49a). Humor, **music** and **dance** are, in fact, forms of worship. **Chasidism** in particular teaches the need to make joy central to worship, and offers techniques for cultivating joyfulness on a daily basis. Sadness is a kind of *satan*, a spiritual obstacle to be overcome daily.

Despite the assumptions of dour puritans of all faiths, both the **Bible** and rabbinic literature brim with humor: puns, wordplays, joke names, and even episodes of *schadenfreude*. The entire biblical book of **Esther** is written in the style of a farce about a very serious subject, anti-Semitism, and through the celebration of Purim, Jewish tradition treats it as an elaborate parody.

Two jesters are mentioned in the **Talmud** as spiritual agents of God (Tan. 22a). The **Baal Shem Tov** particularly praised the work of clowns in opening people's hearts to God. Chasidic masters employed witty stories, jokes, and even outright pranks in order to instruct their disciples, a custom still markedly evident in rabbinic sermons to this day.

Jubilees, Book of: This retelling of the events of Genesis is a **sefer chitzon**, a book "outside" the biblical canon. It features the story of the **fallen angels**, the **giants**, and a sectarian solar calendar. Multiple copies of it were found among the **Dead Sea Scrolls**, and the priests of **Qumran** may well have been the advocates, or even the authors, of the Jubilees ideology.

Judah: Patriarch and son of **Jacob**, progenitor of the tribe of Judah and therefore of most Jews. His voice was so powerful it could be heard in neighboring countries. He was reported to have fantastic strength, superior to Samson. He could grind an **iron** bar to dust with his teeth (Gen. R. 91–93). The "Angel of Desire" drove him to have **sex** with Tamar (Gen. R. 85).

Judah ben Samuel he-Chasid or Judah the Pious: Founding figure of the **German Pietist** movement and wunder-rabbi (German, ca. 12th–13th century). He could use the **name of God** to constructive ends, from **healing** the sick to capturing criminals, and a number of his **segullot** have been preserved. He could teleport via a **cloud**. He believed that one could learn new insights into the Torah and its interpretations by consulting **angels**, adjuring **demons**, and using the theurgic power of certain Jewish **prayers**, especially the **Sh'ma** (Or Zarua, Eruv. 147; Sefer Me'irat Enayim). In at least one account, he conjured a dead spirit (Sefer ha-Gan). When he became convinced by **divination** that a woman's barrenness was a lifelong condition, he had the woman undergo a simulated burial and resurrection in order to cure her. His major works were Sefer ha-Kavod (which has not survived intact), **Sefer Chasidim**, and Sod ha-Yichud.

Judah Loew ben Bezalel (the MaHaRaL): Rabbi, polymath, and mystic (Czech, ca. 16th century). A great communal leader of the Jews of Prague, Rabbi Judah is most famous in occult circles for the story of the **golem** he created to protect the community against anti-Semitic violence.

Judgment: (*Mishpat; Tzedek*). God is the source and guarantor of justice (Ps. 82). In Genesis, chapter 18, Abraham asks the rhetorical question, "Will not the Judge of all the earth deal justly?" Since, as the book of Job highlights, there is in fact no assurance of justice being meted out in this world, Judaism teaches God's ultimate judgment awaits us in the **World-to-Come**. In the rabbinic understanding, post-mortem judgment comes in three phases: **Chibbut ha-Kever**, **Gehenna**, and Yom ha-Din (the torments of the grave, hell, and the Day of Judgment). The process each soul faces is based on the moral condition of the person; whether he or she is counted among the righteous, the wicked, or the **beinonim**, the "in-betweens" whose life is a mix of sin and merit. Kabbalists divide the afterlife into seven periods of judgment (Zohar III: 127a).

Dying itself is seen as a kind of atonement for one's sins (M. Sanh. 6:2) and the terror of encountering the **Angel of Death** begins it all. This is the start of the Chibbut ha-Kever, and the subsequent separation of the soul from the body is overseen by various angels of judgment, especially **Domah**, the angel of the grave. The newly deceased souls, lingering at the grave, must review their earthly deeds and experience the disintegration of their earthly remains (Lev. R. 4; Sanh. 47b; Tan. 11a; Mid. Teh. 11:6; Chag. 5a). The righteous, by contrast, are spared both the pain of death and the confrontation with the grimmest angels (PR 44:8). Those who gave charity in secret or were diligent in their Torah study will also be spared the worst of this first phase (PR 2; Ket. 104a).

The second, intermediate phase of the rabbinic scheme involves the placement of the soul pending the final Day of Judgment. The souls of the righteous, as well as those who underwent enormous suffering while still in their bodies (Eruv. 41b), go directly to Gan **Eden** or the Treasury of Souls beneath the **Throne of Glory**. The wicked and the *beinonim* descend into Gehenna, where they are assigned to different compartments. For the *beinonim* (that is, the bulk of humanity), Gehenna is a kind of purgatory, purifying their souls of the accreted sins of their lifetime. The process lasts a maximum of twelve months, after which the souls are transferred to Gan Eden to await the Day of Judgment (Shab. 33b; R.H. 17a; Ex. R. 7:4). For the wholly wicked, Gehenna is where they will remain until the End of Days. Some Sages in the **Talmud** try to identify those who will meet such an awful judgment. They include those who utterly deride the teachings of God and who combine adultery with publicly shaming and slandering their neighbors as those they think deserve

the fate of "going down into Gehenna and not coming up." (B.M. 58b). Others add the entire generation of the Flood (M. Sanh. 10:3).

Third, at the Final Judgment at the **End of Days**, all souls undergo **resurrection** and must stand before God, the Judge of Judges (Sanh. 91a). Most souls, even those who were burdened with so many sins that they had to be summoned directly from Gehenna, will then know the final reward of the World-to-Come. Only the utterly and completely wicked will be annihilated and blotted out completely from under heaven and from all memory (B.B. 11a; Ber. 18b; Shab. 152b–156b). *SEE* DEATH; ETERNAL LIFE; JUDGMENT, DAY OF; WORLD-TO-COME.

Judgment, Day of: (*Yom ha-Din, Yom Adonai, Yom ha-Hu, Ait ha-Hee*). A term often applied to the annual observance of Rosh ha-Shanah, when God judges Creation (even the angels are judged—Isa. 24:21; High Holiday Machzor) or to the later tradition that there are actually four days of judgment each year: **Rosh ha-Shanah**, **Sukkot**, **Passover**, and **Shavuot** (PdRK 7:2).

"Judgment Day" is also used to refer to the **eschatological** moment at the end of time when the sleeping dead are resurrected to give a final account for their deeds in life. Many versions of this day appear in Jewish writings, starting with the biblical book of **Daniel** (chapter 7). Some describe it as a day of darkness and wrath when all the nations will be judged (Amos 5, 8; Isa. 1–3). It will be marked by earthquakes and consuming fires. Those who go through it will be purified, like silver in a crucible (Zech. 14). Even as individuals are called to moral account, the nations will also be judged. The nation of Israel will be vindicated, and its suffering at the hands of other nations redressed. The righteous among the nations will be accounted to Israel, and will ascend God's sacred mountain to form the messianic kingdom of God. Some traditions link the day to the coming of the **Messiah**, though others distinguish the two events from each other to varying degrees (R.H. 16b–17b). *SEE* BEINONIM; EDEN; ESCHATOLOGY; ETERNAL LIFE; GEHENNA; JUDGMENT.

K

Kabbalah: "[Occult] Tradition." Historians of Judaism identify many schools of Jewish esotericism across time, each with its own unique interests and beliefs. Technically, the term "Kabbalah" only applies to the form of Jewish occult gnosis that emerged in medieval Spain and Provence from the 12th century on. Jews outside the circle of academia, however, use the term "Kabbalah" as a catchall for Jewish esotericism in all its forms.

Two features particularly distinguish Jewish occultism. The first is the tendency to compose mystical and esoteric works as **pseudepigrapha**—to portray a new revelation as the product of antiquity or of a particular worthy figure of the past. This is characteristic of many prominent mystical texts, such as **Hechalot** texts, the **Bahir**, the **Zohar**, and of the writings of the **Circle of the Unique Cherub**.

The other feature is the tendency for Jewish mystics to be part of social circles rather than lone seekers. With few exceptions, such as Abraham Abulafia, esoterically inclined Jews tend to congregate in mystical brotherhoods and associations. It is not unusual for a single master to bring forth a new and innovative mystical school, which yields multiple generations of that particular mystical practice.

Distinctive esoteric schools include **Ma'asei–Bereshit**, **Ma'asei Merkavah**, the **German Pietists**, the Circle of the Unique Cherub, the **Iyyun Circle**, Zoharic Kabbalah, the ecstatic school of **Abraham Abulafia**, the teachings of **Isaac Luria**, and **Chasidism**. Scholars can break these groupings down even further based on individual masters and their disciples.

There are three ways in which esoteric knowledge is obtained in Jewish tradition: through textual interpreta-tion, through the traditions transmitted orally by a Kabbalistic master, and by means of some sort of direct revelation (examples of this include an angel, Elijah, spirit possession, or heavenly visitation).[1]

There are also three dimensions to almost all forms of Jewish esotericism: the speculative, the experiential, and the practical. The first dimension, that of speculation, involves the quest for gnosis—plumbing the hidden reality of the universe (the nature of the Godhead), understanding the cosmogony (origins) and cosmology (organization) of the universe, and apprehending the divine economy of spiritual forces in the cosmos. This is, technically speaking, an esoteric discipline more than it is a mystical one.

Although it is primarily interested in metaphysics, it would be a grave mistake to say that speculative Kabbalah is anti-rational. All Jewish mystical/esoteric traditions adopt the language of, and expand upon, the philosophic ideas of their time: the Merkavah mystics are influenced by both Platonic ideas and Pythagorean mathematics, the classical Kabbalah was influenced by Neo-Platonism, and Abraham Abulafia was inspired by Maimonidean Scholasticism.

The distinctive perspective that speculative Kabbalists bring to their intellectual enterprise, the one that brings it within the boundaries of mysticism, is the tendency to see the Creator and the **Creation** as on a continuum, rather than as discrete entities. This is especially true with regards to the powerful mystical sense of kinship between God and humanity (Ohr Yitzkhak 182a–b; Zohar I: 94a). Within the soul of every individual is a hidden part of God that is waiting to be revealed. And even mystics who refuse to so boldly describe such a fusion of God and man nevertheless find the whole of Creation suffused in divinity, breaking down distinctions between God and the universe. Thus, the Kabbalist Moses Cordovero writes, "The essence of divinity is found in every single thing, nothing but It exists . . . It exists in each existent."

The second dimension is the experiential, which entails the actual quest for mystical experience: a direct, intuitive, unmediated encounter with a close but concealed Deity. As Abraham Joshua Heschel puts it, mystics ". . . want to taste the whole wheat of spirit before it is ground by the millstones of reason." The mystic specifically seeks the ecstatic experience of God, not merely knowledge about God. In their quest to encounter God, Jewish mystics live spiritually disciplined lives. While Jewish mysticism gives no sanction to monasticism, either formal or informal, experiential Kabbalists tend to be ascetics. And though Judaism keeps its mystics grounded—they are expected to marry, raise a family, and fulfill all customary communal religious obligations—they willfully expand the sphere of their pietistic practice beyond what tradition requires. Many Kabbalists create **hanganot**, personal daily devotional practices (Hanganot ha-Tzadikim). Thus, in his will, one Kabbalist recommended this regime to his sons: periods of morning, afternoon, evening, and midnight prayer; two hours devoted to the Bible, four and a half to Talmud, two to ethical and mystical texts, and two to other Jewish texts; one and a half hours to daily care, time to make a living—and five hours to sleep.

The third dimension is the practical, theurgic, or pragmatic Kabbalah (*Kabbalah Maasit* or *Kabbalah Shimmush*); the application of mystical power to effect change in **Asiyah**, the material world of action. This is both the most attractive and the most dangerous aspect of the mystical enterprise. For that reason, many Kabbalists opt not to pursue this branch of Kabbalah at all (Sha'arei Kedushah). Practical Kabbalah consists of rituals for gaining and exercising power. It involves activating theurgic potential by the way one performs the commandments, the summoning and controlling of angelic and demonic forces, and otherwise tapping into the supernatural energies present in Creation.

The purpose of tapping into the practical Kabbalah is to further God's intention in the world: to advance good, subdue **evil**, heal, and mend. The true master of this art fulfills the human potential to be a co-creator with God

(**Sefer Yetzirah**). But beyond these altruistic purposes, it can also be used to serve the needs of the individual, and herein lies the danger. Thus a person may use it to enhance one's knowledge of Torah, or to give the adept an advantage over another. The same power that can be used to heal can be used to harm. It can make real blessings, but also curses. It is also possible to unintentionally unleash demonic powers (Minchat Yehudah). *SEE* CREATION; EMANATION; MEDITATION; SEFIROT; SUMMONING.

1. Fine, *Physician of the Soul, Healer of the Cosmos*, 99–100.

Kabshiel: Angelic name that appears on **amulets**.

Kaddish: (Aramaic, "Sanctification"). This **prayer** of divine praise, which makes no mention of death, has become inextricably associated with memorializing the dead. In part, this association has arisen from a story told of Rabbi **Akiba**. In Seder Eliyahu Zuta, we learn that Akiba once encountered a **ghost**. The Sage inquired as to why the spirit could not find rest, so the ghost related that it was his punishment for having failed to religiously educate his son. Akiba then took it upon himself to teach the boy the prayer service. When the boy finally recited the words of Kaddish, his father's **soul** was released (also see Sanh. 104a).

Perhaps because of this incident, it has become the practice to recite Kaddish daily for a year after the death of a close relative, in the belief that it will ease the soul's time in **Gehenna**, which can last up to a year. Customarily, a surviving relative says Kaddish for eleven months rather than the twelve of a full year, so as not to suggest to others that one considers the deceased so wicked that he or she deserved a full year of punishment. *SEE* DEATH.

Kaf: Eleventh letter of the **Hebrew alphabet**. The letter represents *keter*, "crown," the first emanation of the **sefirot**. It is also the first letter of the word **karet**, "cut off." Every Jew potentially shares in this supernal crown when he or she chooses to embrace the "crowns" God has provided: the crown of Torah, of kingship, of the priesthood, or of a good name. By contrast, those Jews who utterly reject these crowns are spiritually cut off from both the power and blessings of God.[1]

1. Munk, *The Wisdom of the Hebrew Alphabet*, 133–37.

Kaf: "Hand/Palm." *SEE* FINGERS; HAND.

Kaf Kela: "Sling Pocket." One of the seven compartments of **Gehenna**. The name is derived from a biblical passage, "The souls of Your enemies shall be slung out, as from a *kaf kela*" (I Sam. 25:29). In Kaf Kela, the punishing angels play, so to speak, a relentless game of lacrosse, tossing the souls of the transgressors back and forth as their game balls.

Kaftzefoni: A **demon** and occasional consort of **Lilith** (Treatise on the Left Emanation).

Kaftziel: Planetary **angel** of Saturn (Sefer Yetzirah; Sefer Raziel).

Kahana: Talmudic Sage (ca. 3rd–4th century). In a fit of annoyance, his teacher Rabbi Yochanan slew him with the **evil eye**, but later resurrected him. After that, Kahana opted to leave Yochanan's academy (B.K. 117a–b).

Kalonymus (or Qalonymus) Family: This dynasty of medieval Rhineland Jews produced a line of distinguished rabbis. They also had their own familial collection of esoteric traditions that shaped the teachings of the **German Pietists**.[1]

    1. Green, *Jewish Spirituality*, vol. 1, 356.

Kamia: "Amulet." A charm or talisman. *SEE* AMULET.

Kapkafuni: A demon queen mentioned in medieval Jewish tradition (Shoshan Yesod ha-Olam).

Kapparah: "Expiation." In the theurgic ceremony of kapparah, performed on the eve of **Yom Kippur**, traditional Jews transfer their sins to a bird by waving it around their heads three times while reciting the words, "This bird is my surrogate, my substitute, my atonement; this cock shall meet death, but I shall find a long and pleasant life of peace." Then the **animal**, usually a chicken, is slaughtered and donated to the poor. The practice has enjoyed popular support for centuries, despite the disapproval of many rabbinical authorities. Most modernist Orthodox Jews opt to replace the hen with a sack of cash, which is then given as **charity**. *SEE* COCK; SACRIFICE; SUBSTITUTION; THEURGY.

Karet: "Cut off/Extirpation." A divine punishment mentioned in the **Bible** (Gen. 17:14), usually meted out for acts of gross disrespect toward heaven (desecrating the Shabbat, idolatry) or toward another person (incest, adultery). The Mishnah has a tractate, Keritot, which identifies thirty-six crimes that merit Karet. **Nachmanides** believed being "cut off" referred to the soul being reincarnated in a more degraded body (Commentary to Lev. 18:29). **Isaac Luria** taught it involved the lower soul (*nefesh*) being unable to make the journey into the afterlife and was the cause of **ghosts** and **dybbuks** (Zohar III: 57b, 217a; Sha'ar ha-Gilgulim 4).

Kasdiel: An Egyptian sorcerer, the father-in-law of the biblical **Ishmael** (Sefer Meir Tehillot, p. 91).

Kastimon and Afrira: A pair of demonic shape-changing princes (Zohar I: 9b).

Kastirin: (Greek, "Tormentor"). A class of **demons** mentioned in the Zohar (I: 20a).

Kavanah: "Intention/Concentration." Judaism teaches that proper intention is essential to meaningful prayer (Yad., Tefillah 4:16; Hovot Levavot). The Kabbalists go further, teaching that developing the right state of mind is an absolute prerequisite for any religious act or **ritual** to have *gevurah*, or spiritual energy. Often this kavanah requires extended meditation exercises. There are even techniques called *kavanot* to help achieve this concentration.[1] *SEE* MEDITATION; YICHUDIM.

    1. Scholem, *Major Trends in Jewish Mysticism*, 275–77.

Kavanot, Sefer ha-: A collection of the teachings of **Chayyim Vital**, especially focusing on mystical meditations and prayers and the cultivating of the right intention to make them efficacious.

Kavod: *SEE* GLORY.

Kedushah or Kedushat ha-Shem: A liturgical prayer that appears several times in the prayer book. The text is constructed from the various appearances of **angels** in the **Bible** and the words they spoke. One version, included in the prayer *Yotzer Or*, lists the classes of angels that attend upon God. The goal of the prayer is for the congregation to become one with the angelic choirs in their praise of God. In their astral ascensions, **Merkavah** mystics and **German Pietists** took a particular interest in the music of the angels when they recited their *kedushah* praises to God. The ascendant mystic would learn these melodies to bring them back to earth for use in the synagogue.[1]

1. Schafer, *The Hidden and Manifest God*, 46–49. Also see Wolfson, *Through a Speculum that Shines*.

Kefitzat ha-Derech: "Bounding of the Path." *SEE* TELEPORTATION.

Kelach Pitchei Chochmah: "One Hundred and Thirty-Eight Openings of Wisdom." A Kabbalistic treatise by **Moses Luzzato** giving special attention to the architecture of the soul.

Kelipot: "Husks." Remnants of the cosmic tragedy associated with the fall of **Adam Kadmon**, these husks of **evil** encase the scattered sparks of divine holiness that must be released by humanity and restored to their divine source through the spiritual process of **tikkun** (Sha'ar ha-Gilgulim 3; Sefer ha-Tikkunim). Their existence is utterly dependent upon human action, and they are fed and strengthened by human transgression. Later Kabbalistic thought develops a taxonomy of different types of kelipot, including the **nogah**, an admixture of good and evil that energizes all demonic forces. (**Zohar** I: 1a; Tanya 1–2). The most powerful of all kelipot, their organizing principle, is personified as **Samael**. *SEE* BREAKING OF THE VESSELS; NITZOTZ.

Kelonymus Baal ha-Nes: Wonder-working rabbi (Israel, ca. 17th century). This Jerusalem rabbi miraculously restored a Christian child to life using the **Tetragrammaton**. In doing so, he thwarted an attempt to blame the Jews of Jerusalem for a **blood libel**. Pilgrims still visit his grave on the **Mount of Olives**, believing his merit will ensure their safe return home.

Kemuel: Angel who guards the gates of heaven (Gedulat Moshe). While Moses was receiving the **Torah** in heaven, Kemuel attempted to expel him. Moses was forced to destroy him (BhM 1:58–60).

Kenahora: (Aramaic, "No evil eye!"). An exclamatory incantation used to thwart the evil eye when one feels vulnerable to its attack.

Keshet: "Bow." Sign of the Hebrew **zodiac** for the month of Kislev (Sagittarius). A symbol of both peace (Gen. 9) and war, it signifies the varied interaction of Jews and non-Jews; it symbolizes both **Joseph**, who thrived in a foreign land, and **Chanukah**, which exemplified conflict with gentiles.[1]

1. Erlanger, *Signs of the Times*, 161–98.

Kesilim: "Fools/Imps." Impish spirits. Belief in these creatures is derived from a supernatural interpretation of Proverbs 14, which speaks of the misleading ways of the *kesilim*.

Ketem Paz: A commentary on the **Zohar** by Shem Tov ibn Gaon.

Keter: "Crown." The "highest" of the **sefirot**, it is the first to emerge from the **Ein Sof**. It is the intentionality, the desire of the Ein Sof to bring forth **Creation**. It is usually conceived in terms of **paradox**, such as "hidden light," or *via negativa*, by describing only what it is *not*; it is "no thing." The divine name *El Elyon*, "God most High," is linked to Keter. It is also equated with *Arikh Anpin* in the Lurianic theory of **Partzufim**.

Keter Malchut: "Crown of kingship." A critical, yet undefined mystical attribute of the **Messiah**, it is also the name of a treatise on **astrology** written by **Solomon Gabirol**.

Ketev Meriri: A **demon** (Pes. 111b). *SEE* BITTER DESTRUCTION.

Keturah: The wife taken by Abraham after the death of Sarah (Gen. 22), the Sages teach that she is actually Hagar, Abraham's maidservant and father of his first child, Ishmael (Gen. R. 61).

Key: According to Ta'anit 2a, God possesses three keys: to **rain**, to childbirth, and to **resurrection**. All other keys God has given over to "messengers" (i.e., angels and humanity), but these three remain God's sole prerogative.

In Midrash Pesikta Rabbati, at the time of the Roman destruction of the Second **Temple**, the High Priest cast the keys to the building up toward heaven where they were caught by an angelic hand. The High Priest then offered the sacred Temple vessels (or instruments) to the earth and the ground swallowed them up. When the **Messiah** comes, all these Temple articles will be recovered and restored.

Key of Solomon: (*Mafteach Shlomo*). A medieval magical text devoted primarily to the summoning of **angels** and **demons** and the construction of **amulets**. It describes the use of magical **circles** in some detail. There are Hebrew and Latin versions and the book has Jewish, Hermetic, and Christian influences present.

Khazars: A Turkish-speaking tribe of the Crimean-Central Asian regions that converted to Judaism in the early Middle Ages (ca. 740 CE). This Jewish kingdom survived for over a century until overwhelmed by the expanding Rus peoples from the north, spawning numerous legends.[1]

A popular anti-Jewish myth circulating among anti-Semitic groups is that modern Jews from eastern Europe are not Semites at all, and have no relationship to the ancient Jews of the Bible. Rather, we are all really Turkish descendants of the Khazars (and therefore somehow "pseudo-Jews"), despite historical, demographic, linguistic, and, most recently, genetic evidence that reveal the specious nature of this claim.[2]

  1. Roth, *Encyclopedia Judaica*, vol. 10, 944–49.
  2. Hoffman, *Campaign for Radical Truth in History*, at http://www.hoffman-info.com.

Kiddush: The **ritual** for initiating a **Sabbath** or holiday by reciting a blessing over **wine**. Once blessed, Kiddush wine is believed to have medicinal power (Beit Yosef, Orech Chayyim 269).

Kiddush ha-Shem: "Sanctifying the Name." The act of accepting martyrdom rather than refute one's faith. The willingness to accept death rather than deny a doctrine or commandment of Judaism has been celebrated in Jewish tradition since the example set by **Daniel** and his companions in the **Bible**. Naturally, most Jews facing martyrdom have not enjoyed the miraculous deliverances recorded for those biblical worthies. Nevertheless, anyone who dies to honor God is declared "holy," and by the medieval period, artifacts associated with them, their gravesites, and even their names, were believed to be imbued with great spiritual power. The martyrs themselves can expect an exalted place in **Eden**. SEE LAMED-VAVNIKS; RIGHTEOUS, THE.

Kiddush L'vanah: "Sanctifying/Blessing the Moon." SEE NEW MOON.

Kinder Benimmerins: Bloodlusting **witches** who slay children (Emek ha-Melekh 140b).

Kingdom of God (or Kingdom of Heaven): (*Malchut Shaddai; Malchut Shamayim*). This term has multiple connotations, including the individual act of cleaving to God (Deut. R. 2:31), but usually refers to the advent of the Messiah and the Messianic Era. A brief summary of the main ideas is this: At a time deemed appropriate to God, based on either the radical improvement or the radical decline of the human moral condition, there will be a final reconciliation (*tikkun olam*) of the world's political and social order with the establishment of the Kingdom of God on earth under the leadership of the **Messiah**. The **nations** will be brought into harmony and the recognition of God's dominion will be complete, making an end to war, exploitation, and inequity. This period will mark the restoration of the Davidic dynasty to Israel, the return of **prophecy**, and, for all intents and purposes, the end of history. At some point during this Messianic kingdom, the natural order and human nature will be radically transformed. The dead, having already made preliminary journeys through the afterlife, will be restored to a perfected bodily existence through **resurrection**, brought to final judgment, and those who merit it will live out an ideal life. After death the individual soul will dwell in eternal bliss in the presence of God. *SEE* KADDISH; WORLD-TO-COME.

Kings, Books of: The books Kings I and II contain many of the most famous miracles recorded in the **Bible**, outside those of the **Torah**. The central prophets of the books, **Elijah** and **Elisha**, are conspicuous wonder-workers, doing things as minor as levitating **iron** in **water**, to feats as dramatic as resurrecting the dead.

Kipod: Demon prince; guardian of a gate of **Gehenna** (Masekhet Gehinnom).

Kiss: The kiss as a spiritual act has a long history in Judaism. Students would kiss the hand of their master after a learning session, symbolically acknowledging the hand that "fed" them spiritual sustenance. Masters would kiss disciples on the head as a kind of initiation **ritual** (T. Chag. 2:2). In the **Zohar**, in particular, masters would kiss students, often on the eyes, when they had demonstrated an insight or high attainment of wisdom.[1] In the highest heaven, the angels who serve before the **Throne of Glory** kiss God during the afternoon worship (Hechalot Rabbati). A special category of kiss is the "kiss of God" (*Meitah be-nesikah*). This refers to death directly at the hands of God (or the **Shekhinah**). This easiest of all deaths circumvents the dreaded **Angel of Death**. According to the Sages, only six people have died this way: **Abraham**, **Isaac**, **Jacob**, **Miriam**, **Aaron**, and **Moses** (B.B. 17a; S of S R. 1:2; Tanh., Va-Etchanan). In later Jewish mystical writings, a number of Kabbalistic masters die in ecstasy via the "kiss" (Zohar III: 144b; Sha'ar ha-Gilgulim 39). Jewish mysticism also equated the "kiss" with **devekut**, mystical fusion with God (Zohar II: 53a).

1. Arthur Green, "Introducing the Pritzker Edition Zohar" (lecture, Convention of the Central Conference of American Rabbis, Toronto, June 2004).

Kleidon: Listening to **children** at study to hear **omens** in the verses they recite. *SEE* DIVINATION.

Knives: Knives are a symbol of power and force and as such are sometimes used in magical rites. The fact that they are made from **metal**, especially **iron**, only enhances their magical potential. There seems to be a special relationship between knives and the demonic: the **Angel of Death** wields a knife, and knives are used for summoning demons and as a magical defense against evil spirits.

Knives are often used in the creation of magic **circles**. A knife under a pillow will protect a childbearing woman against demonic attack. Specially constructed blades hum when poison is present. Knives are also used in casting curses.

Knots: Knots represent the power to restrict and restrain. The knotted **fringes** commanded to be worn by the Israelites in the book of Leviticus are symbolic reminders that the Jews have "bound" themselves to God even as the fringes are conduits of divine power. Knots were used in Greco-Roman magic as a sympathetic act in cursing rituals. In Jewish esoteric lore, this constricting capacity especially manifests itself in issues of **fertility**. Therefore, one should avoid knots around brides or women in childbirth. Seven loops of knots can fend off **witchcraft** (Shab. 66a). Knots tied to the left arm combined with **incantations** can curb obsessive behavior and "longing."

Kochviel: The "Prince of Stars," he is an angel that falls from heaven after lusting for the daughters of humanity. He taught humanity the art of **astrology** (I Enoch).

Kohan: *SEE* PRIEST.

Kohen Brothers: *SEE* JACOB BEN JACOB HA-KOHEN; ISAAC BEN JACOB HA-KOHEN.

Kohen, Naphtali: Wonder-working rabbi (German, ca. 17th century). A master in the use of divine names, he magically protected the communities he served from fires. He also possessed a **ring** of power like the one owned by **Solomon**, and used it to exorcise **demons**. At the end of his life, he became mentally unbalanced.

Komm: An angel who guides **Joshua ben Levi** on a tour of **Gehenna** (BhM II: 48–51).

Korach ben Izhar: This biblical rebel against the authority of **Moses** was swallowed up by the earth for his effrontery (Num. 16; 26).

According to the Sages, Korach was so arrogant because of being extraordinarily wealthy, having found treasures which Joseph had concealed. Just the keys of Korach's treasuries burdened three hundred mules (Pes. 119a; Sanh. 110a).

Korach was simultaneously burned and buried alive (Tan., Korach 23). When the ground swallowed up Korach, the earth became like a vacuum, and everything that belonged to him, even his possessions that had been borrowed by persons far away, found their way into the chasm (J. Sanh. 10:1; Num. R. 50). He and his followers burned in **Gehenna** until Hannah prayed for them (Gen. R. 98:3). Because of her merit, Korach will eventually have a place in **Eden** (AdRN. 36; Num. R. 18:11). **Rabbah bar Channah** related that he was shown the place where Korach and his company went down. Listening to the crack in the earth, he heard voices saying: "Moses and his Torah are true; and we are liars" (B.B. 74a).

Kosem Kesamim: "Augurer/Diviner/Magician." The biblical word (Deut. 18) is related to the Arabic, "to divide," i.e., drawing lots. Such individuals are often linked in Hebrew Scriptures with false prophecy. SEE DIVINATION.

Kosher: SEE FOOD.

Kriat Sh'ma al ha-Mitah: "Bedtime Recitation of the Sh'ma." In Deuteronomy 6, every Jew is commanded to meditate upon God's unity when rising and when going to bed. *Kriat Sh'ma al ha-Mitah* is the **ritual** that fulfills that obligation (Siddur). The ritual also includes a number of protective prayers, invoking God's protection against bad **dreams**, illness, nighttime spirits, and asking the **Shekhi-**nah and the four angels of the **Throne of Glory—Michael**, **Gabriel**, **Raphael**, and **Uriel**—to guard the person while asleep. SEE SLEEP.

Kuf: Nineteenth letter of the **Hebrew alphabet**. It has the linguistic value of "k" and the numeric value of 100. It signifies holiness and circularity.[1]

    1. Munk, *The Wisdom of the Hebrew Alphabet*, 194–98.

Kushiel or Koshiel: "Severity of God." A punishing **angel** of **Gehenna**, he governs one of the seven compartments, "Well of Destruction" (Mid. Konen).

Kvittel: A written request for spiritual guidance, healing, or miraculous intervention, sent by a Chasid to a Chasidic master. The text usually has a standard or stereotypical form. It is normally accompanied by a **pidyon nefesh**, a donation meant for the upkeep of the master and his household (some rebbes were famed for refusing such gratuities as corrupting).

Often the kvittel initiated a face-to-face audience, called a *yechidut*, with the **rebbe**. At other times, the tzadik would respond in writing. Their recipients treated such letters as spiritual relics. Kvittels are even written to dead saints and are left on the grave, in the belief that the spiritual intercession of that particular **righteous** individual can transcend even death.[1]

    1. Schachter and Hoffman, *Sparks of Light*, 83–84. Also see Schachter-Shalomi, *Spiritual Intimacy*.

Kvorim Mesn: (Yiddish, "Measuring graves"). The Ashkenazi custom of women measuring **cemeteries** and graves with candlewick. Having been exposed to the sanctity of meritorious **ancestors**, the wicks would then be cut and made into **candles** to be used during the **High Holy Days** in rituals, divinations, and as protection against spirits.[1]

    1. Weissler, "Measuring Graves, Laying Wicks," in Fine, *Judaism in Practice*, 61–80.

L

Laban: Jacob's father-in-law (Gen. 30) was not only the cunning, manipulative person as portrayed in the Bible, he was a master of **witchcraft** (Targum Yerushalmi, RaSHI on Gen. 30:27; Zohar I: 133b, 164b). In one tradition, he is identified as the grandfather of **Balaam** (Tanh., Balak 12).

Labyrinth: Conceptualizing the path to enlightenment as a maze that the spiritual pilgrim must travel is a theme that appears in several religious traditions, including Judaism. The Jewish use of labyrinths is almost entirely limited to storytelling, written narratives, and diagrams. **Maimonides**, for example, tells the parable of the multi-chambered King's Palace to illustrate the journey to wisdom (Moreh Nevukhim). Several of the parabolic tales of Rabbi **Nachman of Bratzlav** feature a quest that involves negotiating mazelike forests and castles. The **Baal Shem Tov** describes the "palace of the King" (the world) as a place of many locked doors and many keys, in which the soul must somehow make its way (Or Yesharim).

A small 18th-century book for Holy Land pilgrims, *Zicharon Birushalayim* ("Memory of Jerusalem"), includes a woodcut illustration of Jericho in which the city sits amidst a seven-walled labyrinth.[1]

The **sefirot** can be understood in terms of a labyrinth. This is made clear by one of the few existing graphic illustrations of a Jewish labyrinth, which consists of a Kabbalistic "perspective diagram," a drawing of the ten first letters of the names of the sefirot nested inside each other, so that the lines of each letter represent the walls and the gaps in empty spaces of each letter represent the openings (Pardes Rimmonim).

1. Karp, *From the Ends of the Earth*, 87.

Lailah: "Night." Not to be confused with **Lilith**, this is the **angel** of conception (and sex). Lailah escorts new souls to their bodies and erases from their memories all the **Torah** they knew in the **Guf ha–Briyot** (Nid. 16b; Sanh. 6b, 96a; Tanh., Pikudei 3; Zohar I: 91b).

Lamed: Twelfth letter of the **Hebrew alphabet**. It has the numeric value of 30 and the linguistic value of "l." The word *lamed* itself derives from the root verb for learning. It also signifies majesty and emotion (*lev* is the Hebrew word for "heart"). Since *lamed* is also used as the sign for the preposition "to/toward," it conveys purpose and direction.[1]

1. Munk, *The Wisdom of the Hebrew Alphabet*, 138–43.

Lamed-Vavniks: "The Thirty-Six [Righteous]." Those people who are the minimum number of righteous people in each generation that are necessary to sustain the **world**. The legend evidently evolved from an earlier tradition of interpreting the "thirty shekels of silver" mentioned in Zechariah 11:12 as an allegory for godly people; God ensures there will always be thirty righteous people in every generation. (Gen. R. 49:3; Zohar I: 105b; Tikkunei Zohar, 21).

In the earliest version, found in Gen. R. 49:3, there are forty-five, "fifteen in Babylon, thirty in the Land of Israel."

There is no firm explanation for how the tradition settled on the number 36 (Sanh. 97b). Perhaps it is because in **gematria**, 18 is the numeric value of the word for *chai*, "life," so 36 (double *chai*) signifies "abundant life." The term *Lamed-Vavnik* is Yiddish, constructed from the Hebrew letters *Lamed* and *Vav* (these two letters have the combined numeric value of 36) and adding the Russian/Yiddish genitive *-nik*. According to the "thirty-six" legend, most of the thirty-six are *nister*, unknown, anonymously doing their good work unnoticed by the world. The reward for their anonymous labors is to be privileged to directly experience the **Shekhinah**. One of them in each generation is suitable to be the **Messiah** (Sanh. 97b; Suk. 45b; Gen. R. 35:2; Mid. Teh. 5:5). *SEE* RIGHTEOUS, THE.

Lamps: In the Bible, lamps are a symbol of enlightenment, wisdom, and the **Torah**.

Both the **Bible** and rabbinic literature assume oil lamps to be the primary means of portable or personal **light**.

The Chanukah **menorah** serves as a reminder of a miraculous event entailing a lamp, the rededication of the **Temple** by the Maccabees, when enough oil for only one day's burning miraculous burned eight days.

Lamps can be used for the divination of death **omens**. A lamp is lit in a house sufficient for the duration of the Ten Days of Awe. If it extinguishes during that time, it is a sign that someone in that house will die within the year (Hor. 12a). In **Sefer he-Razim**, a lamp is used as part of a **ritual** to summon angelic beings.

The use of wicks embedded in wax tapers is relatively recent among Jews. But as the times and places where candles were used for Jewish rituals (Sabbath, festivals, and commemorating the dead) proliferated, so also did the mention of candles in supernatural contexts. They are used in **incantations** (Sefer Raziel), **divination**, **exorcisms** (Shoshan Yesod ha-Olam), and magical defense. The **Zohar** (ca. 13th century) mentions a candle-gazing **meditation** technique. European Jews in the early modern era practiced a custom of measuring out a **cemetery** with thread, then using that thread to make candlewicks for the home. It was believed that the merit of the sainted dead buried there could be transferred to the household using the taper.[1]

1. Zimmels, *Magicians, Theologians, and Doctors*, 147, 255n.

Language: (*Lishon*). "Then God said, 'Let there be light,' and there was light" (Gen. 1:3). In contrast to contemporary thought concerning language, which holds that words are pale and inadequate symbols for the rich realities they try (but fail) to signify, Judaism has traditionally taught just the opposite—words *are* reality, the highest and most divine form to be found in the universe. Often a text will speak of God "hewing" or "carving" the letters, as if they are physical artifacts. Words are constructive—language makes things happen. This is exemplified by the story of Creation found in Genesis, in which God creates the universe solely through speech-acts.[1]

Words, if correctly used, will manifest their latent divine power. Humans, having the same godly power of speech, can tap into this creative potential that exists in language. Because of this, Jewish esoteric teachings place special value on language as a vehicle of occult knowledge and power.[2] *SEE* HEBREW ALPHABET; INCANTATIONS; MAGIC; NAMES OF GOD; YETZIRAH, SEFER. *(SEE ALSO APPENDIX, FIGURE 1.)*

1. Munk, *The Wisdom of the Hebrew Alphabet*, 16–30.
2. Janowitz, *Icons of Power*, 45–61.

Law and the Paranormal: Jewish law (*Halakhah*) has had an ambivalent relationship with both magic and mysticism. The **Bible** itself forbids many magical, mantic, and spiritualist practices (see Ex. 22:18; and especially, Deut. 18). The **Talmud** reconfirms many of these prohibitions (Tos. Shab. 7, 8:4–12). Still, despite some controversy (M. Sanh. 10), Jewish legalists opened the door to many paranormal practices with their liberal attitude toward virtually any method for **healing** illness, as well as their willingness to recognize spiritual visitations, **omens**, and veridical **dreams** (Shab. 67a–b; Ber. 55b–57a).

In time, even as Jewish law continued to emphatically condemn the practice of **witchcraft**, it came to tolerate both **sorcery** and mediumism in various forms: medical **theurgy**, **astrology**, and the **summoning** of and consulting with spirit guides, such as an **angel** or a **maggid**. In the case of one medieval legalist, the enslavement of **demons** for beneficent purposes is also permitted.

Repeated attempts are made in Halakhah to draw distinctions between licit and illicit paranormal practices and beliefs (the so-called **Ways of the Amorites**) (Shab. 61a–b, 67a–b; Rashba, Teshuvah 408, 409, 413), but in the descriptions of the various practices preserved in Jewish texts, it is evident that the boundaries between the permitted and forbidden become quite blurry. Many Hebrew magical manuals of late antiquity and the Middle Ages effectively ignore all rabbinic limits and prohibitions, or honor them only in the most tendentious fashion.[1]

Jewish law also attempts to place severe restrictions on how one engages in mystical pursuits, as well as limiting who may do so (Chag. 12a–b). Over time many of these strictures come to be disregarded. Still, in contrast to the magicians, Kabbalists have almost universally worked within the parameters of Jewish normative practice, and Jewish mysticism has sought to uphold and validate the value of Jewish tradition. This was especially the case in the medieval controversies over rationalist philosophy and how it threatened to undermine normative Jewish practice; mystics almost universally rallied to the defense of the traditionalists. Often Jewish mystics have taught and practiced at the boundaries of Jewish law, but rare is the example of a mystic who crossed over into full-blown rejection of all rules and norms of behavior—**Shabbatai Tzvi** and **Jacob Frank** being the two notable exceptions.

Jewish legal scholars certainly took seriously the reality of paranormal events. Meir of Lublin, in one of his legal opinions, entertained the question of whether a woman seduced by an incubus that appeared to her in a human form (but not the form of her husband) was guilty of adultery (he concluded she was not) (Responsa #116). The place where Jewish law asserts itself most emphatically is on the issue of new revelations or interpretations of the law itself. It rejects decisions that are derived from **visions**, **angels**, or heavenly voices (B.M. 59b). Jewish legalists almost universally refuse to recognize as valid any opinions or edicts that are credited to paranormal sources. The major exception to this was a period of controversy among the medieval Rhineland Jews when **Jacob of Marvege** claimed to receive solutions to legal questions through angelic and dream revelations. **Joseph Caro** also may have drawn upon a paranormal authority to help him in writing his great legal opus, Beit Yosef, though the role of his personal **maggid** in this part of his writings is ambiguous.

Some later legal digests, such as the Aruch ha-Shulchan (ca. 19th century), actually go so far as to claim that certain practices derived from the Zohar and the teaching of Isaac Luria can take precedent over norms established by non-esoteric legal sources.[2] *SEE* KABBALAH; MAGIC; SHE'ELOT CHALOM; SHE'ELOT U-TESHUVOT MIN HA-SHAMAYIM; SORCERY.

1. Fishbane, "Aspects of Jewish Magic in the Ancient Rabbinic Period," in *Solomon Goldman Lectures II*, 25–34. Also see Roth, *Encyclopdedia Judaica*, vol. 11, 708.
2. Rosen, "The Interaction of Kabbalah and Halachah in the Aruch ha-Shulchan." Also see Zimmels, *Magicians, Theologians, and Doctors*.

Lecanomancy: The art of divining by pouring **oil** on **water** and studying the patterns the oil forms on the surface. This is the practice alluded to by Joseph when he accuses his brothers of stealing his divining cup (Gen. 40). This author could find no mention of it in the **Talmud** or early rabbinic literature, but the practice resurfaces in other Jewish texts, such as **Sefer ha-Razim** and Geniza fragment T-S K 1.80, around the Mediterranean in late antiquity. **Chayyim Vital** describes consulting a **witch** who was an expert in "oil gazing" (Sefer ha-Hezyonot 5). *SEE* DIVINATION; OIL.

Lecha Dodi: A mystical liturgical poem composed by **Solomon Alkebetz**. It personifies the **Sabbath** as the bride of Israel. It is recited Friday night, when the Sabbath commences. *SEE* SABBATH QUEEN.

Lechishah: "Whispering/Murmuring," "spell." A healing **incantation**. In the **Talmud**, Rabbi **Akiba** expressly condemns the use of spells whispered over a wound, but the prohibition didn't take hold, even among the Sages (M. Sanh. 10; Shab. 67a–b). When the practice is questioned again in the Middle Ages, one authority prohibits only *lechishot* that involve invoking **demons**, but permits other forms of word spells that, for example, use verses from the **Bible**. *SEE* HEALING; LAW AND THE PARANORMAL; MAGIC; SEGULLAH; SORCERY.

Left: The left side of the **sefirot** structure is the side of power and strict justice. It is also the female side, and represents the principles of separation and distinction. It signifies the fearsome awe of God. The unrestrained dominion of the left side gives rise to **evil**. The **Sitra Achra**, or "Other side" of the divine emanation, is the source of the demonic.

Thus, as in Christian tradition, the left can signify weakness, impurity, or evil. The **Zohar** emphasizes that certain **ritual** acts, like washing the hands, should begin with the right hand. Chasidic pious customs expand this to include always starting any bodily act, such as lacing one's shoes or taking one's first step, from the right side to avoid making oneself vulnerable to the impure powers of the left side. *SEE* FINGERS; PURIFICATION; TREATISE ON THE LEFT EMANATION.

Leiliel: Angel of the night (I Enoch).

Leprosy: Today leprosy is identified as Hansen's Disease, a disease that causes the collapse of soft connective tissue and grotesque physical deformity. In the **Bible**, by contrast, *tzaria*, "leprosy," probably encompassed a whole range of disfiguring skin diseases along with Hansen's. Any such leprosy was a sign from God, whether meant as a manifestation of power, like **Moses** making his hand leprous at will (Ex. 4), or as a sign of divine displeasure, as in the cases of **Miriam** and King Uzziah (Num. 12; II Chron. 26). God miraculously cured the Aramean general **Naaman** of leprosy when **Elisha** instructs him to bathe in the Jordan (II Kings, 5).

According to **Midrash**, Pharaoh was afflicted with leprosy. He attempted to cure it by bathing in the blood of Israelite children (Ex. R. 1:23, 1:34). In one of the most unusual of Jewish myths about the **Messiah**, Leviticus Rabbah describes the Messiah as a leper who sits outside the gates of Rome, waiting for his time to come. While he waits, he only changes one bandage at a time, so that there will be no delay when the moment of his advent arrives.

The **Talmud** teaches that mixing meat and milk makes one susceptible to leprosy. Children born from having intercourse during menstruation will possibly be afflicted with leprosy (Lev. R. 15:5). An adept using the **Book of the Great Name** must not gaze upon a leper for forty days as an act of **purification**.

Letter of Rehoboam: A text of astrological medicine and angelology, probably written by a Hellenized Jew. **Solomon** is the purported author, and it is framed as a letter the great king wrote to his son, Rehoboam, explaining the benefits of gaining power through the use of "plants, prayers, stones, but above all else . . . the seven planetary gods." In style, it fits very much with pagan works written in Greco-Roman times. The letter, divided into seven sections, explains the order of the **planets**, stars, and hours, and their relationship to the **angels** and **demons**. It also lists prayers, incantations, and offerings one can use to influence illness, to heal, and to shape other earthly events. In this regard, it resembles **Sefer ha-Razim**. While the document is superficially monotheistic, it speaks of "planetary gods" (angels?) and also has the unusual feature that most of the prayers and spells are addressed directly to the angelic beings and stars.[1] *SEE* ASTROLOGY; MAGIC; SORCERY; WITCHCRAFT.

1. Ness, *Astrology and Judaism in Late Antiquity*, chapter 4.

Levi: One of the twelve sons of Jacob. Eventually the tribe descended from him became the sacerdotal clan for all Israel; all priests and **Temple** functionaries had to be Levites. Levi himself was especially chosen for this status—**Michael** brought Levi alive to the **Throne of Glory** and God blessed him and ordained the priestly role for his offspring (PdRE 37).

Though he is a minor and ambivalent figure in the Scriptures, Levi is given much more elaborate and loving treatment in **apocalyptic literature**, such as **I Enoch**, **Jubilees**, the **Testament of Levi**, and in the writings of the sectarian priests of **Qumran**, who regarded Levi to be their progenitor and the archetypal priest.

Levi, Testament of: A fragmentary **apocalypse** found among the **Dead Sea Scrolls**, probably composed in the 2nd and 1st centuries BCE, devoted to the centrality and elevation of Levi above his brothers. The work aims to affirm the central role of the priesthood in Early Judaism by projecting priestly authority back to the Patriarchs.

Leviathan: (*Livyatan*). A cosmic sea monster, evidently based on Isaiah 27:1, "God created the great sea serpents," combined with the Canaanite myth of Lotan, a watery chaos dragon-monster. Sometimes Leviathan is portrayed as a whale, other times as a (fire breathing) dragon. **Sefer Raziel** sees Leviathan as the animating spirit of the waters, the "genius" of the abyss that dwells at the center of the sea. Leviathan is a beautiful, if volatile, creature. He is what causes rolling seas. It takes the entire Jordan to quench the thirst of the monster.

Originally, God created two Leviathan creatures, but slew the female (Midrash Konen, 2), which is now salted away for the messianic banquet (B.B. 74b). God then hung the world from the surviving Leviathan's tail. Leviathan may have fathered some heavenly creatures of his own (*SEE* HAMNUNA SAVA, RAV). According to Talmud B.B. 75a, at the time of the resurrection, **Michael** and **Gabriel** will fight against Leviathan and overcome it. In other legends, Leviathan will fight a mortal battle with **Behemoth**. In the end, God will catch Leviathan and serve him as the entrée at the **messianic banquet** (Lev. R. 13:3; Gen. R. 7:4; Zohar I: 46b; II 34b–35a). *SEE* ANIMALS; DRAGONS; SERPENTS.

Levirate Marriage: In the **Bible**, it is mandated that if a man dies childless, his brother must marry his widow and cohabit with her long enough to bear a son, who would then be designated the son and heir of the dead man. This served to ensure that no man's name and lineage would be lost in Israel.

This admittedly odd custom has puzzled generations of Jews in post-biblical times, and eventually the Sages enacted rules to end the practical application of this commandment (Tractate Ketubot). Mystics, however, found occult meaning in the law concerning **reincarnation**; they believe the levirate marriage allows the **soul** of the dead man another incarnation (Sefer ha-Gilgulim).

Levush: "Garment." A container for the soul; a membrane that mediates between the spiritual soul and the physical **body** (Kelach Pitchei Chochmah). It is detectable at the wrist pulse and can be used in making a spiritual diagnosis (Sha'ar ha-Yichudim 16a). *SEE* GUF HA-DAK.

Life of Adam and Eve, the: An apocryphal text that gives an account of the fall of **Satan**.

Light: Light is an archetypal symbol of divinity, enlightenment, and the good. Light is the first of God's creations and, as the **Ma'asei-Bereshit** recognizes, it is also the first occult phenomena. It is so because the Talmudic Sages note that God created light on the first day, but had not yet created the sun, moon, and stars (the sources of visible, terrestrial light), which were created on the fourth. From this they conclude that there is a primordial, supernal light, which God has hidden away. From other passages in the **Bible** (specifically Job 38:15 and Ps. 97:11), they come to believe that access to this first light is a special reward for the **righteous** (Chag. 12a; Gen. R. 3:6, 41:3; Ex. R. 35:1).

These insights help define the logic of Jewish occultism (there is a concealed higher reality that is different from the "reality" we experience day-to-day). It also initiates the Jewish quest to know this higher light and thereby become "enlightened." For supernal light allows ". . . one to see from one end of the universe to the other," achieving total gnosis (Chag. 12a–13b).

Certain artifacts of this light are present with us that we can use in this quest. The most obvious, the one God intends us to use, is **Torah** (Prov. 6:23; Bahir 149). Torah began its supernal existence as ". . . black fire written upon white fire" (Tanh., Bereshit 1).

The **Temple**, properly configured and maintained with the right rituals, also emanates that light into the world. **Angels** exist in a medium of this divine light and are therefore a resource for the mystic seeking to experience it.

Ezra of Gerona taught that doing the **commandments** creates more supernal light and draws the one who performs the *mitzvah* into the **Shekhinah** (Commentary on Song of Songs). Lurianic theosophy teaches that sparks of this light are encased and trapped in the "husks" of ordinary reality and it is the human task to release those sparks through performing the commandments. *SEE* FIRE; KELIPOT; NITZOTZ.

Likutim, Sefer ha-: One of Chayyim Vital's works on the teachings of **Isaac Luria**, expounding Lurianic cosmogony on the **breaking of the vessels**, the fallen sparks, and how to achieve cosmic repair. *SEE* NITZOTZ; TIKKUN.

Lilin: An alternative term for "lilot," aerial night demons (Eruv. 18b). Lilin are bald but have hair covering the rest of their faces and bodies (Emek ha-Melech 140b). *SEE* LILITH.

Lilith: (*Lilit*, "Night [Demon]"). Now regarded to be one of the four **queens of demons**, the nature of Lilith has undergone many reinterpretations throughout Jewish history. The origins of Lilith are probably found in the Mesopotamian *lilu*, or "aerial spirit." Some features of Lilith in Jewish tradition also resemble those of Lamashtu, a Babylonian demoness who causes infant death. There is one mention of *lilot* (pl.) in the **Bible** (Isa. 34:14), but references to Lilith demons only become common in post-biblical Jewish sources. Furthermore, the characterization of Lilith as a named demonic personality really only begins late in antiquity. **Amulets** and magical texts well into the Middle Ages continue to speak of *lilot* as a class of demonic beings. Even the gender of the creature is not fixed. **Incantation bowls**, for example, explicitly protect against ". . . *Lilot*, whether male or female. . . ."

Jewish tradition gradually fixes on Lilith as a female demon. In **Talmud**, she is described as a demon with a woman's face, long hair, and wings (Nid. 24b; Eruv. 100b). In amulet **incantations**, she is addressed as a demon that preys on women in childbirth and as a killer of children (Ber. 8a; Zohar I: 148a–b; II: 267b). Some sources also describe her as a **succubus**, seducing men in their sleep and then collecting their nocturnal emissions in order to breed demonic offspring (Shab. 151b). Lilith does this because her consort, **Samael**, has been castrated by God. She has many demonic children, the most famous being **Ormuzd** (B.B. 73b).

The use of "Lilith" as the proper name of a specific demonic personality first appears in the **Midrash**. The most famous legend of Lilith is the one first appearing in the Medieval satirical text **Alef-Bet of Ben Sira**. In that document, Lilith is identified as the first woman God created along with Adam. The case for there having been two women in the Garden of **Eden** is based on the differing accounts of the creation of woman (Gen. 1:27 versus Gen. 2:19–23). According to AbbS, Lilith immediately quarreled with Adam over having to assume the missionary position during intercourse. When Lilith did not get satisfaction, she invoked the power of the **Tetragrammaton** and flew away. God sent three angels, **Sanoi**, **Sansanoi**, and **Samnaglof**, to bring her back. When she refused, she transformed herself into a demon that weakens children through disease (perhaps diphtheria, whooping cough, or SIDS—probably all three) to take her vengeance on God and humanity. But, the story concludes, if the names of her three pursuing angels are used together on an amulet, she is powerless to harm the person bearing it (see **Sefer Raziel** for the continuation of this tradition). This account, incidentally, is a Jewish variation of a story about a demon curbed by three pursuers that also appears in Greek, Coptic, Arabic, Armenian, and Slavonic legends.

Lilith appears in a very different incarnation in **Treatise of the Left Emanation**, the **Zohar**, and other later mystic texts, where she is one of the four queens, or the four mothers, of demons. She is the most prominent of the four, being queen of the forces of **Sitra Achra**, the impure side of divine emanations, which run loose in the world.

In the Treatise, she and Samael are the evil doppelgangers of **Adam** and **Eve**, coming into existence as a spiritual byproduct of the primordial couple's sin. In the Zohar, she is the evil antipode of the **Shekhinah** (II: 118a–b; III: 97a). There is also a tradition in the Zohar that Lilith was the **Queen of Sheba** who came to test **Solomon**.

Lilith has a mount she rides, **Tanin'iver**, "blind dragon." She can command hundreds of legions of demons. Intriguingly, the Treatise of the Left Emanation starts to come full circle, once again referring to multiple Liliths, as did the ancients. This tradition of there being two (or more) Liliths also appears in **Pardes Rimmonim**.

Defenses against Lilith include providing amulets to women in childbirth and to newborns inscribed with the angelic names Sanoi, Sansanoi, and Samnaglof (or **Sandalfon**), not sleeping alone in a house, and tapping an infant on the nose if he appears to be responding to something the parent cannot see. **Psalms**, particularly Pss. 91, 121, and 126, are effective in driving off Lilith (Shimmush Tehillim). There is also a **ritual** that can be performed during and after intercourse to drive her away (Zohar III: 19).

In modern times, inspired by the singular Ben Sira portrayal of her as a woman who stands up to male domination, Lilith has become a rallying point among feminists in critiquing the overwhelmingly male-oriented perspective of traditional Judaism, and she has been adopted as a symbol of feminist resistance to male spiritual hegemony.[1] It should be pointed out, however, that modern claims that Lilith was an early Hebrew goddess later censored out of the tradition by the authors of the Scriptures has no basis whatsoever in the historical record. This claim appears to depend entirely on appealing to the Ben Sira narrative, but that story is *sui generis*, and there is no precedent for any belief in Lilith as either "Wife of Adam" or "Wife of YHWH" prior to the 10th century CE.

1. "Why is the Magazine Called Lilith?" *Lilith Magazine* Online, at http://www.lilith.org/about.htm.

Lion: (*Aryeh*). Lions are a symbol of the tribe of Judah and therefore appear frequently in Jewish iconography. In the **Midrash**, **Solomon** has a whole pride of lions that surround his throne and serve him. *Aryeh* is one of the houses of the Jewish **zodiac**, the equivalent of Leo. Lion's blood is a useful *materia magica* in potions for controlling powerful people (**Sefer ha-Razim**).

Lippold: Mint-master of Brandenburg (German, ca. 16th century). This court Jew was prosecuted for **witchcraft** and confessed under torture to consorting with the devil, shape changing, and injuring his enemies through magical attack. He later recanted, but again admitted the charges under renewed torture. Finally offered the chance to live as a Christian, in the end he insisted on dying a faithful Jew.

Loew, Judah: SEE JUDAH LOEW BEN BEZALEL (THE MAHA-RAL).

Lost Books: In various places in Jewish literature, existing books will cite other books we no longer possess, books that have been lost to history. The **Bible**, for example, mentions *Sefer ha-Yashar, Sefer Milchamot Adonai,* and *Sefer Rafuot* as books that would be familiar to ancient readers. **Solomon** reportedly composed thirteen books, but today we have only the three Scriptural books that tradition credits to him (Song of Songs, Proverbs, and Ecclesiastes).

Later Jewish tradition, especially esoteric tradition, also refers to books we cannot identify. For example, there are traditions about a "Book of Adam" and a "Book of Noah" that, despite tantalizing fragments found among the **Dead Sea Scrolls**, remain un-recovered. The **Zohar** in particular lists a small library of such books, citing wisdom from *Sefer Adam, Sefer Rav Hamnuna Sava, Sefer Rav Yeiva Sava,* and *Sefer Yeisa Sava.*

Lots: (*Goralot, Purim*). The drawing of lots to uncover occult information or receive divine direction occurs several times in the **Bible**. **Aaron** casts lots over the two **goats** brought for the **Yom Kippur** offering to determine which will be the scapegoat (Lev. 16). Lots are used to divvy up the Land of Israel between the tribes (Num. 26; Josh. 15–19). While the passage is vague, **Joshua** apparently used either lots or the **Urim and Thummim** to determine who sinned against God by taking pillage from Jericho (Josh. 7). Saul is identified as God's appointed king by means of lots (I Sam. 10). Seamen on the ship that was carrying Jonah used lots to identify him as the source of God's wrath toward them (Jon. 2). In the story of Purim, Haman uses lots to determine the most propitious day to attack and annihilate the Jews (Esth. 3).

The use of lots for divinatory purposes faded away in post-biblical Judaism. SEE DIVINATION; ORDEAL; SORTES/SORTILEGE.

Love: (*Ahavah; Chesed; Yedidut; Chaviv*). To be loved is a universal human need. For Jewish magicians, love really can come in a bottle. A variety of love potions and love-inducing **amulets** are documented in medieval Jewish literature.[1] One example involves a **magical square** with angelic names written on a **shell** (it is unclear whether an egg shell, turtle shell, or sea shell is meant) with ink made of spices, using a bronze or copper instrument. Several love **incantations** involve casting a spell inscribed on metal or clay into a fire, using the flames as a magic analogy for burning passion: "just as this pot shard burns, so may burn the heart of...." SEE CAIRO GENIZA; SEFER HA-RAZIM; SWORD OF MOSES.

1. Naveh and Shaked, *Magic Spells and Formulae*, 150, 177, 199. Also see Janowitz, *Icons of Power*, 113.

Lulav: Part of the bouquet of plants that are ritually waved during **Sukkot**. SEE FOUR SPECIES.

Luria, Isaac: Mystic (Egyptian, 1534–1572). He was also known as *ha-Ari* (The [Holy] Lion) and *ha-Ashkenazi* (The German—his family moved to the Middle East from Europe). Luria was one of the most influential men in the history of Jewish mysticism; his teachings shaped the thinking of generations of Kabbalists, triggered at least one messianic movement, and serve as intellectual foundation for much of **Chasidism**.

Luria's family came from Europe and first settled in **Egypt**. As an adult, Luria migrated to Safed in Israel, the epicenter of Jewish mystical studies in the 15th and 16th centuries, in order to study with **Moses Cordovero**.

He taught a highly original mystical theosophy, one that diverges dramatically from the Zohar-based **Kabbalah** taught by his predecessors, especially Cordovero. His Gnostic retelling of the Creation myth served as the center point of his metaphysics. His innovative teachings include the doctrines of **Tzimtzum** (divine self-contraction), Shvirat ha-Kelim (the **breaking of the vessels**), **Nitzotzot** (divine sparks), **Kelipot** (husks of evil), **Tikkun** (cosmic restoration), and **Gilgul** (**reincarnation**).[1]

He taught an equally original form of ecstatic Kabbalah, centered on therapeutic "readings" of the spiritual condition of a **soul** and then offering spiritual direction. He also worked with dead souls. He would sleep on graves in order to commune with the dead spirits of Jewish saints buried there. His method of **Yichudim**, including a form of **incubation**, linked necromantic **divination** with his efforts to mend the cosmic imbalances in the universe. He furthered this effort by performing *tikkun* on impure spirits, exorcizing them and thereby returning them to the proper path toward the afterlife.[2]

Huge numbers of stories and legends about his personality and his occult powers have been recorded. Some believed he was a reincarnation of **Simon bar Yochai**. He could make himself invisible to the spiritually immature. On the other hand, those with the right spiritual capacity saw that a pillar of **fire**, extending up to heaven, was constantly hovering over his head. Luria had the power of a sixth sense—he could immediately determine the spiritual state of a person by studying the lines on their forehead. He also had power over angels and made them do his bidding. He healed the sick and granted extended life.

Given all these powers, it is ironic that Luria himself died young. He left behind many disciples, chief of whom was **Chayyim Vital**. Luria himself wrote very little about his mystical ideas, but his disciples produced numerous (sometimes contradictory) works devoted to his life and his teachings. Much of this material is also embellished with legendary material, and despite a wealth of details, many aspects of his life still remain a mystery.

Major works written by his students that provide insights into his esoteric teachings include Shivhei ha-Ari, Etz ha-Chayyim, Sha'ar ha-Gilgulim, and Sefer Limmu-dei Atzilut.

The influence of Luria on Jewish mysticism is hard to overestimate. Only **Moses de Leon** may be his equal. His mystical interpretations have colored the way all earlier Kabbalistic texts are read. His ideas have been incorporated into both traditional and modernist Jewish philosophies and into authoritative prayer books. He is the spiritual godfather of Chasidism. *SEE* IBBUR OR DEVEKUT; INCUBATION; METOPOSCOPY.

1. Miller, "Rabbi Yitzchak Luria: Basic Kabbalah Teachings," http://www.ascentofsafed.com/cgi-bin/ascent.cgi?Name=ari-teachings.
2. Fine, "The Contemplative Practice of Yihudim in Lurianic Kabbalah," in Green, *Jewish Spirituality*, 64–98.

Luz: There are two distinct meanings to this term:

1. The city of Luz, the ancient name for Beit El, was a city "painted blue" (signifying it is a gateway to heaven?). In Jewish mythic tradition, Luz is the city of immortality. The Angel of Death cannot reach anyone who gained entry there, so long as they remain within the city walls (Gen. 28:19, 35:6, 48:3; Josh. 16:2, 18:13; Judg. 1:23; Sot. 46b; Gen. R. 69:8).

2. Based on Psalm 34:21, the Rabbis teach that there is one indestructible **bone** in the **body** called the "luz," around which God will resurrect every person (Eccl. R. 12:5; Lev. R. 18:1; Ber. 28a). It is the "nineteenth" vertebrae, making the spine to correspond to the nineteen blessings of the daily prayer. *SEE* ANGEL OF DEATH; RESURRECTION.

Luzzato, Moses Chayyim: Ethicalist and Kabbalist (Italian, ca. 18th century). He was regularly visited by a **maggid**, which he summoned by theurgic means, who then revealed secrets of the **Torah** to him and his circle.

He may have believed he was the **reincarnation** of **Moses**, which explains why he declared that his marriage, to a woman named **Zipporah** (corresponding to the name of the wife of the biblical Moses), signaled a mending of a cosmic disruption between the masculine and feminine sides of the **Godhead**. His claims to mystical revelations and his belief that he had a role to play in an unfolding messianic drama were controversial, and numerous rabbis suspected him of being a secret follower of **Shabbatai Tzvi**. He moved several times to escape this controversy, but it always followed him. He died in Israel at a young age.

Aside from his famed work of ethics, Mesillat Yesharim—mystics in Judaism seem particularly attuned to issues of daily morality—he is the author of several mystical works, most of them written under the guidance of his maggid: Kelach Pitchei Chokmah, Tikkunin Chadashim, and Zohar Tinyana.[1]

1. Dan, *The Heart and the Fountain*, 223–30. Also see Jacobs, 167–68.

M

Ma'aseh: "Deed/Ritual." There are many meanings that can be assigned to the word *ma'aseh*, including a "fabulous tale" and a theurgic "act of power" (Sefer ha-Razim; Tan. 19a; Gen. R. 5:5). SEE MAGIC; MASHIVA; RITUAL; THEURGY.

Ma'aseh Book: (Yiddish, *Meisa Buch*). A medieval compendium of Jewish legends. Most of the stories are derived from Talmudic/rabbinic sources, but with fabulous elaborations. It also includes supernatural stories of medieval worthies.

Ma'aseh Merkavah: "Working of the Chariot." The modern name given to a **Hechalot** text, discovered by scholar Gershom Scholem, devoted to achieving ascent into heaven and the **summoning** of **angels**. It is a kind of anthology, with Rabbi **Akiba ben Joseph** and Rabbi **Ishmael ben Elisha ha-Kohen** serving as the central teachers.

Ma'aseh Nissim: A 16th-century collection of folk and fantastic tales set in the city of Worms written by Jeptha Yozpa ben Naphtali.

Ma'aseh Yerushalmi: "Tale of the Jerusalemite." An influential 13th-century fantastic tale of a man who marries a demoness, goes to live in the underworld, and then dies at her hands when he rejects his infernal bride.

Ma'asei-Bereshit: "The Workings of Creation." Starting in antiquity, Jewish disciples of the esoteric have engaged in metaphysical speculation about the powers and events surrounding the creation of the universe. This branch of Jewish occult knowledge is called *Ma'asei-Bereshit*. Because the Talmudic Rabbis are so vague about the exact nature of this field of inquiry, the term "ma'asei-bereshit" has been applied to wildly different intellectual disciplines. The rationalist philosopher Maimonides claimed the term MB really refers to the study of Aristotelian physics, but Kabbalists universally regard it to be a branch of esoteric metaphysics. The Mishnah explicitly cautions against pursuing questions of what preceded **Creation** (Chag. 2:1), though the restrictions they impose on learning MB are slightly less stringent than those surrounding inquiring into the other branch of Jewish esotericism, the **Ma'asei-Merkavah**.

Despite this prohibition, or perhaps because of it, such speculation flourished. The tract **Sefer Yetzirah** is clearly the major work of MB and its influence is so significant that over eighty commentaries on it—philosophical, mystical, and magical—presently exist. Presumably, more were written that have not survived down to the modern era. The ideas of Sefer Yetzirah figure in almost all later Jewish mystical cosmogony. There are a few other works that can be subsumed under this title, like Seder Rabbah de Bereshit (also known as Baraita de Ma'aseh Bereshit) and the cosmogonic ideas of the Lurianic Creation myth. Both qualify as a kind of *Ma'asei-Bereshit*, though they are rarely referred to as such. SEE BREAKING OF THE VESSELS; CREATION; HEBREW ALPHABET; TZIMTZUM.

Ma'asei-Merkavah: "Workings of the [Divine] Chariot." A stream of Jewish mystical tradition extending from classical antiquity into the Middle Ages, though its influence goes far beyond that. Using **Ezekiel**'s vision of the divine **chariot** and Isaiah's enthronement vision as their primary inspiration (Ezek. 1, 10; Isa. 6), the Merkavah mystics combined Torah study, **purification** rituals, and meditative practices to obtain **visions** of the heavenly principalities, the **angels**, and God. People in the Merkavah circles also engaged in the **summoning** of angels who would serve the adept in his (with one anonymous exception Merkavah mystics appear to have all been men) quest for revelation, protection, and personal benefit.[1] The **Hechalot literature** provides the major documentary record of this mystical school, though remarks recorded in the **Talmud** and by later medieval authorities slightly supplement our knowledge of their beliefs and activities.

The study and practice of Ma'asei Merkavah was considered hazardous in the extreme, a threat to the practitioner on both mental and physical levels.[2] It was also not considered appropriate for the masses, as it could lead to confusion and apostasy. For example, there is a pronounced tendency in some Hechalot texts for God and high angels to become confused and conflated. Other texts are clearly infected with a kind of **Gnosticism** bordering on polytheism. As a result, the Talmud cautions that a teacher should never expound the Ma'asei Merkavah for more than two students at a time, and then only to students who are already established Sages, in order that they will be able to distinguish the "wheat" of the Merkavah experience from the "chaff." Even established scholars, as in the case of **Elisha ben Abuya**, could become unmoored from Jewish monotheism by the visions and teachings of the Merkavah (Chag. 12b–16b). The most oft-mentioned figures in connection to this mystical tradition are **Ishmael ben Elisha**, **Akiba ben Joseph**, **Joshua ben Levi**, and **Nechunia ben ha-Kanah**.

The impact of the Merkavah tradition on Jewish esotericism is enormous, and almost all subsequent schools of Jewish mysticism have studied its texts, with its influence being most pronounced among the **German Pietists**, the **Tosafists**, the **Circle of the Special Cherub** and the **Iyyun Circle**.

1. Dan, *The Early Jewish Mysticism*, 7–24.
2. Davila, "The Hekhalot Literature and Shamanism," 4–6.

Machaneh: "Encampment." The angelic host of heaven are divided into "encampments," depending upon their function and/or their principalities. The term echoes the story of the **Exodus**, in which the twelve tribes of Israel marched and camped in tribal formations called *machaneh* for the duration of their forty-year sojourn in the wilderness. Each heavenly *machaneh* is ruled by a princely **angel**. Mystics also refer to the **Kavod** and the **Gevurah**, the full scope of God's power in all its manifestations, as the "encampment" of God (Orach Chaim 18:1–3; Pes. 104a–b; J. Pes. 71). *SEE* ASCENT, HEAVENLY.

Machon: (Aramaic, "site/locale"). One of the **seven heavens**, it is the level that warehouses all celestial precipitations: **rain**, snow, **hail**, **dew**, as well as the **winds**, storms, and vapors (Chag. 12b–13a).

Machpelah, the Cave of: *SEE* CAVES.

Magen David: "Shield of David." A type of **hexagram**, this now-ubiquitous symbol of Judaism actually has its origins in occult circles. It was originally known as the "Seal of Solomon" and first appeared in Jewish esoteric literature. The hexagram was understood by many to be the symbol engraved on the magical **ring** of **Solomon**, linking it to Solomon's reputed power over demonic forces. It first appeared as a magical **seal** on **amulets**, **mezuzahs**, and other talismans. At some point the hexagram merged with another occult tradition about a "shield of David" that apparently came out of Arab magical traditions.[1] The hexagram is also a common device in alchemical texts, but what, if any, connection this has with Judaism is impossible to determine.

The MD emerges as an ordinary symbol in Jewish books and on **synagogues**, probably because as the "Shield of David," it had messianic overtones. In all likelihood, its presumed protective properties enhanced its general appeal.

Not surprisingly, even after its universal adoption as a sign for Judaism, it continues as an anti-demonic symbol. Often magical and mystical representations of the MD incorporate words and names of power. One example found on an amulet has **Psalm** 121 written out in the pattern of the hexagram. Other amulets feature divine names in each of the seven fields created by the lines forming the star.[2]

The most common form of hexagram talisman has one of the seventy-two **names of God**, most often the name Taftafiyah, in the center.

1. Scholem, *The Messianic Idea in Judaism*, 257–81.
2. Roth, *Encyclopedia Judaica*, vol. 2, 914.

Maggid: "Revealer." A *maggid* is an angelic teacher; a spirit guide. The maggid is related to the phenomenon of the **Sar ha-Torah** and to other angels of revelation and dreams, but there does seem to be a meaningful distinction: a maggid is the genius, the animating spirit, or personification of some high attribute or nonpersonal supernal reality like the **Torah**, **Shekhinah**, **Wisdom**, or the Mishnah.[1] Though there is considerable variation in maggid accounts, conventionally a maggid manifests itself as a form of beneficent possession, triggering automatic writing and **xenoglossia**. SEE CARO, JOSEPH; IBBUR OR DEVEKUT; MEDIUM.

1. Goldish, *Spirit Possession in Judaism*, 101–23; Bilu, "Dybbuk and Maggid," 349–50.

Maggid Mesharim: Mystical memoir of **Joseph Caro** that gives detailed accounts of his spiritual possession by the **maggid** of the Mishnah.[1]

1. Fine, *Safed Spirituality*, 54–55.

Magic: (*Kesem; Kishuf*). "Magic" is one of those terms for a phenomenon that is hard to define, yet easy to recognize. For the purposes of this encyclopedia, "magic" is the overarching term for a **ritual** for power involving **incantations**, symbolic behavior, materials, and/or formulae meant to influence events and/or entities.[1]

Within Judaism, there are several ways to further subdivide "magic." There is an informal but real distinction between religious **theurgy** and magic; this is fundamentally an issue of distinguishing between the godly deeds of power that arise from the sphere of Torah and Judaism and the lesser deeds of power performed by foreign adepts. Furthermore, a distinction may be made in the sources between what we today term **sorcery** and **shamanism**, which is to say, between learned, scholarly magic and folk magic. Such distinctions are made on the basis of the presumed formal education required for these respective arts. Finally, there is the issue of **witchcraft**—magic that is regarded to be malevolent in purpose and/or derives its power from infernal sources.

With regards to magic and theurgy, a starting point could be that "magic" is a ritual of power that is self-serving and intended for personal outcomes such as gaining influence over others, cursing enemies, or achieving wealth.[2] Theurgy, by contrast, has a "religious" purpose, such as gaining a better understanding of **Torah**, receiving an apocalyptic revelation, or mending some corruption in God's relations to the universe.

This distinction, however, is difficult to sustain in the case of Judaism. Many Hebrew texts that are obviously "religious" in their orientation, like **Sefer Chasidim**, nevertheless contain examples of self-serving adjurations. By the same token, obviously "magical" handbooks, such as The **Sword of Moses**, also include spells and rites that clearly have "higher" religious motives, such as **summoning** an **angel** to teach the adept Torah. The distinction between "religious" theurgy and "self-serving" magic seems all the more artificial because these texts treat all kinds of spells as equally valid and worthwhile. What is more, a ritual of power can be *simultaneously* religious and self-serving. Taking the example of gaining mastery of Torah through an angelic instructor, it has to be acknowledged in Jewish culture that a demonstrated mastery of religious texts is both spiritually meritorious in its own right *and* a means of enhancing one's personal and social status.

Given this ambiguity, it makes more sense to propose a modification of the taxonomy of prayer and magic first put forth by Sir George Fraser in *The Golden Bough* (1922), which distinguishes both magic and theurgy from **prayer** based on the logic of how one addresses the numinous powers. A prayer is a supplication and appeal; it *asks* a deity for a boon or favor. Magic and/or theurgy, by contrast, commands and adjures. Magic is more purely mechanistic; it assumes that, if the ritual is done properly, there is no volition or favor involved on the part of the numinous entity or power being addressed—the desired outcome will simply occur.

Accepting this distinction between prayer and magic based on who is in control, it is more logical to characterize theurgy and magic as really two aspects of this same phenomenon. Perhaps the only meaningful distinctions between the two is that theurgy is based in an idea of influencing divine (or demonic) forces, whereas magic proper is not tied to any deity or spiritual personality except that of the adept. The theurgist commands divine powers. The logical corollary to the exercise of this power is that the theurgic practitioner must be spiritually and morally fit in the eyes of the deity to arrogate such powers. By contrast, the magician activates what appear to be impersonal forces purely by means of the proper performance of the ritual itself.[3] This distinction between theurgy and magic is first proposed in the Talmud itself by Rabbi Hiyya (Sanh. 67b).

Jewish authorities have had differing attitudes toward the efficacy of "magic" in this sense: some have viewed it as simple illusionist trickery, while others have regarded it as a real paranormal phenomenon (Sanh. 67b). The Sage Judah the Prince, for example, was a great spokesman for the former opinion, ascribing the power of magic to the power of the human imagination, "Only a person who believes in the interpretation of signs is pursued by magic." Many other Rabbis, however, accepted the reality of magical power, believing it was introduced to mortals by the angels (I Enoch 7; Zohar I: 58a).

Even when magic is regarded as a reality, however, Jews have universally treated magic as inferior to the miraculous power of God and the theurgic power of God's agents. This is neatly illustrated by the confrontation between **Moses** and the Egyptian wizards (Ex. 6–8; Sanh. 67b), for the author of Exodus accepted at face value that the Egyptians possessed paranormal powers, yet by the third plague the wizards of Egypt have to admit they have nothing to counter the feats of the God of Israel.

The wondrous powers that God gives to the righteous are always superior to that of mere magic, which brings up the other aspect of magic: Jews have informally distinguished between sorcery, shamanism, and witchcraft and reacted differently to each.

Still, Jews are hardly consistent about these distinctions. Some writers, for example, characterized the wondrous deeds of the Egyptian adepts in Exodus, chapter 7, as sorcery; as an art practiced by the learned elite of any traditional society. Other Jewish texts clearly regarded these magicians to be employing witchcraft—demonic magic.[4]

Moreover, while many of the wonders ascribed to Jewish heroes could be characterized as theurgic or miraculous, some of these feats appear overtly magical, in that they involved no direct appeal to God's power. Nevertheless, it is almost universally assumed by Jewish texts and readers that any supernatural power demonstrated by a Jewish Sage must derive, implicitly, from the power of To-

rah. This, in turn, is rooted in the assumption of righteousness: the Sages can bend the will of God only because they have submitted their will to the divine.[5]

As a result of these assumptions, one of the primary Talmudic rationales for labeling a supernatural ritual as *kesem*, and therefore forbidden, rather than as a *fele*, or divine manifestation, was simply the appearance of it being foreign, alien to Torah, or non-Jewish in origin—*Darkhei Amori*, **Ways of the Amorites**. Likewise, if a "Jewish" supernatural practice clearly aped the magic of gentiles, it was more likely to be suspect (Shab. 66a). Still, the Rabbis permitted colleagues to learn magic on a theoretical level in order to understand what they were up against (Sanh. 17a).

The attitude of those who actually practiced such foreign magic could be harsh; one Sage declared, "He who acquires a single item of knowledge from a sorcerer forfeits his life." Yet unlike in contemporary Roman law, rabbinic law does not include a tort for damages done by sorcery, a fact that suggests the Sages who shaped Jewish law retained serious doubts about whether magic was a real force capable of doing real damage.

Magic—in all forms—continued to have an ambivalent and confusing status in medieval Judaism. In addition to the Talmudic criteria, the medievals eventually developed a working distinction between licit and illicit rituals of power. For the medieval rabbis, "word magic" was permitted while magic involving persuasive objects—rituals involving the use of devices or materials to represent the desired result or the person to be influenced, like a **voodoo doll**—was forbidden. This was a discrimination they shared with the pagan philosopher-theurgist Plotinus. Eliezer of Metz (ca. 12th century) made this distinction explicitly in his discussion of Jewish law on magic.

In practice, the boundaries between what was considered foreign and what was Jewish, what was verbal and what was performative, tended to blur. Thus a work like **Sefer ha-Razim** is virtually indistinguishable from pagan magical texts in the use of *materia magica*. What is more, **amulets** are largely exempted from what otherwise seems to be a blanket ban against using devices of ritual power.

By the Renaissance, a number of religious authorities tolerated, and a few even endorsed, the practice of a kind of scholarly sorcery that overlapped with the then fashionable gentile pursuit of hermetic/astrological magic and **alchemy**. **Johannan Alemanno** and **Abraham Yagel**, for example, considered mastery of the astro-magical disciplines to be the summa of a quality humanist education.[6] No less an authority than Rabbi **Judah Loew of Prague** wrote that sorcery that invokes divine names is, for all intents and purposes, indistinguishable from prayer (B'er ha-Golah 2). By contrast, **Manasseh ben Israel** condemned virtually all magic as demonic—but still exempted medicinal spells (Nishmat Chayyim 253).

In eastern Europe, scholarly Jewish magic came to be overshadowed and co-opted by more shamanistic-charismatic forms. The **Baal Shem**, a practitioner that emerged in the Middle Ages, was the paradigmatic figure of this kind of folk-magical adept. In some ways, these baalei shem are a throwback to charismatic Talmudic wonder-workers like **Chanina ben Dosa** and **Choni ha-Ma'agel**. Thus it was assumed that many of the talents manifested by the Baal Shem (**healing**, **fertility**, paranormal knowledge, teleportation, mystical ascent, **amulet** making, and **exorcism**) were part of the power of being **righteous**, regardless of the adept's level of education or Torah learning. SEE KABBALAH; LAW AND THE PARANORMAL; SUMMONING. (SEE ALSO APPENDIX FIGURE 4.)

1. For a summary of academic theories of magic, see van Binsbergen and Wiggerman, "Magic in History: A Theoretical Perspective, and Its Application to Ancient Mesopotamia."
2. Davila, "Ancient Magic (The Prayer of Jacob)," 1.
3. Idel, *Hasidism*, 83.
4. Neusner, "Miracle and Magic in Formative Judaism: The System and the Difference," in *Religion, Science, and Magic*, 61–72.
5. Bosker, "Wonder Working and the Rabbinic Tradition," 42–92.
6. Idel, "Jewish Magic from the Renaissance Period to Early Hasidism," in Neusner, *Religion, Science, and Magic*, 82–94.

Magic Square: Famous as an element of mystical mathematics from Greco-Roman times, Jewish magic squares involve permutations and **notarikons** of divine names. They are commonplace features on **seals**, **amulets**, and **incantation bowls**. Their magical function seems to be to "enclose," bind, and trap the malevolent force which the amulet is targeted against. In the case of **angel**-summoning devices, the function of the square is analogous, containing and restraining the numinous power of the angel so the adept can remain in control.

MaHaRaL of Prague: SEE JUDAH LOEW BEN BEZALEL.

Mahaway: An antediluvian **giant** who consults with Enoch to have his mantic **dreams** interpreted. He appears in the **Book of Giants**.

Maidens: (*Almaot*). Female angels who attend the **Shekhinah** (Zohar I: 21a; Zohar Chadash 183).

Maimonides (Moses ben Maimon): Jewish philosopher, legalist, and physician (Egyptian, ca. 12th–13th century). The greatest scholastic figure of the Middle Ages, the rationalist Maimonides would be appalled to learn that since his death he has been linked to many fantastic and supernatural events. A whole cycle of wonder tales are now associated with him, including his ominous **birth**, miraculous healings, and his success in fabricating homunculi.

Maklitu: Angel and/or divine being mentioned in some **Hechalot** texts. Maklitu is likely an entity borrowed from Greek magical texts.

Makom, ha-: "The Place/The Primordial One." A rabbinic/mystical name for God, apparently derived from a linguistic oddity in the Bible: *Va'yif'ga ba-makom*, "[Jacob] met the place," with "the place" being interpreted as God (Gen 28:11).

While Judaism does not teach pantheism, that God and the Universe are coequal, it does teach *panentheism*, that God is the "place" of the world; the world does not contain God, God contains the world (Gen. R. 40:6, 68:9). SEE GODHEAD; NATURE.

Malach: "Messenger." An **angel**.

Malach Adonai: Usually translated as "**Angel** of YHWH," a more connotative but accurate translation should be "Artifice of YHWH" or even "Manifestation of YHWH," for the phrases *Malach YHWH* and *Malach El* are terms used in the Bible to designate a moment when the God of Israel becomes visible to humans.[1]

Generally, but mistakenly, interpreted to mean a divine entity distinct from God (i.e., an "angel" as we normally imagine them, however that may be), in every place where "Malach Adonai" appears in the Bible, its usage indicates that God is now visible. The classic case is the binding of **Isaac** (Gen. 22:1–22). God first comes to **Abraham** as a disembodied voice (22:1–2), and even as the "Malach YHWH" appears to him (22:11), the conversation suddenly returns to God speaking to Abraham directly (22:16), indicating that God is even more "present" in the second manifestation than in the first. Tellingly, after this encounter with the Malach, Abraham re-names the locale where it happened "YHWH appears."

The fact that this idiom refers not to an angel but to God momentarily becoming visible explains why in so many passages where the "Malach YHWH" or "Malach El," or **Sar Tzevaot** appears, within a verse or two of the manifestation, God is described as present (Gen. 16:9, 22:11, 22:16; Ex. 3:2, 23:20–21, 31:11–13; Judg. 2:1, 5:13–6:5; Zech. 2–4).

This avatar of God, whose "Name is in him (Ex. 23:21)," becomes the source of the Hechalot tradition about divine entities, seeming "super" angels, all of whom have the **Tetragrammaton** included in their names (most famously Akatriel-YaH, who appears in Talmud Berachot 7a) and all of whom merit the puzzling secondary epitaph, "God of Israel." The solution to this confusion is that such entities are not actually angels in the sense that they are distinct sentient beings subservient to God. Instead they are a visible, personified form of the divine (Shev. 35b and the comments of Rashi and Nachmanides on that passage). *SEE* CHERUB, THE UNIQUE; FACE OF GOD; GLORY OF GOD; META-TRON; VISIONS.

1. Kugel, *The God of Old*, 5–36.

Malach Shareit: (Hebrew, "ministering angel"). *SEE* GUARDIAN ANGELS; MINISTERING ANGELS.

Malachei Chavala: "Destructive Angels." A Kabbalistic term that is sometimes used for **demons**, and other times refers to the manifestations of God's strict justice. *SEE* GEHENNA; PUNISHING ANGELS.

Malkat: One of the four **demon queens**, the mothers of all demons.

Malbush, Sefer ha-: "Book of the Garment." A magico-mystical handbook of the early medieval period, Sefer ha-Malbush describes magical uses of *levishat ha-Shem*, "wearing the Name." This is apparently meant literally, referring to the making of a magical cloak from deerskin.[1] Not only does it describe how to make, activate, and use the cloak, it also teaches the use of **Tzerufim**, utilizing the letters of the **Hebrew alphabet** and the **names of God** in various combinations. ShM teaches that through these, the adept concentrates on divine matters. This technique promises both religious revelations on par with prophecy and the power to influence events and entities.[1] *SEE* MAGIC; PROPHECY; SORCERY.

1. Scholem, *Major Trends in Jewish Mysticism*, 77.
2. Dan, *The Heart and the Fountain*, 101–5.

Malchut: "Kingdom." Also known as **Shekhinah** and/or the **Holy Spirit**, it is the tenth and lowest sefirah, the aspect of God that interacts most intimately with the material world. As a result, **Kabbalah** has more to say about this one divine quality than virtually all the other **sefirot** combined. Many symbols signify Malchut, including Knesset Yisraeil (the mystical body of the Jewish people), the **moon**, the **sun**, and the **Apple Orchard**. It is personified by **David**. As the "**speculum** that does not shine," its associated color is black.

Manasseh ben Israel: Jewish communal leader and Kabbalist (Spanish/Dutch, ca. 17th century). He taught a popular version of mystical ideas concerning **reincarnation** and the **soul**. He is the author of **Nishmat Chayyim** ("The Soul of Life").

Mandrake: (Hebrew: *Duda'im*, Aramaic: *Yavrucha*). A root that grows in an anthropoid shape. In the Bible, the mandrake root is treated as an aphrodisiac and fertility enhancer (Gen. 30). The Talmudic name, *yavrucha*, which means "pursuer/shunner," suggests mandrake has anti-demonic properties also. There appear to be other, more unsavory uses; in a notably cryptic passage, even for the Talmud, J. Eruvin 10:26 forbids reading Bible verses over a mandrake, yet does not state the purpose of the **ritual**, assuming the reader will understand.

Manna: ("Whatchamacallit," derived from *mah*, "what"). Manna is the heavenly **bread** that sustained the Israelites for the **forty** years they wandered in the desert. According to rabbinic traditions, manna was created on the twilight of the sixth day of Creation and is stored in heavenly vaults (Avot 5:9; PdRE 3; Tanh., be-Shallach 22). It fell with the dew each morning, a double portion coming on Fridays to provide for the **Sabbath**, when none would appear. The wind blew each day prior to its arrival, so it wouldn't get dirty. The righteous among the Israelites received it ready-to-eat with front-door delivery; everyone else had to go out to gather it and prepare it for consumption. It had the taste of bread, honey, mother's milk, or oil, depending on who was eating it. When it melted in the noonday sun, animals would come and drink the rivulets it formed. These animals became the most delicious and highly prized game: harts, gazelles, and deer (Yoma 75a; MdRI, be-Shallach). In Yoma 75b, Rabbi Akiba dubs it *lechem adirim*, "Bread of the Powerful Ones [angels]."

Manna stopped the moment Israel entered the Promised Land. A sample nonetheless was displayed before the **Holy of Holies** in the First **Temple**. It will fall again in the Messianic Era. According to the Zohar, the manna narratives are figurative descriptions of the divine emanations that "feed" and sustain the lower worlds.

Manual of Discipline: A text found among the **Dead Sea Scrolls**. It gives an elaborate account of the angelic wars between the angels of darkness and the angels of **light**, wars that mirror those being fought between the **sons of light** and the **sons of darkness** on earth.

Maon: The fifth of the **seven heavens** (Chag. 12b).

Maria Hebraea: Alchemist (Egyptian, ca. 1st century CE). She is credited with the discovery of the properties of hydrochloric acid and the invention of the *Kerotakis* or *Bain Maria* water-bath oven, as well as other standard alchemist's devices. She is also the first to give a formula for making the **philosopher's stone**. She taught that all the diverse elements are derivative of a single hylic substance. Sometime later, alchemical tradition conflates her identity with that of the biblical **Miriam**.[1]

1. Patai, *The Jewish Alchemists*, 60–94; Doberer, *The Goldmakers*, 21–22.

Marriage: A good marriage is a small restoration of the Eden-like perfection we knew at the beginning of time (M.K. 18b; Sotah 2a; Zohar I: 91b). A good match is also a miracle, as difficult as parting the Sea of Reeds, and successful matchmaking has kept God occupied since Creation (Gen. R. 68:4; Zohar I: 137a). Later Kabbalah links successful and unsuccessful marriages to issues of reincarnation and "soul mates" (literally) finding each other (Zohar I: 73b; Sha'ar ha-Gilgulim).

Even God is described as entering into marriage, either with the people Israel (Deut. 3:12) or with the **Shekhinah** (Zohar). SEE ANDROGYNY; SEX; WEDDING.

Masekhet Chibbut ha-Kever: This book documents the soul's journey into the afterlife. SEE BODY; DEATH; ETERNAL LIFE.

Masekhet Gehinnom: "Tractate [on the] Underworld." A Medieval text describing **Gehenna**, it instructs the reader about the earthly sins that cause the soul to be sent there and gives vivid descriptions of the afterlife consequences. **Joshua ben Levi** is the tour guide in these texts. There are a number of variant manuscripts and the information contained in them differs from one text to the next.

Masekhet Hechalot: "Tractate [on Divine] Palaces." Part of the **Merkavah** mystical traditions, it is a text for the adept who wishes to ascend to heaven. SEE HECHALOT LITERATURE.

Mashchit: "Destroyer." It is the name of the entity that slays the firstborn Egyptians at the **Exodus**. Also an alternate name for the **Angel of Death**. In **Tomar Devorah**, *mashchit* is a demonic entity brought into existence as a result of human sin. SEE DEMONS; PLAGUES; PUNISHING ANGELS.

Mashiva: "Binding." An adjuration spell for summoning and commanding angels. The language of adjuring angels in Jewish texts often mimics legal language. SEE CIRCLES; GET; HECHALOT LITERATURE; MAGIC SQUARE; SUMMONING.

Massachet Hechalot: A short but relatively intact text of **Hechalot literature**, it describes the heavenly palaces and, in particular, God's **Throne of Glory**.

Mastemah: "Enmity." A demonic prince, perhaps an alternative name for **Satan**, Mastemah is mentioned as the leading demonic entity opposing **Moses** in the Book of **Jubilees**. *SEE* APOCALYPTIC LITERATURE; DEMONS.

Masturbation: *SEE* NOCTURNAL EMISSION.

Mataniel: A **punishing angel** of **Gehenna** (Mid. Konen).

Matariel: The **angel** of **rain** and precipitation (I Enoch).

Matriarchs: The "mothers of Israel" (even the concubines and "informal" consorts, like Tamar) were prophets (Gen. R. 67:9, 72:6, 85:9), and their names have protective powers. *SEE* MOTHER; PATRIARCHS AND MATRIARCHS; RACHEL; REBECCA; SARAH.

Matronit: Another title for the **Shekhinah** (Zohar Chadash). She is the aspect of the divine Presence that mourns for **Jerusalem** and seeks constantly to reunite with the masculine aspect of divinity, the Holy One.

Matzah: Unleavened bread. *SEE* BREAD; UNLEAVENED BREAD.

Mavet: "Death." *SEE* ANGEL OF DEATH.

Mayyim Dukhrin/Mayyim Nukvin: "Male waters/Female waters." Idiomatic terms for the divine energies that flow between the higher and lower **Partzufim**, harmonizing them and thereby fructifying and sustaining life in the universe. *SEE* PHALLUS; WATER.

Mazal: "Planet/Constellation." In Jewish esotericism, it is commonly associated with astrology. And while the word has never lost its literal meaning of "planet," it now has a much more familiar connotative meaning of "luck" or "fortune." From this word is derived the expression of well-wishing, *Mazal Tov*, "Good Star/Good Fortune!" (Sot. 12b; Shab. 156a; B.K. 2b; M.K. 28a). **Sefer Chasidim** personifies mazal and describes it as a type of guardian **angel** (1162). *SEE* ASTROLOGY; FATE; GAD; PLANETS; ZODIAC.

Mazzamauriello: "Tellurian Demon." An Italian-Jewish term for a *kesil*, an imp or mischievous spirit.

Mazzik: "Damager." A class of malevolent spirits or **demons**.

Mechasef: "Sorcerer/Wizard." *SEE* MAGIC; SORCERY; WITCHCRAFT.

Meditation: (*Hitbonenut; Hitbodedut; Histakelut; Yichudim*). Contemplation, meditation, and trance-inducing practices are a feature of Judaism from biblical times. These practices, which vary greatly from one mystical text to another, include breath control, mantralike chanting, reciting divine names, silence, self-isolation, yogalike stress positions, creative visualization, and/or concentrating on a symbol, color, or object.

Meditation techniques can also be incorporated into prayer practices in order to produce **kavanah**, and so invigorate and activate the potential divine power of the traditional liturgy.[1]

The goals of Jewish meditation vary, depending on the particular school. Some promote it as a means to experiencing divine visions or accessing supernal knowledge. Others emphasize, in association with *kavanah*, the theurgic power of meditation to "arouse" a divine response, affect an object, or influence a person or event.

Meditation methods can be found in the writings of **Abraham Abulafia**, **Azriel of Gerona**, **Moses Cordovero**, and **Chayyim Vital**. Many Chasidic masters also emphasize meditation, both as an adjunct to prayer and as a separate discipline.

1. See Kaplan, *Mediation and Kabbalah*.

Medium: A medium is someone who invites voluntary possession (Hebrew, *Ibbur Tov*) by a spirit, usually the soul of a **righteous** ancestor or saint, in order to commune with them.

Genesis posits that human life itself is only possible so long as the "spirit" of life occupies the body (2:7, 5:3). Certain high attributes have their own genius; Elders in the Israelite camp were seized by the spirit of **Prophecy** (Ex. 24) and Joshua by the spirit of **Wisdom** (Deut. 34).

Biblical **necromancers** could summon the dead to answer questions, but it is unclear from the biblical accounts whether this actually entailed physical **possession**. The Gospels provide several examples of Jews being possessed by the **Holy Spirit**.

There are disapproving allusions in the **Talmud** to those who fast in order to attract "unclean spirits" and attempt a séance with the dead (Sanh. 65b; Shab. 152b–153a). **Merkavah** mystics would **summon** an **angel** of revelation called **Sar ha-Torah**, possibly to possess their bodies and speak through them, in order that they could accelerate their mastery of Torah study. The first references to summoning **demons** and enslaving them for beneficent purposes appear in magical texts at this time, such as the **Testament of Solomon**.

Many mystics record accounts of voluntary spirit possession. Notables who testify to such experiences include **Abraham Abulafia**, **Moses Cordovero**, **Joseph Caro**, **Isaac Luria**, and **Chayyim Vital**. As the preceding list suggests, benevolent possession was particularly a major interest among the Kabbalist brotherhood of Safed. Possessing spirits could include the **ibbur** (the virtuous dead), an angelic being, or a **maggid** (a personified aspect of Torah). **Solomon Alkabetz** claims to have been possessed by the **Shekhinah**, the immanent divine Presence that the mystics regarded to be in "exile" on earth alongside Israel.[1]

Achieving a beneficent possession usually involves a multi-step process. The Safed mystics give us the most detailed accounts of how to have a mediumistic experience. First, the potential **medium** must be morally upright and fully conversant with the Written and **Oral Torah**. Repeated **purification**, involving physical mortification through **fasting**, or occasionally even more extreme measures, is also a prerequisite. He (the medium is usually a he) must also work toward mindfulness, purifying even his thoughts. Many will recite texts from Jewish tradition in a mantralike way. The mystic intensifies his practices as he approaches transition to mediumship. Most practitioners will arrange for some conditions of isolation from the distractions of the world. Luria's **incubation** practice of

yichudim involved being at the grave of a righteous man, literally laying over the tomb in order to "animate" the spirit, and in effect "reversing" the death by using one's own body to house the dead soul. This was apparently inspired by the example of the prophet Elisha in II Kings.

Reports of mediumistic possession include **xenoglossia** (automatic speech), automatic writing, and radical changes in behavior and speech patterns. Firsthand accounts describe what we today might label a dissociative experience. *SEE* DIVINATION; ITZTZIM; YEDDIONI.

1. Bilu, "Dybbuk and Maggid," 341–66.

Megillat Ahimaaz: *SEE* AHIMAAZ, MEGILLAT OR SEFER.

Megillat Setarim: "Book of Secrets." The mystical-magical memoir of Isaac Safrin of Komarino.

Meir ha-Baal Nes: Saintly medieval rabbi and wonder-worker (Israel, ca. 15th–16th century). He vowed not to lie down until the advent of the **Messiah**. As a result, he is buried upright in a tomb outside Tiberias. To this day, thousands of pilgrims go there every year, and reportedly many miracles have been wrought for them.

Meir of Rothenberg: Rabbi and communal leader (German, ca. 13th century). Meir ben Baruch was a saintly and beloved rabbi. When he was imprisoned by gentile authorities in order to extract a ransom for the Jewish community, Rabbi Meir ordered the ransom not be paid, and he died in prison after many years. A number of miraculous stories are told about his imprisonment. In one such legend, he received a heavenly **Torah** written in **Moses's** own hand to comfort him during his incarceration. After his death, his body was left in its cell for fourteen years, until a pious disciple bribed his way to retrieving the body. When the cell was finally opened, the body was found perfectly preserved.

Meirat Eynaim: A mystical-magical tract written by **Isaac ben Samuel of Acre**.

Mekubbal: A person trained in the practical **Kabbalah**: amulet making, protective **incantations**, and folk healing.

The term first appears in the early modern era. Such figures still function in the traditional communities of modern Israel and America. At times it is used to refer to any Kabbalist. *SEE* AMULET; BAAL SHEM; HEALING.

Melaveh Malchah: "Escorting the Queen." A **ritual** involving prayers and songs performed at the close of the **Sabbath**, usually an extension of the "third meal" (**Seudah Sh'lishit**) and **Havdalah** at the conclusion of the holiday in order to extend the length of the day of rest. The ritual strengthens the **Shekhinah** for the week ahead. According to one esoteric tradition, the souls of sinners in **Gehenna** are spared punishment for the duration of the Sabbath. Performing the Melaveh Malchah is understood to be a way of easing their suffering.[1] *SEE* SABBATH QUEEN.

   1. Ginsburg, *The Sabbath in Classical Kabbalah,* 277; Rabinowicz, *The Encyclopedia of Hasidism,* 309.

Melchizedek: The mysterious Priest/King of Salem, who welcomed **Abraham** in the name of El Elyon, "God Most High" (Gen. 14), and receives cryptic mention in Psalm 110. In the **Midrash**, he is identified with **Shem**. In another source, he is one of four eschatological figures linked to the "four smiths" mentioned in Zechariah 2. In I Enoch (Slavonic) and in a **Dead Sea Scroll** fragment devoted to him, Melchizedek is a nephew of Noah translated to heaven to serve as a priest on high until the advent of the Messianic Era. In another DSS text, he appears as the "Angel of Light" (Song of the Sabbath Sacrifice). In Christian lore, he is a prefiguration of **Jesus**.

Mem: Thirteenth letter of the **Hebrew alphabet**. It has the numeric value of 40 and the vocalic value of "m." As the first letter in words like *Moshe* (Moses), *Miryam* (Miriam), *Mashiach* (Messiah), and *Malchut* (Kingdom), it signifies majesty and power. It is one of the five letters that also has a *sofit,* or end-form, a totally enclosed shape symbolizing the mysterious, concealed nature of such power.[1]

   1. Munk, *The Wisdom of the Hebrew Alphabet,* 143–50.

Memory, Book of: (*Sefer ha-Zicharon*). The celestial book in which the deeds of every person are recorded, it may or may not be the same as the Sefer ha-Chayyim, the **Book of Life** (Ezra 4:15; Targum Esther 6:1; Zohar I: 8a; II: 70a).

Memra: "Speech/Logos/Word." In **Targum** (Aramaic translations of biblical texts), the translator will often add the word *Memra* before a divine action, as in "The *Memra* of YHWH did. . . ." The exact function of this term is a matter of controversy. Some say it is meant to soften in translation the more anthropomorphic, less philosophical language the Hebrew Bible uses in describing God. Others posit that it is meant to signify an intermediate stage of divine emanation, a form of the divine **Glory** that allows the perfect, unchanging God to interact with an imperfect and changing Creation. Or, as the term itself implies, it may signify the creative and theurgic power present in divine speech (MdRI, be-Shallach 10).[1] *SEE* HEBREW; INCANTATION; NAME OF GOD; SPECULUM.

   1. Burkett, "Memra, Shekinah, Metatron," in the *Journal of Theological Studies,* 158–59. Also see Roth, *Encyclopedia Judaica,* vol. VI, 464–65.

Memuneh: "Deputy." The genius or angel that energizes every discrete phenomenon in the universe. Thus every star, planet, month, day, human being, nation, land, and even abstractions like justice and love, have their own *memuneh*. Only hinted at in rabbinic literature, it is a belief that becomes much more prominent in the Middle Ages. *SEE* ANGELS; MINISTERING ANGELS.

Men, Male: (*Ish; Adam; Gever; Zachar*). There are three archetypes of masculinity in Judaism: **Adam Kadmon**, the primordial man; **Adam Rishon**, the ordinary man; and the **Messiah**, the perfected man of the **World-to-Come** (Philo, *De Opificio Mundi,* 134–42; B.B. 58a; Tanh., Tzaria 2).[1]

In traditional Jewish thought, men are considered the human norm. **Women**, by contrast, present the Sages with many of the exceptional and problematic issues involving Jewish observance and thinking. As feminist critics of traditional Judaism have observed, women represent "the other"—which is not to say men were considered more virtuous than women. There is a theme of women having a greater innate capacity for piety than men that is woven throughout Jewish tradition, as exemplified by the legend that women refused to participate in the Golden Calf incident (Tosafot to Rosh Hashanah 23a).

Men could occupy any position or role of religious authority in Israelite and later Jewish society. The priesthood of Israelite religion was exclusively a masculine office. The same was true of the Levitical functions. This was not the case, however, when it came to charismatic leadership roles, such as that of prophet or judge, where women could also rise to places of authority. The role of rabbi has been a solely male one until the 1970s, when the first women were ordained by a Jewish seminary.

Despite his normative status in Jewish literature, a man is considered an incomplete human without a woman. Men are also be more vulnerable to spiritual assault than women. Men are considered particularly vulnerable prior to circumcision (Ex. 4) and during a wedding.[2] Circumcision in particular is a powerful transformative ritual, for it creates a more proper balance between the masculine and feminine sides of men (Gen. R. 46:4).[3]

1. Schwartz, *The Tree of Souls*, 125–126.
2. Trachtenberg, *Jewish Magic and Superstition*, 121.
3. Eilberg-Schwartz, *God's Phallus*, 170–173. Also see Wolfson, *Through a Speculum that Shines*.

Menachem: The given name of the **Messiah** ben David (Sanh. 98b; Lam. R. 1:51; Sefer Zerubbabel).

Menachesh: "Augurer/Diviner." Derived from the Hebrew root for "snake," a *menachesh* is someone who reads signs and **omens**. Scripture specifically applies this term to Joseph's **hydromancy**, or "cup reading," mentioned in Genesis 44:5. The **Talmud** regards the *menachesh* to be a professional diviner and interpreter of omens, someone who studies the behavior of **animals**, such as **birds**, **snakes**, and weasels, for mantic information (Sanh. 65b–66a).

Mene, Mene, Tekel, Ufarsin: The modern idiom "The writing on the wall" comes from this phrase, which according to the book of Daniel appeared in the palace of King Belshazzar, written by a supernal **hand** (Dan. 5:25). The Bible itself does not give a fully satisfactory explanation of the phrase; it is usually rendered "He has measured, measured, weighed, and divided." The puzzle is deepened by the fact that the book of Daniel, when it repeats the phrase, changes how it is read (5:26). Subsequently, it has become the subject of esoteric speculation. The **Talmud** proposes that it is some kind of **atbash**, a substitution code (Sanh. 22a).

Menorah: The menorah is a golden oil-lamp candelabra used in the **Temple** in **Jerusalem**. Built according to a pattern revealed by God to **Moses**, its appearance is that of a stylized bush with six curved branches coming off of its central stem (Ex. 26). It thus resembles a kind of cosmic tree, and the appearance is probably meant to remind the viewer of the burning bush (Ex. 3). It is by far the most ancient symbol of Judaism. The menorah of which we speak is not to be confused with the nine-branch *chanukiyah*, a menorah used exclusively to celebrate the miracle of Chanukah.

According to legend, the menorah of the First Temple was hidden from the Babylonians and restored to the Second Temple (Ginzberg, *Legends of the Jews*, 4:321). At the destruction of the Second Temple, it was swallowed up by the earth and its whereabouts will be revealed only in the time of the **Messiah**.

The spiritual significance of the menorah is multifold. Some see the six branches as representing the six-winged fiery serafim angels (Isa. 6). Its seven lamps symbolize the seven days of Creation. It can also be seen as an inverted tree, with its roots in heaven. The **Kabbalah** teaches that the menorah is a stylized representation of the **sefirot**, with the seven branches signifying the lower seven sefirot that interact with the world of action.

The menorah is a popular image to include on an **amulet**. Paper amulets may have an image of a menorah made from **microscript**, usually using verses of Psalm 67. According to one amulet manual, David inscribed Psalm 67 in the form of a menorah on his battle shield. Amulets made in this pattern are very common among Jews of the East. *SEE* FIRE; LIGHT; PSALMS; SYNAGOGUE.

Menstruation: From the earliest times in Israelite history, women's monthly cycle of menstruation was viewed with awe and considered an extraordinary phenomenon. Because they have the power to render everything they touch *tamei* (impure/uncanny), menstruating women are isolated to varying degrees in traditional communities, usually by simply avoiding physical contact, but sometimes by sleeping apart from their husbands, limiting their handling of communal objects, etc. Menstruating women were a particular concern for the priesthood, as contact with them temporarily rendered a priest unfit to perform his duties.

Many Kabbalists likewise believed that contact with menstrual blood had the potential to interfere with their mystical practices.

There is one document, Baraita de-Masekhet Niddah, which ascribes all kinds of negative effects to menstruation. As a result, some medieval Jewish authorities went beyond mere issues of ritual purity/impurity, believing menstruants to be powerful carriers of a variety of ills, including boils, **leprosy**, and other malevolent effects. Menstruation apparently enhanced the effects of **witchcraft**, making it more lethal.

On the flip side, Genesis Rabbah interprets Sarah's reaction in Genesis 18:12 as enthusiasm, not for her husband's carnal attention or even for the prospective **birth** of a son, but at the return of her menstrual cycle—she literally calls it a "delight" (48:17, also see PdRE 36; B.M. 87a).

Meonen: "Soothsayer." One who can make apparitions appear. The word may be derived from the Hebrew *anan*, "cloud," suggesting someone who reads **omens** in the sky or interprets smoke patterns, a common form of **divination** in Mesopotamia. The Talmudic Sages differ on the meaning of this term, some saying a *meonen* is a user of **witchcraft**, while others claim it refers to an astrologer. The Talmud also accuses the meonen of using illusions and sleight of hand to deceive observers (Sefrei Deut. 171; Sanh. 65b).

Merkavah: "Chariot." *SEE* CHARIOT; MA'ASEI-MERKAVAH.

Merkavah, Ma'asei-: "Workings of the [Divine] Chariot." *SEE* MA'ASEI-MERKAVAH.

Merkavah Rabbah: A manuscript text of the **Hechalot** literature, probably belonging to the cluster of **Sar ha-Torah** traditions for **summoning angels** of revelation.

Meshiv, Sefer ha-: "Book of the Responding Entity" or "Book of Answering." A medieval manual for summoning both angelic and demonic spiritual entities. As is the case with many other magical books, **Moses** appears as a central figure.

The only legitimate purpose for summoning supernatural forces, according to the book, is to destroy the power of **evil** in the world. Written in Spain between the 14th and 15th centuries, it exists only in manuscript form.[1] *SEE* ANGELS; CIRCLES, MAGIC; DEMONS; REINA, JOSEPH DELLA; SUMMONING.

1. Idel, "Magic and Kabbalah in the 'Book of the Responding Entity,'" in *The Solomon Goldman Lectures VI*.

Meshulahel: A demoness. (Pardes Rimmonim).

Messiah: (*Mashiach*). God's eschatological anointed king; the central figure of Jewish eschatological beliefs.

In ancient Israel, the kings and the High Priests, and even sometimes prophets, were anointed with oil when they ascended to their office. A person so anointed was called a *mashiach*.

In II Samuel 7, God promises **David** that his seed will hold the throne of Israel for all eternity. Out of this royal theology emerges the belief that an ideal king, a descendant of David, will arise and restore the fortunes of Israel at the end of time, defeating its enemies, bringing back its exiles. The prophets taught that the influence of this end-times Messiah would be international—war and oppression will cease, there will be a universal **healing**, and all the peoples and nations will acknowledge the authority of the one God. But unlike Christian theology, Judaism does not regard the Messiah to be an incarnation of God; the Messiah is entirely human. Still, there are many supernatural elements, both subtle and overt, to Jewish Messianism.

Because the doctrine of the Messiah is based on ambiguous biblical texts, there are multiple, at times conflicting, traditions about him.

In the **Dead Sea Scrolls**, there is a tradition of *two* messiahs, a priestly and a royal one, "the messiahs of Aaron and of Israel." There are parallels to this in **apocalyptic literature**, and even some faint echoes in rabbinic literature. Reflecting the priestly bias found in other books of the DSS, the Priestly or Aaronide Messiah is treated as superior to the Royal Messiah, a theme that does not carry over into rabbinic traditions. There are also a number of other messianic figures mentioned in the Qumran texts. One entire DSS text, the **Messianic Apocalypse** (4Q521), is devoted to messianic teachings.

There is also a minor tradition about a second Messiah, descending from the line of **Joseph**. This messianic figure is usually designated the Messiah ben Ephraim (after Joseph's eldest son). This figure is presented as the commander of the messianic army. In most versions of the "two messiahs" tradition, the Messiah ben Ephraim dies in battle, only to be avenged and resurrected by the Messiah ben David (Suk. 52a; Sefer Hechalot; Sefer Zerubbabel). One text even argues there will be no less than seven messiahs. At least one Talmudic Sage expressed doubts about the whole concept of an eschatological Messiah (Sanh. 98b).

While the concepts of a priestly Messiah and a Messiah ben Ephraim do not completely vanish from rabbinic traditions, the overwhelming interest of rabbinic literature is upon the Davidic Messiah, or "King Messiah."

Though the "name" of the Messiah has been known since before Creation (PR 31:10, 33: 6), he is still a product of human procreation, so in every generation there are potential messiahs among us, awaiting the right conditions to be revealed (Lam. R. 1:51). Remarkably, the Messiah is the descendant of several "unusual" relationships; through his great-grandmother Ruth, he is a product of the incestuous union of Lot and his daughters (Gen. 19:30–37) and through his great-grandfather Boaz, he is the offspring of Tamar's act of prostitution (Gen. 38:1–30). In the Zohar, the Messiah is simultaneously a physical descendant of David *and* David reincarnated (I: 82b).

The King Messiah will appear on the ninth of Av, the day that Israel mourns the destruction of the Temple. According to Talmud Yevamot 62a, the Messiah cannot come until every soul that is destined to be born is born, a legend that foreshadows Franz Kafka's statement that the Messiah will not come until he is no longer needed. Varied (and somewhat contradictory) criteria for the coming of the Messiah are given by various Sages in Sanhedrin 98a–b.

Different names derived from Scripture were offered as the proper name of the Messiah, such as Menachem (Comforter) and Immanuel (God is with us), but most Jews simply speak of the *Mashiach ben David* (Messiah, son of David) or *Mashiach ha-Melech* (King Messiah).

There are two very different scenarios concerning the advent of the Messiah: a conflict-driven vision of the end, and a peaceful, yet radically transformative, unfolding. The first idea, that there will be a cataclysmic war accompanying the advent of the Messiah, first emerges in the biblical book of **Zechariah** and the apocalyptic literature of Greco-Ro-

man times. Early rabbinic literature does not emphasize this aspect of the messianic traditions. But by the Middle Ages, perhaps influenced by Christian eschatology, the theme of a war at the end of time once again becomes a prominent feature of Jewish Messianism. The biblical tradition of the apocalyptic **Gog and Magog** reemerges, while for the first time **Armilius**, a mysterious Antichristlike figure, appears as a character in messianic accounts.

There are a number of mystical testimonies, beginning with **Joshua ben Levi** and continuing on to the **Baal Shem Tov**, of personal encounters with the Messiah during mystical **ascent**.

All Jewish holidays, prayers, and rituals have a messianic dimension to them. Today there are two major veins of thought about the Messiah. Traditionalists still hold to the notion of the Messiah as a single person. Many liberals, drawing upon mystical traditions, teach that the whole body of the Jewish people is the Messiah and it is our collective efforts that will bring the world to its final reconciliation.

Certain periods of Jewish history (the Second Temple period; the Napoleonic Wars; after the 1967 Six Day War) have been more susceptible to messianic excitements and expectations. There are many figures in Jewish history that have had messianic ambitions and pretensions. The most famous include **Jesus** of Nazareth, **Simon bar Kochba**, **David Reubeni**, **Abraham Abulafia**, **Isaac Luria**, **Chayyim Vital**, **Shabbatai Tzvi**, **Nachman of Bratzlav**, **Moses Luzzato**, Joel Titelbaum (the first Satmar Rebbe), and **Menachem Mendel Schneerson** (the seventh Lubavitcher Rebbe). Chasids seem particularly inclined to see their own **rebbes** as either messianic contenders or messianic precursors. Yet all have failed to fulfill the messianic prophecies.

Messiah, Summoning the: Several tales exist in Jewish literature of great mystics and sages trying to "force the hand" of God into sending the Messiah. The Talmud (B. M. 85b) teaches that the prayers of the righteous have the power to trigger the coming of the Messiah. In another Talmudic passage, the Sage **Joshua ben Levi** interviewed the Messiah to find out when he would come (he didn't get a satisfactory answer), but it is not until the Middle Ages that there are tales of actual attempts to calculate the coming or theurgically summon the Messiah. Abravanel, Levi Yitzkhak of Berdichev, and Malbim all offered approximate dates for the advent of the Messiah.

Later Jewish literature features a number of stories about efforts to force the Messiah's coming. Perhaps the two most famous tales of Messiah summoning are the attempts of the 15th-century mystic/magician **Joseph della Reina** and the 19th-century Chasidic master, **Jacob Isaac, the Seer of Lublin**. The consequences for both men were disastrous, with della Reina carried off by demons and Jacob Isaac defenestrated.

Messianic Apocalypse: A fragmentary document (4Q521) found among the **Dead Sea Scrolls**, it provides insight into some of the early Jewish beliefs and traditions concerning the Messiah. In it, the Messiah will heal the wounded, restore sight to the blind, and revive the dead—ideas that would later be echoed in the Christian Gospels.

Metal: Because of their mysterious underworldly qualities, metals have been linked to the occult from time immemorial. According to the Bible, Tubal-Cain is the discoverer of metal-smithing (Gen. 4).

All metals, but especially silver and **iron**, play a role in Jewish magical praxis. Silver is the preferred medium for the making of **amulets**, though **gold**, copper, and lead also can be used in specific cases (Sefer ha-Razim). **Sefer Raziel** also requires that plates of silver and gold be used for protective spells. Often it requires the casting away or the destruction of the inscribed plate to trigger its power. Iron, too, has special anti-demonic properties. Copper amulets, inscribed with the name of a missing person and buried at four compass points, will bring word of their whereabouts. Copper plates worn under the heels drive away wild beasts.

Metatron: A **Sar** (Princely Angel) who features prominently in Jewish esoteric literature. The name "Metatron" itself is a puzzle, being a Greek-derived word meaning either *meta-thronos*, "beyond the throne," *metator*, "guide," or *meta-tetra*, "beyond the four [Angels of the Countenance]." Metatron has many other names and titles. Among the most common are **Sar ha-Panim** (Prince of the Countenance), *Sar ha-Olam* (Prince of the World), *ha-Naar* (the

Youth), *Marei de-Gadpei* (Master of Wings), and Yahoel. The very name "Metatron" is spelled differently in different documents. In the **Merkavah** traditions, we learn that Metatron has twelve names, corresponding to the twelve tribes. This may account for why there are so many overlapping names and titles in the Metatron traditions (Sanh. 38b; Zohar I: 21a).

Metatron's place in the angelic host is truly unique for several reasons. So exalted is his status that in some sources he is referred to as the "Lesser YHWH" (Yev. 16b; Sanh. 38b). He is also unique in that he alone among the angels sits upon a throne, as does God. Because of this, Elisha ben Abuyah mistakes Metatron for a god and concludes there are "two powers in heaven" (Chag. 15a). The other remarkable fact about Metatron is that he was once human—the antediluvian hero **Enoch** (Gen. 5; Jubilees 4:23; Sefer Hechalot 12:5). In **III Enoch**, Metatron describes to Rabbi Ishmael how he was transubstantiated from mortal to angelic form: under the direction of **Michael** and **Gabriel**, he grew in size until his body filled the whole universe (signaling a reversal of the "fall" of **Adam Kadmon**). He sprouted 72 wings (for each of the 72 names of God), grew 365,000 luminous eyes (indicating he had became omniscient, symbolized by acquiring 1,000 eyes for each day of the year), and his material body burned away to be replaced with a form of pure fire. According to the Zohar, he has the appearance of a rainbow (I: 7a). Finally, he is given a crown resembling the crown worn by God.

Metatron has a very prominent role in Hechalot literature, where he appears as a guide to human adepts visiting heaven, (except in Hechalot Rabbati, where that role is filled by **Anafiel**). At times, Metatron is described as the High Priest in the heavenly Temple, a role ascribed to **Michael** in other texts. In Sefer Zerubbabel, he is explicitly identified with Michael. He also functions as the heavenly scribe, writing 366 books. In addition, Metatron teaches Torah to the righteous dead in the **Yeshiva** on high (A.Z. 3b; Seder Gan Eden). He is involved in events on earth as well as in heaven. He led Abraham through Canaan, delivered Isaac from his father's knife, wrestled with Jacob, led the Israelites in the desert, rallied Joshua, and revealed the End of Times to Zerubbabel (Sefer Zerubbabel). Even so, he is only rarely adjured in angel summoning incantations.

He continues his function as heavenly tour guide in medieval works like **Gedulat Moshe**, though Metatron does not enjoy the singular prominence in later **Kabbalah** that he does in early **Ma'asei-Merkavah**. In the **Zohar**, Metatron is the first "offspring" of the supernal union of God's feminine and masculine aspects (I: 143a, 162a–b). *SEE* SUMMONING.

Metempsychosis: Transmigration of souls. *SEE* REINCARNATION.

Metoposcopy: (*Chochmat ha-Partzuf*, "Face augury"). A number of ancient, medieval, and modern texts have reported on this technique for deriving occult information from studying other people's foreheads (DSS 4Q186; Hakkarat Panim l'Rabbi Yishmael; Zohar II: 71a–78a; Sefer Ruach ha-Kodesh, 15–22). This talent is especially credited to **Isaac Luria**. According to **Chayyim Vital**, Luria literally saw letters emanating from the soul on the faces of other people. *SEE* DEAD SEA SCROLLS; DIVINATION; FACE.

Mezuzah: "Doorpost." In order to fulfill the commandment that Israel put ". . . the commandments I give you this day . . . upon your doorposts (*mezuzot*) and upon your gates" (Deut. 6), the practice arose of placing a container filled with Scriptural passages on the doorframe of a Jewish home. As early as the 4th century BCE, there is archaeological evidence of the use of mezuzot (pl.) on Jewish homes.

Doorways have always been understood to be liminal zones between the protected space of the home and the vulnerable outside, where malevolent spirits move freely. The practice of placing a text of power in a tube at the doorway closely parallels the Greco-Roman practice of amulet making (Sefer ha-Razim).

Rabbinic literature makes reference to a mezuzah being used as an **amulet**, though many prominent Sages objected to treating it as such (Gen. R. 35:3; A.Z. 11a). By the Middle Ages, a number of Kabbalistic and talismanic additions started to appear on mezuzot—an **Atbash** code version of the first sentence of the Sh'ma, *Kozu be-Machsaz Kozu*, is usually written on the reverse side of the biblical text. Angelic names, hexagrams, **magic squares**, fish, and other protective symbols are also incorporated into some mezuzot. The Chasids are emphatic in their belief that mezuzot have a critical role in keeping spirits and bad fortune out of a house (Shivhei ha-Besht, 186).

A relatively recent phenomenon is the actual *wearing* of mezuzot on the body, often without a text, as a protective charm. This practice evidently arose in the modern era when Jewish mothers started sending their sons to serve in gentile armies. Now mezuzah-like charms are also made to be put into cars, boats, and airplanes.

Michael: "[One] who is Godlike." A princely **angel**, the guardian angel of the people Israel. Michael first appears to **Daniel** (chapter 10) as the defender of Jews, a role that he remains closely identified with in rabbinic literature. This is why he also functions as the High Priest in the ideal heavenly Temple, for he is constantly making offerings before God on Israel's behalf. He is also frequently invoked on protective amulets. Sometimes he is identified with the element of fire, at other times with the element of air.[1]

He is one of the four angels (along with **Gabriel**, **Uriel**, and **Raphael**) who attend upon God's throne. He is one of the generals commanding the **host of heaven**. He is one of the angels God sends to discipline the **fallen angels** (I Enoch 10), and he will play a prominent role in the eschatological battle at the end of time (DDS, Sefer Melchizedek). He is made of snow, air, and/or light (Deut. R. 5:12; DSS War Scroll). He is accompanied everywhere by the **Shekhinah** (Ex. R. 2:5). He holds the keys to heaven and escorts the righteous souls to God's presence (III Baruch). **Sefer Zerubbabel** identifies him with **Metatron**. He is also the "Angel of the right [side]" of the sefirot (Zohar I: 98a).

As an angel of revelation, Michael has had many earthly manifestations and he is linked to many of the encounters between biblical figures and the divine, even if he is not mentioned by name in the biblical text: witnessing the marriage of Adam and Eve (Gen. 2), the visitation of Abraham (Gen. 18), the rescue of Abraham from Nimrod's fiery furnace (Gen. R. 44:13), and accompanying Abraham's servant Eliezer (Gen. R. 59:10). Michael intervenes to prevent Laban from killing Jacob (PdRE 36). He is the fiery manifestation in the burning bush (Ex. 2:5), descends with God on Mount Sinai (Gen. R. 2:34), and accompanies

Moses's body for his burial (Deut. R. 11:10). He was the angel that smote the armies of Sennachrib (Ex. R. 18.5). He assisted Esther in her struggle with Haman (Est. R. 7:12).

Michael also serves God outside the context of Israel. He established the place where Rome would be built (S of S R. 1:6). Michael is frequently paired with Gabriel in rabbinic texts.

There is a fragmentary text among the Dead Sea Scrolls, the "Michael" text, in which Michael addresses the angelic host, which is the only Jewish record of Michael speaking in the first person.

1. Verman, *The Books of Contemplation*, 206.

Microcosm: The belief that the key structures of the universe are replicated and epitomized in critical entities, such as the Tabernacle (Ex. R. 35:6; Num. R. 12:13) and/or the human form. In the case of the human, the idea is most often expressed in the belief that **Adam Kadmon**, the primordial human, once filled and was co-equal with the universe (Gen. R. 3:7, 19:8–9). The idea that the human being, in particular, encapsulates the universe is very appealing to the mystic because it implies that one may draw closer to God by going deeper into oneself. *SEE* BODY; GODHEAD; IMAGE, DIVINE. *(SEE ALSO APPENDIX FIGURE 3.)*

Microscript: Tiny lines of scriptural verses made into images, faces, and symbols. Microscript is a common feature of paper **amulets**. The Psalms, especially Pss. 67, 91, and 121, are the texts most used in microscript amulets. Protective images most often constructed out of microscript include **menorahs**, **eyes**, **faces**, **hands**, and the **Magen David**.

Midnight: In Judaism, midnight is a propitious time for prayer, study, and ritual. At midnight, the ascending power of evil is turned back. God attends to the righteous dead at this time (Zohar I: 92a–b). For these reasons, midnight is an auspicious time to begin Torah study (Chag. 12b; Ber. 3b). Anyone who makes a habit of studying at that time secures eternal life for him- or herself.

In Chasidic spiritual practice, there is the custom of *Tikkun Chatzot*, the Midnight Mending for the destruc-

tion of the Temple, with the hope it will speed its restoration. This is mainly observed in the winter, when nights are longest (Likutei Moharan I). *SEE* ABRAHAM BERUCHIM; DARKNESS; NIGHT.

Midrash: Rabbinic commentaries on the Bible, characterized by their concentrated interest in the close reading of phrases, words, even letters, often at the expense of the contextual meaning. At the same time, Midrash is daring, eclectic, and highly imaginative in its interpretations. As a result, it becomes a repository for many fabulous and supernatural traditions.

There are many, many documents of the Midrash. Among the most fruitful texts for those interested in Jewish fantastic traditions are Genesis Rabbah, Leviticus Rabbah, Midrash Tehillim, Midrash Konen, Pirkei de-Rabbi Eliezer, and Yalkut Shimoni. Some Kabbalistic works, particularly the **Bahir** and the **Zohar**, are partly written in the style of a mystical Midrash.

Midrash Eleh Ezkerah: "Midrash 'These things I Remember.'" A martyrology of the **Ten Martyrs**. It contains accounts of their great piety and extraordinary powers.

Midrash ha-Gadol: An anthology of later Midrashic material. It incorporates many later rabbinic legends.

Midrash ha-Nelam: "Esoteric Midrash." The first part of the **Zohar**, it is a mystical commentary on Genesis and Exodus.

Midrash Konen: A Midrash on Creation. It popularizes many esoteric non-biblical teachings concerning Jewish cosmogony.

Midrash Mishlei: "Midrash on Proverbs." This quasi-Midrash includes some longer narrative passages, such as the stories of **Solomon** and the **Queen of Sheba** and the death of **Rabbi Akiba**.

Midrash Rabbah: The great collection of classical Midrashim on the five books of Moses. There is a "Rabbah" for each book of the Pentateuch. Each has fantastic elements in it, though **Genesis Rabbah**, with the many stories of the mythic origins of the world, is the richest.

Midrash Samuel: A medieval collection of Midrashim and legends about the Sages.

Midrash Tanhuma: A collection of medieval Midrashim on the five books of Moses. It has many longer narrative elements. There are two major versions, the other being known as "Midrash Tanhuma (Buber)" for the modern scholar who discovered and published it.

Midrash Tehillim: "Midrash on Psalms." An early medieval Midrash collection focused on Psalms, it includes many supernatural traditions about David and other biblical heroes. It is sometimes printed with **Midrash Samuel**.

Miflaot Elohim: A text devoted to medical astrology and magic attributed to either **Naftali Katz** or Yoel ben Uri Halperin.

Mikvah; Mikvaot: "[Ritual] Pool." SEE IMMERSION; PURIFICATION; WATER.

Milchamot Adonai, Sefer: A **Lost Book** mentioned in the Hebrew Scriptures (Num. 21:14–15).

Milham Bird: A mythical creature that is a hybrid of a **bird**, a crocodile, and a **lion**. It refused to join Adam and Eve in eating from the fruit of the Tree of the Knowledge of Good and Evil. For that obedience, it is immortal and dwells in the city of Luz (Ginzberg, *Legends of the Jews*, 1:28–9). SEE PHOENIX; ZIZ.

Ministering Angels: (*Malachei ha-Shareit*). Personal guardian angels. Divided into those who minister to God on high and those who serve humanity below, the latter can help, support, and protect individuals, though their effectiveness varies according to circumstance. They cannot prevent their mortal wards from committing willful sins, however, and such behavior actually diminishes their powers (PdRE 15; SCh 1162; Siddur).

Minyan: "Quorum." Ten Jews is the minimum number needed to constitute a "community." A minyan is needed to convene a public worship service, or to serve as a representative body. The number ten is derived from the ten spies who determined the Land of **Israel** was too dangerous to invade and the ten righteous men God needed to find in **Sodom** in order to spare the city (Num. 14:27; Gen. 18:32). There are situations when a minyan is also required to deal with a paranormal phenomenon, such as the **exorcism** of a possessed person (Zera ha-Kodesh).

Miracle: (*Fela, Nes, Mofet, Ot*). A paranormal sign or wonder. Strictly speaking, miracles are events that cannot be explained by normal causality, but are instead credited to divine intervention into the normal course of the world. There are many, many such signs and wonders recorded throughout Jewish literature.

The Bible makes a point of identifying God as the source of all miraculous feats, even when the miracle occurs through the agency of a human being. **Moses** is explicitly rebuked for having failed to acknowledge God while performing the miracle of **water** at Meribah (Num. 20). Other paranormal actions taken without divine sanction, such as the snake charming of the Egyptian wizards (Ex. 7), are mere **magic**.

The **Talmud** is less stringent in ascribing miracles directly to God; it assumes that when a Sage or godly Jew performs a wonder that power comes from God, even if it is not expressly said so. By the same token, for all their blasé attitudes toward the frequent supernatural events that happened around them, the Sages pointedly observe, "One must not rely on miracles" (Kid. 39b; Shab. 32a; Pes. 50b), even as a source of revelation (B.M. 59b). Some voices in the **Midrash** are uncomfortable with the concept of the interruption of normal causality, arguing instead that all the miracles reported in the Scripture were actually natural events pre-programmed into Creation to coincide with critical moments in the history of Israel (AdRN 5:6; PdRE 19).

While Jewish rational philosophers have also attempted to "naturalize" the miraculous, many Jewish pietists and mystics accept the reality of miracles with little evident angst or reservations. The Chasids, particularly, credit their **rebbes** with performing many miracles (Shivhei ha-Besht, 21–23; Or ha-Emet 55b; Midrash Pinkas 16:5a).

Miriam: Prophetess and sister of **Moses** and **Aaron**. The Sages claim she had multiple names and titles, including Helah, Azubah, Efrat, and Naarah (Ex. R. 1:21). She was the third member of the prophetic triumphirate that led the Children of Israel through the **Exodus**. Unlike her brothers Aaron and Moses, nothing miraculous is explicitly credited to Miriam in the biblical text. Post-biblically, however, she is associated with a number of miraculous feats.

Through her, God manifested the **miracle** of the **well of Miriam** (Ta'anit 9a), a supernatural water source that appeared whenever the Israelites encamped during the forty-year sojourn in the desert. The death of Miriam at the end of the book of Numbers causes the well to disappear. The Sages credit this deprivation with causing the confrontation between Moses and the people at Meribah (Num. 20:2).

In one tradition, she is identified as the mother (or grandmother) of **Bezalel**, the mystical artisan (Ex. R. 1:17). She died by the **kiss** of God (B.B. 17a) and her **body** remains perfectly preserved to this day.

Practitioners of Hermetic arts believe she was an alchemist, though this may arise from confusing the biblical figure with **Maria Hebraea** of Greco-Roman times.

Mirror: (*Rei; Marah*). A mirror is both a kind of window and a buffer between worlds. It can be used as a divination device by having a child sit in front of it and looking for figures or objects that convey ominous import. As a buffer, it can be used in divine encounters (RaSHI's commentary, Sukkah 45b). **Chayyim Vital**, for example, repeatedly used a mirror to scry angels and demons, apparently in order to avoid looking them directly in the face (Sefer ha-Hezyonot 23, 24). Mirrors can also be used as aids to meditation. Because the mirror is an object of vanity, its use can attract the **evil eye**. Scrying mirrors occasionally appear in Chasidic miracle tales. *SEE* DIVINATION; SPECULUM; WATER.

Mishkan: "Dwelling Place." The portable sanctuary built by the Israelites at God's direction. Medieval writers often referred to the body of the righteous as a "mishkan." *SEE* MICROCOSM; RIGHTEOUS, THE; TABERNACLE.

Mitzvah: "Commandment." *SEE* COMMANDMENT.

Mochin: According to Lurianic thought, *mochin* is the consciousness God suffuses through all Creation; it is the awareness the universe has of its connection to divinity (Sha'ar ha-Kavvanot).

Molokho, Solomon: Kabbalist and failed messiah (Portuguese, ca. 16th century). Born into a family of **Crypto-Jews**, Molokho returned to his ancestral faith and immersed himself in mystical studies, including cultivating a **maggid**, a spirit guide. He had numerous excellent adventures with **David Reubeni**, and eventually proclaimed himself Messiah. He was arrested by the church for his trouble and was eventually burned at the stake for abandoning **Christianity**.

Moon: (*Levanah; Yerach*). From biblical times, it has been believed that the moon has influence over humanity (Ps. 121). The ancient terms used in describing its cycle, *ibbur* and *moled*, "conceived" and "born," suggest that the Israelites believed it to be a living entity. The **Talmud** believes that the moon has a consciousness, or animating genius. The principle **angel** that governs the moon is **Gabriel**, though some texts identify another angel, such as Yarchiel, as its controlling genius.

According to the **Midrash**, the moon began as a celestial luminary equal to the sun, but God reduced it to a lesser light because of its arrogance. God did, however, compensate it for the loss by giving the moon a greater role in human affairs. Thus the moon is crucial in determining the Jewish **calendar**. According to the **aggadah**, its original glory will be restored in the Messianic Era (Chul. 60b).

According to the Sages, the moon is a symbol of Israel, for though both wax and wane, they also both endure eternally. It is also a symbol of **women**. According to the Talmud, Jewish women are granted an extra monthly day without labor, the **new moon**, because of their loyalty to God during the **Golden Calf** incident (Tanh., Ki Tissa 19; PdRE 45; Tosafot; R.H. 23a).

Moonlight repels demons (Ber. 43b). Lunar eclipses are considered a bad **omen** and a sign of God's anger over moral lapses. There is a theurgic **ritual** preserved in the Talmud, intended to ensure good fortune, called the Blessing for the New Moon.

Medieval Jewish works of astrology list a variety of human spheres that the moon affects with its waxing and waning. The ideal time for sexual intercourse is the new moon, because it would have a positive influence on a child conceived at that time. The best time to construct an **amulet** is determined by the phases of the moon; the same is true for performing certain medical procedures. The moon represents **Malchut/Shekhinah** in the sefirotic Godhead (Sof. 4:5; Suk. 29a; Sanh. 42a; Zohar I: 236b). *SEE* ASTROLOGY; ZODIAC.

Moon, New: *SEE* NEW MOON.

Mordecai: The uncle of **Esther**, the Jewish queen of Persia (Esth. 2). According to the Sages, Mordecai was a prophet. According to legend, when he took in his infant niece, Esther, God caused his breasts to issue milk and he nursed the child himself. He lived four hundred years and spoke every language in the world (Sefer Yuhasin).

Moriah, Mount: "Mountain of Vision." The mountain mentioned in Genesis (22:1–22) where **Abraham** and **Isaac** were tried by God. *SEE* ZION, MOUNT.

Moses: Redeemer, lawgiver, and greatest of all the prophets. His sister **Miriam** prophesied the birth of Moses to her father Amram. The diviners of Pharaoh also detected the threat of the newborn liberator, which is what triggered the killing of the Israelite infants (Sot. 11b–12a). Not only was Moses exceptionally beautiful, he could walk at birth (Sefer ha-Yashar). In one tradition, Moses was born completely circumcised. In a variant tradition, when his circumcision was performed the room was filled with divine light. When **Batya**, the daughter of Pharaoh, found the basket holding the baby, she was cured of **leprosy** the moment she touched it (Ex. R. 1:27).

Angels guarded the child during his time in Pharaoh's court (Ex. R. 1:28), at times protecting him from his own precocious wisdom. When Pharaoh learned that young Moses killed one of his taskmasters, he ordered him beheaded. God, however, turned his neck to marble. The angel **Michael** then immediately teleported him to safety in Midian.

A medieval tradition found in Sefer ha-Yashar relates that Moses fled first to Cush, where he became a general in the army and married the daughter of the king. He himself became king of Cush after the death of his own father-in-law. His own wife later deposed him in a coup d'etat and he was forced to flee to Midian.

Once he was welcomed into the home of **Jethro**, he discovered a marvelous **rod** implanted in Jethro's courtyard. When Moses was able to pull the rod from its place, Jethro knew he was the man destined to liberate Israel and immediately gave his daughter **Zipporah** to Moses in marriage.

While Moses was returning to **Egypt**, **Satan** attacked Moses in the form of a **serpent**. The attack was possible because Moses was spiritually vulnerable, having neglected to circumcise his eldest son. The serpent swallowed Moses up to his penis. His wife Zipporah recognized the significance of this, so she immediately circumcised the boy, causing Satan to withdraw (Ned. 31b–32a).

Once back in Egypt, the angel **Gabriel** teleported Moses past the guards and brought him before Pharaoh (Yalkut, Shemot 175).

When Moses ascended Sinai, he was garbed in a cloak made of **rainbow**, providing him with a prism through which to view all of heaven (Zohar II: 99a). Another tradition described him garbed in the **Holy Spirit** (Yoma 4a). In Gedullat Moshe, he was briefly transubstantiated into fire. In yet another version, he rode to the top of Sinai in a **cloud** (BhM 1:58).

From the top of Sinai, Moses was drawn up into heaven. He dwelt there forty days, fed by the Glory of the **Shekhinah**. Though the angels were hostile to his presence, God granted Moses authority over them, a tradition that forms the basis for the occult belief that Jews can summon angels (Shab. 88b; Sanh. 109a; Gen. R. 118:6; PR 20; ChdM). In one version of this legend, Moses actually has to slay **Kemuel**, a guardian angel at the gates of heaven in order to obtain the Torah. With the giving of the **Torah**, Moses was healed of his speech impediment.

In perhaps the most extraordinary legend concerning Moses, the **Midrash** interprets one of his titles, *Ish Elohim*, to mean "husband of God" (a perfectly valid, if exceptional, interpretation of the phrase, which is normally translated as "man of God"). As a kind of "consort" to God, Moses ceases to have intimate relations with his mortal wife, and instead unites with the Shekhinah (Tanh., Tzav 13; Sifrei Numbers, 99; Shab. 87a). This gives Moses the power to dictate God's actions, even annul divine **decrees** (PdRK, Mishpatim, Vot ha-Brachah; Mid. Teh. 90:5; Zohar I: 148a).

When Moses descended from Sinai, his face glowed with divine **Glory** (Ex. 34). One particularly charming legend asserts that this was the result of using the fiery supernal ink provided by God. As he wrote, Moses would, in the custom of scribes, occasionally wipe off his pen in his hair. The residue produced the glow (Ex. R. 47:6).

Since the **Angel of Death** cannot claim a soul that is engaged in Torah study, on the day Moses was ordained to die he wrote out thirteen complete Torahs. Frustrated, the Angel had to ask God to claim Moses's soul, which God did when the last scroll was completed. Of those thirteen Torahs, Moses intended one for each tribe. The final one was taken back up to heaven with him. That most perfect thirteenth Torah is brought down from heaven and given to a worthy person for use in his lifetime, and then reclaimed by heaven.

In another version of his death, Moses defeated Samael/the Angel of Death by wielding his miraculous rod against the angel. Finally, God Himself had to intervene and take Moses via the "**kiss** of God." Three angels—Michael, Gabriel, and Zagzagel—escorted Moses to his death by laying him upon a kingly couch (Deut. R. 11:10).

In the theosophical system of the **sefirot**, Moses represents the reconciliation of the divine antipodes of **Hod**, majesty, and **Netzach**, victory.

There are additionally a number of texts outside the biblical canon that are ascribed to the authorship of Moses or are purported to be an additional revelation given to Moses, such as: **Jubilees**, Divrei Moshe (DSS), The Temple Scroll (DSS), Pseudo-Moses (DSS), Apocryphon of Moses, and **Gedulat Moshe**. Because of his life in the mysterious courts of Egypt and his close involvement in miraculous events (though they may have come from God), Moses has been widely regarded to be a premier sorcerer. A number of magical manuals are ascribed to him, including **The Sword of Moses** and the **Eighth Book of Moses**. Moses is credited with the knowledge of **alchemy** by both Christians and alchemists. SEE RIGHTEOUS, THE.

Moses of Alexandria: An Egyptian alchemist of late antiquity, nothing of his work has been preserved except his excellent reputation. Later generations of alchemists sometimes conflate him with the biblical Moses. SEE ALCHEMY.

Moses (Shem Tov) de Leon: Spanish Kabbalist and alchemist (Spanish, ca. 13th century). He was likely the principle author of the seminal work of **Kabbalah**, the **Zohar**. De Leon wrote pseudepigraphically, attributing authorship of the Zohar collection to **Simon bar Yochai**, the 2nd-century Talmudic Sage and mystic. He may have produced much of the work via **automatic writing**. He also composed several mystical tracts in his own name.

De Leon was less famous as an alchemist, but his interest in the Hermetic Arts finds expression in his mystical writings.

Moses, Eighth Book of: A magical handbook, probably the product of Greek-Egyptian pagans and/or Christians of late antiquity. Though clearly influenced by Jewish beliefs and practices, the book has far more in common with pagan Greco-Egyptian magical texts than with rabbinic mystical traditions, and is a signal example of religious syncretism in the Greco-Roman world. The text at times conflates the God of Israel with **Helios**, the Sun God. It also identifies "Aion" (another name for Helios?) as the high god who controls all the other divine entities. Its various adjurations invoke Zeus, Michael, Artemis, Gabriel, and Persephone.

Moses, Five Books of: The Pentateuch; the first five books of the Bible and the foundational document of Judaism. SEE TORAH.

Moses, Sword of: SEE SWORD OF MOSES.

Mother: (*Ima*). In order for an incantation for healing to be effective, it must include the name of the ailing person's mother (Shab. 66b). In **Kabbalah**, *Ima* is also a synonym for **Binah**. SEE MATRIARCHS; PARTZUFIM.

Mountain: (*Har*). The place where heaven and earth meet, a mountain is an archetype of the human-divine encounter. There are two cosmic mountains in Jewish tradition: **Sinai** (or Horeb) and **Zion**. Respectively, these represent the revelation of pilgrimage, or spiritual quest, and the revelation of habitation, or sacred space. In both locales, God's numinous presence pierces the veil between divine and mortal realms and becomes, for a while, radically manifest. **Sefer Zerubbabel** identifies the five sacred **mountains** of Israel: Tabor, Carmel, Sinai, Zion/Moriah, and Hermon. The eschatological **Temple** will span all five of these peaks.

In biblical tradition, major events of revelation, life, and death, all occur upon mountains. **Abraham** and **Isaac** are tested by God (Gen. 22); **Moses** and the Children of Israel receive their theophanies on Mount Sinai (Ex. 3, 20). Both Moses and **Aaron** die upon mountains. In the case of Aaron, God placed one mountain on top of another as a token of the miracles God had performed during his lifetime (Tanhuma). God commissions the Temple to be built atop Mount Zion in Jerusalem. **Elijah** fights a miraculous battle with the priests of Baal on Mount Carmel and later experiences a major theophany while in a cave on Mount Horeb. Some thousands of years later, the Baal Shem Tov will fight a magical duel on a mountain (Shivhei ha-Besht 125).

Mythical mountains are also topographic features on the celestial planes. Enoch on his heavenly journeys saw mountains of fire that burn day and night. He also saw seven mountains of supernal beauty surrounded by fragrant trees that will be a reward for the righteous, for they will bestow eternal life on Judgment Day (I Enoch 24–25).

There are also the Mountains of Darkness, located in **Gehenna**, to which the **fallen angels** Uzza and Azazel are chained for all eternity (Agaddat Bereshit).

The concept of the cosmic mountain continues to resonate well into the Middle Ages. **Sefer Raziel** describes a mountain of white fire that separates the Garden of **Eden** from the **World**. A hidden mountain upon which an invaluable **white herb** grows is a recurrent theme in **alchemy**.

Mount of Olives: SEE OLIVES, MOUNT OF.

Mount Sinai: SEE SINAI, MOUNT.

Mount Zion: SEE ZION, MOUNT.

Mouth: Noxious spirits, such as **dybbuks** and possessing **demons**, often gain entry into a person's body via the mouth. **Vampires** can be rendered harmless by stuffing **earth** in their mouths.

Moznayim: "Scales"/Libra: The **zodiac** sign for the month of Tishrei. This sign signifies creation, repentance, balance, and **judgment**. The world was created and the **High Holy Days** occur in this month.[1]

1. Erlanger, *Signs of the Times*, 121–44.

MTzPTz MTzPTz: An **Atbash** code version of the Tetragrammaton (Zohar I: 20a). It is doubled in imitation of the repetition of the Tetragrammaton that occurs in Exodus 34, when God's attributes of mercy are revealed. It is used in incantations to activate that attribute.

Music: Music and Judaism are inseparable. God only created the world for the sake of music (BhM 3:12–13). Music is indispensable to the worship of God (Ar. 11a). The heavens overflow with celestial music and the **earth** sings constant hymns (BhM 3:12), but it is the songs of the Jewish people that move the angels to sing also (Chul. 91b). The presence of the **Holy Spirit** inspires a person to sing, and those who sing passionate hymns to God have their iniquities forgiven (Tos. Sot. 6:1; Yalkut, be-Shallach 254). David was the greatest of all composers, singing songs to God even in the womb (Ber. 10a).

Music has been a weapon against **demons** since biblical times, when David's music drove off Saul's evil spirit (I Sam. 16). Music was also one of the mechanisms used to induce **prophecy** (I Sam. 10; II Kings 3; Likkutei Aytzot). **Elisha** in particular had the "hand of God rest upon him" when musicians played. Some prophets burst into song in response to the prophetic spirit (Ex. 31:1).

Hearing music during a visitation to heaven is a common experience for **Hechalot** mystics. Sometimes the adept will bring melodies back to earth. The **angels** are also sources of musical melodies. Sometimes a **baal ha-chalom** will reveal a heavenly tune in a dream (Sefer Or Zerua 2:276; RaSHI's comment on Yev. 24b; SC 324, 382). The Zohar testifies that "There are heavenly gates that can only be opened by music."

The Chasidic movement is famous for its a capella music. Their *niggunim* (wordless melodies) are a preferred meditative device for pursuing **devekut**, union with God.

It is David singing again in the World-to-Come that will rouse the dead from their graves, but it is Moses who will lead the redeemed in song for eternity (Ex. R. 23:11).

Mussafia, Benjamin: Legalist, scientist, and alchemist (Spanish, ca. 17th century). He is the author of the Latin-language (but bilingually titled) alchemical book *Mezahab Epistola*, "The Epistle 'from Gold.'"

Myrrh: An aromatic balm popular in the Middle East. Abraham is identified symbolically with myrrh in Song of Songs Rabbah. For this reason, it is also equated with the sefirotic quality of **Chesed**, divine love (Zohar III: 3b). *SEE* PHARMACOPOEIA.

Myrtle: A plant common to the Land of Israel. As part of the **four species** (the lulav bouquet—Lev. 23:40), the myrtle represents the phallic, masculine force at work in the universe. For this reason, myrtle branches were sometimes given to the bridegroom as he entered the nuptial chamber after a **wedding** (Tos. Sot. 15:8; Ket. 17a). Myrtles are both the symbol and scent of **Eden** (BhM II: 52; Sefer ha-Hezyonot 17). The Hechalot text Merkavah Rabbah requires one to suck on myrtle leaves as an element of a theurgic ritual. Kabbalists link myrtle to the sefirah of **Tiferet** and use sprigs in their **Sabbath** (especially **Havdalah**) rites to draw down its harmonizing power as the week is initiated (Shab. 33a; Zohar Chadash, S of S, 64d; Sha'ar ha-Kavvanot, vol. 2, pp. 73–76).

Because of the Edenic connection, they are also associated with the **afterlife** (Zohar II: 208b–209a). Bodies were sometimes buried with myrtle branches, and to this day branches are displayed as a welcome to the **Ushpizin**, the spirits of the ancestors who visit on **Sukkot**.

Mystery: (*Sod; Raza; Nistar; Saiter; Kabbalah; Middah*). *SEE* KABBALAH; PARDES; SECRET.

Mysticism: *SEE* KABBALAH.

N

Naamah: One of the four **Queens of the Demons**. She dwells in the sea. In one strand of the tradition, she is the daughter of Tubal-Cain who copulated with **angels**, producing demonic children. In another, she is a **succubus** who seduces sleeping men. She and **Lilith** had intercourse with **Adam** in order to bear **demon** children. Once aroused by her, even if a man has **sex** with his wife instead, any children from that conception will be inclined toward her (Gen. 4:22; Tanh., Chukat; MhG; Zohar I: 9b; III: 76b–77a).

Naaman: Aramean general in the **Bible** who receives a miraculous cure of his leprosy from **Elisha**. The cure is effected when Naaman immerses himself in the Jordan at Elisha's direction (II Kings 5).

Nachash: "Serpent." *SEE* SERPENT.

Nachman of Bratzlav: Chasidic master, Kabbalist, and messianic figure (Ukrainian, ca. 19th century). Great grandson of the **Baal Shem Tov**, the charismatic and eccentric Nachman developed a devoted circle of followers. He was most famous for his intricate and enigmatic parables. He was a controversial figure in his lifetime. After his death, his followers attributed many miracles to him. To this day his followers are often referred to as the "dead Chasids," because they never found a living spiritual leader worthy to succeed Nachman.

Nachmanides: **Bible** commentator, ethicist, and mystic (Spanish, ca. 14th century). While he revealed very little of an esoteric nature in most of his writings, his commentary on the **Torah** is considered a classic of Kabbalistic literature.

Nachum Gam Zu: Mishnaic Sage (ca. 1st–2nd century). He was the archetypal cheerful soul in the face of adversity. He was so sensitive a soul that at one point he cursed himself with blindness for causing the death of a person (Tan. 21a). Crippled and cripplingly poor, his merit kept his decrepit house from collapsing until he was moved out of it. **Elijah** wrought miracles in order to save him from Roman wrath (Sanh. 108b–109a).

Nadav and Abihu: The sons of Aaron the High Priest who are struck down by God when they introduce "alien fire" into the sanctuary of the **Tabernacle** (Lev. 11). The Talmud offers a number of theories as to the exact nature of their transgression, but the topic continues to be speculated upon to this day. According to the Zohar, the souls of these two men transmigrate into their nephew **Pinchas**, who performs a **tikkun** for their error by defending Israel against idolatrous worship in a decisive action (Parashas Tzav 14b).

Naftali Bacharach: Kabbalist (German, ca. 17th century). He is the author of Emek ha-Melech ("Valley of the King"), a work notable for its demonologies, especially regarding **Lilith**.

Naftali Katz: Kabbalist and Baal Shem (Polish, ca. 17th–18th century). A well-known wunder-rabbi, he performed numerous feats, including raising someone from the dead.

Nagaf, Sagaf, and Agaf: Three destructive angels, usually mentioned together, found in medieval texts. Noting that each demon's name ends with the letter *fayh*, it is taught that reciting prayers in the liturgy that have no final *fayh* letters in the words can neutralize their powers.[1]

  1. Kanarfogel, *Peering through the Lattice*, 155–56, 156n.

Nahar Dinur: *SEE* RIVER OF LIGHT.

Name, the Book of the: A 13th-century treatise on the secret power of the divine names written by **Eleazer of Worms**. Besides being on of the most comprehensive works on the magico-mystical nature of God's name, it is also intriguing in that it reveals the actual process of esoteric transmission from master to disciple, a **ritual** that involves being immersed in **water**. *SEE* NAMES OF GOD.

Name, Hebrew: In Hebrew thought, a name is part of the defining essence of a person, and as such is a source of power and influence over that person (Ber. 7b; Yoma 83b; SCh 244). Like Native Americans, biblical parents often named their children after omens or circumstances surrounding their **birth** (see Gen. 26, 30; I Sam. 1). Many Hebrew names also incorporate full or abridged names of God, like Uri*el* (God is my light) or Yesha*yahu*, (YHWH is my salvation).

God changes the names of biblical heroes to mark spiritual transformation: Abram and Sarai have the letter *hay* (from the Tetragrammaton) added to their names, making them **Abraham** and **Sarah**. **Jacob**'s name is completely changed to **Israel**, which also incorporates a divine name within it.

Every Jewish child is given a Hebrew name, usually a name separate and distinct from that which serves as his or her "legal" name. It is one's Hebrew name that is used when one participates in synagogue **rituals** or lifecycle events.

It is considered bad luck among Ashkenazi Jews to name a child after a living relative. Often newborns are not given a name until the ritual **circumcision** or ritual naming, in order to disorient the **Angel of Death** and prevent Death from finding the infant. It is believed changing the name of an ill or dying child likewise will confuse Death (R.H. 16b; SCh 245, 247). These name change customs are still practiced to this day in some circles.

It is bad luck for two people with the same name to live in the same town (SCh 224, 447). It is also an ill **omen** for a man to marry a woman with the same name as his mother. Jewish dream interpretation also finds ominous meaning in names. Thus if one sees a cat (Arabic: *shunra*) in a dream, it signifies *shinui ra* (Hebrew), "a change for the worse."[1]

The ability to recall one's Hebrew name is the first test the **soul** undergoes after **death**. Therefore, some Jewish sects are emphatic about children learning and memorizing their names. Chasidic Jews learn to conclude their daily prayers using a biblical verse that begins with the first initial and ends with the last initial of their names, in order that the soul will be able to respond with its name when summoned to **judgment**.

Angels' names are the key to accessing their divine powers. Angel-summoning texts began appearing in Greco-Roman times that provide long lists of angelic names. According to one book, the Chronicles of **Chanameel**, the book's namesake actually shielded Jerusalem from the Babylonians, using his knowledge of angelic names to call down heavenly hosts in the city's defense and so thwarting the will of God. That continued until God changed the names of all the angels—sort of like changing a PIN number and password—undermining Chanameel's efforts.

The names of the **righteous** also possess power, and they are often incorporated into **amulets** and spells of protection. *SEE* ANGELS; CHIBBUT HA-KEVER; DEATH; DUMAH; HEBREW ALPHABET; LANGUAGE.

  1. Fishbane, "Aspects of Jewish Magic in the Ancient Rabbinic Period," in Stampfer, *The Solomon Goldman Lectures II.*

Names of God: "By the word 'YHWH,' were the heavens made" (Ps. 33:6). The ancients believed that a name conveyed something of the essence of the person who bore it. More than that, a person's name was an avenue to the power of and power over that person. The same assumptions apply to God and God's names. God's name coexisted with God prior to Creation (PdRE 3). This world and the next were made using the first letters of the Tetragrammaton (Men. 29b; Gen. R. 12:10). For many Jews, God's name is a stand-in for God's presence. To know the names of God is to be able to access divine power (Gen. R. 12:10; PdRE 40; SCh 471, 484).

The study of these divine names is a central science of Jewish mysticism. These names are used as maps to divine nature, as tools of **meditation**, and as sources of supernatural power that can be harnessed by the adept.

Over the centuries, Jews have identified many names, titles, and epithets for God. The **Bible** contains fourteen names (though Midrash ha-Gadol Gen. 46:8 claims to find seventy), most of them based on the root Hebrew word (*alef-lamed-hay*) for deity: **Elohim**, *El, Eloha* (God); *El Shaddai* (God of Mountains/Breasts); *El Elyon* (Most High God); *Elohei Yisrael* (the God of Israel); *El Olam* (Eternal God); *El Roi* (God of Vision); *El Brit* (God of the Covenant); *Adonai* (My Lord); *Koneh* (Creator); *Melech* (King); *Av* (Father/Source); and of course, *YHWH* (or *YHVH*), the **Tetragrammaton**. The Sages teach that each name represents a different divine attribute: *Elohim* is the "name" of God's justice, *Adonai* signifies God's compassion, etc. Naturally, one must choose the right name for the right circumstance when one invokes God's assistance.

Rabbinic tradition adds more names for God, such as *Ha-Makom* (The Place [of the World]/Omnipresent One), **Shekhinah** (The Indwelling), *Ha-Kadosh Baruch Hu* (The Blessed Holy One), *Ribbono shel Olam* (Master of the Universe), and *Ha-Rachaman* (The Compassionate One). Mystics added further to the list with terms such as **Ein Sof** (Without End), *Atika de-Atika* (The Most Ancient), and *Temira de-Temira* (The Most Hidden).[1]

Aside from these names and epithets for God, Jews also found names for God by abbreviating certain power phrases. Thus words from a phrase in the prayerbook, *Atah gibor l'olam Adonai . . .* , "You are eternally powerful, Adonai," becomes *Agla*. The rabbinic superlative *Ha-Kadosh Baruch Hu* becomes *Hakabah*. Names so constructed pop up in different texts, but are not widely used for theurgic or magical purposes.

Then there are some truly esoteric names—names that are present in the Bible, but recognizable only by occult tradition. These include the following:

The eight-letter name of God, which consists of merging the letters of the Tetragrammaton with the letters of the title "Adonai." This combination name makes a limited appearance in esoteric writings.

The twelve-letter name of God is derived from the **Priestly Blessing** (Num. 7:6–9). One version is simply a combination of the three times YHWH is repeated in the blessing. A more complex version is really the twelve-*word* name of God. In **Sefer Raziel**, twelve divine names are made out of permutations of four letters of the Tetragrammaton.

The fourteen-letter name of God, which appears on the back of a **Mezuzah** parchment, is one revealed by **temurah**, or letter substitution of the phrase *Adonai Eloheinu Adonai* that appears as part of the **Sh'ma** (Deut. 6:4).

The twenty-two-letter name of God corresponds to the twenty-two letters that make up the alphabet, though this name is not constructed from the complete alphabet. It appears in many Kabbalistic texts, in **incantations** and on amulets. It also appears in an acrostic prayer in some prayer books. Here the name is revealed by the technique of temurah applied to the first five Hebrew words of the Priestly Blessing, which are (translated) "Adonai bless you and guard you, [Adonai] cause illumination. . . ." It is this source text that makes the name particularly appealing for protective spells and charms.

The forty-two-letter name of God, which is the name Kabbalists most associate with the theurgic power of Creation, is derived entirely from the first chapter of Genesis. It is woven into the Jewish prayer book as an acrostic prayer, *Ana Bekoach*. **Tzeruf** and **gematria** techniques applied to this name yield several angelic names and phrases of power and protection.

The seventy-two-word name of God is also a significant tool in performing rituals of power. Books like **Sefer ha-Malbush** and an unpublished manuscript labeled *Techilat ha-Yetzirah* are devoted to explaining the significance and power of this particular name. Its proper use fills one with the **Holy Spirit**, grants power over **angels** and **demons**, and gives clairvoyant sight. The seventy-two-word name is derived from Exodus 14:19–21, which describes the angel that cursed and battled against Pharaoh's army and the parting of the sea by Moses. Each of these three verses consists of seventy-two letters. Tzeruf hermeneutics yields a name of seventy-two three-letter words. Using permutations of the seventy-two-word name of God in the proper state of mind can also result in a minor revelation, called a **bat kol**. (Gen. R. 44:19; S of S R. 2:2; Zohar II: 132b; III: 150b; Pardes Rimmonim, 27:2).[2]

Finally, there is an esoteric tradition that the Torah text, in its entirety, is actually one long name of God. This is one reason why a **Sefer Torah** is sometimes employed in protective **rituals**, such as invoking supernatural assistance for a woman in childbirth, or exorcising a demon.[3]

According to **Shi'ur Qomah**, the heart of God is inscribed with seventy names. SQ provides a list of those names, which includes many familiar names and titles, but also many novel names not previously appearing in biblical or rabbinic sources. SQ also teaches that every limb of God has a divine name. One should perhaps understand the text to be saying that every such name is a limb of God—the shape of the Godhead in actuality consists purely of the many divine names.

The theurgic attitude of Jewish mystics toward divine names can be misinterpreted. It seems at times they view the names of God as separate from God Himself. It is more accurate to say that Jewish mystics view the names as "access codes" that allow them to tap certain aspects of divine power (Mid. Teh., 3.2). To invoke God's name in the world means you can invoke God's presence—if you are in the appropriate moral and spiritual condition. **Moses** killed the Egyptian taskmaster with God's name (Ex. R. 1:29), **Solomon** subdued demons (Git. 68b), and Sages can make life (Sanh. 107b).

That is the "religious" view. By contrast, the purely magical view is that, like the power of the atom, God's names are imbued with power intrinsic unto themselves, and anyone, saint or sinner, righteous or wicked, can make use of the power of the names by means of **sorcery**. The only thing that really matters is simply the technical knowledge of how to activate their power.

This, in fact, is the attitude of medieval magicians, Jewish and gentile, whose interest in divine names focused on the quest for power, ignoring the theology of divine unity that grounds all Jewish theurgy. As can be imagined, many Jewish authorities found such belief appalling and regarded the magic assumptions on which such practice are based to utterly contradict fundamental teachings of Judaism. Still, consistency is not a notable virtue of the human mind, and even some religiously educated Jews have ac-

cepted the premise that the power of God and the power of God's names are in some way separate phenomena. This is exemplified by Rabbi Eliezer's comments in Midrash Tehillim (3:2) that if people only knew the proper order in which to read the Torah, they would be able to perform countless miracles.

Because of their potential for both power and abuse, the names of God are treated with great care in Jewish tradition, and there are many rules governing the speaking, writing, and disposal of objects containing divine names. Seven of God's names need to be treated with special care when written: *El*, *Elohim*, *Adonai*, *YHWH*, *Ehyeh-asher-Ehyeh*, *Shaddai*, and *Tzevaot*. The power inherent in the names meant that they had to be protected from falling into irresponsible hands. Thus, for example, the **Talmud** places limits on who could be taught the twelve- and forty-two-letter **names of God** (Kid. 71a; A.Z. 17b). SEE AMULETS; EXPLICIT NAME OF GOD; HEBREW ALPHABET; LANGUAGE; MAGIC; SEGULLAH. *(SEE ALSO APPENDIX FIGURE 4.)*

1. Dr. Samuel Cohen identifies some one hundred and twenty names, titles, and figurative terms for God in his "The Names of God: a Study in Rabbinic Theology," 602.
2. Ibid., 592–98; Singer, *The Jewish Encyclopedia*, vol. 9, 160–65; also see "Holy Letters: The Names of God" online at http://www.atomick.net/fayelevine/pk/letters03.shtml.
3. Dan, *The Heart and the Fountain*, 101–5.

Names of Impurity: (*Shemot Tumah*). A mysterious power that the **Talmud** reports **Abraham** bequeathed to the gentile children of his concubines (Sanh. 91a). These became the fabled **Children of the East**, the masters of **magic** and **astrology**. This story is offered as an explanation for why non-Jews are able to perform efficacious magic. **RaSHI** identifies *shemot tumah* as knowledge of **witchcraft** and demonology. Later sages relate this term to some of the techniques used in **exorcisms** (Minchat Eliyahu).

Nasagiel: The angelic guardian of **Gehenna** (Gedulat Moshe).

Nathan of Gaza: Prophet and publicist for Shabbatai Tzvi (Israel, ca. 17th century), he experienced numerous **maggid** possessions and mystical visions, including the one that led him first to Tzvi.

Nations: In Jewish mythic imagination, the peoples of the world are represented by a symbolic seventy nations. Every nation of the world has its own **language** (Shab. 88b) and own princely **angel** to be its celestial advocate (Dan. 10:20; Jubilees 15:31–32; Tanh. Re'eh 8; PdRE 24; Zohar I: 146b). These angels will, in parallel with their mortal counterparts, form alliances, conspire, and/or fight one another. Most often, rabbinic literature portrays them involved in efforts to discredit, overthrow, or thwart Israel (MdRI, Shirata 2; Gen. R. 56; Ex. R. 21:5; Zohar I: 86a).

In biblical thought, Israel is apportioned to God directly (Deut. 32). In various rabbinic texts, angelic guardians of the Jewish people start to appear, such as **Michael**, or the eponymous angel, **Israel**.

Seven prophets were appointed to the nations to give them the message of monotheism (Lev. R. 2:9). These nations first emerged in the aftermath of the Tower of **Babel** debacle.

At **Sukkot**, seventy bulls were sacrificed in the **Temple** for the sake of each of the gentile nations (Suk. 55b; Lam. R. 1:23; PdRK 28:9).

Any gentile can become a Jew, but the **Holy Spirit** can rest upon a gentile as it can upon a Jew, depending on his (or her) deeds (TdE 48). Those gentiles who engage in the study of Torah are held to be spiritually equal to a High Priest of Israel (B.K. 38a; Ex. R. 19:4).

The **Zohar**, on the other hand, takes a more negative view of the nations and believes that the souls of non-Jews derive from the **left** side of the sefirotic tree, and therefore they are under the sway of the demonic (Zohar I: 131b).

Natronai, Mar Rav: Scholar and communal leader (Iraqi, ca. 9th century). According to legend, he teleported between Iraq and Spain to teach **Torah** to the Jews of Iberia (Otzer ha-Geonim).

Nature: At first appearances, the **Bible** presents a view of nature that is radically de-spiritualized compared to that of the Israelites' pagan contemporaries.[1] There is God, who is the animating spirit of the world, but who stands "above" and "outside" Creation. Yet in fact, the Bible stubbornly refuses to radically divorce God from nature. Even in the famous Kedushah prayer of the angels in Isaiah 6, the very moment when the Bible affirms God's radical "otherness"

and transcendence from Creation, the **serafim** simultaneously declare, *Melo kol ha-aretz kevodo*, "His **Glory** fills the whole earth" (i.e., the world is an extension of God). This belief that God is simultaneously in *and* beyond the world, is fundamental to Judaism (Jer. 23:34; Tanh., Naso 6).

Taking the biblical position one step further, Jewish mystics affirm what philosophers of religion call *panentheism*, the belief that the universe is *within* God, even though the universe is not equal to God (Etz ha-Chayyim 2). The natural world, the Kabbalists like to say, is like a wave in the ocean. It is both part of the ocean, yet distinguishable from it. Thus **Moses Cordovero** writes in his classic work of systematic Kabbalah, **Pardes Rimmonim**, "The essence of divinity is found in every single thing, nothing but It exists . . . It exists in each existent."

Midrashic imagination ascribes the orderly workings of nature to the power of genius or animating **angels**, which oversee the function of all natural phenomena (Ps. 104:4). Thus there are named angels, like **Baradiel** (Hail of God) and **Barakiel** (Lightning of God) that control all these natural forces.

Rationalist Jewish philosophy, following the course of Western thought, especially "natural law" arguments, has argued for a radically desacralized universe. This is a direction utterly rejected, however, by Jewish mysticism to this day.[2]

1. Wiggerman, "The Mythological Foundations of Nature," in Meijer, *Natural Phenomena*, 289–293.
2. Cohen and Mendes-Flohr, *Contemporary Jewish Religious Thought*, 663–77.

Nazirite: An ancient Israelite institution in which a layperson could deepen his dedication to God, either temporarily or permanently. Becoming a nazirite simply involved taking a vow to become one, but maintaining the status of nazirite required that one abstain from wine, grow one's hair uncut, and avoid all contact with corpses.

Most people would become a nazirite for a specified limited duration of time after taking the vow. The judge **Samson** and the prophet **Samuel**, however, are examples of two individuals who were nazirites from **birth** to **death**. Both possessed paranormal powers—extraordinary strength in the case of Samson, divinatory and clairvoyant powers in the case of Samuel. No such powers are credited to the temporary nazirite.

Nebuchadnezzar: This king of ancient Babylon who destroyed Jerusalem (II Kings), the Rabbis claim, was a descendant of the union between **Solomon** and the **Queen of Sheba**. Another tradition identifies him as the direct descendant of **Nimrod**. He was a mythic figure to the Rabbis, a kind of world-striding witch-king who rode a **lion** with a **snake** as a bridle (PdRE 11; Shab. 150a). God finally decided to humble the king and turned Nebuchadnezzar into a monstrous animal (Chronicles of Jeremeel).

Nechemiah ben Hushiel: The given name of the **Messiah** ben Joseph, the precursor to the Messiah ben David (Sefer Zerubbabel).

Nechiah: "Cleanliness." The spirit of prosperity. The Talmud claims maintaining a clean home ensures the presence of this spirit (Pes. 111b). *SEE* UNCLEAN SPIRITS.

Nechunia ben ha-Kanah: Mishnaic Sage (ca. 2nd century). Along with **Ishmael ben Elisha**, **Akiba**, and **Simon bar Yochai**, Nechunia is one of the "big four" mystics of the Talmudic era. He appears repeatedly in **Hechalot** texts.

Necromancy: (*Yeddione, Ov, Doresh ha-Metim*). The mantic practice of consulting dead spirits. It is a form of divination that is harshly condemned by the **Bible** (Deut. 18:10–12). That being said, it was clearly quite attractive to Israelites (Isa. 8:19–22, 19:3). The story of the woman of Endor (I Sam. 28) is the only account of a necromancer in Scriptures. The Sages themselves believed that the dead could hear what goes on "behind the curtain" of heaven and therefore ghosts have access to paranormal information (PdRE 34).

According to the **Talmud**, there are two methods for achieving communion with the dead: by the use of a medium, who would be possessed by a **ghost**, or by having a dead **soul** speak through a skull (Sanh. 65b; Ber. 59a; Shab. 152b–153a). Both of these practices are explicitly condemned by rabbinic tradition.

On the other hand, beneficent ghosts who address the living via **dreams** or other unsolicited means are to be heeded. And even though trying to induce ghostly voices or making offerings to the dead is forbidden, some Kabbalists did in fact practice **incubation**, sleeping at the graveside of a great sage or holy person in the hopes that the person's spirit would possess them. **Isaac Luria** is a signal case of someone who actively pursued communion with *ibburim*, benevolent dead spirits, by means of a technique he called **yichudim**. As is the case with so many other paranormal practices, the demarcation line between what can be considered permitted and prohibited forms of communication with the dead can become blurred. Contemporary **Chasidism** and other Jewish pietists still occasionally observe the practice of incubation. *SEE* BAAL OV; IBBUR OR DEVEKUT; MEDIUM; XENOGLOSSIA.

Nefesh, Nefesh Behemit: "Animal Soul/Life Energy." *Nefesh* is the fundamental vitality animating all sentient life. This is the lowest part of the triad structure of the human **soul**, the higher souls being **ruach** and **neshamah**. After death, the nefesh is the part of the soul that remains in the world, able to commune with the living (Zohar I: 224b; III: 70b). Kabbalists teach that the interest of demons in human affairs results from the demonic need to feed upon this energy.

Nehushtan: (*Nechushtan*). This bronze image of a serpent was made by **Moses** at the instruction of God in order to miraculously cure wounds from serpent bites (Num. 21). Its name, *Nechushtan*, is a double pun—a word play on both "serpent" (*Nachash*) and "bronze" (*Nechoshet*). It was preserved in the **Temple** until King Hezekiah decided to destroy it after it had become an object of idolatrous worship.

Nephalim: "Fallen [Ones]." *SEE* GIANTS.

Neshamah: The "highest" part of the triad composition of the human **soul**, the Neshamah is the divine, indestructible aspect of the spirit, the seat of intellect.

Neshiyya: The place of forgetfulness. This strange zone of the lower worlds is the home to pygmies (Sitre Torah, Zohar I: 253b–254a).

Netzach: "Endurance." The seventh sefirah, it is the **speculum** through which **prophecy** flows. It is personified by **Moses**.

New Jerusalem: Also known as 11Q18, this document found among the **Dead Sea Scrolls** describes the eschatological battle between Israel and the **nations**, and the colossal dimensions of messianic **Jerusalem**.

New Moon: The new moon marks the beginning of a Hebrew month and, historically, it was determined by the independent report of two witnesses to rabbinic authorities (PdRE 7; Sanh. 37a). It is greeted with prayer and ceremony.

According to esoteric tradition, correctly performing the new moon **rituals** protects one from dying in the month that follows. In Tractate Sanhedrin, the Sages offer a protective ritual to be performed at the beginning of each month: *Kiddush l'vanah*, the sanctification of blessing of the new moon (Sanh. 42a). The ritual can be performed from the third evening after the appearance of the new moon until the fifteenth day, but only if the moon is visible. The ritual is done outside, and one performing the rite must be presentable and in a good mood (Sof. 20:2). Blessing the moon invites the presence of the **Shekhinah**.

In some places, the ritual grew more elaborate over time. In medieval Europe, the ritual of *Kiddush L'vanah* consisted of **dancing** or jumping and reciting the following **incantation** at the **moon**: "Just as I dance toward you but cannot touch you, so shall the **Yetzer ha-Ra** not touch me." Participants also flapped the corners of their clothing in a gesture intended to shake off bad luck.[1] Then the person was to declare it a *siman tov*, a "good sign," three times. This writer has never observed anything like this at a contemporary *Kiddush L'vanah* ceremony, though others report it is still done. SEE ASTROLOGY; GOLDEN CALF; MOON.

1. Roth, *Encyclopedia Judaica*, vol. 12, 291.

New Year: (*Rosh ha-Shanah*). According to the **Talmud**, there are actually four "new years" in the Jewish calendar: the New Year for kings and counting the months (1 Nisan), the New Year for the world and calculating the years (1 Tishrei), the New Year for tithing cattle (1 Elul), and the New Year for tithing trees (Shevat 15). SEE ROSH HA-SHANAH.

Nicanor: According to the **Talmud**, Nicanor was a pious individual who commissioned ornamental doors for the Temple, which he then had specially built in **Egypt**. While on their way via boat to Israel, a storm forced the crew to throw the metal doors overboard. Nicanor insisted on going overboard with his gifts. Miraculously, the metal door Nicanor clung to floated and bore him to Jaffa. When the ship arrived in port, the other door miraculously floated to the surface of the harbor (Yoma 38a). Eventually they were both installed as Nicanor intended and were thereafter known as "The doors of Nicanor" (Sefer Yuhasin). SEE GATES; MEZUZAH.

Niddui: A type of temporary excommunication, it could be used to exorcise a **dybbuk** (SA, Yoreh Deah, 334; Zafnat Pa'aneah). SEE EXORCISM; GET.

Niflaot Maharal: "Wonders of the MaHaRaL." A collection of fantastic tales about Rabbi **Judah Loew** of Prague, including his **golem** adventures. It was written by Judah Rosenberg.

Night: (*Lilah*). The Sages compare night to life in this world and dawn to the **World-to-Come** (PdRE 34). It is at night, when the body is at rest, that the soul is liberated. According to the Sages, during sleep the soul ascends to heaven to give an account of its deeds before it is returned to the body, purified (*Odeh la El* prayer).

Night is the time when the demonic is most active. The **Zohar** identifies the period of nightfall to **midnight** as the time when the forces of the **Sitra Achra** are ascendant. After midnight, the wall between the celestial and terrestrial worlds becomes permeable and the **waters** of **Eden** infuse new life into the sublunar world and **evil** recedes; this is the time when it is most propitious to rise from bed and study **Torah**. SEE DARKNESS; DEMONS; SLEEP.

Nimrod: Identified in Genesis as a "mighty hunter," the Sages describe Nimrod as the archetypal wicked king. As a young man, Nimrod made his reputation as a hunter by supernatural means: he possessed the **garments of Adam**, which gave him the power to subdue any animal (PdRE 24). He later claimed the throne of Cush by feat of arms. Nimrod is credited with being the king who initiated the **Tower of Babel** project (Chul. 89a; Pes. 94a–b) and had himself worshipped as a god (A.Z. 53b).

When his diviners told him of the pending birth of **Abraham**, he sought to kill the child. In the end, Nimrod killed seventy thousand infant boys in his quest to slay the newborn Abraham (Ma'asei Avraham Aveinu). Abraham's father **Terach** hid his son with the help of the angel **Gabriel**. Nimrod continued to persecute Abraham as an adult. At one point, he captured Abraham, and when the Patriarch refused to renounce the one God, Nimrod had him thrown into a furnace (Gen R. 38:13, 42:5), but Abraham walked away from the inferno unharmed. Nimrod was finally slain by **Esau** (Gen. R. 63:13, 65:16; PdRE 24).

Nine Who Entered Paradise Alive: According to Derekh Eretz Zuta 1, there have been nine worthies who will attain Paradise without tasting death: **Enoch**, **Elijah**, the **Messiah**, **Hiram**, **Ebed Melech**, **Batya**, Jaabez (son of Judah the Prince), **Joshua ben Levi**, and **Serach bat Asher**.

Nippur: Archeological site in Iraq that yielded the greatest horde of **incantation bowls** (forty) now in the possession of modern scholars.

Nishmat Chayyim: "The Soul of Life." Tract composed by **Manasseh ben Israel** containing references to reincarnation, demons, spiritual possession, and many other occult beliefs.

Nistarot shel Rabbi Shimon ben Yochai: "The Mysteries of Rabbi Simon bar Yochai." A medieval book that details the supernal secrets that Bar Yochai plumbed during the twelve years he hid in a **cave** with his son.

Nitzotz: "Spark." According to Lurianic **Kabbalah**, *nitzotzot* (pl.) are fragments of divine force or **light**, dispersed into the created universe by the **Breaking of the Vessels**, the cataclysmic collapse of the primeval divine order. These sparks, the creative "word" of God, are contained in everything, but are shrouded from our sight by "husks" of profane reality. Humans must now reveal these sparks, which are concealed in every aspect of Creation, and restore them to God (Zohar I: 4a). This **tikkun**, rectification, or cosmic repair project, is achieved by the proper theurgic performance of all the commandments, both

moral and ritual.[1] *SEE* KELIPOT; LURIA, ISAAC; MITZVOT; THEURGY.

1. Green, *Jewish Spirituality*, vol. 2, 65–70.

Noah: "Comforter." When God decided to undo Creation and release the waters of the **abyss**, the Holy Blessed One chose Noah as the man who would build an ark and save specimens of all avian and terrestrial creatures (Gen. 6–9).

According to **I Enoch**, Noah was totally white, perhaps indicating he was an albino. He came out of the womb white as snow, eyes shining, and already circumcised (AdRN 2). A precocious newborn, he even got up and walked away from his midwife. He invented many of the essential tools of civilization (Tanh., Bereshit 5, 11). Through his three sons, Noah is considered the second father of all humanity.

He also possessed a magical book (Jubilees 10). The introduction to **Sefer ha-Razim** also claims that it was passed down through generations of biblical figures, including Moses and Solomon. It also claims that it was by the power of that book that Noah built the Ark, fed the **animals**, and survived all the hazards of the great Flood.

Some creatures that were meant to be exterminated by the **Flood** survived. The **giants**, for example, survived because one of them, **Og**, clung to the exterior of Noah's Ark. The interior of the Ark was illuminated by the **Tzohar**, the glowing stone filled with the light of Creation that Noah had inherited from **Adam** (Gen. R. 31).

After the Flood, Noah planted the first vine and taught himself how to make wine. Noah immediately became drunk from his innovative beverage, and his son Ham "uncovers his nakedness" while he was besotted. The **Midrash** elaborates on this cryptic expression by explaining that **Satan** seduced Noah into planting the vine and Ham either raped or castrated his father (PdRE 23). Noah then cursed Ham and his descendants for the offense (Gen. 9).

Besides Sefer ha-Razim, Noah is sometimes associated with another book, The **Book of Noah**, a manual of healings based on what the angel **Gabriel** taught him about combating demonically induced illness (Jubilees 10).

In both the **Zohar** (Bereshit 254b) and Lurianic thought, Noah failed to lead his generation to repentance. As a result, his soul was reincarnated as **Moses**.

Noah, Book of: A number of books have been designated "the Book of Noah." Within Jewish apocalyptic, Midrashic, and magical literature, there is a continuing tradition that Noah had a book of magical incantations, which has sometimes been identified with **Sefer Raziel** or **Sefer ha-Razim**. Another candidate is the magico-medical book **Sefer Asaf ha-Rofe**.

A fragmentary text found among the Dead Sea Scrolls, 1Q19, has been offered as a candidate for an ancient "Book of Noah." It is closely related to the Enochean textual tradition.

Another DSS fragment, 4Q534, is an alternative candidate for the magical lost book, given that it appears to be a kind of horoscope of Noah. SEE FLOOD, THE; GIANTS, BOOK OF; NOAH.

Nocturnal Emission: (*Tumat keri*). The Sages regarded the spontaneous emission of semen triggered by erotic dreams as a sign of demonic attack. The succubae **Lilith** and **Naaman** are the **demons** traditionally credited with such nighttime molestations. They seduce men in their sleep and extract their sperm in order to procreate demonic offspring (*Nigei benei Adam*, "harmful sons of Adam"). In commentaries to the **Zohar**, it is even taught that Lilith lurks around the bed during normal intercourse between men and women and gathers any stray droplets of semen. To counter this possibility, there are a number of post-coital **incantations** that can be recited.

In a related matter, Jewish mysticism finds masturbation to be a grave offense for precisely the same reason: the spilling of semen outside of coitus allows demons to procreate. (Tanh., B., Bereshit 26; Gen. R. 20:11; Eruv. 18b; Zohar I: 55a, 57a; II: 231b; III: 76b). SEE BANIM SHOVAVIM; NIGHT; SEX; SLEEP.

Nogah: "Glowing light/Glimmer." *Nogah* is a Kabbalistic term referring to the divine energy that allows what we mortals term "evil" to persist in the universe. In keeping with Jewish monotheism, the **Zohar** teaches that all things emanate from God, including the **Sitra Achra**, the demonic. **Evil** has its purpose in God's Creation also. Because of this spiritual reality, even the most evil things have a *klipah nogah*, "a glowing husk," a mix of evil and divine energy. **Kabbalah** teaches that the **righteous** can learn to recognize and harmlessly release any *nogah* and return it to its divine source. This can usually be achieved by means of **tikkun**, redeeming or transforming some evil thing or situation into something good (Etz ha-Chayyim; Tanya).

North: (*Tzafon*). North is the direction signifying **Gevurah**, the divine emanation of severity (Zohar I: 14b, 77a). It is also the direction linked with impurity, from which **evil** emanates (Jer. 1:14; Ezek. 8; Midrash Konen 2:30). Later Midrashic collections suggest that God somehow left the "north side" of Creation incomplete, a situation that allows the demonic to enter the world (PdRE 3). In the **Zohar**, **Lilith**, the mother of demons, is also called the "Northerner."

Northerner, the: Another title for **Lilith**. SEE NORTH.

Notarikon: (Greek, "Combination"). This is a hermeneutic technique involving dividing words or merging adjacent words in the Torah to yield concealed messages. To give a famous example, by dividing the first word of Genesis, *bereshit*, into two words, *bara shit*, the exegete reveals the Aramaic phrase, "He [God] created six." Six what? Six things, crucial to God's plan of Creation, which had to exist in the mind of God before the universe was formed. These six things are: The **Torah**, the **Throne of Glory**, the **Patriarchs**, the people **Israel**, the **Temple**, and the name of the **Messiah**.

Notarikons can also be acronyms that reveal **names of God**. Thus it is taught that the final letters of the first five verses of Genesis form the divine name *TZaMaRCHaD* (M. Shab., Shabbat 105a, 12:5; MdRI, Bo 8). SEE ENCRYPTION; SIX PRIMORDIAL THINGS; TEMURAH; TZERUF.

Numbers: The practice of **gematria**, or the spiritual interpretation of numbers, is an important hermeneutic technique for understanding sacred Scripture and tapping theurgic powers. Important symbolic and/or sacred numbers:

> 1—One indicates unity, divinity, and wholeness, as exemplified by God.
>
> 3—Three signifies completeness and stability, as represented by the three Patriarchs and the

three pilgrimage festivals—Passover, Shavuot, and Sukkot (I Kings 17:21; Dan. 6:10).

3+1—This is a number cluster that signals the fulfillment of God's plans (Amos 1; Dan. 7:25).

4—Four is a recurrent number in both exoteric and esoteric Jewish traditions. The **Passover** Seder is particularly structured around fours: the Four Questions, the Four Sons, and four cups of **wine**. There are four cardinal **directions** and there are four Matriarchs. Four is also a common factor in esoteric interpretations: four angels surround the **Throne of Glory**, there are **four kingdoms** of the eschaton, and the famous **four Sages** who enter Paradise.

5—There are five books of Moses, and five divisions to the **Psalms**. Magical/mystical texts are also sometimes separated into divisions of five. Five is the number of protection, as symbolized in the **chamsa**, the talismanic hand.

7—Seven is one of the greatest power numbers in Judaism, representing Creation, good fortune, and blessing. The Hebrew word for "luck," **gad**, equals seven in gematria. The other Hebrew word for luck, *mazal*, equals seventy-seven. The **Bible** is replete with things grouped in sevens. Besides the Creation and the exalted status of the **Sabbath**, the seventh day, there are seven laws of Noah and seven **Patriarchs and Matriarchs**. Several Jewish holidays are seven days long, and priestly ordination takes seven days. The Land of Israel was allowed to lie fallow one year in seven. The **menorah** in the **Temple** has seven branches. The prophet Zechariah describes a strange celestial stone with seven eyes (chapter 4). This emphasis on seven continues post-biblically with seven **wedding** blessings, seven circuits performed about a groom, and seven days of mourning after the **death** of a close relative. Events, prayers, and esoteric observances that involve multiples of seven are also common. Entities both natural (gold) and supernatural (angels) are often grouped by sevens (I Enoch 20; II Enoch

19). Seven is a factor in many occult elements and events. The first verse of the Torah consists of seven words and seven is the recurrent number in Pharaoh's divinatory **dreams** in Genesis. The walls of Jericho fall after the Israelites encircle it seven times. In the **Zohar**, the seven lower **sefirot** are those aspects of God that are present in **Asiyah**, our world of action. Seven is also the preferred number in **spells**, **magic squares**, **amulets**, and the like (Gen. 7:2; I Kings 18:43; Deut. 16:9; Pes. 54a; Sot. 10b).

8—Eight is the number of completion. The **Tabernacle** was dedicated in an eight-day ceremony. Male children are circumcised on the eighth day (Gen. 17). Chanukah is an eight-day holiday.

10—Ten is a symbol of good luck and power: there are **ten commandments**, God requires ten righteous individuals in Sodom to avert divine punishment, and ten men constitute a **minyan**, a spiritual community (Gen 18, 24:10; Ex. 26:1; Dan. 7:7–24).

12—Twelve represents totality, wholeness, and the completion of God's purpose. There are twelve tribes of Israel (ten of which must be restored), twelve months in the year and twelve houses of the **zodiac** (Gen. 27:20, 25:16; Ex. 24:4, 25:27; Ezek. 43:16; Yoma 75b, 77b; Tan. 25a; Chul. 95).

18—Eighteen is the value of the Hebrew letters *Chet* and *Yod*, which together spell the word *chai*, life. For this reason, eighteen is considered the luckiest number. God is mentioned eighteen times in both Psalm 29 and the Song of the Sea (Ex. 15:1–21), giving these verses special protective power.

24—The number twenty-four symbolizes abundance. At its prime, **Jerusalem** once had twenty-four dream interpreters you could consult, twenty-four main thoroughfares with twenty-four side-streets leading to twenty-four alleys each containing twenty-four houses (Lam. R. 1).

32—According to **Sefer Yetzirah**, thirty-two is the number of the "Wonderful ways of wisdom," the number of organizing principles that underlie the universe. These are the twenty-two letters of the **Hebrew alphabet** plus the decimal numbers that form the basis for the sefirotic tree.

40—Forty appears many times in the Bible, usually designating a time of radical transition or transformation. Among the most famous examples are these: It rained for forty days and forty nights during the **Flood** (Gen. 7). Exodus records that **Moses** spent forty days on Mount **Sinai** with God. Forty is the number of years the Israelites were required to wander in the wilderness until they were allowed to enter Canaan. Corporeal punishment in the Torah involved forty lashes. **Elijah** fasted for forty days prior to receiving his revelation on Mount Horeb. Multiples of forty are also common: forty thousand men rallied to Barak in the book of Judges. The **Talmud** also reports wondrous phenomena occurring in units of forty. It also appears in mystical texts, usually as an element of **purification**. Thus the **Book of the Great Name** advises its readers to abstain from sleeping in one's own bed for forty days and nights after using the book, mimicking the time Moses spent away from camp while he received the Ten Commandments (Gen. 7; Ex. 24; I Sam. 17:16; I Kings 19:8; Git. 39b, 40a; Sot. 34a).

70—This number symbolizes the world. There are seventy **nations** in the world, seventy languages, and seventy princely angels. The Greek translation of the Bible, the first to make it available to the gentile, was done by seventy Jewish scholars, who, though working separately, produced seventy identical translations.

Finally, it is important to note that odd numbers are lucky; even numbers (especially **pairs**) are bad luck.

Numbers Rabbah: A **Midrash** on the biblical book of Numbers, it preserves several esoteric traditions.

Nun: Fourteenth letter of the **Hebrew alphabet**, it has the vocalic value of "n" and the numeric value of 50. It is one of the five letters that have a *sofit*, or end-form when it appears as the last letter of a word. Then it takes the shape of a long tail. *Nun* signifies faithfulness, light, submission and rest (the regular bent shape) and uprightness and action (the long *sofit* form). Mysteriously, the traditional text of the Torah includes two inverted nuns (Num. 10:35–36) that appear in a passage describing the transport of the Ark of the Covenant. Several esoteric explanations have been offered for this curiosity.[1]

   1. Munk, *The Wisdom of the Hebrew Alphabet*, 151–58.

Nuriel: "Fire of God." Angel of beauty and passion (Cairo Geniza T-S K 1.73; Zohar II: 42).

Nut: (*Egoz*). A nut is an important esoteric symbol in Judaism, representing concealed **secrets**. The "garden of nuts" mentioned in Song of Songs (6:11) becomes the focus of considerable mystical speculation. Some understand it as a symbol of the secret **Torah** concealed beneath the plain sense of the words. Others see it as illustrating the spiritual reality of the divine sparks trapped in husks of evil that characterize the lower worlds (Zohar I: 44b; II: 15b; Etz ha-Chayyim). **Eleazer of Worms** understood it as a symbol of the divine chariot.[1]

It is customary to abstain from eating nuts in the weeks leading up to the High Holidays because the **gematria** value of *egoz* is the same as *chet*, the word for sin.

   1. Wolfson, *Along the Path*, 2.

O

Obed-Edom: The man who sheltered the **Ark of the Covenant** for several months for King **David** after the Ark slew one of David's servants (I Sam. 6). The Bible reports Obed-Edom was greatly blessed by the presence of the Ark on his property. According to the Sages, his daughters-in-law bore him grandchildren on a monthly basis during that time (Num. R. 4:21; Ber. 63b).

Obizoth: A demoness that strangles children (Testament of Solomon).

Odd Numbers: *SEE* NUMBERS.

Ofan, Ofanim: "Wheeled [Ones]." A class of chariot/throne angels mentioned in Ezekiel 1. It is the revolving *Ofanim* that create thunder and lightning (PdRE 4). According to **Midrash Konen**, the Ofan **Sandalfon**, whose dimensions reach from earth to the very **Throne of Glory**, is the angelic link between God and Israel (2:25). The circularity of the Ofan symbolizes the reciprocating bond and flow of spiritual energy between the upper and lower worlds.

Og: The biblical king of Bashan was a **giant** who tried to prevent the Israelites from crossing his territory (Deut. 3). One of the antediluvian giants, he survived the **Flood** by clinging to the outside of Noah's Ark (Pseudo-Jonathan, Gen. 14:13; Zev. 113b; PdRE 23). He was so huge that one of his teeth was the size of a throne (Masekhet Sofrim). Because he plotted against **Abraham**, God cursed him to be slain by one of Abraham's descendants (Gen. R. 41–42,

53). In Masekhet Sofrim, he is actually identified as Eliezer, Abraham's servant (Hosafah 1:2; Yalkut 765).

During the time of the **Exodus**, he cast the **evil eye** on the Children of Israel, to no effect (Deut. R. 1:22). Eventually, he went out to battle Israel directly, attempting to hurl a rock at them as big as their entire encampment (Ber. 54b). God caused a miraculous team of ants to eat a hole through the middle of the rock, which then fell like a yoke around his neck. God then grew **Moses** to the height of ten cubits, tall enough to smite the giant in the ankle and kill him (Pseudo-Jonathan Num. 21:35; B.B. 54a–b)

Ohel: "Tent." Pre-Israelite Canaanites believed that the gods assembled in the sacred tent of El, the supreme god. Thus the idea that the God of Israel would command Moses to build a tent-sanctuary, the **Tabernacle**, must not have seemed too odd to the Children of Israel. Psalm 15 describes God's celestial tent sitting atop a sacred mountain.

In a more modern practice, pious Jews will construct a canopy over the grave of a beloved **rebbe**, sometimes with a *ner tamid*, or perpetual light, turning it into a sanctuary. This, too, is called an *ohel*, and pilgrims will gather there to pray for the intercession of the **righteous** dead person and to leave a petitionary note, called a *pitka* or **kvittle**.

In the **World-to-Come**, the righteous enjoy the comfort of dwelling in seven canopies (B.B. 75a; Seder Gan Eden). *SEE* ADAT EL; ANCESTORS; TENT OF MEETING.

Oil: (*Shemen*). Oil is a source of power, both combustible and spiritual. It is a symbol of divine **emanation** (Zohar I: 88a). As the fuel used to light the **menorah** and religious lamps, oil is a symbol of the divine spirit. In ancient Israel, oil—mostly olive oil—was a multi-purpose product, used for many mundane, religious, and magic purposes. Oil was used in the sacrificial cult. It was poured on **nazirites** and those afflicted with **leprosy** that were ready to reenter the Israelite community. It was also used to anoint sacred shrines (Gen. 29) and those elevated to high office, principally the king and High Priest (I Sam. 16; Lev. 8). The most famous miracle associated with oil is the miracle of **Chanukah**, when a one-day supply of oil burned for the full eight-day rededication ceremony for the **Temple**, though there is also a legend of oil miraculously flowing down from heaven for Jacob (PdRE 35).

Oil is used in **hydromancy** (or lecanomancy); there is a guardian spirit in oil that may be consulted for purposes of **divination**. One spills some oil, most likely in a bowl or cup of **water**, and studies the resulting pattern. The Sages do not consider this a reliable form of augury (Sanh. 101a). Nevertheless, Chayyim Vital repeatedly consulted witches skilled in this form of divination (Sefer ha-Hezyonot pp. 120, 125). In magical handbooks like **Sefer ha-Razim** it is used as an ingredient in magical potions. SEE FOOD; MESSIAH.

Oil, Festival of the First: A holiday, unknown to the normative Jewish **calendar**, mentioned in the **Temple Scroll**. It may have its basis in the biblical list of priestly privileges, however (Num. 18:12–13; Neh. 10:34–40). It is not known whether the holiday was actually ever observed outside the circle of the **Dead Sea Scrolls** community.

Olam: SEE WORLD.

Olam ha-Ba: SEE WORLD-TO-COME.

Olam ha-Tohu: "The World of Chaos." A term that appears frequently in Chasidic thought, but in such different contexts, it is difficult to fix its precise meaning. In some places, it seems to be a temporal dimension, the universe prior to the creation of the primordial vessels of light (see **Breaking the Vessels**). In the writings of **Nachman of Bratzlav** (Likutei Moharan), it is the nether region between this **world** and the **World-to-Come**, where ghostly souls wander, seeking a resting place. In **CHaBaD** metaphysics, on the other hand, it is the higher realm from which human-sustaining life "food" (i.e., plants, animal meat) emanates (Likutei Torah). SEE DYBBUK; FOOD; FOUR WORLDS OF EMANATION; GHOST.

Olive: (*Ziyit*). The olive tree is a symbol of peace and, because olive trees can live upward of a thousand years, longevity. The Rabbis believed that eating olives enhances one's ability to memorize **Torah**.

Most overtly magical practices involve the leaves of the olive tree. **Chai ben Sherira Gaon** describes the belief that throwing olive leaves inscribed with divine names at bandits will paralyze them. One Hechalot formula requires the adept to eat olive leaves in preparation for summoning the **Sar ha-Torah**. SEE FOOD; HERBS; OIL.

Olives, Mount of: (*Har Zait*). A **mountain** ridge directly **east** of **Jerusalem**, across the Kidron Valley. It was over the Mount of Olives that the **Shekhinah** began its journey into exile after the destruction of the Temple, and it is over that same mountain ridge that the Presence of God will return at the End of Days. At the advent of the **Messiah**, **Elijah** (or **Gabriel**) will sound the **shofar** from its summit, at which moment the mountain will split asunder and give up the dead buried in it (Ezek. 11:23; Zech. 14; Lam. R., Petikhta 25; AdRN 34).

Omen: (*Siman, Ot*). Stories involving signs and portents of things to come are recorded in the **Bible**, **Talmud**, and throughout subsequent Jewish tradition. Jews find serendipitous omens in **names**, accidents, overheard words, unusual births, the behavior of children and **animals**, weather, heavenly prodigies, and dreams (Sefer ha-Hezyonot and Shivhei ha-Besht provide numerous illustrations of how attentive Jews are to omens). Omens can be good or bad, and there are many methods for ameliorating bad omens. SEE DIVINATION; DREAM.

Omer: The forty-nine-day period between the holidays of **Passover** and **Shavuot** is a period of spiritual vulnerability. It marks the period of the Israelites' ascent from the impurity of Egypt to the purity and power of the revelation of Sinai. Therefore, Jews observe the "counting of the omer," making the countdown to Shavuot, the holiday which celebrates the giving of the Torah, a time of spiritual preparation and precaution. Because of the dangers associated with this period, traditional Jews eschew weddings, playing music, holding parties, or other joyous occasions. Some pietists will use a chart decorated with protective verses, like **Psalm** 67, which has seven verses of seven words each, to keep track of the count. The mystic and purported author of the **Zohar, Simon bar Yochai,** died a miraculous death on Lag B'Omer (the thirty-third day of the Omer) (Idra Zuta).

Oneiromancy: The art of divining through dreams. Joseph and Daniel were famed for their talent at this form of augury. Tractate Berachot (55a–57a) devotes considerable discussion to it. Women were considered both receptive to ominous dreams and skilled oneiromancers (Sefer ha-Hezyonot I: 17, 18; III: 7, 8, 12). *SEE* DIVINATION; DREAM.

Oniel: "God is my Power." A punishing **angel** of **Gehenna** (Mid. Konen).

Onoskelis: A **succubus** mentioned in the **Testament of Solomon**.

Ophites: Alternately known as the Naasenites, they were a Gnostic movement linked to Judaism in late antiquity. *SEE* GNOSTICS AND GNOSTICISM, ANCIENT.

Oral Torah or Law: The term *Torah she-b'al Pei,* "Oral Law," is used to refer to either (1) the rabbinic hermeneutics of how to interpret the Written **Torah,** or (2) to the whole body of rabbinic traditions and lore. According to rabbinic tradition, Moses received both the written and the Oral Torah at Mount **Sinai** (Avot 1; PdRE 46). It is the Oral Torah that is the source of the bulk of Jewish fantastic and esoteric teachings. *SEE* MIDRASH; TALMUD.

Orchard of Holy Apples: *SEE* APPLE ORCHARD, THE HOLY.

Ordeal: God puts certain biblical figures to the test by asking them to do something difficult, as in the case of **Abraham** having to sacrifice his son, or as a means to determine who is suitable for a certain office or task (Num. 17; Judges 7). **Joshua** employs some sort of trial by lot (or **Urim and Thummim**) to determine who violated God's proscription against pillage being taken from Jericho (Josh. 6–7).

Despite these examples, the human use of trial by ordeal or divine test is not a regular part of Jewish jurisprudence, excepting one special situation: the Sotah. In this trial for a wife suspected of infidelity, she is required to drink a potion made up of **earth** taken from the **Temple** grounds combined with a written **curse**—possibly written in the earth itself—that has been dissolved in living **water**. If she is in fact guilty of adultery, she will die and so "return to the dust." If innocent, the power of the potion will make her pregnant and the resulting child will be "like Abraham." This link to Abraham is apparently because of his righteousness, and because he once trod on the ground of the Temple site, infusing that earth with his holiness (Num. 5; M. Sot. 2:2; Sot. 17a).

The ordeal of the Sotah subsequently becomes the model for many magical potions and formulae, which often require the adept to write a divine name or incantation on an edible object or dissolve the words in water and drink them.

Origen: This Church Father noted that Jews are especially adept at the use of **magic**, and gave particular credence to the idea that certain Hebrew terms, particularly the names of the Patriarchs and **angels**, have magical power (Contra Celsum).

Orlah: "Uncircumcised." In the Bible, the foreskin is used as a symbol of the imperfect, the profane, and the foreign. But it also makes a great wedding gift (I Sam. 18; II Sam. 3). Rabbinic tradition notes that the term *orlah* can refer to several parts of the body, each signifying a part of the body that may be vulnerable to spiritual shortcoming: an uncircumcised penis, ears, lips, or heart (PdRE 29). In Jewish mysticism, it comes to signify the demonic (Zohar I: 13a, 18a, 91b).

Ormuzd: A **demon**, the child of **Lilith** (B.B. 73b).

Ornasis: A vampiric demon mentioned in the **Testament of Solomon**.

Ornias: An **incubus** mentioned in the **Testament of Solomon**.

Orot: The Hebrew word for "light" has an almost infinite number of esoteric connotations. The most complex taxonomy of light may well be the teachings of Isaac Luria. His system, for example, differentiates three types of primeval light. *Or Achudim*, "Unified Light"—this the highest emanation of light flowing from head of **Adam Kadmon**. From this light, the highest stages of the **sefirot** formed. *Or Nekudim*, "Speckled Light," streams from the navel of the Primordial Man and forms the intermediate structures of the sefirot. *Or Berudim*, "Dappled/Showering Light," flows from the **phallus** of Adam Kadmon and gives form and life to the lower worlds.[1] *SEE* LIGHT.

  1. Fine, *Physician of the Soul, Healer of the Cosmos*, 133.

Orpah: The Moabite sister-in-law of Ruth (Ruth 1). In the Midrash, she is the mother of the giants **Goliath** and **Ishbi-benob**. It is unclear whether she herself was a giantess (Midrash Ruth). *SEE* GIANTS.

Oshaya, Rabbi: Talmudic Rabbi and theurgist (ca. 3rd century). He used his knowledge of **Sefer Yetzirah** to make a golem calf to eat on the Sabbath (Sanh. 67b).

Osiris-Michael: An angelic name found in the magical text, **The Prayer of Jacob**. The linking of the pagan god Osiris with the high angel **Michael** is indicative of a kind of "inclusive monotheism" circulating in the Greco-Roman world. The gods of polytheistic pantheons are thus acknowledged as real but "demoted" to angelic status, making them subordinate to the one God of Israel.

Ot, Sefer ha-: "Book of the Letter." Abraham Abulafia's prophetic-apocalyptic revelation that provides much of the biographical information available on his life. It is one of the few mystical tracts that survived to this day that describes his mystical-prophetic experiences. *SEE* ABULAFIA, ABRAHAM.

Ottiyot ben Sirach: *SEE* ALEF-BET OF BEN SIRA.

Ottiyot da Rabbi Akiva: *SEE* ALEF-BET OF RABBI AKIVA.

Otiyyot ha-Mashiach: "Signs of the Messiah." Portentous events that herald the coming of the **Messiah**. While several Jews filled with messianic fervor have, over the centuries, written about the conditions that will signal the end of times, Jewish tradition in general evinces an ambivalent attitude toward all attempts to anticipate the advent of the eschatological Messiah, especially given that all predictions so far have proven wrong. The rationalist Maimonides articulates the most widely accepted summary of the circumstances that will surround the Messiah (Yad, Hilchot Melechim), and many messianic contenders and movements since his day have attempted to hitch themselves to his wagon, but to no avail.

Ov: Either a dead spirit or a necromancer. *SEE* BAAL OV; YIDDIONI.

Ozhiya: Angel summoning texts identify Ozhiya as **Sar ha-Panim**, "the Prince of the **Countenance**," indicating this may be an alternative name for **Metatron**.

P

Padkaras: An **angel** of the Divine **Countenance** (**Sar ha-Panim**) mentioned in **Ma'aseh Merkavah**. It is unclear whether this is just an alternate name for **Metatron**, or an angel in its own right.

Pairs: (*Zugot*). The doubling of a variety of things is a source of bad luck. According to the **Talmud** (Pes. 109b–110b) activities done twice in a row or in pairs, such as eating, drinking, or copulation, invites the attention of evil spirits once the person leaves his or her home. Thus, one should neither celebrate a double joy (like two weddings), nor perform the same onerous task twice, such as a judge passing the same sentence, all on the same day. Even drinking from two cups, one after the other, invites bad luck or the **evil eye**. (Pes. 109b; En Yaakov). On a different but related note, the **Book of the Name** warns the adept not to look in the face of a twin for **forty** days after reading the book.

Asmodeus is the demon that has power over this vulnerability. The **Talmud** passage explains how to militate against this: by crossing thumbs in the palms of the opposing hands and reciting, "You and I, that is three!"

Palace: (*Heichal*). In the Bible, the term is used interchangeably for both the **Temple** and a king's palace. Starting in apocalyptic writings and early Jewish mysticism, *heichal* becomes a standard term for a plane, level, or principality of heaven; often **Eden** is specifically mentioned (PdRE 12). There are seven *Hechalot* (pl.) that constitute the divine residence, a kind of vast celestial compound.

Modern writers will sometimes refer to the **Hechalot** literature traditions as "Palace Mysticism," though probably in the minds of these ancient mystics they are really more focused on the archetype of the Temple when they were describing each heavenly *heichal*. In later medieval thought, the palatial theme becomes more evident, with the *Hechalot* of heaven being described in terms of walled gardens, splendid chambers of repose, and other images more associated with noble residences.

Portraying God as a king dwelling in a palace is a common parabolic image in **Midrash** and Chasidic stories (Gen. R. 15:22; Tales of Rabbi Nachman). There are a number of esoterically important "palaces," both literal and metaphoric, in Jewish literature. *SEE* PALACE OF THE BIRD'S NEST; PALACE OF THE NUT; PALACE OF SPLENDOR; SEVEN HEAVENS; THRONE OF GLORY.

Palace of the Bird's Nest: (*Heichal Kan ha-Tor* or *Kan Tzippor*). The hidden dwelling place of the **Messiah** once he leaves the Garden of **Eden**. From there, he is able to view the suffering of Israel in preparation for his coming. The Bird's Nest is the celestial launch pad for the Messiah's entry into the world. (Zohar II: 8a–9a; III: 196b; Seder Gan Eden; ShB 42) *SEE* DOVE, GOLDEN; PALACES; SEVEN HEAVENS.

Palace of the Nut: (*Heichal ha-Egoz*). One of the **palaces** within **Eden**, this one is derived from a verse in Song of Songs, "let us go down into the nut garden" (S of S 6:11). It is regarded to be the place of the **Yeshiva**

shel Malah, the academy on high, where the **righteous** dead gather to study Torah. In some sources, it is synonymous with the messianic Palace of Splendor (SGE).

Palace of Splendor (or Glimmering Palace): (*Heichal Nogah*). One of the many **palaces** of the **Messiah**, it is built from supernal letters and is found in the precincts of the Garden of **Eden**. There the Messiah and the **righteous** dead gather on the Sabbath (Zohar I: 7b; BhM, vol. 3, 135–36).

Panentheism: *SEE* NATURE; EMANATION; MAKOM.

Papyri, Magical: Greco-Roman documents of late antiquity containing magical formulae, **rituals**, and designs for **amulets**. Almost universally written in Greek, they often combine Jewish, Christian, and pagan divine names in the **incantations**. The magical papyri have many parallels to Hebrew magical texts from the same period, texts like **Sefer ha-Razim, Sword of Moses,** and the magical recipe books of the **Cairo Geniza,** and both Greek and Hebrew texts clearly arise out of the same milieu, though the degree of resemblance varies according to how much the Jewish authors take seriously the rules and admonitions of the Sages. Thus the gentile papyri put a premium on adjuring a wide range of pagan deities (along with the God of Israel), using magical props and materials, and on spells for cursing or binding one's enemies. Depending on the scruples of the author, Hebrew magical books will incorporate these same features to some degree, but may at times substitute the names of angels for deities, or avoid nonkosher ingredients, or emphasize the role of the magical word by reducing or avoiding entirely the use of magical objects and devices.[1] *SEE* INCANTATIONS; MAGIC; NAMES OF GOD; PERMUTATIONS; SORCERY; SYMPATHY; WITCHCRAFT.

1. See Betz, *Greek Magical Papyri in Translation.* Also see Kern-Ulmer, "The Depiction of Magic in Rabbinic Texts."

Paradox: (*Hashva'ah; Yesh v'Ain*). Jews find great value in considering the truths encompassed by paradoxes, or seemingly contradictory ideas. Paradox creates a polarity between two teachings, resulting in an instructive tension. It also helps illustrate the limits of human language in describing the ineffable truths of existence. Of course, on high all paradoxes are reconciled (*Tikkun; Yichud*), though in ways beyond human comprehension. The role of paradox in the religious life gets its most sophisticated treatment in Chasidic mystical theology.[1]

1. Green, *Jewish Spirituality,* vol. 2, 164–73.

Paralyzation: Certain Jewish saints were credited with the power to paralyze evildoers. The great Babylonian scholar **Chai ben Sherira Gaon** discusses a belief among Jews that **olive** tree leaves inscribed with divine names could immobilize bandits. **Jonathan Eybeschitz** also claimed the power to paralyze those who threatened him (Otzer ha-Geonim; Beit Yonatan ha-Sofer).

Pardes or PaRDeS: (Persian, "Paradise"). This term has multiple meanings.

1. Exoterically, this is a conventional locution for either the Garden of **Eden,** or of the heavenly afterlife.

2. Because the term is forever associated with the cryptic Talmudic story of the four Sages who entered Pardes (Chag. 14b), it is also a metonym for the phenomenon of the mystical experience.

3. *PaRDeS* can also be read as an acronym for four methods of Scriptural interpretation: **P**ashat (authoritative), **R**emez (allegorical or philosophic), **D**rash (homiletical or Midrashic), and **S**od (esoteric or mystical). It also carries the connotation of sacred study *in toto*. *SEE* BIBLE; FOUR SAGES; MIDRASH; NUT; ORAL LAW; SECRET; TALMUD; TORAH.

Pardes Rimmonim: "Garden of Pomegranates." The mystical magnum opus of Safed Kabbalist **Moses Cordovero**. It is perhaps the most comprehensive and systematic presentation of classical **Kabbalah** ever written. It also contains many teachings about mystical theosophy, angel- and demonology, and theurgy.

Pargod: "Curtain." The supernal **curtain** that separates God from the rest of heaven. Those who can overhear the voices behind it, such as the dead or the ascendant mystic, can learn the future. (Chag. 16a; Yoma 77a; Ber. 18b; PdRE 4, 6). *SEE* SEVEN HEAVENS; THRONE OF GLORY.

Partzufim: (Aramaic, "Countenances"). First outlined in the **Zohar**, this metaphysical concept is more fully developed by **Isaac Luria**. According to the Lurianic cosmogony, after the catastrophe of the **Breaking of the Vessels**, the shattering of the primeval structure of light, the **Ein Sof** reconstitutes the fragments of the cosmic order into five "countenances" or "visages" that are able to mediate between supernal and material realities in a way the primordial vessels were not. Think of the Partzufim as analogous to a "patch" for a faulty computer program.[1]

The Partzufim interact with humanity in the work of **tikkun**. These countenances also constitute and encompass the personal dimensions of God that are described in biblical and rabbinic writings. This aspect of Lurianic thought has a complex relationship with the sefirotic structure of classic **Kabbalah**, not unlike the "wave/particle" phenomenon in quantum physics. Thus whether the divine structure manifests itself as the **sefirot** or as the Partzufim depends on certain conditions, but they are essentially two aspects of the same divine force. The five countenances are:

> *Arikh Anpin*: The "long/great countenance," also called the *Atik Yamim*, "Ancient of Days."
>
> *Abba*: "Father," the male aspect of the divine *gamos* is linked to the sefirot of **Keter** and/or **Chochmah**.
>
> *Ima*: "Mother," the celestial mother is tied to **Binah**.
>
> *Zer (or Zaur) Anpin/Ben*: "The short/lesser countenance." Product of the union of *Abba* and *Ima*, it is tied to the lower six sefirot: **Chesed**, **Gevurah**, **Tiferet**, **Netzach**, **Hod**, and **Yesod**.
>
> *Kalah/Malcha/Bat*: "Bride/Queen." The feminine counterpart to *Zer Anpin*, she is linked to **Malchut**.

The Partzufim, like their sefirotic counterparts, are also integral to the notion of the restoration of the **Adam Kadmon**, the cosmic human. In a kind of inverted "imitatio dei," all human actions that advance the cause of cosmic restoration are mimicked by the Partzufim.[2] Thus humans help to activate them and ensure the healing flow of divine energies between higher and lower worlds. *(SEE APPENDIX FIGURE 2.)*

1. Scholem, *Kabbalah*, 140–44.

2. Faierstein, *Jewish Mystical Autobiographies*, 28–29. Also see Green, *Jewish Spirituality*, vol. 2, 65–70.

Passover: (*Pesach, Chag ha-Aviv, Chag ha-Matzot*). The holiday of Passover, which is celebrated every spring, is based on the miraculous events of the **Exodus**.

All of the elements of the Passover are thought to have spiritual-theurgic power. The burning of all leaven on the eve of Passover, for example, is meant to symbolize the destruction of the **Yetzer ha-Ra** in oneself, a task which, like removing all leaven, can never be perfectly achieved (J. Ber. 4:2, 7d).

Much of the Seder **ritual** is constructed around groupings of fours: four questions, four sons, and four cups of wine. In practice, there are a number of theurgic and magical customs that have become associated with the holiday and the apparatus of its observance. The most famous of these is the medieval **incantation** known as the **Sixteen-Sided Sword of the Almighty**, which, interestingly enough, is also a multiple of four. *SEE* PRAYER; UNLEAVENED BREAD; WINE.

Patriarchs and Matriarchs: (*Avot and Imahot*). Declared by the Sages to be the "Pillars of the World," Jewish mystics also assign great metaphysical significance to the first ancestors of the Jews, primarily **Abraham**, **Sarah**, **Isaac**, **Rebecca**, **Jacob**, Leah, **Rachel**, and **Joseph**, but sometimes others, also.

God created the world only for the sake of Abraham coming into existence. The Patriarchs are the "**chariots**" of God in the world; in effect they were a kind of "incarnation" of God's presence. The **Zohar** calls Abraham the "four legs" of the **Throne of Glory** (Gen. R. 47:6; Zohar I: 5, 78a).

Because of their merit, God continues to forgive the sins of the people Israel, their children. Often the dead ancestors are portrayed as intervening in heaven on behalf of their living descendants (PdRE 44). The Matriarchs can be appealed to in prayer and supplication to intercede before the **Throne of Glory** on behalf of both individuals and the whole people. The names of the Matriarchs are considered particularly powerful, and are invoked in healing prayers and protective **amulets**.[1]

In the Zohar, Abraham and Isaac represent antipodal divine forces, Love and Fear; these forces are reconciled in balance through Jacob. Out of that balancing of cosmic energy, the people Israel sprang into being (Zohar, Ki Tissa 54). *SEE* ANCESTORS; IRON; RIGHTEOUS, THE; ZECHUT AVOT.

1. Kanarfogel, *Peering through the Lattices*, 137–38, 143; Roth, *Encyclopedia Judaica*, vol. 2, 910 figure 8b.

Payh: Seventeenth letter of the **Hebrew alphabet**. It has a dual vocalic value, being a "p" if a diacritical mark is placed in its middle, or an "f" if one is not. Payh also has a *sofit* form, in which the curved bottom of the letter is straightened into a vertical line. It has the numeric value of 80. The word *payh* itself means "mouth," which the shape of the letter resembles. The letter therefore symbolizes speech and, because we are the "speaking animal," humanity.[1]

1. Munk, *The Wisdom of the Hebrew Alphabet*, 180–89.

Pelotit: The daughter of Lot. In both the **Bible** and rabbinic literature, Lot is portrayed as an unsavory character, so it is not clear why he deserves to be rescued from doomed Sodom; perhaps the merit of Abraham protected him. His daughter, on the other hand, was a noble figure. Despite the laws of Sodom that prohibited hospitality to the needy, she secretly fed the hungry by various clever subterfuges. When she was finally caught, she was burned alive by the inhabitants of Sodom. It was her cry for justice (Gen. 18:21) that brought God's wrath down upon the cities (PdRE 25; Sanh. 108b; Gen. R. 49:6; Sefer ha-Yashar, Va-Yera).

Pentagram: The five-pointed star so familiar to Western occult practitioners is first linked to **Solomon** in the Greek-language document, The **Testament of Solomon**, where it is revealed to have the power to subdue demons. Non-Jewish sources sometimes refer to it as the "Seal of Solomon," while later Jewish sources use the same title for the **hexagram**. Pentagrams reappear from time to time in Hebrew magical and alchemical texts, and on **amulets**, but very little written lore about their significance in Jewish occultism exists. The hexagram takes on much greater significance for Jews. *SEE* MAGEN DAVID.

Perek Shirah: A poem, purportedly by **Solomon**, recounting the praises that animals, plants, and all Creation utter for their Creator. All who recite it daily will be delivered from the fires of **Gehenna**.

Permutations: Jewish magical and mystical texts frequently feature long strings of permutated letters. Most often these permutations are derived from the letters that make up a **name of God**. Reciting these repetitions aloud as part of a spell presumably had some kind of mantralike hypnotic effect. An example of this would be an incantation of angel **summoning** found in the **Sword of Moses** that has a string of permutation based mostly on the four letters of the **Tetragrammaton**, *yod*, *hay*, *vav*, and *hay*. Transliterated, the passage looks like this: *HU HI HHI HU HH AH UH IH IH HUI HU HI HU NA HUH IHU IA HU HU IH IHU HI HU IA IH UH HU IA HU HUA HU IH UH HU HUH IHI HU IH AHIH MH UH.* The logic by which these permutations are ordered, and the rationale for introducing other letters into the mantra, is now lost to us. Permutations also appear in Jewish **meditation** practices and, in less esoteric form, in Jewish liturgy in hymns like "Ein Keloheinu."[1] *(SEE APPENDIX FIGURE 5.)*

1. Kaplan, *Meditation and Kabbalah*, 76–92.

Perush Sodot ha-Tefillah: "Commentary on Secrets of the Prayer [Service]." A collection of esoteric teachings concerning the statutory prayers and **rituals** of Jewish worship written by **Eleazer of Worms**.

Pesach: "Passover." The spring festival that celebrates the **Exodus** from **Egypt**. *SEE* PASSOVER.

Pesak ha-Yira'ah v'ha-Emunah: "Opinion on the Awe and the Faith." This treatise, purportedly written by Joseph ben Uziel but actually a work of the **Circle of the Special Cherub**, is devoted to the mystical significance of prayer and to experiencing a vision of God akin to those described in the Bible.[1] *SEE* CHERUB, UNIQUE.

1. Dan, *The 'Unique Cherub' Circle*, 101–24.

Pesher: A style of **Bible** interpretation found in the **Dead Sea Scrolls** that treats biblical prophecies of the past as referring to events contemporary to the interpreter. *Pesher* interpretations have all but vanished from Jewish hermeneutics in the past two thousand years, but a form of *pesher* is alive and well in some circles of Christianity, where books like Hal Lindsey's *The Late Great Planet Earth* still treat ancient apocalypses as blow-by-blow accounts of current world events.

Pesikta de-Rav Kahana: An early medieval **Midrash** devoted to the Sabbath cycles that especially focuses on stories of the destruction and future redemption of Jerusalem. It preserves some Jewish fantastic beliefs.

Pesikta Rabbati: Medieval **Midrash** on the holidays that records some Jewish fantastic traditions.

Pesikta Zutarta: Medieval **Midrash** on the **Torah** that is a source of Jewish fantastic traditions.

Petachiah of Regnesburg: Medieval adventurer (German, ca. 12th century). In his travels around the Jewish world, he recorded many wonders: miraculous tombs of Jewish heroes, wells that refused to provide water on the Sabbath, and fabulous traces of biblical events throughout the Holy Land.[1]

    1. Unterman, *The Dictionary of Jewish Lore & Legend*, 154–55.

Petayah, Judah: Rabbi and exorcist (Iraqi, ca. 19th–20th century). He is the author of Minchat Yehudah, a book that includes his interviews with spirits, conversations that provided detailed accounts of the spirit world and how it interfaces with the human world.[1]

    1. Goldish, *Spirit Possession in Judaism*, 177.

Petihat ha-Lev: "Opening the Heart." A type of magical **ritual** meant to speed the memorization and mastery of **Torah** teachings. The ritual involves writing a magical **incantation** on either a **cake** or a hard-boiled **egg**, the first ever laid by a hen, and then eating the enchanted object. This conjures the angelic **Sar ha-Torah** and/or the **Sar ha-Panim**, who comes to the aid of the spellcaster. SEE ANGELS; METATRON; SUMMONING.

Phallus: The phallus as a symbol of the source of life and of salvation has a long established history in Jewish interpretation (See Gen. 17; Ex. R. 1:20; Shab. 152a; Zohar I: Lech Lecha).

More controversial than the role of the human penis in Jewish thought is the idea of God having a kind of spiritual analog to a phallus. A few modern scholars have attempted to argue that there was a "cult of the Divine Phallus" pres-

ent in biblical religion. This argument has usually hinged on the special place of **circumcision** as a "mark of the covenant." Such theories have proved largely unpersuasive. Quite a number of pagan cults existed in the ancient world that explicitly celebrated the cosmic phallus, such as the cults of Osiris and of Thor, but did not require their male devotees to modify their own penises. On the flip side, Israel is not the only culture that has the custom of circumcision, and there seems to be no obvious correlation across cultures between ritual circumcision and penis adoration. Arguments that there are veiled references to God's phallus in the Bible are even more tendentious. Rabbinic texts are likewise almost entirely bereft of such sacro-erotic speculations. One **Hechalot** text, however, **Hechalot Rabbati**, features a brief description of a sexually charged dance performed by the angels before the **Throne of Glory**.

Zoharic **Kabbalah**, however, is centered on a blatantly erotic interpretation of the Godhead, dividing the functions of the **sefirot** into male and female sides. The **Zohar** includes multiple interpretations built around a concept of God's "genitals." Using a phrase in Isaiah, "behold the King in his beauty" (33:17) as its springboard, the Zohar interprets the word for *yofi*, "beauty," as a euphemism for a divine member. **Tikkuni Zohar** explicitly claims the "divine image" that God bestowed upon man (but not upon woman) is the penis (I: 62b, 94b). The Zohar also interprets a passage from Job, "In my flesh I see God," as a reference to the human penis being in "the image of God." Depending on the interpretation one reads (the Zohar is often difficult to track on this topic), this supernal phallus is manifest in one or the other of two sefirot, **Tiferet** (Beauty) and **Yesod** (Foundation) (Zohar I: discussion throughout Lech Lecha and Va-yera).

To add to the confusion, apparently unlike the human member, the supernal "phallus" is actually an androgynous entity (Sefer Bahir 61). Specifically, the corona of the divine member represents the **Shekhinah**/Yesod, the feminine aspect of divinity, while masculine Tiferet is identified with the circumcised penis [shaft?]. Once Yesod unites with Tiferet, the feminine "waters" (read: "vaginal fluid") of Malkhut/Shekhinah flow "upward." This in turn triggers the flow of masculine "waters" (read: "semen") into her, thereby receiving its seed. Through these commingled divine male and female principles comes the outpouring of the supernal waters that enliven and fructify the lower worlds, sustaining Creation.[1]

This vivid mystical ideology of a sexually charged deity has been a scandal to more philosophically minded Jews and a public embarrassment even to mystically inclined yet prudish Jews who have come after the Zohar. As a result, to this day it is very difficult to get a clear statement about this aspect of Zoharic metaphysics from even the most committed Kabbalists. *SEE* GODHEAD; ZER ANPIN.

1. Wolfson, *Through a Speculum that Shines*, 326–80; Scholem, *Kabbalah*, 225–28; Scholem, *On the Mystical Shape of the Godhead*, 106–15.

Pharaoh: According to rabbinic legend, the Pharaoh of the Exodus did not die with his troops. Instead, he left Egypt and became the king of Nineveh. There he finally submitted to God's will when the prophet Jonah appeared (PdRE 43).

Pharmacopoeia: Jews of the ancient and medieval world used a wide variety of materials for homeopathic, medical, and magical purposes. A comprehensive list is beyond the scope of this work, but here is a partial list of compounds and objects taken from **Sefer ha-Razim**:

ashes	frankincense	ox brain
bay leaves	glass	precious stones
blood	gold	roots
bronze	herbs	silver
cake	honey	spices
chicken	ink	spikenard
cloth	iron	sulfur
coal	lead	sweat
copper	lizards	tin
dog meat	musk	water
fat	myrrh	wax
flour	myrtle	wine
flower	oil	

When a Hebrew magical text does include rituals involving materials and/or objects, they are usually deployed in one of two ways: either as sacrifices—burning incense, or throwing a gold plaque into the sea, for example—or as material analogies for the reality being influenced, such as

breaking a bowl to break the power of a demon or using human sweat to make love potions.[1]

Chasidic **rebbes** have their own updated arsenal of products: unleavened bread; foods, etrogs, and oil previously used in religious rituals; or potions made from ingredients like those listed above.[2] *SEE* FOOD; HEALING; HERBS; MAGIC; POISON; SEGULLAH.

1. Janowitz, *Icons of Power*, 70–78.
2. Zimmels, *Magicians, Theologians, and Doctors*, 136, 147–48.

Philosopher's Stone: An object, sometimes described (when it is described at all) as a rock or mineral, that can serve as a catalyst for the transformation of metals and other, even greater, feats. At times the stone is interpreted as an allegory for something more abstract, such as the mind, or a specific theosophical insight.

This key device in the work of **alchemy** is closely associated with a number of Jewish figures, starting with biblical characters. Alchemists theorized that the long life spans credited to the **Patriarchs** were a result of their mastery of alchemical sciences, and specifically, their possessing a philosopher's stone. It is this stone that Jacob slept upon when he had his angelic **dream**. Some have speculated that the **Urim and Thummim** is connected to it. Both **David** and **Solomon** have been credited with possessing one.[1]

1. Schwarz, *Kabbalah and Alchemy*, 13, 23, 50–51. Also see Patai, *The Jewish Alchemists*.

Phineas: *SEE* PINCHAS.

Phoenix: (*Hol; Milham*). This fiery mythological **bird** stirs with the sun each day and lives for a thousand years, after which it is consumed by **fire**, only to rise from its own ashes and live again (Midrash Samuel). The phoenix achieved this unique status as an immortal bird because it refrained from bothering the overburdened **Noah** during the **Flood** voyage (Sanh. 108b; Gen. R. 19:5).

Physiognomy: The study of a person's physical features (face, hands, hair, gait) as a means to understand their soul or character (Ben Sira 19:29–30). This is not a widely known practice in Jewish circles, though we have several examples: two documents among the **Dead Sea Scrolls**

(4Q186 and 4Q561) are physiognomic texts that teach that a person's spiritual and moral state is revealed by the shape of his or her teeth, eyes, and other body parts. A **Hechalot** text, called Hakkarat Panim l'Rabbi Yishmael, uses physiological criteria to determine if one is suited to learning mystical knowledge.[1] In a most unusual variation, **Sefer Chasidim** teaches that various ticks, itches, tingles, and other bodily irritations without obvious causation are actually omens of future events (162). The **Zohar** also takes some interest in the art (I: 96b; II: 71a–78a; Zohar Chadash 35b–37c). **Isaac Luria** and various Baalei Shem, such as **Jonathan Eybeschitz**, also had the ability to judge a person's character based on examining the **face**.[2] SEE BAAL SHEM; FACE; METOPOSCOPY.

1. Gruenwald, *Apocalyptic and Merkavah Mysticism*, 218–24. Also see Scholem, *Major Trends in Jewish Mysticism*, 48.
2. Scholem, ibid.

Pidyon ha-Ben: SEE RANSOM.

Pidyon Nefesh: A donation for the support of a spiritual virtuoso, a **baal shem**, or a righteous person. SEE KVITTEL.

Pikulin: A term found in the **Zohar** for a mystical explanation regarding the purpose of a commandment.

Pillars: (*Amud*). Cosmic pillars form the foundation upon which the world rests. The Bible suggests they sit upon the floodwaters of the abyss (I Sam. 2:8; Ps. 104:3). The **Zohar** states that they stand upon *rucha*, divine spirit, which in turn stands upon the Torah (Zohar I: 77a). Each pillar is made up of the fiery divine substance called **chashmal** (Mid. Konen 2:32–33).

Some say there are twelve such pillars, others say there are seven (Chag. 12b). In Pirkei Avot, it is said the world stands upon three metaphorical pillars: worship, Torah, and acts of love (1:2). Elsewhere in the **Talmud**, basing his argument on Proverbs 10:25, Rabbi Eleazar claims there is only one pillar upon which the world stands: Righteousness. Taking this logic one step further, he declares the Patriarchs to be the pillar that sustains the universe (Shab. 88a, 119b). In the Zohar, the pillar, symbolizing the phallus, also takes on great metaphysical significance (Chag. 12b; Zohar I: 186a). SEE PATRIARCHS AND MATRIARCHS; PHALLUS; RIGHTEOUS, THE.

Pinchas: High Priest and grandson of **Aaron**. He achieved fame by thwarting a plague sweeping the Israelite camp in a most extraordinary manner—by impaling an Israelite prince and his Moabite paramour while they engaged in illicit (perhaps ritual) sex (Num. 25). **Zohar** teaches that his soul was possessed by the dead sons of Aaron, Nadab, and Avihu, who led him to bold action as a **tikkun** for their sins (2:26b). He was one of the spies Joshua sent into Jericho, where he demonstrated the power to make himself invisible (Num. R. 26:1). He ascended to heaven, like Elijah, by pronouncing the **Tetragrammaton** (J. Targum Numbers 31:8). Later tradition claims **Elijah**, also an exemplar of zealousness, was Pinchas reincarnated (PdRE 29, 47; Num. R. 21:3). One tradition claims he and Elijah were actually incarnations of the **ofan** angel **Sandalfon**.

Pinchas ben Yair: Talmudic Sage and wonder-worker (ca. 3rd century). Either the son-in-law of **Simon bar Yochai** (Talmud), or his father-in-law (Zohar), Pinchas was famous for his miraculous feats. He communed with animals and natural entities. He once caused a river to split in order that he and those traveling with him could cross on dry ground. He even resurrected the dead (Chul. 7a–b; J. De. 1:3).

Pirkei de-Rabbi Eliezer (PdRE): A **Midrash**, credited to the Talmudic Sage Eliezer ben Hycanus, which contains many fantastic traditions and esoteric teachings. It is arranged as a continuous narrative, giving an account from Creation to the coming of the **Messiah**. It focuses extensively on the events of Creation, and includes esoteric traditions about the **angels**, **Adam Kadmon**, and the expulsion from **Eden**.

Pirkei de-Rabbi Ishmael (PdRI): An alternative name for **Hechalot Rabbati**.

Pirkei Hechalot: An alternate title for Hechalot Rabbati.

Pishon: One of the four rivers that flowed from **Eden** (Gen. 2). In the **Zohar**, it signifies the "right side" of the divine emanations flowing through the **sefirot** (I: 181b).

Pitron Chalomot: The most comprehensive Jewish book on **dream** interpretation and oneiromancy, *Pitron Chalomot* was written by **Solomon Almoli**.

Piznai: A lilot/**succubus** who seduces men and breeds demon children from their semen (Ginzberg, *Legends of the Jews*, 5:166). *SEE* NOCTURNAL EMISSION.

Plagues: The ten plagues that God employed to humble Pharaoh and Egypt (Ex. 4–12) are repeatedly called "great and awesome signs and wonders" and are the archetypal manifestations of divine judgment. The ten plagues are as follows:

1) Blood
2) Frogs
3) Lice (or gnats)
4) Wild beasts (or flies)
5) Cattle disease
6) Boils
7) Hail
8) Locusts
9) Darkness
10) Death of the firstborn

In Deuteronomy, God assures Israel that the "plagues of the Egyptians" will never be visited upon them if Israel harkens to God's word. The initials of the ten plagues were inscribed on the **rod** that Moses used to unleash them (S of S R. 8). Rabbi **Akiba** taught that in fact the Egyptians were actually smitten with no less than two-hundred and fifty plagues (Haggadah for Passover).

In the time of **Abraham**, the pharaoh who took **Sarah** into his harem (Gen. 12:6) also suffered ten plagues, a fore-shadowing of what would happen to Egypt during the **Exodus** (PdRE 26). *SEE* DISEASE; HEALING; PASSOVER.

Planets: (*Mazalot*). In the Bible, there are oblique hints of the idea that celestial objects can influence or affect humans (see especially Ps. 121). By the 6th century BCE, the prophets are railing against Jews being involved in astral cults, but presumably this is a variation of Ancient Near Eastern polytheism. It was not until the rise of Greco-Roman influence, with its enthusiasm for **astrology** as we think of it today, that the "natural" influence of planets starts to be taken seriously in Jewish circles. Thus Jacob Asher regards the word *MaZaL*, "planet," as an acronym for *Mazria Zera L'minehu*, "plants that reproduce according to their kind," signifying that the celestial spheres govern the growing season (ha–Tur).

By the medieval period, Jewish astrologers were earnestly discussing how the planets in their motions hold sway over specific spheres of life in the sublunar world. Thus, one can read in Jewish texts like **Sefer Raziel** how Mars influences matters of blood, war, wounds, and iron, while Mercury influences matters pertaining to writing, arts, and learning. Presumably, knowing this allowed the practitioner to choose propitious times to engage in these matters. As the Middle Ages progressed, both Hermetic traditions and Arab theories of planetary emanations became increasingly accepted by Jewish thinkers.[1] With the rise of modernity, however, Jews just as rapidly assimilated the new celestial-mechanical worldview, so the Jewish spiritual traditions related to the planets continues to spark interest only in the most traditional segments of Jewish society. *SEE* ASTROLOGY; BRONOTOLOGY; MAGIC; MAZAL; ZODIAC.

1. Langerman, "Jewish Magic and Astrology," in Grendler, *Encyclopedia of the Renaissance*, vol. 3, 18–22.

Planets, Seven Angels of the: The angels who govern the heavenly bodies (visible to the naked eye) are **Michael**, Barakiel, **Gabriel**, Dodeniel, Chesidiel, Tzadikiel, and A'aniel.

Poison: In the popular gentile imagination of the Middle Ages, Jews were masters of the occult science of poisons (along with **sorcery**, **healing**, and **alchemy**). According to one anti-Jewish legend, Jewish physicians took a vow to poison every tenth Christian patient under their care. The reality that some Jews, as international traders, handled and sold exotic spices, herbs, drugs, and other substances no doubt contributed to this calumny.

A variation on this theme is that of well-poisoning. According to this pernicious myth, in their satanic hatred of humanity, Jews would poison wells used by Christians. Popular hysterias about Jewish mass poisoning swept various regions of Europe. This accusation peaked in the 14th century, when such accusations occurred in many places, usually in the wake of a plague.[1]

Variations on the theme of poisoning continue to this day. In contemporary America, radical groups and conspiracy theorists claim that AIDS is a part of a Jewish plot to destroy the African-American community.[2] Similar accusations have been made regarding the prevalence of drugs in minority communities. A popular belief in the Middle East is that Jews have put sterility drugs into chewing gum with the purpose of weakening the Arab world.[3] SEE BLOOD LIBEL; PHARMACOPOEIA.

1. Ben-Sasson, *A History of the Jewish People*, 486–87. Also see Ben-Sasson, *Trial and Achievement—Currents in Jewish History*, 251–56.
2. *Chicago Sun Times*, May 10, 1988.
3. *Al Quds*, June 7, 1997; *Al Usbu Al Adabi*, Jan. 1 1998; *Al Ahbar*, Oct. 20, 2000.

Pomegranate: SEE FRUIT.

Possession, Demonic: (*Ibbur Ra; Nichpeh; Achuz Sheid; K'fao Sheid*). Seizure by evil spirits or **demons** is a phenomenon going back to biblical times. Unlike some other cultures, Jews do not usually regard demons as synonymous with the malevolent dead (although there are exceptions). Rather, they are regarded as pre-existent spirits, or as spiritual byproducts of human criminal and immoral sexual activity.

While there are numerous references in the **Bible** to people being filled with divine spirit (Eldad and Medad) or the spirit of Wisdom (Joshua), there is only one reference to evil spirit possession in the Hebrew Scriptures: **Saul** (I Sam. 16:23, 18:12). This spirit could evidently be temporarily exorcised by means of **music**, but it never permanently left Saul. The apocryphal book of Tobit is devoted to a story of demonic haunting and **exorcism** (though it is not about a "possession" in the sense we are using here, of a living soul being bodily taken over).

In historical documents from outside Jewish tradition, there are several references to the phenomenon of demon possession among Jews. The Gospels make repeated mention of demon possession. Jesus reportedly exorcised several people, including Mary Magdalene (Mark 1:24). He himself was accused of being possessed by a demon (John). Josephus also records a case of demonic possession (Ant. 8:2, 8:5). Even given the doubtful historical reliability of these stories, they at least suggest that belief in demon possession was part of the intellectual landscape of 1st-century Jewish Palestine.[1]

The Dead Sea Scrolls include several exorcism liturgies. There are a few references to demonic possession in the **Talmud** and classical **Midrash** (Me. 17b; Num. R. 19.8; PdRK 1:74; Tanh., Hukat 8). Interestingly, there are discussions about how to judge the moral culpability of a person who is possessed (PdRE 12). **Incantation bowls** and medieval texts found in the **Cairo Geniza** link various illnesses to demonic attack, indicating that at the level of popular Jewish culture, possession (at least in the form of invasive illness being seen as demonic) was taken seriously.[2]

There is a marked upsurge in accounts of possession starting in the 16th century, though these are mostly reports of spiritual rather than demonic possession. Yet, incidents of possession by evil spirits are recorded in Jewish literature up to this day, almost exclusively in traditional Jewish circles (see the next article).

Many symptoms are linked to possession, including compulsive deviant social, sexual, and religious behaviors. An outstanding feature of all forms of possession is **xenoglossia**, an alien voice speaking from within the possessed person. Numerous authorities have attempted to distinguish *ibbur ra* from mental illness, though many others, from Jesus in the 1st century up to people in the present, regarded insanity to be a sign of demonic possession. SEE BONES; EXORCISM; POSSESSION, GHOSTLY.

1. See Twelftree, *Jesus the Exorcist*.
2. Bar-Ilan, "Exorcism by Rabbis: The Talmudic Sages and Magic," 1–14; Goldish, *Spirit Possession in Judaism*, 73–98.

Possession, Ghostly: (*Achuz Dibbuk; Ibbur ra*). Belief that a spirit of the dead can possess the living is a surprisingly modern phenomenon in Judaism. While stories of demonic possession appear as early as biblical times, there are no unambiguous reports of possession by dead spirits until the 16th century.[1] There are three related forms of possession described in the literature: beneficent possession by either an angelic being, usually termed a **maggid** (guide), or a righteous ancestor (ibbur),[2] or malevolent possession by a poltergeist. An evil spirit is usually referred to as a **ruach** (spirit), **dybbuk** (clinging ghost), or **tzeruf** (changling or additional soul). This entry concentrates on the latter phenomenon.

In most of the accounts preserved in Judaism, souls of the dead seek to possess people either as a way of finding refuge from the punishments inflicted on them in the afterlife, or out of a desire for sexual gratification (a variation on the tradition of the incubus). According to **Judah Petayah** of Baghdad, many spirits find themselves adrift in the world of the living because of sex; their ghostly existence is a punishment for gross licentiousness while they were living (Minchat Yehudah). Lurianic theory developed a very elaborate model of how a soul may have its transmigrations impeded by unresolved sins. Such souls must find a material host to enter and any human is far preferable to an animal, plant, or inanimate object.

Based on recorded incidents, many victims of possession are (young) women, while almost all possessing spirits are male.[3] An outstanding feature of all forms of possession is **xenoglossia**, an alien voice speaking from within the possessed person (Zera Kodesh).

While literary accounts of ghostly possession peak in the 17th–18th centuries, periodic reports of spiritual possession continue across Jewish cultures up to this day, with the most recent publicly revealed incidents occurring (on videotape) in Israel.[4]

Jewish communities at different times employed different methods of **exorcism**, though the most consistent Jewish strategy appears to be simply to talk the spirit to death.[5] *SEE IBBUR OR DEVEKUT; MEDIUM.*

1. Chajes, "Judgments Sweetened: Possession and Exorcism in Early Modern Jewish History," *Journal of Early Modern History*, 1:2, 1997, 124–69.
2. Goldish, *Spirit Possession in Judaism*, 101–24.
3. Ibid, 41–72.
4. *Jerusalem Post*, April 22, 1999.
5. See Patai, "Exorcism and Xenoglossia among the Safed Mystics."

Potah: The angel (or demon) of forgetfulness frequently mentioned in medieval texts. He is the nemesis of the **Sar ha-Torah** (Machzor Vitry, 115–16; Havdalah de Rabbi Akiva; Sefer Assufot).

Prayer: (*Bakash; Tefillah, Berachah*). What, if anything, distinguishes prayer from **incantation** is a topic of ongoing debate among academics. Since Sir James George Fraser's taxonomy first appeared in *The Golden Bough* in 1922, popular convention regards prayer to be a supplication, an appeal for favor from a deity, knowing that the god is free to ignore the plea. By contrast, an incantation is both mecha-

nistic and coercive; if the rite is performed correctly, the deity must fulfill the wish of the initiate. But even given this distinction, prayer in Judaism is regarded to be very powerful in affecting all kinds of change, including the miraculous (B.B. 116a; ShB 50).

Many Jewish sages have believed in and taught *sodot ha-tefillah*, that Jewish liturgy has an esoteric dimension and secret power that can only be tapped by those with the occult knowledge and right **kavanah**.[1] The Circle of the Unique Cherub formulated an esoteric rationale for prayer (Pesak ha-Yirah). For another example, the Pietists of Germany used to draw out the prayers recited for the conclusion of the Sabbath for the benefit of the dead, because it was believed that the souls being punished in **Gehenna** were released for the duration of the Sabbath.[2] Medievals also believed that many destructive angels had names ending in the letter **payh** (the "p" or "f" sound) and that reciting a prayer text that contained no words with final payhs, such as the *Yotzer Or* prayer, would protect against such demons.

Over time, the function of prayer also evolved in Jewish esoteric thought. The **Zohar**, for example, treats prayer not so much as a means for dialogue with the divine, but rather as a **ritual** leading to **devekut**, union with God. It even characterizes the process of giving the soul over to God in prayer as a kind of (temporary) death (II: 201a, 213b; III: 21a–b). *SEE MAGIC; THEURGY.*

1. Idel, *Hasidism*, 157–58.
2. Kanarfogel, *Peering through the Lattices*, 143. Also see Dan, "The Emergence of Mystical Prayer," in *Studies in Jewish Mysticism*, 85–120.

Prayer of Jacob: A magical text of antiquity, it describes how the Patriarch **Jacob** invokes God for wisdom and divine powers. There are a number of pagan themes in the text, so it is a matter of controversy whether the author was a Jewish syncretist or a pagan.[1]

1. Davila, "Ancient Magic (The Prayer of Jacob)."

Preida, Rabbi: Talmudic Sage (ca. 4th century). He was rewarded with a lifespan of four hundred years because of his devotion to teaching Torah. His merit was such that because of him, his entire generation was vouchsafed eternity in **Eden** (Eruv. 54b; Sefer Yuhasin).

Priesthood and Priest: (*Kehunah; Kohan*). The priests of ancient Israel were in charge of the sacrificial cult in the **Temple** and as such were spiritual conduits between Israel and God. They also functioned as diviners, diagnosticians, and possibly as healers.

The priesthood was a hereditary affair, all priests being descendants of the clan of **Aaron**. They also possessed no land of their own, but depended on the Temple donations and **sacrifices** for their upkeep.

In order for the priests to function within the sacred grounds of the Temple without risk of transgressing or polluting the divine space, they were governed by an elaborate set of physical requirements, dress codes, and purity rules. In time, the clothing items and purity practices used by the priests in preparation for approaching the holy became archetypes that would later evolve into the kind of **purification** rites used by subsequent generations of mystics and magicians seeking to access divine power.[1]

The High Priest controlled the **Urim and Thummim**, by which he could address questions to God of national import. *SEE* ALTAR; PINCHAS; SACRIFICES; TABERNACLE.

1. Metzger and Coogan, *Oxford Companion to the Bible*, 608–11.

Priestly Blessing: (*Birkat Cohanim*). A three-fold blessing, "May YHWH bless you and guard you/May YHWH cause His countenance to shine upon you and be gracious to you/May YHWH lift up His countenance toward you and grant you peace," said by the priest over the whole Jewish people at the times of festival gatherings. The **ritual** is performed with the hands of the priest held "Vulcan style," with the thumb and fingers forming three prongs, the shape of a "shin."

The Priestly Benediction includes characteristics of an **incantation**, being made up of progressive verses of three, five, and seven words. It invokes God's power to protect the person and grant material prosperity and enlightenment. Each line contains the **Tetragrammaton**. From its words, mystics have uncovered the esoteric twelve-part and twenty-two letter **names of God**. It can counteract bad **omens** and **dreams**.

Priluka, Isaac: Rabbi and exorcist (Ukranian, ca. 19th century).

Prince of the Congregation: A messianic moniker that appears in the **Dead Sea Scrolls**. The Prince is the war leader of Israel in the great eschatological battle against evil (CD VII, 19–20; 4Q161; 4Q285).

Prince of Fire: *SEE* PRINCES OF FEAR.

Prince of the Sea: (*Sar Yam* or *Sar shel Yam*). Possibly either an angel or a demon, the Sar Yam is at times identified with **Leviathan** or **Rahav** (Ex. R. 34:1; B.B. 74b). Some Jews in Talmudic times evidently sought to placate this numinous entity by throwing sacrifices into water, a practice denounced by the Sages, who could exercise some authority over the Prince (Chul. 41b; J. Sanh. 13a–d).

Prince of the World: (*Sar Olam; Sar ha-Olam*). An angelic title, sometimes applied to **Metatron**, sometimes to **Michael** (Yev. 16b; Chul. 60a).

Princes of Envy and Enmity: An array of **demons**, each the commander of a demon legion, mentioned in **Treatise on the Left Emanation**.

Princes of Fear: These **punishing angels** will descend on anyone who misuses the power of divine names and/or theurgic rituals. They are mentioned in **Hechalot** texts and in the stories of **Israel ben Eliezer**, the Baal Shem Tov.

Privy Demon: (*Sheid beit ha-Kissei*). Tractate Berachot tells us demons like to lurk in places of impurity. This particular demon likes toilets and spreads plagues to mankind (Zohar III: 76b). Talmud Shabbat 67a provides a magical spell to exorcise such an unclean spirit. *SEE* EXCREMENT; TOILET; UNCLEAN SPIRITS.

Prophecy, Prophets: (*Neviut*). Unlike the Eastern Semites, who favored **omen** reading and impetrated **divination**, among many Western Semitic peoples (including the Israelites) the preferred source of augury and revelation was the intuitive human oracle. So unlike the *baru* diviners of Mesopotamia, who were essentially technicians and observers, the prophets of the West were individuals with mediumistic, mystical, and occult predispositions.[1]

The most common method of inducing a vision among early Semitic prophets appears to have been achieving a state of ecstasy by means of **music**, **dance**, or even self-mutilation (I Sam. 10, 19; I Kings 18).

While biblical prophecy clearly has its roots in these Semitic practices, the nature of prophecy seems to have evolved in the biblical period.[2] Early in Israelite history, there was a distinction between a prophet (*navi*) and a seer (*roeh* or *chozeh*), the distinction being that the prophet was a shamanlike ecstatic who communed with divine forces while in a trance, while the seer relied on dreams and visions in the **darkness** (I Sam. 9:1–10:6). This distinction doesn't apply to the case of **Moses**, who appears to have his prophetic experiences without being in a mind-altering state.

In later Israelite culture, this distinction vanishes and the terms are used interchangeably (II Sam. 14:11; Isa. 29:10), though the classical prophets continue to rail against various forms of "false prophecy," among which they include using wine to induce drunken dream visions (Isa. 28), ecstatic trances (Zech. 13), consulting spirits, or experiencing **automatic speech** (Isa. 8).

According to the Sages, there are ten types of prophets: envoys, men of faith, men of God, servants, seers, messengers, angels, visionaries, sentinels, and prophets. Prophecy comes in ten forms: parable, metaphor, **riddle**, speech, saying, **dream**, command, pronouncement, prophecy, and **vision** (Mishnat R. Eliezer 6; AdRN 34; Gen. R. 44:6). By tradition, there were forty-eight prophets and seven prophetesses in Israel (Shab. 104a). All the prophets perceived the divine only through the medium of the **speculum**, filters that shielded them from the reality-annulling power of pure spirit (Lev. R. 1:14; Mishnat R. Eliezer 6). Later mysticism equated these speculi with the **sefirot**. Most prophets had to view the divine reality through the filter of up to nine specula. Only Moses experienced prophetic visions through the special clarity of just a single speculum (Yev. 49b).

The mechanism of prophecy among the classical prophets is much debated, and the prophets themselves do not give detailed accounts of how their prophetic experiences unfold.[3] **Isaiah**, **Ezekiel**, and **Zechariah** describe vivid visions full of light and symbols. Zechariah described his vi-

sions as like a dream, and it has been suggested that Isaiah's vision in the **Temple** (Isa. 6) was the result of **incubation**, though there is no explicit testimony to this in the text itself. Moreover, elsewhere in the book of Isaiah, the practice of incubation is condemned (8:19–22, 19:3). Ezekiel is physically bowled over by the Spirit of God, which then enters him (Ezek. 1–2). While it has been popular to argue that all prophets experienced their revelations in a state of ecstasy, the evidence for this is spotty. In the accounts of Moses, Amos, Hosea, and **Jeremiah**, evidence of ecstasy is utterly absent. It is also not at all clear that the classical prophets were "taken over" or that they simply "channeled" a divine voice (enthusiasm), as there are ample examples of the prophets conversing with God, indicating they retained their own consciousness and their own will during the prophetic experience. The **Talmud** claims the spirit of prophecy only descends upon one who is in a state of joy; anger causes prophecy to depart (Pes. 117a; Shab. 30b).

According to some, true prophecy can only happen in the Land of Israel, though there were a few exceptions which only occurred because of the purifying presence of **water** (MdRI, Bo, Pisha 1). Still, there are enough exceptions to this rule found in Scripture that this claim is hard to sustain. This is especially the case because the tradition teaches that the gentile **nations** were also sent prophets, seven in total—Job, **Jethro**, Eliphaz, Bildad, Zophar, Elihu, and **Balaam**—with Balaam, son of Beor, being the greatest (B.B. 15b; Num. R. 14:20). Gradually, as the **Shekhinah** came to reside among Israel, the spirit of prophecy disappeared among the nations (Lev. R. 1:12). In a related vein, the **Zohar** suggests **circumcision** is a prerequisite to prophecy (I: 89a), even though this claim flies in the face of the biblical and rabbinic traditions of both female and gentile prophets. The Kabbalists also teach that prophecy flows from the feminine side of the Godhead.[4]

After the Babylonian exile, the institution of prophecy fades from Israel, perhaps because it reverted to the older ecstatic mode and Jews of the time found such prophecies unreliable (Zech. 13). From about 300 BCE on, the **Bible** itself, supplemented by **omens**, becomes the preferred source of divine revelation. Haggai, **Zechariah**, and Malachi were the last of the recognized prophets. Prophecy, it is said, had now been given over to children and the insane (Sanh. 11a; B.B. 12a–b).

The Talmudic Sages insisted God's will is only made known through a **Bat Kol** or a visitation by **Elijah**. Yet numerous mystics have believed attenuated forms of prophecy can be experienced through ecstatic mystical practices (Sha'arei ha-Kedushah), and a number of Kabbalists and Chasidic masters have been given the title "prophet" or "seer," though any claim to true prophecy made in post-biblical Judaism is highly controversial and generally dismissed by all but a few true believers.[5] Certainly no one since the 3rd century BCE has been universally recognized in Israel as a prophet. Prophecy will truly return to Israel with the final appearance of Elijah and the advent of the Messianic age. *SEE* DIVINATION; HOLY SPIRIT.

1. Oppenheim, *Ancient Mesopotamia*, 206–28.
2. Bamberger, "The Changing Image of the Prophet in Jewish Thought," *The 1966 Goldenson Lecture, Hebrew Union College, Cincinnati.*
3. Heschel, *The Prophets*, 324–425.
4. Wolfson, *Through a Speculum that Shines*, 70–317, 343–44.
5. Heschel, *Prophetic Inspiration after the Prophets.* Also see Fine, *Physician of the Soul, Healer of the Cosmos*, 296.

Protocols of the Elders of Zion: An anti-Semitic tract that purports to reveal a secret cabal of Jewish elders striving for world domination. This rambling fabrication of the Czarist Russian secret police has some quaint aspects. For example, it reviles Jews for undermining aristocracy, promoting liberal ideas, and spreading democracy as a means to take world control.

Providence: *SEE* FATE; FREE WILL.

Psalms: The 150 poems/hymns, ascribed to the authorship of **David**, which make up the biblical book of Psalms. There are also several psalms that appear in other books of the Bible, most notably the books of Samuel and Jonah. Non-canonical psalms have been found in the Dead Sea Scrolls collection (11Q11; 4Q435–38).

The use of the biblical psalms for **prophecy**, for **divination**, for protection, and even for magical purposes is very ancient. The earliest evidence of this appears in the Dead Sea Scrolls (*SEE* PSALMS, APOCRYPHAL) and continues to this day. In the Middle Ages, an anonymous author wrote **Shimmush Tehillim** (Practical Psalms), a workbook for using various psalms in amulets, rituals of protec-

tion, and theurgy. There is a similar list of magical applications found in a Judeo-Arabic translation of the Psalms by Ezekiel Shemtov David. Examples of psalms that can be used for practical benefit include:

Ps. 1 can help counteract a potential miscarriage.

Ps. 9 can be used for healing an ailing child.

Pss. 16 and 19 are most useful in uncovering a thief. The psalms are recited as part of a divining ritual in which the names of the suspects are written in clay and then dissolved with living **water**.

In a **Cairo Geniza** fragment, Ps. 23 is included in a **ritual** for asking **dream** questions of the angel **Michael**.

Ps. 29 is recited over a body of water as part of a ritual to make revelations appear in the reflecting surface (Pes.112a; Sefer Tagi; Perush ha-Merkavah).

Ps. 31 is used to combat the **evil eye**.

Ps. 49 is recited to reduce a fever.

Ps. 67, which consists of precisely 49 words, is read during the 49 days of the **Omer**. Done with the proper **kavanah**, it protects one against imprisonment (Abraham Galante).

Ps. 91, based on the language of verses 7 and 10, is identified by the Talmud as "a song of afflictions" (Shev. 15b) and is without a doubt the most frequently cited psalm for defense against illness and demons.

Ps. 109, especially verse 6, is useful in performing exorcisms when recited in **reverse**.

Ps. 119, the longest psalm, and one constructed on an acrostic structure, has protective uses for every letter-verse.

Ps. 121 is an excellent tool for protecting against threats that come in the night.

The Chasidic master Yehiel Meir Lipschitz, the *Tehillim Yid* ("Psalm Jew") believed that any Jew with troubles who came to him could be saved from any hardship, given appropriate psalms to recite. *SEE* AMULETS; BIBLE; BIBLIOMANCY; DEAD SEA SCROLLS.

Psalms, Apocryphal: Four psalms (the canonical Ps. 91 and three noncanonical psalms) found in the **Dead Sea Scrolls**. All four are attributed to **David** and are intended to be used in exorcising disease-causing **demons**. The psalms are to be recited over the victim as he responds "amen" and "selah" to their adjurations.

Pseudepigrapha: Religious literature, usually containing some form of divine revelation, which is (falsely) credited to a worthy figure of antiquity. In Israelite religion, before the creation of the biblical canon, people received their divine communications primarily through the phenomenon of living oracles—prophets. In Early Judaism, as canonized written accounts of those prophetic oracles (Scriptures) came to increasingly be regarded as the only reliable source of God's will, those who continued to experience revelatory moments and wanted to share these new oracles found it more and more difficult to be taken seriously. Because of this, the phenomenon of ascribing such insights to ancient authorities arose.[1]

Deuteronomy, a book which purports to be from the hand of **Moses**, yet was not known of until centuries after Moses, may be the oldest example of pseudepigrapha in Judaism.[2] Other biblical books suspected of being pseudepigraphic include Daniel and Ecclesiastes.

The vast majority of such writing, however, arose during the Greco-Roman period, once the biblical canon was closed. The number of works ascribed to biblical figures, both important and peripheral, multiplied exponentially. They include such works as the Apocalypse of Isaiah, the **Testament of Levi**, and, of course, the many Enochean books. Magical books, too, can achieve a greater aura of authority by claiming ancient authorship, as exemplified by works like the **Testament of Solomon**, **Sefer ha-Razim**, the **Eighth Book of Moses**, and **The Sword of Moses**.

Mystics, too, will use this strategy to reach a wider audience with their novel and radical metaphysics. The **Bahir** and the **Zohar**, for example, both claim to be works of greater antiquity than they in fact are.[3]

1. Metzger and Coogan, *Oxford Companion to the Bible*, 629–31.
2. Tigay, *The JPS Commentary: Deuteronomy*, xix–xxvi.
3. Dan, *The 'Unique Cherub' Circle*, 1–16.

Pseudo-Sa'adia: A mystical-magical commentary on **Sefer Yetzirah** that is wrongly attributed to Sa'adia Gaon, the 10th-century Babylonian polymath. It is instead the composition coming out of a group of little-known medieval mystics, possibly the **Circle of the Unique Cherub**. It is most notable for providing further details on the **golem** traditions.[1]

1. Dan, *The 'Unique Cherub' Circle*, 125–41.

Pulse: The arterial pulse of the wrist has long been held to reveal the spiritual condition of a person. Tikkunei ha-Zohar identifies ten pulse patterns and their spiritual implications. **Chayyim Vital** describes in detail how to use a pulse in performing an **exorcism**.[1]

1. Chajes, *Between Worlds*, 75–76; 213, n. 71.

Punishing Angels: In keeping with Jewish monotheism, the spirits that oversee **Gehenna** are rarely characterized as **demons**. Rather, Jewish texts assume that hell, like heaven, is completely under divine control. This being the case, the numinous creatures that operate Gehenna are in fact angels. These angels execute a near infinite variety of horrific punishments upon the souls of the wayward. These include being hurled across the universe, being flogged with rods of burning coals, flaying, dismemberment, and a host of other vividly unpleasant experiences. Different angels oversee the punishment of different classes of people, with the worst being reserved for the few wholly unredeemable wicked souls (Masekhet Gehinnom; Seder Gan Eden).

Purification: While **ritual** purification is a regular feature of traditional Jewish observance, purity also plays a prominent role in Jewish mysticism and magic. Some sort of purification is usually required before performing these acts: a mystical **ascension**, making an **amulet**, or **summoning**. Most specifications of magical purification are modeled on the purification rites required of the Israelites before they received the **Torah** at Mount **Sinai** (Ex. chapter 19) and on the priestly purity system of the ancient **Temple**. Thus, in **The Sword of Moses**, a Hebrew manual for angel summoning, we read: "If you wish to use this Sword . . . the man who decides to use it must first free himself three days earlier from accidental pollution and from everything unclean, eat and drink [but] once every evening, and must eat the bread from a pure man or wash his hands first in salt and drink only water . . . on the first day when you withdraw [from potential pollutants] bathe [in a mikvah] once and no more, pray three times daily, and after each prayer recite this blessing. . . ."

The most common elements of such purification instructions are: **immersion** in a **mikvah** (sometimes with accompanying **incantations** and reciting secret **names of God**) or a river (both **Jacob** and **Ezekiel** had encounters with God at a riverside), fasting, prayer, abstaining from sex, and withdrawal from normal activities and human contact. Having a **nocturnal emission** will require one to begin the period of purification over again. Fasting or reducing the kinds of foods one eats also makes it easier to move in divine realms and/or deal with divine beings, for it makes you less human and more angelic (angels don't eat).[1] In **Hechalot Rabbati**, it is recommended that one also abstain from smelly food because angels can distinguish a human in their midst by the smell.[2]

Part of purification also involves donning clean clothes. When one is purifying oneself in preparation of performing a theurgic **ritual**, the clothing worn is usually required to be white (Hechalot Rabbati).

1. Lesses, 119–60.
2. Swartz, "The Book of the Great Name," in Fine, *Judaism in Practice*, 340–47.

Purple: *SEE* COLOR.

Q

Qabbalah: While this is a linguistically reasonable way to transliterate "Kabbalah," this spelling has become associated with Christian and Western Spiritualist/Occultist offshoots of Jewish mysticism that strip those teachings of their specifically Jewish/rabbinic content and attempt to fuse them with Christian doctrine and non-Jewish esoteric traditions, such as Hermeticism. For this reason, it is useful to maintain a distinction between Jewish "**Kabbalah**" and non-Jewish "Qabbalah."

Queen of Demons: *SEE* LILITH.

Queen of Sheba: The mysterious figure of the Queen who comes to test the wisdom of **Solomon** (I Kings 10:13) truly captured the Jewish imagination. In most early stories, she is a figure of exotic sexuality and intellectual acumen who tests Solomon with a variety of cunning puzzles and **riddles** (Mid. Mish., 1:1). In later Jewish literature, she comes to be regarded as a **demon**, a **suc-** cubus that seduces men, even weds them, in order to lead them to their eventual ruin. Medieval **Midrash** regard "The Queen of Sheba" to be a moniker for **Lilith**.

Queens, the Four Demon: They are **Lilith**, **Igrat**, **Malkat**, and **Naaman**.

Qumran: A mysterious ancient habitation along the Dead Sea that is the closest ruin to the caves that contained the **Dead Sea Scrolls**. Archaeologists believe the DSS were the library of Qumran, but still argue over fundamental questions, such as whether the site was a communal center for the **Essenes** or a personal retreat for a wealthy Jerusalemite.

Qumrin Tehirin: Night **demons** who interfere with the efforts of the **soul** to commune with the Godhead (Zohar I: 83a).

R

Ra'aya Meheimna: A subsection of the **Zohar** devoted to the mystical rationales for the divine **commandments**.

Raba bar Joseph: Talmudic Sage, demonologist, and theurgist (ca. 4th century). According to the **Talmud**, he created a **golem**. He first did this with the help of Rabbi **Zeira**. On the second occasion, Zeira disapproved of his actions and destroyed Raba's golem (Sanh. 65b). He saw the workings of demons in all kinds of human misery (Ber. 6a).

Rabbah bar Channah: Storyteller (ca. 3rd century). A kind of Jewish Baron Munchausen, Bar Channah told tall tales of his travels, mostly sea journeys that are filled with **demons**, fantastic feats, mysterious locales, and giant **animals**. He once heard the voice of **Korach** emanating from the place where the earth swallowed him up (B.B. 72b–73b; Yoma 39b; EY).

Rabbah bar Nachmani: Talmudic Sage (ca. 3rd–4th century). According to legend, God became embroiled in a dispute over a point of law with the **righteous** dead while they studied together in the **Yeshiva shel Malah**, the academy on high. God then ordered the **Angel of Death** to fetch Rabbah bar Nachmani to heaven to adjudicate the argument. But since he was constantly engaged in the study of **Torah**, Rabbah was beyond the reach of the Angel. It only caught him when he momentarily interrupted his studies because he thought he was being pursued by hostile mortals. Heaven proclaimed his purity at his **death** (B.M. 86a; Nega. 4:11).

Rabbah ben Abuha: Talmudic Sage (ca. 3rd century). After encountering **Elijah**, he ascended to the Garden of **Eden** while still alive. When he returned to earth, all of his clothing bore the fragrance of Eden, a scent so enchanting that he made a fortune by selling his **garments** (B.M. 114a–b).

Rabbi and Sage: (*Rabbi; Rav; Rov; Chacham*). "Master/ Teacher/Wise [one]." The office of the rabbinate is not a biblical institution, though it has its prototype in the biblical figure of the sage. The title begins being used in the first centuries of the Common Era. The first Rabbis (or "Sages" with a capital "S," also known as Chazal) envisioned their authority as analogous to that of the biblical *shofet* (judge). As such, the Talmudic Sages believed they had the biblical authority to lead the people, wage war, interpret and adjudicate the **commandments** found in the **Torah**, and administer all its sanctions, including capital punishment. This was based on the belief that the divinely established system of transmitting authority through *s'michah*, "laying of hands/ordination," continued uninterrupted from Moses and Joshua (see Deut. 34:9; M. Avot 1:1) until their own day. Since around the 3rd century CE, the Sages lost confidence in the reliability of this chain of transmission and all rabbis ordained since that time have been regarded as having far less authority.

Rachamim: "Compassion." Another title for the sefirah of **Tiferet**. *SEE* SEFIROT.

Rachel: One of the four Matriarchs of the Jewish people, she was the beloved second wife of **Jacob** and mother of **Joseph** and Benjamin. In the **Bible**, Rachel's magical activities are limited to the use of **mandrake** as a fertility enhancer (Gen. 30). She stole the **terafim** of her father, **Laban**. The Rabbis conclude her death shortly after that incident was punishment for dabbling with these idols (Gen. R. 74:5, 74:9; PdRE 36).

Because of her own struggle with barrenness, after her death Rachel came to be the spiritual intercessor of choice for Jewish women having trouble with childbirth. Her tomb outside of Bethlehem is a popular destination for Jewish pilgrims. Sometimes a **red** cord will be unwound around the shrine as part of the supplications for Rachel's intercession.[1] *SEE* ANCESTORS; FERTILITY; PATRIARCHS AND MATRIARCHS.

1. Roth, *Encyclopedia Judaica*, vol. 13, 1486–90.

Rachel Aberlin ha-Ashkenazit: Visionary and oneiromancer (Greco-Turkish, ca. 16th century). **Chayyim Vital** admired her sensitivity to paranormal apparitions, angels, and ghosts (Sefer ha-Hezyonot).

Ragshiel: The angel of **dreams**, he is sometimes equated with the **Baal ha-Chalom/Sar ha-Chalom**. He can be summoned to answer dream questions. *SEE* DIVINATION; INCUBATION; MERKAVAH.

Rahab: The prostitute living in Jericho who assisted Joshua and the Israelite spies prior to their siege of the city (book of Joshua). She was so beautiful the mere mention of her name inflamed men's desire. After the siege, she converted to Judaism and married **Joshua**. Three prophets, **Ezekiel**, **Jeremiah**, and **Huldah**, were her descendants (Meg. 14b–15a; Tan. 5b; Deut. R. 2:19; Yalkut, Josh. 10)

Rahav: A cosmic sea monster first mentioned in the biblical book of Isaiah (51:9; Ps. 89:10; Job 26:12). Talmud called him the **Prince of the Sea**, echoing the Canaanite name for their sea god, "Prince River." God slew him when he refused to help in creating the **earth**. The oceans conceal the lethal stink of his carcass, which is why sea water smells so strange (B.B. 74b; Tan. 10a). Rahav may be an alternative name for **Leviathan**, though some sources treat them as two different entities.

Rain: "Greater is the falling of rain than the giving of Torah, for the giving of Torah was a joy to Israel, but the falling of rain is a joy for all the world" (Mid. Teh. 117:1). A critical force in the life of the **world**, rain is the focus of many Jewish myths, prayers, and theurgic rituals. According to the **Bible**, God is the sender of rain and may withhold it as punishment for idolatry, bloodshed, and lawlessness (Deut. 11). Rain is also an **omen** of divine favor. For example, the Sages interpret rain at a funeral as a sign of the righteousness of the deceased.

One of the powers of a **righteous** person is to intercede with God to make it rain. The Rabbis not only mandated supplication prayers for rain, they would impose fasts in time of drought and/or appeal to rainmakers, like **Choni ha-Ma'agel**, to intervene with God. Later figures, such as the Baal Shem Tov, also were remembered as wondrous rainmakers (ShB 21).

According to the mystics, rain is the masculine principle in the **fertility** cycle of the earth; it must mix with the feminine force of subterranean waters and dew in order for the lower worlds to fructify and the ground to yield its bounty (Tan. 10a). Together they symbolize the proper union of male and female principles at work (Zohar I: 17b, 29b; II: 28b).[1] The Water Libation ritual performed on Sukkot is a theurgic ceremony meant to activate this fusion (Tan. 25b; Suk. 49a). *SEE* DEW; WATER.

1. Green, *Guide to the Zohar*, 67.

Rainbow: According to Genesis, after the **Flood**, God created the rainbow as a promise to the descendants of **Noah** to never again reverse the creative order (Gen. 9). The rainbow is therefore a symbol of God's forgiveness and reconciliation with **Creation**.

The Sages regarded a rainbow to be a miraculous sign rather than a natural phenomenon. Hechalot literature suggests the earthly rainbow is a reflection of a supernal rainbow in heaven (III Enoch 22). In the **Zohar**, a rainbow is a form of the divine **Glory** and is an emanation of either **Malchut** or **Yesod**. Other mystical sources declare all the colors of the **sefirot** are expressed in the rainbow. **Moses** wore the "garments" of a rainbow in order to shield himself during his encounter with God on **Sinai** (Zohar II: 99a). **Elijah** tests the righteousness of individuals by asking if they have ever seen a rainbow. Since the truly **righteous** person sustains the world on his or her own merit, such a person never sees one. This is because it is a reminder of God's graciousness toward those of us who otherwise don't merit redemption (Ket. 77b; Zohar II: 15a). A particularly splendid rainbow will herald the coming of the **Messiah** (Sefer Chasidim 1445; Bachya commenting on Gen. 9:13).

Rakia: "Firmament." One of the **seven heavens**, Rakia contains all the celestial luminaries, the sun, the moon, the stars, and constellations (Chag. 12b–13a).

Ram: (*Iel*). A symbol of both power and forgiveness, rams were a favored sacrificial offering in the **Temple**. A ram's **horn** is the type most commonly used to make a **shofar**, and its hide is used to make **Torah** scrolls and **tefillin**.

The ram that Abraham slaughtered in place of his son Isaac (Gen. 22) was a miraculous creature, made by God even before the creation of the **world**. From this ram were made the strings of David's **harp**, the loincloth of **Elijah**, the shofar that sounded at Mount **Sinai**, as well as the shofar that will be sounded at the return of the exiled tribes of Israel in the Messianic Era (PdRE 31; R.H. 16a; Eccl. R. 10:8).

A ram's head is sometimes used as the centerpiece of the **Rosh ha-Shanah** festive meals, in order to invoke good luck for the coming year. *SEE* ANIMALS; NEW YEAR; SACRIFICE.

Ransom: (*Pidyon*). The spiritual ransoming of souls is an ancient practice. One of the oldest forms of spiritual ransom in Judaism is the custom of *Pidyon ha-Ben*, ransom of the **firstborn** son. Since all that "opens the womb" belongs first to God, the firstborn male in every Jewish family must be "redeemed" in a ceremony where the father makes a **charity** (*tzedakah*) donation in the presence of a priest to reclaim the child for himself.

Based on the biblical adage "Charity saves from death" (Prov. 10:2), the giving of *tzedakah* to aid the ill sometimes takes on a magical dimension. Specifically, ransoming ceremonies can be performed on behalf of the sick and dying. Often such protective charity involves donating money in symbolically significant amounts (45, for example, equal to the numeric value of the **Tetragrammaton**). Aside from money donations, the ill person's clothing was often given away, not only to placate numinous forces, but with the additional hope that it would confuse the **Angel of Death**.

There also exist Kabbalistic rituals (reciting the **names of God**, symbolically arranging the donation) to accompany such acts, which are deemed necessary for the ransom to be efficacious.[1]

> 1. Klein, *A Time to Be Born*, 107–8, 147.

Raphael: "God is a Healer." One of the four princely **angels** that attends upon the **Throne of Glory**. Raphael is also a warrior angel, having battled against the **fallen angels**, then casting them into the netherworld (I Enoch 10). Raphael can also directly assist righteous mortals, as he does when he assists the boy Tobiah battle a **demon** (Tobit 3–6). Despite his name, he is only occasionally linked to **healing**. **Midrash** identifies him as one of the three angels that visited Abraham after his self-circumcision (Gen. 18). He is one of the four guardian angels who protect a sleeping person.

Raphael Anav, the Daughter of: This **medium**, whose name was not preserved, was frequently possessed by angels and the spirits of dead sages. Through her they revealed many secret sins of the Jewish community of Damascus and so brought many to repentance (Sefer ha-Hezyonot 22–24).

RaSHI: Bible and Talmud commentator (French, ca. 11th century). RaSHI is an acronym for **Ra**bbi **SH**imon ben **Y**itzchak. While Rashi's writings reveal a familiarity with **Hechalot literature** and **Sefer Yetzirah**, only a very few esoteric references appear in his writings. A few occult traditions exist surrounding the person of Rashi, mostly in tales that the deceased sage appeared to his disciples in dreams to reveal secrets of the **Torah**.[1]

> 1. Kanarfogel, *Peering through the Lattices*, 67, 144–45, 160n.

Raven: This unclean bird is a bearer of bad **omens**. For this reason the roof of the **Temple** in **Jerusalem** was covered with spikes to keep ravens away. **Rabbah bar Channah** claims to have seen a giant raven, a **bird** bigger than the "fort of Hagronia" (B.B. 73b; EY).

Raza/Razim: (Aramaic, "secret/secrets"). This term refers to occult knowledge in general, but the construction of **amulets** in particular. In fact, as evidenced by the texts of some **incantation bowls**, the word is sometimes used as a synonym for "amulet" or "protective charm." *SEE* RAZIM, SEFER HA-.

Raza de-Mehemenuta: "Secret of Faith." The lower seven **sefirot** are collectively known by this term.

Raza ha-Razim: "Mystery of Mysteries." A section of the **Zohar** partly devoted to **divination**, especially **physiognomy**.

Raziel: "Secret of God." An angel of revelation, he gave a book of magical power to **Adam**. One text identifies Raziel as an alternative name for the angel **Galitzur**. He shields the guardian angels from the fiery breath of the **Chayyot** as they stand arrayed around the **Throne of Glory** (BhM 1:58–61). *SEE* RAZIEL, SEFER; RAZIM, SEFER HA-.

Raziel, Sefer: An influential book of sorcery. Tradition credits it with being given to **Adam** by the angel **Raziel**. Heavily indebted to Greek magical **papyri**, the title itself is mentioned in another magical work of late antiquity, The **Sword of Moses**. Still, critical historians consider SR a medieval work—though sections of it are no doubt older—probably having origins among the Jews of Rhineland, for citations from it begin to appear only in the 13th century.[1] The likely compiler of the medieval version is **Eleazer of Worms**. It draws heavily on earlier works, **Sefer Yetzirah** and **Sefer ha-Razim**. There are multiple manuscript versions, containing up to seven tractates. The printed version of Sefer Raziel, like the **Torah**, is divided into five books, some of it in the form of a mystical **Midrash** on **Creation**. It features an elaborate angelology, magical uses of the **zodiac**, **gematria**, the **names of God**, protective spells, and instructions on how to write **amulets**.

1. Roth, *Encyclopedia Judaica*, vol. 13, 1592.

Razim, Sefer ha-: "The Book of Secrets" or "The Book of Amulets." A Jewish magical manual that has circulated in a number of fragmentary versions, including a manuscript found among the documents of the **Cairo Geniza**. Other parts have been recovered and from them a larger

text reconstructed. Elements of the book were published in 1701 as part of **Sefer Raziel**.[1]

The book attests that it was revealed to **Noah** by the angel **Raziel**. The book then passed through the generations of worthies until it became Solomon's most prized book of **magic**. Other sources credit **Solomon** with its authorship.

ShR is mostly focused on astral magic, the power that can be derived from planetary forces and their associated angels. It is divided into seven sections, mirroring the seven days of Creation and the **seven heavens**. It describes in great details the **host of heaven**, the angelic commanders, and their powers. It also delineates the twelve months, their **zodiacs**, governing angels, and the like. It is particularly interested in the power of the **sun** as a numinous source of revelation.

It also provides a menu of useful **incantations**. These spells are very characteristic of Greek magical **papyri** texts of late antiquity—they feature repetitions, **reversed** language, foreign and nonsense words, and names.

More surprising for a Hebrew book is the number of references to Greek gods, such as **Helios**, Hermes, and Aphrodite. Disregarding the stricter biblical and rabbinic attitudes toward idols, the approach of Sefer ha-Razim seems to be to simply demote these pagan gods to another class of angels subordinate to the God of Israel.

Like the **Hechalot literature**, ShR emphasizes the need for performing all deeds in a state of strict ritual and spiritual purity. But unlike the Hechalot texts, ShR includes magical practices that these other texts eschew, such as the use of ritual objects (lamps, knives) and animal **sacrifices**. There is also virtually no use of biblical verses of power such as is seen in many other Hebrew magical manuals, nor are any rabbinic figures mentioned. All of this suggests that the author of Sefer ha-Razim, though Hebrew literate, was perhaps marginal to, or marginalized from, the Judaism of his time. *SEE* ASTROLOGY; SORCERY.

1. Morgan, *Sepher ha-Razim*, Introduction. Also see Janowitz, *Icons of Power*, 85–108.

Rebbe: The charismatic leader of a Chasidic community, alternately called *Tzadik*, "Righteous One." Rebbes are usually, though not always, ordained rabbis. Being a rebbe is often a hereditary position, for after a beloved rebbe dies, his Chasids will look first to immediate relatives for a replacement. This convention is naturally subject to abuse and sometimes yields uneven leadership. Rebbes are often credited with miraculous powers such as precognition, **metoposcopy**, **teleportation**, and **healing** (See all of Shivhei ha-Besht). *SEE* CHASIDISM; RIGHTEOUS, THE; TZADIK.

Rebecca: Wife of Isaac and matriarch of the Jewish people. No fabulous traditions associated with Rebecca have been found by this author.

Red: In the Bible, red is a symbol of life and power. The presence of **blood** on the lintels of Israelite houses averted the **Angel of Death** during the tenth plague. In the ancient **Temple**, a **scarlet cord** was hung up on Yom Kippur and its miraculous change to white signaled that the nation had been forgiven its sins. According to the book of Numbers, one overcomes the ritual impurity of contact with a dead body by being sprinkled with the ashes of a red heifer burned with cedar wood, a crimson compound, and hyssop (Num. 19:2–10). A barren woman will wrap a red cord around the tomb of Rachel as a **ritual** to restore her fertility. This cord is then cut into strands and tied to cribs, children, or the sick as a protective amulet.[1]

Red also has anti-demonic properties. As a result, there are a number of amulets that are made incorporating red materials: thread, coral beads, or henna. In sefirotic theosophy, red is the color of **Gevurah**. As part of the recent enthusiasm for Kabbalah among celebrities, many people have adopted the custom of wearing a red thread bracelet to protect against the **evil eye**. *SEE* COLOR.

1. Goldin, *Studies in Midrash and Related Literature*, 118; also see Roth, *Encyclopedia Judaica*, vol. 13, 1590.

Reed Sea: (*Yam Suf*). Long mistranslated in Western tradition as the "Red Sea," the parting of the Reed Sea is a paradigmatic miracle of salvation in the Hebrew Scriptures, a feat performed through the agency of the greatest of all prophets, **Moses** (Ex. 14). The fact that both **Joshua** and **Elijah** performed later similar miracles with the Jordan River signifies their special status in the eyes of the biblical authors.

According to one Midrash, God did not actually part the waters; instead Mount **Sinai** was transported to the spot and the people crossed over on its crest (Gen. R. 55:8).

At the moment of the parting, a great apocalyptic revelation occurred, witnessed by all Israel (MdRI, Be-shallach), the **Glory** of God becoming fully manifest. Others teach the sea actually parted into twelve pathways, one for each tribe (PdRE 42).

Re'em: A mythic giant oxlike beast with horns (Ps. 22:22). It is an untamed creature of great agility and strength. It is so big that its horns touch the clouds and its droppings are capable of damming the river Jordan (Yalkut II: 97d). Created on the sixth day, there are only two re'ems at a time; one dwells in the furthermost west, the other in the east. After mating once in seventy years, the female kills the male. The next pair of re'ems gestates in the female for a minimum of twelve years. The female dies while giving birth. **Noah** preserved them by bringing the two calves on board when they were still small enough to fit inside the vessel. Another legend claims that the adult re'ems swam the entire time, tied to the back of the Ark (Zev. 113b). King **David** also had a misadventure in his youth by inadvertently mistaking a re'em for a mountain and climbing on it (B.B. 73a; Mid. Teh. 22:28; EY). In medieval writings, the re'em is conflated with the unicorn myth. *SEE* ANIMALS; BEHEMOTH.

Refuot, Sefer: "The Book of Cures." A book mentioned in the **Bible**. King Hezekiah destroyed it, apparently as part of his campaign to snuff out pagan practices (II Kings 20). *SEE* HEALING.

Reina, Joseph della: Kabbalist and sorcerer (Spanish, ca. 15th century). Della Reina is most famous for attempting, with the help of ten adepts, to summon and enslave the **demon** princes **Samael** and **Ammon of No** in order to have them help bring the **Messiah**. The attempt went awry because della Reina introduced an alien magical practice into the ritual. Consequently he suffered a most supernatural punishment when the demons broke their bonds and escaped.[1] Della Reina may also be the author of the magico-Kabbalistic **Sefer ha-Meshiv**. *SEE* MESSIAH, SUMMONING THE.

1. Idel, "The Story of Rabbi Joseph della Reina," in *Studies and Texts on the History of the Jewish Community in Safed*.

Reincarnation: (*Gilgul*). The belief that a **soul** migrates from one body to another is an occult Kabbalistic teaching that first explicitly appears in the **Bahir**, a mystical text of the late 12th century, basing its claim on the verse from Ecclesiastes, "One generation *passes* so another generation comes." Within a century, it was being widely mentioned in Kabbalistic literature. It gets serious elaboration in the 16th-century book, **Galya Raza**. **Chayyim Vital** followed shortly thereafter with the highly influential books **Sefer ha-Gilgulim** and **Sha'ar ha-Gilgulim**. Though the idea only surfaces in the Middle Ages, these sources find additional references to it in the **Bible** itself (specifically Job 33:29–30), but also in the custom of **levirate marriage**. The fundamental assumption underpinning reincarnation is that each soul must properly fulfill every mitzvah and will undergo transmigration until that task is complete. Transgressions and failure to perform a commandment retard the soul's progress.[1]

The specific metaphysics of reincarnation have varied widely from teacher to teacher. Unlike other schools of reincarnation, the Bahir assumes that human souls may only transmigrate to other humans. Later works, especially Chasidic writings, hold that souls may pass between human, animal, and even inanimate bodies (ShB 108). Like in Hinduism, reincarnation in a nonhuman life reflects a kind of punishment, but reincarnation is generally viewed positively, as multiple opportunities to help others and acquire merit for the self.[2]

For those who accept that souls can transmigrate into animals, plants, and the foods that are made from them, it follows that one must take care to treat every morsel according to the prescriptions of tradition, for doing so helps liberate that soul to continue its journey (Sha'ar ha-Gilgulim, Mavo; Kav ha-Yashar 1).

Exactly how reincarnation dovetails with the concept of **Gehenna** has been much discussed. Kabbalists believe that the soul is polypsychic and different aspects of the triad soul (**neshamah**, **ruach**, and **nefesh**) have separate paths in the afterlife. This model has the virtue of encompassing all other afterlife scenarios (**resurrection**, **eternal life**) found in tradition.

The concept of the **dybbuk** and the **ibbur** are tied to this aspect of reincarnation. The Tanya offers gilgul as an explanation for conversion to Judaism: all converts are re-

ally lost Jewish souls trapped in gentile bodies who have now found their way back to Torah.

The number of possible reincarnations for a soul could be as few as three (based on the Job verses cited above) or as many as a thousand. All souls, but especially a righteous soul, can subdivide and occupy multiple bodies. Based on the account found in Exodus, which declares that six hundred thousand "souls" stood at Sinai, there exists the belief that there are only six hundred thousand "root" souls in Israel. These have subsequently split, spread out, and reunited in millions of Jewish bodies across the generations. We can see this manifest in the ideology surrounding *tzadikim*, **righteous** individuals. Such people possess a full soul, a soul that is close to completing its cycle of transmigrations, yet remains bound to a body long enough to help lift up the other souls around it. The righteous know the secrets of their own and of other people's reincarnations. Such saints also have the power of **tikkun**: they can "correct" certain errors in the transmigration of a given soul and set it on its proper course. **Exorcism** is such a reparative mechanism, benefiting both the possessed person and the dybbuk. The souls of the saintly are also transmigrated into fish, which is one reason why it is meritorious to consume fish on the Sabbath. Thus a person can, as it were, "embody" and absorb some of the virtue of saintly souls (Sha'ar ha-Gilgulim; Yesod V'Shoresh Ha'Avoda, sha'ar 7).

1. Fine, *Physician of the Soul, Healer of the Cosmos*, 192.
2. Green, *Jewish Spirituality*, vol. 2, 77.

Reishit Chochmah: Mystical text written by Elijah de Vidas (1518–1592). It includes accounts of spirit **possession** and veridical dreams.

Reiyat ha-Lev: "Visions of the Heart." The term for **visions**, more than imaginative, less than factual, that account for anthropomorphic descriptions of God. SEE CHERUB, THE UNIQUE; FACE OF GOD; IMAGINATION.

Resh: The twentieth letter of the **Hebrew alphabet**. It has the vocalic value of "r" and the numeric value of 200. It signifies the head, wickedness, and evil.[1] SEE LANGUAGE.

1. Munk, *The Wisdom of the Hebrew Alphabet*, 199–206.

Resh Lakish: Talmudic Sage (ca. 2nd–3rd century). A reformed highwayman and gladiator, he was the Samson of the rabbinic period, performing great feats of strength (Git. 47a; B.M. 84a).

Reshef: "Plague." A demon first mentioned in the Bible (Hab. 3:5).

Resurrection: (*T'chayyat ha-Metim*). The doctrine that the dead will undergo an embodied restoration in the **World-to-Come**. First mentioned explicitly in the book of **Daniel**, resurrection has been a central concept of the afterlife in Judaism (Siddur); **Maimonides** regarded it to be one of the thirteen doctrines a faithful Jew must believe in.

On **Judgment Day**, all the dead will be resurrected with the blast of a **shofar** and be judged for their actions in life. Those buried in the Land of Israel will be the first to rise from the grave (Gen. R. 74:1; Tanh., Va-yichi 3). Those who died outside the land will have to journey there first through subterranean conduits (Ket. 111a). The **righteous**, as well as those who have atoned for their sins through time spent in **Gehenna**, will know an afterlife in a perfected body. Those who constitute the incorrigible sinners will be annihilated, body and soul, and their memory blotted out from under heaven. Some sources treat resurrection as an intermediate phase before the souls go on to a disembodied existence in eternity (Gen. R. 95:1; Pes. 68a; Sanh. 91b; Eccl. R. 1:4; Tanh., Va-yigash; Zohar I: 130b).

Eleazer of Worms suggested that the truly **righteous** have the power to resurrect the dead, as demonstrated by the examples of **Elijah**, **Elisha**, and **Ezekiel**. This power to resurrect is an autonomous power that results from the saint's own knowledge of how to manipulate the mystical power of the **alphabet**, especially the seventy-two-word name of God (Zohar I: 7b), the same power that can be used to construct a **golem**.

Reubeni, David: Adventurer (ca. 16th century). Appearing from whereabouts unknown, Reubeni came to Italy claiming to represent a Jewish kingdom in the east and asking the Pope to assist him in a crusade against the Turks. He reportedly received a favorable hearing. His mission to Portugal was less successful and he was expelled from there, but not before triggering renewed persecutions by the Inquisition against the Portuguese "New Christian" community that had welcomed him. While in Iberia, he met **Solomon Molokho**, a Crypto-Jew and aspiring **messiah**. Molokho publicly reconverted to Judaism and followed Reubeni back to Italy. Together they toured various Christian kingdoms announcing the impending end of the world. Christian authorities eventually arrested both men, and Reubeni died in prison after several years.[1]

1. Roth, *Encyclopedia Judaica*, vol. 14, 114–15.

Re'uyot Yehezkel: "Visions of Ezekiel." RY is one of the earliest **Merkavah** texts in existence. The work enumerates the various things that **Ezekiel** saw in his vision of the divine chariot (Ezek. 1). It gives one of most detailed description of the **seven heavens** found in Jewish literature, describing all their dimensions and functions.[1]

1. Gruenwald, *Apocalyptic and Merkavah Mysticism*, 134–41.

Reversal (Magical): (*L'mufra*). The concept of symbolic analogy is fundamental to the logic of **magic**. Likewise, reversing or inverting a symbolic analogy—doing something backward—whether it be by performing a task or reading a word, frequently appears in magical literature. It is held to have the power to reverse the natural order, to undo something, or to achieve a counter-magical effect. The most infamous example in Christian circles is the "black Sabbath," in which many Christian rituals and objects are used contrary, upside-down or backward to the prescribed manner, or with a completely contradictory purpose to the "authorized" version. Common Jewish examples of magical reversal include: reciting potent biblical verses forward and then backward, changing the order of a name, or performing an act of reversal as part of a **ritual** (backing out of a room, for example). A large number of medieval **incantations** have been preserved that were written wholly or partly in reverse.[1]

1. Kern-Ulmer, "The Depiction of Magic in Rabbinic Texts," 299.

Rhabdomancy: Divination using sticks or rods. *SEE* BELOMANCY; DIVINATION ROD.

Riddle: (*Chidah*). Riddles and word puzzles have had a role in Jewish life since **Samson** first used them against the Philistines (Judges). **Solomon** specifically honors them as spiritual tools and claims that the Scripture frequently speaks in riddles and enigmas (S of S R. 1.5). **Gematria**, of course, is treated as an elaborate form of numeric riddles woven into the very fabric of the universe. The **Zohar** has a strong inclination toward numerical puzzles (I: 32b, 72b, 77a, 151b; II: 12b, 95a). Some Chasidic tales weave spiritual lessons into elaborate allegorical riddles. SEE PARADOX; SECRET.

Righteous, the: (*Tzadikim, Kedoshim, Amudat ha-Olam*). While Judaism has no notion of "Saints" in the sense that it is used in Roman Catholicism, Judaism definitely recognizes "saints" (with a small "s"). These are exceptionally pure and righteous individuals.

The truly righteous, such as the **Patriarchs and Matriarchs**, have an awesome status in the eyes of God. They are called the "Pillars of the World," i.e., their righteousness sustains existence (Chag. 12b; Yoma 38b; Bahir 71). In Genesis Rabbah, the righteous are called the "divine **chariot**"; they are God's vehicle in this dimension of reality (47:6). The righteous bring the **Shekhinah** back into the world, which is why they are also called the "altar of God" (Gen. 33:20; Zohar I: 150a). One text even posits that **Jacob**, as the most perfect of the **Patriarchs**, achieved quasi-divine status on earth through his righteousness (Meg. 18a; Gen. R. 79:8; Zohar I: 138a).

In keeping with Judaism's esteem for sacred text and learning, most are understood to be masters of **Torah** and the tradition—when a righteous person studies Torah, he or she is on par with the **angels** (Zohar I: 12b; Ned. 20b; Kid. 72a). However, it is also possible for non-scholarly individuals to be recognized as *tzadikim*.

Jewish saints are not automatically associated with wonder-working, but it is also not unusual to have reports of the righteous performing wonders and miraculous **healings**. The **Talmud** teaches this is so because of a **paradox**: having submitted his or her will to the will of God, God in turn fulfills the will of the righteous (Shab. 59b). Based on a verse in II Samuel, "The righteous rule the awe of God" (23:3), Talmud M.K. 16b quotes God as declaring, "I rule over humanity. Who rules over Me? The righteous. . . ." This becomes the basis for explaining the miraculous powers sometimes displayed by the righteous.[1] So great is the power of the righteous through their piety and ethical mastery that they can, at times, reverse even a divine **decree**, as Ezekiel did when he annulled the Toraitic decree that God would "visit the guilt of the parents upon the children" (Suk. 42a).

Unlike **witchcraft** or scholarly **sorcery**, the wondrous powers of the righteous are directed to the benefit of others: individuals, communities, all Israel, or the entire world. The most extraordinary *tzadikim* are declared *kedoshim*, "holy ones," but the righteous are not to be called "holy" in their own lifetime. Upon death, the souls of the righteous descend into **Gehenna** and gather up damaged souls to ascend with them (Chag. 15b; Sha'ar ha-Mitzvot, p. 112).

Once dead, even the mere **name** of the righteous one possesses its own power. The names of Rabbi **Eleazar** or Rabbi **Joshua ben Perachya**, for example, are invoked for healing and protection on **incantation bowls**. Writing the name of the **Baal Shem Tov** on an **amulet** makes it effective (Shivhei ha-BeSHT). The bodies of the righteous dead do not decay, or decay only slowly, and smell fragrant (B.M. 84b). Mystical adepts visit the graves of the righteous dead in the hopes of receiving a revelation or healing (B.M. 85b). In ancient Antioch, the locals felt their synagogue was a place of power because it was built over the graves of Jewish martyrs.[2]

God exults in the righteous dead and gathers with them in **Eden** at **midnight** to study Torah (Ber. 3b; Zohar I: 10b, 60b). SEE OHEL; SEGULLAH.

1. Lauterbach, "The Belief in the Power of the Word," 290–92.
2. Levine, *The Ancient Synagogue*, 275.

Rigyon: A fiery river that flows in heaven. Every day **serafim** issue forth from it and the other angels purify themselves by immersing in it (BhM 1:60). SEE NAHAR DINUR; RIVER.

Rings: Rings, in a way akin to **seals**, can grant one power over the spirits. Solomon enslaved demons with a magical ring (Testament of Solomon). Josephus describes how an **exorcism** was performed with a ring containing a special root (Ant. 8). Rings incorporating protective **amulets** were frequently made in Greco-Roman times. In **Hech-**

alot literature, rings feature prominently, both as objects of power held by **angels** (Hechalot Rabbati) and as seals used by human adepts for accessing the heavenly precincts (Merkavah Rabbah).

A fragment from the **Cairo Geniza** describes how to make a magic ring (cover an **egg** first with **semen** and then with **incantations**, bury it in cow **excrement** for **forty** days, recover the egg and find an image of a **bird** on it, then sacrifice that part of the egg over a **coin** and make the coin into a ring), but the part of the text explaining the purpose of the ring did not survive. If one assumes there is a magical analogy involved, this ring was probably intended either for a **love** charm or for **fertility**.

Ritual: Judaism is often characterized as a "performative religion," a tradition that emphasizes action, both ethical and ritual, over the quest for correct doctrine. It is a faith of "deeds, not creeds," as one wag put it. And ritual action, in all forms, is a major element of living Jewishly.

This book defines a ritual as any conscious symbolic behavior involving verbal and/or performative action that is directed toward a cosmic structure and/or numinous presence (adapted from Evan Zuesse). For the purposes of this book, Jewish rituals can be categorized as follows (with some inevitable overlap):

> *Lifecycle rituals*: Ceremonies acknowledging transitions and liminal/transitional moments in life. Examples in Judaism include rituals of **birth**, coming of age, **marriage**, and **death**.
>
> *Calendaric rituals*: Rites that mark seasonal and historic moments of sacred significance, such as **Rosh ha-Shanah**, **Yom Kippur**, **Passover**, **Sukkot**, **Shavuot**, Purim, and **Chanukah**.
>
> *Protective rituals*: Rituals that prevent or reverse negative events or influences. Examples in Judaism include **purification**, **healing**, **segullah**, **exorcism**, mourning, and **blessings**.
>
> *Communion rituals*: Rites that bring one (or the community) into the presence of the divine. In Judaism these include blessing, **circumcision**, **prayer**, **ascent**, and **incubation**.
>
> *Exchange/Substitution rituals*: Ceremonies that involve an offering to divine forces, usually in

the hope of receiving some benefit or to gain power, such as **sacrifice**, **fasting**, **kapparah**, **divination**, or **incantation**.[1]

1. This list is a modified version of the taxonomy of Catherine Bell as described in Davila's "Ritual in the Jewish Pseudepigrapha."

River: (*Nahal, nahar*). In Jewish mythology, a river represents either a channel of life and bounty, or an obstacle and/or point for transformation (a "liminal" zone). Examples of the first archetype include the four rivers that flowed out of **Eden** and in the birth narrative of **Moses** and the purifying river that will flow from **Jerusalem** in messianic times (Zech. 14; Ezek. 47:1–12). The latter idea appears in the incident of Jacob wrestling with the angel. Similarly, in **Midrash** Tanhuma it is reported that **Satan** transformed himself into a river to keep **Abraham** from fulfilling God's command to sacrifice Isaac.

Rivers also flow in both heavenly and subterranean realms. "The Throne [of Glory] is established upon seven rivers corresponding to the seven clouds of Glory (Reuyot Yekhezkel; J. Sukkah 5:1, 55a)." Gedulat Moshe claims there are only four rivers. Underground rivers, sometimes related to the currents of the **abyss**, are the conduits through which the supernal "female" waters flow (Tanh., Kedoshim 10; Zohar I: 78a).

There are various ways to use the supernatural power of rivers here on earth. Torah study by a riverside helps learning to flow continuously, just as the water flows continuously (Hor. 12a). Immersion in a river is both a means of **purification** and a way to experience a revelation or vision. *SEE* SAR HA-TORAH; SUMMONING; WATER.

River of Light or Fire: (*Nehar Dinur; Rigyon*). This river is the passage from lower to higher realms and is the conduit for **angels** to move between heaven and **earth** (Dan. 7:10; Seder Gan Eden). Angels spring daily from its flow (Chag. 14a). The stars, too, emerge from this river, which surrounds the firmament (Sefer Raziel). Created on the first day, it flows from the sweat of the **serafim** who carry the **Throne of Glory** (Gen. R. 1:3). The souls of the dead must immerse themselves in this river before they can enter the **World-to-Come**. The river ceases to flow on the Sabbath (Ex. R. 15:6; Lam. R. 3:8; Gedulat Moshe 5; Zohar II: 252b). *SEE* RIGYON.

Robe: *SEE* GARMENT.

Rock: (*Tzur; Sela*). As a totem of permanence, endurance, and stability, God is sometimes called "the Rock" in the **Bible** and rabbinic tradition. In **Jerusalem**, the **Foundation Stone** seals away the waters of the **abyss**, keeping the world from reverting to a state of **chaos**.

Rocks also have power. The **Tzohar** was a healing stone owned by the **Patriarchs**. Likewise, **gemstones** in general have been held to have healing properties. Jewish **incantation bowls** frequently mention a particular evil spirit known as a "pebble demon."[1] **Geomancy**, the use of pebbles or sand for the purposes of divination, also appears in Medieval Jewish literature.

    1. Naveh and Shaked, *Magic Spells and Formulae*, 68.

Rod: Jewish tradition tells of staffs endowed with miraculous powers. Specifically, the staff of **Aaron** was transformed into a **serpent** and was the instrument for summoning the first three **plagues** against **Egypt**. Aaron's rod, however, also delivered signs when not in his hands, as when it budded and blossomed overnight as part of a trial by **ordeal** (Num. 17:8). **Moses** also possessed a rod he used in performing miraculous deeds.

Later tradition claims all biblical references to staves actually allude to a single magical rod that was given to Adam, then traveled with the **Patriarchs**, prophets, and kings of Israel across history (Num. R. 18:23; PdRE 40; Sefer Zerubbabel). This rod, created on the eve of the sixth day, was made of either sapphire or almond wood and bore an inscription of the **Tetragrammaton** as well as an acrostic phrase constructed from the initials for the ten plagues (Mid. Teh. 9:1; Avot 5.6; Pes. 54a). It radiated light from the divine name (Zohar I: 9a). Like Excalibur, only the rightful owner could withdraw the rod once it was planted in the ground.

Hidden away by **Elijah**, in time the staff will reappear as a **weapon** in the hands of **Hephzibah**, the mother of the **Messiah**. It then pass from her to the Messiah ben Joseph and then to the Messiah ben David, who will wield it in end-times struggles (Sefer Zerubbabel; PdRE 40; Yalkut Ps. 110 #869; Buber Tan., Yaeira 8).

Christianity developed additional magical traditions about this legendary staff, regarding it to be a relic from the **Tree of Life** and linking it closely to various biblical figures and finally to Jesus, for whom the staff served as the crossbeam of his crucifix.

Rogziel: "God is my Wrath." A **punishing angel** of **Gehenna** (Mid. Konen).

Rokeah, Sefer ha-: "Book of the Perfumer." Written by the **German Pietist** Eleazar ben Judah of Worms, it is mostly an ethical tract, but does contain some information as to the fantastic beliefs and practices of Eleazar and his contemporaries.

Rose: A symbol of **Kabbalah**, according to the **Zohar**, the "thirteen-petalled rose" is the mystical body of the people Israel, through whom God's thirteen attributes are activated in **Creation**.

Rosh ha-Shanah: "Head of the Year." The Jewish New Year. On this day, Israel performs a ritual of divine "enthronement," acknowledging God as its king, accompanied by the blasts of the **shofar**. This is also the anniversary of the creation of the world, which began on the first of Tishrei. On this day, the whole world is judged and those who merit another year of life are written in the **Book of Life**.

There are a variety of practices Jews around the world engage in during the holiday in order to ensure good fortune, such as eating certain vegetables: leeks, pumpkins, fennels, and dates. Some Jews serve the heads of **fish**, or even **goats** and calves, to ensure that the family "will be at the head and not at the tail" in the year ahead. By the same token, nuts should be avoided, because in gematria the Hebrew word for "**nut**," *egoz*, numerically equals "*chet*," sin. *SEE* NEW YEAR.

Rosh Hodesh: Prayers are said for each new moon on the Sabbath before they begin. The only exception is the month of Tishrei. Because **Rosh ha-Shanah** begins that month, and that is the time when God judges the world and determines who will live and die, it is believed that not proclaiming the beginning of the month will confuse **Satan** and the **Angel of Death**.

Ruach: "Wind/Spirit." *SEE* WIND.

Ruach Chayyim: A 16th-century tract containing actual accounts of ghostly possession and exorcisms.

Ruach Elohim: *SEE* HOLY SPIRIT.

Ruach Tumah: *SEE* UNCLEAN SPIRIT.

S

Sabbateanism: A messianic heresy of the 17th century. *SEE* SHABBATAI TZVI.

Sabbath: (*Shabbat*). The Jewish day of rest. The seventh day of the week, *Shabbat* (derived from the Hebrew verb "to rest") is declared by God to be holy, a day commemorating the six days of **Creation** (Gen. 1).

The human observance of this holiday is repeatedly mandated by the Torah. It has long been understood in Jewish tradition that the right to Sabbath rest reveals a divine aspect of humanity; we, like God, are to rest one day in seven and must extend that same privilege to the creatures dependant upon us (Ex. 20). Attentive observance of the Sabbath is even regarded to be equal to the observance of all the other commandments of the Torah (Ex. R. 25:12).

The idea of the Sabbath was one of the six things that preceded Creation, even though it was the last thing to actually be created (Shab. 10b; MdRI, be-Shallach). The universe itself is constructed around the Sabbath, for there will be six ages that precede the seventh, messianic age. The Sabbath is therefore described as a "foretaste" of messianic times (Ned. 3:9; Ex. R. 25:12; Zohar II: 88a–89a; Sha'arei Gan Eden 12c). Since customarily a day begins at sunset, the Sabbath is observed from sunset Friday to sunset on Saturday.

Besides tropes of creation and rest, there is a recurrent theme of pairing that finds many echoes in Sabbath traditions, echoing the pattern of paired creations that occurred during the six days of active creation (Bet. 15b–16a; Bahir 57). Aside from lighting a minimum of two lights, serving two challot breads and other rites involving doubles, there

is a Talmudic tradition that two guardian angels accompany each person on the Sabbath, a good one and a destructive one. If the person honors the Sabbath properly, the good angel declares "May it be so next Sabbath" and the destructive angel must respond "Amen." If the person desecrates the Sabbath, the destructive angel gets to say, "May it be so next Sabbath," and the good angel is compelled to say "Amen" (Shab. 119b). A song to greet these angels, *Shalom Aleichem*, eventually became a fixed part of Sabbath liturgy. In a similar vein, it is taught that a Jew is given a second, additional soul for the duration of the Sabbath (Bet. 15b–16a; Tan. 27b).

In Lurianic mystical tradition, the **number** twelve becomes significant, and in many Chasidic communities, twelve loaves will be provided for a Kiddush meal.

The Sabbath is often personified as the consort of the people Israel, the **Sabbath Queen** (B.K. 32b). The Sabbath is also envisioned as God's daughter, just as Israel is characterized as God's "firstborn son" (Gen. R. 11:8; PR 23:6).

Many aspects of the Sabbath are considered healing, protective and spiritually rejuvenating. The fact that the **Bible** speaks of the seventh day as *nofesh*, "refreshing," but literally "re-souling," helps emphasize the special power of the Sabbath. **Havdalah**, the ceremony marking the end of the Sabbath, in particular, is associated with rituals of **divination**, protection, and power.

The Sabbath looms so large in Jewish imagination that it even has a role in the **World-to-Come** (Mid. Teh. 73:4; Zohar II: 252a–b). Even the souls being punished in **Gehenna** enjoy Sabbath rest. Only those who were Sabbath desecrators in life do not get to participate in the Sabbath respite of Gehenna (Zohar II: 251a).

Sabbath Queen, the: Starting in **Talmud**, the day of rest becomes personified as *Shabbat ha-Malka*, the Sabbath Queen, Israel's consort, comfort, and companion (Shab. 119a; B.K. 32b). In **Midrash**, we read:

> Rabbi Simon bar Yochai said: "The Sabbath said before God:'Master of the worlds! Each day has its mate, but I have none! Why?' The Blessed Holy One answered her:'The Community of Israel is your mate.' And when Israel stood before Mount Sinai, the Blessed Holy One said to them:'Remember what I told the Sabbath:'The Community of Israel is your mate.' Therefore, remember the Sabbath day to keep it holy'" (Gen. R. 11:8, PR 23:6).

This feminine figure comes to occupy a prominent position in Judaic mythology. Kabbalists find even more profound implications in these Sabbath metaphors and practices. For them, this image of the Sabbath as a regal bride alludes to a divine process of cosmic/erotic significance. So when Jews joyously welcome the Sabbath with feasting and celebration, and subsequently have marital intercourse on Friday night, they are actually fulfilling a critical role in facilitating the *hieros gamos*, the conjoining of the masculine and feminine aspects of God, which in turn unleashes a downflow of vital energy and blessings into the lower worlds.[1] This is because the Sabbath is also identified with the **Shekhinah**, the female aspect of the Godhead and the consort of the masculine **Yesod/Holy Blessed One** (Zohar II: 88b–89a, 131b, 135a–b).

Many mystical customs observed during the day are meant to facilitate this cosmic union. Mystically minded Jews sing songs directly to her on Friday afternoon before the Queen "descends" to grace the world for twenty-four hours (Siddur). The home, like a bridal chamber, must be made worthy for her temporary presence. **Zohar** declares:

> One must prepare a comfortable seat with cushions and decorative covers, from all that is found in the house, like one who prepares a canopy for a bride. For the Sabbath is a queen and a bride. This is why the masters of the Mishnah used to go out on the eve of Sabbath to receive her on the road, and used to say: "Come, O bride, come,

O bride!" And one must sing and rejoice at the table in her honor . . . one must receive the Lady with many lighted candles, many enjoyments, beautiful clothes, and a house embellished with many fine appointments (Zohar III: 272b; also see Shabbat 119a–b; B.K. 32b).

On Friday night, Jewish mystics will also sing songs with allusions to the "**Apple Orchard**," the mystical realm where the masculine side of God and his consort Shekhinah unite. Clearly, the human coupling that happens following the Sabbath evening celebrations is the apex of this cosmic drama, and there are a number of mystical prayers and practices that can accompany coitus. (Hekhalot Rabbati 852; Zohar II: 88b, 131b, 135a–b). *SEE* SABBATH; SEX.

1. Ginsburg, *The Sabbath in Classical Kabbalah*, 106–16.

Sacrifice: (*Avodah, Korban*). The Bible describes a variety of sacrificial offers made by the Israelites on different occasions: *Olah* (Burnt, or Total), *Shlamim* (Well-being), *Chet* (Sin), *Minchah* (Meal), *Chagigah* (Festival), and *Asham* (Guilt). Human sacrifice, while honored among the other Semitic peoples of the Ancient Near East, is expressly forbidden for Israelites.

Scholars argue over the degree to which the Israelite sacrificial cult served a magical function in biblical religion. Clearly, the Israelites did not believe that their offerings sustained the God of Israel, as their neighbors believed they were doing with their gods. Some of the most notable magical elements found in neighboring cults, such as reciting incantations over sacrifices, are almost completely absent from Israelite practice.[1]

Many Israelites, however, believed that making material sacrifices in the form of meal, oil, salt, water, and especially animals, was the key to pleasing YHWH. So while there was no evidence of a theology of "dependant deity," or that there was a notion of divine-human mutual dependence, there were clearly some theurgic assumptions underlying the Israelite ideology of sacrifice. Moreover, there are in the Bible remnant indications of earlier, more clearly magical beliefs. These are preserved in Hebrew idioms and early stories about the sacrifices. Thus the Torah speaks of sacrifices as "making a pleasing odor" to God's nostrils (Gen. 8). And we have an example of a "sacred meal" being shared with the deity, alluded to in the story of Moses and the elders ascending Mount Sinai (Ex. 24).

It is also evident that ancient Israelites did not have one shared understanding of what the sacrifices represented. The writers of the Bible have very specific notions about the limited role of sacrifices in the life of God (they are an external sign of our internal desire to draw close to God, but mean little or nothing to God qua God). Still, the fact that there are prophetic complaints that their contemporaries misunderstand the meaning of their offerings reveals that many Israelites continued to see the sacrifices in more frankly magical terms than the biblical authors.

After the sacrifice cult ceased following the destruction of the Temple, the Rabbis spiritualized the concept of physical offerings to God by declaring **prayer** to be the "sacrifice of the heart." Magical traditions, by contrast, continued to use modified forms of material sacrifice. SEE ALTAR; ANIMALS; BLOOD; FIRE; INCENSE; MAGIC; SUBSTITUTION; TEMPLE.

1. Kaufmann, *The Religion of Israel*, 110–15.

Sadness: Judaism, especially **Chasidism**, teaches that melancholy, bitterness, anger and depression separate one from God and interfere with spiritual communion. SEE JOY AND HUMOR.

Safed: One of the four holy cities of Judaism, this Galilean hilltop city in Israel has long been associated with mystical movements and activities. **Simon bar Yochai** is buried nearby in Meron, as are other ancient and medieval Jewish luminaries. In the 16th and 17th centuries, Safed became the home of several mystical brotherhoods. **Moses Cordovero**, **Isaac Luria**, **Joseph Caro**, and **Chayyim Vital** were among its more famous denizens. They too, in turn, were buried in the area, and in time their graves have become the focus of pilgrimage and veneration.[1]

1. Fine, *Safed Spirituality*, 1–37; Goldish, *Spirit Possession in Judaism*, 124–58.

Sahriel: A **fallen angel** who teaches mankind lunar astronomy. (I Enoch).

Salt: Salt is essential to life and a symbol of vitality, fitness, and the sea. The most famous fantastic salt tale is that of Lot's wife being transformed after gazing at the destruction of Sodom (Gen. 20; Gen. R. 50:4, 51:5). Salt was used in the **sacrifices** of the **Temple** (Lev. 2:13). Bread and salt provide spiritual protection against the **evil eye**. Thus newborns may be rubbed with salt as a defense against **demons**. For the same reason, newlyweds will be sprinkled with salt.[1] Conversely, the Shulchan Aruch warns that handling salt with one's thumb could bring bad luck.

1. Trachtenberg, *Jewish Magic and Superstition*, 122–23, 160, 173.

Samael: This prince of **demons** and/or destructive angel has had many incarnations in Jewish literature. In several texts, "Samael" seems to be the name of the **Angel of Death**. At least once in the **Zohar**, he is declared the "shadow of death," a kind of consort to Death (I: 160b). In other texts, he is regarded as synonymous with **Satan**, but almost as often he is treated as a separate entity (BhM 1:58–61; Ex. R. 21:7). Elsewhere, Samael is called "chief of all the satans" (Deut. R. 11:10; III Enoch). In **Midrash Konen**, Samael is the prince of the third gate to **Gehenna**, the gate that opens on **Jerusalem** (2:30). One text designates him the guardian angel of Rome, the nemesis of Israel. He sits in the celestial palaces with Satan and **Dumiel** and plots the overthrow of Israel (R.H. 8a–b). When he rejoiced over God's decree that the **Ten Martyrs** should die at Roman hands, God punished him by afflicting Rome with all the diseases of Egypt.

Samael has made many earthly appearances. In Pirkei de-Rabbi Eleazer (13), he is described as the greatest angel in heaven, who out of jealousy over the creation of humanity, decided to tempt **Eve**. Appearing in the form of the **serpent**, he actually copulated with her (Targum Jonathan, Gen. 4:1; Zohar I: 37a). He is one candidate that the tradition has identified to be the angel who wrestled with Jacob (Zohar, I: 148a–b). Satanlike, he accused Israel of idol worship while they dwelt in Egyptian slavery (Ex. R. 21:7). He attempted to claim the soul of **Moses**, who fended him off with his miraculous **rod**. In The **Treatise of the Left Emanation**, Samael is the animus of Adam; the **evil** doppelganger of the first man that came into being with the first human transgression.

The Zohar has the most extensive, if sometimes confusing, description of Samael. The Zohar builds upon the image of Samael found in the Treatise on the Left Emanation: he is the demon king and consort of **Lilith**; together they are the evil counterparts of Adam and Eve. He is the tempting angel from whom the **Evil Inclination** emanates. When he copulates with Lilith, the male and female principles of the "left side emanation" are united and achieve their full potential and demon souls are spawned, so he is in effect the evil left-side counterpart of **Tiferet** in the sefirotic system.

In later Chasidic thought, Samael is the organizing force of the **kelipot**, the garments of evil that enshroud the divine sparks contained in all things. *SEE* DEMONS.

Sambatyon, the River: A mythic river in the East, beyond which the ten tribes of the northern kingdom of Israel were taken by God to protect them from their Assyrian captors.

The Sambatyon is no ordinary **river**. Various legends describe it as wide as a sea or flowing with all kinds of fantastic hazards: rolling boulders and flowing **fire** and/or a **Cloud of Glory**. The river ceases to flow on the **Sabbath** in honor of the divine command to rest that day. There are tales of individual adventurers who have reached the lost tribes by crossing at that time, but the Sabbath-observant Israelites will not cross back. The **ten lost tribes** will dwell there on the far side of the river until the coming of the **Messiah** and the ingathering of all Jewish exiles (War 7:5; Sanh. 65b; Gen. R. 11:5, 73:6).

Samech: The fifteenth letter of the **Hebrew alphabet**. It has the vocalic value of "s" and the numeric value of 60. It is an enclosed loop in shape, signifying the feminine, enclosure, secrecy, protection, and support.[1]

    1. Munk, *The Wisdom of the Hebrew Alphabet*, 159–70.

Samech Mem: A euphemism for **Samael**, used to avoid saying his name and thereby attracting his attention.

Samkhiel: "God is my Support." A destructive angel in charge of the **beinonim**, the "morally divided" souls sent to **Gehenna**. He oversees their **purification** from sin through fiery torments, and then their eventual return to God. (III Enoch; BhM 5:186).

Samriel: According to the **Zohar**, he is a fearsome **angel** who serves as guardian of the gates of **Gehenna** (I: 62b).

Samson: This biblical hero, a *shofet* (judge/chieftain) of ancient Israel, he is remembered for his remarkable strength. As a redeemer of Israel, his **birth** was heralded to his mother and father by an **angel** (Judg. 13). He was dedicated to God from birth, and lived his entire life as a **nazirite**. God blessed him with extraordinary physical strength, which he demonstrated in a series of amazing feats.

Nevertheless he was easily distracted from his dedication to God's purpose. This made him vulnerable to the schemes of his enemies, the Philistines. Eventually he was shorn of his long hair, which the Philistines believed was the source of his power, after which he was blinded and enslaved. Both his faith in God and his hair grew during his servitude, and he eventually was able to ambush the Philistines while in their temple, bringing the building down upon everyone inside, including himself (Judg. 13–17).

Given the already fantastic nature of the biblical account, there is surprisingly little additional rabbinic material about him and his adventures.

Samuel: Biblical prophet, seer, and judge. Dedicated to be a lifelong **nazirite** by his mother, Samuel first heard the voice of God as a child. He heard God calling him as he slept in the **Tabernacle** compound, suggesting he had an **incubation** revelation. From that time on, he regularly communed with God. Most memorably, God commissioned him to anoint kings over Israel—first Saul, and later, David. After his death, his **ghost** was summoned from the grave for a séance with his former protégé, King Saul (I and II Samuel). *SEE* PROPHECY.

Samuel ben Isaac: Talmudic Sage and angelologist (ca. 3rd century). It is Samuel who taught that ministering angels are temporary creations that emerge every day from the Nahal Dinur, the heavenly **River of Light**, to sing God's praises and then vanish (Chag. 14a). He also taught that angels oversee all aspects of both life and death (Gen. R. 9:10). According to the Talmud, when Samuel passed away, heaven acknowledged his death with a miraculous sign: uprooting all the cedar trees in Israel (M.K. 25b; J. A. Z. 3:1).

Samuel ben Kalonymus he-Chasid: Mystic and theurgist (German, ca. 13th century). A member of the circle of **German Pietists**, Samuel was able to use the divine names to achieve all kinds of wonders: **healing** illness, illuminating a darkened room, and **summoning** and controlling animals. There is one story of Rabbi Samuel fighting a magical duel with a gentile sorcerer (Ma'aseh Buch).

Sandalfon: A princely **angel**. Sandalfon is an **ofan**, a flaming cosmic-sized wheel-shaped angel that stretches from heaven to earth ("five hundred years' journey" taller than any other angel, according to Beit ha-Midrash 1:58–61). He is the wheel **Ezekiel** described seeing on God's **chariot** (Ezek. 1:15). He stands behind the **Throne of Glory** and every day he weaves a crown for God from the prayers of Israel (Chag. 13a–b). Some mystical sources claim Sandalfon is the angelic name of **Elijah** and that he is the *psychopomp*, the gatekeeper of heaven. Other sources identify him as the angelic ruler of **Asiyah**, the World of Action (PR 20:4; Mid. Teh. 19:7).

Sanegor: "Advocate." An **angel** or one of the ancestral dead (such as Abraham) who argues against **Satan** when the Adversary criticizes Israel in the heavenly court (Meam Lo'az). *SEE* ANCESTORS; RIGHTEOUS, THE.

Sanoi, Sansanoi, and Samnaglof: Three guardian angels frequently invoked on amulets. They are the nemesis of **Lilith** and have the authority to turn her away (AbbS).

Santriel: A **punishing angel** who has authority over the souls of Sabbath desecrators (Zohar II: 25a).

Sar, Sarim: "Chieftain/Prince," "Archon." Sometimes used to refer to a class of angels, such as the *Sarei ha-Panim*, "the Angels of the Countenance," at other times it is a synonym for angels in general. Thus in **Midrash Konen**, it is written, "There is not a single [blade of] grass or tree that does not have its sar who . . . makes it grow."

Sar ha-Chalom: "Prince of Dream." An angel of revelation specializing in dream visions. *SEE* DREAM; INCUBATION; MAGGID.

Sar ha-Cos and Sar ha-Bohen: "Prince of the Cup" and "Prince of the Thumb." Angels of **divination** that, when summoned, make images appear in reflections on water and on fingernails. Later in the Middle Ages, Jewish tradition starts speaking of "Demons of the Cup and of the Thumb." Evidently, this change is the result of a simple spelling mistake in transmission (*Sar*, "Prince/Angel," ends in a *resh*, which closely resembles a *dalet*. *Shin-Dalet* spells *Sheid*—an imp or **demon**. It is an object lesson in the importance of good penmanship).[1] *SEE* FINGER; HAVDALAH; HYDROMANCY; WATER.

1. Dan, "Samael, Lilith, and the Concept of Evil in Early Kabbalah," in *AJS Review*, vol. 5, 1980, 17–40.

Sar ha-Panim: "Prince of the [Divine] Presence." This angel of revelation is often identified with **Yofiel**, or **Metatron**. He is also associated with the **Sar ha-Torah**, and the titles may in fact be synonymous. Some texts treat Sar ha-Panim as a class of angels.[1] There are several related texts known to modern scholars, such as **Hechalot Rabbati**, manuscripts such as **Merkavah Rabbah**, and a **Cairo Geniza** fragment, that describe the **summoning** rituals for this angel in detail.[2] *SEE* MAGGID.

1. Lesses, *Ritual Practices to Gain Power*, 221.
2. Schafer, *Synopse Zur Hekhalot Lituratur*, 563, 566.

Sar ha-Torah: "Prince of the Torah." An angel of revelation associated with the memorization and recall of Torah and Jewish teachings. From late antiquity, there are Jewish mystical traditions of an angel who could be summoned to help the student of Torah master the text and grant oracular and apocalyptic visions.[1] Sometimes the Sar is identified as **Metatron** or **Yefafiah**. One **Hechalot** text describes the angel as enshrouded "in flames of fire, his face the appearance of lightning." *SEE* GALITZUR; MAGGID; MEDIUM; SUMMONING.

1. Dan, *The Early Jewish Mysticism*, 139–68.

Sar Tzevaot: "Prince of Hosts." The warrior angel that appeared to Joshua outside of Jericho, providing the Israelite leader with the ritual of **circles** and **shofar** blasts that eventually toppled the city walls (Josh. 5:13–6:5). In some rabbinic traditions, the Sar Tzevaot is identified as **Michael**. In one tradition, he is said to be **Metatron**. *SEE* MALACH ADONAI.

Sarah: "Princess." Matriarch and wife of Abraham. The Rabbis regarded her to have been a greater prophet than her husband (Ex. R. 1:1; Meg. 14a). A **cloud** of **Glory** hovered over her tent (Gen. R. 60:16). She was the most beautiful woman of her age (and at her age); she was as radiant as the sun (Tanh., Lech Lecha 5; Gen. R. 40:5). Miraculously, she gave birth to Isaac in her nineties. When Isaac was born, the milk in Sarah's breasts was so bountiful she was able to nurse all the infants, numbering in the hundreds, at Isaac's birth feast. (Baba Metzia; PR 43:4). Sarah died in anguish after Satan revealed that Abraham had gone to sacrifice Isaac without telling her that her son would be spared (Tanh. Va-year 23).

Sariel: "Chieftain of God." This **angel** is mentioned only in passing in I Enoch, but in **Kabbalah**, he is the prince of the demons of the air and he serves **Lilith**.

Sartan: "Crab"/Cancer. The **zodiac** sign for the month of Tammuz. It is a sign of weakness and vulnerability. Indicative of this is the fact that Tammuz has no festivals or holidays. Rather, it is a month of ill fortune, with a number of Jewish tragedies (the **Golden Calf** incident, the besieging of **Jerusalem** by the Babylonians) occurring within this sign.[1]

1. Erlanger, *Signs of the Times*, 73–83.

Satan, ha-Satan: "Adversary/Accuser." The angel of temptation and sin. From his first appearance in the book of Job (chapter 1) as one of the *B'nai Elohim*, the "Sons of God," he has been the most provocative and intriguing angel in Jewish mythology. Satan has been understood and represented in many diverse ways in Jewish literature.

Unlike in Christian mythology, where Satan is often regarded as a kind of "anti-God," leading the forces of rebellious angels/demons against God's rule, in Jewish tradition Satan is totally subservient to God. In Jewish myth, he functions as God's "prosecuting attorney," indicting sinners before God and demanding their punishment. As the angel of temptation, he is also conducting perpetual "sting operations" against mortals, setting them up in situations meant to lead them into transgression. But at no point in normative Jewish literature is there any indication that Satan can act contrary to the will of God (B.B. 16a; Zohar I: 10b).

That being said, the identity and nature of Satan is quite variable at different times and in different texts. In some sources, Satan is identified as Samael, or as the **Angel of Death** (B.B. 16a), but at other times they are regarded as separate entities (Sefer Hechalot). "Satan" is sometimes understood to be a proper name, but at other times it is simply an epitaph: *ha-Satan*, "the adversary." Several Sages even speak in the plural of *satanim*, as if "adversaries" were a class of destructive angels, rather than a named personality. This reflects a confusion arising from the **Bible** itself, which at times treats him as a distinctive personality (Job 1), but at other points uses the word *satan* as if referring to an anonymous entity or impersonal force (Zech. 3; Num. 24).

In **Talmud** and **Midrash**, Satan is portrayed as particularly preoccupied with the sins of Israel. He appears in many guises, intent on luring the upright from the straight and narrow. There are famous episodes of Satan tormenting **Noah**, **Abraham**, **Sarah**, **Joseph**, **Moses**, and other ancient worthies. He introduces Noah to wine, creating endless mischief to this day (Tanh. Noah 13). He is responsible for provoking the **Golden Calf** incident (Shab. 89a). He can also place humans in mortal danger, as he did when he lured David into a confrontation with **Ishbi-benob**, the brother of Goliath (Sanh. 45a).

According to Sefer Hechalot, Satan sits in consultation with **Samael** and **Dumiel**, compiling a ledger of Israel's sins. God in his gracious love, however, sends fiery **serafim** every day to receive those records, only with the result that they are burned to a crisp (8a–b).

Satan makes frequent appearances in medieval writings. At times he seems to approach the status of being an autonomous force of evil, but such readings are ambiguous at best. Much more common are the portrayals meant to make logical sense of Satan's role in a monotheistic worldview. SEE DEMONS; EVIL; FALLEN ANGELS.

Satyr: SEE GOATS.

Saul: The first king of Israel. At first favored by God and anointed by the prophet Samuel, he was filled with a prophetic spirit. When he disobeyed God, however, an evil spirit settled upon him and only the music of **David**, the man ordained to replace him, could give him temporary relief. Cut off from God, in desperation he engaged a necromancer to arrange a séance with the dead, only to be confronted by the dead spirit of the prophet Samuel and to be informed of his own doom (I Sam. 9–II Sam. 4).

Not many fantastic tales of Saul appear in subsequent rabbinic literature, which mostly devotes itself to better understanding the nature of Saul's fall from grace. *SEE* NECROMANCY; SPIRITUAL POSSESSION.

Scapegoat: *SEE* AZAZEL; GOAT; YOM KIPPUR.

Scarlet Cord: In the **Temple**, a scarlet strap hung by the sanctuary. At the conclusion of each **Yom Kippur**, it would miraculously turn white, signaling that God had forgiven Israel its sins (Yoma 39a).

Schneerson, Menachem Mendel: Chasidic master and failed **messiah** (American, 1902–1994). The charismatic seventh rebbe of the Lubavitch movement, Menachem Mendel was born in eastern Europe, studied engineering in France, but became a Chasidic leader after relocating to America. He was credited with many miraculous healings. Some of his Chasids even claim he revealed auguries to the Israeli army that helped turn the tide in the 1973 war. In the 1990s, his Chasids started to publicize their belief that he was the Messiah, a claim he himself never made but never refuted. In 1994, he died.[1] By all indications, he is still dead. *SEE* CHABAD; CHASIDISM.

1. See Berger, *The Rebbe, the Messiah, and the Scandal of Orthodox Indifference*.

Scrolls: *SEE* SEFER.

Sea: (*Yam*). According to Hebrew myth, the land mass of the world is entirely surrounded by sea. There are upper and lower waters with a primordial ocean of the abyss below them both (Mid. Konen 2:32–33). Prior to Creation, waters covered the universe (Gen. 1:1; Gen. R. 13:6; PR 48:2).

The ocean contains primordial monsters, like **Leviathan** and **Rahav**. Rabba bar Chana tells tales of the many fantastic denizens the sea contains, as well as many the many treasures that will eventually serve as rewards for the righteous (B.B. 74a–b). *SEE* ABYSS; WATER.

Sea of Glass/Marble: Human visitors to heaven describe a mysterious supernal watery substance spread out before the **Throne of Glory**. This substance is a threat to those who would draw closer to God, so it is important not to gaze upon it, lest it destroy the mind of the viewer (III Enoch). *SEE* ASCENT, HEAVENLY; HECHALOT LITERATURE; YORED MERKAVAH.

Sea Goat: A mythical horned **fish**, three hundred parasangs in length (B.B. 74a). *SEE* ANIMALS.

Sea, Prince of the: (*Sar Yam*). *SEE* PRINCE OF THE SEA.

Seal of Solomon: In the ancient **Testament of Solomon**, the seal was identified as a pentagram. In medieval alchemical texts, this was the name given to the **hexagram**. Later it was the hexagram that became known as the **Magen David**, the "shield of David." This term also refers to Solomon's magic **ring**. *SEE* SEAL, MAGICAL.

Seal, Magical: (*Chatimah; Taba'at*). In different Hebrew texts, seals refer to different phenomena. In some, they indicate an object, usually an **amulet** or **ring**, inscribed with the names of **angels** or God (III Enoch; Ma'aseh Merkavah). In others, it seems to be a temporary tattoolike inscription written on parts of the body, probably contained in a magic **circle** or **magic square** (M. Makk. 3:6; Tosefta Makk. 4:15; M. Yoma 8:3). In either case, the seal is used as a kind of "key" or, more aptly, an "access code" for a mystical ascent or a **summoning** ritual.

Just like the tattoo variety, the metallic, parchment, or paper seals are apparently placed on the body, either as rings or pendants, for protection and for gaining authority over angels. One text indicates that the adept simply holds the seals in his hands during the ritual. **Sefer Raziel** details various seals that have magical power, including the "seal of heaven and earth." One such seal is diagrammed in the book, though the illustration doesn't specify precisely what this particular seal is to be used for.

The most famous magical seal in Jewish occult tradition is the **Seal of Solomon**, a brass and iron ring inscribed with a **pentagram** (Testament of Solomon) and the **Tetragrammaton** (Git. 68a), given to Solomon by

Michael, that gave the king the power to communicate with **animals** and to summon and control demons. Rabbinic tradition also interprets **circumcision** as a kind of protective seal (Tosefta Ber. 6:24; Shab. 137b). *SEE* ASCENT, HEAVENLY; MA'ASEI-MERKAVAH.

Seasons: (*Tekufaot*). Each season has its own principal **angel**. According to Jewish **astrology**, the period marking the transition from one season to another is a liminal time when the new angel may not yet be in place, the stars lack governance, and malevolent forces are in ascendance. **Amulets** can counter these effects. *SEE* CALENDAR; ZODIAC.

Seclusion: (*Hitbodedut*). Usually this refers to physical isolation from others. According to Chasidic teachings, it is part of a contemplative method to achieve **devekut**. *SEE* MEDITATION.

Second Day of Creation: The only one of the six days of **Creation** that God does not affirm as "good," it is considered a bad luck day. One tradition teaches **Gehenna** was created on that day, which is why God refused to bless it (Gen. R. 4:6, 11:9).

Secret: (*Sod; Nitrah; Middah*; Aramaic: *Raza*). "The secret things belong to the Eternal our God: but those things that are revealed belong to us and to our children forever, that we may do all the words of this Torah forever" (Deut. 29:29). With regard to occult knowledge, a "secret" has meant different things to different Jewish communities.

In the Hechalot texts, *Middah*, the great "Mystery," is the knowledge of how to use divine names for theurgic purposes.[1] The **German Pietists** taught about *Sod ha-Tefillah* and *Sod ha-Torah*—the concealed truths within prayers and Scriptures. According to **Sefer Raziel**, there are three categories of secret knowledge: secrets of Creation, secrets of the chariot, and the secrets of the commandments. The medieval philosophers speak of how all Jewish teachings can be compared to "golden **apples** [concealed] in silver filigree," that while all Torah is precious, there are more valuable teachings hidden within that most people can only glimpse beneath the surface.

About the only thing that all agree on is that Judaism has (at least) two dimensions of spiritual teachings that co-exist together, the exoteric (the commonly revealed) and the esoteric (the concealed).

1. Schafer, *The Hidden and Manifest God*, 110–17.

Seder: *SEE* PASSOVER.

Seder Eliyahu (or Tanna de Eliyahu): A potpourri of fables, stories, and teachings, loosely strung together by periodic appearances of **Elijah**.

Seder Gan Eden: "The Order of Paradise." A medieval text describing the realm of the afterlife. *SEE* EDEN.

Seder Olam: A medieval chronology of the world, including many miraculous and fantastic elements from Jewish tradition.

Seder Rabbah de Bereshit (also known as Baraita de Ma'aseh Bereshit): A text devoted to the secrets of Creation. *SEE* CREATION; MA'ASEI BERESHIT; SEFER YETZIRAH.

Sefer: "Scroll/Book." The Hebrew word *Sefer* technically refers to a "scroll," a document made up of many pages sewn end-to-end and then rolled up. After the invention of the *codex*, in which pages are all bound together along one edge, the term comes to mean "book" in the most generic sense.

Jews continue to use the older technology of the scroll for **ritual** purposes: Scriptures, especially the **Torah**, continue to be preserved in hand-written scrolls to this day. Such scrolls are used mostly for liturgical reading.

Because of their unusual nature and the sanctity surrounding them, *sifrim* (pl.) can be used from time-to-time for theurgic purposes as well. It is customary, for example, to recite petitionary prayers for the sick while a Torah scroll is open and being read, based on the belief that God will look more favorably on a supplication offered while one is engaged in a meritorious activity. Sefer Torahs have also been used in **exorcisms** and in rituals to ease a difficult childbirth.[1] In the latter case, the Torah scroll is unbound in the presence of the travailing woman, in the expectation that there will be a sympathetic "unbinding" of her womb.

1. Klein, *A Time to Be Born*, 114, 148.

Sefer XXXX: All books in this encyclopedia will be listed under their unique titles. Thus "Sefer Yuhasin" will be found under **Yuhasin, Sefer**.

Sefirot: "Numbers." The sefirot are the ten archetypal attributes or structures of the Godhead manifest in the universe (SY 1:4–6). They are the "ten crowns" of God (Zohar III: 70a). The doctrine of the ten sefirot is the single most distinctive aspect of Jewish mystical speculation and forms the very heart of all Kabbalistic theosophy.[1]

The idea of ten archetypal forces of Creation is first alluded to in the **Midrash**:

R. Zutra bar Tobiah said in the name of Rav: "The world was created by means of ten capacities and powers: by wisdom, by understanding, by reason, by strength, by rebuke, by might, by righteousness, by judgment, by love, and by compassion" (Gen. R. 1).

The term *sefirot* first appears in **Sefer Yetzirah**. A more detailed account is found in the **Sefer Bahir**. As Kabbalah developed, additional meanings have been revealed and increasingly complex designations added to each sefirah, with each later development incorporating the earlier ones.

To understand the sefirot, it is first important to understand that a distinction is made in **Kabbalah** between the **Ein Sof**, the infinite and unknowable God, and the knowable qualities of God, as represented by the sefirot. These ten knowable attributes of God can be "mapped," and conventionally they are graphically arranged as a structure of interconnected networks, a kind of "flow chart," as we would say today. The ten sefirot—**Keter, Chochmah, Binah, Gevurah, Chesed, Tiferet, Hod, Netzach, Yesod,** and **Malchut**—are connected by twenty-two "pathways" that go both down and across the pattern. The sefirot are configured graphically so that they form "left," "right," and "center" groupings, corresponding to the "feminine," "masculine," and "harmonizing" principles within God. They also can be seen as three hierarchical triads terminating in Ein Sof at the "upper" end and the material universe at the "lower" end. The sefirot are often equated with spatial (e.g.,

"palaces"), temporal (e.g., "days"), and personalistic (e.g., "Jacob") phenomena, though in fact they transcend all time, space, and material entities. This two-dimensional stylized map of the divine attributes is, of course, simply a kind of graphic/spatial metaphor for an extra-dimensional reality. The sefirot *en toto* is a complex and rich image; it is simultaneously a map, a flow chart, a mandala, and a **labyrinth**.

Proper understanding of the sefirot and their relationship to each other not only allows the adept to understand the divine order, but also to influence divine actions through theurgic acts (Pardes Rimmonim 10:1; Cheshek Shlomo, p. 145). The wise adept can, for example, apply the workings of the sefirot to any situation and, by introducing the appropriate complimentary sefirah quality into that situation, positively influence the outcome.[2] Kabbalists often applied the model of the sefirot to biblical narratives and practices to better understand the underlying divine dynamics present in the text.[3]

Not only have the sefirot undergone multiple varied interpretations, the schema of sefirot also exists alongside several other models of divine **emanation**, most notably the concept of the **four worlds of emanation** and the Lurianic models of **Partzufim** ("[Divine] Countenances"). Later Kabbalists synthesize and harmonize these models.

There are a few examples of the sefirot being illustrated in configurations different from the familiar "tree of life" pattern. These include concentric circles and labyrinths formed from nesting the first letters of each sefirah, one inside the next. (*SEE APPENDIX FIGURES 2 AND 3.*)

1. Holtz, *Back to the Sources*, 318–27.
2. Idel, *Hasidism*, 66. Also see Twersky and Septimus, *Jewish Thought in the Seventeenth Century*, 369.
3. Green, *Guide to the Zohar*, 28–59; Scholem, *On the Mystical Shape of the Godhead*, 39–46.

Segullah, Segullot: "[Concealed] Treasure." A medical remedy; a charm, folk remedy, or potion, often made of herbal/homeopathic ingredients. The Hebrew word itself has the connotation of something with a hidden or occult benefit. The practice of using segullot is most closely linked to the healing figure of the **Baal Shem** and with **Chasidism**.

A complex example of a Chasidic segullah would be one intended to overcome infertility. It might involve multiple elements: a combination of incantation prayer (usually from the Psalms), intercessory prayer, propitious times for copulation, dietary changes (fish and garlic are held to enhance both semen and ardor), "psychological" advice to improve harmony between the couple, and a suitable amulet.[1] Examples of a segullah amulet could include an object handled by a **rebbe**, a written note (containing the segullah instructions), an **etrog** left over from **Sukkot**, or oil used for **Chanukah** celebrations.

  1. Zimmels, *Magicians, Theologians, and Doctors*, 136, 147.

Segullot, Sefer: "Treasure/Charm book." A general term for any manual of practical Kabbalah emphasizing methods of magical healing, divination, and/or amulet making. The term is usually applied to works composed from the 17th century onward.[1]

  1. Elkes, *The BeSHT: Magician, Mystic, and Leader*, 5, 25–33.

Se'ir: A satyr or goat **demon** mentioned in the **Torah** (Lev. 17:7; Isa. 13:21) that lurks in the wilderness and in ruins.

Semen: (*Zera; mayyim; onah*). With few exceptions, the Bible and rabbinic literature gives little attention to the mechanical particulars of procreation. An emphasis on various forms of "erotic theology," however, is a prominent feature of mystical systems, both Eastern (Tantric Hinduism; Taoism) and Western (Bernard of Clairvaux; John of the Cross). This can be seen in Judaism by how its mystics regard the processes of human union and procreation as reflections of the divine processes that unfold within the **Godhead**.[1] Thus, when they speak of the upper and lower "waters" that must unite in order to energize and sustain the universe, the mystics are euphemistically describing the constant spiritual "insemination" that occurs between the masculine and feminine aspects of God, the *yichud Kedusha Baruch Hu u'Shekhinto*, "union between the Holy Blessed One and His Shekhinah" (Bahir 51, 86; Zohar I:17b–18a; Sefer ha-Hezyonot, 212–17).[2]

Jewish mystical practice allows the mystic to participate in this process in various ways. Some Kabbalists teach that through engaging in licit intercourse here on earth, we theurgically stimulate the analogous divine process on high. Others see themselves as a receptacle impregnated by divine light (or the Active Intellect), giving birth to new spiritual insight.[3]

In the medieval mystical-sexual manual, **Iggeret ha-Kodesh**, the sexual union of a man and woman is "in the likeness of heaven and earth." Human semen is envisioned as the vehicle through which divine energy is transferred into new life, creating a permanent umbilicus between the individual and the higher realms through which the divine light continuously flows. *SEE* MARRIAGE; NOCTURNAL EMISSIONS; PHALLUS; SEX; ZIVVUGA KADDISHA.

  1. Idel, "Sexual Metaphors and Praxis in Kabbalah," 207, 210.
  2. Schwartz, *Tree of Souls*, 104–5.
  3. Idel, *The Mystical Experience in Abraham Abulafia*, 190–203.

Serach bat Asher: This daughter (or step-daughter) of the biblical **Patriarch** Asher lived through the entire four hundred years of enslavement in Egypt, from the time of Joseph until the generation of the Exodus, and beyond; she is a sort of personification of Jewish memory (Gen. 46:17; Num. 26:46; Ex. R. 5:13; Num. R. 20:19).

A master of the harp, she revealed to **Jacob** that his son **Joseph** was still alive through song to soften the shock (Mid. Avot; Sefer Yashar). She was a prophetess who foretold the major events of the **Exodus**, from the coming of **Moses** to the location of Joseph's bones (Sot. 13a; PdRK II: 12; Num. R. 5:13; PR 17:5; PdRE 48; MdRI, Beshallah 1). She is mentioned again as the "wise woman" who protects the town of Avel in the time of King **David** (II Sam. 20; Eccl. R. 7:11; Mid. Sam. 32; Gen. R. 94:9).

She is one of the select few, along with **Elijah** and **Enoch**, who was translated to heaven without dying, because Jacob blessed her with eternal life for informing him that Joseph was alive (Targum Yonatan, Vayigash; Me'am Loez, Yalkut 2:267). There she governs one of the heavenly palaces (Zohar III: 167b). Like Elijah, she continues to make earthly visitations (PdRK 11:12). A tradition among Persian Jews holds that Serach lived until the 12th century CE, but finally did die. Her tomb there is a pilgrimage destination.

Seraf, Serafim: (*Saraf, Serafim*, "Fiery Ones"). A class of angels first described in the apocalypse experienced by Isaiah in the Temple (Isa. 6). There are four serafim, corresponding to the four winds. The appearance of the seraf is truly awesome. It has six wings, sixteen faces, and is the height of all **seven heavens** combined. Serafim are born anew each day, rising from the **river of light** that flows from under the **Throne of Glory** (Sefer Hechalot).

Serpent: (*Nachash*). The serpent, or snake, is a symbol of cunning, **evil**, and **healing**. There are a number of mythic serpents in Jewish tradition: the creature that tempts Eve and the cosmic monsters, **Leviathan**, **Rahav**, and **Tanin'iver**. Often destructive angels, like **Samael** and **Satan**, will appear on earth in the guise of a serpent or **dragon** (Zohar; Emek ha-Melekh, 84b–84c).

The most famous such incident is the serpent in the Garden of **Eden**. In one **aggadah**, **Samael** takes the form of the serpent and as such he physically seduced **Eve**, impregnating her with demonic seed. This accounts for **Cain** and the generations of increasingly degenerate people leading up to the **Flood**. In the **Zohar**, the serpent is a mythic representation of false gnosis, of misapprehension of the Godhead (I: 83a). Interestingly, Zohar also gives one of the few positive images of a serpent found in Jewish tradition by teaching that there are two cosmic serpents, the "serpent of the death of the world" and "the serpent of life" that accompanies each person (Zohar I: 52a; Tikkunei Zohar 43a). Seeing a serpent in a **dream** is a good **omen**.

Earthly, yet still numinous, serpents appear in the **Bible**: Moses uses snakes in his preliminary bout with the sorcerers of **Egypt**. By way of explaining the mysterious incident of the spiritual attack on **Moses** as he traveled to Egypt (Ex. 4:20–26), a rabbinic tradition explains that Satan in the shape of a serpent attacked Moses in order to prevent him from fulfilling his mission. The serpent swallowed him from his head to his penis, but could not swallow "the sign of the covenant." Seeing this, his wife **Zipporah** immediately circumcised their son and cast the blood and foreskin on the serpent. Like a vampire splattered by holy water, Satan immediately spit Moses out and retreated (B. Ned. 32a; BhM 1:43).

Equally cryptic is the incident in the book of Numbers where the people find themselves being bitten by fiery snakes. To combat this, God commands Moses to make a bronze image of a serpent. Whoever gazes on it is healed. This image, known as **Nehushtan**, was part of the **Temple** furnishings until King Hezekiah destroyed it. In an oft-repeated rabbinic wonder-story about **Chanina ben Dosa**, we learn that the righteous who study Torah are both oblivious to and invulnerable to the deadliest of snakes.

Poisonous snakes, the **aggadah** assures us, can be used by heaven as punishing emissaries. In one story, Rabbi Eleazer stops and turns away a snake that was on its way to bite a Jew who had since repented (Zohar Chadash 107a–108a). The snake went off and slew a gentile thief instead.

In the Middle Ages, the starry belt of the Milky Way became known as **Teli**, the heavenly Dragon, because of its serpentine appearance.

Seudah Sh'lishit: "Third Meal." Mystical tradition elevates the third meal of the Sabbath (Shab. 118a), the one eaten before the end of the day, to a special moment. It is a liminal time, often compared to the moment of death, when God and humanity are particularly close. Some teach that the additional soul given to each Jew on the Sabbath now departs again for the higher realms. It is therefore an opportune time for **devekut**, cleaving to God. Extending the length of the meal helps those souls already suffering in **Gehenna** and gains future forgiveness in the **World-to-Come** for the living participant. Keenly observed in **Chasidism**, the meal entails Torah discourses, food, and ecstatic song and dancing. SEE HAVDALAH; MELAVEH MALCHAH.

Seven: SEE NUMBERS.

Seven Heavens: SEE HEAVEN.

Seven Primordial Things: According to Talmud Pesachim 54a, seven things were created prior to the world: the **Torah**, Repentance, the Garden of **Eden**, **Gehenna**, the **Throne of Glory**, the **Temple**, and the name of the **Messiah**. SEE CREATION.

Seven Qualities: Seven reified qualities stand in attendance around God's **Throne of Glory**: Faithfulness, Righteousness, Justice, Love, Compassion, Truth, and Peace (Vilna Gaon commentary on AdRN 37). SEE SEFIROT.

Seven Species: There are seven species of **food** mentioned in the **Bible** (Deut. 8:8) specifically symbolizing the fruitfulness of the Land of Israel: wheat, barley, olives, grapes, pomegranates, dates, and figs. A **meonen** can use them in creating illusions. Today, traditional Jews will display these fruits or their products in the sukkah and then, having soaked up the holy energy of the holiday, will use them in the following months to bring blessing and good luck (Zohar I: 157b).

Seventy Faces of Torah: Every verse of Torah has seventy legitimate interpretations (Num. R. 13:16).

Seventy Names of God: The Midrash claims there are seventy names for God in the Bible (Num. R. 14:12). The complete list appears in Midrash ha-Gadol, Gen. 46:8. *SEE* NAMES OF GOD.

Seventy Nations: *SEE* NATIONS.

Seventy Princes: Each nation has its own princely **angel** to be its advocate on high (Gen. R. 56; Ex. R. 21; Lev. R. 29). *SEE* NATIONS.

Seventy-Two: A magical number of power found in **Sefer Raziel**. The seventy-two-word name of God is one of particular power. *SEE* NAMES OF GOD; NUMBERS.

Sex: (*Shimush; Min; Be'ah; Be'elah; Zuug*). Judaism endorses the central role of sex in human life. The first commandment God gives to humanity is "be fruitful and multiply." The **Talmud** views properly disciplined sex (within marriage, with due consideration to modesty) in a very positive light. It is, in fact, a sacred obligation, even if done for pleasure rather than procreation (Shev. 18b; Yev. 63b).

Because of the centrality of sexuality to the human experience, esoteric practices and fantastic beliefs about sex often do appear in Jewish tradition, and can be divided into three areas: extreme practices in human sexuality, sexuality as a theurgic practice, and mystic-sexual mythology.

With regards to the first category, Jewish sectarian groups are often distinguished from more normative Judaism by their more restrictive or negative view of sex. Thus, both the **Damascus Document** and the **Temple Scroll**, found among the **Dead Sea Scrolls**, include prohibitions against having sex anywhere in Jerusalem, for such unclean behavior undermines the holiness of the **Temple**. The Qumran sect may also have required celibacy among its higher circles of initiates. Likewise, the early Jesus-sect espoused a more negative view of marriage and human sexu-

ality in general (I Cor. 7:9; Matt. 19:10–12) than did rabbinic Judaism, which advocated that one should sanctify oneself through everything that is permitted.

With regards to theurgic practice, in Merkavah mysticism issues of purity in performing certain mystical-magical rites require that the adept refrain from sex for a period prior to performing such a **ritual**. Early **Kabbalah**, by contrast, actually promoted sex as its own spiritual discipline. Thus, according to **Iggeret ha-Kodesh**, a mystical-magical sex manual purportedly written by **Nachmanides**, sexual intercourse between a husband and wife can be used as a vehicle for mystical ascent. What is more, with the proper **kavanah**, divine light can be drawn down into the semen released in coitus, imbuing it with the power to produce righteous and beautiful children. The Zohar makes sacred sexuality a central theme of its teaching, but as part of that also views sexual transgression as a cosmic affront (Zohar I: 55a, 57a; II: 89a–89b, 231b; III: 76b).

The Safed mystics, especially **Isaac Luria**, expounded a more disengaged, somewhat joyless attitude toward sex, a point of view that undermined the more positive attitudes of earlier sages. **Chasidism** somewhat reversed that trend, though Safed-tainted puritanical attitudes still find expression in some Orthodox sects.[1]

Most startling and shocking to contemporary Jews, steeped as we are in modernity and rationalist Jewish philosophy, is Kabbalah's mystic-sexual mythology; much of Kabbalah revels in ideas of the "sexual life" of God. Regarding human sexuality to be part and parcel of the "image of God," the Zohar divides the sefirot into male and female forces, and regards ensuring successful *hieros gamos*, the proper universe-sustaining union of these divine forces, as a major human task. This internal process within the Godhead is often described in the most explicit terms, with semen, vaginal lubrication, and other sexual phenomena serving as vivid metaphors for the spiritual dynamics going on on high.[2]

By linking conjugal desire and passion to the divine realms, Kabbalah also interprets the mystical experience of **devekut** as a kind of mystico-sexual event. The **righteous** individual seeks unification with God, "arousing" a response from the Holy One in the form of an "emission" of divine effluence with its beneficent vitality that the meritorious mortal (the "female" receptacle) can then use (Degel Machaneh Efraim 168). SEE PHALLUS; SEFIROT; SHEKHINAH; SONG OF SONGS; ZIVVUGA KADISHA; ZOHAR.

1. Fine, *Physician of the Soul, Healer of the Cosmos*, 199–200.
2. Idel, "Sexual Metaphors and Praxis in the Kabbalah," in Kraemer, *The Jewish Family*.

Sha'ar ha-Gilgulim: "Gates of Reincarnation." Treatise by **Chayyim Vital** on reincarnation and the metaphysics of the various components of the soul. Not to be confused with another book on the same topic by the same author, **Sefer ha-Gilgulim**.

Sha'ar ha-Kavanah la-Mekubalim ha-Rishonim: Modern name for an early medieval text on mystical prayer rediscovered by Gershom Scholem.

Sha'ar ha-Razim: Mystical treatise on the **sefirot** by Todros Abulafia.

Sha'arei Binah: A 13th-century book by **Eleazar ben Judah of Worms** on **gematria** and the numerical codes of the **Bible**.

Sha'arei-Mavet: "Gates of Death." One of the seven compartments of **Gehenna**, Maktiel is its principal angel.

Sha'arei Orah: "Gates of Light." The Kabbalistic-theosophical masterwork of **Joseph Gikatilla**.

Sha'arei Ru'ach ha-Kodesh: "Gates of the Holy Spirit." A mystical tract by **Chayyim Vital**.

Sha'arei Tzalmavet: "Gates of the Shadow of Death." A compartment of **Gehenna**. Pariel is its principal angel (Masekhet Gehinnom).

Sha'arei Tzedek: Medieval mystical autobiography of an anonymous Kabbalist, made famous by Gershom Scholem. It describes in detail the author's use and assessment of different techniques for achieving mystical union.

Shabbat: SEE SABBATH.

Shabbatai Tzvi: Turkish mystic and failed messiah (ca. 17th century). Inspired by the teachings of Lurianic **Kabbalah** and encouraged by his disciple and publicist, **Nathan of Gaza**, Tzvi claimed to be the **Messiah**. Word of his claims reached the far ends of Europe, and a messianic panic ensued in many Jewish communities. After enjoying a brief period of phenomenal success, Tzvi's messianic career was cut short by the Ottoman Sultan, who offered him the choice of martyrdom or conversion to Islam. Tzvi chose conversion. Despite this, believers persisted in their faith, causing aftershocks in the Jewish world for decades to follow. A small sect of Sabbateanism, the **Donmeh**, survives to this day.

Shabriri: "Blindness." A demon that causes blindness and/or ocular diseases (Pes. 112a).

Shachakim: One of the **seven heavens**, this is the level at which **manna** is milled to feed the righteous (Chag. 12b–13a).

Shaddai, El: "[God of] Mountains/Breasts." A name of God that appears mostly in the book of Genesis. In Zoharic **Kabbalah**, it is another name for **Shekhinah**.

Shadow: (*Tzel*). Jewish mystics regard the shadow as a kind of aura that can be used for the purposes of **divination**. According to the Talmud, anyone whose shadow lacks a head on Rosh ha-Shanah is destined to die within the year. Samson Bacchi claimed his teacher **Isaac Luria** could discern a person's moral condition, even history of past lives, from his or her shadow.[1] SEE GUF HA-DAK; TZELEM.

1. Fine, *Physician of the Soul, Healer of the Cosmos*, 94.

Shadrach, Meschach, and Abednego: The three companions of **Daniel** (Dan. 1:6), they were thrown into a fiery furnace by King Nebuchadnezzar because they refused to deny the God of Israel (Dan. 3). God sent an **angel** to shield them from the fire. According to the **Midrash** (S of S R. 7:8), other miracles occurred coinciding with this incident. The furnace erupted out of the ground and blew to pieces. As a result of the explosion, the fiasco burned up princes from four idolatrous nations, half-cooked Nebuchadnezzar, and blew down his idolatrous image. At the same moment, **Ezekiel** resurrected the six hundred thousand dead Israelites lying in the valley of bones (Ezek. 37).

Shalgiel: The angel of snow (I Enoch).

Shalshelet ha-Kabbalah: "The Chain of Tradition." A mystical tract by R. Gedaliah ibn Yahia (ca. 16th century). It includes accounts of spiritual possession and **ghosts**.

Shamanism: The practice of controlling spiritual forces through ecstatic rituals and magical objects for the purposes of healing and protection. Throughout its history, Judaism has manifest some shamanistic elements. Shamanistic-charismatic practices are evident, for example, in the case of the **Ma'asei-Merkavah** mystics and in some of the magical and **amulet**-making practices of Greco-Roman Jewry.[1] Occasionally such practices rise to the level of being almost universally accepted, as is the case of folk-healers and rain-makers recorded in the **Talmud**. This is also true of the rise of the **Baal Shems** and the very shamanlike role of the Chasidic **rebbe**.

> 1. Davila, "The Hekhalot Literature and Shamanism," 767–89. Also see Winkler, *The Magic of the Ordinary*.

Shamayim: "Heaven." SEE SEVEN HEAVENS.

Shamir Worm: This miraculous animal, formed on the sixth day of Creation, eats stone. **Solomon** stole the shamir from the mythical **Hoopoe** bird that guarded it, in order to use it to cut blocks for the **Temple**, while fulfilling God's command that no implement of iron be used to construct the altar of God (Ex. 22; Git. 68a–68b). It carved the **Urim and Thummim** of the High Priest's **breastplate**. SEE ANIMALS.

Shamshiel: A **fallen angel** who teaches mankind the secrets of the **zodiac** (I Enoch).

Shavuot: "Weeks." An early summer holiday that comes forty-nine days after **Passover**, at the conclusion of the **omer**, which simultaneously celebrates the barley harvest and God's giving the **Torah** on Mount **Sinai**.

The role of the holiday has been controversial at times. It was very important to the author of **Jubilees** (1, 6, 14, 17,

22, 32, 44, 50). For the sectarian priests who composed the **Dead Sea Scrolls**, *Shavuot* was *the* critical holiday (**Damascus Document**; **Temple Scroll**; Scroll of Priestly Courses). By comparison, the Rabbis treat it with more muted interest—it is not even mentioned by name in the Mishnah, and consequently it is the only festival that does not have a tractate devoted to it in the **Talmud**. Moreover, it is overshadowed by the attention given to other holidays like Passover and Sukkot.

Because of a rabbinic legend that the Israelites were caught sleeping when God first appeared to give the **Ten Commandments**, the Kabbalists instituted a penitential all-night study session on Shavuot, *Tikkun Leil Shavuot*, "Repair of the Night of Shavuot," so that God will see we are both awake for any moment when Torah is given and diligent in our devotion to its study (Zohar, Emor, 98a).

Shedim: SEE DEMONS.

She'elot Chalom: "Inquiry of dreaming." Also called *shailah b'hakeitz*, "an awakening inquiry," it is an **incubation** technique for asking questions of God or **angels** involving a period of **purification**, usually lasting several days, and using or writing an **incantation** that includes several divine names, then followed by **sleep**. Either via a **dream** or upon awaking, the adept should receive a revelation. It is first described in the **Hechalot** literature and subsequently variations appear in Jewish communities around the world (ShB 7; Sefer he-Hezyonot).

She'elot u-Teshuvot min ha-Shamayim: "Questions and Answers from Heaven." A book by **Jacob of Marvege**, in which he recorded the answers to questions of Jewish law that he received from angels by means of dream **incubation**. SEE LAW AND THE PARANORMAL.

Shefa: "Overflow/Emanation" SEE EMANATION; FOUR WORLDS OF EMANATION; PARTZUFIM; SEFIROT.

Shekel ha-Kodesh, Sefer: "The Book of the Holy Shekel." A small mystical tract, only identified and published in the last century, written by **Moses de Leon**. It helps illuminate some of the teachings found in the **Zohar**.

Shekhinah: "Indwelling [Spirit]." That aspect of God that is close to and accessible to Creation. While it often simply means "the presence of God," it is more often treated as a personified hypostasis of the divine. The Shekhinah has been identified with many other supernal entities that are "projections" of God into the lower worlds: the **Holy Spirit**, the Logos (Word of God), the **Glory** of God, and the **Torah**. The **German Pietists** equate the Shekhinah with the Divine Anthropos described in **Shi'ur Qomah**. In classical **Kabbalah**, Shekhinah is equated with the tenth sefirah of **Malchut**. Often it is associated with divine **light**, through phrases like "the radiance of Shekhinah."

Often personified as a **woman**, the Shekhinah appears to mortals in one of three guises: a bride in white, an elderly woman in mourning black, or as a **dove**. In one medieval text that mimics Shi'ur Qomah, her physical dimensions are given, with a single one of her handbreadths exceeding the length of the universe (Otiyyot de Rabbi Akiva).

The most consistent interpretation of the Shekhinah is that it is that aspect of God that eternally adheres to *Kenesset Yisrael*, the Jewish people. It is, in a sense, the "spirit of Israel." Thus, when Israel went into **exile**, the Shekhinah went into exile with them (Me. 29a; MdRI, Pisha 14). Much Kabbalistic thought is devoted to the idea that because the feminine Shekhinah is separated from the masculine Holy One, the One God is, in a sense, fragmented and that the true cosmic unity has to be restored by human action. The alienation of the Shekhinah/Malchut from the masculine side of the Godhead and its recoupling with the Holy One/Tiferet is the preeminent obsession of the **Zohar**. This alienation makes Shekhinah vulnerable to the machinations of the **Sitra Achra**. Such teachings drive much of the theurgic practice of the medieval mystics, especially the Lurianic Kabbalists. Thus Chasids begin the performance of many mitzvot by reciting a kavanah prayer that begins, "For the sake of the unification of the Holy Blessed One with His Shekhinah. . . ."

By the early modern era, some mystics had brought the notion of Shekhinah full circle, so that it once again becomes a Logos-like "word of God" that speaks through the adept. **Solomon Alkebetz**, for example, told of the personified Shekhinah serving as his **maggid**, his spirit guide.

One mystical handbook explicitly equates seeing the Shekhinah with seeing the **face of God**, an experience that can have fatal consequences.

Shell: Various kinds of shells, but especially **egg** shells and turtle shells, have magical uses. For example, inscribed with incantations invoking the four rivers that flowed from **Eden**, a shell could be tied to the belly of a **woman** in difficult labor to ease the **birth**.

Shem: One of the sons of **Noah**, he is the only one not cursed for "exposing the nakedness" of his father. He is the progenitor of all Asians, including the Children of Israel. He learned a number of occult arts from his father, including the use of **herbs** to counter **demons** (Jubilees 10, 12, 21) and **astrology**. According to rabbinic tradition, he established the first House of Study for **Torah** (even though it had yet to be given at Mount **Sinai**).

Shem, ha- : "The Name." A euphemism used by Jews to avoid saying any one of God's powerful names. SEE EXPLICIT NAME OF GOD; NAMES OF GOD; TETRAGRAMMATON.

Shem ha-Kotev: "The Writing Name." SEE XENOGLOSSIA AND AUTOMATIC WRITING.

Shem ha-Meforash: "The Explicit Name." SEE EXPLICIT NAME OF GOD; TETRAGRAMMATON.

Shem, Sefer ha-: SEE NAME, THE BOOK OF THE.

Shem Tov Katan: "The Abbreviated Good Name." (1709). A book of *tikkunei tefillah* (mending prayers) for the treatment of illnesses and afflictions, both natural and supernatural, written by the **Baal Shem** Binyamin Binush.

Shemchazi: An **angel** who became infatuated with the daughters of humanity, and the leader of those **Watchers** who fell from heaven as a result. He was the angel who taught mankind the magical arts (I Enoch).

Shemirat ha-Derekh: "Protection of the Road." A class of protective **incantations** for wayfarers, found in medieval Ashkenazi literature.

Shemot ha-Tzadikim: A text listing the names of all the righteous souls from Adam onward. Recitation of these names grants the reader theurgic powers. SEE NAMES OF IMPURITY; RIGHTEOUS, THE.

Sheol: "Grave." The most common biblical term for the place of the afterlife, in later rabbinic cosmology, it is one of the seven compartments of **Gehenna**, a place of pits and fiery beasts.

Shephatiah, Rabbi: Wonder-working rabbi (Italian, ca. 11th century). According to **Sefer Yuhasin**, he could teleport himself (and his horse) using divine names of power—though one wonders why he needed a horse at all, given this particular talent.

Sherayim: "Leftovers." Food, usually **bread**, which has been blessed by a righteous man is a spiritual treasure and much sought after (Sanh. 92a; J. M.K. 2:3). It is eaten in the belief that the tzadik's touch released its **nitzotz**, its holy potential. Some, however, will keep it as a relic or a **segullah** charm. SEE FOOD; SEUDAH SH'LISHIT; TISH.

Sheva Zutarti: Hechalot text of prayers and angel-**summoning** adjurations.

Shevirat Ha-Kelim: SEE BREAKING OF THE VESSELS.

Shimmush Tehillim: "Practical Psalms." A 16th-century popular compendium of **psalms** that explains their theurgic uses.

Shimmushei Torah: A medieval theurgic text listing the supernatural feats and healings that can be achieved using verses from the **Torah**. **Moses** is presented as the source of these spells and formulae, having wrestled them from hostile **angels** (Otzer Midrashim).

Shimon: Hebrew proper name. Look for all entries under "Simon."

Shin: The twenty-first letter of the **Hebrew alphabet**. Depending on what diacritical marks are included, its vocalic value can be "sh" or "s." (When it is signifying the "s" sound, the letter is called *sin*.) The word *shin* literally means "tooth." It has the numeric value of 300. It can symbolize God (as the letter that begins "**Shaddai**"), the three **Patriarchs** and/or the middle three **sefirot** (because of the three prongs), but it can also symbolize falsehood[1] (Zohar I: 2b, 25b).

1. Munk, *The Wisdom of the Hebrew Alphabet*, 207–13.

Shinnui Shem: "Changing of a Name." The custom of changing one's name in the hope it will change one's fortune or **fate**. SEE NAMES, HEBREW.

Shi'ur Qomah: "Measurement of the Body." One of the most puzzling and disturbing texts in Jewish history, this brief document, ascribed to Rabbi **Ishmael ben Elisha ha-Kohen**, describes the "height of the body" of God, apparently inspired by the description of the masculine "lover" found in Song of Songs, chapter 5. God is outlined here in frankly anthropomorphic terms, with references to God's feet, thighs, neck, etc. The measurement of each limb is extravagantly enormous (often millions of miles), but exact.

Whether these numbers are meant to be taken as factual or as an exercise in awe-inspiring exaggeration is a matter of debate. Often the proportions are nonsensical (the divine big toe is vastly larger than the divine beard, for example). Some passages in the text suggest the author is actually cautioning readers against literalism, because midway into SQ he changes the rules and values of the measurements (are we talking about a human "span" or a divine "span," which alone is equal to the size of the universe?) to the point where they cease to make sense. Likewise, several statements in the text itself suggest that any straight anthropomorphic interpretation of a term like "nose" is misleading, as "no creature can recognize it."

SQ also claims that each divine limb has its own name that is inscribed on it, a parallel to the **Merkavah** mystical practice of writing **incantations** on each limb of the adept attempting to ascend into heaven. The text concludes by presenting this as a secret gnosis and that reciting this text will both protect the initiate in this world and guarantee him or her a place in the **World-to-Come**.

It is interesting to note that despite the exhaustive and specific measurements provided, there is no evidence that any adept has ever attempted to graphically illustrate the divine form. Later mystical readers rejected the notion that this is an actual description of God's body, instead interpreting this anthropomorphic figure to be a divine **emanation**, designating it as part of God's **Glory** or labeling it something angelic, such as the **Unique Cherub**.[1]

1. See S. Cohen, *Shi'ur Qomah: Texts and Recensions.*

Shivhei ha-BeSHT: "In Praise of the Baal Shem Tov." A collection of stories, miraculous tales, and legends that constitute the first document and primary source of information on the life of **Israel ben Eliezer**. There are multiple versions of the book in existence.

Shivitti: A handmade or printed **amulet**, constructed around Psalm 16:8—*Shivitti Adonai l'negdi tamid,* "I have placed the Lord constantly before me." Most versions of the Shivitti include the **Tetragrammaton** surrounded by protective verses and images, especially Psalm 67 and **menorahs**.

Sh'ma: The first word of Deuteronomy 6:4, "Hear O Israel, the Eternal is our God, the Eternal is One." It is recited twice a day by pious Jews, as well as at any moment one anticipates **death** or **martyrdom**. It is called the "watchword of Israel's faith." It sometimes appears on **amulets**. *SEE* KRIAT SH'MA AL HA-MITAH; SLEEP.

Sh'neur Zalman of Laydi: Chasidic master (Russian, ca. 19th century). Sh'neur was the founder of CHaBaD, the most influential of all Chasidic groups today. He is the author of the **Tanya**, an influential book of mystical metaphysics.

Shofar: A simple musical instrument made from the **horn** of any kosher animal (except a cow). Shofars were heard on the mountain of **Sinai** when God gave the **Torah** to the Jewish people. Since then, shofars have been used for many communal and religious purposes. The shofar is sounded each **Rosh ha-Shanah** in order to confound **Satan** (R.H. 16a–b). It may be for this reason that shofars are often used as part of **exorcisms** (Mishna R.H. 3:7)

and are mentioned in some healing **rituals** (Chul. 105a). It may also be because of the combined power of its disturbing loudness and its symbolic role as a summons to God to attend to human needs (Sha'ar Ruach ha-Kodesh).

A heavenly shofar sounds from beneath the **Throne of Glory** whenever Israel is forgiven (Hechalot Rabbati). A unique shofar made from the **ram** that **Abraham** sacrificed in place of **Isaac** awaits the **Messiah**. When he comes, he will sound that particular horn, which will be heard throughout the world, heralding the final redemption (Gen. R. 56; PdRK 23).

Shoftiel: "God is my Judge." A punishing angel of **Gehenna**.

Shoham Stones: The twelve stones mounted on the breastplate of the High Priest (Sot. 36a). *SEE* BREASTPLATE.

Shor: "Bull"/Taurus. The **zodiac** sign for the month of Iyar. It signifies the feminine, fitness, maturity, nighttime, and goodness.[1]

1. Erlanger, *Signs of the Times,* 41–55.

Shoresh ha-Shemot: "The Root of the Names." A Kabbalistic text written by **Moses Zacuto**, it provides a detailed outline for the proper construction of **amulets**.

Shoshan Yesod ha-Olam: "The Rose Foundation of the World." A medieval magical book compiled by Yosef Tirshom, it is a compendium of earlier magical traditions and sources. It exists only in manuscript form.

Shulchan Aruch: The most influential digest of Jewish law, it was composed in the 16th century by the mystic/lawyer **Joseph Caro**. References to theurgic-mystical beliefs and practices are sprinkled throughout its entries, often focusing on how to protect against the **evil eye**. Its description of the protective customs surrounding funerals is a prime example of its interest in the paranormal. *SEE* LAW AND THE PARANORMAL.

Sibylline Oracles: A collection of writing from Greco-Roman antiquity with some Jewish content. The Sibyls were a series of oracular women who prophesied for their contemporaries. At least some of the messages (specifically oracles 4 and 5) were composed by Jews, probably from the Jewish community of Alexandria, Egypt.

Silence: Since words are God's first creation and it is from words that diversity (*Olam ha-Dibur*) unfolds, it follows that silence, which preceded the divine speech, is more primal, more akin to the higher reality of divine oneness.[1]

The **Psalms**, **Talmud**, and mystical texts all praise silence as an appropriate way to worship God. The great Maggid, the disciple of the Baal Shem Tov, even declared, "It is best to serve God by silence." *SEE* HEBREW; INCANTATION; MEMRA.

1. Tishby, *The Wisdom of the Zohar*, vol. 2, 271–72.

Silver: *SEE* COLOR.

Simon (Shimon) bar Kochba: A 2nd-century military leader and failed **messiah**. He was credited with superhuman powers, including extraordinary strength, the ability to catch and return catapult missiles, and the power to breathe fire.

Simon (Shimon) bar Yochai: Mishnaic Sage and mystic (ca. 2nd century). In the **Talmud**, he is portrayed as an awesome spiritual virtuoso. Bar Yochai performed many wondrous feats. He exorcised a **demon** that had possessed Caesar's daughter (Me. 17a–b). In order to escape Roman persecution, Simon and his son hid in a **cave** for twelve years, living off the fruit of a carob tree that grew there miraculously for their benefit. There they sat naked, buried themselves in sand, and studied **Torah** constantly. After twelve years they emerged, only to find that the supernal power they had cultivated in that time set everything mundane they gazed at on fire. A voice from heaven immediately ordered them to return to the cave, where they remained for another twelve months as punishment (paralleling the traditions concerning **Gehenna**) until they were finally reconciled to the imperfection of the material world, and only then did God release them. Still, Simon had to use his powers to heal everyone his son struck down. Bar Yochai himself retained the power to slay with

his gaze, but had the capacity to control it (Shab. 33b–34a).

Rabbi Simon is the purported author of the **Zohar**, but as that document first surfaced in the 13th century, a thousand years after his death, there is controversy concerning that (*SEE* DE LEON, MOSES). Much of the Zohar is a spiritual memoir of Bar Yochai's life and ministry, a kind of mystical gospel. The bulk of the supernatural traditions about him are found there. He learned his Torah directly from an **angel**, who studied with him from behind a **curtain** of fire (Zohar II 14a–15a). By his word, he could fill a wadi with dinars. He performed many other miracles, both great and small. More compelling than that, he regularly conversed with angels, disguised spiritual entities, and other heavenly messengers. His death was a miracle unto itself, a gracious death of celestial illumination.

Simon ben Azzai: *SEE* BEN AZZAI.

Simon (Shimon) ben Halafta: Talmudic Sage and demonologist (ca. 3rd century). He learns from a conversation with the **Angel of Death** that Death has no authority over the **righteous** (Eccl. R. 3:2).

Simon (Shimon) ben Isaac ha-Gadol: Pietist, poet, and mystic (German, ca. 11th century). Rabbi Simon taught such beliefs as the **summoning** of angels and their intercessory power and had communications with the angelic **Baal ha-Chalom**. He also expounded on the theurgic and practical power of the seventy-two letter **name of God**.

Simon ben Zoma: *SEE* BEN ZOMA, SIMON.

Sin: (*Chatat*, "Miss [the target]"). In conventional understanding, sin is any human action that violates God's will for humanity as expressed by the 613 commandments appearing in the Torah. In the Bible, the word carries a connotation of "inadvertent error," of an unintentional transgression.

In Jewish mysticism, sin has greater cosmic import than mere human disobedience: sin ruins the harmony on high, interrupting the flow of divine energy between worlds, even causing fissures in God. The mission of the Jewish people, then, is to perfect our actions, repair (*m'takein*) the ruptures that are caused by sin, and so reestablish the harmony of the cosmos (Zohar I: 87b). *SEE* KELIPOT; SITRA ACHRA; TIKKUN.

Sin: The letter *shin* of the **Hebrew alphabet** can symbolize the sound of either "sh" or "s," depending on the diacritical mark that accompanies it. When it is signifying the "s" sound, the letter is called *sin*. *SEE* SHIN.

Sinai, Mount (alternately, Horeb): The great mountain of God (*Har Elohim*), where Moses brought the people Israel to enter into a covenant and receive the **Torah**. The events that unfolded there provide the archetypal story of theophany in Jewish tradition. The people witnessed God upon the top of the **mountain** in visions of **cloud**, smoke, lightning, and **fire**. They also heard **shofars** and the sound of God's own voice. God descended to the mountaintop accompanied by twenty-two thousand companies of angels. When **Moses** stood upon its peak, God lifted it up so that Moses could behold heaven (Ex. R. 28; Sot. 5a; Tanh., Tzav 16; MdRI, Yitro; PdRE 41). From there he ascended to heaven (Suk. 5a; Yoma 4a; MdRI, Ba-Chodesh). When the people heard God speak the first letter of the first word of the **Ten Commandments**, the entire population fell over dead, and had to be resurrected (Shab. 88b; Ex. R. 29:4, 29:9; PdRE 20). Other **Midrashim** teach that the people each heard God's voice differently, according to their particular capacity to hear (Tanh., Shemot 22; Bahir 45). Prior to the theophany, **Jacob** and **Rachel** met at its foot, and Moses encountered the **burning bush** on its slopes. In one rabbinic tradition, God didn't technically split the Sea of Reeds; he simply moved Sinai to the location and the people walked over the sea on its crest. To this day, no one knows its exact location in the Sinai peninsula.

Sisera: The Canaanite general defeated by the prophetess Deborah and the chieftain Barak was yet another **giant** of extraordinary power: his voice was so powerful it stunned **animals** and toppled city walls. When he bathed in a **river**, he could net enough **fish** with his beard to feed his entire army. He rode into battle on a chariot pulled by nine hundred horses. (Yalkut, Judges 43).

Sitra Achra: (Aramaic, the "Other Side"). The demonic realm, it is ruled by **Samael** and **Lilith**. Born out of the very process of creation, this **left** side of the emanated Godhead is the manifestation of divine severity and wrath. Cosmic strife emerged between it and the Right Side, and from that strife emerged **Gehenna** and the demonic. Like a controlling rod in a nuclear pile, the "Pillar of the Middle" of the **sefirot**—**Tiferet**, **Yesod**, and **Malchut**—moderates the two sides and maintains peace (Zohar I: 17a). Though the Sitra Achra would, under the ideal conditions, be an attenuated expression of the divine emanations, it feeds upon human sin and transgression. The broken nature of our current existence keeps the Sitra Achra a powerful presence in Creation. Only in messianic times will it be reintegrated into a holy dimension.[1] *SEE* CREATION; EVIL; TREATISE ON THE LEFT EMANATION; ZOHAR.

   1. Fine, *Essential Papers in Kabbalah*, 155–60, 248–62; Green, *Guide to the Zohar*, 116–21.

Six Primordial Things: God conceived of six entities that preceded the creation of the world and around which the universe is structured: the **Torah** (the blueprint), the **Throne of Glory** (positive existence), the **Patriarchs** (the pillars that support the world), **Israel** (the purpose of the world), the **Temple** (the link between worlds), and the name of the **Messiah** (redemption and final rectification of the world) (Gen. R. 1:4). *SEE* SEVEN PRIMORDIAL THINGS.

Sixteen-Sided Sword of the Almighty: Also called the Sword of **Moses**, it is a mysterious divine power that can be adjured to protect a person from disease, grant happiness, or defeat even the **Angel of Death**. The existence of this power is derived from a **gematria** interpretation of Exodus 15:3, where God first wielded it in the defense of Israel. It is mentioned several times in the literature of Medieval Jewry and is particularly associated with the **Passover** Seder **ritual**. This mysterious force may be the inspiration for the title of the magical handbook **The Sword of Moses**.[1] *SEE* MAGIC.

   1. Kanarfogel, *Peering through the Lattices*, 137n, 137–139.

Sleep: During sleep, the **soul** leaves the body and ascends to and draws renewed life from the celestial realms

(Gen. R. 14:9). According to the **Zohar**, the soul makes a perilous journey each night, having to confront **demons** and **unclean spirits** as it navigates the **sefirot** (I: 10b, 83a). **Dreams** are the byproducts of these soul ascents. **Incubi** and **succubae** may also seek to molest one through dreams in order to release **nocturnal emissions** to breed more demons.

Because the Sages describe sleep as one-sixtieth **death** and because of the increased physical and spiritual vulnerability of the sleeper, there is a protective ritual one may perform before going to bed, the **Kriat Sh'ma al ha-Mitah** (Ber. 4b; Zohar I: 11a; the Siddur). One can use sleep for the purpose of **divination**. *SEE* INCUBATION.

Snake: *SEE* SERPENT.

Snake Charming: According to the Talmudic Sages, the control of **animals** through magical means is forbidden by the Torah (Sanh. 65b).

Sod: "Secret." One of the four methods of interpreting the **Torah**, usually assumed to be based on occult knowledge. *SEE* PARDES; SECRET.

Sod ha-Sodot: "The Secret of Secrets." A theosophical summary by Rabbi Elchanan ben Yakar of the teachings of the **Circle of the Unique Cherub**.

Sodei Razaya: A collection of occult teachings on Jewish **prayer** traditions by **Eleazer of Worms** (ca. 13th century).

Sodom and Gomorrah: Beyond the sins ascribed to them in the **Bible** (Gen. 13, 19–20; Isa. 19; Ezek. 16), numerous bizarre cruelties were credited to the Sodomites in rabbinic literature, including having laws against hospitality and committing the Procrustean-like crime of stretching or chopping up guests to make them fit a bed. Lot's own daughter was burned for showing kindness to strangers (Sanh. 109b; PdRE 25; Gen. R. 49:6).

Solar Calendar: While the normative Jewish **calendar** is a lunar calendar adjusted with leap months to keep aligned with the solar cycle, the sectarian priests of the **Dead Sea Scrolls** sect adhered to a purely solar calendar based on a 364-day year, divided into four, 13-week seasons. They believed this calendar was a gift of the **angels** and reflected the divine perfection of the cosmos, where it enjoyed a primordial pre-existence inscribed upon "heavenly tablets" (Jubilees 32; I Enoch 81, 93). Some sources claim it was first given to **Enoch**, others indicate it was first taught to **Moses**. *SEE* CALENDAR; ENOCH, BOOKS OF; JUBILEES; SUN.

Solomon: Third king of ancient Israel and son of David. In the biblical accounts, he lives an extraordinary life, but one mostly without fantastic or supernatural elements. One exception is according to I Kings 3:4–15, which records how Solomon made a series of massive sacrifices at a shrine in Gibeon. There he had a dream, perhaps the result of an incubation ritual accompanying the sacrifices. In that dream, God offered him any gift. Solomon chose wisdom. In keeping with the promise of that dream, God gave him wisdom in abundance. I Kings 5:11 describes Solomon as "the wisest of all men."

Solomon subsequently demonstrated this divine gift in his role as a judge. He also built a large military establishment and the First **Temple** to God in **Jerusalem**. His wisdom extended to the natural sciences and he was a master in all matters involving botany and zoology. His wisdom was such that his renown extended far beyond the borders of Israel (I Kings 5:11).

Unfortunately, his **wisdom** failed him in his decision to marry a thousand foreign wives in order to cement political alliances. These women, with their foreign retinues, introduced unwelcome pagan practices back into Israelite society. Presumably, their magical and occult practices also became part of Solomon's repertoire of knowledge.

As the archetypal wisdom figure, Solomon was credited with skill and mastery of esoteric lore. Post-biblical Jewish literature amplified and expanded on this aspect of Solomon's life. The **Throne of Solomon** was a wonder unto itself, a reflection of the **Throne of Glory** on high. He also possessed an enormous flying carpet capable of holding forty thousand people.

Not only did Solomon study **animals**, but he could actually talk with them, through the agency of a magical **ring** that he fabricated (Testament of Solomon; Mid. Tanh.

B., Mavo). The same ring gave him the power to summon and command **demons** (Eccl. 2:8; Testament of Solomon). He enslaved Asmodeus (Belzeboul in other sources), king of demons, to help him construct the Temple by providing Solomon with the **shamir worm**, which could cut the stones without the aid of **iron** tools. Eventually, a whole army of demons assisted in the project (Yalkut, I Kings 182; Ex. R. 52:3). In time, **Asmodeus** tricked Solomon into giving him his magical ring and then teleported the king to the end of the earth, from whence he had to return to Jerusalem by begging. In the meantime, Asmodeus's shape changed and he took the king's place, thus explaining how the wisest king in history seemingly strayed from God (Git. 68a–b). According to some legends, Solomon took three years to return to his throne. In others, he actually died in humble circumstances as punishment for his sins.

He had **eagles** who served as his personal entourage. These eagles would lift up his throne and fly him to the ends of the earth, even into heaven and **Gehenna** (Ruth R. 1:17; Eccl. R. 2:25; Zohar II: 112b–113a).

His bevy of foreign marriages also had cosmic consequences. Since their presence corrupted the Temple, God commissioned **Michael** to raise up a nemesis against Israel from the slime of the sea. This eventually grew into the city of Rome (S of S R. 1:6).

Aside from the three biblical books he purportedly authored (Proverbs, Song of Songs, and Ecclesiastes), a number of magical handbooks are credited to the great king, most notably the **Testament of Solomon, Sefer ha-Razim, Letter of Rehoboam**, and the **Key of Solomon**. A whole array of other books, devoted to alchemy, metallurgy, angelology, and metaphysics, are also **pseudepigraphically** ascribed to him.

Jewish oneiromancers teach that if Solomon appears to someone in a **dream**, the dreamer can expect wisdom to come to him also (Ber. 57b).

Solomon, Testament of: A Greek text of late antiquity devoted to the power of demons and their control, the Testament of Solomon is probably a document with Jewish roots, but has been thoroughly reworked with the addition of Christian beliefs and themes. This book provides the most comprehensive presentation of **Solomon** as arch-magi and summoner of **demons**. In the narrative, he uses a magic **ring** to force thirty-six demons to help him construct the **Temple**. From each demon, he extracts its name, the nature of its malevolent activities, and the angel that is its nemesis. One interesting idea it contains that has some Jewish providence is that demons are the offspring of humans and fallen angels. *(SEE ALSO APPENDIX FIGURE 4.)*

Solomon, Throne of: *SEE* THRONE OF SOLOMON.

Son(s) of God: (*Ben Elohim; B'nai Elohim*). A term variously used to refer to **angels** (Gen.6; Deut. 32; Ps. 82; Job 1), kings of Israel (II Sam. 7; Ps. 2), and the Children of Israel (Ex. 4; Deut. 32).

Son of Man: (*Ben Adam; Ben Enosh*). This idiom for "human being" or "mortal" takes on the meaning of a prophet in Ezekiel, and then messianic overtones in the book of Daniel (7) and the Books of Enoch.

Sonadora: Witch and diviner (Turkish, ca. 16th century). This witch was repeatedly consulted by Chayyim Vital, who relied on her ability to use **lecanomancy** to divine the future (Sefer ha-Hezyonot 2).

Song of Songs, the: Also called "The Song of Solomon" and "Canticles" in Christian tradition, it is a book of the Bible. The Sages of the 1st century debated whether this series of passionate love poems that never mention God should actually be part of the biblical canon. The Song of Songs was accepted, however, on the strength of the argument that it is actually an allegory for the love between God and Israel. Since then, the text has been a fertile ground for mystical speculation. Rabbi **Akiba** and his contemporaries evidently had a whole body of mystical traditions concerning this text, starting with the claim that it was given, along with the Torah, at Mount **Sinai** (S of S R. 1). A number of interpreters understand it as the internal narrative of God's thoughts and feelings during the Exodus. Because of this, most Midrashim on S of S attempt to make its verses correspond to specific incidents in the book of Exodus.

Shi'ur Qomah's description of the supernal body of God is inspired by the Song, as is the mystical liturgical poem *Shir ha-Kavod*, which came out of **German Pietist** circles. It is frequently cited in the **Zohar** and other mystical tracts.

Songs of the Sabbath Sacrifice: Also known as 4Q400–7 and 11Q17, this **Dead Sea Scroll** text is a kind of mystical liturgy that describes how the **priests** and **angels** worship together in the heavenly **Temple** at the **Throne of Glory**. It is built around the sectarian solar **calendar** of **Jubilees**, with the year being divided into four 13-week cycles, with a special liturgy for each week of that cycle. It also is one of the earliest Jewish texts to allude to the **seven heavens**.

Songs of the Sage: Also known as 4Q510–11, it is a fragmentary collection of protective incantations against demonic attack found in the **Dead Sea Scrolls**.

Sons of Light and Darkness: *SEE* CHILDREN OF DARKNESS; CHILDREN OF LIGHT.

Soothsayer: *SEE* DIVINATION.

Sophia: *SEE* WISDOM.

Sorcery: (*Kishuf; Kesem; Nachshaya*). Modern scholars of the occult distinguish between "sorcery" and "witchcraft," arguing that the former is characteristically treated as a "technology," practicable by anyone educated in its methods. It is performed for either beneficent (healing, protection) or selfish (attaining wealth, love, or power) ends, but it is not inherently evil. **Witchcraft**, on the other hand, is the term applied to magical practitioners who derive their power from infernal forces and/or use that power for malevolent purposes. By these definitions, Jews have long tolerated the practice of certain kinds of sorcery, both scholarly and shamanistic, even as they have proscribed witchcraft.

The **Bible** forbids the practice of magic without being very specific in describing what the offending activity entails (Deut. 18). Later authorities seek to clarify exactly what kinds of behaviors are permitted and what are not. The **Talmud** condemns those practices that involve "performance," i.e., manipulating objects or *materia magica*, but permits "word magic." This seems to be one of the distinguishing features of **Hechalot literature**: in some ways it closely resembles the spells and adjurations found in pagan magical texts, yet it lacks the same elaborate use of substances, objects, or sacrifices found in the latter.

In a related vein, medieval Jewish authorities condemn **magic** (the mechanical performance of symbolic behavior with the belief that it will force something to occur, regardless of heavenly powers), but tolerate various forms of **theurgy** (invoking God, angels, and even demons, with rituals and words to achieve a desired end) when performed by figures otherwise recognized for their righteousness and piety. But however it is parsed out, "sorcery" in certain forms is understood to function somehow within the parameters (or at the boundaries) of Judaism.[1] While Jewish authorities regard the practice of sorcery to be dangerous and doubtful, the Christian notion that all sorcerers have allied themselves with the devil is unheard of in Jewish tradition.

Most examples of Jewish sorcery can be classified as "learned" or "scholarly" magic. It is understood to be a byproduct of mastery of other Jewish disciplines (Jewish texts, mysticism, or even medicine) and made possible by the moral rectitude of the adept. As a result, influential rabbis could also have the reputation of being sorcerers or theurgists. Given that a thorough Jewish education is a prerequisite for acquiring such theurgic powers,[2] Jewish adepts of sorcery were, historically, men. Still, though women were most often not in a position to gain the requisite education, they did practice kinds of folk medicine and magic that were also accepted by the community, because in theory, the use of supernal power was open to any **righteous** person who could acquire the knowledge and skill, regardless of education.[3]

Man or woman, there are few cases before modern times of a Jew functioning as a "professional" sorcerer for the community, though the activities of Renaissance and early modern Jewish alchemists employed by gentile patrons do provide several examples of Jews working as professional adepts.

1. Dan, *The Heart and the Fountain*, 101–5.
2. Chajes and Copenhaver, "Magic and Astrology," 21–23.
3. Chajes, "Women Leading Women (and Attentive Men)," in Wertheimer, *Jewish Religious Leadership: Image and Reality*.

Sortes/Sortilege: Any **divination** by means of drawing **lots**, casting arrows (**belomancy**), or randomly selecting biblical passages and interpreting the results (**Bibliomancy**).

Sotah: The term used for the **ritual** trial of a woman accused of adultery (Num. 5). *SEE* ORDEAL.

Soul: "The dust returns to the earth; the spirit returns to God who made it" (Eccl. 12:7). Despite claims to the contrary among some modern scholars, ancient Israelites from the very beginning had a notion that some aspect of the human individual continues to exist after death. It is true, however, that how Israelites, and their Jewish descendants, understood the enduring nature of the human being has varied over time.

As on so many other issues of metaphysics, the Hebrew Scriptures are vague on the nature of the soul, and the Jewish understanding of this mystery has had to be pieced together from diverse parts of the **Bible**. Even the word used for the "soul," the higher consciousness and enduring aspect of human identity, varies throughout Scripture.

The Sages assert that the soul is polypsychic and identify a hierarchy of three dimensions to the human soul from three terms used in the Bible: **Nefesh**, **Ruach**, and **Neshamah**. This triad soul is the basis for virtually all Jewish metaphysics (Sha'ar Ruach ha-Kodesh, p. 39).

The *Nefesh* is the animus, the "animal vitality," that animates all sentient creatures. In the **Zohar**, the *Nefesh* remains bound to the body and close to those who were once close to the deceased. Thus an appearance of the dead in cemeteries, dreams, and apparitions is a manifestation of the *Nefesh*. The **Vilna Gaon**, by contrast, regards this to be the part of the soul that undergoes radical transformation in the process of **reincarnation**.

The *Ruach* is the "spirit," the seat of the emotions and moral capacity, the discerning capacity that makes a human distinct from other animals. This is the part of the soul that must undergo **Gehenna** for the poor choices it made while living, but then also gets to enjoy Gan **Eden** in the afterlife. In some metaphysical models, it then migrates to the Tzror ha-Chayyim, the "Treasury of Souls," from which it will be recycled into a new bodily existence until it has completed all the necessary work that soul must accomplish.

Finally, the *Neshamah*, or "soul," is the highest self, the intellect that allows a person to apprehend God. Since this aspect of the soul is not tainted by the sins committed in this world, it is the *Neshamah* that has an eternal afterlife. It is the interaction of these three elements that give a person his or her distinct personality.

In later mystical traditions, two more dimensions of the soul are discerned, aspects of the soul that are fully developed in only a few people: the *Chayyah* and the *Yechidah*. The former is that which serves as the "sixth sense," the ability to be attuned to divine forces, and the latter is the part of the soul that is the true "spark" of divinity and is capable of complete fusion with God. It is through this part of the soul that some people are able to perform miracles (Zohar II: 94b; Keter Shem Tov, 4a; Sha'ar ha-Gilgulim 1–2; Tanya 1–2).

In **Kabbalah**, the soul is called the "fruit" of the "Tree of Life," the **sefirot** (Bahir 14; Zohar I: 15b, 59a–60a, 115a–b). In the Zohar, the soul is the "child" of the union of Shekhinah and the Holy One, and the angels give the soul its good and evil inclination (Zohar III: 119b–120a). Later mysticism suggests that all souls originate from the one soul of **Adam Kadmon** (Sefer Hezyonot; Sha'ar ha-Gilgulim 1:2).

Souls begin as part of larger *shoresh gadol*, "root souls," in the **Guf ha-Briyot**, the Treasury of Souls or in Adam Kadmon. Initially, souls have no gender (Gen. R. 8:1; Zohar I: 85b). Every soul has an **angel** that teaches it the entire **Torah**. At the moment of ensoulment, the angel strikes the fetus on the upper lip, causing the soul to forget all it has learned (and making the indention under the nose), so the task of each soul is to remember the Torah it learned before **birth** (Nid. 16b) and perform every commandment perfectly. (Also see Sanh. 98a; Yev. 62a–63b; Tanh., Pikudei 3, 9; Ki Tissa 12; Gen. R. 40:3; Sha'ar ha-Gilgulim.) *SEE* ANCESTORS; TZROR HA-CHAYYIM.

South: (*Negev*). One of the four cardinal compass points, it is the direction from which **light**, love, and compassion emanate (Zohar I: 81b).

Speculum: (*Re'i*; Gr., *Espaklarya*). This term is associated with the power of **prophecy**, but it is not clear whether the term refers to a physical scrying device, such as a mirror, or to a paranormal phenomenon. In any case, **Moses** communed with God through a single "clear" speculum, while most prophets only saw their prophetic vision through nine "murky" speculums (Yev. 49b).

Much of Jewish mystical and Kabbalistic thought is devoted to understanding the nature of the prophetic speculum. Some believed the term refers to the **Urim and Thummim**. Others believe that an actual mirror is being described; it was simply a device to avoid looking directly at the divine **Glory**, which—like the gaze of a Gorgon in Greek mythology—could kill. In the **Zohar**, each of the **sefirot** is a different kind of speculum that refracts the divine **light**, transmitting it to the lower worlds (I: 141a). The **righteous** can in turn gaze through the same sefirot and discern the future, divine intentions, and other occult truths.

Speech: *SEE* HEBREW ALPHABET; LANGUAGE.

Spitting: Spitting, essentially an act of expulsion, is a common Jewish defensive act against the **evil eye**. Most often, it is done three times in concert with reciting a protective phrase, such as **kenahora**, or with a passage of Scripture. According to the **Testament of Solomon**, spittle combined with the right **ritual** has the power to drive away demons. Conversely, the Talmud forbids spitting while reciting biblical verses, apparently assuming that the two in combination are intended to perform a magical ritual (Shev. 15b).

It is interesting to note that even as early as the 1st century, saliva was used against spiritual threats; **Jesus** of Nazareth used spit to remove a demon that caused a man to stammer (Mark 7:32–35).

Staff: *SEE* ROD.

Study: **Torah** study is one of the central devotional activities of Judaism, equal to worship (Avot 1:3; Shab. 127b; Pes. 50b). In fact, it is a form of worship. Moreover, it is like a re-experiencing of the revelation at Sinai, even to the point of having some of the visionary elements, like **fire** and heavenly voices, manifest themselves (Lev. R. 16:4; B.M. 59b). Other miracles are triggered by intensive Torah study, such as creating ambulatory trees and destroying interfering

animals (Chag. 14b; Suk. 28a; Zohar I: 243a). If performed with the right **kavanah**, Torah study causes the **Shekhinah** to be restored to its place on high (Zohar I: 10b).

Substitution: Substitution is the belief that one can deflect or redirect a detrimental condition or event by transferring it to a substitute object or entity. This is the logic behind folk beliefs about offering **sacrifices**, but especially the **Yom Kippur** scapegoat offering (PdRE 46). Another prime example in Jewish lore of a substitution **ritual** is **kapparah**, in which one ritually transfers one's sins to a **bird**, slaughters the bird, and then donates the meat to the poor. If one suffers a sudden foreboding about an unknown menace, one should remove oneself from the spot by four cubits and recite the phrase "The he-goat at the butcher's is fatter than I." (B. Meg. 3a). A person suffering a **fever** was directed to go to a crossroad, find an ant carrying a burden, collect it in a copper tube and intone "What you carry on me, that I carry on you" while shaking the tube (Shab. 66b). Medieval Jewish segullot include many remedies that involve affecting a substitution.[1] *SEE* REVERSAL; SYMPATHY.

1. Zimmels, *Magicians, Theologians, and Doctors*, 121, 139–40.

Succubus: A female demon that enters the dreams of sleeping men, arouses them, and causes **nocturnal emissions** (Nishmat Chayyim III: 16). The semen so released is used to breed new demons, a belief that is repeatedly explored in the **Zohar** (I: 19b, 55a; III: 76b).

Anonymous succubae appear in Jewish literature. The most notable are the orgy of demonesses who copulated with Adam for 130 years (Eruv. 18b; Tanh., Bereshit 26; Gen. R. 20:1). Tradition identifies several succubae by name, most famously **Lilith**, **Igrat**, and **Naaman**.

Sukkot: The holiday of Sukkot, which celebrates the harvest and reminds Jews of our forty-year sojourn in the wilderness, has a number of mystical-theurgic elements associated with it.

One of the overarching themes of Sukkot during Talmudic times was to pray for the continued **fertility** of the earth, now that the year's harvest has been gathered. Thus Jews begin seasonal prayers for rain. While the **Temple** stood, there was a corresponding **ritual** to "draw up" the subterranean waters called the **water libation** ritual (Tan. 25b).

Thematically linked is the waving of the lulav, the **four species**. The four plants, held together in a grouping suggestive of a phallus, is waved in the four compass directions, up toward heaven (the upper waters?) and down to the earth (the lower waters?) (Zohar III: 255a).

Finally, there is the famous custom of the **ushpizin**, inviting the ancestral ghosts to sit in the sukkah with us (Zohar III: 121a).

A number of other less conspicuous occult elements are all associated with Sukkot. Perhaps because of the theme of fertility for the whole world, Sukkot is the holiday most focused on the well-being of the entire world. There were other rituals performed that were understood to benefit all humanity, such as the seventy bull offerings made, one for every **nation** in the world (Num. 29; Suk. 55b; Lam. R. 1:23; PdRK 28:9).

Sulfur: A popular component in the practice of **alchemy**. It is also a *materia magica* used in Jewish exorcisms. *SEE* PHARMACOPOEIA.

Summoning: In Psalm 68:19 it is written, "You ascended on high, having taken captives. . . ." Rabbinic tradition understands this to be referring to Moses, and this verse becomes the prooftext for the belief that, like Moses, mortals can summon and harness **angels** to their service. At the root of this practice of power is a tradition that the angels opposed **Moses** receiving the **Torah**. When God and Moses won out and the Torah was given to humanity, the angels submitted themselves to Moses, even giving him their names and revealing incantations that would allow him to command the angelic hosts. These spells Moses then bequeathed to the Children of Israel, and a worthy sage of the Torah can likewise command angels (Sword of Moses).

The actual act of summoning is preceded by a long period of preparatory **purification**. Five elements are present in most mystical/magical purification practices: a set period of time (three to forty-one days), avoiding **sex** and seminal emissions (and in the case of men, avoiding women), **fasting** and **food** restrictions, **immersion**, performing certain rituals/**incantations**, and washing one's clothing.

Besides repeatedly cleansing oneself and one's clothing in the living **waters** of heaven (in at least one case, the

adept must be immersed in water at the time of angelic visitation), fasting or reducing the kinds of foods one eats also makes it easier to move in divine realms and/or deal with divine beings, for it makes you less human and more angelic (angels don't eat).[1]

As the purification rites draw to a close, the time has come to use the **mashiva** or summoning incantation. This involves a series of repetitive commands and praises that incorporate the names of the angels and long strings of *nomina barbara*, apparent nonsense words that were understood to be the "language of heaven," comprehensible on high.

The combination of severe and ascetic purification rites, physical and social isolation, constant concentration, and mantralike repetitions of incantations and divine names evidently induces a trance that allows the adept to commune with the angelic beings (Otzer ha-Geonim 4:2:1).

Once the angel has been successfully summoned, the texts are unclear on the exact nature of the angelic manifestation. One text states the angel will appear "like a man" and converse with the adept "lovingly."[2] Others state that one will hear a voice but see nothing, possibly meaning that the angel possesses the body of the adept, but this is never explicitly stated.[3] Often, the angel will come clothed in a **dream**. Witnessed accounts of angelic possession of humans do not appear before the 16th century.

There are also traditions about religious wunderkinds who could summon **animals** to do their bidding, and stories of attempts to summon the **Messiah** himself. *SEE* MAGGID; MEDIUM; MESSIAH, SUMMONING THE; SAR HA-TORAH.

1. Lesses, *Ritual Practices to Gain Power*, 117–58.
2. Swartz, "The Book of the Great Name," in Fine, *Judaism in Practice*, 340–47.
3. Lesses, 85.

Sun: (*Shemesh*). The sun was widely worshipped as a god in the Ancient Near East. The **Torah** expressly forbids such worship (Deut. 4), but that does not mean that Jews have not regarded the sun as a source of numinous power. The sun is generally considered a benevolent force (Mal. 3), but also has the power to harm (Ps. 121). On two occasions in the **Bible**, God alters the course of the sun: once for the benefit of Israel (Josh. 10) and once as a sign to King Hezekiah (II Kings 20).

For the sectarian priests who authored many of the **Dead Sea Scrolls**, the sun was central to their mystical-priestly ideology. In contrast to the rabbinic tradition, they observed a solar **calendar**. To them the sun signified divine constancy and purity.

In Hebrew magical texts such as **Safer ha-Razim**, the influence of the sun is a matter of some interest. In certain Hebrew magical texts from late antiquity, pagan sun deities, such as **Helios**/Sol, are subsumed into a kind of "inclusive monotheism" that demotes them to the status of angels but still retains their names as numinous beings subservient to the God of Israel.

The **Talmud** suggests that the sun is sentient (Ned. 39b). Rabbinic thought teaches that, like all other celestial bodies, the sun has an animating intellect or **angel**. The sun comes to rest in the Garden of **Eden** each night. It burns red in the morning because its light is seen through the roses of Eden; it burns red at sunset because it passes behind the fire of **Gehenna** (B.B. 84a). An **eclipse** of the sun signifies a bad **omen** for the non-Jewish nations.

The Sages teach that the sun will shine more brightly in the Messianic Era. They also promise that the sun's true supernatural power will become evident in the **World-to-Come**; it will heal the **righteous** and burn up the wicked (Ned. 8b; B.B. 4a; Pes. 12a–b; Eruv. 56a). SEE ALSO ASTROLOGY; ZODIAC.

Suriel: A **Sar** angel mentioned in Berachot 51a and in **Hechalot** texts. He offers advice to mortals to protect them from **demons**.

Susiel: An angel mentioned in amulets.

Sword: A symbol of power, force, and punishment. God has a sword of judgment which is given to the **angels**; this may be the same sword that is wielded by the **Angel of Death**. Right now it "sleeps," but woe to the world should God ever awaken it (Mid. Teh. 80:3). The "sword" may be a figure of speech, referring to divine speech (Deut. 32:41; III Enoch 32). In Jewish magical practice, a sword was a component in a ritual to cure impotence.[1] SEE LANGUAGE; SIXTEEN-SIDED SWORD OF THE ALMIGHTY; WEAPONS.

1. Elkes, *The BeSHT: Magician, Mystic, and Leader*, 15.

Sword of Moses: (*Charba de Moshe*). A medieval manual of **theurgy**. This short book provides the most detailed description available of the rituals used by Jewish sorcerers to summon **angels**. The "sword" in the title is the power God gives over to mortals to fulfill "every desire." The manual begins with its theurgic philosophy, recounting how God adjured the angels to serve all humans who summon them properly, just as the angels served **Moses**. According to the text, the teaching contained in The Sword of Moses was given to Moses at the **burning bush**. The book describes the steps of **purification** and then gives the **incantations** that must be recited to command the angels to "adhere" to the sorcerer.

Like other Hebrew magical texts, The Sword of Moses is crammed with divine names, the names of hundreds of angels, and **permutation** mantras. The book includes an elaborate angelology, though most of the angelic names that appear in it are not names conventionally appearing in rabbinic texts. Even more peculiar is the fact that some of the angelic names are patronymic (they consist of the angel's name and the name of the angel's *father*). On the face of it, this contradicts other authoritative Jewish texts on the origins of angels.

Unlike other Hebrew magical texts that adhere more closely to rabbinic prohibitions against the methods of **sorcery** and **witchcraft**, The Sword of Moses revels in rituals and activities more characteristic of pagan magic—the extensive use of magical materials, animal **sacrifices**, and even the consumption of blood from ritually impure animals. The Sword contains a fine list of the *pharmalogia* of medieval magic. Some of these include rose oil, eggs, live **cocks**, worms, grasshoppers, fingernail parings, donkey meat, dust of ant hills, **olive oil**, camphor oil, **lion**'s blood, gall, human **bones**, and the dura mater of a ram's brain, as well as various broths made from substances soaked in water (hemp, radishes, laurels, etc.).

Some of the powers promised to the adept who employs the power of the Sword include destroying **demons**, **healing** disease, freeing prisoners, stopping a ship at sea, overthrowing kings, killing enemies, communing with the dead, and having supernal secrets revealed. And of course, it offers advice on the construction of **amulets**. It is striking that at one point in the text, the author of the work felt the need to assuage more traditionally-minded Jews by claiming that Moses used the Sword to combat **witch-craft**. *SEE* SUMMONING.

Sympathy: Sympathetic influence is one of the under-pinning assumptions of **magic**. Sympathetic magic is based on the metaphysical belief that divine forces are clothed in ordinary things and like affects like; that there are analogies to be made between symbolic acts and real events and that if things can be mentally associated, they can magically influence each other.

Sympathy is the basis for many forms of Jewish **divination**. **Bones** are used to summon dead spirits to séances. Adepts **summoning** angels will purify themselves in **water** direct from heaven and then dress themselves in **white**. The shapes and patterns in **oil** on water or thrown stones, or smoke curls, or the behavior of animals, are understood to parallel events in the empirical world.

It is also the basis for cursing rituals such as tying or burying figurines representing enemies and for healing practices such as reciting a word of power backwards to **reverse** an illness. Sympathy is clearly the logical basis for Jewish homeopathic remedies and remote **healing** (what in Latin is called *similia similibus curantur*, "like cures like"). Thus one 18th-century Jewish manual advised drinking a solution made from the brain of a hanged man as a treatment for epilepsy (apparently because, unarguably, hanging had quickly cured the executed man of *his* twitching and thrashing). Such examples of sympathetic rationales for Jewish theurgic and healing practices abound, though this is not the only way to think about the symbolic behavior found in Jewish magical traditions.[1]

Sympathy is also at work in the relationships between the higher and lower worlds. Thus when a Kabbalist wishes to effect a change in the divine **sefirot**, for example, he may opt to dress in the **color** of the particular sefirah he seeks to influence. *SEE* CURSES; PHARMACOPOEIA; SORCERY; VOODOO DOLLS.

1. Kern-Ulmer, "The Depiction of Magic in Rabbinic Texts," 291–92; Zimmels, *Magicians, Theologians, and Doctors*, 114–15.

Synagogue: (*Beit Kenesset; Beit Midrash;* Yiddish: *Shul*). Since Judaism does not have the concept of *terra sancta*, with the accompanying belief that such earth provides sanctuary against evil, this means that synagogues are as vulnerable to demonic assault as any other place (ShB 84). Thus archeologists have uncovered several examples of **amulets** being incorporated into synagogue walls, floors, and even placed within the **ark**.[1] At times the ark and other accoutrements and furnishings could themselves become the objects of magical or prophylactic beliefs and practices.

This is not to say synagogues have not been treated as places of numinous power. Synagogues have long served as centers of **healing**. In ancient and medieval times, this would entail the use of **segullot** (quasi-magical remedies), **lechishiot** (healing incantations), and **amulet**-making on or around the synagogue premises (Sword of Moses). Though such activities may have been marginal in the eyes of Jewish authorities, there are very few opinions recorded in Jewish law objecting to such activities. This suggests that these were, at the very least, tolerated uses for the synagogue.[2] Some **golem** traditions specify that earth from a synagogue is a necessary component in making one, while others indicate the actual construction of a golem must take place within a synagogue.[3]

1. Naveh and Shaked, *Amulets and Magic Bowls*, 14.
2. Levine, *The Ancient Synagogue*, 274–75.
3. Idel, *The Golem*, 61.

T

Ta'anit Chalom: "Dream fast." This defensive **ritual** fast meant to avert an evil **omen** is first described in the **Talmud**. When an individual experiences an ominous dream and wishes to escape the fulfillment of the premonition, he or she should fast, usually on the day following the dream. The importance of such fasts to avoid ill omens is considered so great that some authorities permit it to even override the obligation to feast on the Sabbath and festivals (Tan. 11b; Ber. 31b). *SEE* DREAMS; FASTING; PURIFICATION.

Tabernacle: (*Mishkan, Ohel Moed*). The portable sanctuary built by the Israelites while they sojourned in the desert for forty years. It was built at the explicit instructions of God. The building project was overseen by **Bezalel**. The **Cloud** of the **Glory** of God would descend into the tent and address the whole people through **Moses** (Ex. 40:38).

The structure was built out of a vast array of materials—wood, gold, silver, copper; clothes of blue, purple, and red; animal skins—given as freewill offerings by the Israelites. Its design was a **microcosm** of the world (Ex. R. 35:6; Num. R. 12:13). Its dimensions were based on symbolic numbers: sevens and tens. Besides the furnishings demanded by God, the Tabernacle displayed two miraculous items: the **rod** of **Aaron** and a bowl filled with **manna**.

Divided into three zones (the enclosure, sanctuary, and **devir**), it housed the **Ark of the Covenant**, the tablets of the **Ten Commandments**, the **altars**, and the **menorah**, as well as the sacred vessels and instruments of the sacrificial cult. Once the people settled Israel, the tent resided in various locations until **David** brought it to **Jerusalem**. Eventually, **Solomon** replaced it as the central sanctuary of the Jews by building the permanent **Temple**. *SEE* CHERUB; GOLD; OHEL; TENT OF MEETING.

Tahorah: "Purity." *SEE* PURIFICATION.

Taitazak, Joseph: Legalist and mystic (Turkish, ca. 17th century). He was the leading figure among the mystical circle in Salonica that gathered there after the expulsion of Jews from Spain. He experienced numerous revelations through a **maggid** that triggered **automatic writing**. He is possibly the author of **Sefer ha-Meshiv**.[1]

1. Kaplan, *Meditation and Kabbalah*, 173–75. Also see Bilu, "Dybbuk and Maggid," 350.

Takhlit he-Chacham: "Aim of the Wise." A Hebrew version of a popular gentile text of astrological magic, known as *Picatrix* in the Latin version, *Ghayat al Hakim* in the Arabic, that circulated in Jewish magical circles in the Middle Ages.

Taleh: "Ram"/Aries. **Zodiac** sign for the month of Nisan, which falls in the spring. It is a symbol of **fire**, **birth**, and the masculine principle. **Passover**, which occurs during Nisan, once entailed the sacrifice of a **ram** for the Seder meal. Since the Sages believed the Egyptians worshiped a sheep-headed God, this act signified the slaying of the demonic principle of bondage and constriction.[1]

1. Erlanger, *Signs of the Times*, 27–40.

Talmud: Second in authority only to the **Bible**, the Talmud is a vast compendium of Jewish lore made up of sixty-three tractates, each devoted to a different topic. The arrangement of information is more associative than categorical, and it often requires the study of multiple tractates in order to find all relevant information on a single topic. It is made up of several strata of material, composed over the 2nd through 6th centuries.

While the major focus of the Talmud is Jewish law, which is the application of the biblical commandments to everyday life, the Talmud also overflows with **aggadah**, nonlegal materials—stories, proverbs, medical remedies, and much more—of mythological, legendary, miraculous, fantastic, and esoteric nature.

Tamar: Judah's Canaanite daughter-in-law, who tricked him into sleeping with her in order to perpetuate Judah's family line, did so as a prophetess, inspired by the **Holy Spirit**. **Samael** worked to thwart her, but aided by **Gabriel**, she succeeded in her mission (Gen. 38; Gen. R. 85:9).

Tanin: *SEE* DRAGON.

Tanin'iver: "Blind dragon." An evil cosmic entity described in the Kabbalistic teachings of the **Treatise of the Left Emanation**, **Zohar**, **Emek ha-Melekh**, and subsequent writings based on these systems. He is the steed of **Lilith**, so he is a mechanism by which evil is activated. Though Tanin'iver is castrated (echoing legends about **Leviathan** and the **Yetzer ha-Ra**), he is still the catalyst for the coupling of Lilith with **Samael**, a union that brings pestilence into the world. *SEE* DEMON; DRAGON; SERPENT.

Tanna de Eliyahu: *SEE* SEDER ELIYAHU.

Tanya: Formally titled Likkutei Amarim but universally known as "Tanya," it is the magnum opus of Chasidic master **Sh'neur Zalman of Laydi** and the central text of the **CHaBaD** branch of **Chasidism**. Tanya is a large, sprawling fusion of medieval philosophy with Zoharic and Lurianic Kabbalah. It has many teachings regarding the **Godhead**, the **soul**, and **reincarnation**, among other things. Its most radical teaching is that of "acosmism," that the world is an illusion (320). Its most problematic concept is its endorsement of a kind of metaphysical racism, for it teaches that non-Jewish souls emanate from the **Sitra Achra**, the realm of evil, and are fundamentally different from Jewish souls (5).

Targum: Any translation of the Hebrew Bible into Aramaic. Often the translations are highly periphrastic, with explanations and occult interpretations being woven right into the verses. Targum **Song of Songs** is a classic example of this, since the mythic/Midrashic Aramaic "translation" bears only the most tenuous relationship to the plain meaning of the Hebrew original.

Tarot: A set of cards, modeled on playing cards, used for the purposes of **divination**. Tarot cards are a gentile invention of 14th- or 15th-century occult Italy. Despite the presence of Hebrew letters, including the **Tetragrammaton**, on some decks, the relationship of Tarot to Jewish esotericism is largely non-existent. Rather, the letters reflect the general occult enthusiasm for **Kabbalah** that arose in Renaissance culture. Because of their interest in divination, many Jews have become devotees of Tarot reading. *SEE* CHRISTIAN QABBALISTS.

Tarshishim: A class of **angels** mentioned in **Seder Gan Eden** and **Sefer Raziel**.

Tav: The twenty-second and last letter of the **Hebrew alphabet**. It has the vocalic value, depending on the regional dialect, of either "th," "t," or "s." Tav has the numeric value of 400. It symbolizes truth, perfection, and the end.[1] *SEE* HEBREW ALPHABET; LANGUAGE.

1. Munk, *The Wisdom of the Hebrew Alphabet*, 214–20.

Tefillin: "Prayer [Frontlets]." Also known as phylacteries, tefillin are two leather boxes with straps containing biblical verses (Deut. 6:4, 11:13–21; Ex. 13:1–10, 11–16), which are bound to the brow and left bicep with leather straps during Morning Prayers. They are meant to be worn as an *ot*, a "sign" or reminder of God's covenant with Israel. According to Talmud Tractate Berachot, humans wear tefillin in imitation of God, who wears tefillin with the name "Israel" contained in them (6a).

The fact that some early post-biblical literature calls tefillin *kamiaot* (amulets) points to the idea that many perceived them as objects of protection and power. Thus, according to one legend, during a time of persecution, a rabbi wore his tefillin despite the prohibition. When officers came to arrest him, he concealed his phylacteries in his hands. When the authorities demanded to see what he was concealing, the tefillin turned into doves (Shab. 19a).

Tefillin is the one religious article most mentioned in rituals for mystical **ascent** and for summoning angels. Safed mystics thought that the wearing of tefillin was a prerequisite for being possessed by an **ibbur**, a beneficent spirit. Beyond the general potential for tefillin to serve as an **amulet**, tales of miraculous sets of tefillin also appear in Jewish literature (ShB 172). These items gain their wondrous power either because they were previously owned by a righteous person, or because they have supernal origins, like being a gift from **Elijah**.[1]

1. Trachtenberg, *Jewish Magic and Superstition*, 145, 158.

Teleportation: (*Kefitzat ha-Derech*, "Jumping the Way"). Physical teleportation is first mentioned in the **Midrash**, where the saintly Sage **Chanina ben Dosa** is instantaneously transported to Jerusalem by a team of angels (S of S R. 1:4; Eccl. R. 1:1). The **Talmud** lists three biblical figures, **Eliezer**, **Jacob**, and Abishai, who traversed huge distances at miraculous speeds (Sanh. 95a; Chul. 91b). There are several other accounts of angelically assisted teleportation, usually involving religious virtuosos on a particular mission, such as one involving Simon bar Yochai's quest for an audience with Caesar in which angels progressively get Bar Yochai to Rome, past the palace guards, and then directly before the Emperor. Angels cease to be a part of later reports, and instead it becomes one of the wondrous talents available to the enlightened. Reports of teleportation were discussed by early medieval legal authorities. **Chai ben Sherira Gaon** writes about reports of a **Baal Shem** who could appear the same day in two synagogues several days apart (Otzer Geonim). Two medieval German Pietists, **Samuel he-Chasid** and **Judah he-Chasid**, could deploy a cloud to transport them over long distances (Sefer ha-Peliyah). Other sources suggest teleportation is achieved by enslaving demons for the purpose (Biur Maamar l'Rav Chayyim Vital). Both **Isaac Luria** and **Chayyim Vital** are credited with this feat.

Teleportation accounts jump dramatically in Chasidic wonder stories. There is even an account, reminiscent of the "night journey" of Mohammed, of a horse being able to transport a rider with supernatural speed after the **Tetragrammaton** was written on each of its hooves.

Teli: This enigmatic term first appears in **Sefer Yetzirah** (6:3, Long Recension), where it is described as being like a celestial "king on his throne." Some commentators take this to be an astronomical reference to the Milky Way or to the axis on which the celestial spheres turn. In Bahir, it is translated as "axis" and is linked to the divine **hair** (*taltalim*) described in Song of Songs chapter 5. It has also been translated as "dragon" and "serpent." Again, the assumption is that this is a reference to the sinuous appearance of the Milky Way galaxy, though this word and its significance remains a conundrum.

Temple: (*Beit ha-Mikdash, ha-Heichal, Beit Elohim, ha-Bayit, Beit ha-Bechira*). The Holy Temple in **Jerusalem** was one of the seven things God conceived before beginning the creation of the world (Gen. R. 3:9). There is a heavenly Temple to which the earthbound Temple corresponds (Tan. 5a; Ex. R. 33:4).

The building itself was made up of the Court, the Sanctuary and the **Holy of Holies**. The design of the Temple was that of a **microcosm**, a model representation of earth, heaven, and the **Throne of Glory** (Num. R. 12:13; *The Jewish War*, 5:5.4). There is also a strain of Jewish tradition that metaphysically links the Temple with **Eden**.[1] The Temple instruments and objects, decorated in such floral motifs as palms, pomegranates, and almonds, were meant to evoke that "garden" association (I Kings 6; II Chron. 3; I Enoch 29–32; Jubilees 3, 8), as were the decorative cherubim (I Kings 6, 7), known to the Israelites as the guardians of Eden (Gen. 3). The Temple is also understood to be a kind of macrocosm of the human soul, its three-chamber structure reflecting the three levels of the soul: **Nefesh**, **Ruach**, and **Neshamah**.

Many wonders were associated with its building. It only rained at night throughout the building project, the **shamir worm** cut all the stones needed for the work, the stones moved of their own accord from the quarry, and all the workers were immediately transported to the Garden of Eden upon the Temple's completion (Gen. R. 2:5; PR 6). According to the extracanonical **Testament of Solomon**, the great king enslaved the demons of the underworld to assist him in completing the sacred project.

The **Ark of the Covenant** emanated a supernal light that illuminated the interior of the Temple (Yoma 54b; Lev. R. 20:4). The gold **menorah** at the doorway would glow when the time for Morning Prayer came (Yoma 37b).

During the entire existence of the Temple, the rain and wind never put out a single sacrifice. The **fire** of the altar was unlike any other: it was clear, yet its flames were solid; it could consume both dry and wet wood; and the smoke it produced was never affected by the wind. Instead, the movement of the smoke was a kind of continuous omen, and the people could divine whether the future was positive or negative based on which way it flowed (Yoma 21a–b).

God and/or other divine entities such as angels would appear in the Temple precincts. The presence of God could be experienced in auditory and/or visible manifestations (I Kings 8:10–12; Isa. 6; Ber. 7a).

According to most of the prophets, God punished Israel for its many sins by decreeing the destruction of Solomon's Temple. God sent multiple omens to **Nebuchadnezzar**, the king of Babylon, directing him to conquer Judah (Eccl. R. 12:7; Lam. R. petichta 23). Angels even opened the city walls to the invaders (PR 26).

For the forty years preceding its destruction, signs of God's judgment were manifest throughout the building. Doors opened of their own accord, the **Urim and Thummim** did not give a positive answer, and the **scarlet cord** would not turn white (Yoma 39b).

At the time of the First Temple's destruction, objects of power were hidden away, including the **Ark of the Covenant**, the anointing **oil**, a jar of **manna**, Aaron's **rod**, and the treasure of the Philistines (Hor. 12a).

When the Romans destroyed Jerusalem and the Second Temple, the Sages were divided on whether it, too, was a punishment sent from God, or happened for some other, more positive divine purpose. As the Romans looted the building, the High Priest fled to the rooftop. There he took the keys and cast them into heaven, where a supernal hand caught them and took them to be held until the coming of the Messiah. When Titus finally entered the sanctuary, he cut the curtain of the **Holy of Holies**, causing it to bleed. Those Temple vessels he could find he took as prizes to Rome.

As mentioned earlier, there is a heavenly Temple, which the earthly one mirrors. Even though the earthly one is gone, the angel **Michael** continues to make offerings to God in the ascendant Temple (MdRI, Shirata 10; Chag. 12a; Gen. R. 1:4; Tanh., Vayakehel 7, Pikudei 1–3; Ex. R. 33:4). The **Zohar** equates this Temple on high with **Binah** (I: 2b).

At the End of Days, this supernal Jerusalem will descend and will rest upon the tops of the sacred **mountains** of Israel: Tabor, Carmel, Sinai, Zion/Moriah, and Hermon (Isa. 2:2; PdRK 21:4; Sefer Zerubbabel). In the Messianic Temple a mighty **river**, a fountain of purity and life, will flow from the Temple precincts, healing and fructifying the world (Zech. 14; Ezek. 47:1–12).

Much of early Jewish mystical practice revolved around obtaining **visions** of the heavenly Temple.[2] *SEE* ASCENT, HEAVENLY; PALACES; TABERNACLE.

1. Green, *Jewish Spiritually*, vol. 1, 51–52.
2. See Berman, *The Temple: Its Symbolism and Meaning Then and Now* and Elior, *The Three Temples*.

Temple Mount: *SEE* ZION.

Temple Scroll: A document found among the **Dead Sea Scrolls**, it is a revised version of Exodus through Deuteronomy, in which **Moses** is portrayed as mandating the agenda of the sectarian priests of **Qumran**, including the **solar calendar**, the organization of the **Temple**, and the purity of the sacred precincts and the surrounding city. It shares themes and teachings in common with **I Enoch** and **Jubilees**.

Temurah: Letter substitution. This is a popular method for revealing esoteric names of power for God. *SEE* ENCRYPTION; HAFUCH; TZERUF.

Ten Commandments: (*Eser ha-Dibrot*). The two tablets on which God inscribed the commandments were first carved from the **Even ha-Shetiyah**. When **Moses** shattered the first tablets, the letters flew back up to heaven (Avot 5:6; AdRN 2:11; Shab. 146a; Eruv. 54a; Deut. R. 15:17). God required Moses to make the second tablets with mortal hands, so the second stones did not have the same potent power, though the second stones were actually sapphire (PdRE 44). Surprisingly, while the Ten Commandments are a frequently cited text, they are rarely used in Jewish rituals of power.

Ten Lost Tribes: When the biblical northern kingdom of Israel was conquered by the Assyrians, the tribes that made up that nation—Simon, Levi, Gad, Dan, Naftali, Issachar, Reuben, Benjamin, Manasseh, and Ephraim—were carried off into exile. They subsequently vanished from history, but since the prophets repeatedly refer to their eventual restoration, many occult traditions about the whereabouts of the ten "lost tribes" continue to this day. In rabbinic tradition, the tribes dwell in the East, beyond the mythic river **Sambatyon**, which they cannot cross. Periodically, individuals would appear claiming to be from one of the tribes (Sanh. 10:6; Gen. R. 73:6; PR 31).

The ten tribes have been variously identified with the Pathans, the Kurds, the Masai, the Japanese, and Native Americans. A Christian movement, the "Anglo-Israelites," have claimed that the English (and German) peoples are the tribes. The Sefardic Chief Rabbinate of modern Israel has designated the *Beta Yisrael*, the black Jews of Ethiopia, to be descendants of **Dan**.[1]

1. See Segal, "The Ten Lost Tribes: Looking for the Remnants," *Hagshama*, World Zionist Organization Education Center. http://www.wzo.org.il.

Ten Martyrs: (*Aseret Harugei Melachot*). These ten Sages who died during Roman persecution are the archetypal martyrs. Their story is preserved in the collection known as Eleh Ezcharah ("This I Remember") and is recited every Yom Kippur afternoon in the **synagogue**. Many of the stories feature supernatural and miraculous elements. *SEE* AKIBA BEN JOSEPH; DECREES, DIVINE; ISHMAEL BEN ELISHA HA-KOHEN; RIGHTEOUS, THE.

Ten Miracles on the Twilight of the Sixth Day: According to Avot de Rabbi Natan 5:6, ten miracles alluded

to in the **Bible** were already preordained at **Creation** and merely awaited their appointed time to occur:

1) The mouth of the earth that swallowed **Korach** and his companions
2) **The Well of Miriam**
3) The mouth on Balaam's donkey
4) The **rainbow**
5) **Manna**
6) The **Rod** of Moses
7) The **shamir worm**
8) The supernal script on the first tablet of the **Ten Commandments**
9) The divine pen for writing the script
10) The stone tablets able to withstand the script.

Some add **demons**, the grave of **Moses**, Abraham's **ram**, and the first set of tongs (to make other tongs) (Avot 5:6).

Ten Trials of Abraham: God tested his chosen servant by ten trials. These were:

1) Having to leave his home as an old man;
2) Facing the famine in Canaan;
3) The taking of his wife by Pharaoh;
4) His battle with the four kings to rescue his nephew Lot;
5) The infertility of Sarah;
6) Accepting the command to circumcise himself as an old man;
7) The taking of his wife by the Philistine king;
8) Having to send away Hagar;
9) Having to send away Ishmael;
10) Having to offer his son Isaac for a sacrifice

(Jubilees 17:17; Avot 5:5; AdRN 33; PdRE 26–31).

Tent: *SEE* ADAT EL; OHEL; TABERNACLE; TENT OF MEETING.

Tent of Meeting: (Ohel Moed). In most passages of the Torah, this term appears to be a synonym for the **Tabernacle**. In Exodus 33:7–11, however, the Tent seems to be a separate structure, an oracular building outside the camp. God descends upon it in a **pillar** of **cloud** and then addresses the people from its entrance (Ex. 33:9–11; Deut. 31:14–15). *SEE* ADAT EL.

Teomim: "Twins"/Gemini. The Hebrew **zodiac** sign for the month of *Sivan*. It signifies unity, especially the unity of God and Israel, as this was the month in which the revelation at **Sinai** occurred.[1] *SEE* CALENDAR.

    1. Erlanger, *Signs of the Times*, 55–69.

Terach: The father of Abraham, he is alternately portrayed in the **Midrash** as a noble figure and a base idolator. He was witness to several miracles performed on behalf of his son.

Terafim: Terafim were small figurines, evidently representations of either gods or ancestors, kept in the homes by the Semitic peoples of the Ancient Near East. The etiology of the word itself is subject to debate. It may be a derivation of the Hittite *tarpi*, meaning "spirit," or possibly from the Arabic *raffa*, "shine." Terafim were clearly regarded to be objects of power, as illustrated by the determination of Laban to retrieve the terafim removed by his daughter Rachel when she departed with Jacob (Gen. 31:34). Scholars speculate that terafim may have been part of a complex of beliefs concerning the deified dead among the Western Semitic peoples, including the Hebrews.

    The Hebrew Scriptures clearly associate terafim with mantic practices (Judg. 17:5, 18:14; Ezek. 21:26; Hos. 3:4; Zech. 10:2). The exact manner of their divinatory use is unclear, though Ezek. 21:26 raises the possibility that **arrows** or other sticks may have been cast in front of the statues, I Ching fashion. The terafim had some connection to the **Urim and Thummim** used by the Israelite priesthood. Both were used for divination, but some speculate they resembled each other in form as well as function. There is some evidence that some terafim were made from alabaster or some other stone that would interact with light, and may be related to the luminous *elmeshu* stone mentioned in Mesopotamian sources.

    The terafim were the butt of satirical humor in the Bible, such as having a menstruating woman sit on them (Gen. 31) and having Michal, the wife of David, use one as a decoy (I Sam. 19:13). Such stories are intended to denigrate the spiritual value of terafim in the eyes of the reader.

    In the **Zohar**, they are identified as idols specifically used in **witchcraft** (I: 164b). According to **Pirkei de-Rabbi Eliezer**, the terafim were actually enchanted talking skulls (36).

Tesira: A **demon** of the underworld that attacks the ritually lax after the end of the **Sabbath** (Zohar I: 17b).

Testament of Abraham: *SEE* ABRAHAM, TESTAMENT OF.

Testament of Levi: *SEE* LEVI, TESTAMENT OF.

Testament of Solomon: *SEE* SOLOMON, TESTAMENT OF.

Tet: Ninth letter of the **Hebrew alphabet**, it has the vocalic value of "t" and the numeric value of 9.[1]

    1. Munk, *The Wisdom of the Hebrew Alphabet*, 118–24.

Tetragrammaton: (Greek, "The four-letter name"). YHWH (or YHVH) is derived from the Hebrew verb "to be," so it carries the sense of "The Eternal" or "[Ultimate] Being." Also known as the "ineffable name" of God and the "explicit name" of God, it is the holiest of God's names and the archetypal divine name of power.[1] So great was its holiness that eventually the proper pronunciation was concealed to prevent its abuse (Yoma 39b–40a). Even great Sages who misuse the name can expect dire punishments (A.Z. 17b).

    According to one **Midrash**, every **angel** wears a seal with the Tetragrammaton inscribed on it (PdRK 12:22). Using only the first two letters, God created both this world and the **World-to-Come** (PR 21). God revealed it to **Moses** while granting him his prophetic powers (Ex. 4). It was inscribed on Aaron's **rod** of power. **Solomon** inscribed it on his **ring**, giving him control of **demons**. It subsequently appears in countless tales of wonders performed by prophets, sages, and other men and women of God, as it grants virtually unlimited powers to those who know how to properly activate it (Mak. 11a; Git. 68b; PdRK 19). It is used to summon angels, perform healings, teleport, empower **amulets**, and animate **golems**. Inscribed on **weap-**

ons, it made the bearer invulnerable (ChdM; Targum S of S 2:17; Tanh. B. Shelach 1; PdRE 47).

The name, however, is like plutonium and can be used for purposes both good and ill. **Lilith** used it to escape Eden and the reach of the angels. Jeroboam used it to animate the gold calves in his false sanctuary and so deceived the northern tribes into following him (Sot. 47a). **Jesus** used it to gain magical powers (**Toldot Yeshu**).

As mentioned earlier, by long-standing custom, the four-letter name of God is not pronounced. According to one tradition, the Sages would reveal the correct pronunciation of the Name only once in seven years (Kid. 71a). Based on Psalm 29—*kol YHWH al ha-mayyim*, "the sound 'YHWH' is upon the water"—**Eleazar of Worms** taught that a master could only transmit the proper pronunciation of the Tetragrammaton to a disciple while they were both partially immersed in water (**Sefer ha-Shem**).

While in biblical and rabbinic literature the name serves as a metaphor for the presence of God on earth (Ex. 24), in sefirotic metaphysics YHWH is the divine name linked with **Tiferet**. There is also a mystical tradition that the morphology of the letters of the Tetragrammaton are seen as a visual representation of the **sefirot**, when arranged vertically, with *yod* representing Keter, the first *hay* representing the middle sefirot, the *vav* signifying the lower sefirot, and the second *hay* symbolizing **Malchut**. Other configurations and associations are proposed in various mystical tracts, such as the idea that the first two letters signify the negative reality of God (God is "No-thing"), while the last two represent God's positive existence (Kedushat Levi, Bereshit). *SEE* ENCRYPTION; EXPLICIT NAME OF GOD; NAMES OF GOD.

1. Janowitz, *Icons of Power*, 19–31.

Tevel: One of the seven material worlds. According to Seder Gan Eden, it is where the earthly Garden of **Eden** is located. In other sources, it is one of the compartments of **Gehenna**.

Theurgy: Rabbinic thought teaches that humanity has the power to influence the Godhead, and even contribute to its wellbeing, empowering God through our actions (PdRK 26). Conversely, both **Midrash** and later **Kabbalah** also assert that human sin actually "weakens divine power." (Bachya ben Asher, Commentary to Numbers 14:17). By the same token, humans are able to use divine power to influence things in the lower realms. This ability goes beyond the mere power of supplication in prayer; the knowledgeable Jew can, in effect, borrow God's power and use it in what we today would call a "magical" fashion.

Theurgy is, like magic, a **ritual** means to gain and exercise power. Two things distinguish theurgy from magic. First, the power that the theurgist commands/adjures is a personalistic entity—a god, angel, or demon—rather than abstract, impersonal forces, as is the case with magic. Thus, for example, Hechalot texts will command angels to do the work, whereas Greek magical ritual texts will simply say, "I bind so-and-so." Second, theurgy requires spiritual and moral excellence of the adept for it to be effective. Magic is merely a technology that anyone can be trained to use.

There are several ways in which Jewish theurgists have understood how their power works. The most ancient is the belief that **Hebrew** letters and words, being supernatural first creations of God, are repositories of divine energy. This is all the more true of names and, especially, divine names. The adept who knows how to tap the power of words and angelic and divine names can perform mighty acts of power. This idea is first hinted at in the **Talmud** and further developed in **Sefer Yetzirah**. Subsequently, the theurgic power of language is one of the foundational assumptions of Merkavah mystics, **amulet** makers, practical Kabbalists, and sorcerers.

The second assumption comes out of Kabbalah; that the *shefa*, or divine influx that flows from God through the **sefirot** and animates the lower worlds, can be channeled and tapped by the Kabbalist for practical purposes. With the right knowledge, both letters and shefa can be tapped at will, much like one can use the energy of a river to drive a power plant (Pardes Rimmonim; Hesed L'Avraham 15). To use these forces, the human soul is the transformer, and the adept must attune his or her body to these spiritual forces through Jewish rituals, incantations and special practices in order to use them. In a number of mystical systems, these two theories of theurgy are fused together and harmonized (Chayyim ha-Olam ha-Ba).

Over time, the Jewish belief in the human ability to manipulate sefirotic energy also becomes conflated with the astral-magical belief found in the Hermetic traditions that one can harness the power and influence of the stars and constellations. These gentile traditions especially emphasize the use of objects that are in some way analogous to the power being accessed, or represent the force or desired result. Thus we see throughout the Middle Ages both the correlation of **angels** (named entities of power) and sefirot (influx of power) with astrological symbols and the increasing use of sympathetic magic and homeopathic objects in Jewish theurgy.[1]

1. Idel, *Hasidism*, 65–69; Idel, *Kabbalah: New Perspectives*, 165–99; Ginsburg, *The Sabbath in Classical Kabbalah*, 3.

Thirteen Attributes of Mercy: Based on the "revelation of the cleft" given **Moses** (Ex. 34:6), these thirteen attributes of God are symbolized in the thirteen twists found in the last winding of each ritual **fringe** on a tallit. Since God recites them on high when desiring to forgive Israel, any Jew who recites these verses in sincere contrition while wrapped in a tallit will be forgiven all sins. Others insist they must be accompanied with action (R.H. 17b; Tomar Devorah 1).

Thirty-Two Paths of Wisdom: In Sefer Yetzirah, this refers to the supernal power inherent in the twenty-two letters of the **Hebrew alphabet** and the ten **sefirot**. Mastery of the paths gives one both transcendent knowledge and theurgic power. (SY 1:1).

Thread, Blue: *SEE* FRINGES.

Throne of Glory: (*Kisse Kavod, Merkvah*). Both Isaiah and Daniel describe visions of God seated upon a throne (Isa. 6; Dan. 7). As the archetypal symbol of God's *Gevurah*, God's power, the Throne of Glory is one of the six things that preexists **Creation** (Gen. R. 1:4). God threw a chunk of the Throne into the abyss and the cosmos coagulated around it (Midrash Konen 2:24).

The throne is represented on the **Ark of the Covenant** as two **cherubim** whose wings form God's "Seat of Mercy." By contrast, Ezekiel's vision describes God upon a **chariot**, also supported by cherubim. Some understand that both prophets are describing the same entity. As a result, it is sometimes characterized as God's "Throne-Chariot."

There are many vivid descriptions of the Throne and its prominent features. It is a celestial sky blue, the same blue that is part of the **fringes** an Israelite must wear. Another Midrash calls it **chashmal**, amber. Made of half **fire**, half hail, it hovers in the air, is eight hundred thousand parasangs in length and five hundred thousand in width—and that is calculated in the parasang of heaven, which is two thousand cubits of the length of God's arm (PdRE 3, 4, 6; BhM 2:25, 41–46).

When sitting upon the Throne in judgment, God is draped in a supernal robe of purple inscribed with the names of the martyrs of Israel (Mid. Teh. 4:12). The Throne is also inscribed with the image of the Patriarch **Jacob**. Thus the Throne, like God's **tefillin**, represents the metaphysical bond of the people Israel to the Godhead (Hechalot Zutarti).

The angel **Sandalfon** stands over the Throne, weaving the prayers of Israel into God's crown. Four princes surround the Throne: **Michael** (right), **Gabriel** (left), **Uriel** (in front), and **Raphael** (behind). Other texts describe myriads of armies of angels arrayed around it. The earth is the footstool of God's throne.

There is one tradition that there are actually two thrones, the Throne of Strict Justice and the Throne of Mercy. When Israel prays for forgiveness, it moves God to leave the first and sit in the second (Sanh. 38b).

Despite the detailed and exacting descriptions, the exact nature of the Throne is difficult to pin down. It has sentience and at times it speaks—and sings. Some passages suggest the Throne consists entirely of cherubim and **ofanim** (winged and wheeled angels) (Hechalot Rabbati).

Later Kabbalistic teachings tend to understand the Throne as being more metaphorical than concrete. As a result, various sources equate the Throne with the heavens, the divine mind (Mada'ey ha-Yahadut), the supernal first **light** of Creation, or the Torah (Meshiv Devarim Nekhochim). Some Kabbalistic sources coyly intimate that that the Throne is, like the **Shekhinah**, an attribute of the divine feminine principle, so when the Glory of God sits upon it, it signifies a *hieros gamos*, that the male and female principles are unified.

Based on Daniel 7:9, one Sage teaches that there are thrones for the **righteous** beside the Throne. **Abraham**, **Moses**, and **David** sit upon these thrones. **Metatron**, the "lesser YHWH" also has a throne proximate to the Throne of Glory. It is such an enthronement in the presence of God, amounting to a kind of "**angelification**," that is the ultimate desire of the Merkavah mystic.

Akin to this idea that God draws the righteous close to the Throne, there are a number of traditions about what God keeps under the throne, including a Treasury of Souls waiting to be born and a Treasury of Souls of the saintly dead. Four angelic encampments are arranged around the throne, just as the tribes of Israel were once arrayed around the **Tabernacle** while they encamped in the desert (PdRE 4).

According to an oft-repeated legend, the face of Jacob is inscribed upon the Throne, signifying God's special devotion to the Patriarch and to Jacob's children (Gen. R. 68:12; PdRE 35). In the **World-to-Come**, the Throne will become visible and evident to all (J. Shabbat 6:9).

Throne of Solomon: Inspired by the **Holy Spirit**, King Solomon constructed a throne that resembled God's **Throne of Glory** (I Chron. 29:23). The throne had the images of the four faces that Ezekiel saw on God's chariot-throne: a man, an eagle, an ox, and a **lion**. It was engraved with the words of the **Priestly Blessing** and encrusted with precious gems so that it glowed. **Sefer Raziel** states that it resembled ice and that divine names are inscribed upon it.

Behind it was a large wheel back-panel, mimicking the **ofan** angel behind God's throne. A dove hovered over the seat, and it was surrounded by images of **cherubim** and **chayyot** angels. It was mounted on six steps, reminiscent of the six lower levels of heaven. There were twelve golden lions and twelve golden eagles on the steps. Trees grew around the throne, and multi-hued cloths hung above it.

There were also many living animals, clean and unclean, predators and prey, ringing the dais. These animals lived harmoniously together and would serve as mounts, moving Solomon on and off the platform. Some of the animals could speak. At times the animals would raise their voices together in Solomon's honor, imitating the angelic choirs that sing God's praises. Eagles could lift the entire throne complex, moving him from place to place.

Solomon's throne room was filled with seventy thousand chairs. The seventy leaders of Israel were always seated at the forefront. Two chairs nearest the throne were reserved for the prophets who attended Solomon—Gad and Nathan. A golden **menorah** of seven branches, each inscribed with the name of an antediluvian or a Patriarch, stood nearby.

Whenever Solomon uttered a just decision from his throne, the Holy Spirit would confirm the decision and lions would lick his feet.

After the Babylonian conquest, the throne was carried off to the East. Many kings attempted to sit on it, but the beasts surrounding it would prevent them. Finally the Romans broke it into pieces (Es. R., 1:2; Num. R. 12:21; BhM 2:83–85, 5:34–37).

Tiferet: "Beauty." The sixth and central of the **sefirot**. In classical **Kabbalah**, it is usually understood as the masculine principle of the Godhead. It is the sefirah of the written Torah (Zohar I: 77a). It is also the critical harmonizing principle of the Godhead, balancing between the polar "left" and "right" sides of divine emanations. In the **Zohar** it is equated with the divine title **Blessed Holy One**. Jacob and Moses personify this sefirah, and green and purple are the **colors** that symbolize it.

Tihari: "Noon [Demons]." This class of disease-bearing demon is mentioned in Targum Song of Songs 4:6, based on Psalm 91:6.

Tikkun: "Repair/Rectification/Completion." Many magical-mystical practices in Judaism come with the rationale of *tikkun*; that performing a **commandment**, rite, or act correctly will have the theurgic effect of repairing the cosmos and/or strengthening the Godhead. This idea, first fully developed in the teachings of **Isaac Luria**, reflects the notion that humanity exists in order to rebuild **Adam Kadmon**, the quasi-divine anthropos that was God's ideal creation at the beginning of time. Tikkun can take place in virtually any situation; all aspects of the Creation, whether mundane or supernatural, are in need of tikkun. Animals achieved it by being sacrificed in the **Temple** or by being slaughtered in accordance with the laws of Kashrut. People need to continue personal tikkun both in this life and the next. Chasidic exorcists, for example, perform "tikkun" upon ghosts, helping them make the journey into the afterlife.[1] SEE BREAKING OF THE VESSELS.

1. Green, *Jewish Spirituality*, vol. 2, 27–30, 65–69, 107–8, 411–12.

Tikkun Shovavim: "Repairing the mischievous ones." SEE BANIM SHOVAVIM.

Tikkunei Zohar: A late addition to the corpus of the **Zohar**, it is in fact a free-standing work in its own right, a commentary devoted primarily to expounding the mysteries of **Creation**, though it is quite free-ranging in its topic matter.

Tish: (Also *Firen Tish; Farbrengen*. Yiddish, "Table.") Among the spiritual customs of **Chasidism** is the rebbe's *tish*, a mass gathering of Chasids around their spiritual leader, in which the sharing of food and drinking is combined with lengthy discourses on Torah, singing, and ecstatic dancing. These normally occur at Sabbaths, festivals, or commemorative days, and can last many hours.

The food (usually **bread** and/or **fish**) is blessed and distributed through the hand of the rebbe. This food, called **sherayim**, is considered to be imbued with great sanctity. While most will eat it, some participants will keep the morsels as **amulets**.[1] SEE FARBRENGEN.

1. Rabinowicz, *The Encyclopedia of Hasidism*, 495–96.

Tit ha-Yaven: "Miry Clay." One of the seven compartments of **Gehenna**. There slanderers, bribe takers, traitors, heretics, and all those who betrayed the trust of their fellows are punished (Gedulat Moshe).

Tobiah: Pious Israelite boy who is the protagonist of the book of **Tobit**. With the aid of **Raphael**, he battles and exorcises a **demon** that haunts a damsel in distress.

Tobit: This Jewish novella that is included in the Catholic canon of the Apocrypha tells the story of a young man, Tobiah, who is sent on a journey by his father. Meanwhile, a young bride, Sarah, is haunted by the demon **Asmodeus**, who slays seven grooms to the girl on each of their wedding nights. The angel **Raphael** brings these two together and gives Tobiah the tools to defeat the de-

mon and win the girl. It is the first detailed description of an **exorcism** found in Jewish literature.

Toilet: The Talmudic Rabbis actually offer considerable advice on toilet hygiene and the preservation of health during bodily evacuation. There is also a malevolent spirit that lurks in toilets and privies known as the *sheid shel beit ha-kisei*, "the demon of the outhouse." SEE PRIVY DEMON; UNCLEAN SPIRITS.

Toldat Adam: An 18th-century medical/magical book, possibly composed by Yoel ben Uri Halperin.

Toldot Yeshu: "The Chronicle of Jesus." A polemical tract against **Christianity** that gives an alternate version of the life of **Jesus** from that found in the Gospels. Like the Gospels, it is full of fabulous events, but in Toldot Yeshu these are credited to Jesus's talent as a magician. A fragmentary Aramaic copy appears among the **Cairo Geniza** collection. Since the medieval Church would not tolerate any counter-narrative to the New Testament or criticism of Christian traditions, even in parody form, the book was suppressed by Christian censors wherever they had to power to do so.

Tomar Devorah: This 16th-century mystical-ethical treatise by **Moses Cordovero** explains that human transgression produces **mashchit**/destructive entities. It also explains the power of Torah to counteract **Samael** and all forces of **evil**.

Tophet: "Roaster." A high place designated for the sacrifice of children to pagan gods such as Molech. Child sacrifice, mostly in time of national or communal crisis, was an accepted element of Western Semitic paganism and tophets were created not only in Israel and Lebanon (II Kings 3:27, 23:10; Jer. 7:31), but also in Phoenician colonies such as Carthage.[1]

1. Stager and Wolf, "Child Sacrifice at Carthage" in *Biblical Archaeology Review*, Jan./Feb. 1984.

Torah: "Instruction." The Pentateuch, the first five books of the Hebrew Scriptures (Genesis, Exodus, Leviticus,

Numbers, and Deuteronomy). By tradition, all five of the books that constitute the Torah were given to the Jewish people on Mount **Sinai** through the agency of Moses. The term "*Torah*," however, can also be used informally to refer to the entire corpus of Jewish teachings (the phrase, "to study Torah," for example, can mean the study of any sacred Jewish text). At times it is even used as a synonym for "Judaism."

Despite the seemingly "historical" character of the five books (an account going from **Creation** to the death of Moses), in Jewish mythos Torah is a truly timeless supernal entity. It is one of the **six primordial things** (or **seven primordial things**) that predate Creation (Gen. R. 1:4, 8:2; Mid. Teh. 90:12; Mid. Prov. 8). The true Torah, the soul of the Torah, exists in heaven as black **fire** written on white fire (Tanh., Bereshit 1). God used the Torah as a blueprint for ordering the universe (Gen. R. 1:1, 1:4; Tanh., Bereshit 1; PdRE 3). According to Midrash Konen, God drew three drops of water and three drops of fire from the supernal Torah kept in heaven and from them God made the world (2:24). The Torah is the **light** of Creation (Ex. R. 5:3). It is also the **Tree of Life** that grew in the center of **Eden**. Lost after the expulsion of **Adam** and **Eve**, it was restored to humanity at Sinai, liberating humanity from death by serving as the key to the afterlife (Ber. 32b, 61b; Lev. R. 18:3; Zohar I: 132a). Other sources describe it as the *ketubah*, the wedding contract between God and Israel, who have entered into a kind of cosmic **marriage** (Deut. R. 3:12; Pes. 106a).

The medieval German Pietists identified Torah as "The footstool of God," conflating it with God's **Glory** and the **Shekhinah**. Torah, in these terms, is nothing less than the physical manifestation of divinity, a kind of "God inscripted," as it were. To be constantly engaged in its study is the highest form of worship known to Judaism.

The **Zohar** teaches that the Torah we have on earth, the Torah of laws, stories, and theology, is only the "garments of Torah," for material beings could not survive an encounter with the unshielded Torah.

The earthly Torah, however, is still very powerful. King **David** wore a miniature Torah strapped to his right arm in combat and won every battle, thus illustrating that the Torah is also used as an **amulet** (Ps. 16:8). Both the words of Torah and the physical object of the Torah scroll have protective powers.

The **Talmud** notes that at times Torah narratives appear out of order. The Sages go on to explain this is deliberate—for if the Torah were properly arranged according to its heavenly configuration, any person reciting it could perform wonders, even resurrect the dead (Mid. Teh. 3:2; Yalkut 625:3). *SEE* BIBLE; ORAL TORAH; SEFER.

Torat ha-Melachim: "Torah of the Angels." A term for secret meanings to the **Torah**, the **commandments**, and/or Jewish Law that are revealed by **angels** to pious individuals. While most authorities did not recognize angelic revelations as a basis for Jewish observance, some Jews of Medieval Europe and Kabbalists put special stock in such angelic insights (Sefer Or Zerua; She'elot u'T'shuvot min ha-Shamayim). *SEE* LAW AND THE PARANORMAL; MAGGID; SAR HA-TORAH; STUDY; SUMMONING.

Tosafist: "Amender." Medieval French-German Talmudists and Bible commentators (11th–13th centuries). Though the greater bulk of their studies concentrated on Jewish Law and understanding the plain meaning of both the **Bible** and **Talmud**, the Tosafists were not without their own occult beliefs. A number of them engaged in theurgic practices, especially pertaining to adjuring **angels** and **demons** to assist them in their study of Torah. They also made use of **amulets** and mantic techniques.[1]

1. Kanarfogel, *Peering through the Lattices*, 121–231.

Tosefta to Targum Ezekiel: A Hechalot text on angel adjurations.

Totems: An object of nature, usually an animal, taken as a symbol for a people. Ancient Israelites had many totemistic symbols. The tribe of Judah (ancestors of modern Jews) had the lion as their totem, which is why lion iconography appears in synagogues and Jewish art to this day. Other tribes were also identified with plants or animals (Gen. 49; Deut. 33). Israelite mothers would often name their children based on events or phenomena associated with their birth. Animal names (Devorah, "bee"; Nachson, "snake"; Huldah, "weasel") were commonplace. The "Tree of Life" is the totem for the **Torah**. A number of totemistic animals are associated with God (eagles, lions, oxen) (Ezek. 1). *SEE* MENORAH.

Tower of Babel: (*Migdol Bavel*). Already a fantastic tale as recorded in the Bible (Gen. 11), Jewish tradition added occult elements to the story. The Midrash includes the tradition that the builders intended to storm heaven and take it by force. After God confounded the speech of its builders, one-third of the building burned, one-third was swallowed by the earth, and only one-third remained visible above ground. In the apocalyptic tradition, its designers turned into demons and spirits (Sanh. 109a; Apocalypse of Baruch). The peoples then scattered and eventually formed the distinctive seventy **nations** that make up the newly diverse humanity (PdRE 24; Tanh., Noah).

Trance: An altered state of consciousness. Many different forms of trances have been described in Jewish literature, including prophetic, mystical, and mediumistic or possessive types.[1] *SEE* ASCENT; DANCE; MEDITATION; MEDIUM; PROPHECY; VISION; YORED MERKAVAH.

1. Bilu, "Dybbuk and Maggid," 341–48. Also see Davila, "Hekhalot Literature and Shamanism."

Transmigration: *SEE* REINCARNATION.

Treasury of Souls: *SEE* TZROR HA-CHAYYIM.

Treatise on the Left Emanation: This revolutionary and influential text by **Isaac ben Jacob ha-Kohen** offers the first comprehensive mystical interpretation of evil as an integral part of God's emanation of **Asiyah**, the material world. In it, we learn of a demonic universe, later known as the **Sitra Achra**, which parallels and mirrors the angelic structures of the **sefirot**. The book also offers a mystical eschatology.

Treatise of Shem: An astrological almanac, found among the **Dead Sea Scrolls**, for predicting the future (especially agricultural conditions) based on the position of the stars and other conditions at the beginning of each year. The purported author of this work is **Shem**, the son of **Noah**, though internal evidence, like explicit references to the Romans, mark it as a work of late antiquity.

Trees: (*Eitz; Eitzim*). A tree is one of the most potent symbols in Jewish semiotics. It is a bridge between heaven and earth, and can symbolize the Torah, the human being, and the **sefirot** (Bahir 22, 119).

Trees are sentient (Gen. R. 13:2). The trees that grow in the Garden of **Eden** have **healing** powers (BhM II: 53). They sing praises to God (Perek Shirah; J. Chag. 2:1; Zohar I: 77a). The leaves give off a heavenly scent. Rabbi **Abbahu**, who collected such leaves in his gown, was later able to sell the gown for a fortune (B.M. 114a–b). The leaves of Edenic trees can be ground up and eaten for their healing properties. **Solomon** planted a variety of wondrous trees on the grounds of the **Temple** (J. Yoma 41d). They produced **fruits** for those who visited the Temple, but when gentile armies entered the Temple, the trees withered instantly and will not be restored until the Messianic Age (Yoma 38a; Sanh. 100a).

Tree of the Knowledge of Good and Evil: The tree at the center of the Garden of Eden. God forbade the primordial couple from eating its fruit, but at the prompting of the serpent, they did anyway (Gen. 2–3).

Because it is the source of the fall of humanity, it is sometimes also called the "Tree of Death" (Seder Eliyahu Rabbah 5). The exact type of **fruit** that **Adam** and **Eve** ate was a matter of rabbinic debate. Candidates put forward include: grapes, pomegranates, etrogs, and figs. One Sage even argued for wheat, but his colleagues ridiculed him for that claim. Fig has been the most obvious choice, because only a few verses later it is described how they made garments of fig leaves (Gen. 3:7). There is also a Talmudic tradition that the leaves of the Tree contain the knowledge of **magic** and consuming them grants one such gnosis (Ber. 40a; B.M. 114b).

The Tree of the Knowledge of Good and Evil is linked to Atara (**Keter**) in the sefirotic system (Biur al ha-Torah 1:67). In the Messianic Age, God will uproot the Tree from the world and replant it in **Gehenna**.

Tree of Life: The source of immortality (Biur al ha-Torah 1:67–69), the Tree of Life grew in the middle of Eden with the Tree of the Knowledge of Good and Evil. The **Zohar** claims that both trees grew from the same trunk. It is so big that the circumference of its trunk is "five-hundred years' walking" (the ancients like to measure distance by time, see the book of Jonah). All four of the primordial rivers branched out from beneath it (J. Ber. 2c).

One legend claims the **rod** of **Moses** was culled from the Tree. According the rabbinic understanding, the Tree of Life is the **Torah**, and the eternal life that was lost in Eden was restored to humanity with the giving of the Torah at Sinai (Prov. 3:18; Ber. 32b, 61b; Zohar I: 132a). This may explain the enigmatic declaration that the souls of the righteous ascend to heaven via the tree (Midrash Konen). It is **Tiferet** in the sefirotic system, which is also equated to the Torah.

Twilight: This is a liminal time, a time of transition. Most fantastic traditions regarding twilight are associated with the twilight of the sixth day of **Creation**, the eve of the first **Sabbath**. **Adam** and **Eve** committed the sin of disobedience at that time, initiating history (A.Z. 8a). According to Avot 5:6, **ten miracles** mentioned in the Bible were preprogrammed into Creation at that time. A related tradition says that **demons** were created at twilight of the sixth day. *SEE* NIGHT.

Twins: There is one famous pair of twins mentioned in the Bible (**Jacob** and **Esau**) and one in rabbinic literature (Abel and his twin sister, later Cain's wife) (PdRE 21). *SEE* PAIRS.

Tzadi: The eighteenth letter of the **Hebrew alphabet**. It has the linguistic value of "tz/ts." It has the numeric value of 90. It is one of the five letters that has a *sofit* form, a different shape if it appears at the end of a word. It symbolizes righteousness and humility.[1]

    1. Munk, *The Wisdom of the Hebrew Alphabet*, 189–93.

Tzadik: *SEE* REBBE; RIGHTEOUS, THE.

Tzadikiel: "Righteous of God." An angel mentioned in **Sefer Yetzirah** and the **Zohar**. He is the good angel who escorts the individual home on the eve of the **Sabbath** (Shab. 119b) and who assists the dead entering **Eden**.

Tzakadhazy: An angel of the **Countenance** mentioned in **Ma'aseh Merkavah**.

Tzavua: A ferocious beast whose fur contains 365 colors, mostly likely a **hyena** (Gen. R. 7; Josh. 1:3).

Tzedakah: *SEE* CHARITY.

Tzeidah Laderekh: Medieval tract by Menachem ben Aharon devoted to the astrological signs and their influence on humanity.

Tzelanit: (Aramaic, "Shadow [Demon]"). A class of demons frequently mentioned in **amulets** and **incantation bowls**. It also appears in Targum to Song of Songs.

Tzelem: "Image." In the Zohar and later Jewish mysticism, the "image" of God mentioned in Gen. 1:26 is thought to refer to a specific dimension of the human being, a kind of spiritual membrane or aura that mediates between the body and the soul. The shadow cast by the human body is a visible effect of this aura.[1] This *tzelem* may be the same concept that appears in other Kabbalistic works such as the **Guf ha-Dak**. *SEE* SHADOW.

    1. Scholem, *On the Mystical Shape of the Godhead*, 251–73.

Tzeruf/Tzerufim: Acrostic or letter re-combination or **permutation**. As a technique of mystical research, Tzeruf refers to recombining letters in different order both to uncover **names of God** and in constructing **incantations** and other power phrases (SY 2:2, 6:4). It can also refer to incantations involving the combination of **names of God** with elaborate mathematical permutations of letters of the **Hebrew alphabet**. This was the preferred ecstatic practice of **Abraham Abulafia**. The worthy ancients, such as **Moses**, were purportedly especially adept at this practice (Ber. 55a; Zohar III: 2a; Sefer Peliyah 1:17b). Tzerufim incantations are used in a variety of theurgic rites, most notably summoning **angels** and **demons** and constructing a **golem**. *SEE* ABBREVIATIONS; CODES.

Tzimtzum: "[Divine] Self-Contraction/Withdrawal." According to Lurianic cosmogony, the **Ein Sof** of God had to "withdraw" (imagine creating a finite space within infinity, like a bubble or a womb) in order for the universe to emerge from within It as an independent reality. The implication of this is that God is "absent" from the world in a very real sense. On the flip side, there could be no sense of "otherness," or existence outside God, unless God had made this self-contraction (Shem Olam; Tanya 20). This is necessary for the sake of **Creation** itself, for free will, and the fulfillment of God's ultimate will in Creation—that we engage in the **Tikkun**, or repair, of the world and so become worthy partners with God (Etz ha-Chayyim 1). While the cosmic model of God's withdrawal is a novel teaching of Luria, the concept of divine contraction was already taught in rabbinic literature (Tanh., Va-Yakhel 7).

According to one Chasidic theosophy, there is no differentiation or diversity from God's perspective—all is still One. From our perspective, however, God seems more absent than present. This divine-human disconnect in perception is the real nature of Tzimtzum (Tanya).[1] *SEE* EMANATION; EXILE.

1. Drob, *Symbols of the Kabbalah*, 12–154.

Tziyya: "Dry Land." One of the seven realms that makes up the lower worlds, it is a desert/wilderness whose people aspire to the more fertile Tevel (Sitre Torah, Zohar I: 253b–254a).

Tzohar: A luminous **gemstone** holding the primordial light of Creation. Those who possessed it not only had illumination, but access to the secrets of the Torah and all its powers. God created it, but then hid it away for the sole use of the righteous. The angel **Raziel** gave it to **Adam** after the Fall. Adam gave it to his children. **Noah** used it to illumine the Ark (Gen. 6:16). **Abraham** possessed this stone, and used it to heal all who came to him. According to one legend, he returned to heaven and hung it on the sun. But other traditions track its continued use by the righteous of each generation. Joseph used it for his dream interpretations. Moses recovered it from the Bone of Joseph and placed it in the Tabernacle. The **Zohar** claims that **Simon bar Yochai** possessed it in the rabbinic era (Sanh. 108b; B.B. 16b; Lev. R. 11; Gen. R. 31:11; Zohar I: 11; Otzer ha-Midrash).

Tzoreif: "Alchemy." *SEE* ALCHEMY.

Tzror ha-Chayyim: "The Bonds of Life." In Kabbalistic metaphysics, this is the final resting place of righteous souls before they are transmigrated into new bodies. Some describe this as a realm where the highest soul (*neshamah*) dwells in the constant presence of God. Others describe it as a treasury or storehouse beneath the **Throne of Glory**. In either case, it is a place of unsurpassed bliss (Siddur; Etz ha-Chayyim 2). *SEE* GUF HA-BRIYOT.

U

Unclean Spirits or Impure Spirits: (*Ruchei Tamei*). Evil spirits often linked to the priestly purity system (Zech. 13:2). Ritual laxness invites attack by these spirits, which inhabit privies, foods, liquids, beds, and even hands contaminated by *tamei*, ritual impurity (Kid. 72a; Ber. 62b; Zohar I: 83a). They also strike while one sleeps, through inducing **nocturnal emissions** that render a person impure (Shab. 109a; Zohar I: 10b; III: 67a). Since **death** also has strong associations with ritual impurity, a few texts hint that they may be spirits of the dead (Num. R., Chukkat 19:8; 11Q11; Sanh. 65b), but most texts treat them as demons.

The rabbinic attitude toward these spirits at times parallels contemporary attitudes toward hygiene, even to the extent that authorities taught that such spirits "infect" the body by entering through orifices and membranes. Concern about *ruchei tamei* may have had a role in shaping the custom of hand washing after leaving a **cemetery**, but there is no text known that directly links the two (Shab. 108b; Tosafot on Yoma 77b and Chul. 107b; Orah Chayyim 4.3). *SEE* DEMONS; PURIFICATION.

Unicorn: *SEE* RE'EM.

Unleavened Bread: (*Matzah*). A large, crackerlike wafer that is eaten throughout the holiday of **Passover** in place of risen bread. It is eaten to commemorate both the slavery and liberation our ancestors experienced. Matzah is made using only specially supervised (keeping it free from exposure to airborne yeast) wheat and water. It is then baked precisely eighteen minutes (the number symbolizing life).

It is a symbol of **ritual** and spiritual purity; Jews eat matzah free of leaven just as we must free ourselves of the "leaven" of ego, sin, and old habits. It is also a symbol of **paradox**: it simultaneously symbolizes slavery and freedom. At the Seder, three pieces of matzah are prominently displayed, reminding Jews of both the three biblical classes of Jews (Priest, Levite, and Israelite) and the three epochs (the **Garden of Eden**, historic time, and the time of the **Messiah**).

One aspect of unleavened bread that has particular occult symbolism is the afikoman. The afikoman is one-half of a matzah wafer that is publicly broken, only to be hidden away during the Seder. Children must then find it or steal it from the holder in order for the Seder to continue. Originally intended as a pedagogical tool to keep the attention of children during the ceremony, by the Middle Ages the afikoman became a symbol of the occult and started to be used as an **amulet** against the **evil eye**. Customs include preserving a piece at home for good luck, while some may actually carry crumbs of the afikoman in their coat pockets. Pregnant women will sometimes keep a piece of afikoman nearby to ensure an easy labor. According to one tradition, an afikoman kept seven years can avert a flood or other natural disaster.[1]

1. Trachtenberg, *Jewish Magic and Superstition*, 134, 295.

Uraltes Chymisches Werck: "Arcane Chemical Work." A treatise on **alchemy** credited to **Abraham Eleazar**, probably composed in the late 14th or early 15th century.

Uriel: "God is my Light." Uriel is one of the four princely **angels** that surround or form the **Throne of Glory**. He is first mentioned by name in **I Enoch** (chapters 9, 19–20), though he does not appear in a later angelic list in that same book. He is identified as the angel who revealed the secrets of the true, celestial **calendar** to Enoch, counteracting the impure lunar calendar given to humanity by the **fallen angels** (I Enoch 33, 80). In II **Esdras** he brings God's message of rebuke to Ezra (4:1). He appears regularly in medieval angelic lists (PR 46; Num. R. 2:10; Mid. Konen).

Uriel is the patron angel of **Jerusalem** (IV Ezra 10). He has control over earthquakes and thunder. In **Gedulat Moshe**, he is described as being made entirely from **hail**. He could also take on the form of an **eagle**. Midrash Aggadah claims he was the avenging force God sent against **Moses** for failing to circumcise his son Gershom. He announced the birth of **Samson**. In the **Zohar**, he is identified with the lion-faced angel in Ezekiel's **chariot**. In **lion** form, Uriel would descend and consume the sacrifices on the altar of the **Temple** (I: 6b).

Uriel is one of the four guardian angels invoked for protection while sleeping in the bedtime ritual of **K'riat Sh'ma al ha-Mitah**. *SEE* SAR HA-PANIM.

Urim and Thummim: Meaning uncertain, possibly "Light and Perfection" or "Perfect lights." A method of **divination** that was worn as part of the priestly garments (Ex. 28; Num. 27; I Sam. 28). Little is truly known about Urim and Thummim; even the name has been subjected to wildly different translations. The Rabbis understood the Urim and Thummim to be part of the **Breastplate** of the High **Priest** and that its oracular function came from light shining through the twelve gemstones mounted on the breastplate (PdRE 38). This was achieved by having a plate inscribed with the **Tetragrammaton** inserted behind the gemstone mounts. Supernal light radiating from the divine name would illuminate different stones. Since each stone was inscribed with the names of the twelve tribes, the Talmud teaches that it functioned as a kind of Ouija board, with messages being spelled on the Urim and Thummim for the High Priest. In Pirkei de-Rabbi Eliezer, it is taught that the stone representing a tribe would glow if the tribe was involved in a transgression, but then the diviner would

have to discern the specifics himself (38). Some believe the *Urim* were the lights, while the *Thummim* was a device or code that helped in interpreting the message.

Other interpreters suggest that the Urim and Thummim were separate objects that were both kept in a pouch of the breastplate. In the Bible, one individual who made a counterfeit breastplate for his personal cult substituted **terafim** for the Urim and Thummim (Judg. 17–18; Hos. 3:4). This is a tantalizing but frustrating bit of data. Because we also know so little about the terafim, the association of the two objects does not shed much light on either, no pun intended. The best evidence is that the two may have both been made of light-reflecting stone; Mesopotamian sources also mention an *elmeshu* stone used by the gods for oracular purposes.

The context for its mention in Scripture indicates the Urim and Thummim was only used for questions of grave importance, usually connected to the function of the state, such as whether and when to go to war, though there is one passage in Numbers that hints at the possibility it was used for more mundane questions, such as resolving difficult legal questions. While it is not mentioned by name, Joshua may have determined who violated God's decree of proscription at Jericho by means of the Urim and Thummim (Josh. 6–7). The answers given by the device that were recorded in the Bible were full sentences, suggesting either that the device was an aid to prophecy, but did not operate apart from **prophecy**, or that the Rabbis were correct in their claim that it spelled out messages from the letters on the breastplate.

Mention of the Urim and Thummim ceases early in the history of Israel, indicating that it was no longer in use at the rise of classical prophecy (8th century BCE). There is some indication that it was reintroduced briefly during the Persian period, but it again quickly disappears from the records.[1] Post-biblical sources offer numerous elaborations on the history and operation of the Urim and Thummim, but many of the sources contradict each other, making it difficult to fix on any as a legitimate tradition (DDS 4Q376; 4QpIsa; Antiquities 3:8; B. Yoma 73b; Ex. R. 47; Sifrei Num. 141; Targum Pseudo-Jonathan to Ex. 28; Zohar II: 234b; Ramban on Ex. 28). The Urim and Thummim have also become part and parcel of Western occult lore; Joseph Smith, for example, claimed to have used the Urim and

Thummim to read "Reformed Egyptian" language of the golden book given him by the angel Moroni. The seal of Yale University also contains a reference to them.

1. Hurowitz, "New Light on the Urim and Thummim," 263–74. Also see Van Dam, *The Urim and Thummim*.

Urine: Urine is used in magical formulae and **healing** remedies (Shab. 109b).

Ushpizin: (Aramaic, "guests"). The spiritual or ghostly guests welcomed into the festive hut during the holiday of **Sukkot**. The **ritual** first emerged among the Kabbalists of 16th-century Safed. The seven—**Adam** (or **Joseph**), **Abraham**, **Isaac**, **Jacob**, **Moses**, **Aaron**, and **David**—are each a personification of one of the seven lower **sefirot**. A list of seven female counterparts—**Sarah, Miriam**, Deborah, Channah, Abigail, **Huldah**, and **Esther**—also exists. A different one of these guests is invited for each night of the seven nights of the holiday, and the evening is spent expounding on the virtues and the spiritual significance of that night's visitor (Suk. 54b; Zohar II: 256a; III: 103b–104a). *SEE* ANCESTORS; HOSPITALITY; PATRIARCHS AND MATRIARCHS; RIGHTEOUS, THE.

Uzza: Princely and guardian **angel** of the Egyptians (BhM 1:39). In other traditions, he and **Azazel** opposed the creation of humanity. They in time fell in love with mortal women, producing demonic offspring from those couplings. They were punished by being chained to the Mountains of Darkness, yet from there they continue to wreak mischief (Yoma 67b; Aggadat Bereshit; PdRE 22; Zohar I: 9b). *SEE* FALLEN ANGELS; MOUNTAIN.

V

Vampire: (Hebrew: *Arpad, Alukah,* Yiddish: *Estrie*). A bloodlusting monster. The earliest reference to a vampire appears in the **Bible**, where it is called an *alukah* (Prov. 30:15). Jewish traditions about vampires vary over history. Sometimes they are regarded as demonic spirits, other times vampirism is an attribute of a **witch**. The earliest mention of vampires appears in the **Testament of Solomon**, where vampirism is one malevolent activity of demons.

Interesting information on Jewish beliefs about vampirism appears in **Sefer Chasidim**, where the creature is understood to be a living human being, akin to a witch, that can shape-change into a wolf. It can fly (by releasing its long hair) and will eventually die if prevented from feeding on blood for a long enough time. Once dead, a vampire can be prevented from becoming a **demon** by being buried with its mouth stuffed with **earth** (Toldot Adam v'Chavah 28).

Vav: The sixth letter of the **Hebrew alphabet**. It has a vocalic value of "v/w" or "o" and the numeric value of 6. It is one of the letters that make up the **Tetragrammaton**. It denotes physical completion. In the case of some biblical personalities, such as **Jethro** (formerly Jether), a *vav* is added to their name to symbolize a spiritual fulfillment.[1]

1. Munk, *The Wisdom of the Hebrew Alphabet,* 94–103.

Vilna Gaon: Talmudist and Kabbalist (Lithuanian, 1720–1797). Though most famous for his opposition to **Chasidism**, the Vilna Gaon (Elijah ben Solomon Kramer) was a prolific writer on Kabbalistic topics, including commentaries to the **Zohar** and **Sefer Yetzirah**. He also wrote a commentary on the book of Jonah that understands it as an allegory for **reincarnation** of the **soul**. Some admirers ascribed miracles and wonders to him, though the Gaon himself made no such claims for himself.

Vilon: The lowest of the **seven heavens**, it serves only as a membrane between day and night. The name is derived from Isaiah 40:22 (Chag. 12b–13a).

Virility: Potions for virility and potency are commonly found in Hebrew magico-medical texts. One is even mentioned in the Talmud (Git. 70a). *SEE SEX.*

Visions: (*Chazon; Ra'eyah*). There are three kinds of mystical encounters with divinity recorded in Jewish tradition: the ineffable experience, in which nothing experienced is in any way describable; the auditory, in which a voice (a **Bat Kol**, or **Maggid**, for example) addresses the person(s); and the visionary experience, in which the person has some kind of visual impression of the encounter. And since, by definition, the first does not lend itself to be put into writing, it is not surprising that the latter two are by far the best documented in Jewish tradition. Of the latter two, purely auditory experiences, without a visual component, are comparatively rare, but given the comparably few truly visual experiences recorded in biblical **prophecy**, an auditory manifestation is a significant form of visionary experience.

Ocular paranormal visions, whether recorded by prophets, mystics, or ordinary Jews, generally fall into one of these three types: a manifestation of God's **Glory** on earth (Ex. 19–22; Ezek. 1), an angelic or demonic visitation (Gen. 18; Num. 24), or a revelation of the occult cosmos (I Enoch; Sefer Hechalot; Sha'ar Ruach ha-Kodesh, Mavo; Divrei Yosef, p. 364). The three types frequently overlap, as in the case of Isaiah's or Zechariah's visions. These visions can be experienced while asleep or in a waking state.

The most common elements that appear in these visions are **light**, **clouds**, **fire**, numinous beings (whether anthropomorphic or hybrid in appearance), and/or the chariot-throne of God (Ber. 6a; Meg. 24b; Zohar I: 103b). *SEE* AKATRIEL-YAH; CHERUB, THE UNIQUE; DREAM; FACE OF GOD; IMAGINATION; MALACH ADONAI; REIYAT HA-LEV; SHEKHINAH; SHI'UR QOMAH.

Vital, Chayyim: Kabbalist (Turkish, 1542–1620). A leading disciple of **Isaac Luria**, Vital experienced many fantastic visions and personal revelations. **Elijah** and other righteous men of the past appeared to him. He performed **healings**, **exorcisms**, dowsing for water, and at one point declared himself the **Messiah**. He also believed he had undergone multiple incarnations and, for example, had the soul of R. Abika (Sefer ha-Hezyonot, I: 10). His writings, including Etz ha-Chayyim, Otzerot Chayyim, and Sefer ha-Gilgulim, not only provide some of the most complete accounts of Luria's mystical cosmology, but also give us detailed information about **reincarnation**, ghostly possession, **divination**, and **dream** interpretation.

Voodoo or Magical Dolls: The use of figurines for magical ends was known to the Babylonians and was a mainstay of Greek magic. It is a feature of only a very few rituals in Hebrew magical texts. **Sefer ha-Razim**, for example, includes only one **ritual** involving making a figurine as part of a magical incantation to drive away lions.

Wall, Western: (*ha-Kotel*). Alternately called the "Wailing Wall" or simply "the Wall," this retaining wall to the platform of the Temple Mount is the last remaining remnant of the **Temple** in **Jerusalem**, the nexus point of communion between God and Israel (Ber. 32b). As such it is considered the structure closest to the **Holy of Holies** that a Jew can approach without being in danger of stepping on that most sacred ground, an act forbidden to all but the High Priest. It is a place of great spiritual power in Judaism, drawing pilgrims who not only desire the merit of having prayed there, but who also leave prayer petitions, called *kvitlakh*, in the hope that their supplications are more likely to get a positive outcome.

According to legend, the poor of Jerusalem originally built the Wall, the only contribution they could afford to give King Solomon's project. Because of the merit of this act of piety, the **Shekhinah** promised never to depart from the Wall. On the ninth of Av, the anniversary of the day when the Temple was destroyed, a white **dove** will join those gathered in mourning; the Wall itself weeps. Supposedly, there is one stone with an idolatrous image carved into it made by King Manasseh and enchanted with a spell by King Jeroboam that hinders the redemption. It is no longer visible, and several legends relate that the cursed stone was removed by one or another spiritual genius, but no one knows for sure. Miraculous signs of God's mourning for the destroyed Temple are sometimes reported.

War Scroll: This **Dead Sea Scrolls** text, also labeled 1QM and 4QM, details an eschatological war that is to eventually be fought between the **Sons of Light** and the **Sons of Darkness**. *SEE* ANGELS; MANUAL OF DISCIPLINE.

Warrior, Divine: One of the most popular mythic ways to portray the God of Israel in the Bible was as a hero or warrior (Ex. 15; Pss. 2, 9, 24, 29, 46, 48, 98, 104; Isa. 34–35, 42–43; Zech. 9). This "divine warrior" motif usually follows a set literary pattern: threat, combat, theophany, victory, the salvation of Israel, and God's universal reign. The order may vary according to the needs of the poet, with different elements being added or modified to reflect the historic or mythic circumstance. This type of hymn has its roots in Canaanite-Mesopotamian hymns (Baal and Yamm, Enuma Elisha).[1]

1. Cross, *Canaanite Myth and Hebrew Epic*, 91–111.

Wars of the Lord, Book of: (*Sefer Milchamot Adonai*). A **lost book** mentioned in the Bible, it evidently contained accounts of God's victories over Israel's enemies. Not to be confused with the medieval philosophic work of the same name.

Watchers: (*Irinim*, "Wakeful Ones"). A class of high **angels**, sometimes characterized as "archangels," first described in the book of Daniel (4:10–14). In **apocalyptic literature**, these are the **fallen angels** who have intercourse with mortal women (Gen. 6:2, 6:4; I Enoch 6, 19, 64, 69; Jubilees 4, 7). They subsequently corrupt humans with forbidden knowledge and ultimately rebel against God. In **Gedulat Moshe**, these angels perform the celestial music of the sixth heaven. They are central figures in the mythic theology of the Qumran priests (Community Rule II, IV; Damascus Document, II, III; War Scroll XIII). SEE ENOCH, BOOKS OF.

Water: "The Spirit of God hovers over the waters" (Gen. 1:2). From this passage, Jewish esoteric tradition derives the belief that water is a primordial force, a sign of divine energy, and a key component in encountering and invoking divine power (Chag. 12b). Water is also a symbol of Torah (B.K. 82a; Gen. R. 54:1).

Water is the visible manifestation of **chaos**. Order only emerges as God drives back and delimits the watery **abyss** (Ex. R. 15:22). God's separating the waters into heavenly and earthly zones then permits the cosmos to appear (Gen. 1; Tan. 10a; Num. R. 18:22). With the appearance of dry land, God traps the primordial waters under the **earth** and seals them in place with the **Foundation Stone**.

According to the Talmudic Sages, all the water of the universe is divided between the female tellurian waters and the male celestial waters. Their joining together fructifies the earth (Tan. 10a; Gen. R. 4:2–4, 13:11, 13:13). This is the rationale for the **water libation** service performed on **Sukkot**. There is a similar gender distinction made between rain and **dew**. This notion of "gendered" waters plays a crucial role in mystical thought and theurgic practices (J. Ber. 9:3, 14a; Tan. 25b; PdRE 23). According to **Azriel of Gerona**, water was the primeval mother who gave birth to darkness. Water flowing from the heavenly **Eden** sustains life in the lower worlds (Zohar I: 17b, 29b, 46a, 82b; III: 223b).

Though God has tamed them, the waters still possess great and destructive power. Therefore, the appearance of supernal water while ascending through the palaces of heaven was considered a barrier and a danger to the living soul. (Chag. 14b; Hechalot Ms. Munich 22d). When **David** attempted to move the Foundation Stone, he unwittingly unleashed the waters of the abyss, threatening to undo the world.

Water sources are also a favorite lurking place for spirits and **demons**, as exemplified by the incident of **Jacob** wrestling with a spirit being by the river Jabbok (Gen. 39. Also see Lev. R. 24.3; Pes. 112a), a belief that appears to be a hold-over from pagan traditions (the Banyas rapids at the headwaters of the Jordan are named for the Greek god Pan and the ruins of a shrine to him are still visible there).[1]

By the same token, a body of water, because of its association with purity, is a place of revelation (Ezek. 1:3; Dan. 8:2, 10:4; III Baruch; I Enoch 13:7; MdRI, Pisha 1; Kohelet Rabbah 3:16). In the mystical book the **Re'uyot Yehezkel**, the prophet received his prophetic insights by gazing into the reflections on the river Chabar. From that time forward, water was a frequent component in rituals of power and protection.[2] The kings of Israel are anointed standing over water (Hor. 12a). Studying Torah by a stream ensures that one's memorization will "flow like a river." Ecclesiastes Rabbah 3:15 goes so far as to say that if one intends to use the name of God for theurgic purposes, one should do so only over a body of water. In a similar vein, **Sefer ha-Shem** and **Sefer ha-Malbush** teach that one may only transmit the knowledge of the proper pronunciation of the **Tetragrammaton** in a ritual while standing in or over water, based on Psalm 29—*kol YHWH al hamayyim*, "the sound 'YHWH' is upon the waters."[3]

German Pietists would also perform theurgic rituals and transmit occult knowledge over water (**Sefer ha-Malbush**). Among the **Merkavah** mystics, some rituals for drawing down angels required the summoner to be immersed neck-deep in living waters.[4] Perhaps the image of the angel appears in the reflecting surface. Some Jewish **divination** techniques include studying the patterns of oil poured into a bowl of water (Sefer ha-Hezyonot 5).

Without question, the water that has the greatest power is *mayim chayyim*, "living water." This is rainwater that has not yet been drawn from its source by human hands or by artificial conduit. All seas, natural lakes, rivers, and ponds are reservoirs of living water. A source of living water is also the necessary ingredient in a **mikvah**, or ritual bath. The potency of living water derives from the fact that it has fallen directly from the pure state of heaven. In fact, it serves as a kind of reservoir of the heavenly **Eden** here on earth, not unlike how we today think of the embassies in a country as being "foreign soil." As such, **immersion** in it has the power to purify that which it contacts.

Living water of all forms has heavenly, even life-giving, energy. This belief is exemplified by Ezekiel's narrative about the great life-giving river that will flow from the Temple Mount in the days of the Messiah (Ezek. 47:1–12).

For this reason living water is used in many rituals of power, such as constructing a **golem**, divination, **ordeals**, and the preparation of **amulets**. *SEE* MAGIC; MIRIAM; RAIN; RIVER; SUMMONING.

1. Canaan, "Haunted Springs and Water Demons in Palestine," 153–70.
2. Winkler, *Magic of the Ordinary*, 174–75, 227n.
3. Dan, *The Heart and the Fountain*, 104–5.
4. Lesses, *Ritual Practices to Gain Power*, 218–19.

Water Libation or Water Drawing Ceremony: When the **Temple** stood, one of the rituals of the holiday of **Sukkot** would be the Water Libation ritual. This theurgic ceremony entailed gathering a jug of water from the Pool of Siloam (an underground spring) and taking it up to the Temple, where it would be poured over the **altar**. As the drawn water was poured out, this incantation was recited: "Let your waters flow, I hear the voice of two friends [the drawn water calling to its source], as it is said, 'Abyss calls to abyss in the roar of the channels'" (Tan. 25b). The purpose of the **ritual** was to draw the underground waters of the abyss toward the surface of the earth, to trigger the fructifying mingling of tellurian (subterranean) and heavenly (rain) waters that would allow growth in the coming season (Tos. Tan. 1:4; PdRE 23). *SEE* ABYSS; CHAOS; WATER.

Water of Bitterness: (*Mai ha-Marim*). A solution of water, dust from the grounds of the Temple, and the divine name (written either in the dust or on a parchment and then dissolved in the potion) that was a critical element in the **ordeal** the Torah designated as a way to determine if a wife has been unfaithful to her husband (Num. 5; Sot. 8b–9a; Num. R. 9:9). If the woman is guilty, the **ritual** causes her to manifest her guilt through some unpleasant abdominal event, probably either a peritoneal rupture or a prolapsed uterus that renders her barren. *SEE* SOTAH.

Wax: Wax was sometimes used as a *materia magica* in Greek magical texts, such as in the making of magical figurines similar to the popular conception of "voodoo dolls." There are not many parallel references to wax in Hebrew magical documents, **Sefer ha-Razim** being one of the few. In that book, wax is listed only as a method to seal the mouth of dead animals used in magical rituals. *SEE* MAGIC; SORCERY.

Ways of the Amorites: (*Darkhei Emori*). The Amorites were a Western Semitic people related to the Israelites, who lived in the region of what is now Syria/northern Iraq, though it has been proposed that in the Talmudic age, the Sages use the term *Emori* in a deliberate metathesis of the word *Romai*, as an encoded way to offer criticisms of the Romans. Whatever the origins, "Ways of the Amorites" is a rabbinic expression for forbidden ritual practices, but especially magical and divinatory practices (Tos. Shab. 7, 8:4–12). It is often translated as "witchcraft." As a rule, any method of healing, even if it is overtly magical, is exempted from this prohibition (Shab. 67a).[1] *SEE* MAGIC; SORCERY; WITCHES AND WITCHCRAFT.

1. Goldin, *Studies in Midrash and Related Literature*, 117.

Weapons: Tubal-Cain (Gen. 4:22) is credited by the Sages with being the inventor of weapons of war. Apocalyptic tradition claims they were introduced by the **fallen angels**.

There are several weapons of power mentioned in Jewish tradition. The **cherubim** posted to guard the way back to the Garden of **Eden** have a spinning fiery sword (Gen. 3). The sling stones used by David were miraculously enhanced because he inscribed them with the names of the **Patriarchs**. In flight, they formed a single, lethal mass (Mid. Sam. 20:106–8, 21:109).

In the **Midrash**, there is mention of God presenting Israel at Mount Sinai with supernal weapons inscribed with the **Tetragrammaton** (Mid. Teh. 36:8). (This Midrash interprets the Hebrew word for "ornaments" as "armaments"—other Midrashim interpret this same reference as "crown.") These weapons made them invulnerable, even to the **Angel of Death**. The weapons were taken back by God after the **Golden Calf** incident (Gen. 33:5; Targum S of S 2:17; Lam. R. Petichta 24; Tanh. B., Vayera 5). The Zohar suggests these same weapons first belonged to **Adam** and **Eve**, but for what purpose they needed them is not made clear (I: 53b). In the **War Scroll** of the DSS, the Children of Light will go forth to the great eschatological battle against the **evil** Children of Darkness wielding similar weapons.

In dealing with the contradictory statements in I Samuel, first that there were no weapons among the Israelites (13:19–20, 22), but then that Saul and Jonathan had swords, the **Midrash** teaches that **angels** brought down swords from heaven for Saul and his son.

Though not technically a weapon, the miraculous **rod** of the Patriarchs still proved a potent tool against Israel's enemies. So, too, is the **Ark of the Covenant**.

Weather: Divining by means of the weather or the interpretation of cloud formations is mentioned in the Talmud (B.B. 147a). Later traditions teach how to prognosticate on the basis of weather that occurs on certain days or in conjunction with certain astral phenomena. *SEE* AS-TROLOGY; DIVINATION; SEASONS; ZODIAC.

Wedding: (*Erusin; Kiddushin; Nisuin*). The wedding is an important messianic ritual in Judaism, symbolizing a partial restoration of the Edenic ideal, a time when male and female were "one flesh." Jewish tradition teaches that it is only as part of a couple that an individual becomes fully human as God intended (Eruv. 18a; Ber. 61a; PdRE 12; Sotah 2a). Marriage is also an event of cosmic healing, with the linking of a man and a woman in these lower worlds initiating an analogous **tikkun** in the Godhead (Zohar III: 19a, 44b).

Many spiritual forces, both beneficent and malevolent, are in play around a wedding. The most propitious day for a wedding is Tuesday, the third day of the week, the day that God blessed twice (Gen. 1). **Fish** is a favored food at a wedding ceremony, signifying both blessing and fertility. Other foods regarded as imbued with the power of sexual potency, such as **nuts**, are also eaten or thrown at the couple. In Talmudic times the wedding procession would be led by groomsmen carrying a hen and **cock**. Seven blessings are recited over the couple during the ceremony, ensuring good fortune. **Demons**, the **evil eye**, and even the **Angel of Death**, are attracted by the positive energies of the festivities (Ber. 54b).

The state of marriage especially brings a state of spiritual protection to the man (Yev. 62b), but since at least the period of the book of Tobit, it has been believed that the bridegroom is particularly vulnerable to malevolent attack during the liminal period surrounding the wedding. For this reason, the groom often wears a *kittle*, or funeral shroud, during the ceremony in order to confuse the evil eye. Often, both bride and groom fast prior to the ceremony based on the same logic. It is also customary for the bride to walk

in a series of protective circles around the groom before they enter under the chuppah (the wedding canopy) together. The skin of Oriental Jewish brides is decorated with red protective patterns made from henna.

It is considered bad luck to mention any future joyous occasion, such as the **birth** of children, during a wedding (Eccl. R. 3:2). It has been widely argued that the breaking of a glass after the ceremony also has an anti-demonic function, though there is no documented reference to this in traditional literature. *SEE* SEX; WOMEN.

Weeping: (*Bekhi*). Despite the disapproval of some Talmudic Sages (Shab. 30a), weeping is a widely practiced mystical technique for inducing revelations and visions (II Enoch; Zohar I: 4a; III: 166b; Sefer ha-Hezyonot) and inducing God to respond to supplications (Ber. 34b; A.Z. 17a; Zohar II: 20a). Jews ritually weep and mourn for the destruction of the Temple, an act that comforts the **Shekhinah** and draws it down to the worshipper (Reshit Chochmah). Menachem Mendel of Kotzk emphasized the spiritual practice of "holy sadness" in his teachings and the Seer of Lublin encouraged **ritual** weeping at **midnight**.[1]

1. Idel, *Kabbalah: New Perspectives*, 75–88.

Weiberlamden: (Yiddish, "Woman's Scholar"). A spiritual healer specializing in the needs of women. *SEE* BIRTH; HEALING; INTERCESSION; WOMEN.

Wells: Wells are ancient symbols of life, wealth, fertility, salvation, and tellurian power. The Sages identify two miraculous well incidents in the biblical accounts: the well that appeared for Hagar, and the mobile well that the prophet **Miriam** made manifest during the forty years of wandering in the wilderness following the **Exodus** (Avot 5:6; Ginzberg, *Legends of the Jews*, 3:53–54). One tradition claims these were actually the same well, a supernal creation made on the twilight of the sixth day. *SEE* WATER.

Well of Job: A small fountain in the Kidron Valley of **Jerusalem**. Like most **water** sources in the Holy Land, it is credited with miraculous powers. In this instance, its waters once healed Job of his boils, a miracle from which the spring derives its name.

Well of Miriam: This miraculous mobile well was one of the **ten miracles on the twilight of the sixth day**. Created in the form of a **rock**, the well provided Israel with **water** throughout their forty years in the wilderness. These waters also had the power to heal. At the end of each Sabbath, the well replenished itself for the week. Whenever the Israelites moved, Miriam would cause it to materialize in the new campsite (Avot 5:6). When Miriam died, the rock lost its miraculous quality, precipitating the crisis at Meribah in which **Moses** found himself in a confrontation with the children of Israel over the lack of water (Num. 20, 27).

In at least one thread of the tradition, the well actually has appeared in other times and places, particularly for Hagar and Ishmael (Gen. 21).

Well Poisoning: *SEE* POISON.

Werewolf: The Baal Shem Tov did battle with a demonic werewolf (ShB 4). Werewolves are most often mentioned in medieval writings as part of a complex of **witch/vampire**/shape-changing traditions, especially in **Sefer Chasidim**.

West: The direction from which fulfillment and redemption flows (Bahir 110–16). It also signifies the **Shekhinah**.

Wheels: (*Ofannim*). *SEE* OFAN.

White: *SEE* COLOR.

White Herb: A plant used in **alchemy** first mentioned by **Maria Hebraea**. It is probably Moonwart, *botrychium lunaria*. Alchemists find many medicinal and magical uses for this plant. A "white flower" is also an ingredient used in making incense for exorcisms, but it is not clear whether this is the same plant.

Wilderness: Talmud Tractate Berachot identifies deserts, ruins, and other uninhabited areas as the places where demonic and **unclean spirits** like to frequent. This sense of the spiritually untamed wilderness may spring from biblical concepts of **chaos** as a force in opposition to God, as well as the **Yom Kippur** ritual of sending the scapegoat to **Azazel**. *SEE* DEMONS; GOATS.

William of Norwich: Supposed victim of Jewish ritual murder in England (1144). His was the first recorded case of the **blood libel** accusation. The boy's head was allegedly shaven and wounds from a "crown of thorns" were found on his brow. The boy became an instant local martyr. Remarkably, little was done to the Jewish community of Norwich, apparently because the local constabulary judged the popular hysteria surrounding William's death to be unfounded. At the same time, the populous (for once) proved too law-abiding to take matters into their own hands. Subsequent Jewish communities would not be so lucky.

Willow: (*Aravah*). Willow is one of the **four species** that make up the lulav. In the **ritual** of the holiday of Hoshana Rabbah that follows **Sukkot**, the willow branch is separated from the other branches and is used to flog the **earth**, for that is the day "the earth is judged for the **water** to be received." As a plant that thrives near moisture, it is believed that using the willow in this sympathetic theurgic ceremony ensures the earth will be adequately watered. The willow is also seen as a talisman of **fertility** because of its link to the water ritual, and a Jewish couple may keep one under their bed to ensure conception (R.H. 1:2).

Wind: (*Ruach*). Winds coming from the four compass points symbolize the whole, wide world. The winds originate in storehouses of heaven and emanate from the "corners," or cardinal compass **directions**, of the earth (Jer. 49; Dan. 7:2, 11; Zech. 6). According to the Bible, winds are angels that fulfill God's will (Ps. 104:4; Ex. 10, 14; Isa. 26:6; Deut. R. 9:3). Wind is a manifestation of divine Presence (Gen. 1; Isa. 11:2–3; Git. 31b; B.B. 25a).

The word *ruach* is also used to refer to several other phenomena, both natural and supernatural: human breath, the imminent presence of God (*SEE* HOLY SPIRIT), an evil or demonic entity (*SEE* DEMON; UNCLEAN SPIRITS), and one aspect of the **soul**.

Wine: (*Yi'in*). The very existence of wine was an event of supernatural origins. A **Midrash** on Genesis 9:21 claims **Satan** introduced **Noah** to viniculture, with dire consequences (Tanh., Noah 13). Despite this inauspicious start, wine occupies a very positive role in Jewish thought. As a symbol of rejoicing and prosperity, wine is a frequent element in Jewish rituals. Not surprisingly, some theurgic meanings have been ascribed to this practice, and more overtly magical uses for wine have emerged.

The custom of dipping one's finger in the wine cup and removing drops of wine while reciting the plagues at the **Passover** Seder may have its origins in a medieval theurgic ceremony. Rhineland sage Eliezer ha-Gadol taught that removing sixteen drops in this way would trigger the "Sixteen-sided avenging sword of God." This force would thwart the power of **Dever**, the **demon** of pestilence.[1] Sometimes wine was poured on the ground at birth ceremonies and weddings to satisfy the spirits who had been attracted to the joyous occasion.[2] **Havdalah** wine smeared on the eyelids brings good luck in the coming week.

German Pietists believed reciting certain incantations over wine enhanced their memorization of Torah studies. Wine was also used by magical practitioners. Methods found in Hebrew magical texts include using wine to dissolve magical incantations and then drinking the solution to absorb their power (**Sefer ha-Razim**).

1. Kanarfogel, *Peering through the Lattices*, 138–39.
2. Trachtenberg, *Jewish Magic and Superstition*, 166–67, 195.

Wisdom: (*Chochmah*). Wisdom is one of the attributes Jews value most. **Solomon** is celebrated for his wisdom, and he in turn offers many paeans to it in the biblical book of Proverbs. Wisdom was the object most treasured by Solomon, and because he asked for it over gold and silver, those were given to him also, and more. His supernal wisdom allowed him to become a celebrated judge and the archetypal scholarly sorcerer (S of S R. 1:1).

In Solomon's Proverbs, Wisdom is personified as a woman prophet who lives in a palace of seven pillars (1:20, 9:1–6). She is also described as a desirable bride; childbearer and life-giver (Prov. 3:16, 3:18, 3:22, and 4:13). At times, Wisdom takes on a quasi-divine quality.

Arguments have been put forward that Wisdom is really a pagan goddess refashioned for monotheistic sensibilities. There is only little direct evidence for this. Proverbs 3:8 does characterize Wisdom as a "tree of life," which may be a link to the Canaanite goddess Asherah, who was sometimes symbolized by a sacred tree/totem pole. We also now have one piece of evidence, an ancient piece of graffiti, which refers to "YHWH and His asherah." If one then returns to Proverbs starting at 8:22, there Wisdom is

portrayed as a kind of consort to God. If one looks past the fact that Proverbs clearly designates Wisdom as one of God's creations, those inclined to connect these dots can find an occult goddess tradition concealed within.

Personified Wisdom continues to appear in post-biblical Jewish writings like the Wisdom of Solomon (9:1), II Enoch (30:8), and DSS texts. Jewish Gnostics made the female *Sophia* a central figure in their beliefs.

In rabbinic tradition the Sages fuse Wisdom with other divine entities that they explicitly characterized as female: **Torah** and the **Shekhinah**. (Job 28; Mid. Proverbs 8; Gen. R. 1:1).

In **Kabbalah**, **Chochmah** is one of the **sefirot**, the first emanation of **Keter**. It is the highest any human can hope to reach in **devekut**, mystical union with God.

Witches and Witchcraft: (*Mechashef*, "Wizard," *Mechashefah* "Witch"). In most cultures across the world, a witch or wizard is generally regarded to be a nefarious practitioner of magic. In Jewish culture, in contrast to both modern culture, which has reversed most images of evil creatures (vampires are now romantic figures, for example, instead of bloodlusting killers) and Christian culture, which sees them as virtually demonic, the Jewish attitude toward witches has varied considerably over time and geography. The **German Pietists**, for example, did regard them as quasi-demons. In the 17th century, **Manasseh ben Israel** of Holland expressed a view of witchcraft virtually indistinguishable from contemporary Christian demonologists (Nishmat Chayyim 232). The Talmudic Rabbis, on the other hand, while not approving of witches, blithely assume most of their own wives engage in at least some witchcraft practices (M. Sanh. 7:4, 7:11). These differences may well reflect the attitudes of the surrounding cultures in which Jews lived. Mediterranean societies were generally more tolerant of witches than northern European societies.[1]

The formal biblical attitude toward wizards and witches is severe, witchcraft being a capital offense (Ex. 22:17; Lev. 20:27; Sanh. 45b). This seems to spring from its association with idolatry. Both men and **women** are portrayed as engaging in witchcraft, and contrary to the modern distinction made in academic circles between socially empowered sorcerers and socially marginal witches, witches in the Bible are often shown in positions of power, notably the wizards in the employ of the kings of **Babylon** and **Egypt** and the witches in the employ of King Manasseh. Queen Jezebel herself is a witch (Ex. 7:11; Dan. 2:2; II Kings 9:22, 21:2).

Little is known about biblical witchcraft. There is an oblique reference to "voodoo-like" practices (Ezek. 13:19), but the Bible almost universally opts to remain silent on the particular practices of the witch. The Woman of **Endor**, often identified as a witch in Jewish post-biblical literature, is not designated so in the Bible itself, so it is not clear whether **necromancy** was considered a discipline of witchcraft, or a wholly separate offense (Deut. 18:10–12; Isa. 8:19–22, 19:3).

Jewish sources offer several accounts of the origins of witchcraft. According to I Enoch, witchcraft was first taught by the **fallen angels** to their mortal wives. This presumably explains the special association between women and witchcraft that marks subsequent Jewish literature. In the medieval text Alef-Bet ben Sira, the first woman, **Lilith**, transforms herself into a demon/witch by the power of using the **Tetragrammaton**.

While Jews were generally regarded to be exceptional magicians and even some Rabbis use **incantations, potions**, and **healing** rituals, in rabbinic literature witchcraft is most associated with women. Though there is an explicit statement that both men and women can engage in witchcraft, the fact that Exodus 22:17 prohibits *machasefah* (the feminine form of the noun) is taken as a prooftext that witchcraft is a particularly feminine activity (Sanh. 67a). And this is despite the existence of magical manuals such as The **Sword of Moses**, which is clearly written with the assumption that the adept using it will be a man. Perhaps a distinction between learned **sorcery** (practiced mostly by men), and folk magic (practiced mostly by women) starts to emerge here. Several passages of Talmud make a point of linking witchcraft with women (Avot 2:7; Eruv. 64b; J. A.Z. 1:9). In one citation, none other than **Simon bar Yochai**, a Sage who is reported to have once used the **evil eye** to slay a man, makes this linkage. The practice of witchcraft was considered so pervasive among women that even the children of great Sages could be involved (Git. 45a).

In general, witches in biblical and rabbinic literature are thought to be engaged mostly in malevolent activities, from interfering with **fertility** and healthy **births** (Otzer

ha-Geonim, Sotah 11) to **cursing** rivals and killing the unsuspecting. This stands in contrast with beneficent sorcery, such as healing rituals and **amulet** making, which Jewish tradition tolerates. While there are examples recorded of "witchcraft" that serves purely utilitarian purposes (the ability to stir a boiling pot with one's bare hand, for example), in general it is assumed witchcraft is used mostly for nefarious ends. The motivation for such behavior is rarely explicitly stated in the texts, but can be inferred. Witches seem to be a source of the evil eye, indicating they are motivated by envy and jealousy. Others use their powers for personal profit.[2]

Witches are sometimes portrayed as having idiosyncratic powers: one may be able to materialize bread, another drink, etc. The Talmud recounts that Rabbi Simeon ben Shetah defeated a coven of eighty witches. First, he tricked them into demonstrating their powers, then he gained the upper hand by appealing to their lusts. He brought eighty men before them, each of whom lifted a witch from the ground, thereby robbing each of her power (a piquant detail linking ancient witchcraft with earth or, perhaps, underworld power). Enforcing the biblical penalty, ben Shetah eventually had all of them hung. While dramatic in scale, this incident is actually the only such capital punishment of witches mentioned in the entire vast rabbinic corpus, and given its particularly legendary features, many scholars have held the historicity of the story suspect.

Aside from this one story, witches in rabbinic literature are rarely portrayed as demonic creatures, though it is not clear exactly what they are. In a virtually indecipherable tale found in the Jerusalem Talmud, Rabbi Chanania pulls the head of a witch from flax (Sanh. 7:13a). In general, though, witchcraft is seen more as a vice that virtually every woman will indulge in. With few exceptions, it is regarded rather just as something inappropriate that women do.

In medieval Jewish literature of northern Europe, by contrast, the image of the witch as a purely malevolent entity comes to the forefront, perhaps reflecting the greater hostility toward witches found in Christian culture at that time (Nishmat Chayyim 232). In **Sefer Chasidim**, witches share attributes with **werewolves** and **vampires**: they shape-shift, fly, have bloodlust, and can become the undead

(456, 465). Yet despite this more alarming view of witches, there is no record of any large-scale witch hunts among the Jews of Europe to mirror the witch-hunting mania that seized gentile society. Perhaps the popular Christian notion of the Jew as a satanic agent made Jewish authorities leery of giving fuel to such talk with the spectacle of Jews trying other Jews on such charges.

Among the Jews of the Ottoman Empire, witches were viewed with more acceptance. Even an established Kabbalist like Chayyim Vital would seek the expertise of such wise women (Sefer ha-Hezyonot 4, 120).

The threat of a witch may be deterred by reciting the following curse: "May boiling excrement in a sieve be forced into your mouth, [you] witches! May your head go bald and carry off your crumbs; your spices be scattered, and the wind carry off the new saffron in your hands, witches!" (Pes. 110a). Seven loops of knots [tied to the left side of the body] are also a good defense against illness caused by witchcraft (Shab. 66b).

1. Homza, *Religious Authority in the Spanish Renaissance*, 176–209.
2. Bar Ilan, "Witches in the Bible and Talmud," 1–12.

Women: Despite the clearly patriarchal nature of traditional Jewish culture, Jewish tradition provides a wide range of images of women: wives, mothers, daughters, harlots, warriors, prophets, leaders, entrepreneurs, **witches**, seductresses, and sages. In the Bible, women personify both **wisdom** and witchcraft. While women are often portrayed as especially devious, indirect, and manipulative, that quality is often used for godly purposes (Rebecca in Genesis, Yael in Judges, the Wise Woman of Tokea in I Samuel, and Bathsheba in II Samuel all being signal examples). Women are also a source of discord among men because of male lust—the first murder, Pirkei de-Rabbi Eliezer claims, was actually a fight over Abel's **twin** sister (21). It is also the case that some Sages show a marked misogyny (Gen. R. 18:2).

The Talmud identifies seven biblical women upon whom "the **Holy Spirit** rested"—i.e., they were prophets. Those were **Sarah**, **Miriam**, Deborah, Channah, Abigail, **Huldah**, and **Esther**. According to the Zohar, there are four women who have been translated living into heaven and each of them governs one of the seven heavenly palaces (other sources speak of six palaces for women). There the souls of righteous women are rewarded. The women are Yocheved, the mother of Moses, Miriam, his sister, and the prophetesses **Serach bat Asher** and Deborah. Other versions of this list of ascendant women include **Batya**, the daughter of Pharaoh, Moses's adoptive mother (Seder Gan Eden; Zohar III: 167a–b; Midrash Yashar).

Jewish women have functioned as folk healers throughout history. Generally excluded from the scholarly circles that produced "physicians" in the learned tradition, women nevertheless were the avid practitioners and teachers of folk **healings**, midwifery, divination, clairvoyance, and **amulet** making.[1]

Because of the monthly cycle of menstruation, women are considered a potential source for *tamei*, ritual impurity. At least one extreme sectarian Jewish group believed the ritual impurity of women was such that women should not be allowed permanent residence in Jerusalem, lest their presence undermine the holiness of the **Temple** (Temple Scroll).

This was also a concern with women in theurgic and magical practices. Most handbooks of mystical-magical practices instruct the adept to avoid even talking to women for three days prior to performing a summoning or an ascent, apparently out of concern that even the most innocuous contact could trigger sexual arousal and seminal discharge.

In Jewish accounts of spiritual possession, women are predominantly (though far from exclusively) the hosts for possessing spirits, both beneficent and malevolent. Women could also be the targets of *incubi*, lustful spirits (Nishmat Chayyim). From the 16th century on, women became prominent mediums. Some, such as the daughter of **Raphael Anav**, were possessed by the spirit of a great sage with insight into the supernal realms (**maggid** or **ibbur tov**). Intriguingly, possession by such an ibbur granted the possessed woman an authoritative religious "voice" she might not otherwise have enjoyed in the Jewish community[2] (Sefer ha-Hezyonot 23–24; Divrei Yosef 319–24).
SEE MENSTRUATION; POSSESSION, GHOSTLY.

1. Chajes, "Women Leading Women (and Attentive Men)," 9–40.
2. Faierstein, "Maggidim, Spirits, and Women in Rabbi Hayyim Vital's 'Book of Visions,'" in Goldish, *Spirit Possession in Judaism*, 188–95.

Wood: *SEE* TREES; WILLOW.

Wood Offering, Festival of: A holiday mentioned in the **Temple Scroll** of the **Dead Sea Scrolls**. It is a holiday unattested to anywhere else in Jewish tradition and may have been simply part of an idealized, rather than actual, calendar featured in that text. There is some biblical basis for it, though (Neh. 10:34–40).

Word Mysticism: *SEE* HEBREW.

Words of Gad the Seer, The: (*Divrei Gad ha-Chozen*). A little-known manuscript, it purports to be the work of Gad, a prophet who served King **David**. In it, Gad describes an apocalypse of heaven and the End of Days granted him by God.

World: (*Olam*). The word *Olam* means both "world" (in the planetary sense) and "universe" (the sum total of Creation). *Olam* also has both spatial and temporal connotations. Thus *ha-olam* is "the world," while *le-olam* means "forever." The word itself is derived from the root *ayin-lamed-mem*, "hidden," reflecting the mystical teaching that the universe is the "garment" of God. Like heaven and **Gehenna**, the material world is divided into seven levels (AdRN 37; Lev. R. 29:10–11). It is a common locution to divide the universe into "Upper" and "Lower" Worlds, the celestial (*Elyonim*) and the terrestrial (*Tachtonim*). The lower universe is like a shadow cast by the upper world, and all things manifest below are reflections of higher, greater realities. *SEE* ADAM KADMON; CREATION; EARTH; FOUR WORLDS OF EMANATION.

World-to-Come: (*Olam ha-Ba*). A general term for those spiritual realms in which humanity will one day be a part. Sometimes it refers to a perfect reality that is temporally in the future, i.e., the messianic **Kingdom of God**, which will follow the advent of the **Messiah**, a period of interregnum between the advent of the Messiah and the end of the world (Pes. 68a; Ber. 34b; Sanh. 91b). Its duration is indeterminate, with periods as short as forty and as long as a thousand years being proposed (Sanh. 99a). In this renewed Creation, ten things will change: The supernal light of first Creation will return, living waters that **heal** will flow forth from **Jerusalem**, fruit-bearing **trees** with healing powers will sprout from those waters, all the ruined cities will be rebuilt, Jerusalem will be completely rebuilt out of precious materials, harmony will reign in the animal kingdom and between animals and humans, suffering will be swept from the world, **death** will be swallowed up, and all human beings will know wholeness and contentment (Ex. R. 15:2).

At other times, the World-to-Come refers to a temporally current spiritual world that surrounds the material world and is the place of the afterlife (Shab. 152a). In this interpretation, it is mysterious and beyond our understanding (Ber. 17a; Ex. R. 52:3). It is a place of unending bliss, though some contrary Sages express some dialectic tension over this. They apparently thought the World-to-Come was less interesting and rewarding than this world, since there will be little to do there and no **commandments** to fulfill (Ber. 17a).

Whatever its true configuration, the **righteous** of every nation have a portion in the World-to-Come (J. Yev. 15:2; Ber. 17a; B.B. 75a; Shab. 152b; Sanh. 90a; Tos. Sanh. 13:12). *SEE* ETERNAL LIFE; HEAVEN; SOUL.

Wunder-rabbi: (Yiddish). A term, sometimes used pejoratively, for a faith healer or Baal Shem.

X

Xenoglossia and Automatic Writing: (*Maggid; Shem ha-Kotev; Shem ha-Doresh*). Xenoglossia is the phenomenon of alien spirits speaking through or out of a possessed person while in a **trance**; "channeling." Such experiences may have been part of some prophetic trances, though evidence for this in the Hebrew Bible is sparse and elliptical at best. The first explicit accounts appear in the Christian New Testament, where there are descriptions of both demonic spirits addressing Jesus and seizure by the Holy Spirit resulting in people "speaking in tongues." Later Jewish sources also equate automatic speech with prophecy (Sha'ar ha-Gilgulim). Xenoglossia is a defining characteristic of ghostly and angelic possession in most Jewish reports after the 15th century. **Joseph Taitazak** provides the first detailed account of this phenomenon.[1] Perhaps the most famous Jew to experience it was **Joseph Caro**.

A parallel phenomenon is that of "automatic writing," composing while in an altered state of consciousness. **Moses de Leon** is a notable example, as there are indications he wrote parts of the **Zohar** while in a trance.[2] Medieval mystics label this phenomenon the *shem ha-kotev*, "the writing Name." This divine name can be invoked to trigger the trance-induced writing (Sha'arei Tzedek). Sources mention the practice, but do not record the actual "name" or how it was used.

Samson Ostropoler also described the *Shem ha-Doresh*, the "Interpreting Name," a form of automatic speech.[3] *SEE* DEVEKUT; IBBUR OR DEVEKUT; MAGGID; MEDIUM; POSSESSION.

1. Patai, "Exorcism and Xenoglossia among the Safed Mystics," 314–25. Also see Bilu, "Dybbuk and Maggid," 255–57.
2. Matt, *The Zohar: Pritzker Edition*, vol. 1, lxxv, xxiv.
3. Twersky and Septimus, *Jewish Thought in the Seventeenth Century*, 221–55.

Y

Yachad: "Togetherness/Community/Union." This is the term that the sectarian priests of the Dead Sea Scrolls sect used to describe themselves. The term, however, refers to vertical as well as horizontal unity, for the Qumran priests believed that they experienced periodic mystical unity and intermingling with angels through their **ritual** and liturgy (4Q405). *SEE* SONGS OF THE SABBATH SACRIFICE.

Yagel, Abraham: Renaissance physician and sorcerer (Italian, ca. 16th century). A proponent of scholarly magic in the style of the non-Jewish Hermetic schools, Yagel reconciled those ideas with many Jewish esoteric traditions. He believed knowledge of **sorcery** to be the apex of a philosophic education. He wrote extensively on spiritualism—demonology, spiritual **healing**, **dreams**, and the influences of the stars on human health—as it relates to medicine and the sciences. He is the author of Beit Yaar ha-Levanon, which exists only in manuscript form.[1] *SEE* ASTROLOGY; MAGIC; SORCERY.

> 1. See Ruderman, *Kabbalah, Magic, and Science: The Cultural Universe of a Sixteenth-Century Jewish Physician.*

Yah, Yahu: A shortened version of the **Tetragrammaton**, it appears occasionally in the **Bible**, as in *hallelu-Yah*, and in Hebrew names, like *Eli-Yahu*. It is a divine name that is frequently integrated into **incantations** and **amulets**. *SEE* NAMES OF GOD.

Yalkut Shimoni: Medieval **Midrash** containing many supernatural and fantastic elements.

Yannai, Rabbi: Talmudic Sage and theurgist (ca. 3rd century). He once caught a **witch** who tried to poison him with scorpions that had been magically disguised as a beverage. Turning the tables on her, he gave her a potion that shape-changed her into a donkey, which he then rode to the marketplace (Sanh. 67b).

Yashar, Sefer: A **lost book** mentioned in the Bible. Sefer ha-Yashar (or Toldot Adam) is also a chronology of history from Adam until the Exodus. It incorporates many rabbinic legends and fantastic elements.

Yechidut: A Chasidic spiritual consultation.

Yeddioni: "Wizard, medium." Derived from the Hebrew "know," the name has the sense of one "familiar with" spirits or the dead. Such a person is punishable by death in the Bible. According to the Talmud, a Yeddioni is a **medium** who places a bone in his mouth and then channels the voice of the dead spirit (Sanh. 65b). *SEE* GHOSTS; IBBUR OR DEVEKUT; MEDIUM; NECROMANCY; POSSESSION, DEMONIC; POSSESSION, GHOSTLY; XENOGLOSSIA.

Yefeiyah: "Beautiful One of God." This angel may be identical with the **Sar ha-Torah**. He is the angel who actually presented the **Torah** to **Moses** (BhM 1:61). **Gedulat Moshe** also identifies him as the angel **Zagzagel**. He is one of the instructors who teach Torah to the righteous dead. *SEE* YESHIVA SHEL MALAH.

Yehoel: "Yah is God." A powerful **angel** that appears in **Hechalot literature** and on protective **amulets**.

Yenne Velt: (Yiddish, "Another World/Out of this World"). This is a generic term for anything far out of the mainstream, but is also used to refer to spiritual dimensions, forces, and the occult.

Yeshiva shel Malah: "The Academy on High." One of the rewards awaiting the righteous in the afterlife is to study and understand Torah in its supernal completeness. The realm where this takes place is known as the *beit ha-midrash ba-olam ha-ba*, "The House of Study in the World-to-Come," or *yeshiva shel malah*, "the seminary on high." The righteous dead will study there under the instruction of the angelic **Sar ha-Torah** known as **Zagzagel**, or under God's own tutelage (A.Z. 18; Gen. R. 49:2; B.M. 86a; Gedulat Moshe; Zohar I: 4a–b). *SEE* DEATH; EDEN; PARADISE; RIGHTEOUS, THE.

Yesod: "Foundation/Phallus." The ninth sefirah. It is the conduit of divine **emanations** that flow into the material universe. It is also known as *Tzadik*. As the divine **phallus**, it is the source of the vitality and sexuality that energizes this plane of existence, the world of **Asiyah** (Zohar, everywhere). It is associated with the person of **Joseph**.

Yetzer ha-Ra: "The Evil/Selfish Desire." Every human being is created with two impulses, the Good Impulse and the Evil Impulse (Ber. 61a; Kid. 30b). Every human must learn to manage his or her impulse toward selfishness and evil, but a person should not seek to utterly destroy his or her Yetzer ha-Ra, for the Evil Impulse also motivates a person to pursue worthwhile goals: creativity, marriage, and creating a family. The Yetzer ha-Ra is therefore a critical component in God's plan for humanity to be co-creators in the world. A person should love God with both Yetzers (Gen. R. 9:7; Sifrei Deut. 32). According to one legend, the Sages once captured the Yetzer ha-Ra and were about to destroy it when they realized that without it, the world would end. So instead, they blinded it in order to reduce its power over humanity, but then let it go (Yoma 69b). The Talmud (Suk. 52a)

teaches that the greater the person, the more powerful the Yetzer ha-Ra is within that person.

One tradition equates the Yetzer ha-Ra with seven terms in Scripture: "evil," "uncircumcised," "unclean," "the enemy," "stumbling block," "stone," and "the hidden." Other traditions personify it by identifying it with **Satan** and/or the **Angel of Death** (B.B. 16a). Like death, the Yetzer ha-Ra will finally be overthrown in the **World-to-Come** (also see Suk. 52a–b; Gen. R. 21:5). *SEE* EVIL.

Yetzirah: "Formation." The third of the **four worlds of emanation**. This is the source of all material forms, the domain of angels, and the place from which emotion emerges.

Yetzirah, Sefer: "Book of Formation/Creation." The most influential book of the **Ma'asei-Bereshit** mystical tradition, Sefer Yetzirah, was written sometime in late antiquity (probably between the 3rd and 6th centuries). Over eighty commentaries to it have come down to us across the centuries, many of them composed by prominent rabbinic figures. The book describes the "thirty-two paths of wisdom," consisting of the twenty-two letters of the **Hebrew alphabet** and the ten **sefirot**. The book teaches that the letters of the alphabet are the building blocks out of which God constructs creations. The adept who masters the secret knowledge of the letters can also become a "lesser creator" even able to make a **golem**, or man-made anthropoid. Sefer Yetzirah is also deeply engaged by mystical mathematics. Tradition credits **Abraham** as its author, though there is no internal evidence for this. *(SEE APPENDIX, FIGURE 1.)*

YHWH or YHVH: *SEE* TETRAGRAMMATON.

Yichud/Yichudim: In Zoharic and Lurianic Kabbalah, *yichud* is any action or spiritual practice (**mitzvah**, **kavanah**, or **hanganot**) that theurgically affects or enhances the unity of God, either in the lower worlds, or on high. It results in a **tikkun**, an act of cosmic repair. It usually entails an action or **ritual** that harmonizes the forces of the **sefirot**. **Isaac Luria** would use the term to refer specifically to a ritual of incubation that was often performed at the grave of a **righteous** man for the purpose of communing with

him (Sha'ar Ruach ha-Kodesh, p. 75).[1] SEE IBBUR OR DEVE-
KUT; INCUBATION; MEDIUM; POSSESSION, GHOSTLY; THEURGY.

> 1. Fine, "The Contemplative Practice of Yihudim in Lurianic
> Kabbalah," in Green, *Jewish Spirituality*, vol. 2, 79–80.

Yochanan bar Nappaha, Rabbi: Talmudic Sage and faith
healer (ca. 3rd century). The Talmud repeatedly tells of his
spectacular beauty; he literally lit up a room. Pregnant
women would come to gaze on him in the belief that a
measure of his beauty would be transmitted to their un-
born children (Ber. 20a). He also had the power to heal
with his touch (Ber. 5B). He taught on a wide array of esoteric topics: **angels**, **creation**, **astrology**, **dreams**, and the
World-to-Come.

Yod or Yud: Tenth letter of the **Hebrew alphabet**, it has
the numeric value of 10. Its linguistic value is variable, as
it is a diphthong. Sometimes it is "y," other times it represents a short or long "e," or even a long "i" sound. It is
one of the letters that make up the Tetragrammaton. It is
a "form" or "foundation" letter, because other letters are
made from its form.[1]

> 1. Munk, *The Wisdom of the Hebrew Alphabet*, 125–32.

Yofiel: "The Beauty of God." An angel of revelation, sometimes identified as the **Sar ha-Torah** (Gedulat Moshe).
SEE DINA; YEFEIYAH.

Yoga: Though the term "yoga" derives from Hinduism,
the use of posture as a meditative technique is ancient to
Judaism. Most famous of these is placing one's head between the knees for extended periods of time, the so-
called "prophetic posture" (I Kings 18:42; Ber. 34b; A.Z.
17a; Hechalot Zutarti). Kneeling and prostrating oneself
are other examples. Judaism also makes extensive use of
body movement in prayer.

Yohani bat Retivi: A Jewish **witch**. Using acts of sympathetic **magic**, she tormented **women** in childbirth by
shutting their wombs, only to come to them in their distress and reap rewards for alleviating the condition that she
herself created. She was exposed when a person visiting in
her home unwittingly unstopped an enchanted bottle,

thereby releasing her victim (Otzer ha-Geonim 11; Rashi).
SEE BIRTH; WITCHES.

Yom Kippur: "Day of Atonement." Regarded by many
to be the holiest day of the Jewish sacred calendar, it is a
time of judgment, contrition, and renewal.

In biblical times, Yom Kippur entailed the dramatic
ritual of the High Priest entering the **Holy of Holies**
and making an incense offering while speaking the **Tetragrammaton**. It is also the day on which the scapegoat
ritual is performed. Two identical **goats** are brought before the High Priest. By means of **lots**, one is selected to
be sacrificed, while the other is sent to **Azazel** (Lev. 16).
Whether Azazel is an entity, a locale or something else
entirely is never resolved in Jewish tradition (RaSHI's and
Nachmanides' comments on 16:8; Zohar I: 114a).

According to the Sages, Yom Kippur is the only day
when **Satan** is completely powerless (Yoma 20a). In one
Midrash, the scapegoat ritual is explained as a bribe meant
to co-opt **Samael**/Satan, who comes every Yom Kippur
to accuse Israel before the **Throne of Glory**. The gift of
the goat forces the Adversary (not unlike Balaam) to speak
positively of the Jewish people instead (PdRE 46; Me'am
Loez).

The ritual of **Kapparah** is performed on the eve of the
day as an act of **substitution** expiation. A **lamp** or candle
can be used to divine whether a person will live through
the coming year (Hor. 12a). If one dreams of Yom Kippur,
it is an **omen** that the dreamer should **fast** in order to prevent some evil future event.

Yored Merkavah: "One who Descends [upon] the [Di-
vine] Chariot." This is the term used in **Ma'asei-Merkavah** to describe a practitioner who makes a spiritual ascension into the heavenly realms. Scholars have been puzzled
by the idiom itself; why does one not "go up" in the **chariot**, rather than "go down?" Certainly the preferred spatial
metaphor in **Hechalot literature** is that heaven is "upward." There are three proposed answers. First, the idiom
may allude to a meditative/trance act that triggers the
journey—one must "go down" into one's self in order to
make the ascent. Another explanation is that the mystic
uses water as a medium for seeing the **vision** (the Israelites

saw an awesome vision of God while surrounded by water, Ex. 15), so "descending" refers either to looking down at, or partially immersing in, water.[1] Finally, it may be that the term does not actually refer to the ascent itself, but only to the moment when the adept is welcomed into the divine Presence and, having achieved a temporary angelic status, is invited to be enthroned in a Chariot-Throne like the one upon which God sits.[2] If this latter explanation is correct, then to be designated a "Yored Merkavah" is more than simply being a mystical adept—it is to be counted among the spiritual virtuosos of Torah, a truly elite title.
SEE ASCENT, HEAVENLY; MEDITATION; MERKAVAH; THRONE OF GLORY.

1. Halperin, *Faces of the Chariot*, 237. Also see Schwartz, "Book of the Great Name," in Fine, *Judaism in Practice*, 340–47.
2. Wolfson, "Yeirdah ha-Merkavah: Typology of Enthronement and Ecstasy in Early Jewish Mysticism," in Herrera, 13–44.

Yossi, Abba: Exorcist (ca. 2nd century). One of the few Sages credited with performing an **exorcism**, he drove an evil spirit from a water source with the help of townspeople. The exorcism involved shouting the phrase, "Ours triumphs!" and beating the water with **iron** implements (Lev. R. 24; Tanh., Buber).

Yuhasin, Sefer: Also known as **Megillat Ahimaaz**, this medieval memoir of the life of Ahimaaz ben Paltiel includes accounts of **exorcisms**, shape changing, **zombie** making, and spellcasting. It is not to be confused with a later work of the same name by **Abraham Zacuto**.

Z

Zaamiel: "Rebuke of God." The **angel** of whirlwinds.

Zaapiel: "God is my Wrath." A destructive **angel** in charge of the utterly wicked souls in **Gehenna**. He torments them with rods of burning coal that turn their flesh black. He is also identified as the angel of storms (III Enoch; BhM 5:186).

Zacuto, Abraham: Astrologer (Spanish, ca. 15th–16th century) who served in the court of Manuel I of Portugal from 1494 until the expulsion of Jews from the country in 1497. He is the author of Sefer Yuhasin (The Book of Descent), a history of the Sages of Israel, an account that includes many of the miracles associated with them.

Zacuto, Moses: Kabbalist and poet (Italian, ca. 17th century). His interest in ghostly possession and his accounts of performing exorcisms helped popularize these ideas in the Italian Jewish community. He was actually a sophisticated diagnostician and attempted to distinguish between genuine possession and mere mental illness. He is the author of **Shoresh ha-Shemot**. *SEE* EXORCISM; POSSESSION, GHOSTLY.

Zagzagel: Another name for the angelic **Sar ha-Torah** (**Gedulat Moshe**).

Zakiel: "Comet of God" (?). A **fallen angel** who teaches mankind the art of divining through the study of clouds (I Enoch).

Zambri: A mythical medieval Jewish sorcerer appearing in Christian tradition. He fought (and lost) a magical duel with Pope Sylvester.

Zar: A possessing evil spirit mentioned in Ethiopian Jewish traditions.

Zayin: The seventh letter of the **Hebrew alphabet**. It has the vocalic value of "z" and the numeric value of 7. It signifies the **Sabbath**, the **World-to-Come**, and the wholeness of reality: the six cardinal points of the physical world (north, south, east, west, up, down) plus the dimension of spirit. The word itself also means "penis."[1]

1. Munk, *The Wisdom of the Hebrew Alphabet*, 104–11.

Zebulon: One of several mythical Jewish magicians of extraordinary prowess who feature prominently in Christian medieval legends.

Zechariah: The name of several people in the Hebrew Scriptures, most notably the post-exilic prophet and author of the biblical book that bears his name. The prophet Zechariah was a seer-like figure who experienced numerous vivid, highly encoded apocalyptic-style night visions. It is impossible to say specifically whether these were dreams or waking visions.

There is a conflated tradition of a righteous figure named Zechariah who was murdered on the **Temple** grounds by killers unknown. In some versions, this was the prophet Zechariah, in others it was a noble pre-exilic person also named Zechariah. Whoever this particular Zechariah was historically, after his murder in the Temple his **blood** continued to bubble out of the earth as a reproach to his murderers. After he captured the Temple grounds, the Babylonian king **Nebuchadnezzar** tried to stop the eruption by spilling the blood of thousands of Jews over the spot, but this blood atonement proved fruitless, since the descendants of the killers were not among the victims (Zech. 1; J. Tan. 69a).

Zechut Avot: "Merits of the Ancestors." In gauging the moral worth of any generation of the people **Israel**, God adds the merit of the **Patriarchs and Matriarchs** to their descendants. The worth of the ancestors makes it easier for God to more readily forgive any failings of the children. Being directly descended from a particular person, such as **Joseph**, brings even more benefit (Siddur, Avot Prayer; Lam. R. proem; Ber. 20a).

Zeira, Rabbi: Talmudic Sage (ca. 4th century). Working with **Raba bar Joseph**, he created a **golem**. In another incident mentioned in Talmud, Raba sent a golem to Zeira, who immediately turned the creature back to dust. On another occasion, an ominous **dream** caused him to make a pilgrimage from Iraq to Israel (Ber. 57a).

Zeiri, Rabbi: Talmudic Sage (ca. 2nd century). This Sage was a talented diagnostician of **witchcraft**. He restored to human form a person who had been shape-changed into an ass (Sanh. 67a).

Zer Anpin: In Sefer **Bahir**, this is the aspect of God's generativity, God as Creator. It is understood to be the androgynous divine source of life that is mirrored in the human genital forms (Bahir, Part 2, 30; 168–74). Later sources, perhaps euphemistically, identify the Zer Anpin as God's "beard." It eventually forms one element in the Lurianic concept of the **Partzufim**. *SEE* PHALLUS.

Zera Kodesh: "Seed of Holiness." A 17th-century handbook that explains the procedures for exorcizing spirits of the dead. *SEE* DYBBUK; EXORCISM.

Zerubbabel, Sefer: An apocalyptic text of late antiquity ascribed to the authorship of the post-Exilic Jewish leader Zerubbabel, which describes the end of the world. Many of the traditions concerning **Armilius**, an "Antichrist"-like figure, appear here, as do tales of **Hephzibah**, the mother of the **Messiah**.

Zevul: "Dwelling." One of the **seven heavens** (Chag. 12b–13a), it is the plane on which the Heavenly Temple exists and the angelic priests continue their sacrifices in God's honor. The name is derived from Hab. 3:11.

Zion, Mount: (*Har Tzion, Har ha-Bayit*). Also known as Mount Moriah and the Temple Mount, it is historically the eastern hill of Jerusalem situated between the Valley of Hinnom and the Valley Kidron, which is the site of the First and Second Temples. It is the point where God first created **light** and began the **creation** of the universe (Ps. 50:2; Eccl. R. 1:1) and the *Even ha-Shetiyah*, the **Foundation Stone** that holds back the waters of the **abyss**, first emerged from primordial **chaos**. It is the center of the universe (Tanhuma, Kedoshim 10). **Adam** was created from the dust of the mountain, from the spot where the **altar** would eventually rest (Mid. Konen 2:27). Noah made his offerings to God there after the **Flood**. When the Children of Israel needed to cross the Reed Sea to escape **Pharaoh**, God transported Mount Moriah to the bottom of the sea, and the Israelites walked across on it (MdRI, be-Shallach).

The mount is a place of revelation. According to Pirkei de-Rabbi Eliezer, it was miraculously formed from several hills to be the place where the *Akedah*, the trial of Isaac would take place (15). There **Abraham** almost sacrificed his son **Isaac**, when an **angel** appeared, telling him not to kill his son (Gen. 22). **Jacob** also had his dream/vision of angels while sleeping on the mount (Gen. 28:11).

In recent centuries, the term "Mount Zion" has been transferred to a spur of the western ridge of Jerusalem, across from the original Mount Zion. This is a modern misnomer.

Zipporah: The Midianite wife of **Moses**. When her father **Jethro** first encountered Moses, he threw Moses into a pit. She kept him alive ten years by secretly feeding him until her father relented (Sefer Zichronot, 46:9). She protected her husband from supernatural attack by circumcising their son Gershom and then throwing the detached foreskin in front of Moses while reciting verses of power (Ex. 4). *SEE* CIRCUMCISION; SATAN; SERPENT; WOMEN.

Ziviel: "Affliction of God" (?). An angel mentioned in the **Book of the Great Name**.

Zivvuga Kaddisha: (Aramaic, "Holy Union"). The concept of a *hieros gamos*, of divine union, between the masculine and feminine aspects of God. This is a major theme in Zoharic Kabbalah. **Isaac Luria** taught that there are five types of Zivvuga that occur within different levels of the Godhead (Sefer ha-Hezyonot, pp. 212–17). He believed that humans engaging in sex at different times, with different intentions (such as procreation versus companionship) mirrored and influenced these higher unions.[1]
SEE SEFIROT; SEX; SHEKINAH.

1. Fine, *Physician of the Soul, Healer of the Cosmos*, 196–205.

Ziz: A giant mythological bird, sometimes called the Queen of Birds (Ps. 50:11). It is so enormous that it can stand in the heart of the sea and the water would reach only its ankles while her head pierces the sky. When Ziz rides on the back of **Leviathan**, the bird can see the **Throne of Glory** and sing to God. The beating of its wings can change the direction of the winds. Like Leviathan and **Behemoth**, Ziz is destined to be served at the Messianic banquet (B.B. 73a–74a; EY). *SEE* ANIMALS.

Zodiac: The system of dividing the night sky into zones for the purpose of astrological reading and interpretation.

Zodiacs are quite ancient and may be alluded to in the Bible as early as the 7th century BCE, where a reference to *mazzalot* (stars, or perhaps, constellations) is understood by some scholars as a term for a zodiac (II Kings 23:5). Others speculate an earlier reference to the zodiac appears as graffiti on a tomb site at Khibet el Qom in Israel (8th century BCE). Based on their order the four initials written there, *alef, bet, mem*, and *alef*, suggest they may be referring to four signs of the zodiac.

Jewish zodiac systems derived from, or at least influenced by, the Western traditions of **astrology** are evident by late antiquity, when the mystical manual **Sefer Yetzi-**

rah makes repeated references to Greco-Roman zodiac houses such as the Gedi (Capricorn), the Shor (Taurus), and the Dagim (Pieces) (SY 4:6–5:10, Short Recension). More surprising, a magnificent mosaic zodiac featuring all the familiar houses is the decorative centerpiece of the floor of the 5th-century Bet Alfa synagogue that was unearthed in northern Israel. By this time the names of the twelve zodiac signs (*mazzalot*) are established: **Taleh** (Aries), **Shor** (Taurus), **Teomim** (Gemini), **Sartan** (Cancer), **Aryah** (Leo), **Betulah** (Virgo), **Moznayim** (Libra), **Akrav** (Scorpio), **Keshet** (Sagittarius), **Gedi** (Capricorn), **D'li** (Aquarius), and **Dagim** (Pisces) (Yalkut 418).

By the early Middle Ages, the zodiac was an accepted part of Jewish astrology and had been fused with traditional Jewish angelology, with each house having its own principal angel and heavenly host (Ber. 32b). One Midrash uses the zodiac signs as an allegory to chart the progress of a man's life (Mid. Tanh., Ha'azinu 1). For each of the houses of the zodiac, God created thirty hosts of angels; one host for each of the 360 degrees of the heavenly circumference (Ber. 32b).

Sections of Hebrew magical manuals such as **Sefer ha-Razim** ("The Book of Mysteries") and **Sefer Raziel** ha-Malach ("The Book of [the Angel] Raziel") are devoted to the influence of the zodiac over the universe.

Mainstream figures in medieval Jewry were more divided on the issue of astral influences than the Jewish populous, who generally accepted the power of the stars. The rationalist philosopher **Maimonides**, for example, utterly dismissed the value of astrology, while others, like the Bible exegete **Abraham ibn Ezra**, gave it great credence. The physician **Abraham Yagel** (Italian, ca. 16th century) even used the zodiac in his diagnosis and treatment of his patients. Interest in the supernatural influence of the zodiac has faded among Jews, but has never entirely gone away. *(SEE APPENDIX FIGURE 6.)*

Zohar, Sefer ha-: "The Book of Radiance." This massive masterwork of Spanish Kabbalah is the single most influential work of esotericism in Judaism. Part esoteric commentary, part medieval romance, and part mystical gospel, the Zohar is ostensibly the work of the 2nd-century Galilean Sage **Simon bar Yochai**. In fact, most of the collection is the work of **Moses (Shem Tov) de Leon** of Guadalajara (ca. 13th century). Rabbi Moses composed the Zohar, partly through **automatic writing**, in a series of booklets he sold and distributed over his lifetime. As a result, the Zohar text we have today is actually an anthology of the surviving booklets.

The core of the published book (18th century) consists of three sections: commentaries on Genesis, Exodus, and the last three books of the Torah. In addition, these are usually published with several related compositions: partial commentaries on Song of Songs, Ruth, and Lamentations, the early **Zohar Chadash**, the later **Ra'aya Meheimna**, and the much later **Tikkunei Zohar**.

Written in an eccentric, poetically charged Aramaic, the Zohar is at turns lyrical, fantastic, and downright cryptic. At times the text revels in **paradox**, riddles, and obscure and elliptical pronouncements. It is also charged with erotic themes throughout.

The single most outstanding idea in it is its elaborate and complex concept of the **sefirot** (the pleroma of divine powers). These ten divine forces, unfolding at different levels, revealing rungs of divine purpose and function, are the centerpiece of the Zohar's theosophy. The workings of these sefirot are then applied to the **Bible**, simultaneously revealing the inner workings of the Godhead and illustrating the divine energies at play in all aspects of the biblical narratives. Every figure and event in the Bible is correlated to the sefirot, highlighting the analogous movement of forces both divine and earthly.

The Zohar also gives a highly mythological view of the cosmos, with the forces of the sefirot also expressed through **demons**, heavenly beings, and mythic locales. Most startling of all is the frankly sexual interpretation the Zohar applies to the Godhead. God has both masculine and feminine aspects that are engaged in a dynamic divine drama of ongoing *hieros gamos* in order to achieve perfect unity. The people **Israel** is a crucial element of the lowest of the sefirot, **Malchut**, and has a central role in sustaining this divine process of unification. Mortals effect this ongoing divine unification through diligent observance of the mitzvot, bringing the right intention to their performance, and by other specific acts of *imitatio dei*.

Another outstanding aspect of Zoharic theosophy is its interpretation of **evil**. Drawing on the teachings of **Treatise on the Left Emanation**, the Zohar teaches that evil is really an emanation of the sefirah **Gevurah**, of divine justice, that becomes sustained and distorted by human wickedness.

The work devotes surprisingly little attention to the personal mystical experience or how to achieve it. The one distinctive mystical pursuit mentioned in the Zohar is **devekut**, "cleaving," or erotic-passionate attachment to God.[1] Mostly this is achieved through the mystical revelations that unfold in sacred study, though other mystical customs—intensive prayer and meditation, self-denial, and ecstasy-inducing practices, like sleep deprivation—also play a role. Most importantly, Zohar consistently sees humanity (specifically Jews) and the lower sefirot on a kind of continuum, blurring the distinction between Israel and its God. This is why Jews both facilitate and participate in the ongoing **tikkun** of **zivvuga kaddisha**, "Holy Union."

The impact of the Zohar on subsequent Jewish mysticism is unparalleled. Its importance soared in the aftermath of the catastrophic expulsion of Spanish Jewry, as those exiles found meaning for their plight in the complex interplay of the sefirot. In some segments of the Jewish community, the Zohar eventually stood on par with the Bible and Talmud as an authoritative text. It also had a profound impact on **Christian Qabbalists** of the Renaissance and later, who combed the murky language of the Zohar for secreted references to the Trinity and other Christian doctrines.

1. Matt, *The Zohar: Pritzker Edition*, vol. 1, lxix-lxxi.

Zohar Chadash: "New Radiance." Paradoxically, this "new" section of the **Zohar** is one of the oldest parts of the collection, a section including many esoteric Midrashim.

Zombies: While there is not a large tradition of stories about people reanimating dead bodies (as opposed to fully resurrecting a person), there are a few medieval and early modern European stories of how one may make a zombie by writing the secret **name of God** on a parchment and inserting it under the tongue of a corpse, or into an incision in the skin. Removing the parchment reverses the effect (Sefer Yuhasin). This description closely parallels traditions on the construction of a **golem**. In one account, the dead, driven by a need unfulfilled during life, can spontaneously start to walk the earth again (Shivhei ha-Ari). Virtually all other traditions assume that zombies must be animated by an adept (Ma'aseh Buch 171). *SEE* RESURRECTION.

APPENDIX OF ILLUSTRATIONS

Letter	Name		Sound	Value	Designation	Phonetic Family
א	Alef	אלף	silent	1	mother	guttural
ב	Bet	בית	B, Bh	2	double	labial
ג	Gimel	גמל	G, Gh	3	double	palatal
ד	Dalet	דלת	D, Dh	4	double	lingual
ה	Hay	הא	H	5	elemental	guttural
ו	Vav	וו	V (W)	6	elemental	labial
ז	Zayin	זין	Z	7	elemental	dental
ח	Chet	חית	German ch	8	elemental	guttural
ט	Tet	טית	T	9	elemental	lingual
י	Yod or Yud	יוד	Y (I)	10	elemental	palatal
כ,ך	Kaf	כף	K, Kh	20	double	palatal
ל	Lamed	למד	L	30	elemental	lingual
מ,ם	Mem	מם	M	40	mother	labial
נ,ן	Nun	נון	N	50	elemental	lingual
ס	Samech	סמך	S	60	elemental	dental
ע	Ayin	עין	silent	70	elemental	guttural
פ,ף	Payh	פא	P, Ph	80	double	labial
צ,ץ	Tzadi	צדי	Tz	90	elemental	dental
ק	Kuf	קוף	K (Q)	100	elemental	palatal
ר	Resh	ריש	R, Rh	200	double	dental
ש	Shin	שין	Sh (S)	300	mother	dental
ת	Tav	תיו	T, Th	400	double	lingual

Figure 1: The Hebrew alphabet.
See Hebrew; Incantations, Spells, and Adjurations; Language; Yetzirah, Sefer.

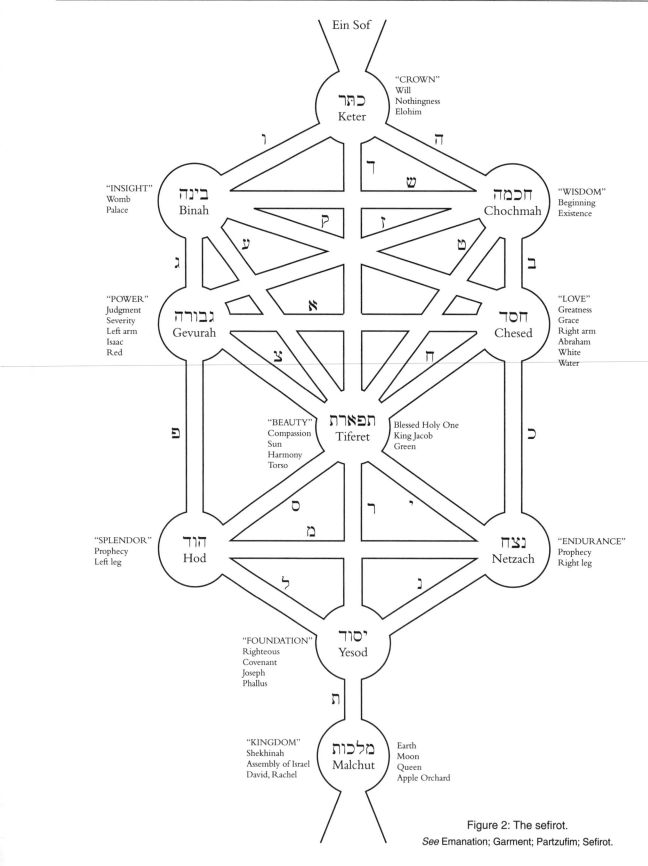

Figure 2: The sefirot.

See Emanation; Garment; Partzufim; Sefirot.

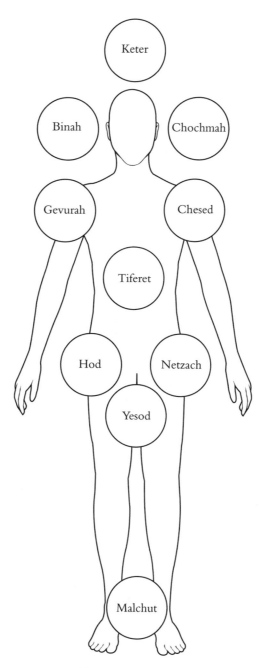

Figure 3: Microcosm.
See Adam Kadmon; Body; Microcosm; Sefirot.

Figure 4: Magen David amulet.
See Amulet; Hexagram; Magic; Names of God; Solomon, Testament of.

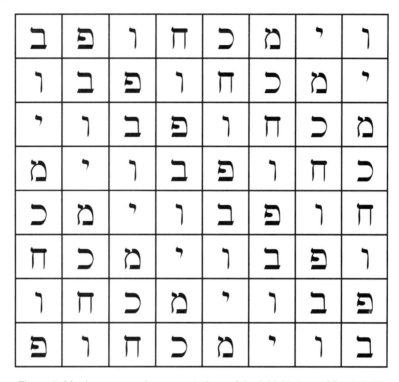

Figure 5: Magic square using permutations of the initial letters of Deut. 7:15.
See Amulet; Bible; Hebrew; Permutations.

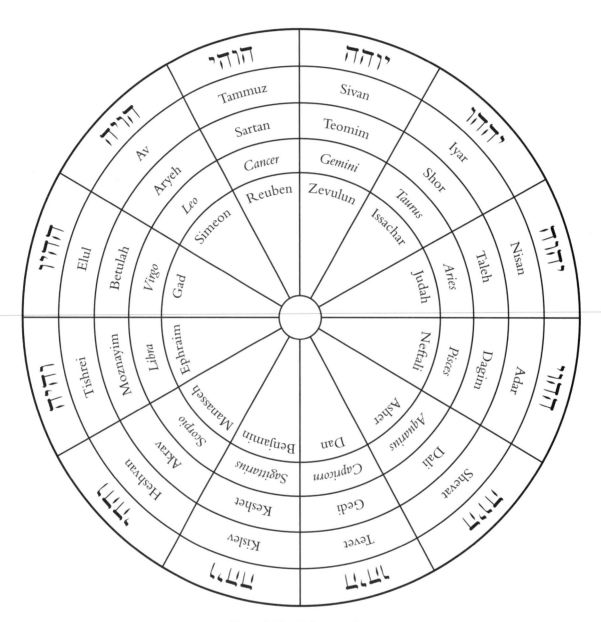

Figure 6: The Hebrew zodiac.
See Astrology; Calendar; Zodiac.

ABBREVIATIONS OF CITATIONS FROM TRADITIONAL TEXTS

Abbreviation of Biblical Books

Gen.	Genesis	*Ezek.*	Ezekial	*Prov.*	Proverbs
Ex.	Exodus	*Hos.*	Hosea	*Job*	Job
Lev.	Leviticus	*Joel*	Joel	*S of S*	Song of Songs
Num.	Numbers	*Am.*	Amos	*Ruth*	Ruth
Deut.	Deuteronomy	*Jon.*	Jonah	*Lam.*	Lamentations
Josh.	Joshua	*Mic.*	Micah	*Ecc.*	Ecclesiastes
Judg.	Judges	*Nah.*	Nahum	*Esth.*	Esther
I Sam.	I Samuel	*Hab.*	Habakkuk	*Dan.*	Daniel
II Sam.	II Samuel	*Zeph.*	Zephaniah	*Ez.*	Ezra
I Kings	I Kings	*Hag.*	Haggai	*Neh.*	Nehemiah
II Kings	II Kings	*Zech.*	Zechariah	*1 Chr.*	I Chronicles
Isa.	Isaiah	*Mal.*	Malachi	*2 Chr.*	II Chronicles
Jer.	Jeremiah	*Ps.* (pl. *Pss.*)	Psalms		

Abbreviation of Talmud Tractates

Ar.	Arakin	*Ker.*	Keriot	*Pes.*	Pesachim
Avot	Avot	*Ket.*	Ketubot	*R.H.*	Rosh Hashanah
A.Z.	Avodah Zarah	*Kid.*	Kiddushin	*Sanh.*	Sanhedrin
B.B.	Baba Batra	*Kin.*	Kinnim	*Sem.*	Semahot
Bech.	Bechorot	*Kut.*	Kutim	*Shab.*	Shabbat
Ber.	Berachot	*Mak.*	Makkot	*Shek.*	Shekalim
Betz.	Betzah	*Makh.*	Makhshirin	*Shev.*	Shevuot
Bik.	Bikkurim	*Me.*	Meilah	*Sof.*	Sofrim
B.K.	Baba Kama	*Meg.*	Megillah	*Sot.*	Sotah
B.M.	Baba Metzia	*Men.*	Menahot	*Suk.*	Sukkah
Chag.	Chagigah	*Mez.*	Mezuzah	*Tam.*	Tamid
Chal.	Challah	*Midd.*	Middot	*Tan.*	Ta'anit
Chul.	Chullin	*Mik.*	Mikvaot	*Tem.*	Terumah
De.	Demai	*M.K.*	Moed Katan	*Toh.*	Toharot
Ed.	Ediyyot	*Ned.*	Nedarim	*Yad.*	Yadayim
Eruv.	Eruvin	*Nega.*	Nega'im	*Yev.*	Yevamot
Git.	Gittin	*Nid.*	Niddah	*Yoma*	Yoma
Hor.	Horayot	*Oh.*	Ohalot	*Zev.*	Zevahim
Ka.	Kallah	*Or.*	Orlah		
Kel.	Kelim	*Pe.*	Peah		

Midrash, Kabbalah, and other Traditional Sources

AbbS	Alef-Bet ben Sira		*Mid. Teh.*	Midrash Tehillim (Psalms)
AdRN	Avot de-Rabbi Natan		*Num. R.*	Numbers Rabbah
Ant.	Antiquities of the Jews (Josephus)		*PdRE*	Pirkei de-Rabbi Eliezer
B.	Babylonian Talmud		*PdRK*	Pesikta de-Rav Kahana
Bahir	Sefer ha-Bahir		*PR*	Pesikta Rabbati
BhM	Beit ha-Midrash		*Ruth R.*	Ruth Rabbah
ChdM	Charba de Moshe		*SA*	Shulchan Aruch
Deut. R.	Deuteronomy Rabbah		*SCh*	Sefer Chasidim
Eccl. R.	Ecclesiastes Rabbah		*SGE*	Seder Gan Eden
En.	Enoch (I, II, III)		*ShB*	Shivchei ha-Besht
Es. R.	Esther Rabbah		*ShR*	Sefer ha-Razim
Ex. R.	Exodus Rabbah		*Sif.*	Sifra
EY	Ein Yaakov		*Sif. D.*	Sifrei Deuteronomy
Gen. R.	Genesis Rabbah		*S of S R.*	Song of Songs Rabbah
J.	Jerusalem Talmud		*SY*	Sefer Yetzirah
Lam. R.	Lamentations Rabbah		*Tanh.*	Midrash Tanhuma
Lev. R.	Leviticus Rabbah		*Tanh. B.*	Midrash Tanhuma (Buber)
M.	Mishnah		*TdE*	Tanna de Eliyahu
MdRI	Mekhilta de Rabbi Ishmael		*Tos.*	Tosefta
MG	Masekhet Gehinnom		*T.Z.*	Tikkunei Zohar
MhG	Midrash ha-Gadol		*War*	The Jewish War (Josephus)
Mid. Avkir	Midrash Avkir		*Yalkut*	Yalkut Shimoni
Mid. Konen	Midrash Konen		*ZCh*	Zohar Chadash
Mid. Mish.	Midrash Mishlei (Proverbs)		*Zohar*	Sefer ha-Zohar
Mid. Sam.	Midrash Samuel			

Systems for citations vary from one Jewish document to the next. Citations such as "8a" and "8b" refer to the front and flip side of a folio page. Hebrew citations following the title of a Midrashic work, such as "Yitro," refer to the *parshiyot*, or traditional divisions of Torah, which run many pages and will require further browsing. Short documents will often not include more page-specific citations.

QUICK REFERENCE GLOSSARY
OF FREQUENTLY USED TERMS

Aggadah: Stories, narratives, and legends; all the non-legal materials in rabbinic literature.

Apotropaic: Protective.

BCE/CE: "Before the Common Era/Common Era." These dating designations coincide with the Christocentric dating system of "BC/AD." Thus, 1497 CE is the same as 1497 AD.

Bible: For the purposes of this encyclopedia, "Bible" refers to the Hebrew canonical Bible, also called TaNaKH, consisting of thirty-nine books and being effectively identical to the Christian "Old Testament."

Classical Antiquity: For the purposes of this encyclopedia, the period from about 500 BCE–200 CE.

Early Judaism: The spiritual expressions of the Jewish people from the end of the Babylonian exile (516 BCE) until the rise of the Sages (200 CE).

Gloss: An interpretation, clarification, or comment inserted into an earlier text by a later copyist. This phenomena occurs throughout classical Jewish literature, making every document, including the Bible, a work of composite authorship.

Greco-Roman Period: For the purposes of this encyclopedia, from 300 BCE–500 CE.

Hermetic: Refers to the teachings and disciplines of Western non-Jewish magic most closely associated with alchemy and the Islamic-Renaissance fusion of astronomy and magic.

Kabbalah: A Jewish mystical movement of the 12th–16th centuries, but also used as a catch-all term for Jewish mysticism.

Medieval Period: For the purposes of this encyclopedia, the period from the Muslim conquests (8th century) until the Reformation (16th century).

Midrash: Homiletic and legal interpretations of the Bible, usually collected into books.

Mishna, or Mishnah: The core document of the Talmud and the first great text of rabbinic Judaism, compiled around 200 CE.

Modern: For the purposes of this encyclopedia, the 17th–20th centuries.

Numinous: Spiritual forces and entities of an awesome and/or terrifying aspect.

Parsha, Parshiyot: The traditional/medieval system of dividing the Torah into fifty-four sections.

Persian Period: A period lasting from 500–300 BCE.

Prophylactic: Preventative protection.

Rabbinic Literature: All literary writings of the Sages and their immediate successors (100 BCE–1100 CE), such as Mishnah, Talmud, and the Midrashim.

Rabbinic Period: The period when the Sages came to define Jewish spiritual practice. Though the first of the Sages emerged around 200 BCE, their influence really peaked from about 200 CE to the Islamic conquests of the 8th century. This roughly coincides with the period dubbed "late antiquity."

Renaissance: For the purposes of this encyclopedia, the 15th through early 17th centuries.

Sages: The Rabbis of the Talmudic and immediate Post-Talmudic eras who defined rabbinic Judaism.

Talmud: The Mishnah combined with its vast commentaries (Gemara). There are two versions of the Talmud, the Babylonian and the Palestinian (or Jerusalem) versions, compiled over the 5th and 6th centuries CE.

Targum: An early translation of the Bible from Hebrew, usually into Aramaic. The translations are often packed with interpretative glosses, paraphrases, and unusual readings.

Tellurian: Of subterranean, underground, or underworld origins.

Theosophy: Any philosophic system based on mystical or extra-rational insight into the nature of God and the universe.

Theurgy: The word *theurgy* comes from the practices of Egyptian Neo-Platonists. For the purposes of this encyclopedia, I distinguish theurgic from magical practices when the ritual or act involves invoking/adjuring sentient spirits (including angels, demons, or even a name of God).

Torah: The Five Books of Moses; the first five books of the Bible, and the spiritual "Constitution" of the Jewish people. The word can also be used as a metonym for the full scope of all Jewish teachings, or even as a synonym for "Judaism."

BIBLIOGRAPHY

English Reference Works

Avi-Yonah, M. *The Encyclopedia of Archaeological Excavations in the Holy Land*. London: Oxford University Press, 1975.

Ben-Sasson, H. H. *A History of the Jewish People*. Cambridge: Harvard University Press, 1976.

Betz, H. D. *Greek Magical Papyri in Translation*. Chicago: University of Chicago Press, 1996.

Bialik and Ravnitzky, eds. *The Book of Legends*. Translated by William Braude. New York: Schocken, 1992.

Buxbaum, Yitzhak. *Jewish Spiritual Practices*. Northvale: Jason Aronson, 1990.

Cohen and Mendes-Flohr. *Contemporary Jewish Religious Thought*. New York: Free Press, 1987.

Epstein, I., ed. *The Talmud*. London: the Soncino Press, 1939.

Frankel, E. and B. Platkin Teutsch. *The Encyclopedia of Jewish Symbols*. Philadelphia: JPS, 2000.

Ginzberg, L. *Legends of the Jews*. 7 vols. Philadelphia: JPS, 1968.

Glick, H. S., trans. *Legends of the Talmud/Ein Yaakov*, H. S. Glick, 1923.

Green, A. *Jewish Spirituality*. 2 vols. New York: Crossroad, 1986.

Grendler, P. *Encyclopedia of the Renaissance*. Vols. 1–6. New York: Charles Schribner's Sons, 1998.

Hallo and Younger, ed. *The Context of Scripture*. Vols. 1–3. Leiden, Netherlands: Brill, 2000.

Marcus, J. R. *The Jew in the Medieval World*. New York: Atheneum, 1938.

Pritchard, J. B., ed. *Ancient Near Eastern Texts Relating to the Old Testament*. New Haven: Yale Press, 1969.

Rabinowicz, T., ed. *The Encyclopedia of Hasidism*. Northvale, NJ: Jason Aronson, 1996.

Rawlinson, H. *Cuneiform Inscriptions of Western Asia*, 5 vols. London: British Museum, 1894.

Roth, C., ed. *Encyclopedia Judaica*. 14 vols. Jerusalem: Keter, 1974.

Schiffman, L., and J. VanderKam. *Encyclopedia of the Dead Sea Scrolls*. 2 vols. New York: Oxford University Press, 2000.

Seltzer, R. *Jewish People, Jewish Thought*. New York: Macmillan, 1980.

Singer, I., ed. *The Jewish Encyclopedia*. 12 vols. New York: KTAV, 1901.

Sperling and Simon, trans. *The Zohar*. 5 vols. London: Soncino Press, 1956.

Hebrew Sources

Bialik and Ravnitzky. *Sefer Ha-Aggadah*. Tel Aviv: Davir, 1987.

Eisenstein, J. D. *Otzer D'rushim Nibcharim: Yalkut*. New York: Hebrew Publishing Co., 1929.

Horowitz and Rabin, eds. *Mekhilta d'Rabbi Yishmael*. Jerusalem: Sifrei Wehrmann, 1970.

Jellenik, A. *Beit ha-Midrash*. Vols. 1–6. Jerusalem: Wahrmann Books, 1967.

The Judaic Classics Library: The Deluxe Edition. CD-ROM. Chicago: Davka Corporation, 1995.

Klein, M. L. *Genizah Manuscripts of Palestinian Targum*. Cincinnati: HUC Press, 1986.

Mikraot G'dolot: Neviim ha-Rishonim, Neviim ha-Achronim, Ketuvim. Jerusalem: Ha-Masorah, 1975.

Schafer, P. *Synopse Zur Hekhalot Lituratur* [in Hebrew/German]. Tuebingen: Mohr/Siebeck, 1981.

Shimon ha-Darshan. *Yalkut Shimoni l'esrim v'arbaah Sifrei Torah, Neviim, v'Khetuvim*. Berlin: Horeb Publishing, 1878.

Steinsaltz, A., ed. *Talmud Bavli*. Vols. 1–23. Jerusalem: Ha-Machon Ha-Yisraeli L'farsumim Talmudiyim, 1989.

Torat Chayyim. Jerusalem: Mossad Ha-Rav Kook, 1991.

Online Reference Material

The Comprehensive Aramaic Lexicon. A linguistic and textual resource online at http://cal1.cn.huc.edu/aramaic_language.html.

Jewish Heritage Online Magazine. http://www.jhom.com.

Levine, F. *Practical Kabbalah & Related Folklore*. http://www.atomick.net/fayelevine/pk/.

Noegel, Scott B. "General Jewish Magic." An online bibliography at http://faculty.washington.edu/snoegel/generaljewishmagic.htm.

Soc.Culture.Jewish Newsgroups at http://www.scjfaq.org.

English Monographs, Anthologies, and Articles

Abrams, D. "From Divine Shape to Angelic Being: The Career of Akatriel in Jewish Literature," *Journal of Religion* 76 (1996).

Arbusch, R. "The Figure of Rabbi Ishmael in the Hekhalot Literature and in Jewish Martyrology as Competing Models of Heavenly Ascent." Paper for 2001 SBL Convention. Published online at http://www.iwu.edu/~religion/ejcm/SBLbirthoral.html.

Armstrong, A. H. *Classical Mediterranean Spirituality*. New York: Crossroad, 1986.

Austin, J. L. *How to Do Things with Words*. Oxford: Clarendon Press, 1962.

Bamberger, B. J. "The Changing Image of the Prophet in Jewish Thought," *The 1966 Goldenson Lecture, Hebrew Union College, Cincinnati*.

———. *Fallen Angels: Soldiers of Satan's Realm*. Philadelphia: JPS, 1952.

Bar Ilan, M. "Exorcism by Rabbis: Talmud Sages and Their Magic," *Bar Ilan University Online Articles*, http://faculty.biu.ac.il/~barilm/exorcism.html.

———. "Magic Seals on the Body among Jews of the First Centuries CE," *Tarbiz* 57 (1988).

———. "Witches in the Bible and in the Talmud," *Approaches to Ancient Judaism*. Atlanta: Scholars Press, 1993.

Barker, M. "Beyond the Veil of the Temple: The High Priestly Origin of the Apocalypses," *Scottish Journal of Theology* 51, no. 1 (1998).

———. *An Extraordinary Gathering of Angels*. London: MQ Publishing, 2004.

Ben-Amos, D., and J. Mintz. *In Praise of the Baal Shem Tov [Shivhei ha-Besht]*. Bloomington: Indiana University Press, 1970.

Ben-Sasson, H. H. *Trial and Achievement: Currents in Jewish History.* Jerusalem: Keter Publishing, 1974.

Benton, C. "An Introduction to the Sefer Yetzirah," *The Maqom Journal*, published online at http://www .maqom.com/journal/paper14.pdf.

Berger, D. *The Rebbe, the Messiah, and the Scandal of Orthodox Indifference.* Oxford: The Littmann Library of Jewish Civilization, 2001.

Berman, J. *The Temple: Its Symbolism and Meaning Then and Now.* Northvale, NJ: Jason Aronson, 1995.

Bilu, Y. "Dybbuk and Maggid: Two Cultural Patterns of Altered Consciousness in Judaism," *AJS Review* 21, no. 2 (1996).

Blumenthal, D. *Understanding Jewish Mysticism.* New York: KTAV, 1984.

Bosker, B. M. "Wonder Working and the Rabbinic Tradition: The Case of Hanina ben Dosa," *Journal for the Study of Judaism* 16, no. 1 (1985).

Braude, W. *Pesikta de-Rab Kahana.* Philadelphia: JPS, 1975.

———. *Pesikta Rabbati.* Vols. 1–2. New Haven: Yale University Press, 1981.

———. *Tanna Debe Eliyyahu.* Philadelphia: JPS, 1981.

Bregman, M. "The Four Who Entered Paradise: The Evolution of a Talmudic Tale," in *First Harvest: Jewish Writing in St. Louis: 1991–1996*, ed. H. Schwartz. St. Louis: Brodsky Library Press, 1997.

———. "Mordecai the Milkman," Unpublished lecture given at Hebrew Union College-Jewish Institute of Religion, 1996.

———. "Seeing with the Sages," in *Agendas for the Study of Midrash in the 21st Century*, ed. M. L. Raphael. Williamsburg, VA: College of William and Mary, 1999.

Breslauer, S. D., ed. *The Seductiveness of Jewish Myth: Challenge or Response?* Albany: SUNY Press, 1997.

Brichto, H. "Kin, Cult, Land and Afterlife—A Biblical Complex," *HUCA* 54 (1983).

———. *The Problem of "Curse" in the Hebrew Bible.* Philadelphia: JBLMS 13 (1963).

Brigg, C. V. *The Encyclopedia of Angels.* New York: Plume Books, 1997.

Buber, M. *Tales of Angels, Spirits, and Demons.* New York: Hawk's Well Press, 1958.

Burkett, F. C. "Memra, Shekinah, Metatron," *Journal of Theological Studies* 24 (1923).

Canaan, T. "Haunted Springs and Water Demons in Palestine," *Journal of the Palestine Oriental Society*, no. 1 (1921).

Chajes, J. H. *Between Worlds: Dybbuks, Exorcists, and Early Modern Judaism.* Philadelphia: University of Pennsylvania Press, 2003.

———. "Judgments Sweetened: Possession and Exorcism in Early Modern Jewish Culture," *Journal of Early Modern History* 1, no. 2 (1997).

———. "Women Leading Women (and Attentive Men): Early Modern Jewish Models of Pietistic Female Authority," in *Jewish Religious Leadership: Image and Reality*, ed. Jack Wertheimer. 2 vols. New York: Jewish Theological Seminary, 2004.

Chajes and Copenhaver, "Magic and Astrology," in *Encyclopedia of the Renaissance*, ed. P. Grendler. New York: Charles Scriber's Sons, 1998.

Chajes, Z. "Demons, Witchcraft, Incantations, Dreams, and Planetary Influences: Medical Prescriptions and Curative Methods in the Aggadah," *The Student's Guide to the Talmud.* Jerusalem: Hebrew University Press, 1960.

Ciraolo and Seidel, eds. *Magic and Divination in the Ancient World.* Leiden, Netherlands: Brill/Styx, 2002.

Cohen, A. "'Do the Dead Know. . .' The Representation of Death in the Bavli," *AJS Review* 24, no. 1 (1999).

Cohen, M. *Shi'ur Qomah: Texts and Recensions.* Tuebingen: J. C. B. Mohr, 1985.

Cohen, S. S. "The Name of God, a Study in Rabbinic Theology," *HUCA* 23 (1950).

Cohen, S. J. *The Holy Letter: A Study in Jewish Sexual Morality*. New York: KTAV, 1976.

Conybeare, F. C., trans. "The Testament of Solomon," *Jewish Quarterly Review*, Oct. 1898. Published online by Joseph Peterson at http://www.esotericarchives .com/solomon/testamen.htm.

Coogan, M. D., trans. *Stories from Ancient Canaan*. Louisville, KY: Westminster Press, 1978.

Couliano, I. P. *The Tree of Gnosis: Gnostic Mythology from Early Christianity to Modern Nihilism*. San Francisco: Harper-Cross, 1990.

Cross, F. *Canaanite Myth and Hebrew Epic: Essays in the History of the Religion of Israel*. Cambridge: Harvard University Press, 1973.

Dan, J. *The Early Jewish Mysticism*. Tel Aviv: MOD Books, 1993.

———. *The Heart and the Fountain: An Anthology of Jewish Mystical Experiences*. New York: Oxford University Press, 2002.

———. "Samael, Lilith, and the Concept of Evil in Early Kabbalah," *AJS Review* 5 (1980).

———. *The 'Unique Cherub' Circle*. Tubingen: J. C. B. Mohr, 1999.

Dan, J. and R. Kiener. *The Early Kabbalah*. Mahwah, NJ: Paulist Press, 1986.

Davila, J. "Ancient Magic (The Prayer of Jacob)," Lecture online at http://www.st-andrews.ac.uk/~www_sd/ magic.html.

———. "The Hekhalot Literature and Shamanism," Society of Biblical Literature 1994 Seminar Papers, Atlanta, GA: Scholars Press, 1994.

———. "Ritual in the Jewish Pseudepigrapha," Draft article online at http://www.st-andrews.ac.uk/ academic/divinity/ritual_pseud_paper.htm.

Deacy, S. and K. Pierce, eds. *Rape in Antiquity: Sexual Violence in the Greek and Roman Worlds*. London: Duckworth, 2002.

Doberer, K. K. *The Goldmakers: Ten Thousand Years of Alchemy*. London: Nicholson & Watson, 1948.

Dodd, E. R. *The Greeks and the Irrational*. Berkley: University of California Press, 1951.

Drob, S. *Symbols of the Kabbalah: Philosophical and Psychological Perspectives*. Northvale: Jason Aronson, 1996.

Eilberg-Schwartz, H. *God's Phallus, and Other Problems for Men and Monotheism*. Boston: Beacon Press, 1992.

Eliade, M., ed. *The Encyclopedia of Religion*. New York: Pantheon, 1964.

Elior, R. "Mysticism, Magic, and Angelology: The Perception of Angels in Hekhalot Literature," *Jewish Studies Quarterly* 1 (1993).

———. *The Three Temples: On the Emergence of Early Jewish Mysticism*. Oxford, OH: Littmann Library of Jewish Civilization, 2004.

Elkes, I. *The BeSHT: Magician, Mystic, and Leader*. Waltham: Brandeis University Press, 2004.

Erlanger, G. *Signs of the Times: The Zodiac in Jewish Tradition*. Jerusalem: Feldman Publishing, 1999.

Eskenazi and Harrington. *The Sabbath in Jewish and Christian Traditions*. New York: Crossroad, 1971.

Faierstein, M. *Jewish Mystical Autobiographies: Book of Visions and Book of Secrets*. Mahwah, NJ: Paulist Press, 1999.

Feher, M., ed. *Fragments for a History of the Human Body*. 3 vols. Cambridge: Zone Books, 1989.

Fine, L., ed. *Essential Papers on Kabbalah*. New York: NYU Press, 1995.

———, ed. *Judaism in Practice: From the Middle Ages through the Early Modern Period*. Princeton, NJ: Princeton University Press, 2001.

———. *Physician of the Soul, Healer of the Cosmos: Isaac Luria and his Kabbalistic Fellowship*. Stanford: Stanford University Press, 2003.

———. *Safed Spirituality: Rules of Mystical Piety, the Beginning of Wisdom*. Mahwah, NJ: Paulist Press, 1989.

Fine, S. *This Holy Place: On the Sanctity of the Synagogue during the Greco-Roman Period*. Notre Dame, IN: Notre Dame Press, 1997.

Finkel, A. Y. *In My Flesh I See God: A Treasury of Rabbinic Insights About the Human Anatomy*. Northvale, NJ: Jason Aronson, 1995.

Fishbane, M. "Arm of the Lord: Biblical Myth, Rabbinic Midrash, and the Mystery of History," in *Language, Theology, and the Bible*, ed. S. Balentine. Oxford: Clarington Press, 1994.

———. "Aspects of Jewish Magic in the Ancient Rabbinic Period," in *The Solomon Goldman Lectures II*, ed. N. Stampfer. Chicago: Spertus College of Judaica Press, 1987.

———. "The Holy One Sits and Roars: Mythopoesis and the Midrashic Imagination," *Journal of Jewish Thought and Philosophy* 1 (1991).

Flannery-Daily, F. *Dreamers, Scribes, and Priests: Jewish Dreams in Hellenistic and Roman Eras*. Leiden: Brill Academic Publishers, 2004.

Frymer-Kensky, T. *In the Wake of Goddesses: Women, Culture and the Biblical Transformation of Pagan Myth*. New York: Macmillan, 1992.

Gaster, M. *The Chronicles of Jerahmeel*. New York: KTAV, 1971.

———. *The Ma'aseh Book: Book of Jewish Tales and Legends Translated from the Judeo-German*. Philadelphia: JPS, 1934.

———. *The Sword of Moses*. New York: KTAV, 1971.

Ginsburg, E. *The Sabbath in Classical Kabbalah*. Albany: SUNY Press, 1989.

Goldberg, S. A. *Crossing the Jabbok: Illness and Death in Ashkenazi Judaism*. Berkley: University of California Press, 1996.

Goldin, J. "The Magic of Magic and Superstition," *Studies in Midrash and Related Literature*. Philadelphia: JPS, 1988.

———. *Studies in Midrash and Related Literature*. Philadelphia: JPS, 1988.

Goldish, M. *Spirit Possession in Judaism: Cases and Contexts from the Middle Ages to the Present*. Detroit: Wayne State University Press, 2003.

Gottstein, A. G. "The Body as Image of God in Rabbinic Literature," *Harvard Theological Review* 87, no. 2, 1994.

Green, A. *Guide to the Zohar*. Stanford: Stanford University Press, 2002.

———. "Introducing the Pritzker Edition Zohar" Lecture, Convention of the Central Conference of American Rabbis, Toronto, June 2004.

———. "The Song of Songs in Early Jewish Mysticism," in *Song of Songs*, ed. H. Bloom. New York: Chelsea Publishing, 1988.

Greenspahn, F. E. *Essential Papers on Israel and the Ancient Near East*. New York: NYU Press, 1991.

Gruenwald, I. *Apocalyptic and Merkavah Mysticism*. Leiden: E. J. Brill, 1980.

———. *Rituals and Ritual Theory in Ancient Israel*. Leiden: E. J. Brill, 2003.

Halperin, D. *Faces of the Chariot*. New York: SUNY Press, 1986.

Hammer, R. *The Jerusalem Anthology: A Literary Guide*. Philadelphia: JPS, 2000.

Herrera, R. *Mystics of the Book: Themes, Topics, and Typologies*. New York: Peter Lang, 1993.

Heschel, A. J. "The Mystical Element in Judaism," in *Understanding Rabbinic Judaism*, ed. J. Neusner. New York: KTAV, 1988.

———. *Prophetic Inspiration After the Prophets.* New York: KTAV, 1985.

———. *The Prophets.* Philadelphia: JPS, 1962.

Hoffman, M. *Campaign for Radical Truth in History.* http://www.hoffman-info.com.

Holtz, B., ed. *Back to the Sources: Reading the Classic Jewish Texts.* New York: Summit, 1985.

Homza, L. A. *Religious Authority in the Spanish Renaissance.* Baltimore: Johns Hopkins University Press, 2000.

Hurd, P. *Icons of Erotic Art.* London: Prestel, 1997.

Hurowitz, V. A. "True Light on the Urim and Thummim," *Jewish Quarterly Review* 88, Nos. 3–4 (Jan.–April 1998).

Idel, M. *The Golem: Jewish Magical and Mystical Traditions on the Artificial Anthropoid.* New York: SUNY Press, 1990.

———. *Hasidism: Between Ecstasy and Magic.* New York: SUNY Press, 1995.

———. *Kabbalah: New Perspectives.* New Haven: Yale Press, 1988.

———. "Kabbalistic Prayer and Color," in *Approaches to Judaism in Medieval Times,* ed. D. Blumenthal. Chicago: Scholar's Press, 1985.

———. "Magic and Kabbalah in the 'Book of the Responding Entity,'" in *The Solomon Goldman Lectures VI,* ed. M. Gruber. Chicago: Spertus College of Judaica Press, 1993.

———. *The Mystical Experience in Abraham Abulafia.* New York: SUNY Press, 1988.

———. "Sexual Metaphors and Praxis in Kabbalah," in *The Jewish Family: Metaphor and Memory,* ed. D. Kraemer. New York: Oxford University Press, 1989.

———. "The Story of Rabbi Joseph della Reina," *Sefunot: Studies and Texts on the History of the Jewish Community in Safed* [in Hebrew] 6 (1963).

Isaacs, R. *Ascending Jacob's Ladder.* Northvale, NJ: Jason Aronson, 1998.

———. *Divination, Magic, and Healing.* Northvale, NJ: Jason Aronson, 1998.

———. *Miracles: A Jewish Perspective.* Northvale, NJ: Jason Aronson, 2000.

Jacobs, L. *Jewish Mystical Testimonies.* New York: Schocken Books, 1976.

———. *The Jewish Mystics.* London: Kyle Cathie, 1990.

Janowitz, N. *Icons of Power: Ritual Practices in Late Antiquity.* Oxford, OH: Littmann Library of Jewish Civilization, 2004.

———. *The Poetics of Ascent: Theories of Language in a Rabbinic Ascent Text.* New York: SUNY Press, 1989.

"Jewish Magic: a Perspectives Symposium," *AJS Perspectives,* Fall 2001.

Jonas, H. *The Gnostic Religion.* Boston: Beacon Press, 1979.

Kanarfogel, E. *Peering through the Lattices: Mystical, Magical, and Pietistic Dimensions in the Tosafist Period.* Detroit: Wayne State University Press, 2000.

Kaplan, A. *The Aryeh Kaplan Anthology.* 2 vols. New York: NCSY Press, 1998.

———, trans. *The Bahir.* Northvale, NJ: Jason Aronson, 1995.

———. *Meditation and Kabbalah.* York Beach: Samuel Weiser, 1982.

———. *Sefer Yetzirah: The Book of Formation.* New York: Samuel Weiser, 1978.

———. *Tzitzith: A Thread of Light.* New York: NCSY/ Orthodox Union, 1984.

Karp, Abraham. *From the Ends of the Earth: Judaic Treasures of the Library of Congress.* New York: Rizzoli, 1991.

Karr, D. *Collected Articles on the Kabbalah.* Vol. 1. Ithaca, 1985.

Kaufmann, Y. *The Religion of Israel: From Its Beginnings to the Babylonian Exile.* New York: Schocken Books, 1960.

Kern-Ulmer, B. "The Depiction of Magic in Rabbinic Texts: The Rabbinic and Greek Concept of Magic," *Journal for the Study of Judaism* 27, no. 3 (1996).

Kertzer, D. *The Popes Against the Jews: The Vatican's Role in the Rise of Modern Anti-Semitism.* New York: Alfred A. Knopf, 2001.

Klausner, J. *The Messianic Idea in Israel.* New York: Macmillan, 1955.

Klein, M. *A Time to Be Born: Customs and Folklore of Jewish Birth.* Philadelphia: JPS, 1998.

Koch, K. *The Prophets.* Vols. 1 and 2, Philadelphia: Fortress Press, 1992.

Kosman, A. "The Story of a Giant Story," *Hebrew Union College Annual* 73 (2002).

Kugel, J. *The God of Old: Inside the Lost World of the Bible.* New York: Free Press, 2003.

Lauterbach, J. "The Belief in the Power of the Word," *Hebrew Union College Annual* 14 (1939).

Lesses, R. *Ritual Practices to Gain Power.* Leiden: Brill, 1998.

Levenson, J. *Creation and the Persistence of Evil.* Princeton, NJ: Princeton University Press, 1988.

———. *Sinai and Zion: An Entry into the Jewish Bible.* San Francisco: Harper San Francisco, 1985.

Levine, L. *The Ancient Synagogue.* New Haven, CT: Yale University Press, 2000.

Lex, B. "Recent Contributions to the Study of Ritual Trance," *Reviews in Anthropology* 11, nos. 44–51 (1984).

Maccoby, H. *Judas Iscariot and the Myth of Jewish Evil.* New York: Free Press, 1992.

Martinez, F. G. *The Dead Sea Scrolls Translated.* Leiden, the Netherlands: Brill/Eerdmans, 1994.

Mathieu, P. *Sex Pots: Eroticism in Ceramics.* New York: A & C Black, 2003.

Matt, D., trans. *The Essential Kabbalah: The Heart of Jewish Mysticism.* San Francisco: HarperSanFrancisco, 1995.

———, trans. *Zohar: The Book of Enlightenment.* New York: Paulist, 1983.

———, trans. *The Zohar: Pritzker Edition.* Vols. 1 and 2. Stanford: Stanford University Press, 2004.

Mazar, A. *Archaeology of the Land of the Bible 10,000–586 B.C.E.* New York: Doubleday Publishing, 1992.

Metzger and Coogan, eds. *The Oxford Companion to the Bible.* New York: Oxford Press, 1993.

Miller, M. "Rabbi Yitzchak Luria: Basic Kabbala Teachings," http://www.ascentofsafed.com/cgi-bin/ascent.cgi?Name=ari-teachings.

Monford, H. *Studies in Jewish Dream Interpretation.* Northvale, NJ: Jason Aronson, 1994.

Morgan, M. *Sepher Ha-Razim.* Bloomington, IN: Scholars Press, 1983.

Munk, M. *The Wisdom of the Hebrew Alphabet.* New York: Mesorah, 1983.

Naveh, J. and S. Shaked. *Amulets and Magic Bowls: Aramaic Incantations of Late Antiquity.* Jerusalem: Magnes Press, 1985.

———. *Magic Spells and Formulae: Aramaic Incantations of Late Antiquity.* Jerusalem: Magnes Press, 1991.

Ness, L. J. *Astrology and Judaism in Late Antiquity* (Dissertation, Miami University, 1990), published online at http://www.smoe.org/arcana/diss.html.

Neulander, J. "The New Mexican Crypto-Jewish Canon: Choosing to be 'Chosen' in Millennial Tradition," *Jewish Folklore and Ethnology Review* 18, no. 12 (1996).

Neusner, J., ed. *Religion, Science, and Magic: In Concert and in Conflict.* New York: Oxford University Press, 1989.

Nickelsburg, G. "The Experience of Demons (and Angels) in 1 Enoch, Jubilees, and the Book of Tobit," *Minutes of the 1988 Philadelphia Seminar on Christian Origins*. Online at http://ccat.sas.upenn.edu/psco/year25/8803a.shtml.

Nigal, G. *Magic, Mysticism, and Hasidism*. Northvale, NJ: Jason Aronson, 1994.

Oppenheim, A. L. *Ancient Mesopotamia*. Chicago: University of Chicago Press, 1977.

Patai, R. "Exorcism and Xenoglossia among the Safed Mystics," *The Journal of American Folklore* 91, no. 361 (1978).

———. *Gates to the Old City: A Book of Jewish Legends*. New York: Avon Books, 1980.

———. *The Jewish Alchemists: A History and Source Book*. Princeton, NJ: Princeton University Press, 1994.

———. *The Messiah Texts*. New York: Avon Books, 1979.

———. *On Jewish Folklore*. Detroit: Wayne State Press, 1983.

Petrovsky-Shtern, Y. "The Master of the Evil Name: Hillel Ba'al Shem and his Sefer ha-Heshek," *AJS Review* 28, no. 2 (2004): 217–48.

Raphael, P. S. *Jewish Views of the Afterlife*. Northvale, NJ: Jason Aronson, 1996.

Robson, J. E. "Bestiality and Bestial Rape in Greek Myth," *Rape in Antiquity: Sexual Violence in the Greek and Roman Worlds*, ed. S. Deacy, and K. Pierce. London: Ducksworth, 2002.

Rosen, M. "The Interaction of Kabbalah and Halachah in the Aruch ha-Shulchan," *The Maqom Journal*, published online at http://www.maqom.com/journal/paper22.pdf.

Ruderman, D. B. *Kabbalah, Magic and Science: The Cultural Universe of a Sixteenth-Century Jewish Physician*. Cambridge: Harvard University Press, 1988.

Rudolph, K. *Gnosis: The Nature and History of Gnosticism*. San Francisco: HarperSanFrancisco, 1987.

Schachter-Shalomi, Z., and E. Hoffman. *Sparks of Light: Counseling in the Hasidic Tradition*. Boulder: Shambala, 1983.

Schachter-Shalomi, Z. *Spiritual Intimacy: A Study of Counseling in Hasidism*. Northvale: Jason Aronson, 1996.

Schafer, P. *The Hidden and Manifest God: Some Major Themes in Early Jewish Mysticism*. New York: SUNY Press, 1992.

———. *Judeophobia: Attitudes Toward the Jews in the Ancient World*. Cambridge: Harvard University Press, 1994.

Schmidt, B. *Israel's Beneficent Dead: Ancestor Cult and Necromancy in Ancient Israelite Religion and Tradition*. Lake Geneva: Eisenbraun, 1996.

Scholem, G. *Kabbalah*. New York: Meridian Books, 1974.

———. *Major Trends in Jewish Mysticism*. New York: Schocken, 1961.

———. *The Messianic Idea in Judaism*. New York: Schocken Books, 1971.

———. *On the Kabbalah and Its Symbolism*. New York: Schocken, 1965.

———. *On the Mystical Shape of the Godhead*. New York: Schocken, 1991.

———. *Zohar: The Book of Splendor*. New York: Schocken, 1963.

Schwarz, A. *Kabbalah and Alchemy: An Essay on Common Archetypes*. Northvale, NJ: Jason Aronson, 2000.

Schwartz, H. *Gabriel's Palace: Jewish Mystical Tales*. New York: Oxford University Press, 1993.

———. *Lilith's Cave: Jewish Tales of the Supernatural*. New York: Harper & Row, 1988.

———. *Tree of Souls: The Mythology of Judaism*. New York: Oxford University Press, 2004.

Segal, A. "The Ten Lost Tribes of Israel: Looking for the Remnants," *Hagshama*. The World Zionist Organization Education Center, http://www.wzo.org.il.

Singer, S. A. *Medieval Jewish Mysticism: Book of the Pious.* Wheeling, IL: Whitehall Co., 1971.

Smelik, K. *Writings from Ancient Israel: A Handbook of Historical and Religious Documents.* Louisville: Westminster/John Knox Press, 1991.

Spiegel, S. *The Last Trial: On the Legends and Lore of the Command to Abraham to Offer Isaac As a Sacrifice: The Akedah.* New York: Schocken Books, 1967.

Stager, L. E. and S. R. Wolff. "Child Sacrifice at Carthage," *Biblical Archaeology Review* (Jan./Feb. 1984).

Steinsaltz, A. *The Thirteen Petalled Rose.* Northvale, NJ: Jason Aronson, 1998.

Stern, D. and M. Mirsky. *Rabbinic Fantasies: Imaginative Narratives from Classical Hebrew Literature.* New Haven: Yale University Press, 1990.

Tigay, J. *The JPS Torah Commentary: Deuteronomy.* Philadelphia: JPS, 1996.

Tishby, I. *The Wisdom of the Zohar.* 3 vols. New York: B'nai Brith Books, 1989.

Trachtenberg, J. *The Devil and the Jews.* Philadelphia: JPS, 1943.

———. *Jewish Magic and Superstition: A Study in Folk Religion.* Philadelphia: JPS, 1939.

Travis, Yakov. "The Aural Effect of Mitzvot in Early Kabbalah." Lecture presented at the 2004 Conference of the Association of Jewish Studies, December, 2004.

Twelftree, G. *Jesus the Exorcist: A Contribution to the Study of the Historical Jesus.* Tuebingen: J. C. B. Mohr, 1993.

Twersky, I. and B. Septimus, eds. *Jewish Thought in the Seventeenth Century.* Cambridge: Harvard University Press, 1987.

Tzadok, A. B. *The Rise and Fall of Rabbi Yosef della Reina.* Yeshivat Benei N'vi'im Online, 2003. http://www.koshertorah.com/PDF/Della-Reina.pdf.

Unterman, A. *Dictionary of Jewish Lore & Legend.* London: Thames and Hudson, 1991.

Valantasis, R., ed. *Religions of Late Antiquity in Practice.* Princeton, NJ: Princeton University Press, 2000.

Van Binsbergen, W. and F. Wiggermann. "Magic in History: A Theoretical Perspective, and its Application to Ancient Mesopotamia," published online at http://www.shikanda.net/ancient_models/gen3/magic.htm.

Van Dam, C. *The Urim and Thummim: A Means of Revelation in Ancient Israel.* Winona Lake, IN: Eisenbrauns, 1997.

Veltri, G. "Defining Forbidden Foreign Practices: Some Remarks on the Halakhah of Magic," *Proceedings of the Eleventh World Congress, vol. 1: Rabbinic and Talmudic Literature,* 1994.

Verman, M. *The Books of Contemplation: Medieval Jewish Mystical Sources.* New York: SUNY Press, 1992.

Vilnay, Z. *Legends of Jerusalem.* Philadelphia: JPS, 1975.

Werblowsky, R. J. Z. *Joseph Karo, Lawyer and Mystic.* Philadelphia: JPS, 1977.

Wertheimer, J., ed. *Jewish Religious Leadership: Image and Reality.* 2 vols. New York: Jewish Theological Seminary, 2004.

Wiggerman, E. "The Mythological Foundations of Nature," in *Natural Phenomenon,* ed. D. J. W. Meijer. Amsterdam: North Holland Press, 1992.

Winkler, G. *Magic of the Ordinary: Recovering the Shamanic in Judaism.* Berkley, CA: North Atlantic Press, 2003.

Wolfson, E. *Along the Path: Studies in Kabbalistic Myth, Symbolism, and Hermeneutics.* New York: SUNY, 1995.

———. *Through a Speculum that Shines: Vision and Imagination in Medieval Jewish Mysticism.* Princeton, NJ: Princeton University Press, 1997.

Zimmels, H. J. *Magicians, Theologians, and Doctors.* Northvale, NJ: Jason Aronson, 1997.

LLEWELLYN ORDERING INFORMATION

Order Online:

Visit our website at www.llewellyn.com, select your books, and order them on our secure server.

Order by Phone:

- Call toll-free within the U.S. at 1-877-NEW-WRLD (1-877-639-9753). Call toll-free within Canada at 1-866-NEW-WRLD (1-866-639-9753)
- We accept VISA, MasterCard, and American Express

Order by Mail:

Send the full price of your order (MN residents add 7% sales tax) in U.S. funds, plus postage & handling to:

**Llewellyn Worldwide
2143 Wooddale Drive, Dept. 0-7387-0905-0
Woodbury, MN 55125-2989, U.S.A.**

Postage & Handling:

Standard (U.S., Mexico, & Canada). If your order is:
$24.99 and under, add $3.00
$25.00 and over, FREE STANDARD SHIPPING

AK, HI, PR: $15.00 for one book plus $1.00 for each additional book.

International Orders (airmail only):
$16.00 for one book plus $3.00 for each additional book

Orders are processed within 2 business days.
Please allow for normal shipping time. Postage and handling rates subject to change.

The New Encyclopedia of the Occult

JOHN MICHAEL GREER

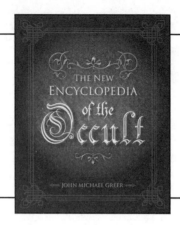

From "Aarab Zereq" to "Zos Kia Cultus," it's the most complete occult reference work on the market. With this one text, you will gain a thorough overview of the history and current state of the occult from a variety of North American and western European traditions. Its pages offer the essential knowledge you need to make sense of the occult, along with references for further reading if you want to learn more.

You will find the whole range of occult tradition, lore, history, philosophy, and practice in the Western world. *The New Encyclopedia of the Occult* includes magic, alchemy, astrology, divination, Tarot, palmistry, geomancy, magical orders such as the Golden Dawn and Rosicrucians, Wiccan, Thelema, Theosophy, modern Paganism, and biographies of important occultists.

1–56718–336–0
608 pp., 8 x 10   **$29.95**

The Kabbalah Tree
A Journey of Balance & Growth

RACHEL POLLACK

Kabbalah's most famous symbol, the Tree of Life, has become the organizing principle behind our human efforts to understand the world. Using Hermann Haindl's lush depiction of the Tree of Life, Rachel Pollack examines the message behind this ancient symbol. She takes a non-denominational approach—drawing upon unusual sources such as tribal and shamanic traditions, modern science, contemporary Kabbalists, tarot interpreters, and a comic book writer—to explore the Tree's meaning. Along the way, we learn more about Kabbalah's history, texts, mystical concepts, and why this esoteric tradition has sprung up again in the twenty-first century.

0-7387-0507-1
192 pp., 6 x 9, illus., includes Haindl's *Tree of Life* poster   **$16.95**

To order, call 1-877-NEW-WRLD
Prices subject to change without notice

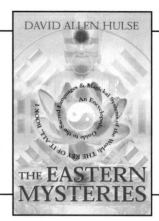

The Eastern Mysteries
An Encyclopedic Guide to the Sacred Languages & Magical Systems of the World

DAVID ALLEN HULSE

The Eastern Mysteries series clarifies and extends the knowledge established by all previous books on occult magick. Book One catalogs and distills, in hundreds of tables of secret symbolism, the true alphabet magick of every ancient Eastern magickal tradition. Unlike the current rash of publications which do no more than recapitulate Regardie or Crowley, The Eastern Mysteries series establishes a new level of competence in all fields of magick both East and West.

Cuneiform—the oldest tradition ascribing number to word; the symbolism of base 60 used in Babylonian and Sumerian Cuneiform; the first God and Goddess names associated to number.

Hebrew—a complete exposition of the rules governing the Hebrew Qabalah; the evolution of the Tree of Life; an analysis of the Book of Formation, the oldest key to the symbolic meaning of the Hebrew alphabet.

Arabic—the similarity between the Hebrew and Arabic Qabalahs; the secret Quranic symbolism for the Arabic alphabet; the Persian alphabet code; the philosophical numbering system of G. I. Gurdjieff.

Sanskrit—the secret Vedic number codes for Sanskrit; the digital word-numbers; the symbolism of the seven chakras and their numerical key.

Tibetan—the secret number lore for Tibetan as inspired by the Sanskrit codes; the secret symbols for the Tibetan alphabet; the six major schools of Tattva philosophy.

Chinese—the Taoist calligraphic stroke count technique for number Chinese characters; Chinese Taoist number philosophy; the I Ching, the Japanese language and its parallels to the Chinese number system.

1-56718-428-6

672 pp., 7 x 10 $39.95

To order, call 1-877-NEW-WRLD
Prices subject to change without notice

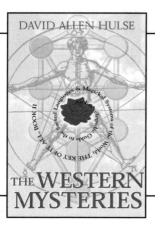

The Western Mysteries
An Encyclopedic Guide to the Sacred Languages & Magical Systems of the World

DAVID ALLEN HULSE

The Western Mysteries series clarifies and extends the knowledge established by all previous books on occult magick. Book Two catalogs and distills, in hundreds of tables of secret symbolism, the true alphabet magick of every ancient Western magickal tradition.

Greek—the number codes for Greek; the Gnostic cosmology; the Pythagorean philosophical metaphors for the number series.

Coptic—the number values for Coptic, derived from the Greek; Coptic astrological symbolism; the Egyptian hieroglyphs and their influence in the numbering of Hebrew and Greek.

Runes—the ancient runic alphabet codes for Germanic, Icelandic, Scandinavian, and English Rune systems; the modern German Armanen Runic cult; the Irish Ogham and Beth-Luis-Nion poetic alphabets.

Latin—Roman Numerals as the first Latin code; the Lullian Latin Qabalah; the Germanic and Italian serial codes for Latin; the Renaissance cosmological model of three worlds.

Enochian—the number codes for Enochian according to John Dee, S. L. MacGregor Mathers, and Aleister Crowley; the true pattern behind the Watchtower symbolism; the complete rectified Golden Dawn correspondences for the Enochian alphabet.

Tarot—the pictorial key to the Hebrew alphabet; the divinatory system for the Tarot; the two major Qabalistic codes for the Tarot emanating from France and England.

English—the serial order code for English; Aleister Crowley's attempt of an English Qabalah; the symbolism behind the shapes of the English alphabet letters.

1-56718-429-4

705 pp., 7 x 10   **$39.95**

To order, call 1-877-NEW-WRLD
Prices subject to change without notice

Garden of Pomegranates

Skrying on the Tree of Life

ISRAEL REGARDIE

ED BY CHIC CICERO AND
SANDRA TABATHA CICERO

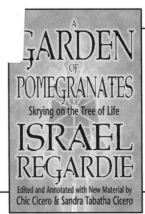

When Israel Regardie wrote *A Garden of Pomegranates* in 1932, he designed it to be a simple yet comprehensive guidebook outlining the complex system of the Qabalah and providing a key to its symbolism. Since then it has achieved the status of a classic among texts on the Hermetic Qabalah. It stands as the best single introductory guide for magicians on this complex system, with an emphasis on direct experience through meditation on the twenty-two paths.

Now, Chic Cicero and Sandra Tabatha Cicero—Golden Dawn adepts and personal friends of the late Regardie—have made the book even more useful for today's occult students with full annotations, critical commentary, and explanatory notes. They've added practical material in the form of pathworkings, suggested exercises, and daily affirmations—one for each Sephirah and each path. Brief rituals, meditations, and Qabalistic mantras complement Regardie's section on gematria and other forms of numerical Qabalah.

1-56718-141-4
552 pp., 6 x 9 $17.95

To order, call 1-877-NEW-WRLD

Prices subject to change without notice